S0-FJD-401

THE FRONTIER

of

RESEARCH IN THE CONSUMER INTEREST

Proceedings of the International Conference on
Research in the Consumer Interest

Edited
by

E. Scott Maynes
Cornell University

and

The ACCI Research Committee:

Monroe P. Friedman
Eastern Michigan University

Jean Kinsey
University of Minnesota

Carole J. Makela
Colorado State University

Nancy M. Rudd
Ohio State University

Roger M. Swagler
University of Georgia

William L. Wilkie
University of Notre Dame

Assisted by

Peggy H. Haney
American Express Company

W. Keith Bryant
Cornell University

Daria Sheehan
Chesebrough-Pond's Inc.

Folke Olander
Aarhus School of Business
Administration and Economics

Published by
American Council on Consumer Interests
240 Stanley Hall
University of Missouri, Columbia
Columbia, Missouri 65211

WITHDRAWN
LUTHER L. GOBBEL LIBRARY
LAMBUTH COLLEGE
JACKSON, TENNESSEE

104994

22/Net

© AMERICAN COUNCIL ON CONSUMER INTERESTS, 1988

All rights reserved. No part of this publication may be reproduced, stored in a retrieval system, or transmitted, in any form or by any means, electronic, mechanical, photocopying, recording, or otherwise, without the prior written permission of the publisher.

ISBN 0-945857-00-4

DEDICATED TO:

COLSTON E. WARNE

1900-1987

Founder of:

Consumers Union, 1936

American Council on Consumer Interests, 1953

International Organization of Consumers Unions, 1960

Papers By:

Alan R. Andreasen
California State University,
Long Beach

Robert W. Crandall
Brookings Institution

David J. Curry
University of Iowa

Rachel Dardis
University of Maryland

Claes Fornell
University of Michigan

Jennifer L. Gerner
Cornell University

Loren V. Geistfeld
Ohio State University

H. Keith Hunt
Brigham Young University

Pauline M. Ippolito
Federal Trade Commission

John E. Kushman
University of Delaware

Robert J. Lampman
University of Wisconsin

James N. Morgan
University of Michigan

Folke Olander
Aarhus School of Business
Administration and Economics

George L. Priest
Yale University

Michael R. Reich
Harvard University

Jean R. Robinson
Cornell University

J. Edward Russo
Cornell University

Hans B. Thorelli
Indiana University

FINANCIAL SUPPORTERS OF THE CONFERENCE

THE JOHNSON FOUNDATION
Wingspread Conference Center, Racine, Wisconsin

CHESEBROUGH-POND'S INC.
Greenwich, Connecticut

AMERICAN EXPRESS FOUNDATION
New York City

With Additional Funding From:

SHELL OIL FOUNDATION
Houston, Texas

CONTENTS

Chapter | Page

THE RIGHT TO BE INFORMED

THE RIGHT TO BE HEARD

THE RIGHT TO REDRESS

OVERVIEW

Chapter 1

ABOUT THE AUTHOR

E. Scott Maynes is Professor in the Department of Consumer Economics and Housing at Cornell University. A consumer economist, Maynes received his Ph.D. from the University of Michigan in 1956. Maynes was a member of the Economics faculty at the University of Minnesota for 18 years. At Cornell he served as Department Chairman from 1976 to 1981.

Active in the consumer movement, Maynes served on the Board and Executive Committee of Consumers Union for 9 years. He is author of Decision-Making For Consumers (Macmillan, 1976). Maynes has been Chairman of the ACCI Research Committee since 1983. He has served on the editorial boards of the Journals of Consumer Affairs, Consumer Research, and Consumer Policy.

THE FIRST WORD, THE LAST WORD

E. Scott Maynes

The first part of this chapter -- The "First Word"-- introduces the reader to this Book and to the Conference from which it springs. The last part -- The "Last Word" -- is a look back, expressing appreciation to those who helped make both Conference and Book possible and assessing the impact of the Book.

I. ABOUT THIS BOOK

As its title indicates, the purpose of this Book and the Conference on which it is based is to delineate "The Frontier" of research in the consumer interest: what we know, what we don't know, what we need to know. Simultaneously, this book should lay a foundation in research for consumer economics, consumer education, and "consumer affairs," i.e., the profession in business, government, and consumer organizations that seeks to respond to the needs of consumers.

The Consumer Interest

The notion of "the consumer interest" has evoked several alternative interpretations. We will consider four.

The first interpretation is due to the ACCI Research Committee, the planners of the Conference on which this book is based. Necessarily, our Committee had to wrestle with the problem of just what *is* the "consumer interest." The answer, proposed by

Monroe P. Friedman, adopted by our Committee and embodied in the Table of Contents of this book: anything that furthers the attainment of The Consumer Rights. Seven Consumer Rights have been widely accepted. They are:

1. The Right to Safety -- to be protected against the marketing of goods that are hazardous to health or life;

2. The Right to Be Informed -- to be protected against fraudulent, deceitful, or grossly misleading information, advertising, labeling, or other practices, and to be given the facts needed to make an informed choice;

3. The Right to Choose -- to be assured, wherever possible, of access to a variety of products and services at competitive prices; and in those industries in which competition is not workable and government regulation is substituted, an assurance of satisfactory quality and service at a fair price;

4. The Right to Be Heard -- to be assured that consumer interests will receive full and sympathetic consideration in the formulation of government policy, and fair and expeditious treatment in its administrative tribunals;

5. The Right to Recourse and Redress -- to be entitled to a correction of consumer grievances.

6. The Right to Consumer Education.

7. The Right to a Healthy Environment.

A second interpretation, that of the author of this chapter, is based on the approval of informed consumers. In this view the consumer interest consists of "those policies, practices, institutions, ideas of which most consumers would approve were they fully informed and fully understanding." This is a refinement of a definition first proposed in 1976 [12].

A third approach is embodied in James Morgan's thoughtful and seminal paper, "What Is In the Consumer Interest?", the 1985 Colston E. Warne lecture to the American Council on Consumer Interests (hereafter ACCI) [14]. While Morgan does not propose a succinct definition of "the consumer interest," he regards two concepts as critical in delineating the consumer interest: (1) cost-benefit assessments of proposals or institutions as a means of assessing "efficiency," and (2) considerations of "fairness" (which he does not define).

A fourth approach is implicit in the various surveys conducted to document "consumer concerns," "consumer problems," or "consumerism." Remove these concerns and problems and, presumably, you have served the consumer interest. The most ambitious of these investigations was the Survey of Consumer Concerns conducted for the National Consumer Council, London in 1979 with reinterviews in 1981 [16]. For a probability sample of consumers, it probed "concerns" over an extraordinarily wide range of domains. The most highly regarded and most cited survey of this type in the U.S. was the 1982 Consumerism in the Eighties survey conducted by Louis Harris for Atlantic Richfield [1]. It had the advantage of comparing changes over time between "low" and "high" points of the consumerism movement: 1982 versus 1976. The 1983 Whirlpool Study, America's Search for Quality [21], delved different and fascinating topics. Unfortunately, some of its data may have been biased and misleading. You can test this allegation yourself. Turn to the questionnaire in its Appendix and try to answer the questions posed, using the fixed categories offered. If some of your responses -- like those of the author -- fit none of the fixed response categories offered, then you are facing a biased survey instrument that will yield biased data.

What are we to make of these alternative approaches to "the consumer interest?" First and foremost, they lay bare the potential division between leaders of the consumer movement and researchers in the consumer interest. Consumer leaders and most "activists" will usually concern themselves with perceived problems -- Definition #4 -- while researchers will want to assess the consumer interest under assumptions of full information and full understanding. Sometimes this difference of viewpoint is of no consequence. For example, both activists and researchers would agree that such palpable concerns as appliances that don't work are consumer "problems" and that their elimination or correction is in the consumer interest. Similarly, both would agree on the desirability of consumer representation in the determination of public policy.

But two other examples show how the difference in concepts may lead to conflict. Many consumer "advocates" -- Consumers Union, for example -- support interest rate ceilings on consumer credit. Their purpose is clear. They feel that credit markets are working badly and they wish to assure credit to most consumers, particularly low income consumers at lower, "fair" rates. They see ceilings as an effective instrument for achieving these goals. Not so, most researchers. By their analysis, "too low" interest rate ceilings will make insufficient allowance for the bad debts of "poor" risks (often low-income consumers) and thus lead lenders to deny credit to low-income consumers, the very group that Consumers Union wishes to help. A second example is informationally imperfect consumer markets, i.e., markets characterized by a low or near-zero correlation between product price and quality. Loren Geistfeld's chapter of this volume [Ch. 7] concludes that most local consumer markets are informationally imperfect. This contrasts with the views of most consumers, as suggested in data from the survey conducted for Atlantic Richfield by Louis Harris [1].

Given this analysis, we should not be surprised when consumer leaders and consumer researchers line up on different sides of a policy issue.

But the discussion above suggests appropriate roles for researchers, educators, and consumer leaders. Clearly it is the responsibility of researchers to ascertain, under the most demanding conditions (full information and full understanding) what truly <u>is</u> in the consumer interest. And it is their responsibility, and that also of consumer educators, to communicate these insights to all consumers, whether involved in the consumer movement or not. As for consumer leaders, the above discussion would seem to imply the recognition that what is "in the consumer interest" is not always obvious and that researchers can play a useful role in answering this question.

The consumer movement is of course political and social in nature, energized by felt consumer dissatisfaction. Consumer leaders fully realize that they must respond to perceived consumer dissatisfaction. If researchers want the support of the consumer movement, they must recognize and react, in part at least, to perceived consumer dissatisfaction. But consumer leaders should recognize that the determination of the consumer interest is complex and that researchers have an important role in working out what is truly in the consumer interest.

Turning back to the four interpretations of the "consumer interest," it seems clear that there may be no simple, generally accepted of the consumer interest. Instead, it could be argued that each of the interpretations cited offers some worthwhile elements.

<u>The Conference and Its Book</u>

This book represents the "Proceedings" of the International Conference on Research in the Consumer Interest, held at the Wingspread Conference Center, Racine, Wisconsin on August 16-19,

1986. The "Wingspread Conference" brought together 75 researchers and consumer leaders from all over the world. A few words regarding the Conference will help the reader understand this book.

As stated earlier, the purpose of the Wingspread Conference was to spell out "the frontier" of research in the consumer interest: what we know, what we do not know, what we need to know. Following a suggestion of Monroe Friedman, the Conference Sessions and Papers were organized around the Seven Consumer Rights.[1]

Examine the Table of Contents and you will see for yourself how Consumer Rights provide the skeleton that holds together the Conference and its Book. The Book starts with a singularly interesting paper by Robert Lampman that tells a story never told before: how Lampman and his colleagues in the Federal Government in 1962 concocted the speech that became President Kennedy's "Consumer Address." This was the influential speech that, somewhat expanded, has become the ideological keystone of the World Consumer Movement.

The other 18 major papers and 54 comments are organized under the Six Consumer Rights.

Why this organization? There were two reasons. The first was that this represented a reasonable way of defining the "consumer interest": to what extent and in what ways have we attained or not attained each consumer right? A second reason was that the Consumer Rights provide a durable framework for assessing over time the progress of research in the consumer interest. This is an important property because the ACCI Research Committee viewed the Wingspread Conference as the first of a series of conferences, to be held every 4 or 5 years, each designed to evaluate progress made in achieving the consumer rights since the last conference.

Note that our selection of the Consumer Rights as the unifying framework clearly focused the Conference and its Book on policy. This means that some topics, typically dealt with by consumer economists and family economists are excluded. Models and empirical research that seek to explain and predict consumer behavior individually and aggregatively are included only to the extent that they are related to policy. Among other topics excluded from this volume are the economic organization of the household,

---

[1]There were no sessions dedicated explicitly to "The Right to a Healthy Environment." It could be argued that this was a concern that permeated many sessions.

time use, the consumption/saving function, demand analysis, research on particular products -- cars, videotex, consumer credit, research on normative behavior, i.e., optimal search procedures.

In seeking to evaluate progress towards the achievement of the consumer rights, the ACCI Research Committee decided to recruit as participants at Wingspread the best people it could identify, regardless of discipline, professional affiliation, geographic location. Following this principle and recognizing that consumer problems are irrevocably cross-disciplinary in nature, it should not surprise the reader to discover that our roster of authors is highly variegated, including consumer leaders as well as researchers. In this respect this Conference and this Book differ greatly from the Federal Trade Commission's Conference on Consumer Protection, whose participants were drawn almost exclusively from mainstream Economics [11].

Let me urge the reader of this book to pay equal attention to major papers and to the comments of panelists or discussants. There are three reasons for this recommendation. First, discussants and panelists were selected to represent divergent views. Only by reading all views will the reader obtain a balanced view of a topic. Speaking personally, in several cases I found myself drastically revising my judgments of particular major papers as I digested the comments of the discussants. Second, these comments were much more carefully prepared than is customary. All the discussants received the papers on which they were to comment three months before the Wingspread Conference. Further, all but four of the panelists and discussants brought written comments to the Conference. These comments, like the major papers, have been reviewed by two editors and then revised by the authors. Finally, Wingspread discussants were invited to follow either the traditional role of commenting on the major paper or, alternatively, to present at lesser length comments or research results on related topics they felt to be important. The titles of discussants' comments should reveal the cases where a discussant paper deals with a topic quite different from that of the major paper.

While the Wingspread Conference is the largest and most comprehensive conference ever to deal with research in the consumer interest, it is not the first to deal with the topic. We list below, for the interested reader, conferences whose purpose overlapped that of the Wingspread Conference.

Year	Place/Name of Conference	Citation
1972	Williamsburg Conference on Family Economic Behavior	[19]
1974	Berlin-I Conference on Consumer Action Research	[17]
1975	Berlin-II	[18]
1977	Carnegie-Mellon Conference on Effects of Information on Consumer and Market Behavior	[13]
1978	MIT Conference on Research for Consumer Policy	[9]
1981	European Workshops on Consumer Law, University of Louvain, Belgium	[4]
1982	University of Maryland Conference on Consumerism and Beyond	[3]
1982	Wisconsin Conference on Consumer Education	[20]
1984	Federal Trade Commission on Consumer Protection	[11]
1986	Heiligkreutzal Symposium on Consumer Policy	No Proceedings
1986	Iowa State Symposium on Human Resources Research	[8]

My Last Word looks back, paying tribute to Colston Warne, expressing "thanks" to those who made book and conference possible, and seeking to assess the significance of both conference and book.

A TRIBUTE TO COLSTON E. WARNE

First, I want to express our debt to and appreciation of the friend and mentor of us all, Colston E. Warne, Father of the World Consumer Movement. Without Colston Warne, it is unlikely that this book would have come into existence. Concerned as much with organizations as with ideas, Colston Warne was founder of several of the important organizations sponsoring and contributing to The Frontier. I note those in which Colston Warne exerted a pivotal influence.

First and foremost is the American Council on Consumer Interest (ACCI), originally named the Council on Consumer Information. Colston Warne was Founder and Charter Member of ACCI. He was instrumental in obtaining from Consumers Union financial support that would sustain ACCI in its first decade. The goal of ACCI was to provide the information and education that would enable consumers and the market economy to function more effectively. What the Wingspread Conference and The Frontier does is to further these goals by providing a research foundation for consumer education, consumer affairs, and consumer economics.

The second organization to benefit from Colston Warne's ministrations was the Association for Consumer Research (ACR), co-sponsor of the Wingspread Conference. Here Warne's influence was indirect. Colston was prescient in recognizing the importance of research, especially in the consumer interest. Through his influence, Consumers Union along with the Social Science Research Council sponsored a series of Conferences on Consumer Behavior at the Survey Research Center of the University of Michigan with George Katona and his colleagues as hosts. These conferences resulted in a series of volumes, edited mainly by Lincoln Clark appearing under the title, Consumer Behavior [5, 6, 7, 10]. The conferences could be properly regarded as antecedents of ACR and the books as antecedents to ACR Proceedings, Advances in Consumer Research [2].

The participants and topics considered at the first Conference on Consumer Behavior in 1954 should interest readers of this book. Present at that first Conference was Ruby T. Morris, a pioneer in our field whose later paper in the Journal of Marketing [15] first noted the "chaos of competition" in local consumer markets. It was at this conference that George Katona and Eva Mueller reported on their landmark piece of research, "A Study of Consumer Purchases" [5]. James Tobin, the Nobel prizewinner, was a discussant. Also present was James Morgan, the author of a major paper in this book, and E. Scott Maynes (a graduate student). At the next Conference Morgan and John B. Lansing presented a seminal paper on the "Family Life Cycle" [6]. Another familiar figure involved in these conferences was Robert Ferber, so well known to so many of us both in Consumer Economics and in Consumer Behavior. Ferber later became the founding Editor of the Journal of Marketing Research and served terms as Editor of the Journal of the American Statistical Association and the Journal of Consumer Research.

Colston Warne is better known as the founder of two major consumer organizations. Most notably, he was Founder and President of Consumers Union, represented in this volume with contributions by R. David Pittle, Technical Director, and Charlotte Baecher, Educational Director. Warne was also Founder and first President of the International Organization of Consumers Union (IOCU). IOCU is represented in this book by a number of contributors: Jean-Pierre Allain, Special Assistant from IOCU's Penang Office, Roland Huttenrauch from Stiftung Warentest in Berlin, Jeremy Mitchell from the National Consumer Council in London, Peter Sand and Michael Warren from Consumers' Association in London, Mitsuaki Imai from the Japanese Association of Consumer Education, Robert Kerton from the Canadian Association of Consumers, and -- again -- by David Pittle and Charlotte Baecher from Consumers Union.

Prior to the International Conference on Research in the Consumer Interest, Colston Warne's daughter, Barbara Warne Newell, wrote me that Colston was "thrilled" by the plans for the Conference. He would have been even more thrilled by the reality of this book based on the Conference. It is a pleasure for me to remind you of the extent to which the consumer movement and "researchers in the consumer interest" are in debt to Colston E. Warne.

A Lack of Accents

For the Editor, this book represents a first exercise in "desktop publishing." Unlike traditional publishing, this form of publication requires a selection of type font at the very outset. So the font in which this book is rendered was chosen by the Editor in Fall, 1986. Recognizing and respecting the various accent marks appropriate to the Danish, French, German, Norwegian, Swedish, and Spanish languages, I intended to render each of these languages with its appropriate accents. But I did not explore whether my candidate type font contained the desired accents. Later, to my dismay, I discovered that it did not.

The upshot is that most non-English names and words are printed in anglicized form, lacking the accents appropriate to their language. For this I apologize. And I alert future editors and desktop publishers to this problem, inherent in this new technology.

WORDS OF THANKS

As Chairman of the 1983-87 ACCI Research Committee and Editor of this Book, it is my pleasant duty to say "Thanks" to those individuals and organizations who contributed to the Conference and its Book.

First I say "Thank You" to our hosts for the Conference, The Johnson Foundation, operators of the Wingspread Conference Center. Ours was one of the longest and largest conferences ever supported by The Foundation. Those participating in the Conference were loud in their praise of The Foundation -- its exquisite facilities, its caring hospitality, the knowing advice and ministrations of its excellent staff. Individuals who merit our thanks include Richard Kinch, Program Director, who helped us in the planning of the Wingspread Conference; Kay Mauer, who organized logistics at Wingspread.

Second, I thank our Financial Supporters: Chesebrough-Pond's Inc., American Express Foundation, The Johnson Foundation and Shell Oil Foundation.

Our appreciation extends not only to these organizations, but also to certain key individuals: Grace E. Richardson, formerly Director of Consumer Affairs at Chesebrough-Pond's; Meredith M. Fernstrom, Senior Vice President-Public Responsibility, American Express Company; Peggy H. Haney, Vice President of Consumer Affairs, American Express Company; Daria Sheehan, Manager, Corporate Affairs, Lever Brothers.

Grace Richardson and Meredith Fernstrom were pivotal in helping us obtain financial support for the Conference. Peggy Haney and Daria Sheehan participated actively and fruitfully in the detailed planning of the Conference though, of course, control of the Conference rested with the ACCI Research Committee. Kenneth R. Lightcap, Vice President, Corporate Affairs, Unilever, United States, contributed useful advice. Barbara Slusher, Executive Director of ACCI, handled the business aspects of both Conference and Book punctiliously and expeditiously.

Presidents of ACCI during the planning period for both Conference and Book included Jean Kinsey, Karen P. Goebel, Geraldine Olson, Nancy M. Rudd, Mel Zelenak. All were enthusiastic and helpful supporters of this enterprise. But I speak somewhat ruefully of one of them -- Jean Kinsey. It was she who persuaded me to take on the Chairmanship of the ACCI Research Committee in

1983, a task that has involved considerably more work than I anticipated.

We in ACCI have been well served by the wholehearted support of several Presidents of our co-sponsor, the Association for Consumer Research. The relevant Presidents were Kenneth L. Bernhardt, Jagdish N. Sheth, Peter L. Wright, Russell W. Belk, and Richard J. Lutz.

Let me say "Thank You" to the most important group of all, the 1983-87 ACCI Research Committee. They served three major roles: as Planners of the Conference, Chairs of Conference Sessions, Second-Stage Editors of The Frontier. The members were Monroe P. Friedman, Jean Kinsey, Carole J. Makela, Nancy M. Rudd, Roger M. Swagler, and William L. Wilkie, a former President of the Association for Consumer Research who served as the ACR representative on the ACCI Research Committee. In my career I have chaired many committees. None surpassed this Committee in terms of work (1983-87!!), constructive discussion, felicitous spirit. Like their Chairman, they have perhaps worked more than they expected. I --and you -- owe much to them.

Thanks are due also to my department, the Department of Consumer Economics and Housing at Cornell University. Their contribution has been greater than you may think. For five years (!), on an increasing scale, they furnished secretarial and staff support, first to the planning of the Conference and then, more intensively during the last year, to the preparation of this Book. My own commitment to the Conference and its Book may have been at the expense of projects to which my Department would have attached a higher priority.

Let me express my appreciation of the support given me by my colleagues in Consumer Economics and Housing. Over the 5-year gestation period for both Conference and Book, they have contributed generously with both highly valued counsel and with support. My debt is particularly great to Keith Bryant, Jean Robinson, Jenny Gerner, and Ramona Heck. The arrangements for printing The Frontier were greatly facilitated by the knowing advice and help of Richard Gingras, Assistant Director of Graphics Purchasing, at Cornell.

Finally, I express my deep appreciation of someone whose help on both Conference and Book was indispensable: my Secretary, Patricia Baker. She is a secretary beyond compare: competent in all respects, enthusiastic, uncomplaining even under pressure, foresighted anticipating problems before they occurred, hardworking.

All told, the Conference and its Book have pre-empted 1 and 1/2 years of her professional life. I -- and you -- are deeply in debt to Patricia Baker.

THE SIGNIFICANCE OF THIS VOLUME

The questions come naturally: What have we achieved by the Wingspread Conference and this Book? What, if any, will be their long-run effect? These are questions that only history can answer. But we can record our hopes and expectations with respect to their ultimate impact.

As Conference Chairman and Editor of The Frontier, I turn to this task.

I hope and expect that:

1. This Conference and Book will represent an inflection point with respect to the quantity and quality of research in the consumer interest -- that people will remark that "After The Frontier" consumer policy research "took off";

2. This Conference and Book will establish an intellectual fraternity/sorority of consumer policy researchers whose knowledge of one another, whose knowledge of the others' work and whose easy relations will contribute to the expansion of research in the consumer interest;

3. This Conference and Book will establish an agenda of challenging and important consumer policy issues that will attract the best minds of the next generation;

4. After Wingspread and The Frontier, those in consumer policy, consumer education and consumer affairs will increasingly turn to consumer researchers, both to pose questions in need of answers and in seeking answers to questions posed earlier;

5. We researchers in the consumer interest will have a better understanding -- after Wingspread and The Frontier -- of when to turn and when not to turn to our fellows in adjacent disciplines for answers to questions and for help in our own research;

6. This Conference and Book will help to identify policies, institutions, practices that are in the consumer interest, thus advancing the welfare of all consumers;

7. This Conference and Book will have mapped the "frontier" of research in the consumer interest -- that, as a result of Wingspread and The Frontier, (1) we will know what we know, (2) we will know what we do not know, and (3) we will know what we need to know;

8. Wingspread I will give birth to Wingspread II, III . . . N, all with the same goal of furthering society's movement toward the attainment of the Seven Consumer Rights.

Finally, as a sentimental concession to those privileged to attend Wingspread, I close this First and Last Word by repeating the parting words with which I closed the Wingspread Conference. They come from an old Welch benediction, often used by President Frank Rhodes of Cornell University:

> May the sun shine gently upon your face,
> May the wind be at your back;
> May the road rise to meet you;
> May the Lord hold you in hollow of his hand;
> Until we meet again.

REFERENCES

1. ATLANTIC RICHFIELD COMPANY (1976), Consumerism in the Eighties, Report of a Survey Conducted by Louis Harris Associates, Los Angeles: Atlantic Richfield Company.

2. ASSOCIATION FOR CONSUMER RESEARCH (Annually), Advances in Consumer Research, Provo, Utah: Association for Consumer Research.

3. BLOOM, PAUL N. and RUTH BELK SMITH, eds., (1986), The Future of Consumerism, Lexington, Mass.: Lexington Books.

4. CENTER FOR CONSUMER LAW, (Annually), Proceedings of European Workshops on Consumer Law, Louvain, Belgium: Center for Consumer Law, University of Louvain.

5. CLARK, LINCOLN, ed. (1954), Consumer Behavior, The Dynamics of Consumer Reaction, New York: New York University Press.

6. ________ (1955), Consumer Behavior, Vol. II, The Life Cycle and Consumer Behavior, New York: New York University Press.

7. ________ (1958), Consumer Behavior, Research on Consumer Reactions, New York: Harper.

8. DEACON, RUTH E. and WALLACE E. HUFFMAN, eds., (1986), Home Economics Research, 1887-1987, Proceedings, Ames, Iowa: Iowa State University, College of Home Economics.

9. DENNEY, WILLIAM MICHAEL and ROBERT T. LUND, eds., (1978), Proceedings of the Conference on Research on Consumer Policy, Cambridge, Mass.: Center for Policy Alternatives, Massachusetts Institute of Technology.

10. FOOTE, NELSON N., ed., (1961), Household Decision-Making, New York: New York University Press.

11. IPPOLITO, PAULINE M. and DAVID T. SCHEFFMAN, eds. (1986), Empirical Approaches to Consumer Protection, Washington: Bureau of Economics, Federal Trade Commission.

12. MAYNES, E. SCOTT (1976), Decision-Making For Consumers, An Introduction to Consumer Economics, New York: Macmillan.

13. MITCHELL, ANDREW A. (1978), The Effect of Information on Consumer and Market Behavior, Chicago: American Marketing Association.

14. MORGAN, JAMES N. (1985), "What Is In the Consumer's Interest?" pp. 1-7, in Karen P. Schittgrund, ed., Proceedings, 31st Annual Conference of the American Council on Consumer Interests, March 27-30, Columbia, Missouri: ACCI.

15. MORRIS, RUBY T. and CHARLOTTE S. BRONSON (1969), "The Chaos in Competition As Indicated by Consumer Reports," Journal of Marketing, 33, July, pp. 419-426.

16. NATIONAL CONSUMER COUNCIL, An Introduction to The Findings of the Consumer Concerns Survey, London: National Consumer Council, 1981.

17. PROCEEDINGS OF THE FIRST WORKSHOP ON CONSUMER ACTION RESEARCH, OCTOBER 9-12, 1974 (1974), Berlin: International Institute of Management.

18. PROCEEDINGS OF THE SECOND WORKSHOP ON CONSUMER ACTION RESEARCH, APRIL 9-12, 1975 (1975), Berlin: International Institute of Management.

19. SHELDON, ELEANOR BERNERT, ed. (1973), Family Economic Behavior, Problems and Prospects, Philadelphia: J.P. Lippincott.

20. STAMPFL, RONALD W., ed., (1983), Consumer Science in Institutions of Higher Education, Proceedings of the National Invitational Symposium, July 5-9, 1982, Madison, Wisconsin: University of Wisconsin, School of Family Resources and Consumer Sciences.

21. WHIRLPOOL CORPORATION (1983), America's Search for Quality, Report of A Survey by Research and Forecasts, Inc.,, Benton Harbor, Michigan: Whirlpool Corporation.

KEYNOTE PAPER

Chapter 2

ABOUT THE AUTHOR

Robert J. Lampman has spend much of his long and productive career in the Department of Economics at the University of Wisconsin, exploring various facets of inequality. His 1962 book, Top Wealth-Holders Share of National Wealth dealt with the upper end of the income distribution while his 1984 book on Social Welfare Spending focuses on matters of poverty and its alleviation.

Most relevant for us, Professor Lampman spent the 1962-63 year on the staff of the Council of Economic Advisors in Washington where he ghostwrote President Kennedy's famous Consumer Message proposing Consumer Rights.

JFK'S FOUR CONSUMER RIGHTS: A RETROSPECTIVE VIEW

ROBERT J. LAMPMAN[1]

SUMMARY

This paper tells "the story" of President Kennedy's 1962 address, proposing Four Consumer Rights. Before Kennedy's address, formal consumer representation in the Federal Government was non-existent (except for the Consumer Advisory Council under the National Recovery Act in the 1930's); after Kennedy, some kind of consumer representation has always existed. Lampman's paper describes the political environment in which the President's consumer "message" was given precedence over competing political initiatives and explains how the goals of the consumer movement came to be presented as "rights." The paper also looks for connections between the enunciation of the four consumer rights and subsequent legislative and regulatory actions on behalf of consumers. The author discusses the social benefits and costs of consumer protection. Professor Lampman was the "speech architect" who put together President Kennedy's much remembered consumer message.

* * * *

[1]The following people were helpful to me in preparing this paper: Charles Cavagnaro, Christian Jorges, Stewart Lee, Michael March, E. Scott Maynes, Richard L.D. Morse, Helen E. Nelson, and David Swankin.

Where did President Kennedy's Bill of Consumer Rights come from? What did these rights mean in 1962? What significance have they had since? My credentials for talking about these rights is that I was a participant in the work that led to the March 15, 1962 Special Message on Protecting the Consumer Interest, the first one by a president on this topic [8]. For a little over two years, beginning in the fall of 1961, I was associated with the Council of Economic Advisers (CEA) either as a part-time consultant or as a full-time staff member. During part of that period I served the Consumer Advisory Council and helped to prepare the first and only published report of that Council [6].[2] That was almost twenty-five years ago but, as Maurice Chevalier sang, "I remember it well."

My credentials for a discussion of what has happened in the field of consumer protection since 1963 are not so strong. Since then I have worked largely in the related fields of public finance and labor economics with a special interest in poverty. So what I have to say about recent developments should be thought of as coming from a person interested in but outside the field of consumer economics.

BACKGROUND OF THE 1962 PRESIDENT MESSAGE

In his 1960 campaign JFK promised that, if elected, he would give a high priority to consumer protection issues and would bring consumer representatives into the upper reaches of government.[3] In 1961 steps were taken to reorganize and revitalize several of the independent regulatory agencies. And approximately a year after the election the wheels started to turn to fulfill this promise of 1960. A somewhat reluctant CEA was identified as the home base for what was to become the Consumer Advisory Council and steps were taken to name special assistants for consumer affairs in selected departments and agencies. William Cannon of the Bureau of the Budget was a key figure in developing this pattern of consumer representation as he was later in designing "community action" in the War on Poverty.

Many others were involved in early discussions of the possible directions the Administration might take in consumer protection.

---

[2]A number of other reports were published in later years by successor consumer councils that were not affiliated with the CEA.

[3]Richard L.D. Morse pointed out to me that excerpts of JFK's November 5, 1960 speech on consumers and correspondence between Morse and JFK are to be found in [4, pp. 100-104].

Chairman Walter W. Heller and his fellow CEA member, Kermit Gordon, along with Meyer Feldman of the White House staff, played particularly strong roles. Other people from inside government, such as Wilbur Cohen (Assistant Secretary of Health, Education and Welfare) and Hazel Guffey (Bureau of the Budget), and from outside government, such as Persia Campbell, Helen E. Nelson, Carolyn Ware, and Colston Warne, made important contributions.

The Bureau of the Budget set up an interdepartmental task force to collect and review a "laundry list" of proposals for action on consumer issues. This list included ways to strengthen almost every existing program of consumer protection as broadly defined. Some of the specific items on that list were efficacy-testing of prescription drugs, truth-in-lending, fair packaging and labeling, unit pricing, the metric system of weights and measures, new rules on food additives and food supplements, performance testing of household appliances, publication of more consumer information bulletins by the Government Printing Office, and plans for local ombudsmen and citizens' advice bureaus.

The White House decided to put its weight behind certain of the items on this laundry list and to do so by means of a message to Congress. The development of such a message was, of course, a team effort. Requests went out to members of the afore-mentioned task force and to others for "language" to describe and justify each of the specific proposals selected for presidential backing. Because of this procedure it is right to say that there were many drafters of the message. The last step of the procedure converted the laundry list into a message having historical and thematic context. Michael March, who was Assistant Chief of the Labor and Welfare Division of the Bureau of the Budget, and I started the last step by classifying and organizing the wide range of ideas and concepts that had emerged up to that point.[4]

THE FOUR CONSUMER RIGHTS

The two of us devoted several long meetings over a period of a couple of weeks to "thinking out loud" about an organizing principle or frame for the message. We noted that most of the measures then under current consideration had their historic roots in the two decades preceding World War I, with the establishment of the

---

[4]One document that we found useful was a 1961 publication of the Congressional Committee on Government Operations entitled <u>Consumer Protection Activities of Federal Departments and Agencies</u> [15].

Interstate Commerce Commission in 1886 and the National Bureau of Standards in 1901 and the passage of the Sherman Antitrust Act of 1890, the Pure Food and Drug Act of 1906 and the Clayton Act of 1914. We looked for parallels between governmental promotion of the consumer interest and promotion of worker or farmer interests. We sketched out the types of consumer protection activities then being carried out in federal departments and agencies. We considered alternative ways of classifying such activities, one of which would relate to the stated goals of each program and would point to overlapping and contradictory activities of government. (In this regard we were thinking along the lines of what would later be called the Planning Program Budget System). While thinking in such broad terms we hit upon the idea of consumer <u>rights</u> as distinct from goals--a Bill of Rights, if you will. Under each right we could list specific items from the laundry list.[5]

We identified (1) The Right to Safety--to be protected against the marketing of goods which are hazardous to health or life; (2) The Right to Be Informed--to be protected against fraudulent, deceitful, or grossly misleading information, advertising, labeling, or other practices, and to be given the facts needed to make an informed choice; (3) The Right to Choose--to be assured, wherever possible, of access to a variety of products and services at competitive prices; and in those industries in which competition is not workable and government regulation is substituted, an assurance of satisfactory quality and service at a fair price; and (4) The Right to Be Heard--to be assured that consumer interests will receive full and sympathetic consideration in the formulation of government policy, and fair and expeditious treatment in its administrative tribunals. (This is an abridgement of what appeared in the message. See [8].)

Our draft statement of these four rights was intensively reviewed and redrafted by Kermit Gordon. It then moved on via Chairman Heller to the White House and was reflected in the message as finally sent to the Congress by the President.

Precedent for the rhetorical use of the term "rights" is to be found in the enabling clauses of such landmark statutes as the National Labor Relations Act, the Social Security Act, and the Housing Act, and the G.I. Bill of Rights. However, the consumer

---

[5]March's memory is that it was he who first thought of casting the discussion of terms of "rights." He was led in this direction by earlier experience with similar documentary writing, including some on legislation for veterans.

message was well in advance of the flood of claims for rights and entitlement on behalf of racial and religious minorities, women, mentally ill and handicapped persons, welfare recipients, prisoners, tenants, and even students that were put forward in subsequent legislation. Like some earlier and some later statements, the consumer message, with it vision of a fair society that balances the interests of the consumer with those of the producer, expressed a faith in the integrity and capacity of the federal government to promote economic and social justice.

It is interesting to recall that JFK's boost for the consumer interest was one of only a few moves he made on the domestic agenda of FDR and Harry Truman. He was a disappointment to some of his liberal backers who saw him as unwilling to challenge the conservative coalition in Congress. His narrow margin of victory in 1960 made him hostage to the fear of being identified as anti-business. He was willing to accept heavy criticism from labor and farm groups if he could thereby win business support for the Keynesian-style tax cut which he decided to promote over the strenuous objections of his Republican Secretary of the Treasury. Even the tax cut was seen by Galbraith-type liberals as a sell-out of the alternative expansion strategy of deficit creation via more spending on domestic programs.

By the middle of the 1963 White House planners were assuming that Congress would pass the tax cut soon and that this would "get the economy moving"--to use Kennedy's phrase. They were looking for issues that followed logically from that macroeconomic policy and which would be suitable in the campaign for reelection. Area re-development, manpower retraining, and federal aid to education had some claims, as did the idea of a war on poverty. Other rivals for special attention were the environmental issue of conservation and the issue of safety for consumers and workers. Political advisers assigned heavy weight to the strength of an issue to attract support of independent or swing voters. No selection of campaign issues had been made before the assassination in November. Shortly after that LBJ announced that the flag issue for his 1964 election campaign would be a war on poverty.

ACTION FOLLOWING THE PRESIDENTIAL MESSAGE

In July of 1962 JFK appointed a Consumer Advisory Council. Members of this council were:

Person	Affiliation
Helen Canoyer, Chair	Dean, College of Home Economics, Cornell University

David Angevine	Public Relations Director, Cooperative League of the USA
Persia Campbell	Professor of Economics, Queens College, New York
Stephen M. DuBrul, Jr.	Partner, Lehman Brothers, New York
Mrs. John G. Lee	Past President, League of Women Voters
Edward S. Lewis	Executive Director, Urban League of Greater New York
Walter F. Mondale	Attorney General, State of Minnesota
Richard L.D. Morse	Professor of Consumer Economics, Kansas State University
Helen E. Nelson	Consumer Counsel, State of California
Carolyn E. Ware	Consultant, Vienna, Virginia
Colston E. Warne	President, Consumers Union

This group, which worked with special assistants for consumer affairs in twenty-two departments and agencies, met regularly in 1962 and 1963. President Johnson dropped the CEA out of the picture as he and succeeding presidents used the alternative device for consumer representation of a Special Assistant to the President. In the early 1970s Congress considered but never adopted the idea of an executive department of consumer affairs (or protection).

It should be noted that the expression of the right to be heard was one of the more radical parts of the consumer message. It was based on the notion that the consumer interest tends to get lost in departments designed to express a producer interest such as those of Labor, Agriculture, and Commerce and even in the independent regulatory agencies addressed to the problems of specific industries such as transportation and banking. Consumer advocates in those days were keenly aware of the tendency for regulatory agencies to be captured by those regulated and for ostensibly pro-consumer legislation to be perverted to serve pro-business ends. There was a clear understanding that a principal barrier to the realization of the consumer rights to safety, to be informed, and to choose was government itself, as distinct from business. What was needed, in the view of several members of the Consumer Advisory Council, was a shift in the structure of government to make it more responsive to the priorities of consumers. It is still a matter of controversy whether the consumer right to be heard requires a separate executive department or other structural change [12]. In retrospect, it seems that some lasting advance in consumer representation in the government was accomplished during the Kennedy years.

Congress did, in 1962, act favorably on some of the legislative proposals endorsed by JFK, most notably the Kefauver-Harris drug efficacy amendments. Later Congresses enacted other laws urged by JFK or his Consumer Advisory Council. These included the Douglas truth-in lending law, the Hart fair packaging and labelling law and several laws involving hazardous materials and appliances. Some writers speak of a "consumer decade" which ended in 1972 with the adoption in that year of the Consumer Products Safety Act. This Act set up an omnibus commission to enforce several laws, three of which were adopted in 1966, 1967, and 1968 [13]. Other consumer laws of the decade were the Cigarette Labeling and Advertising Act of 1965 and the National Traffic and Motor Vehicle Safety Act of 1966. Other writers identify "social regulation" as broader than the consumer legislation listed above and including laws of the same decade dealing with civil rights, environmental pollution, occupational safety, and energy. Contemporary observers seem to have difficulty in determining whether the partial deregulation in the 1970s and 1980s of markets for transportation, financial services, communication, and, most recently, energy is a reversal of a trend or merely an in-course correction by the so-called social regulation movement. Those who support the latter idea tend to emphasize that deregulation was first emphasized by President Carter and Senator Edward Kennedy. As I indicated above, consumer advocates in 1962 had strong beliefs about the need for certain kinds of deregulation.

Maynes asserts that JFK's consumer rights have been "...repeatedly and widely invoked as justifications for various consumer protection measures" [10, p. 99]. However, it is hard to know how much credit to give to JKF for the substantial list of pro-consumer laws of the consumer decade. The possibility that such laws would have been enacted without any leadership from a president is supported by the theory that the precondition for safety legislation is consumer outrage over a tragic event, followed by the effort of a strategically placed legislator to focus attention on a specific legislative remedy as responsive to that event. Thus, the Kefauver-Harris amendments passed only after the occurrence of the thalidomide tragedies [11, Chapter 1]. Recent developments suggest that it is possible to mobilize consumer energy in some cases by dramatizing the potential benefits from deregulation. My own view is that JFK did pave the way for at least some of the legislative activity that followed his consumer message.

However, it is useful to think of a three-link chain of policy making, from presidential announcement of right or need, to legislation on specific wrongs to be righted, and then to still more specific administrative rules. One critic notes that:

> In 1962, President Kennedy managed to capture the spirit of the newborn (consumer) movement and embody its tenets in his widely noted presidential proclamation of a Consumer Bill of Rights... Despite their overt simplicity, so comprehensive was their thrust that the four spanned all causes of relief that the consumers have since or are ever likely to demand... In essence, the Consumer Bill of Rights was a bill of principles rather than a blueprint for practice. None of the four enumerated rights was self-executing dogma. Yet the proclamation set forth a comprehensive, albeit generalized, platform of consumer rights and demands that now had been legitimized by presidential announcement. Lawmakers were thus faced with the challenge to design equitable formulas for safeguarding and enforcing the now acknowledged rights [2, p. 185].

Another critic emphasizes that even the Congress paints only with a broad brush and that "Many of the consumer laws enacted in the 1960s (and early 1970s) consisted essentially of the legislative naming of wrongs to be righted. To the regulators were left the remedies" [11, p. 138].

All of this suggests that in order to evaluate the consumer message we need to consider not only the legislation but also the specific rules which followed. I will return to that later, but first I want to respond to another line of criticism, one that is implicit in a resolution by the International Organization of Consumer Unions, namely, that the JKF message should have included two more rights, specifically the rights to redress, to consumer education, and to a healthy environment [7, 10].[6] A similar expansion of the list of consumer rights is to be found in measures adopted by the European Economic Community [3].[7]

SHOULD OTHER CONSUMER RIGHTS BE ADDED?

There can be no doubt that consumers who are denied either the right to be informed or the right to safety should have the right to redress of such denials. It is axiomatic in law that a right granted to one party imposes an obligation on some other person. Rights do not exist except by their remedies and a right is mere rhetoric if no one can or will enforce it either by private litigation or public prosecution.

Thus a consumer who buys a product that does not conform to standards or perform as advertised should have a way to get restitution of the purchase price. This could be added to the JFK message either as a separate right or as a corollary of the right to be informed.

JFK's message did say that consumers had a Right to Safety, but failed to say that they have a Right to Redress for damages arising out of use of an unsafe good or service. It is arguable that such redress is a way to assure that only safe goods will be produced and is hence a step in implementing the right of safety. Alternatively, it may be argued that such redress is better classified under the heading of "social security" than under "consumer protection". Courts, through case by case interpretation of the law of contract and the law of torts, can give redress to consumers and at the same time create a financial incentive to produce a safer good. JFK may have had no influence on court thinking, but it is

---

[6]Stewart Lee has pointed out to me that President Nixon identified "the right to register dissatisfaction and have a complaint heard and weighed" on October 30, 1969 and that President Ford recognized "the right to consumer education" on November 19, 1975. I do not discuss the latter right in this paper. Apparently the right to a healthy environment was added by IOCU.

[7]The Consultative Assembly of the Council of Europe adopted a 28-article "Consumer Protection Charter" in 1973. The Council of Ministers in 1975 and 1981 adopted resolutions which grant consumers five basic rights, namely, the right to protection of health and safety, to protection of economic interests, to redress of damages, to information and education, and to representation (the right to be heard) [3, pp. 176-197].

interesting to note that his message was coincident with a marked shift by courts in favor of the consumer. This shift is most clear in the imposition of strict liability rules on producers and sellers which was first enunciated by Justice Robert Trainor of the California Supreme Court and adopted in 1965 in the Federal Restatement of Torts (2nd), Section 402A [1]. Such rules have been applied across a wide range of markets from automobiles, household appliances, and asbestos, to medical services.

The importance of this shift in the burden of proof should not be understated in any historical account of advances in consumer well-being. However, there is a question of whether this policy on redress should be thought of as a measure of consumer protection or as a measure of income support. Perhaps drawing a line between the two turns on one's view of the effectiveness of redress in inducing preventive safety measures.

It is relevant here to note that workers' compensation statutes express the theory that giving workers a clear and certain route to payment for damages arising out of work accidents will not only spread the cost of accidents equitably but will also, by differential insurance charges, lead to employer efforts to create a safer work place. The alleged ineffectiveness of workers compensation in regard to prevention is often cited as a reason for the enactment of the federal Occupational Safety and Health Act of 1970. It can be said that something akin to "consumer compensation" is found in laws providing cash or health care benefits to the victims of nonwork-related accidents or illnesses. Such benefits are provided by federal disability insurance and the disability component of Supplemental Security Income and by Medicare and Medicaid and voluntary health insurance. By tradition these forms of redress for workers and for consumers are considered under the heading of income support or social security rather than consumer protection. It is a fine line that divides these two fields.

In the same spirit one may justify the exclusion from the consumer message of a right to a healthy environment. Environmental threats were not yet well understood by the general public in 1962, although Rachel Carson's Silent Spring was published in that year. But even for a later year one can argue that environmental factors are subsumed by the right to safety as only one of numerous causes of potentially unsafe food or other consumables. However, the protection of the quality of air and water starts from a rather different basis than protection of most marketable goods. We, as individuals, do not customarily buy ambient air and water in the way we do meat or bicycles. Pollution may be supplied to us without our requesting it and we benefit from our neighbors' efforts to control it. This public goods character of the environment is, of course, found in other forms of collective consumption, including law and order and national defense. Most collective consumption is by convention left out of the field of consumer protection. By that rather mysterious statement I have reference to the fact that the curriculum in economics and in legal studies seems generally to reserve a special place for the study of environmental issues. But as all of you who are academics know, curriculum design is the most divisive of topics.

Social Benefits and Social Costs of Consumer Protection

To evaluate the merits of a piece of consumer protection legislation, one needs to consider the specific administrative rules or court decisions that give concrete meaning to the statute. Then one has to determine, with reference to each rule, whether or not there is an achievement of a recognizable goal. Then one has to ask whether the social benefit of such goal achievement is greater or less than whatever social costs are generated by the rule.

JFK's four consumer rights are relevant to the identification of goals and social benefits. The consumer right to safety is more substantive than the other three. It is aimed at the goal of reducing such measurable bads as consumer injury, illness, and fatality resulting from goods purchased. The counterfactual is a world with less as opposed to more safety rules, all other things remaining the same. Identifying and measuring the goal achievement of such regulation on the number and market (or other) value of such bads prevented is difficult, but not so difficult as in the case of the rights to be informed, to choose, and to be heard.

The rights to information and choice are presumably related to the goal of improving the level of consumer satisfaction from a given level of expenditure. Here again the comparison is between a world with and without a specific rule. One needs to take account of the fact that safety rules may have a negative effect on the right to choice. But measuring changes in the level of consumer satisfaction takes one into the realm of the subjective and hypothetical.

The right to be heard refers to the process of policy-making and suggests that consumer participation will change the rules and that those rule changes will produce more goal achievement with respect to the rights to information and choice and safety. Evaluation of the change in consumer participation is then more remote from the ultimate benefits to consumers than evaluation of the other changes but the problems of quantification are not different unless one wants to claim that such participation is an end in itself rather like the right to vote and is hence beyond verification as instrumental of any higher purpose. Such a claim makes the right to be heard what Ronald Dworkin calls a "right in the strong sense," by which he means a right which it is wrong for the government to deny to a person even though it would be in the general interest to do so [5, Chs. 7, 12].

With regard to the social costs of a consumer protection rule, the methodology is the same for all four rights. These costs include the resources used up in developing, enforcing, and complying with the rule plus the excess burden of any price changes arising from the rule, and what can be called indirect or side effect costs on willingness of producers to work, invest, or introduce new technologies.

A final step in evaluation of a rule calls for a comparison of the social benefits and the social costs that flow from the rule. But each evaluator will tend to put different weights on the several types of benefits and costs. As Barton puts it with respect to the ex ante evaluation or a rule:

> In sum, the desirability of regulation is a function of projected immediate and long-term benefits balanced against correlative costs, tempered by due regard to enforcement costs and probable alternative behavior were regulation to be imposed. A conscious choice of values must be made in deciding how to weight each factor, including the primacy of individual or societal interests, and who in particular should bear the brunt or benefits of regulation [2, p. 191]. For an essay on benefits and costs in a related field, see [9].

While a full evaluation which ends up with a single number for a benefit-cost ratio is seldom developed, more general use is made of cost-effectiveness comparisons of alternative rules aimed at a particular level of achievement of a particular specified goal.

Benefit-cost analysis is viewed by many policy-makers across the broad field of social regulation as unacceptable because it appears to put the burden of proof on the advocate of a rule, it places a premium on quantification, and it relies on numerous assumptions about what causes what. But the broad method of economists in approaching evaluation has gained ground. Pertschuk, the former Chairman of the Federal Trade Commission, says he was gradually persuaded by his work at the Commission that economists asked questions that needed to be asked but that lawyers and consumer advocates did not ask. These include, he says,

> What do you think you are accomplishing with this rule; who will benefit, who will pay? What else will happen as a result of this rule? Who among competitors will be the winners and who the losers? In curing this market place failure, what others may you inadvertently cause, and what healthy market signals will you distort?
> Is there a less intrusive, less costly way to remedy the problem? [11, p. 138].

SUMMARY COMMENT

JFK's four consumer rights emerged out of unique political circumstances. These included (1) a presidential campaign promise to the consumer movement (2) a process of surveying currently live proposals to advance the consumer interest, and (3) a search for new departures that merited presidential sponsorship. The four rights amount to a way to define and limit the field of consumer protection and to identify legitimate policy choices vis à vis consumer markets. They endorse the value to the consumer of a competitive market with special modifications to assure adequate information and protection on safety grounds. They give cautious support to the idea that consumers need to have more political influence to offset the influence of entrenched producers in making government policy. Thus, they reflect the idea that consumers can suffer from government failure as well as market failure.

This declaration of rights has been widely used for pedagogic purposes. It probably has had some influence in favor of the passage of a number of statutes, including some that deregulate, in the years since 1962. Scott Maynes tells us that JFK's Consumer Rights have become the ideology ("aims that constitute a sociopolitical program") or rallying cry for the consumer movement the world over.

JFK's assertion of four consumer rights was thought of in 1962 as a guide to future action in pursuit of the consumer interest. Now it may also be read, twenty-five years later, as a guidepost appraising what in fact happened in the name of consumer protection over that period. These rights have been useful to evaluators of specific rules by helping them identify socially beneficial goals. These consumer rights are parallel with and sometimes overlap other rights. Examples are the right to security against the risks of income loss, and ofsecurity vis-à-vis irregular and extraordinary expenditure; the right to goods, such as a healthy environment, that can only be purchased collectively. Moreover, the four consumer rights are to some extent contradictory in the sense that one can sometimes be advanced only at the expense of another, e.g., more safety may mean less choice. This means that evaluators have to assign weights to the several goals.

In the same sense, evaluators must identify and seek ways to minimize the social costs of enforcement and compliance as well as undesirable side effects. One can, in retrospect, criticize the statement of the four rights for not being more explicit about the need for careful design of consumer protection measures to take account of the social costs involved, and for failing to specify the need for routine collection of data for use in cost-effectiveness comparisons of alternative ways to achieve the goals implicit in the rights [14].

REFERENCES

1. AMERICAN LAW INSTITUTE (1965), Restatement (Second) of Torts. Topic 5, 402A, Also see 1977. Topic 4, 552C. Washington.

2. BARTON, BABETTE B. (1976), "Private Redress for Consumers: Redress or Rape." In Robert N. Katz, (ed.), Protecting the Consumer Interest: Private Initiative and Public Response. Cambridge, MA: Ballinger Publishing Co.

3. BOURGOIGNIE, THIERRY M. (1984), "Consumer Law and the European Community." In Thierrry M. Bourgoignie and David M. Trubeck, Consumer Law, Common Markets, and Federalism in Europe and the U.S. Madison, WI, mimeo.

4. COUNCIL ON CONSUMER INFORMATION (1961), Proceedings. Seventh Annual Conference. St. Louis, MO. [CCI was the early name of ACCI.]

5. DWORKIN, RONALD (1977), Taking Rights Seriously. London: Gerald M. Duskworth and Co.

6. EXECUTIVE OFFICE OF THE PRESIDENT (1963), Consumer Advisory Council First Report, October, Washington, D.C.: Government Printing Office.

7. INTERNATIONAL ORGANIZATION OF CONSUMER UNIONS (1984), Consumer Rights.

8. KENNEDY, PRESIDENT JOHN F. (1962), Special Message on Protecting the Consumer Interest, March 15, Washington, D.C.: Government Printing Office.

9. LAMPMAN, ROBERT J. (1984), Social Welfare Spending: Accounting for Changes from 1950 to 1978. Orlando, Florida: Academic Press.

10. MAYNES, E. SCOTT (1979), "Consumer Protection: the Issues, and Consumer Protection: Corrective Measures." Journal of Consumer Policy, vol. 3, No's. 2 and 3 + 4.

11. PERTSCHUK, MICHAEL (1982), Revolt Against Regulation: the Rise and Pause of the Consumer Movement. Berkeley: University of California Press.

12. ROTHSTEIN, LAURA F. (1986), "Presentation of the Consumer Viewpoint in Federal Administrative Proceedings--What is the Best Alternative?" University of Pittsburgh Law Review, 41:565-594.

13. SCHWARTZ, TERESA M. (1982), "The Consumer Products Safety Commission: a Flawed Product of the Consumer Decade." George Washington Law Review, 51:32-95.

14. RIVLIN, ALICE M. (1971), Systematic Thinking for Social Action. Washington, D.C.: The Brookings Institution.

15. U.S. CONGRESS (1961), Consumer Protection Activities of Federal Departments and Agencies. 8th Report of the Committee on Government Operations. Washington: Government Printing Office.

THE RIGHT

OF

SAFETY

Chapter 3

ABOUT THE AUTHOR

Jennifer L. Gerner is Associate Professor in the Department of Consumer Economics and Housing at Cornell University. An economist, she received her Ph.D. from the University of Wisconsin in 1974.

Professor Gerner's research interests center on product warranties, the problems of two parent-households, and of course, product safety. Relevant to this paper, Professor Gerner teaches a course on "Consumer and the Law." Gerner has served as Director of Graduate Studies in her Department since 1984.

PRODUCT SAFETY: A REVIEW

JENNIFER L. GERNER

SUMMARY

This paper maps out the frontier of knowledge on product safety. It focuses particularly on the frontier between how much safety we have already achieved and how much more we might want. Written by an economist, the paper reviews the economics of product safety. It then goes on to assess, through a review of the relevant theoretical and empirical literature, the effects of the main levers for achieving safety: product liability law in its various regimes, regulation, and the exercise of care by consumers. The author points out that no one has undertaken analyses that simultaneously take account of product liability and safety regulation. An underresearched topic is the way the courts function in implementing product liability laws.

This paper does not deal with data on safety achieved, either as compared with other countries or with the U.S. in earlier times.

* * * *

Provision of product safety is a complicated business. Since President Kennedy proposed the "Consumer's Bill of Rights" in 1962 asserting the consumer's right to safe products, a considerable amount of policy attention has focused on mechanisms by which this might be attained. Some of this attention has culminated in federal and state legislation aimed at intervention in private market decisions on matters of safety. It has ranged from mandatory testing of drugs to setting safety standards for consumer products and also safe work places to requiring seat belts that be used in automobiles. More recently policy attention has focused on liability issues.

Despite these new regulatory initiatives, there remains the question of the extent to which safety has been assured to consumers. This paper examines what we know about safety, both theoretically and empirically. Despite the considerable theoretical literature empirically we remain relatively uninformed about how much safety there is, how much is enough, and how well various techniques for achieving product safety perform.

A considerable and diverse literature exists dealing with product safety. Cornell, Noll, and Weingast [12] provide an excellent overview of the history and institutional setting in which product safety regulation occurs. Others have provided detailed descriptions of the most prominent agencies--the Food and Drug Administration [24, 26, 70], the Consumer Product Safety Commission [3, 25, 48, 68], and the Occupational Safety and Health Administration [69]. In this paper I will not deal in detail with the institutional background except when it is relevant to other issues.

A considerable literature also exists on cost-benefit assessments of particular standards [38, 40, 64). Robert Crandall's paper in this volume deals with these studies. I will refer to them only in passing.

THE ECONOMICS OF PRODUCT SAFETY

Accidents happen. Because we cannot fully specify the properties of materials and human interaction with materials, consumer products sometimes fail in a way that causes injury. Even if the appropriate safety features are built into the products, it is unrealistic to believe that all accidents involving consumer products can be prevented.

Nevertheless, there are some accidents that are probably preventable. The extent to which consumer products are safe can be controlled by two means: (1) consumers taking additional care in the use of products and (2) manufacturers introducing safety features into the products. Both of these actions are costly. If consumers are to be careful, they need information about the proper use of the product and of its potential hazards. Using the product carefully may necessitate additional time or inconvenience. For the firm, building additional safety features into the product is costly. It may require research into hazards associated with the product or into alternative technologies. It may also require additional parts or equipment to assure safety.

The problem for the economist is to identify the level of safety features and consumer care that is most efficient, simultaneously minimizing the cost of accidents and the cost of accident prevention.[1] Since specifying the most efficient level of safety features, consumer care, and accidents is often difficult, the economist searches for a system which, when it operates, yields the most efficient level of safety and accidents. When there are alternative ways of assuring product safety, the efficient solution will be the one that requires the fewest resources.

Injury as a result of the operation of a consumer product has consequences for the distribution of economic well being as well. When product safety issues are discussed, the distributional consequences are not always explicitly examined. But they are central to the concern for safe products. Should a particular consumer be forced to bear the cost of an unlikely injury or death caused by a consumer product? Or should the producer of that product be forced to provide compensation to the consumer? If the producer provides compensation, this is equivalent to imposing a mandatory insurance policy on all purchasers of the product. The price of the product, as well as the output will reflect the extent of the insurance built into the price of the product. Thus all consumers will bear a part of the cost [29]. Much of the current policy debate over the reform of the tort system focuses on the compensation aspects of liability suits rather than on the incentives set up by such suits.

In the research on questions of product safety, there is analysis of a variety of mechanisms in place or that might be put in place that have an impact on the extent of product safety in the market. These include (1) the liability system that is part of tort law, (2) direct regulation of product safety through setting standards, (3) requiring testing and disclosure, (4) banning products completely, and (5) a variety of voluntary action that might be taken in the private market. The remainder of this paper is devoted to an overview of each of these mechanisms.

---

[1]A number of issues arise here that I will not deal with except tangentially. Among them are the problems of valuing life or loss due to injury. Although this is an extremely important empirical issue when trying to determine the actual level of product safety that is optimal, it is dealt with extensively elsewhere. See, for example, Michael Jones-Lee, ed., <u>The Value of Life and Safety</u> [41].

PRODUCT SAFETY AND PRODUCT LIABILITY: THE THEORY

One technique for achieving safe products is the liability system. Most of the economic work which considers the impact of liability rules on product safety is theoretical in nature. Theoretical treatment of the economics of product safety through the tort system begins with Coase [10]. The possibility that a product fails in a way that causes injury introduces an externality into an otherwise simple market transaction. This idea is further developed by McKean [47], Calabresi [6, 7, 8] and others [5, 42] who examine market behavior under various liability rules. McKean puts it best when he writes, "Alternative [property] right assignments may have different impacts on equity and, since there are transaction costs, different impacts on production processes and costs, insurance carried, the allocation of resources among uses, and the options open to consumers" [47, p. 612]. The focus of this research is to understand the implications on market outcomes of various liability assignments. This has been undertaken in the context of an apparent shift toward strict liability and away from negligence during the decade of the 1960s and early 1970s.[2]

McKean does not set out a formal model of products liability, but he does identify the fundamental elements of an analysis of market behavior under three conditions: (1) caveat emptor, (2) producer liability with defect, and (3) producer liability without defect. He argues that under caveat emptor the consumer always has the option of "hiring producers to make safer products and issue warnings and instructions" via the market mechanisms. Particular consumers might suffer disappointments and injuries. To the extent that these disappointments occur to many customers, the market provides a mechanism by which consumers can turn to alternative producers. Thus one would expect consumers to pay lower prices for less safe goods and higher prices for safer goods. Moreover, consumers have knowledge of and control over the use to which they put the product. To the extent that consumer actions themselves affect product safety, the caveat emptor approach gives consumers incentives to use the product carefully at minimum cost.

McKean recognizes the difficulties associated with consumer acquisition of information about products. He notes, "With high

---

[2]McKean provides a historical overview of tort law treatment of liability. Recent popular discussion again has focused on liability issues. George Priest's paper in this volume [Ch. 32] deals with liability in general. Here I focus on liability only because it is central to understanding the research dealing with product safety.

[information] costs, potential buyers settle for relatively little information and either forego exchanges that might be mutually advantageous or accept risks that would be rejected if information costs were lower." [47, p. 619] Alternatively, he suggests that if information about the product is sufficiently costly--as it might be with new, changing, or complex products, or items that consumers do not buy frequently--a case might be made for a different liability assignment, such as producer liability with defect.

McKean identifies several effects on the market that would occur as the liability system moved from a consumer liability to a producer liability system. He predicts that there would be more court cases and court costs. This would arise since under caveat emptor the possibility of consumer compensation is not present while under producer liability some court determination of the presence of defects and the extent of the injury must be made. Under producer liability there is the possibility of moral hazard, leading consumers to exercise less care, resulting in an increased accident rate would rise. This would lead producers to turn increasingly to insurance. Since adjusting insurance premiums to reflect the safety features of the products would be difficult, some of the incentives for production of safe products would be lost. Consumers, compensated for losses due to product defect, would be less reluctant to purchase unsafe products. But, because the insurance against injury is tied to the purchase of the product, the price of the more hazardous products would rise relative to the safer products. Thus there would be a shift toward safer products.

Subsequent theoretical work examining the impact of various liability rules on the market has formalized this model, examining the impact of variations in assumptions on the market outcomes.[3] Nevertheless, the broad outlines of the liability model identified in McKean remain intact.

---

[3]Extensive subsequent work has provided formal models of the market consequences of various liability arrangements with various amounts of information available. This work began with Brown [4] who offered a formal model of liability with various standards of care required by the court. Diamond [16], Diamond and Mirrlees [17], and Green [28] have all offered formal models of liability law, examining the impact that the standard of care has for the optimal liability rules under various assumptions about the distribution of accident costs. None of these models are explicitly developed for the case of product liability, although clearly they are meant to apply to such cases. Cooter, Kornhauser, and Lane [12] modify the model by allowing for precedent setting behavior by courts.

It was Oi [52] who developed the model of product liability that deals explicitly with product safety. In Oi's model a consumer must choose a product for which there are various levels of risk. The full price of the product includes the expected value of the cost associated with injury. In his analysis Oi assumes the consumer is fully informed about the risk associated with the product and about the cost arising from an accident. In addition, product risks are assumed to be exogenous to consumers' actions as well as producers' actions, although products vary with respect to the degree of risk. Oi shows that under a regime of consumer liability there will be a positive demand for both risky and less risky products. A ban of the riskier product will reduce accident cost but not necessarily increase welfare since some consumers would have preferred the riskier product available at a lower price.

Under a regime of producer liability, the producer is required to offer a tied sale that includes the product itself plus insurance against accident costs. Oi shows that under some conditions, in particular when the average loss for all consumers is less than the loss incurred by the marginal consumer, safer products will no longer be produced. In addition, there is a redistribution of income inherent in the change to producer liability, shifting income away from consumers with low accident costs and toward consumers with high accident costs.

Although Oi does not formally incorporate the possibility of consumer care into his model,[4] he notes that safety may be partially the outcome of consumer activities. In his discussion of the role of regulatory activity he implies that in his view the liability system is better equipped to handle the problem of product safety in part because of the role of consumers in taking care.

Oi's model adopts a number of assumptions, most particularly, that all the parties are fully informed. This assumption will lead to the optimal level of safety and output. Goldberg [23] criticizes Oi's model on these grounds. Subsequent models of liability have incorporated various sorts of limits on the amount of information available to various parties.

Spence [65] casts the model in a signalling framework and specifies consumers who underestimate failure probabilities. In his

---

[4]As noted earlier, subsequent work has focused on theoretically modelling the impact on the market of various liability rules when safety is not fully exogenous, but rather under the control of the injurer or the injured. See Green [28] for one such model.

framework safety is undersupplied by the market, assuming risk-neutral consumers. This outcome can be corrected by imposing producer liability. When consumers are risk averse, a more complicated liability system is needed that includes producer liability to the consumer and also producer liability to the state.

Epple and Raviv [21] come to a similar conclusion. They show that no single liability rule will universally assure optimal safety and output. Rather, the particular rule of choice will depend on the amount of information available, the market structure of the industry in question, and the extent to which insurance is available.

Polinsky and Rogerson [59] also introduce the possibility of market power into the model,[5] showing that when consumers are risk neutral, underestimate the risk, and there is no market power, producer liability leads to the optimal level of safety and output. When there is market power and consumers do not underestimate the risk, then caveat emptor, strict liability and negligence are equally capable of reaching the optimal level of safety and output. Finally, if there are consumer misperceptions of the risk, and market power, some mixed system is necessary. Such a system would use strict liability if market power is not too great, but negligence when market power is large. Introducing the possibility that consumers can affect the probability of accident complicates this analysis because consumers who misperceive the risk may not take the optimal level of care. The comparison across liability rules remains correct, however.

These models are important in identifying the impact of liability rules and the predicting how product safety might be affected should liability rules change. However, many salient aspects of the real liability system that are not yet incorporated into these models.

The liability system is part of Common Law. Although there is some legislative authority for some aspects of the liability system, much of it is based on precedent. Indeed, until recently changes in the location of liability occurred exclusively as a result of changing legal interpretations manifested through court decisions. Thus there is a great deal of uncertainty as to how courts interpret standards of care, negligence, and so on. How court behavior affects the

---

[5]Market power may play an important role in determining industry response to both changes in the liability system. Market structure may partially explain industry attitudes toward standards as well. This is discussed in more detail in a later section of this paper.

liability system has been treated theoretically only by Cooter, Kornhauser, and Lane [11].

The liability system varies from state to state. The decisions in one state may have some influence on other states, but there remain considerable variation across states. This diversity of treatment of liability from state to state juxtaposed against national markets introduces the possibility that firms and consumers may be misinformed about the liability rules they face. It also provides the opportunity for strategic behavior by both firms and consumers. What impact this might have on the amount of safety available is unknown.

In most product liability models the amount of the liability is generally shown to be equal to the actual losses experienced.[6] Such losses presumably include the economic loss, including medical bills and lost wages, as well as the monetary value of any inconvenience, pain or suffering that might have occurred. But real liability awards often include punitive damages as well. The impact of a liability exceeding the actual loss is not explicitly taken into account in the liability models. It should be straightforward to introduce this modification.

PRODUCT SAFETY AND PRODUCT LIABILITY: EMPIRICAL EXAMINATION

One objection that could be made to this relatively large body of theoretical work is that it focuses on identifying the relatively simple liability rules that will yield optimal product safety and consumer care. It pays little attention to whether the liability system in fact operates as the models suggest. There is very little research, either theoretical or empirical, assessing how liability rules affect the care taken by risk averse firms. Nor has much research been examined on how care taken by consumers and firms be evaluated by the courts. No attention is given to the effects of various liability rules on product innovation.[7] Little empirical work has been done concerning the income distribution consequences of various liability rules. Although the role of liability insurance is recognized in this literature, little attention has been paid to the impact of insurance on safety when premiums are not experience

---

[6]Only Spence's model suggests that the liability should exceed the loss the consumer experiences. See the above discussion.

[7]This contrasts with the extensive empirical investigations examining the impact of regulation on product innovation.

rated. In the same vein there has been little empirical work evaluating the operation of the liability system. This is particularly surprising in view of the intense public debate currently in progress over tort reform [20].

Proposals for reform currently being considered in the Congress would have several important effects on the liability system. They would make the liability system a matter of Federal legislation, eliminating differential treatments across states. Several of the proposals would provide for a no fault compensation system where injured parties could waive their rights to sue in exchange for relatively speedy compensation, restricted to economic losses. Other proposals would cap liability awards under most circumstances. These proposals are likely to have important effects on product safety, although empirically we have little evidence to suggest what these effects might be. There are six studies which shed some empirical light on some of these issues.

The most comprehensive descriptive study available was that of the Interagency Task Force on Product Liability in 1975 [31]. Ascertaining that existing data were unsatisfactory, the Interagency Task Force undertook a study of liability decisions in eight states that had generated a substantial number of post-1965 reported products liability decisions. In each case studied injuries were alleged to have been sustained as a result of a defective product. The data, covering 655 cases, provide information on (1) the product involved, (2) the court in which the case was tried, (3) the parties involved, and (4) the disposition of the case. The data show an increase between 1965 and 1976 in the number of reported cases and in the total damages awarded in each of the eight states. These increases conform to McKean's predictions of what should happen as the liability system moves from a regime of consumer liability to producer liability.

While the data of the Interagency Task Force make a modest beginning, they do not provide enough information to reveal reliably the impact of either producer or consumer liability on product safety. The reasons are straightforward. Most cases never go to verdict. Even if they do, they may not be reported. Thus, the extent to which these data are representative of the functioning of the liability system over time is not clear. In addition, these data provide no information about the nature of the product defects that generated the liability cases in the first place.

A much more comprehensive empirical study is that of Danzon [14] who reviews a 1974 sample of medical malpractice cases[8] from California hospitals in which negligence might reasonably have been found. Fewer than 10% of these actually generated a liability claim. Danzon examined court records of these cases, and found that the legal system, as it operates in medical malpractice, conforms roughly to what is expected under a model of liability of the sort suggested above. Danzon was unable to determine how much malpractice was avoided as a result of the liability system. But her evidence suggests that the system is cost effective if it reduces incidents of malpractice by 20%.

Some evidence on how no-fault systems compare with a tort liability system is provided by Landes [37] in her study of the adoption of no-fault systems in automobile accidents. Between 1971 and 1976 sixteen states adopted some kind of no-fault system for automobile insurance, the systems varying in the extent to which they limited tort liability.

The liability model predicts that restricting tort liability will result in more automobile accidents. Modifying the liability model, Landes shows that compulsory insurance offsets the desirable effect of tort liability in reducing accidents. On the other hand, Landes found that the restricting tort liability with a no fault systems substantially increases accident losses, using fatal accidents as a measure of the loss. Her empirical investigation confirmed the expected effect of compulsory insurance--that it increased losses.

A similar natural experiment arose in the case of Outer Continental Shelf (OCS) oil leasing. The Outer Continental Shelf Lands Act of 1978 makes firms responsible strictly liable for damages arising from oil spills. Opaluch and Grigalunas [54] argue that the strict liability rule should increase the bid price for offshore leases. An examination of the December 1979 lease sale in the North Atlantic (Georges Bank) confirms their expectations.

Two empirical studies provide some evidence on the extent to which the assumptions of the liability model are met. The first is a study done by Eads and Reuter [19]. They examine the impact of products liability and product safety regulation on the organization of firms. This is a case study, examining seven firms chosen for

---

[8]The separate literature dealing with medical malpractice is not discussed here. Danzon's work is reviewed because it provides one of the few examples of a comprehensive empirical examination of a liability issue.

their obvious organizational responses to product safety regulation. It is difficult to generalize from seven firms. Further, Eads and Reuter do not undertake a statistical analysis. Nevertheless, their report suggests that products liability cases are often handled by the legal sections of firms with little communication between the legal and product design offices. They conclude that the firms they examined made little connection between products liability and safety design. If liability rules are to play an important part in assuring product safety, such communication is crucial.

In the second study Wittman [71] examines how the behavior of juries changes as liability rules change. In November 1975 the California system of negligence was changed from with contributory negligence to comparative negligence. Under contributory negligence the plaintiff had to prove that the defendant was negligent <u>and</u> that the plaintiff was not contributorily negligent. Under the comparative negligence rule the plaintiff needs only to show that the defendant was negligent. The award is then apportioned across the two parties in proportion to the relative negligence of each party.

Using data from 582 civil cases involving rear end automobile accidents in California between 1974 and 1976, Wittman finds juries to be sensitive to the liability rules. Furthermore, jury behavior seems to be consistent across cases, and negotiated out-of-court settlements are consistent with jury behavior. This conclusion is congruent with the Danzon study of medical malpractice cases which reported that jury awards are proportional to actual economic loss.

It is unfortunate that there has been so little empirical research on how the liability system works. Current public policy affecting product safety is largely focused on liability <u>rules</u> and how they might be changed. The theoretical work laying out optimal liability rules and examining the impact of liability assignment on safety and output does not provide much guidance about how effective liability rules are in the real world in assuring product safety, particularly as compared with alternative mechanisms for obtaining safe products. Since much of the current policy debate focuses on the incentives the liability system sets up for product safety, informed policy making requires considerable attention to this issue. Danzon has provided a model worthy of emulation in other areas of product safety.

Wittman's study of jury awards, taken with Danzon's overview of awards in medical malpractice cases, is reassuring. If liability assignment is to matter in determining the amount of product safety available in the market, the incentives set up by the liability assignment must be the ones we expect. Not only must the liability awards be the ones we expect, but firms must respond to these awards. The research of Eads and Reuter suggests, however, that the internal organization of firms may not allow the liability incentives to feed into the design process. This is an alarming result which, if supported in further research, will limit the impact of liability rules on product safety. These studies only begin the inquiry into what difference liability rules in fact make to product safety.

PRODUCT SAFETY AND REGULATION: THEORETICAL CONSIDERATIONS

Another approach to assuring product safety is direct regulation. Regulation has taken several forms. Safety standards can be set, as is done by the Consumer Product Safety Commission. Product testing can be made mandatory and may be coupled with marketing restrictions, as occurs in the drug testing requirements of the Food and Drug Administration. Products can be banned altogether, an option mandated by the 1968 Delaney amendments to the Food, Drug and Cosmetics Act.

The theoretical research on these techniques is limited. To examine the impact of product testing and standards it is useful to treat product safety as a characteristic of a product, that is, as a component of product quality. Of the diverse literature dealing with the provision of information about product quality [51, 15], one of the most relevant for providing guidance on how to think about product safety is Akerlof's notion of a market for "lemons" [1]. ("Lemons" are examplars of products that are substantially and irremediably flawed, e.g., a new car that can't be fixed.) Products may be good or bad, but at the point of purchase there is an asymmetry of information about the quality of the product. Sellers tend to have more information about product quality than buyers. For at least some aspects of quality, including safety characteristics, buyers can determine the nature of the characteristics only after some experience with the item in use. Moreover, consumers, concerned that they will purchase a "lemon," and unable to distinguish between items of various quality, will be unwilling to pay a higher price for an item of uncertain quality. Therefore, sellers respond to this lower price by providing lower quality products. If mechanisms could be identified to certify quality reliably, both consumers and producers could be made better off. Consumers, willing to pay for certifiably higher quality products, could identify and purchase such products. Producers, willing to produce or sell higher quality products at a higher price, would be able to do so.

Akerlof does not apply his model to product testing and standards. Leland [39] elaborates and formalizes the Akerlof model to explicitly deal with the imposition of minimum quality standards. He shows that when there is asymmetric information between buyers and sellers there will be too much or too little produced. In such cases minimum quality standards will be desirable if quality is sufficiently important to consumers relative to the cost of provision of quality.

Akerlof and Leland establish the case for market failure when there is asymmetric information. But neither of them develop the argument for regulatory activity in such cases. In fact, Leland directly applies his model to the case of voluntary certification or licensing by a professional group rather than mandatory standards or testing by a government agency.

Metzger [49] modifies the Leland model to examine the case of used car certification, warranty, or disclosure requirements contemplated by the Federal Trade Commission. The requirements proposed by the FTC concerning certification of used cars pertained to dealers, not to private sellers. This introduced the possibility of segmentation of the market which is the key feature of the Metzger analysis. He shows that when minimum quality standards are imposed partially on sellers, the standards do not necessarily yield an improvement in welfare.

Taken together, the Akerlof, Leland and Metzger models of product standards or certification suggest that a good case can be made for imposing minimum standards, appropriately chosen, and, by implication, banning products below the minimum standard. The case turns on whether the consumer's valuation of the benefits from the higher quality exceed the costs of production of that quality, a requirement that might be met for at least some minimum level of safety. But it is also important that the minimum standard be imposed across all sellers.

Matthews and Postlewaite [44] posit a model which examines the conditions under which firms will voluntarily test products and inform consumers honestly of the outcome of the tests. They show that if firms can credibly claim ignorance of product characteristics a requirement to disclose test results (but no mandatory testing) will result in firms choosing not to perform tests. They qualify their model to cover only cases where there is no independent use for the information, which limits its use in examining cases of product safety. However, it does provide the beginning of a useful model for considering product testing.

Another approach is suggested in the work by Kinsey, Roe, and Sexauer [35]. In an significant elaboration and formalization of a model suggested by Peltzman [56], Kinsey, Roe, and Sexauer incorporate the possibility of ex ante imperfect information into the determination of consumer product demand. Once the product is purchased and used, the error in information becomes known, resulting in known errors in choice, evaluated ex post. This leads to a loss in consumer surplus over what would have been the case had the information been available prior to the demand decision.

Peltzman used the rudiments of a model like this to evaluate the impact of drug testing on consumer surplus. Roe, Sexauer, and Kinsey [61] have used this model to evaluate the consumer surplus loss associated with mistakes in the EPA mileage ratings on new cars. A model of this type is useful for empirical work, providing a framework which would allow comparative evaluation of various types of standards or other techniques for providing information about safety features as well as other aspects of product quality.

PRODUCT SAFETY REGULATION: EMPIRICAL ISSUES

Whether product testing and standards should be mandatory and carried out by some government agency is an issue that has concerned many researchers, although formal modelling is limited. Oi's model of the impact of various liability assignments [52] was motivated by an interest in evaluating the report of the National Commission on Product Safety, which recommended the establishment of the Consumer Product Safety Commission. Oi [53] is concerned that standards reduce the incentives for the user of the product to take appropriate care in use.

This concern is a common theme throughout evaluations of regulatory activity designed to achieve product safety. Peltzman [58] in his evaluation of the impact of the National Traffic and Motor Vehicle Safety Act of 1966 argues that automobile safety and "intensity of driving," are joint products. If safety devices are mandated, the risk price of driving intensity falls. The response to the reduction in price of driving intensity is an increase in demand. It is possible that the increased demand for driving intensity carries with it an increase in automobile deaths. This theoretical point is surely right. Peltzman argues that whether the mandated safety devices in fact result in increased or reduced deaths in automobile accidents is an empirical issue. His own empirical work shows an increase in automobile accident deaths of about 10000 over what they would have been had safety devices not been mandated (as compared with 45,000 deaths per year in recent years).

Not surprisingly this research by Peltzman has been quite controversial.[9] It is generally agreed by economists that consumer responses to safety requirements partially offset the additional safety that might be achieved. Evidence of such behavior is found in other activities as well [67]. The relevant issue for policymakers, however, is how large is this response [13]. If the intent of policymakers is to reduce deaths or accidents, and if offsetting behavior is large, the safety requirements may result in the opposite of the intended increase in safety.[10]

How much offsetting behavior might be expected depends in part on how rational consumers can be taken to be. Buchanan [5] and Oi [53] note that consumers can choose their "risk portfolios" by selectively choosing various products and activities with varying amounts of risk. To the extent that this happens, consumers are taken to be rational beings, trading off accident risks against other goods which are desirable. Changes in risks are registered in the decision-making calculus of the consumer. When safety features are added to products, the consumer adjusts his "risk portfolio" to take the added safety (reduced risk) associated with these features into account.

On the other hand, when probabilities are small and consequences unpleasant there is some evidence that consumers underestimate the probabilities [36]. To the extent this is true, the offsetting behavior that might be expected will be limited.

In the automobile safety case there is disagreement over the extent of such behavior. Peltzman [55] and others [9] find evidence of offsetting behavior which overwhelms the additional safety attributable to the safety devices. Crandall and Graham [13] and

---

[9]See H. G. Manne and R.L. Miller, eds., Auto Safety Regulation: The Cure or the Problem [43] for a collections of papers addressing this issue.

[10]Although the safety requirements could result in increases in accidents, the increased accident rate could be consistent with increases in the consumer welfare. Consumers are better off because they no longer need to take costly safety precautions. The total cost of accidents and accident prevention may also be minimized, if the safety precautions previously taken by consumers were costly relative to the provision of the safety features on the product. Note that this behavior is exactly the same as the behavior one would expect in the perfectly informed world postulated by those who consider optimal liability rules.

Graham and Garber[11][27], using similar models with some plausible respecification and refinement, find the offsetting behavior to be modest in size.

Viscusi [68] has carried out the most comprehensive examination of product standards. In his evaluation of the Consumer Product Safety Commission he has examined the mattress flammability standard, child-resistant bottle caps, crib regulations, swimming pool slide standards, carpet and rug flammability standards, and bicycles standards. In no case does he find evidence that the standard is associated with reduced accidents--a striking and perhaps unexpected finding.

Another issue suggested in the empirical literature relating to testing and standards is the impact of such regulatory activity on the product markets involved. Peltzman [56, 57] in his examination of the 1962 Kefauver-Harris Amendments to the Food, Drug, and Cosmetics Act as well as follow-up studies [2, 24, 26] suggests that the testing requirements of the Kefauver-Harris Amendments reduced innovation and limited the number of new drug introductions in the U.S. market. Grabowski [24], reviewing the evidence on this issue, notes that the studies investigating the decline in drug innovation incorporate a number of different analytical approaches. They consistently find a significant negative effect of regulation on the rate of innovation [24, p. 37]. The size of this effect is a matter of dispute, but all agree that such an effect exists.

Although there is no comparable examination of other industries where standards or testing has been imposed, it is reasonable to postulate a similar effect. This follows because the standard or testing imposes a cost on production that would otherwise not be present. Hence, output should be reduced. This effect is similar to the effect that is expected as a result of the optimal liability rule.

A final issue worth mentioning here is the distinction between behavioral and technological standards. This issue is raised by

---

[11]The Graham and Garber work catalogue the dangers in empirical work which is so inherently controversial. They show that Peltzman's results can be reversed simply by changing the functional specification from logarithmic to linear. Moreover, there is no theoretical justification for the logarithmic specification. They also discuss the impact on Peltzman's results of omitted variables and measurement error. Both, if corrected, would reduce the estimated impact of offsetting behavior.

Mayer and Zick [45] in their examination of consumer preferences for air bags and seat belts. Their study ascertained the characteristics of consumers who express a preference for one or the other of these safety features. Behavioral requirements, such as seat belt laws, or restrictions on smoking, may provide a way of requiring consumer care, thus limiting offsetting behavior. Whether such requirements can work remains an issue for empirical investigation.

VOLUNTARY STANDARDS AND TESTING

There is little literature dealing exclusively with voluntary standards and testing.[12] One type of voluntary standard has been examined. This is the grading system used by the United States Department of Agriculture (USDA) for beef, pork, milk, eggs, wool, lumber, and other commodities. It is argued that grading of commodities benefits both consumers and producers. From the consumer's point of view grading is beneficial because it provides information about the quality of the commodities. It is beneficial to producers because it increases revenues associated with the products through product differentiation.

Zwart [73] has developed a model of consumer choice under various market conditions and grades that allows evaluation of benefits of grading. He shows that consumers and producers do not always benefit from grading. However, under typical conditions for the marketing of agricultural commodities, benefits should accrue. Others have suggested changes in the grading scheme that would improve the information provided to consumers [50] or increase revenues to producers [60].

Hemenway [30], in the most comprehensive study of voluntary product standards, suggests why grading is welcomed in the agricultural sector, but fought elsewhere. Grades help firms lacking differentiation advantages while decreasing the value of long-standing reputations and trade names. In addition, grading is advantageous in industries where quality assurance has been difficult to establish. Thus, in agriculture where brand names are not

[12]Much of the theoretical work dealing with testing and standards makes no distinction between mandatory and voluntary standards. These models can be applied to either case. Indeed, Matthews and Postlewaite [44] examine whether a professional group can be expected to set appropriate standards. The review here is meant to identify issues that seem puzzling, given the other literature dealing with safety.

important, standards such as those imposed by USDA help differentiate an otherwise homogeneous product. Agriculturalists may disagree over the exact form standards should take, but there is little objection to standards in principle.

PRODUCTS LIABILITY AND SAFETY REGULATION AS A COMPLETE SYSTEM

A final set of issues arise when products liability and safety regulations of various sorts are considered simultaneously as a comprehensive system. Both in fact exist side by side. In general those who have considered product liabilities or safety regulation have acknowledged the effects of the other [52, 68]. But until recently there has been little explicit consideration of how each operates to complement or substitute for the other.

Recently a small theoretical literature treating this issue has developed [62, 63, 72, 33]. Shavell [63] shows that regulatory safety requirements are superior to liability if (1) producers would not be able to fully pay for harm done _or_ if (2) they would not be sued for it. But liability would be superior to regulatory solutions if the regulatory authority's information about risk is poor. If both of these problems exist, so that neither is by itself optimal, a case can be made for the two techniques to stand side by side.

Johnson, Kolstad, and Ulen [33] introduce uncertainty about the determination of the care taken by the defendant relative to the standard required by the court system. When such uncertainty exists, the introduction of regulation can achieve the efficient amount of safety. They also show that the minimum standard set by the regulatory mechanism should be below the social optimum, a conclusion consistent with the results of the Shavell model.

This research is quite new, and there is no empirical work to suggest the extent to which a real life system incorporating both _ex post_ liability and _ex ante_ regulation approximates the optimal mix as suggested by the models. Nevertheless, this line of research begins to address some of the complications actually present in our legal and regulatory systems.

AN EVALUATION OF RESEARCH IN PRODUCTS LIABILITY AND REGULATION

In this paper I have reviewed much of the literature dealing with product safety. In doing so, I have raised a number of issues confronted in the literature and also a number of concerns not yet addressed.

Product liability and regulation concerning product safety are the two main techniques for assuring product safety. There is a striking contrast between the literature dealing with these two techniques. The product liability literature is primarily theoretical, focusing on a description of the liability rule that will achieve optimal safety and output under various conditions of information and transaction costs. There is very little discussion of the court system that operates the liability system. It is taken to operate mechanically. Its presence, while necessary, has no independent impact on how the liability system operates. Only the recent work by Johnson, Kolstad, and Ulen take account of the uncertainty introduced by the functioning of the court itself. They show that the standard of care used by the court might introduce imperfections into the market.

On the other hand, the research dealing with regulation for product safety is primarily empirical, focusing on the imperfections in markets that are likely to arise because of regulation. These imperfections include reductions in innovation and new product development as well as changes in the behavior of consumers in response to the regulations that frustrate attempts to increase product safety. Lying behind these imperfections is the difficulty in identifying the optimal level of safety. If the level of firm-produced safety that minimized the sum of accident costs and accident prevention costs were known, this level could be set by regulators. Regulations would have negative effects on innovation and might be offset by undesirable behavior by consumers as compared to the unregulated situation. But the overall effects of regulation would be optimal.

Economists have a natural preference for solutions involving liability rules. Given the optimal set of liability rules, the economic actors--consumers and producers--choose the appropriate level of accident prevention activity. Regulatory activity which sets standards reduces that choice. Consumers cannot buy and producers cannot produce items which are less safe than the minimum standard requires. But so far the comparison of regulation and product liability has not provided sufficient grounds for choice. Examination of liability rules has failed to consider the crucial uncertainties involved in the process. Examination of regulatory activity has failed to provide a coherent theoretical background against which to frame the comparison. How liability rules affect innovation, research and development, and consumer behavior has not been examined empirically. Since both liability rules and regulatory activity are used as a matter of policy, and since both have advantages and disadvantages, how they work--whether together or at cross-purposes--must be understood.

If we want to understand how much product safety there is, whether there is more now than there was at some time in the past, and what price we have paid for product safety, we must complete the work that has been begun with the research reviewed here.

REFERENCES

1. AKERLOF, GEORGE A. (1970), "The Market of 'Lemons': Quality Uncertainty and the Market Mechanism," Quarterly Journal of Economics, Vol. 84, pp. 488-500.

2. BAILY, MARTIN NEIL (1972), "Research and Development Cost and Returns: The U.S. Pharmaceutical Industry," Journal of Political Economy, Vol. 80 (1), pp. 70-85, January/February.

3. BROUSSALIAN, V. (1975), "Risk Measurement and Safety Standards in Consumer Products," in Nestor E. Terleckyj, ed., Household Consumption and Production, National Bureau of Economic Research, pp. 491.

4. BROWN, JOHN P. (1973), "Toward an Economic Theory of Liability," Journal of Legal Studies, Vol. 2 (2), pp. 323-349.

5. BUCHANAN, JAMES M. (1970-71), "In Defense of Caveat Emptor," University of Chicago Law Review, pp. 64-73.

6. CALABRESI, GUIDO (1970), The Costs of Accidents: A Legal and Economic Analysis, New Haven, Conn.: Yale University Press.

7. _________ (1969), "Does the Fault System Optimally Control Primary Accident Costs?," Law and Contempory Problems, pp. 429-463, Summer.

8. CALABRESI, GUIDO, and KENNETH C. BASS III (1970), "Right Approach, Wrong Implications: A Critique of McKean on Products Liability," The University of Chicago Law Review, Vol. 37, pp. 74-91.

9. CANTU, OSCAR R. (1980), "An Updated Regression Analysis on the Effects of the Regulation of Automobile Safety," Working Paper No. 15, School of Organization and Management, Yale University.

10. COASE, RONALD (1960), "The Problem of Social Cost," Journal of Law and Economics, Vol. 3 (1).

11. COOTER, ROBERT, LEWIS KORNHAUSER, and DAVID LANE (1979), "Liability Rules, Limited Information, and the Role of Precedent," The Bell Journal of Economics, Vol. 10 (1), pp. 366-373, Spring.

12. CORNELL, NINA W., ROGER G. NOLL, and BARRY WEINGAST (1976), "Safety Regulation," in Setting National Priorities: The Next Ten Years, H. Owen and C. Schultze, ed., Washington, D.C.: Brookings Institution, pp. 457-504.

13. CRANDALL, ROBERT W. and JOHN D. GRAHAM (1984), "Automobile Safety Regulation and Offsetting Behavior: Some New Empirical Estimates," American Economic Review Papers and Proceedings, Vol. 74 (2), pp. 328-331, May.

14. DANZON, PATRICIA M. (1985), Medical Malpractice: Theory, Evidence, and Public Policy, Cambridge, Mass.: Harvard University Press.

15. DARBY, MICHAEL R., and EDI KARNI (1973), "Free Competition and the Optimal Amount of Fraud," Journal of Law and Economics, pp. 67-88, April.

16. DIAMOND, PETER A. (1974), "Accident Law and Resource Allocation," The Bell Journal of Economics and Management Science, Vol. 5 (2), pp. 366-405, Autumn.

17. DIAMOND, PETER A., and J. MIRRLEES (1975), "On the Assignment of Liability: The Uniform Case," The Bell Journal of Economics, Vol. 6 (2), pp. 287-516, Autumn.

18. DORFMAN, ROBERT (1970), "The Economics of Products Liability: A Reaction to McKean," University of Chicago Law Review, Vol. 37, pp. 92-102.

19. EADS, GEORGE, and PETER REUTER (1984), "Designing Safer Products: Corporate Responses to Product Liability Law and Regulation," Journal of Products Liability, Vol. 7, pp. 263-294.

20. EISMAN, DEBORAH E. (1983), "Product Liability: Who Should Bear the Burden?," American Economist, pp.54-57, Spring.

21. EPPLE, DENNIS, and ARTHUR RAVIV (1978), "Product Safety: Liability Rules, Market Structure, and Imperfect Information," American Economic Review, Vol. 68 (1), pp. 80-95, March.

22. EUROPEAN CONSUMER LAW GROUP (1983), "Non-Legislative Means of Consumer Protection," Journal of Consumer Policy, Vol. 6, pp. 209-224.

23. GOLDBERG, VICTOR P. (1974), "The Economics of Product Safety and Imperfect Information," The Bell Journal of Economics and Managements Science, Vol. 5 (2), pp. 683-688, Autumn.

24. GRABOWSKI, HENRY G. (1976), Drug Regulation and Innovation, Washington, D.C.: American Enterprise Institute for Public Policy Research.

25. GRABOWSKI, HENRY G., and JOHN M. VERNON (1978), "Consumer Product Safety Regulation," American Economic Review, Vol. 68, pp. 284, May.

26. GRABOWSKI, HENRY G., and JOHN M. VERNON (1983), The Regulation of Pharmaceutical: Balancing the Benefits and Risks, Washington, D.C.: American Enterprise Institute for Public Policy Research.

27. GRAHAM, JOHN D., and STEVEN GARBER (1984), "Evaluating the Effects of Automobile Safety Regulation," Journal of Policy Analysis and Management, Vol. 3 (2), pp. 206-224.

28. GREEN, JERRY (1976), "On the Optimal Structure of Liability Laws," The Bell Journal of Economics, Vol. 7 (2), pp. 553-574, Autumn, 1976.

29. HAMADA, KOICHI (1976), "Liability Rules and Income Distribution in Product Liability," American Economic Review, Vol. 66 (1), pp. 228-234, March.

30. HEMENWAY, DAVID (1975), Industrywide Voluntary Product Standards, Cambridge, Mass.: Ballinger Publishing Company.

31. INTERAGENCY TASK FORCE ON PRODUCT LIABILITY, FINAL REPORT (1978), U.S. Government Printing Office.

32. JENSEN, WALTER, JR., EDWARD M. MAZZE, and DUKE NORDLINGER STERN (1973), "The Consumer Product Safety Act: A Special Case in Consumerism," Journal of Marketing, pp. 68-71, October.

33. JOHNSON, GARY V., CHARLES D. KOLSTAD, and THOMAS S. ULEN (1986), "Ex Ante Regulation and Ex Post Liability: Substitutes or Complements?," Institute for Environmental Studies Staff Paper No. 29, University of Illinois, March.

34. KELMAN, STEVEN (1974), "Regulation by the Numbers--A Report on the Consumer Product Safety Commission," The Public Interest, No. 36, pp. 83-102, Summer.

35. KINSEY, JEAN, TERRY ROE, and BENJAMIN SEXAUER (1980), "Imperfect Information, Consumer Theory, and Allocative Error in Consumption," Department of Agricultural and Applied Economics Staff Papers Series, P80-8, University of Minnesota, April.

36. KUNREUTHER, HOWARD (1976), "Limited Knowledge and Insurance Protection," Public Policy, Vol. 24, pp. 229-261.

37. LANDES, ELISABETH M. (1982), "Insurance, Liability, and Accidents: A Theoretical and Empirical Investigation of the Effect of No-Fault Accidents," Journal of Law and Economics, Vol. 25 (1), pp. 49-66, April.

38. LAVE, LESTER, and W. WEBER (1970), "A Benefit-Cost Analysis of Auto Safety Features," Applied Economics, Vol. 2 (4), pp. 215-275.

39. LELAND, HAYNE E. (1979), "Quacks, Lemons, and Licensing: A Theory of Minimum Quality Standards," Journal or Political Economy, Vol. 87 (6), pp. 1328-1346.

40. LINNEMAN, PETER (1980), "The Effects of Consumer Safety Standards: The 1973 Mattress Flammability Standard," Journal of Law and Economics, Vol. 23 (2), pp. 461-480, October.

41. JONES-LEE, MICHAEL, ed. (1980), The Value of Life and Safety, Amsterdam: North-Holland Publishing Co.

42. MANNE, HENRY G., ed. (1970), "Edited Transcript of AALS-AEA Conference on Products Liability," University of Chicago Law Review, Vol. 37, pp. 117-141.

43. MANNE, HENRY G., and R. L. MILLER, eds. (1976), Auto Safety Regulation: The Cure or the Problem, Glen Ridge: Thomas Horton and Daughters, pp. 83-88.

44. MATTHEWS, STEVEN, and ANDREW POSTLEWAITE (1985), "Quality Testing and Disclosure," Rand Journal of Economics, Vol 16 (3), pp. 328-340, Autumn.

45. MAYER, ROBERT N., and CATHLEEN D. ZICK (1986), "Mandating Behavioral or Technological Change: The Case of Auto Safety," The Journal of Consumer Affairs, Vol. 20 (1), pp. 1-18, Summer.

46. MCGUIRE, THOMAS, RICHARD NELSON, and THOMAS SPAVINS (1975), "'An Evaluation of Consumer Protection Legislation: The 1962 Drug Amendments': A Comment," Journal of Political Economy, Vol. 83 (3), pp. 655-662, June.

47. MCKEAN, R. N. (1970), " Products Liability: Implications of Some Changing Property Rights," Quarterly Journal of Economics, Vol. 61 (4), pp. 611-626, November.

48. MEINERS, ROGER E. (1982), "What to Do about Hazardous Products," in Robert W. Poole, Jr., ed., Instead of Regulation: Alternatives to Federal Regulatory Agencies, Lexington, Mass.: Lexington Books.

49. METZGER, MICHAEL R. (1983), "Cherries, Lemons, and the FTC: Minimum Quality Standards in the Retail Used Automobile Industry," Economic Inquiry, Vol. 21, pp. 129-139, January.

50. MILLER, JOHN A., DAVID G. TOPEL, and ROBERT E. RUST (1976), "USDA Beef Grading: A Failure in Consumer Information?," Journal of Marketing, Vol. 40, pp. 25-31, January.

51. NELSON, PHILLIP (1970), "Information and Consumer Behavior," Journal of Political Economy, Vol. 78, April.

52. OI, WALTER Y. (1972), "The Economics of Product Safety," The Bell Journal of Economics and Management Sciences, Vol. 4 (1), pp. 3-28, Spring.

53. _________ (1977), "Safety at Any Price?," Regulation, November/December.

54. OPALUCH, JAMES J., and THOMAS A. GRIGALUNAS (1984), "Controlling Stochastic Pollution Events Through Liability Rules: Some Evidence From OCS Leasing," The Rand Journal of Economics, Vol. 15 (1), pp. 142-152, Spring.

55. PELTZMAN, SAM (1975), "The Effects of Automobile Safety Regulation," Journal of Political Economy, Vol. 83 (4), pp. 677-726, August.

56. _________ (1973), "An Evaluation of Consumer Protection Legislation: The 1962 Drug Amendments," Journal of Political Economy, Vol. 81 (5), pp. 1049-1092, Sept./Oct.

57. _________ (1975), "'An Evaluation of Consumer Protection Legislation: The 1962 Drug Amendments': A Reply," Journal of Political Economy, Vol. 83 (3), pp. 663-668, June.

58. _________ (1974), Regulation of Pharmaceutical Innovation, Washington, D.C.: American Enterprise Institute for Public Policy Research.

59. POLINSKY, A. MITCHELL, and WILLIAM P. ROGERSON (1981), "Products Liability, Consumer Misperceptions, and Market Power," The Bell Journal of Economics.

60. PURCELL, WAYNE D., and KENNETH E. NELSON (1976), "Recent Changes in Beef Grades: Issues and Analysis of the Yield Grade Requirement," American Journal of Agricultural Economics, Vol. 58 (3), pp. 475-484, August.

61. ROE, TERRY, BENJAMIN SEXAUER, and JEAN KINSEY (1981), "The Cost of Inaccurate Consumer Information: The Case of the EPA Mileage Figures," Staff Paper P81-23, Department of Agricultural and Applied Economics, University of Minnesota, August.

62. SHAVELL, STEVEN (1984), "Liability for Harm Versus Regulation of Safety," Journal of Legal Studies, Vol. 13, pp. 357-374.

63. _________ (1984), "A Model of the Optimal Use of Liability and Safety Regulation," Rand Journal of Economics, Vol. 15 (2), Summer.

64. SMITH, BETTY F., and RACHEL DARDIS (1977), "Cost Benefit Analysis of Consumer Product Safety Standards," Journal of Consumer Affairs, Vol. 22 (1), pp. 34-46, Summer.

65. SPENCE, MICHAEL (1977), "Consumer Misperceptions, Product Failure and Producer Liability," Review of Economic Studies, Vol. 44 (3), pp. 561-572.

66. VISCUSI, W. KIP (1985), "Consumer Behavior and the Safety Effects of Product Safety Regulation," Journal of Law and Economics, Vol. 23 (3), pp. 527-554, Oct..

67. _________ (1984), "The Lulling Effect: The Impact of Child-Resistant Packaging on Aspirin and Analgesic Ingestions," American Economic Review Papers and Proceedings, Vol. 74 (2), pp. 324-327, May.

68. _________ (1984), Regulating Consumer Product Safety, Washington, D.C.: American Enterprise Institute for Public Policy Research.

69. _________ (1983), Risk by Choice: Regulating Health and Safety in the Workplace, Cambridge, Mass.: Harvard University Press.

70. WEIMER, DAVID LEO (1982), "Safe--and Available--Drugs," in Robert W. Poole, Jr., ed., Instead of Regulation: Alternatives to Federal Regulatory Agencies, Lexington, Mass.: Lexington Books.

71. WITTMAN, DONALD (1986), "The Price of Negligence Under Differing Liability Rules," Journal of Law and Economics, Vol. 29 (1), pp. 151-163.

72. _________ (1977), "Prior Regulation Versus Post Liability: The Choice between Input and Output Monitoring," Journal of Legal Studies, Vol. 6, pp. 193-212.

73. ZWART, A. C. (1984), "The Economics and Welfare Impacts of Grading Schemes," mimeo, Cornell University, October.

Chapter 4

ABOUT THE AUTHOR

Robert W. Crandall is a Senior Fellow in the Economic Studies Program at The Brookings Institution, Washington. Crandall received his Ph.D. from Northwestern in 1968. Within Economics his specialties are industrial organization, regulation, and antitrust policy.

Before going to Brookings in 1978, Crandall was first a member of the Economics faculty at M.I.T. and then an administrator in the Council on Wage and Price Stability. He is the author of Regulating the Automobile, Controlling Industrial Pollution, and The Scientific Basis of Health and Safety Regulation, all available from Brookings.

THE USE OF COST-BENEFIT ANALYSIS IN PRODUCT SAFETY REGULATION

ROBERT W. CRANDALL

SUMMARY

Robert Crandall starts his discussion of the use of cost-benefit analysis in product safety regulation by first scrutinizing the basis for undertaking regulation in the first place. Are externalities necessary to justify regulation? Crandall's answer is "No." There are other factors that might justify regulatory intervention: the inability of consumers to identify unsafe products, situations where an information approach is relatively inefficient, the problems posed by irreversible choices that are potentially disastrous, and the possible inability of some to react rationally to low probability risks.

Since 1974 every administration has purported to use cost-benefit analysis in monitoring regulation. But in fact it has been little used in health-safety-environmental regulation. Why? It has not yet achieved public acceptance. Crandall reviews the reasons for this at length: the difficulties in assessing the exposure-risk relationship, the difficulties in putting a value on serious injury or premature death, the choice of an appropriate discount rate, "conservatism" in carrying out the analysis. Conceptual problems aside, cost-benefit analysis often conflicts with political goals or hidden "agendas" of bureaucrats.

Crandall notes that the National Highway Safety Administration has carried out numerous cost-benefit analyses while EPA and CPSC have done almost nothing. But cost-benefit studies are enough: they must mesh appropriately with the goals and instruments of regulatory policy. Crandall "makes the case" for retrospective cost-benefit analysis, something seldom done at present.

Summing up, Crandall, while sanguine about what cost-benefit analysis could do to make regulatory activities more productive, is not optimistic as to greater future use of this instrument.

* * * *

The mere mention of cost-benefit analysis is likely to evoke strong emotional reactions from some proponents of government regulation, particularly from noneconomists. These reactions may reflect a misunderstanding of this analytical method. They may derive from a basic philosophical rejection of the basic tenets of welfare economics. To some critics, cost-benefit analysis is inappropriate in health-safety regulation because it allows society callously to trade dollars for lives and to forego "essential" regulation.[1] To others, it is too crude a tool to be used by regulators to guide extremely important social decisions.

In this paper, I will suggest that these concerns are substantially overstated. Nevertheless, I share some of the concerns about the potential for excessive use of cost benefit analysis in regulatory proceedings. Many of today's problems in regulation derive from inappropriate regulatory strategies. Cost-benefit analysis can help regulators make some difficult choices, but it is not very useful if the appropriate choice is not to intervene in the first place. Nor is this technique useful if the political choice of regulatory technique is hopelessly ineffective or inefficient. It makes little difference if a proposed regulation passes a cost-benefit test if in fact it cannot be implemented and enforced. Finally, while cost-benefit analysis may be used in determining whether to regulate and in choosing the technique of regulation, it simply cannot be used as an explicit guide for every regulatory decision without an enormous expenditure of resources. Even analysts have opportunity costs!

THE PHILOSOPHICAL BASIS OF REGULATION

There is a range of views about the appropriate role of regulation in controlling risks to health and safety. To most economists, regulation is clearly called for where there are

---

[1]There are many noneconomists who hold such views. See [2].

externalities in production processes or consumption activity.[2] If these externalities are present, and an effective regulatory mechanism exists, an economist would generally evaluate the efficiency of health-safety regulation by comparing the incremental benefits of regulatory control, measured by the willingness of the protected consumers or workers to pay, with its incremental costs, measured by the value of social output foregone.

Some argue that a regulation is worthwhile if its incremental benefits are greater than its incremental costs regardless of the presence of externalities. In this view, regulation is defended not only to correct for externalities but to protect consumers or workers from their own irrationality or myopia. Alternatively, it may reflect a view that consumers and workers should not be allowed to take risks voluntarily. In its most populist form, this argument reduces to the view that "poor" consumers or workers should not be forced to take risks forced upon them by powerful, "wealthy" employers or capitalists.

Finally, there is the view that no individual should be exposed to undue risk from externalities regardless of the cost of protecting him from such risk.[3] The regulation of an externality should not depend upon the number of people exposed, according to this argument, but upon whether any people are exposed to "undue" risk. In essence, this view dismisses standard economic welfare analysis that weighs costs and benefits unless the victims are actually compensated. It is not sufficient to say that the benefits of regulation are outweighed by the costs because the losers from regulation could compensate the gainers and still be better off without the regulatory regime. As long as the compensation is not paid, social justice requires regulation, according to this view.

Throughout this paper, I shall use the traditional welfare-theoretic approach of maximizing total social product, but one should be clear that important issues remain concerning the distributional impacts of risk and regulation.

---

[2]For a statement of this "market-failure" justification for regulation, see [2, Ch. 1].

[3]See [10, Ch. 2] for a discussion of alternative approaches to the regulation of risk.

ARE EXTERNALITIES NECESSARY TO JUSTIFY REGULATION?

It is all too simple to examine a safety problem, to conclude that accidents could be reduced, and to prescribe a government response. Such "problems" may well be the result of risks voluntarily assumed by individuals with full knowledge of their consequences. A society that tells me I may not take the risk of losing a finger by buying a less expensive electric saw, but allows me to climb dangerous rock faces on weekends is being quite inconsistent in its approach to my welfare. I know that climbing rocks and cutting boards with a high-speed saw are both dangerous activities. In neither case am I placing anyone else's welfare at risk. Therefore, why do I need the protection of the government in either activity?

There are several reasons why it is sound economically to regulate product safety without any clear indication of market failure from externalities. First, individuals may not be able to distinguish safe from unsafe products in some cases. All consumers might prefer that all of the power saws on the hardware shelves be insulated against electric shocks because we cannot easily examine a saw's internal wiring. The benefits of such a regulation must be measured in terms of the increase in the information afforded consumers or in the reduction in uncertainty that they face.

Second, there may be situations where labelling is sufficient to forewarn consumers of risks, but only at a very large consumer cost of time spent reading the labels. For instance, it may be more efficient to regulate the contents of prepared foods than to require everyone to read each label at the supermarket to be sure that the various prepared foods one buys are free from toxic contaminants. Obviously, there is no reason why we need to allow these toxic materials to be offered as one of the options for purchase and consumption.

Third, a somewhat weaker case can be made for disallowing free choice when the outcome from an unfortunate choice is irreversible and even catastrophic. This is at least one of the reasons for regulating pharmaceuticals with potentially harmful side effects.[4]

In each of these cases, one could argue that regulation is not required because the tort system should induce producers to supply

---

[4]For a discussion of tragic outcomes, see [4].

the "correct" level of safety even in the face of imperfect consumer information. Recently, however, regulation has been preferred as an alternative to a costly and ineffective tort liability system [9]. This argument presupposes that the political-administrative process that guides regulation works better than the tort system.

Finally, there is an argument for regulation that derives from the assumed inability of individuals to react rationally to low-probability risks [1, pp. 307-319]. Worker safety and automobile safety are two examples. Workers may understand the evidence on the probability of cancer in a given work environment, but view this risk as too distant or too remote to take seriously. Similarly, people may not buckle their automobile seat belt because they cannot translate the low probabilities of an automobile accident occurring to them.

Whatever the case for it, regulation in the absence of clear externalities may well mean that cost-benefit analysis cannot be very useful. If the analyst values costs and benefits at market prices and if the regulation simply thwarts the operation of markets in which there are no externality problems, it is quite likely that regulation cannot be shown to be welfare enhancing. No amount of sophistication in cost-benefit analysis can alter this fact.

ISSUES IN THE APPLICATION OF COST BENEFIT ANALYSIS TO GOVERNMENT REGULATION

Every administration since 1974 has purported to use cost-benefit analysis in overseeing the work product of its regulatory bureaucracies.[5] Despite this fact, it is difficult to find any area of health-safety-environmental regulation where cost-benefit analysis is used routinely to guide decisionmaking and to defend the resulting standards in the courts or in the court of public opinion. Nor is it possible to argue that the Office of Management and Budget and its predecessor have had notable success in reducing the inefficiency of regulation.

To a great extent, the failure of cost-benefit analysis as a tool for improving regulation derives from the lack of public acceptance of it. Part of this problem reflects the obvious political difficulty that an agency administrator or a Congressman has in explaining that another turn of the regulatory screw is not "worth it" because

---

[5]For a review of the various approaches to regulatory oversight and regulatory reform, see [11]; and [20, Ch. 10].

the costs are too great in comparison with the few lives that are saved.

But the issues are more than simple public relations. In fact, most of the controversies in cost-benefit analysis derive from four sources: (i) the difficulty in translating imperfect information on risk-exposure levels into meaningful projections of the threat to human safety; (ii) the difficulties in evaluating the expected value of an increase in the risk of serious injury or premature mortality; (iii) the choice of the appropriate discount rate for future benefits and costs; and (iv) "conservatism" in carrying out the analysis. In addition, there are a number of more subtle issues that complicate cost-benefit analysis, but that are not at the center of the current policy debate. These are covered in the next section of this paper.

Measuring Risk

The most common argument against using cost-benefit analysis is that the dose-response or exposure-risk relationship is so imperfectly understood that precise, quantitative techniques cannot be used to evaluate alternative regulatory strategies.[6] The fact that there is truly no substitute for some estimate of regulatory outcomes in establishing rational regulation is often not sufficient to deflect this argument in the political arena. A regulator's "judgment" is invoked as the solution, presumably to be guided by his notion of the "public interest," but often influenced by political pressures that would not be an integral part of a formal cost-benefit analysis.

There is an enormous literature on decisionmaking under uncertainty.[7] This literature suggests that safety regulators should first establish a loss function and assign probabilities to various outcomes. It is insufficient simply to estimate the expected values of benefits and costs from each alternative and to choose that one with the highest ratio of expected benefits to expected costs. The social management of risk often involves guarding against the low-probability of very large losses. There is no reason to assume that the benefits of avoiding such risks are linear in the magnitude of the risk or in the probability of adverse outcomes. Nevertheless, linearity is often assumed in combination with "conservative" estimates of the risk in carrying out the analysis. This technique is discussed below.

---

[6]For examples of this argument, see [7]. For a more general analysis, see [10].

[7]A good introduction is to be found in [12], Part VI.

The practical, political problem involved in extrapolating societal risks from incomplete information is obvious [10]. Formal cost-benefit analysis requires that the nature of the risk and the evidence supporting its existence be clearly documented. This opens up the regulatory process to endless controversy, ridicule, and--inevitably -- litigation. Of course, such public exposure makes it more difficult to regulate against low-probability risks with relatively small losses, and perhaps it also allows more attention to be paid to those risks with potentially disastrous consequences. Transparency has its benefits!

Ultimately, regulators must use the best available evidence on risk and extrapolate from it to the outcome under various regulatory regimes or standards. For some risks, such as the risk of death in an automobile accident, the results of exposure will be observable in a relatively short period of time. In these instances, retrospective analyses can be helpful in iterating to a reasonable solution.

In other instances, the latency period between exposure and adverse outcome may be very long indeed. Disposal of certain hazardous wastes, such as spent nuclear fuels, is an obvious case in point. Most carcinogens have a very long latency period. In these cases, regulators can and must use imperfect information on the dose-response relationship without the benefit of an early reading on the wisdom of their choices. There is little alternative to estimating expected outcomes in these situations although the careful regulation will want to know something about the distribution of these outcomes about their mean.

The Value of Reducing Risk of Injury or Early Death

It is very difficult to say anything new on this subject. Mishan [12, Part V], Schelling [16], Zeckhauser [21], Thaler and Rosen [18], Bailey [3], and others have provided a lively and compelling literature on this subject. That the topic remains controversial is a reflection of some of the difficult issues involved and, of course, the emotional nature of the subject.

Most economists would use some variant of the willingness to pay criterion to establish the benefits of reducing the risk to life and limb. This is easily stated, but difficult to implement in practice. Obviously, different people are likely to place different values on avoiding the same risk, depending on their age, family status, income level, and degree of risk aversion. Equally important is the fact that all risks are not likely to be viewed equivalently by the same person. The distribution of risks about its expected level matters. So apparently does the source of the risk. Some studies have shown that people react quite differently to risks depending upon whether they believe that they have some control over the outcome [17, pp. 1232-38]. For this reason, many people are apparently willing to pay more to avoid death in an airplane than in a car because of the feeling that they have some control over the latter risk.

Under a strict potential Pareto improvement criterion, the ability-to-pay valuation procedure requires regulators to value low-income lives at less than those with higher incomes. Philosophically, this may be an untenable approach for evaluating risks caused by externalities and therefore not willingly assumed by the poorer person. It may also be difficult to justify politically lower values for those persons who have a lower degree of risk aversion and therefore choose a risky line of work. Once again, one must distinguish between risks assumed voluntarily and those imposed upon others involuntarily through various externalities.

Despite all of these difficulties in estimating the value of reducing death, there are very few cost-benefit analyses of regulation that depend critically upon the magnitude one uses for the value of extended life or reduced morbidity. most regulatory decisions are relatively insensitive to choices over a fairly wide range of values for these essential parameters. In most cases, uncertainty over the risk-exposure relationship is by far more important than the uncertainty over the appropriate "value of life."

Discounting Benefits

In general, all benefits and costs of regulation must be discounted back to the present at some discount rate if costs and benefits with different time profiles are to be compared. Expenditures today can be used to generate returns tomorrow--returns that cumulate because capital is productive in generating private and social product. Similarly, we value income today more highly than income tomorrow because at the margin capital is productive.

There is little controversy over discounting for most social investment decisions. In those involving health and safety, however, there is considerable debate about whether it is reasonable to discount the future savings of statistical lives. Mishan has shown that this is not a problem for decisions involving overlapping generations, but when decisions today create losses for individuals several generations hence, the discounted present value criterion fails [13]. Unfortunately, Mishan does not provide an alternative criterion for such distant outcomes.

For most health-safety problems, however, standard present value criteria are appropriate. Few safety regulations confer their benefits principally upon those unborn. Even carcinogens, with their long latency periods, have their principal effects upon those currently living unless they create genetic changes that damage future generations.

"Conservatism" in Risk Assessment

This brief catalogue of issues in performing cost-benefit analysis completely ignores the problems in calculating the costs of regulation. This is not because such calculations are easy, but because the inherent problems in making such calculations are rather routine and mundane. Learning and scale economies, joint and common costs, the rate at which resources can be transferred from one use to another, and the separation of transitory dislocation costs from long-run effects pose significant problems for the analyst. But these are neither interesting problems nor a particular obstacle to the implementation of cost-benefit analysis. The difficult and interesting problems lie on the benefits side of the ledger.

Given the difficulties in assessing the probable risk of exposures to life- or health-threatening substances or situations and the controversial nature of attempting to place a value on the reduction in early deaths or excess morbidity, regulators are likely to use conservative assumptions in performing the risk assessment that enters into the cost-benefit analysis. For this reason, the actual cost per expected life saved in regulating uncertain risks such as carcinogens is often very high compared to the cost of reducing fatalities through more certain and mundane product safety regulation.

Some students of regulation, such as Nichols and Zeckhauser [14], argue that regulators may well be spending so much per expected life saved on a given regulation that they actually sacrifice lives. The resources mandated by these regulations could actually improve health safety by much more if allocated to other regulations, medical care, improved nutrition, or even safer consumer durables. For instance, it is not fanciful to suggest that the purchasing power absorbed by some of Occupational Safety and Health Administration's (OSHA) more expensive regulations would actually generate greater improvements in mortality if simply left to consumers to spend on food, shelter, medical care, and new (safer) automobiles.

THE PRACTICAL OBSTACLES TO IMPLEMENTING COST-BENEFIT ANALYSIS

Most discussions of the role of cost-benefit analysis in regulation focus upon many of the narrow methodological concerns detailed in the first few sections of this paper. Debate usually centers on the value of life, the extrapolation of risk, or the choice of discount rates. What is often lost in this discussion is whether the regulatory program is well designed in the first place. One can spend countless millions of dollars analyzing the validity of alternative standards for, say, particulates from steel industry coke ovens. But if these regulations cannot be enforced or if they affect only a small fraction of total particulate emissions, it may be futile to conduct such an analysis when other sources are uncontrolled or not analyzed.

Nor can cost-benefit analysis induce efficient regulation if Congress has chosen the wrong targets or required the wrong instruments to achieve its targets. While cost-benefit analysis can be used in the choice of targets, this choice is often preempted by the Congress which gives very little attention to formal cost-benefit tests. And if regulation itself induces offsetting behavior that nullifies the potentially beneficial aspects of the regulatory rule, cost-benefit analysis may prove to have analyzed only a subset of the problem. To illustrate some of these problems, it is useful to turn to a few of the more prominent regulatory programs for examples.

The Choice of Targets

A frequent criticism of health-safety regulation is that Congress or the delegated agency has chosen its regulatory targets poorly. Often this is the result of legislative deliberations in reaction to a recent catastrophe, such as Three Mile Island or Love Canal. The recent alarm over hazardous wastes is an obvious case, giving rise to the Superfund legislation that may well reduce the amount of dangerous wastes, but may also result in the expenditure of billions of dollars to move wastes around with little practical effect. At this juncture, few in Congress are asking whether such clean-up activity will actually work. Nor are they comparing any quantitative estimates of prospective benefits with the enormous costs they are mandating in this effort.

In 1969, the Congress reacted to concern about air pollution by drafting a bill that required the elimination of 90 to 95 percent of new-car emissions of hydrocarbons, carbon monoxide, and nitrogen oxides. Very little study went into the decision to control these emissions tightly while ignoring other pollutants, such as airborne lead. No amount of subsequent analysis showing that these pollutants are only a limited threat to human health has moved Congress to reconsider despite the enormous cost of the mobile-source program [8, ch. 5]. In this situation, The Environmental Protection Agency (EPA) is helpless. No amount of cost-benefit analysis can reverse the statutory goals. Indeed, EPA has found it so difficult even to set ambient standards for these pollutants that it is now four years behind the legislated schedule for revising them.

Simply placing the decisions in the hands of an expert agency may not be the solution either. In 1966, Congress established a government agency, now the National Highway Traffic Safety Administration (NHTSA), to set safety standards for new automobiles. Even though the legislation does not require that standards pass a cost-benefit test, such analyses are routinely done by the agency. Overall, the regulations that NHTSA has promulgated are rather few in number and appear to be quite effective in reducing automobile fatalities [8, Ch. 4]. Of course, political pressures have had a restraining influence on the agency's agenda. For instance, it has grappled for nearly 20 years with the passive restraint issue, but has not been able to withstand the political pressures against it.

On the other hand, the Consumer Product Safety Commission (CPSC) has also had considerable latitude in choosing regulatory targets, but Viscusi contends that data limitations and procedural problems have led to a poor choice of regulatory targets [19]. Even with a limited mandate and agenda, the CPSC has not undertaken systematic cost-benefit analyses of its prospective standards. This has led the agency to choose the wrong targets, according to Viscusi. Why the performance of NHTSA and the CPSC should differ so substantially in this regard is difficult to understand.

The Choice of Regulatory Instruments

No amount of cost-benefit analysis will help to guide a regulatory agency if Congress has saddled it with the wrong choice of regulatory instruments. Economists often criticize detailed engineering standards because they are likely to be inefficient. Regulators are less likely to be able to measure the incremental costs of control across sources than decentralized firms facing pressures to minimize costs.

In fact, detailed engineering standards suffer from another serious limitation -- they place too heavy a burden on the regulatory agency's resources. In regulating air and water pollution,

EPA must set literally thousands of point-source standards. It is not feasible to perform a cost-benefit test on each one. In fact, it is often impossible to promulgate, defend, and enforce all of these standards. Nor does EPA have the resources to engage in retrospective studies of the costs and benefits of these standards [6].

In contrast, the NHTSA standards for automobile safety are largely performance standards. Ex ante analyses of each are based upon engineers' estimates of the likely choice of technology, but this technology is not forced upon the manufacturers. In this environment, cost-benefit analysis of prospective standards and retrospective analyses of existing standards are conducted regularly. The program simply works much better than the Gosplan-like air and water pollution programs.

The Anticipated Costs of Safety Regulation

One might find instances in which estimates of the present value of risks avoided (premature deaths or serious injuries) are greater than the estimated costs of the regulation, but where it is appropriate to reject regulation as a desirable activity. If the regulations serve to reduce choices among products of varying degrees of "safety" and if the safety of the products is at least partly dependent upon consumer care in using them, regulation may force costs upon the careful in order to protect the careless.

The reduction in choices for the careful members of society is not likely to be considered in the regulatory process. A regulator is unlikely to defend his failure to protect the careless from themselves as desirable because it allows others greater freedom of choice. Moreover, these costs are often difficult to quantify in a cost-benefit analysis since any available demand estimates are likely to be difficult to use in evaluating the loss of consumer welfare as the price of the "unsafe" commodity or service essentially becomes infinite.

Regulation itself may dull the incentives for risk avoidance. Thus, it may be circular to argue that the risks "avoided" are worth the costs if avoidance itself is blunted by individuals' knowledge that the state will protect them from themselves. This "moral hazard" problem is now becoming a central element of the economic analyses of regulation, social insurance systems, and private insurance.

Examples of these feedback effects or "offsetting behavior" are found in Peltzman's analysis of automobile safety [15, pp. 677-725] and Viscusi's analysis of childproof bottle caps [19, ff. 76]. In each case, regulation is identified as a cause of increasing precisely the type of risk that it is designed to avoid. Proponents of these regulatory policies, rather than addressing such problems, simply deny that they exist.

Regulation may also dull managerial incentives for innovation. Proponents of government regulation are quick to point to new products or processes that appeared as the serendipitous result of regulation. But when managers and engineers spend their energies on compliance and on lobbying for regulatory advantage, they are less likely to be pursuing new products or technologies.

Prospective Versus Retrospective Cost-Benefit Analysis

Most of the debate over cost-benefit analysis of regulation concerns prospective analyses of proposed rules. It is these "regulatory impact analyses" that generate the tumult and the shouting in the political arena. Yet rarely does one see retrospective analyses of regulations. (NHTSA's series of evaluations of its standards is an exception.)

There is considerable evidence that many of the health-safety-regulatory policies are not even effective in reducing the risks they are designed to combat. Obviously, they were not designed to fail, and even if prospective cost-benefit analyses had been conducted, the analyses would surely not have reflected the inefficacy of the regulation. Optimistic assumptions about the prospective reduction of exposure to risk that drive the regulation will also be built into the prospective cost-benefit analysis.

It would obviously be useful to conduct analyses of how regulations have actually worked several years after their promulgation. Of course, this would require that someone monitor the effects of the rules, a requirement that is often missing, particularly in the environmental area. For some forms of product safety regulation, such as automobile safety, the data are much more readily available. For carcinogens, however, a detailed longitudinal data base is required if useful epidemiological studies are to be conducted twenty or thirty years after the fact.

THE POLITICS OF REGULATION

Even assuming that the practical obstacles to the use of cost-benefit analysis in health-safety regulation can be overcome, one should not be too optimistic that this tool can be used to make regulatory policies effective and efficient. It would be naive to think that each regulatory program was designed solely for the purpose stated in the preamble to its authorizing legislation. Surely, the Occupational Safety and Health Act was not passed simply to improve worker safety. Nor were ludicrously tight new-source standards in the Clean Air Act imposed simply to improve air quality. Nor perhaps to improve air quality at all.

The potential contribution of cost-benefit analysis of regulation is that it provides a careful documentation of the public benefits of a regulatory rule and its opportunity costs. This presumably makes it difficult for bureaucrats or politicians to squander our social product in the pursuit of ineffective assaults upon threats to human health and safety. But this transparency may also undermine the hidden agendas behind various regulatory policies. I remarked earlier that transparency has its benefits. To some, it may also be very costly.

REFERENCES

1. AKERLOF, GEORGE A. and WILLIAM T. DICKENS (1982), "The Economic Consequence of Cognitive Dissonance," The American Economic Review, June.

2. BARAM, MICHAEL S. (1979), Regulation of Health, Safety and Environment and the Use of Cost-Benefit Analysis, Final Report to the Administrative Conference of the United States.

3. BAILEY, MARTIN J. (1980), Reducing Risks to Life: Measurements of the Benefits, Washington, DC: The American Enterprise Institute.

4. BEYER, STEPHEN (1982), Regulation and Its Reform, Cambridge, MA: Harvard University Press.

5. CALABRESI, GUIDO and PHILIP BOBBITT (1978), Tragic Choices, New York: W.W. Norton Co.

6. CRANDALL, ROBERT W. (1983), Controlling Industrial Pollution, Washington, DC: The Brookings Institution.

7. CRANDALL, ROBERT W. and LESTER B. LAVE (1981), The Scientific Basis of Health and Safety Regulation, Washington, DC: The Brookings Institution.

8. CRANDALL, ROBERT W., HOWARD K. GRUENSPECHT, THEODORE E. KEELER, and LESTER B. LAVE (1986), Regulating the Automobile, Washington, DC: The Brookings Institution.

9. EADS, GEORGE and PETER REUTER (1983), Designing Safer Products: Corporate Responses to Product Liability Law and Regulation, Santa Monica, CA: The Rand Corporation.

10. LAVE, LESTER B. (1981), The Strategy of Social Regulation: Decision Frameworks for Policy, Washington, DC: The Brookings Institution.

11. LITAN, ROBERT E. and WILLIAM D. NORDHAUS (1983), Reforming Federal Regulation, New Haven: Yale University Press.

12. MISHAN, E.J. (1976), Cost-Benefit Analysis, New York: Praeger.

13. ________ (1981), "Distributive Implications of Economic Controls," in Allen R. Ferguson and E. Phillip LeVeen, eds., The Benefits of Health and Safety Regulation, Cambridge, MA: Ballinger.

14. NICHOLS, ALBERT L. and RICHARD J. ZECKHAUSER (1985), "The Dangers of Caution: Conservatism in Assessment and the Mismanagement of Risk," Harvard University, Energy and Environmental Policy Center, Working Paper E85-11, November.

15. PELTZMAN, SAM (1975), "The Effects of Automobile Safety Regulation," The Journal of Political Economy, August.

16. SCHELLING, THOMAS C. (1968), "The Life You Save May Be Your Own," in Samuel B. Chase, Jr., ed., Problems in Public Expenditure Analysis, Washington, DC: The Brookings Institution.

17. STARR, CHANNING (1969), "Social Benefit versus Technology in Risk," Science, September.

18. THALER, RICHARD and SHERWIN ROSEN (1976), "The Value of Saving a Life: Evidence from the Labor Market," in N. Terleckyj, ed., Household Production and Consumption, New York: NBER.

19. VISCUSI, W. KIP (1984), Regulating Consumer Product Safety, Washington, DC: The American Enterprise Institute.

20. WEIDENBAUM, MURRAY L. (1986), Business, Government and the Public, Englewood Cliffs, NJ: Prentice-Hall, Inc., Third Edition.

21. ZECKHAUSER, RICHARD J. (1975), "Procedures for Valuing Lives," Public Policy.

Chapter 5

Panel: Issues in Product Safety

ABOUT THE AUTHOR

Eric B. Ault is a career professional in safety regulation. Taking an undergraduate degree from Ohio State University in Zoology and and MBA from the Keller Graduate School of Management at Chicago, Illinois, Ault spent two and one-half years with FDA in Cincinnati before joining CPCS at its inception in 1973. He is currently Acting Regional Director of the Midwestern Regional Office of CPSC.

CPCS'S VOLUNTARY STANDARDS: AN ASSESSMENT AND A PARADOX

THE PARADOX OF VOLUNTARY STANDARDS FOR CONSUMER PRODUCTS

Eric B. Ault

THE LEGISLATIVE MANDATE FOR VOLUNTARY STANDARDS

It is Section 7 of the Consumer Product Safety Act that provides the legislative mandate for Consumer Product Safety Standards. The current version of Section 7 differs drastically from the 1981 version. Both the 1981 and current versions of this Section specify (1) requirements for Standards and (2) means of promulgation. One of the unique features of Section 7 in 1981 was the Offeror Process. In promulgating Standards, CPSC had the option of (1) developing the rule in-house or (2) accepting an offer to do the work, from an outside party.

Today the same Section of the Consumer Product Safety Act is markedly different. Six sub-sections have shrunk to three; 4 3/4 pages have become two-thirds of one page. Clearly, something important has happened to Consumer Product Safety Standards. Gone is all the detail surrounding the Offeror Process and the Commission Development Process. In its place one finds Section 7(b) which states:

> "The Commission shall rely upon Voluntary Consumer Product Safety Standards rather than promulgate a Consumer Product Safety Standard prescribing requirements described in sub-section (a) whenever compliance with such Voluntary Standards would eliminate or

> adequately reduce the risk of injury addressed and it is likely that there will be substantial compliance with such voluntary standards."

Clearly, Congress has given the Consumer Product Safety Commission (CPSC) a mandate to pursue Voluntary Standards.

A PARADOX OF VOLUNTARY STANDARDS: CONSUMER GAINS COUPLED WITH BURDENS FOR INDUSTRIES ADOPTING THEM

Voluntary Standards Expand CPSC's Scope

This turn by CPCS towards Voluntary Standards has produced a fascinating paradox: it has produced advantages for the consuming public while at the same time yielding disadvantages to the very groups whose cooperation was essential to the voluntary approach. The discussion that follows elaborates on this.

Certainly, reliance on the voluntary process helps conserve scarce CPSC resources. This is salutary since the struggle to cut Federal deficits has reduced CPCS funding and manpower. Development of mandatory standards is an expensive and time consuming business. By promoting voluntary standards or monitoring them, CPSC staff can exert influence over a considerable number of products or areas rather than concentrating on one or two hazards, as in a mandatory process. As examples, we are currently reviewing an updated voluntary bunk bed safety guideline. We are also working with the American Society For Testing and Materials on ways to address crib strangulation as well as problems of entrapment and mechanical integrity on home playground equipment. CPSC is collaborating with Underwriters Laboratories standards designed to avoid electrocutions in the use of portable electric heaters and hair dryers. Altogether we are currently involved in over 40 voluntary standards activities. Relying solely on its own resoruces, CPCS would probably lack the resources to tackle more than one or two such projects.

Reliance on the voluntary process also affects resources in other ways. It may in effect increase the enforcement resources of CPSC. Many "Voluntary Standards" such as model building codes have been adopted by local jurisdictions. By removing controversial glazed panel requirements from its Architectural Glazing Standard, CPSC was able to obtain the "enforcement" services of thousands of building inspectors. This horde of building inspectors contrasts with the 19 investigations CPCS has to cover the ten states of its

Midwestern Region. A great deal of enforcement was gained by reaching a compromise via voluntary standards.

Voluntary Standards Stricter Than Mandatory Standards

It is yet another paradox that in some ways the use of Voluntary Standards can actually lead to stricter requirements than those embodied in Mandatory Standards. (Certainly, product liability concerns have helped the Consumer Product Safety Commission to force the issue on increased Voluntary Standards coverage as well.) A review of the eight Consumer Product Safety Act Standards currently in force shows that several have had to be modified in response to various challenges. For example, portions of the Swimming Pool Slide Standard and the Matchbook Standard were revoked as a result of court challenges. Congress, for better or for worse, changed the blade stopping requirements in the Walk-Behind Lawn Mower Standard to permit use of an engine stopping device that would be activated when the user leaves the mower.[1] We have already seen how the Architectural Glazing Standard failed to meet the "enforcement challenge". In newer Voluntary Standards efforts the Commission has been able to push for more stringent requirements that might not have withstood a legal challenge under the mandatory standard regime. As yet another example, the National Electrical Code was recently modified to require Ground Fault Circuit Interrupters in kitchen and basement circuits. It is questionable whether all portions the changes would have survived a challenge under the mandatory regime.

An additional paradox of Voluntary Standards is produced by their voluntary character. Being voluntary makes them attractive to businesses but it may also produce problems for businesses. Let us see how.

Voluntary Standards appear to lack the clout of mandatory compliance. This is a feature about which consumer advocates have complained. I suspect that complying businesses will complain too as non-complying competitors emerge. The extent to which this will occur has yet to be revealed and may vary greatly, depending upon the industry. For example, many local jurisdictions forbid the sale of electrical products lacking the seal of approval of independent test laboratories. This prohibition should tend to encourage compliance with these Standards. In addition, voluntary standards should work well in industries that are well organized or have a

---

[1]CPSC's original standard called for a more expensive blade clutch.

very limited number of manufacturers or importers. An example is the chain saw industry. CPCS and the industry have worked closely to develop a Voluntary Safety Standard. We are currently in the process of checking comformance with this voluntary chain saw standard. Since there are a few firms in this industry and the expense of entry is great, it seems unlikely that a non-complying competitor could start production of chain saws.

Some industries are more fragmented as is the case with the bunk bed industry which has many small competitors. In inspecting these firms, CPSC discovered that many were ignorant of work on the current industry standards for bunk beds. In fact, many were also manufacturing bunk bed mattresses and were totally unaware of the Mattress Standard established in the early 1970s under the Federal Flammable Fabrics Act. Once the current effort to improve the Voluntary Standard for Bunk Beds has been finished, it will be interesting to determine the extent of industry comformance. As indicated above, this will be a noteworthy test because many manufacturers are not aware of the Voluntary Standard now in place. Further, it is an industry in which new firms can enter easily and cheaply.

Who Preempts Whom? -- CPSC's Voluntary Standards Vs. State/Local Regulations

The final paradox of CPCS's Voluntary Standards from the business viewpoint relates to their possible preemption by conflicting state or local regulations. In 1986 Massachusetts enacted legislation, banning the sale or use of unvented liquid-fueled space heaters. This action was challenged in the U.S. District Court by the National Kerosene Heater Association which contended that the Massachusetts Ban was preempted by CPSC as far as "new generation" kerosene heaters were concerned. They argued that the preemption clause of the Consumer Product Safety Act held because the Commission had chosen to rely on the Underwriters Laboratory Standard (UL 647) as a Voluntary Consumer Product Safety Standard. In its arguments the Commonwealth of Massachusetts stated that CPSC must follow appropriate procedures and publish a notice in the Federal Register stating that it will rely on the Voluntary Standard before preemption can occur. The court, supporting CPCS on this substantive case, stated that preemption occurs whenever a Consumer Product Safety Standard is in effect. However, the court declared that this test is not met when the Consumer Product Safety Commission informally relies on a Voluntary Standard. The court therefore let the Massachusetts ban stand. In its opinion the court noted that the preemption issue was raised by Congress when it amended the Consumer Product Safety Act to place greater reliance on Voluntary Standards. Unfortunately, while Congress discussed the preemption question, no specific language was included in the Act providing for preemption by Voluntary Standards. It is interesting to note that the Court did not decide whether a CPSC-recognized Voluntary Standard would be entitled to preemption. Currently the National Kerosene Heater Association is considering whether to ask the Commission to formally recognize the Voluntary Standard. Thus, we see another paradox where, an industry's efforts to obtain recognition of a desired Voluntary Standard is thwarted by state legislation.

We have seen how the move toward Voluntary Standards which appeared to favor business has proved to provide a number of problems for business as well. It will be interesting to see how these and other problems which may emerge over time will be resolved as the Commission continues its reliance on the Voluntary Standards Process.

ABOUT THE AUTHOR

Robert N. Mayer is Associate Professor in the Department of Family and Consumer Studies at the University of Utah. A sociologist, Mayer received his Ph.D. from the University of California, Berkeley, in 1978. Widely published, Mayer's research has had the sociology of consumption, consumerism and its implications, and consumer socialization of children as continuing themes.

In 1985-86 Mayer spent a sabbatical in Paris studying the development of on-line videotex systems in France. A monograph, Videotex in France, is due for early publication. Rob Mayer will be Chairman of the next International Conference on Research in the Consumer Interest to be held in 1990.

CONSUMER SAFETY AND THE ISSUE EMERGENCE PROCESS

Robert N. Mayer

Consumer researchers justifiably focus a great deal of their attention on how best to solve consumer safety problems. For example, Jennifer Gerner in Chapter 3 of this volume compares product liability and regulation as alternative means of promoting consumer safety. Similarly, Robert Crandall's discussion in Chapter 4 of how to apply cost-benefit analysis presupposes that a consumer safety problem has reached the stage of the public policy process in which solutions are being considered.

Much less attention has been given to the initial step in the policy process: how consumer safety problems emerge as "important" and compete for a place on the governmental agenda. This step is variously described as "issue emergence," "agenda building," and "agenda setting" [5, 7, 8]. The purpose of this paper is to examine the question of how consumer safety issues manage to achieve a place on a nation's policy agenda.

The social and relativistic nature of the issue emergence process is underscored by differences among industrialized countries in what constitutes a pressing consumer safety issue. (One would expect major differences between more and less developed nations.) Safety issues that are at the top of the political agenda in certain European countries are not necessarily perceived as pressing in the United States, and vice versa. In France, for example, the presence of hormones in beef has stimulated consumer boycotts on more than one occasion, although this issue has failed to stimulate much public action in the United States. Conversely, the French are completely oblivious to passive smoking, an issue that has received a serious hearing at virtually all levels of government in the United States.

Understanding the processes by which consumer safety issues emerge (or fail to emerge) in various societies should be valuable to both public policy makers and consumer safety activists. Researchers in this area should be able to identify those social mechanisms that are most effective in rapidly and reliably placing consumer safety issues on a nation's political agenda. Ultimately, when the emergence of consumer safety issues is understood, attention can be focused on the processes which produce an "efficient" consumer safety agenda: one in which risks that are most substantial and/or amenable to reduction at reasonable cost receive the greatest attention.

CONSUMER SAFETY ISSUES AS A SPECIAL CASE

The number of social problems competing for public attention is always great. So it is difficult for any type of social problem to capture a place on the public policy agenda. Consumer safety problems are particularly handicapped in achieving the status of public issues.

One difficulty has to do with the fact that consumer safety policy usually entails the protection of <u>unknown</u> individuals against <u>uncertain</u> risks in the <u>future</u>. Contrast this with protecting known individuals against a clear and present danger. Consumer safety is likely to be the loser if two such problems compete for public attention and resources. For example, when American automobile industry jobs and profits were endangered in the early 1980's, the Reagan Administration was quick to propose regulatory relief in the form a weakened standard for the strength of bumpers and the elimination of the passive restraint standard.

Consumer safety's ability to achieve a place on the public policy agenda is further hampered by the fact that safety policies are usually public goods. That is, all consumers benefit from a safety policy, regardless of their level of effort in establishing that policy. Therefore, few consumers are willing to expend time, money, and effort in lobbying for such policies because the benefits to the lobbyist are small as compared with benefits to others. Of course, if everyone takes the attitude that someone else will do the work, nothing will be accomplished. This "free- rider" problem in the provision of public goods is most common for issues which (1) affect large numbers of people and (2) are not among the most intensely-felt concerns of individuals [17, 20]. These conditions apply strongly to consumer safety problems.

A FEW DEFINITIONAL AND METHODOLOGICAL ISSUES

There has been virtually no research on the issue emergence process as it pertains to consumer issues in general or consumer safety in particular. Hence, a host of definitional, methodological, and substantive questions remain to be answered. Fortunately, studies conducted with respect to public issues such as environmental protection [9], child abuse [18], and nutrition [27] have had to tackle many of the same definitional and methodological problems. For example, what is an issue and how can issue-ness be measured? What type of research design is appropriate and feasible for studying the issue emergence process? These questions cannot be resolved easily and will not be treated here. Rather, the assumptions that guide the discussion below will be made explicit.

The key point in defining an issue is distinguishing it from the much larger set of social problems. Agenda-setting research is based on the assumption that "the number of potential public issues far exceeds the capabilities of decision-making institutions to process them" [6]. Thus, an issue is "any unresolved matter recognized by the general public and/or public officials as requiring an authoritative decision." [7]

Some researchers distinguish between two types of policy agendas. One consists of those issues that have achieved a high degree of salience and visibility among members of the general public. This may be called the "public agenda." The second type of agenda is the "formal agenda." It consists of those items which public decision makers have accepted formally for serious consideration [6]. The approach adopted here is to focus on the process by which issues reach the formal agenda. Public concern is viewed as an extremely powerful and common means of placing issues on the formal agenda, but only one of several such factors.

Issue-emergence research need not be based on the assumption that issues are always initiated by groups outside of government. Nor does public agenda status necessarily precede formal agenda status. Issues may be initiated by governmental actors such as legislators and regulators. In these cases formal agenda status may precede public agenda status.

The measurement of issue-ness poses further difficulties. One problem is distinguishing the different stages of the issue emergence process. Another is deciding when the issue emergence process ceases and the process of responding to an issue begins [18]. Most studies of issue emergence have been qualitative and descriptive in nature. Yet, some attempts at quantification have been made. For example, evidence of issues being on the public agenda may come from public opinion polls, consumer complaints, or discussion by non-government interest groups. Similarly, the existence of an item on the formal agenda may be indicated by court calendars, legislative and regulatory dockets, and political party platforms.

A final methodological problem in studying issue emergence is finding a strong research design. Case studies are the most common way of studying the agenda-setting process, but such studies can only suggest the general dynamics of the agenda building process. Comparative research on this subject requires studying several geographical units (nations, states, or cities) at a single time, the same geographical unit at different times, or both.

Perhaps because of these conceptual and methodological challenges, there have been only a few studies [10, 23] of the emergence of consumer issues. Nevertheless, some research exists which can be used to generate a working model of how consumer safety problems achieve issue status. This model (Figure 1) is presented below along with a discussion of some of the research upon which it is based.

A Model of the Emergence of Consumer Safety Issues

Figure 1 has a number of obvious limitations as a model of the issue-emergence process. First, it takes the determination of several variables as given. For example, it does not try to explain variation in the strength of non-governmental consumer safety activists. Second, the model is intended to apply to all western, industrialized countries, but it is probably most descriptive of the United States. Third, it does not acknowledge the diffusion of consumer safety issues from one country to another. Fourth, it is based on studies of consumer policy at the national level and may not pertain to states or local governments. Finally, it does not include feedback loops, most notably from formal issue status to public concern. Still, the model includes those variables that have been shown to influence the issue emergence process.

The Nature of the Risk

There is an emerging body of research on the relationship between risk characteristics and public policy [16]. The characteristics of risks affect issue emergence in at least two ways. First, some types of risks are more likely than others to result in the kinds of accidents and scandals that force their way into the public's awareness and the formal policy agenda (e.g., Bhopal).

Second, independent of their likelihood of resulting in newsworthy accidents, some types of risks are systematically overestimated by members of the general public while others are consistently underestimated [13, 28, 29]. For example, risks which threaten a group of people (e.g., a coal mining disaster) are more likely to capture public attention than risks posed to the identical number of isolated individuals (e.g., lumberjacks). Consequently, some risks are easier for consumer safety activists to sell the general public and government officials.

Figure 1

PRELIMINARY MODEL OF THE ISSUE EMERGENCE PROCESS FOR CONSUMER SAFETY PROBLEMS

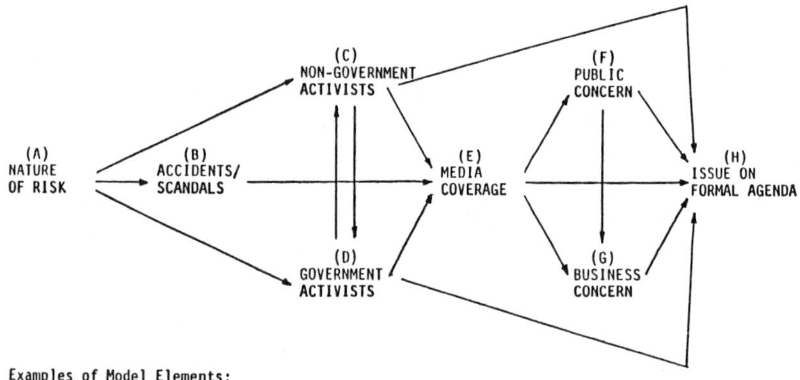

Examples of Model Elements:

A. age, sex of likely victims degree of conscious risk acceptance
B. Thalidomide-related birth defects Chernobyl; drug tampering
C. product test results; exposes; boycotts; class action suits; petitions; lobbying
D. speeches; press conferences; leaks; hearings
E. news reports; documentaries; consumer columns
F. public opinion polls; referenda; complaints
G. fear of stiff regulation; need to reassure public
H. legislation filed; cases filed rule-making initiated;

TRAGEDIES AND SCANDALS

Certain consumer safety problems have the "benefit" of a major accident or scandal to help them become public issues. Examples would include birth defects resulting from thalidomide, nuclear accidents at Three Mile Island and Chernobyl, and the Tylenol poisonings. However, the role of accidents and scandals in issue emergence can be exaggerated.

First, such dramatic events are neither sufficient nor necessary for the emergence of a consumer safety issue. For example, the dangerously high levels of pesticides found in watermelons in 1985 did not result in any new regulation of pesticide use. Conversely, many consumer safety problems have become issues without a dramatic disaster (e.g., flammable furniture or carcinogens like radon gas). Second, the impact of accidents and scandals is highly dependent on the degree of media coverage they receive. The drug, thalidomide, provides an illustration. Even though thalidomide's disastrous side effects were mentioned in Congressional hearings nearly two months before surfacing as a major issue, the hearings received no press coverage. The issue caught the public's attention only after Senator Estes Kefauver and his staff alerted the press to the Subcommittee's hearings as part of their strategy to get a stronger drug bill [17]. In some instances, then, tragedies can be thought of as managed events.

While tragedies or outrageous corporate conduct (e.g., deliberately concealing safety defects) can help consumer safety problems reach the policy agenda, reliance on such events would severely constrain the ability of consumer safety advocates to raise issues. Other mechanisms must exist by which consumer safety issues can be placed on the policy agenda.

NON-GOVERNMENT CONSUMER SAFETY ACTIVISTS

Consumer groups play a major role in bringing consumer safety problems to the public's attention and in transforming these problems into issues demanding government action. There are many techniques by which the "consumerism industry" [3] sells issues and places them on the public policy agenda. For instance, comparative product testing organizations like Consumers Union not only uncover safety problems but also lend credibility to the consumer voice by virtue of the relatively objective nature of product testing. Legislative committees devoted to consumer affairs also serve as forums for safety activists to air consumer safety problems in public. Liberal rules for initiating shareholder resolutions [30] and class action suits provide additional avenues for bringing consumer safety problems to public attention. Two additional mechanisms will be considered here briefly--the petition process and consumer boycotts.

The Right to Petition

Even though private citizens do not usually have the right to initiate legislation, it is possible in several nations for interested individuals and organizations to petition regulatory agencies to initiate action. Thus the petition mechanism makes it possible to place an issue on the policy agenda without generating either media coverage or support from the general public.

The right to petition can be more or less effective depending on the exact provisions of the petition process. In the United States, for example, the Administrative Procedure Act allows interested parties to petition for the issuance of a product safety rule. If an agency declines to start rule-making proceedings, the petitioner is only entitled to prompt notice of denial and a brief explanation.

Until 1981, the Consumer Product Safety Commission had a much more liberal petition process. Under Section 10 of the Consumer Product Safety Act, individuals or organizations could request that the Commission begin a rule-making proceeding. The petitions did not have to be technically sophisticated. Rather, petitioners only needed to state why Commission action was needed and what type of standard they envisioned. In the event that a petition was denied, the Commission had to publish its reasons in the Federal Register. Further, a unique provision of the statute gave a petitioner whose petition was denied the right to file an action in a United States District Court to require CPSC to initiate action! During the first three years of the CPSC's existence, petitions accounted for seven of the nine safety standards initiated by CPSC, an indication of the power of this mechanism for allowing outsiders to influence agency priorities [25].

Consumer Boycotts

Consumer boycotts have been long used to bring about social change [11]. Although boycotts have rarely cut deeply into the sales of a business or the price of its stock [22], boycotts have become a successful method of focusing public attention on a consumer problem, thus stimulating responses by either businesses or government [30].

In the United States, the right to boycott is essentially unlimited as long as no laws are broken in the process. This unlimited right is not enjoyed in all countries. A recent court decision in France, for instance, restricted the right of consumer groups to organize a boycott against meat containing high amounts of hormones. Thus, the right to boycott must be treated as a variable in research on issue emergency, and the conditions under which boycotts are most successful in placing consumer safety problems on the public policy agenda need to be identified.

GOVERNMENT CONSUMER SAFETY ACTIVISTS

Recent research has emphasized the extent to which the action's of members of government are rooted in self-interest [2, 4]. Accordingly, executives, legislators, and regulators often try to capitalize on risks that are salient and compelling to the general public, thereby playing an important role in the emergence of consumer safety issues.

Executives

One of the jobs of a national leader is to promote national solidarity. When this solidarity is threatened by a divisive issue (e.g., an unpopular war or increasing disparities between rich and poor citizens), executives may call for correction of widely-experienced problems such as risks posed by hazardous products.

Nadel [17] explains the rise of consumer safety issues in the United States during the late 1960's with just such an argument. According to Nadel, President Lyndon Johnson placed consumer protection high on the presidential policy agenda in order to offset domestic division regarding the Vietnam War without further straining a tight government budget. Nadel observes, "To champion an issue as inherently popular as consumer protection was an irresistible opportunity for a President concerned both with getting new programs and with achieving consensus" [17, p. 41].

Legislators

Legislators, perhaps more than presidents and other political executives, must constantly worry about being re-elected. Accordingly, a legislator may champion consumer safety issues as a means of revitalizing a flagging political career. Former Chairman of the FTC, Michael Pertschuk attributes this motivation to his mentor, Senator Warren Magnuson:

> ....in the election of 1962, Magnuson ...came within 50,000 votes of losing his Senate seat to a political novice, a young Methodist minister who had never before run for political office. He...turned for guidance and leadership to a brilliant young Yale and Harvard lawyer from the state of Washington, Gerald Grinstein....I do not know when Magnuson and Grinstein determined that a strong pro-consumer record of achievement would be a major component of the political revitalization of Warren Magnuson,

> but in the fall of 1964, Grinstein....asked me to join the staff of the Senate Commerce Committee in the newly created capacity of consumer counsel....My assignment: to help build a consumer record for Magnuson....and make certain that Magnuson received appropriate acknowledgement for his achievements....By 1968, eight new consumer laws bore Magnuson's name as principal author [almost all pertaining to consumer safety] [21, pp. 24-5].

Mark Nadel [17] contends that Magnuson's successor as Chairman of the Senate Consumer Subcommittee, Frank Moss of Utah, used a similar strategy. Moss, a Democrat in a predominantly Republican state, may have owed his 1970 re-election to his support of consumer protection. Citizens may react negatively to the abstract concept of "regulation," but public opinion polls show consistent support for specific instances of safety regulation [1, 26].

Nadel cautions against too readily accepting the idea that consumer advocacy produces political victories. Indeed, championing consumer protection can result in increased campaign contributions by business to one's opponent. For example, Senator George McGovern's failure to win reelection in 1980 has been attributed to his attack on chlesterol levels in the American diet and the resulting alienation of cattle ranchers [15].

Attempts by legislators to achieve popularity through promoting consumer safety issues may be especially evident when political parties are weak in terms of their ability to influence electoral outcomes. When parties are relatively strong, as in contemporary Europe, three conditions pertain: (1) members occupy a relatively clear position within the party hierarchy, (2) the party controls key political resources (e.g., safe seats), and (3) members typically run on the party's platform. When political parties are fairly weak, as in contemporary United States, candidates must be more entrepreneurial in raising resources and seeking out issues, like consumer safety, that will build their individual popularity. By the same logic, in a situation where one political party is strong and another is weak, candidates belonging to the weaker party are more likely to raise consumer safety issues in their campaigns.

Regulators

Few regulatory agencies are explicitly charged with the task of identifying consumer safety issues. Even the consumer ombudsmen found in many European countries and American states are largely engaged in reactive rather than proactive measures. Agencies typically implement laws that have already been passed in response to an issue. Nevertheless, because of their broad mandates and rule-making authority, agencies charged with promoting consumer safety often have opportunities to raise issues if they so choose. The propensity of a government agency to raise a consumer safety issue depends on many factors, including idiosyncratic ones such as the political sentiments of its leaders and the morale of its personnel. Perhaps a more systematic influence on an agency's tendency to raise safety issues is its degree of responsibility for its actions.

One might hypothesize that, holding other factors constant, the staff of agencies with a high degree of responsibility for their actions will be most likely to raise consumer safety issues. Responsibility promotes risk aversiveness among regulators because the political costs of failing to recognize a safety problem are likely to be greater than the costs of impeding some potentially-risky activity (e.g., the introduction of a new product). In contrast, when regulators have little freedom of action and simply carry out legislatively-mandated procedures, they will have less incentive to seek out new threats to consumer safety. They can always say that they were "just doing their job."

In the United States, subtle differences in political aggressiveness exist between safety agencies located within departments directly accountable to the President and those which have a greater degree of institutional independence. Indeed, the so-called independent agencies like the FTC and CPSC have been accused of overstepping their powers, and they have paid the wages of zealotry [21]. Still, most regulatory agencies in the United States operate under broadly-defined mandates and exercise a high degree of responsibility. Consequently, regulators tend to err on the side of caution rather than leave themselves open to the charge of ignoring their safety responsibilities [12, 19].

Closely related to an agency's degree of responsibility is the extent to which safety is its only goal. Some agencies are free-standing and pursue only consumer safety (e.g., CPSC). Others, while having safety as a major goal, are embedded within organizations with additional, sometimes conflicting goals (e.g., NHTSA). Still others promote safety simultaneously with other goals. A classic American example of the latter is the Atomic Energy Commission. It was originally charged with both insuring nuclear safety and promoting this new form of energy--two goals with the potential for conflict. Only with the creation of the

Nuclear Regulatory Commission did safety become somewhat disentangled from the goal of industry development.

The Netherlands provides another example of the effect of agency structure on the tendency to raise consumer safety issues. Consumer product safety functions are currently housed in a division of the Ministry of Welfare, Health, and Culture. Buried within a ministry grappling with containment of medical and public assistance costs, the consumer safety division is less able to pursue an aggressive safety agenda than when it was previously located within the more activist Ministry of Environmental Affairs [31].

In all, a variety of governmental actors--executives, legislators, and regulators--may on occasion become consumer activists, but rarely does the task constitute one of their primary responsibilities. More knowledge is needed with respect to the conditions that promote consumer activism by members of the government and the successful placing of consumer safety issues on the policy agenda.

Mass Media Coverage

In virtually every western nation, the broadcast and print media assist consumer groups in publicizing their concerns. At a minimum, the mass media carry reports of accidents and scandals and amplify the activities of consumer activists both within and outside government. Yet, the mass media can play a much more active role. For example, muckraking reporters and journalists often uncover consumer safety problems on their own. Similarly, the mass media may provide time or space to consumer groups. In France, the Institut National de la Consommation, a product testing agency, is provided with 24 minutes of prime-time television access per week.

It is likely that the media must enjoy a high degree of independence if they are to pursue consumer safety problems. At the most basic level, the media must be independent from control by business interests. Because of their frequent dependence on advertising revenues, the media cannot afford to alienate sponsors with exposes on product hazards. Sponsors may shift their business to competing media. Given this fact, Nadel [17] observes that the national media can cover consumer safety problems more aggressively than local media because the former rely less heavily on any single sponsor.

Control by political parties can also compromise pro-consumer coverage by the mass media. To a greater degree in Europe than in the United States, newspapers are associated with particular political parties. When a consumer safety problem stems from government action (or inaction), newspapers loyal to the party in power may not investigate the problem to the fullest (although opposition newspapers would have an incentive to do so). And when a problem conflicts with the policies of all major parties, coverage may be practically non-existent. An example is the minimal coverage of the Chernobyl nuclear accident by the French media. Though the relative silence of the mass media may have been partly due to a lack of concrete information and scientific expertise, the support of France's massive commitment to nuclear power by both major political parties was probably an important factor.

The mass media clearly play a critical role in amplifying the efforts of consumer safety activists and, on occasion, play an independent role in transforming safety problems into pubic issues. However, the supportive role of the mass media should not be treated as constant but rather as variable across time and place. Nor should this role be overemphasized. Nadel [17], for example, found that media attention, as measured by articles in the Reader's Guide, was not common until 1966, one of the busiest years for Congressional consumer protection in the United States. Perhaps media coverage plays a relatively more important role with respect to consumer safety issues than consumer protection issues in general, but media coverage cannot be considered either a necessary or sufficient condition for issue emergence.

Concern by Powerful Constituencies

Studies of the agenda-setting process typically give substantial weight to public opinion. As noted above, many researchers speak of a public agenda and a formal agenda and examine the relationship between the two. The assumption is that policy makers are sensitive to the concerns of the public and often respond to them, even in the absence of mobilized mass support. Yet, the general public is only one of several powerful constituencies whose policy agenda may be considered in the creation of the formal agenda. In the area of consumer safety policy, business is likely to constitute such a constituency. Indeed, Crenson [7] argues that the business agenda will be heeded by policy makers even in the absence of explicit lobbying efforts.

Businesses have little interest in raising consumer safety issues. Rather, businesses are likely to enter the issue-emergence process after an issue has already reached the stage of mass media coverage. In certain instances, businesses will contribute to the emergence of an issue instead of trying to hinder it. For example, businesses may regard government action as necessary for restoring public confidence and trust in a product. Similarly, businesses may jump on an issue's bandwagon in the hope of steering it in a direction that minimizes damage to them (e.g., more lenient or flexible regulation). Thus, both public concern and business concern are likely to play an important role in whether an issue attains a place on the formal policy agenda.

CONCLUSION

This paper has sought to identify the conditions under which consumer safety problems attain a place on a nation's public policy agenda. A few consumer safety problems are so dramatic or intense that they attain issue status almost spontaneously. More commonly, issues are either "pushed" by mobilized interest groups or aroused public opinion or they are "pulled" by policy makers who choose particular issues according to the needs of the situation [5, 32].

Based on an examination of the United States and Great Britain, Flickinger [10] concludes that the "pull" pattern is by far the most characteristic of consumer issues. It is possible that both the "spontaneous" and "push" patterns are slightly more important in the case of safety issues, with their often dramatic qualities. Nevertheless, the general pattern that appears is that consumer safety problems must pass through a number of filters before they reach the public policy agenda. These filters include the potential for dramatic portrayal, the role of risk perception, the political and institutional imperatives faced by activists, the independence of the mass media, and the attempts at redirection by powerful constituencies such as business.

All of these factors suggest that the consumer safety problems that reach a society's policy agenda may not be those which impose the highest objective risks to consumers, even holding constant differences in the cost of reducing various risks. Yet, consumer activists and public policy makers alike would prefer a ranking of consumer safety problems that gives greatest attention to a society's "real" safety problems.

Therefore, research on issue emergence should have two goals if it is to be in the consumer interest. First, it should identify those social mechanisms that assist the emergence of consumer safety issues in general. Second, research should analyze differences among nations in their ability to place truly significant threats to consumer safety on the policy agenda while delaying action on less important safety problems. In particular, how do different societies manage to awaken (or reawaken) interest in truly dangerous products like cigarettes, alcohol, firearms, and automobiles? In these latter cases, issue emergence tends to be short-circuited by the fact that there is no quick and easy technological solution to the problems posed by these products. So a large proportion of the social impulse for safer products gets redirected toward such relatively minor dangers as artificial sweeteners and irradiated food. Our research should strive to uncover mechanisms for placing on the public agenda consumer safety issues that can be defended in terms of both their need for action and their prospects for efficient resolution.

REFERENCES

1. ATLANTIC RICHFIELD COMPANY (1983), Consumerism in the Eighties.

2. BARTLETT, RANDALL (1973), Economic Foundations of Political Power, New York: Free Press.

3. BLOOM, PAUL N. and STEPHEN A. GREYSER (1981), "The Maturing of Consumerism," Harvard Business Review, 59:130-139, (November-December).

4. BUCHANAN, JAMES M., ROBERT D. TOLLISON, and GORDON TULLOCK (eds.) (1980), Toward a Theory of the Rent-Seeking Society, College Station, Texas: Texas A&M University Press.

5. COBB, ROGER W. and C.D. ELDER (1972), Participation in American Politics: The Dynamics of Agenda Building, Boston: Allyn and Bacon.

6. COBB, ROGER W., JENNIE-KEITH ROSS, and MARC HOWARD ROSS (1976), "Agenda Building as a Comparative Political Process," American Political Science Review, 70:126-138, (March).

7. CRENSON, MATTHEW A. (1971), The Un-Politics of Air Pollution, Baltimore: Johns Hopkins Press.

8. DOWNS, ANTHONY (1972), "Up and Down with Ecology--The Issue Attention Cycle," Public Interest, 32:38-50, (Summer).

9. ENLOE, CYNTHIA H. (1975), The Politics of Pollution in a Comparative Perspective, New York: David McKay.

10. FLICKINGER, RICHARD (1983), "The Comparative Politics of Agenda Setting: The Emergence of Consumer Protection as a Public Policy Issue in Britain and the United States," Policy Studies Review, 2:429-444, (February).

11. FRIEDMAN, MONROE (1985), "Consumer Boycotts in the United States, 1970-1980: Contemporary Events in Historical Perspective," Journal of Consumer Affairs, 19:96-117, (Summer).

12. GOODMAN, JOHN C. and EDWIN G. DOLAN (1979), Economics of Public Policy, St. Paul: West Publishing.

13. KUNREUTHER, HOWARD (1978), Disaster Insurance Protection: Public Policy Lessons, New York: Wiley.

14. LAVE, LESTER (1980), "Health, Safety, and Environmental Regulations," in Joseph A. Pechman, ed., Setting National Priorities: Agenda for the 1980's, Washington, D.C.: The Brookings Institution.

15. LEVINE, JANET M. (1986), "Hearts and Minds: The Politics of Diet and Heart Disease," in Harvey M. Sapolsky (ed.), Consuming Fears, New York: Basic Books.

16. LOWRANCE, WILLIAM W. (1976), Of Acceptable Risk, Los Altos, California: William Kaufmann, Inc.

17. NADEL, MARK V. (1971), The Politics of Consumer Protection, Indianapolis: Bobbs-Merrill.

18. NELSON, BARBARA J. and THOMAS LINDENFELD (1978), "Setting the Public Agenda: The Case of Child Abuse," in Judith V. May and Aaron B. Wildavsky, eds., The Policy Cycle, Beverly Hills: Sage.

19. NICHOLS, ALBERT L. and RICHARD J. ZECKHAUSER (1986), "The Perils of Prudence," Regulation, 10:13-24, (November/December).

20. OLSON, MANCUR, JR. (1968), The Logic of Collective Action, New York: Schoken Books.

21. PERTSCHUK, MICHAEL (1982), Revolt Against Regulation, Berkeley, University of California Press.

22. PRUITT, STEPHEN W. and MONROE FRIEDMAN (1986), "Determining the Effectiveness of Consumer Boycotts: A Stock Price Analysis of Their Impact on Corporate Targets," Journal of Consumer Policy, 9:375-388, (December).

23. ROSE, LAWRENCE E. (1981), "The Role of Interest Groups in Collective Interest Policy Making: Consumer Protection in Norway and the United States," European Journal of Political Research, 9:17-45, (January).

24. SAPOLSKY, HARVEY M. (ed) (1986), Consuming Fears, New York: Basic Books.

25. SCHWARTZ, TERESA M. (1982), "The Consumer Product Safety Commission: A Flawed Product of the Consumer Decade," George Washington Law Review, 51:32-112, (November).

26. SENTRY INSURANCE, Consumerism at the Crossroads, 1977.

27. SIMS, LAURA S. (1983), "The Ebb and Flow of Nutrition as a Public Policy Issue," Journal of Nutrition Education, 15:132-136, (November).

28. SLOVIC, PAUL, BARUCH FISCHHOFF, and SARAH LICHTENSTEIN (1979), "Rating the Risks," Environment, 21:14-20, (April).

29. TVERSKY, AMOS and DANIEL KAHNEMAN (1981), "The Framing of Decisions and Psychology of Choice," Science, 211:453-458, (January 30).

30. VOGEL, DAVID (1978), Lobbying the Corporation, New York: Basic Books.

31. VON BREMEN, HUBERT (1986), personal interview, Leidschendam, The Netherlands, July 14.

32. WALKER, J.L. (1977), "Setting the Agenda in the U.S. Senate: A Theory of Problem Selection," British Journal of Political Science, 7:423-445, (October).

ABOUT THE AUTHOR

Helen E. Nelson has been a long-time leader in the consumer movement. She was Consumer Counsel of California from 1959 through 1966. She was one of the consumer leaders who put "truth-in-lending" and "unit pricing" across. In the 1970's Nelson was Director of the Center for Consumer Affairs at the University of Wisconsin in Milwaukee. For 15 years she was a member of the Board of Directors of Consumers Union. Currently she is President of the Consumer Research Foundation in California and a member of the Federal Reserve Board's Consumer Advisory Council. She is a Distinguished Fellow of the American Council on Consumer Interests.

REFLECTIONS ON RESEARCH IN THE CONSUMER INTEREST

HELEN EWING NELSON

THE NATURE OF THE CONSUMER INTEREST

The title of this Conference is a delight to me: Research in the Consumer Interest!! The Conference and the research on which it reports has a purpose: to serve consumers. Often researchers, in their zeal for objectivity, shun discussing or even defining the purpose of their research. Objectivity, however, does not imply purposelessness. The U.S. Department of Labor in the United States conducts research in the interest of labor just as the Department of Agriculture conducts research in the interest of agriculture. This is not to say that they are not objective in their reading of the data. It is to say that they have thought through the purpose of doing the research and intend the results to be helpful to their constituencies.

Consumers Union in the U.S. and Consumers' Association in the U.K. are examples of non-government organizations with a commitment to purposeful research. A clear and straightforward sense of purpose helps conceptualize the project or program wisely.

In formulating our consumer research projects, we can benefit from what I call "bottom-line thinking." Industry, in making its decisions, typically asks: "What is the bottom line?" Bluntly they are asking, "What do we, as entrepreneurs, get out of it?" As yet, consumer researchers are not thinking so purposefully. We need to begin doing just that.

"What is the 'bottom line' for the world's billions of consumers in the year 2010?" That is a research question worthy of the very best of us. Bottom-line thinking forces us to begin to define the consumer interest. To the extent that we can identify the consumer interest in particular cases and maintain our awareness of it, we will be able to ensure that the modest amounts of money and resources available for consumer research will serve the consumer interest most effectively.[1]

THE PURSUIT OF RESEARCH ON SAFETY

In the United States, the Federal Food and Drug Administration (FDA) continues to be the primary consumer safety assurance body. Goaded occasionally by the Congress and provided by Congress with strong legislative authority, FDA conducts research itself and requires potential suppliers to conduct research on safety, efficacy, wholesomeness, and a broad range of public policy issues relating to the sale of foods, drugs and medical devices.

Another heartening contribution of research to product safety has been the data collection from hospitals. It was the analysis of these data that preceded, and practically mandated, the passage of the Consumer Product Safety Act in the United States, which established CPSC. The amassing of the data on injuries occurring in households as reported and treated in the country's hospitals provided incontrovertible evidence of the need for surveillance over products in common use in America's households. This research continues to guide decision making at CPSC.

A concern that researchers need to address is: how is the consumer position on safety developed? How is it formulated? How can it be formulated? Occasionally one person "plants the standard," sounds the rallying cry, and the public joins in. Ralph Nader certainly planted the standard for auto safety in this country, and taught us to abhor the slaughter on the highways to which we were previously insensitive.

The Center for Research in Auto Safety came later, and continues to monitor the products of automobile manufacturers. Similarly, Michael Jacobson planted the standard and uttered the rallying cry about hazards such as red dye and undesignated amounts of salt in packaged food. His Center for Science in the Public Interest continues to provide a focus and a searchlight upon hazards in the food supply in the United States and point the way to their correction.

---

[1]See Morgan [1] for a deep and sophisticated exploration of "the consumer interest".

A critical review of some of our successes in consumer product safety would be a worthy research project. For example, how are these two Centers financed? How do they make their influence felt? Such an evaluation might lead us to understand ways in which we might replicate them and improve upon them.

As yet, our academic establishment, in the United States at any rate, lacks a focal center or institute whose single purpose is research in the consumer interest. We do have the Economic Behavior Program of the Survey Research Center within the Institute for Social Research at the University of Michigan. However, its research program is focused mainly on consumer behavior, and only incidentally on research in the consumer interest. The University of California at Davis has a tiny, underfunded Center for Consumer Research. For a large and rich state, it is hardly a focal point for research in the consumer interest. Wisconsin, Florida, and Utah also have University Centers, but in each case (as at Davis) the center represents, at best, a toe-hold. By no measure do they represent focal points for research in the consumer interest.

Yet a model for achieving a focal point in academia for research in the consumer interest does exist--in another interest area. The field of labor management relations provides a model for achieving an academic "focal point" for research. The most conspicuous variant is the School of Industrial and Labor Relations at Cornell where a large academic unit is focused exclusively on instruction, research, and extension in Labor-Management relations. A more common variant has been the creation of industrial and labor relations units within the business administration schools of major universities, notably Minnesota, Wisconsin, and Colorado. Similar units at Illinois and Michigan State are restricted to research and instruction at the graduate level. The Industrial and Labor Relations Centers at the Universities of California at Berkeley and at Los Angeles stand as independent units.[2]

Can -- will -- a similar development take place in the many Colleges of Liberal Arts, Home Economics, Human Ecology, Human Development across the country? It would be propitious for the consumer and the U.S. economy.

---

[2]Caroline Ware's 1946 monograph [2] on the development of such centers makes for fascinating reading.

SOME CAVEATS FOR CONSUMER RESEARCHERS[3]

I feel compelled to add a few caveats. First, when we analyze product safety from the consumer interest, we tend to treat "consumer" and "buyer" as synonymous. They are not. Increasingly the consumers who need product safety as much as anyone are not buyers and have no relationship with the vendor. They are the users of a product that someone else bought. They live in a rented apartment or a mobile home. They drive a company car or a rented one. He or she is a "consumer" of the product but has no relationship with the vendor of that product. Modeling these consumers in a vendor-buyer relationship is erroneous.

Second, the consumer right to safety is much larger than product safety. Researchers in the consumer interest will need to be dealing with a larger conception of safety than is conventional. They must ask: How "safe" is a consumer who has no access to health care services? How "safe" is the consumer who has no entitlement to the delivery of medical services?

The third, caveat is directed especially to colleagues from other countries regarding our U.S. tort system and product liability laws. In the U.S., we have not one government, as many of you do, but rather fifty-one! The courts and laws that govern torts are instruments of the 50 states and can --but actually don't--differ as much as the states do. Hence readings on legal matters may vary widely depending on the state in which they are taken. If you want to get a sense of the tort system's workings, you may learn more from the Boston Globe, the Los Angeles Times and The Chicago Tribune than from the Congressional Record.

Further, as one who participated in the consumer movement in the 1960's, let me comment on the origins of the "Consumer Rights." Professor Lampman's reminiscences of the origins of President Kennedy's Consumer Rights Message may have sounded to you as if it were an immaculate conception. What went unstated, but needs to be understood, is that prior to President Kennedy's Consumer Message, some of the states--notably Massachusetts, New York, California, and Wisconsin--had pioneered consumer representation in their state governments. In this arena as in many others, changes in public policy have an evolutionary development in the states

[3]Some of Helen Nelson's writings on the consumer interest may be found in the Helen Ewing Nelson Papers at the Bancroft Library of the University of California at Berkeley.

before being addressed by the Federal Government. Some matters continue to be wholly or primarily dealt with by state government. Indeed, this is what I expect in the case of product liability torts system.

Finally, on a globe whose economies are becoming increasingly socialized and where all inhabitants face certain health hazards in common, researchers in the consumer interest are going to need to address some problems on a world scale such as products and practices contributing to depletion of the ozone layer, and the possibility of nuclear disaster. If we fail to do so, we will be perceived--and probably rightfully so--as straining at the gnat and swallowing the camel.

REFERENCES

1. MORGAN, JAMES N. (1985), "What Is In The Consumer Interest," in Karen P. Schittgrund, (Ed.), The Proceedings of ACCI, 1985, Colubmia, MO.: ACCI), pp. 1-12.

2. WARE, CAROLINE F. (1946), Labor Education in Universities: A Study of University Programs, American Labor Education Science, N.Y.

ABOUT THE AUTHOR

R. David Pittle is Technical Director of Consumers Union, a position he has held since 1982. Pittle was trained in engineering, receiving his Ph.D. in Electrical Engineering from the University of Wisconsin in 1969. He served on the faculties of the University of Wisconsin and Carnegie-Mellon University. Pittle was a Commissioner of the Consumer Product Safety Commission from 1973 to 1982 when he moved to Consumers Union. On the Commission he was viewed as a staunch advocate of the consumer viewpoint, his service being recognized with a Philip Hart Public Service Award.

PRODUCT SAFETY: THE VIEWS OF A FORMER REGULATOR

R. David Pittle

This comment seeks to make the case for regulation as a route to achieving safety in consumer products.

Some words about my background may help you understand where I come from. For many years I was a member of the electrical engineering faculty of a university. I am also a slightly used Commissioner who spent nine years on the Consumer Product Safety Commission. At present I am Technical Director of Consumers Union, a position in which I pay considerable attention to safety. As will be clear from my discussion, I am not an economist.

The mission of the Consumer Product Safety Commission since its inception is to reduce or eliminate unreasonable risks in consumer products. This is a mission that Congress has reaffirmed again and again. It is not a mission that has been concocted by a self-appointed do-gooder or a faceless Washington bureaucrat. It is a mission with which I emphatically agree.

Perceptions of "safety" vary greatly, depending upon the role of the observer and the data available to that person(s). Economists study their literature and models and draw conclusions from them. Others study death certificates and injury reports. Still others focus on people needing "instant repairs" in emergency rooms. Reconstruction surgeons and trauma mechanics--whom I encountered at a recent conference--become very impatient at having so many patients. So different people are sensitive to different aspects of product safety.

In assessing product safety, it is important to have an open mind, being willing to consider and weigh fairly challenging and new information.

In contrast to the assumptions in some economic models, consumers are in no position to assess quality. They can never begin to appreciate the electrical, mechanical, chemical, and even logical aspects of the thousands of products available in the market. Ironically, some rarely have time to consider carefully even the color they want!

Consider me as an example. In my professional life I am an information provider. But, as a consumer, I am an information seeker. I find that my professional background confers hardly any advantage at all. Take video cassette recorders as an example. I would never expect to walk into a store full of recorders and think I could choose "the best" just by looking at them or asking questions of the salesperson. Consumers simply lack expertise.

But it is my view that consumers are entitled to a minimal level of safety in any product they purchase. And it is my belief that most consumers assume that <u>any</u> product on the shelf is minimally safe. They feel that "somebody" is protecting them and Sears (or other reputable retailer) would not sell them a product that is "dangerous." Some research that I conducted some years ago showed that most consumers believe that they have "somehow" delegated to "somebody" the responsibility for assuring safety. Thus, they feel secure that the elevator they enter has been inspected, that a can of peas will not be harmful, that an electric drill will be free of electrical shock.

SOME DOUBTS ABOUT PRODUCTS LIABILITY LAWSUITS

In my judgment the doctrine of product liability and product liability lawsuits have had little to do with the attainment of this ambient level of safety. Let me say why. First, it is true that, far too often, the designer and marketer of a product, separated by space and organizational table, rarely interact with the company's legal office or insurer. These relationships are improving, but there still remains an enormous gap.

When I hear (over and over again!) that product liability lawsuits will induce manufacturers to undertake major improvements in product design, I think of the many examples where this did not occur, numerous lawsuits notwithstanding. Lawnmowers provide an instructive example. Despite the large number of lawsuits, the basic design of power lawnmowers did not change over 25 years. Why? A conversation I had with the president of a very large chain store is revealing. The nub of the conversation was that his firm was sued frequently, but never successfully. The reason lies deeply embedded in lawnmower technology and in both consumer and producer behavior.

Chain saws are plagued by what is called chain saw "kickback." This occurs when the chain catches in the wood being cut as it goes around the tip. The driving chain occasionally becomes blocked, driving the saw back toward the user. If it hits you in the neck or the chest, it can cause death by serious bleeding. It can certainly "do a job" on your face. Kickback accidents occur about 23,000 times a year! What can be done to avoid these horrendous accidents? One technically feasible alternative is offered by several manufacturers: they supply the purchaser with a "safety tip" that you screw on to the saw. The rub: with the safety tip in place, you can only saw "very small" logs. Thus, the safety tip drastically undercuts the utility of the chain saw to the user and hence becomes undesirable to the user. A second alternative--followed by most--is to provide clear instructions to purchasers. The rub here: many purchasers do not read instructions; many who read do not understand or, understanding, fail to follow the proffered advice. Is it any surprise that the distributor of chain saws has never been sued successfully by any of the 23,000 users who are injured annually by chain saws?

Shower stalls are another example. The shower stall in my home and in many of the motels I have visited lack soap racks. Some of us will be tempted to put the soap on the flat side of the tub. And we will be thwarted: usually it will fall to the floor of the stall. And a certain random number of us will slip on the soap and sustain injuries. Is the threat or actuality of a lawsuit going to lead Mr. Motel Chain to replace all those rackless shower stalls with new, better designed stalls that hold your soap safety? It seems unlikely. Again, do we try to change (1) people's behavior, or (2) product design. Let me discuss each further.

It was my former belief that people who know more, behave better. And, some time ago when I was a university professor, I received a grant from the National Science Foundation to try to educate consumers to technical safety problems with an eye to avoiding injuries. Today I view the education approach as unworkable. Indeed, I have become very vocal against the idea of wasting taxpayers' money to print and distribute bulletins/coloring books/demonstrations/other devices designed to teach people about the sudden kickback of chain saws. It is a waste of funds. For most people, there is no way that I can <u>now</u> warn you <u>effectively</u> against the possibility that, three years from now, the tip of your chain saw might hit a log and bounce back, seriously injuring you in a split second. This is not to deny the general value of consumer education. I am simply skeptical of the effectiveness of consumer education in such specific areas as training people to the proper use of power lawnmowers, chain saws, gas appliances, some toys, ladders, blenders, toasters, etc.

WHEN TO REGULATE

Turning directly to the regulation of product safety in the consumer interest, I suggest that there are three major steps in deciding whether to regulate. The first step is to obtain accurate information regarding the frequency and the seriousness of the problem. As part of this, the regulator should seek to understand the problem and, in particular, to be able to judge to what extent injuries are attributable to defects in the product itself vs. errors in users' judgment. Skiing illustrates this latter point. A ski binding that results in an unreasonably high number of injuries is an appropriate candidate for surveillance by CPSC. Not so skiing itself. Here the individual can judge for him/herself whether the undeniable pleasure of skiing exceeds the undeniable riskiness of the activity.

The second step is to determine whether the regulator can develop an intervention strategy that will protect the consumer from product hazards that he/she has reasonably accepted, e.g., the use of chain saw instead of a hand saw. One unworkable strategy is to rely on the "invisible hand" of competition. First, it is not clear that consumers, on their own, can distinguish "safe" from "unsafe" products. Second, it is difficult to think of instances where consumer demand has shifted from an "unsafe" to a "safe" product, penalizing and rewarding sellers in the Adam Smith mode.

What obstacles does the regulator face in pursuing change? A major obstacle is the emotional attachment that product designers and manufacturers sometimes develop for the product they have created. The sense of pride and achievement that is embedded in "their" product may make them resistant to change, no matter how meritorious.

Another obstacle is the vested interest that various participants develop in a particular production process or production line. Manufacturers have a vested interest in the plant, the machines, the organization of the process. Changes will inevitably involve dislocations, delays, costs. Foremen and supervisors have vested interests in a process and/or teamwork that is working well. In Bert Lance's immortal phrase: "If it ain't broke, why fix it?" Finally, workers on a line have attained skills that yield good wages, that are easy because they are practiced, and in which they may take pride. These vested interests constitute obstacles that must be overcome. That's why, when you propose regulations that imply drastic change, they will fight you tooth and nail.

Eric Ault's paper makes the case for voluntary standards. Let me first note that voluntary standards are hardly every truly "voluntary." From the viewpoint of the foreman running the production line, they are mandatory. It makes little difference to the foreman whether his process conforms to a voluntary or mandatory standard set by CPSC: he and his process must conform. There is very little that is "voluntary" about many voluntary standards. If you wish to sell an electrical appliance in this country, you had better be sure that it conforms to the voluntary standard set by the "national code" established by Underwriters Laboratories. Otherwise, you will not be permitted to sell it in some jurisdictions and would be a fool to try in others.

What leads to the acceptance of voluntary standards is the threat of mandatory standards. With voluntary standards a company does not have to keep a lot of records, thus reducing costs and bother.

A final obstacle to the setting of voluntary standards is manufacturers' attitudes. The very first day that CPSC opened its store, the first question that the Commission put to his staff was: "What is the industry willing to do voluntarily?" The invarying answer: they don't believe there is a "problem." This was what the chain saw industry told us. Alternatively, some firms, willing to adopt a standard on their own, refused to go along because two or three firms in their industry were unwilling. For a given firm to accept a cost-increasing standard that others rejected would place it at a disadvantage. What is needed here is the threat or actuality of regulatory intervention.

The final step (finally!) in deciding whether to regulate is to decide whether it is worth it. The enabling legislation for CPSC has a clear provision that requires the Commission to undertake an economic analysis. A prescribed solution must bear a reasonable relationship to costs imposed by it on producers and consumers. For every move made by CPSC, I can attest that it was never a close issue.

We could not tell you whether the gains from a regulation exceeded costs by (say) $47,000 or $121,000. Nor did our legislation require formal cost-benefit analysis. Nonetheless, I can tell you that--kind or unkind remarks about cost-benefit analysis aside--I found cost-benefit analysis to be a very valuable tool and continue to believe in it. Indeed, it is indispensable. The easiest part of course is the estimation of costs. Manufacturers will tell you about costs until the cows come home. It is the benefits that are most difficult and elusive to estimate. I urge you researchers to collaborate with people possessing the relevant technical background. Find a doctor or engineer who believes a product should be made safer and collaborate with him/her. I can imagine a paper co-authored by someone deeply knowledgeable in cost-benefit analysis and a technical expert. That would be a truly fine and convincing paper.

THE RIGHT

TO

BE INFORMED

Chapter 6

ABOUT THE AUTHOR

David J. Curry is a Professor in the Department of Marketing at the University of Iowa. His research interests embrace price-quality competition, consumer information processing, international marketing, and -- as this paper reveals -- the domain of measurement and scaling.

Professor Curry began his career at Iowa after receiving a Ph.D. in Marketing from the University of California, Berkeley. Curry has published in a wide variety of marketing and psychology journals and has been a visiting professor at the University of Colorado and a consultant in both Europe and Australia. Of particular interest to readers of this volume, Curry and Professor David Faulds, the University of Tennessee at Knoxville, have created and maintain a computer archive of product tests published by sixteen consumer products testing organizations.

THE CONCEPT OF QUALITY: NEW INSIGHTS, UNANSWERED QUESTIONS

David J. Curry

SUMMARY

This essay analyzes the most important influences on product quality and its measurement. The essay consists of three parts: an analytical framework, answers to questions derived from this framework and recommendations to consumer product testing agencies. The framework identifies three groups whose actions and interactions determine the "true" quality levels of consumer products as well as their indexed or measured quality levels.

The questions addressed through the analytical framework relate directly to current practices that members of the International Organization of Consumers Unions (IOCU) use to measure and index product quality. These are questions that appear to be particularly troublesome and for which new theory, evidence and solutions are now available. For example, the correlation structure among measured attributes is a key force affecting the reliability of a weighted composite quality scale. Nearly 400 such corrrelation structures are summarized from recent studies by Curry and Faulds [4] and by Hjorth-Andersen [15]. The results provide direct answers to the following questions:

** How sensitive are published quality scales to different weighting vectors?

** In theory, can the process of indexing product quality be improved by one or more of the following actions on the part of members of the International Organization of Consumer Unions (IOCU):

- using non-additive rules
- selecting attributes differently
- applying statistical normalizations
- changing report formats or media.

The analysis of these questions leads to a series of broader recommendations directed at improving the consumer product testing process.

* * * *

FACTORS INFLUENCING PRODUCT QUALITY AND ITS MEASUREMENT

Product quality and its measurement have been studied from a variety of perspectives, including consumer welfare [14, 21, 32, 37], quality control in manufacturing [19], consumer decision-making, e.g., price-quality tradeoffs [10, 11, 18, 22, 23, 28, 33] and aesthetic judgment [17]. The framework presented here summarizes the interaction of three agents who have different perspectives and who, therefore, bring different agendas to the product testing process.

The Agents

Although in principle more elaborate models might be devised to account for the forces affecting product quality, three key agents appear to be primarily responsible. These are the firms that manufacture branded products, the organizations that test these brands and publish test results and the consumers who consider, choose and consume these brands. The roles of these three agents are discussed in turn, and an inventory is created of factors that require subsequent analysis. The discussion begins with an idealized synopsis of the product testing process. The reader is directed to Pittle [27] and Maynes [22, 23] for greater detail about these steps.

Consumer Products Testing Organizations

The product testing process involves a complicated series of steps including construct definitions (e.g., what is quality?), operational definitions (e.g., how do we define quality for the purposes of this test?), sampling plans, test designs, measurement processes, test and financial administration and reporting. These steps are outlined and labeled in Exhibit 1 and are briefly reviewed below. The review highlights the key constituents of indexed product quality, those that interact with similar constituents to be identified in the manufacturing and consumption processes. These factors are, subsequently, drawn together in a unified model of the product quality environment.

EXHIBIT 1

MAJOR STEPS IN THE CONSUMER PRODUCT TESTING PROCESS

	STEP	LABEL(S)
1.	Select product category(s) to test	category delineation operational definition sampling process
2.	Select a set of varieties which are members of a category	implement operational definition
3.	Select particular item(s) for testing	sampling frame sampling process sample size
4.	Determine test procedure	test design(s) test administration
	4.1 Select attributes	definition/sampling
	4.2 Transform raw values to utility	define a scoring rule for each attribute
	4.3 Conduct test	procedure reliability; true score/observed score
	4.4 Combine results from separate attributes	composition rule
5.	Interpret and report test results	numeric/linguistic transforamtions & format selection

Questions of Statistical Inference

A testing organization must decide which product categories to test, which brands within these categories to include, which particular items to evaluate and where to obtain these items [23, 26, 36]. These decisions identify a population, sample from it, define constructs to measure and carry out these measurements on the sample. As technical decisions, they ensure that the testing organization draws appropriate inferences from the statistical evidence.

These decisions achieve both managerial and scientific objectives. For example, Consumer Reports publishes studies about product categories that are of interest to a broad spectrum of consumers. Thus, the sampling of categories is weighted by an implicit measure of consumer interest and is driven primarily by managerial, not scientific forces. However, once a category is selected and operationally defined, the decision of which varieties to include in the category becomes a question of scientific merit. The operational definition of the category may use price, geographic area and product specifications so restrictively that it becomes feasible to test all varieties meeting these specifications. In such cases the issue of sampling is replaced by the issue of category definition. For example, specifications that distinguish portable AM-FM radios from non-portable AM-FM radios may result in category boundaries that exclude all but 8 to 15 brand/model combinations. Every member of this small universe can be evaluated, rendering moot the question of statistical inference.[1] These decisions constitute an important area of control in the testing environment summarized in steps 1 and 2 in Exhibit 1.

Test Procedures

In steps 3 and 4 shown in Exhibit 1, the testing organization selects specific items for testing and selects protocols for conducting the tests. The issue of which item(s) to test clearly involves problems of statistical inference because the organization

---

[1]If all varieties in a category are included in a test, then there is no inductive leap to those not included. However, because only particular items are tested, there remains the inductive leap from these to nontested items of the same variety. Further complicating matters, CU and other testing organizations typically test only one item from a particular variety resulting in what Maynes [22] calls the sample-of-one problem.

must generalize about all items of a given variety available from a particular manufacturer.

These tests are usually conducted piecemeal; the organization defines attributes which will be measured and then designs and administers a test specific for each attribute. This typically involves transforming test results from one form (numeric or categorical) to another (numeric, categorical or verbal). Finally, the resulting subscores are combined into an overall index of quality. This unidimensional composite index must be interpreted for readers and the test procedures must be organized in a format suitable for the lay public, as well as for academicians, federal officials and others with technical interests.

Decisions of considerable impact are made during this series of steps. For example, a physical product may be viewed as a particular combination of attribute levels, yet the set of attributes used in the characterization is not unique. Attribute sets can be defined operationally in any number of ways. Experiments on perception, for example, note that people respond differently regarding the comparative size of boxes if the boxes are characterized by three scores (length, width, height) rather than by one score (volume). Which attribute decomposition is more basic, more practical or more reportable?

A step notable both for its degree of difficulty and for its lack of practical guidelines is step 4.2: utility transformations. Most comparative product test studies report scores for physical attributes such as interior volume (microwave ovens, refrigerators), gross weight (bicycles, air conditioners), or cycle time (dishwashers, clothes dryers). Yet the relationship between these physical scores and overall quality is at best inexplicit and at worst illusory.

The Meaning of Quality

In transforming engineering levels of a product to a single-valued index, testing organizations must confront the definition of product quality. Is quality related to consumption utility or is it an intrinsic property of an object? If quality is related to consumption utility, then it represents a relationship between a physical object and a person. If quality is an intrinsic property of an object, then it can be described and measured by machines without human intervention and without explicit recognition of the relationship between a product's physical properties and people. This mechanical approach would seem possible for properties such as durability, hardness or weight. Consumer product testing agencies, however, should adopt the point of view that quality is related to consumption utility. Quality then represents a relationship between an object and a person. It follows that physical measures on single attributes must be transformed to scales that one might call "quatility" scales or "partworth quality" scales, to distinguish them from overall composite scales of purely aesthetic or consumptive utility. These quality transformations would indicate that equal spacing on a physical scale may not represent equal contributions to overall quality.

The issue of appropriate transformations is extremely complex. Theory should be developed that suggests how a physical attribute, alone or in combination with other attributes, contributes to a product's use and enjoyment potential.

Combining Test Results

Steps 4.3 and 4.4 in Exhibit 1 represent the process of conducting a test and combining results from the separate attributes tested. At present, combination rules are usually additive, although non-additivities are sometimes introduced by safety thresholds on certain attributes [23]. This paper will later examine the particular conditions under which additive composite scales are sensitive to the weights chosen and whether non-additive rules would improve matters.

Interpretation and Reporting

Finally a consumer products testing organization interprets and reports test results. Although one might argue that this step is largely determined by editorial principles, consumer product testing organizations must do more than display journalistic skill. In their role as information agents, they must integrate the rules of scientific reporting into a lay format. These tenets include the use of neutral words and an explicit rather than implicit judgment of which results and interpretations to report and which to withhold. Silber [32] describes the style as follows (p. 122):

> The language...was chosen to sound authoritative and neutral. CU reminded its readers of the impartiality of its researchers and its meticulous process of checking and rechecking each report. The scholarly apparatus of footnotes was missing, but all of CU's arguments were expressed in an objective, unambiguous, confident, scientific style that made accessible the findings of CU's researchers and eliminated pretentious or exaggerated jargon.

Product Manufacturers

The firms that design, manufacture and market consumer products are responsible for the quality of these products. These firms, however, operate in an environment of economic, technological and natural forces that constrain their sphere of quality control. Although the connection is not obvious, some factors that affect product design and manufacturing processes are inherently tied through statistical laws to questions of indexing product quality.

Exhibit 2 outlines three categories of forces -- economic tradeoffs, design standards and natural laws -- that influence the manufactured realization of an item as a combination of physical attributes. These three are discussed in turn with particular emphasis on how they influence the correlation structure among product attributes. As will be demonstrated, this correlation structure strongly influences the reliability of a product quality index.

EXHIBIT 2

MAJOR STEPS IN MANUFACTURING AND MARKETING

	STEP	LABEL(S)
1.	Develop the product idea	product design
2.	Decide how the product will be manufactured	
	2.1 Determine the product's design including the choice of materials, the choice of components,... etc.	objective attribute scores
	2.2 Determine the manufacturing process including the product's labor content, process design, capital equipment requirements and quality control programs	economic tradeoffs design standards natural laws
3.	Decide how the product will be marketed, including its price, package, position and distribution program	
	3.1 Set price 3.2 Define position	economic tradeoffs attribute levels: desired and advertised

Economic Tradeoffs

To sustain profitability manufacturers must concentrate on the interaction between price and quality (product value) rather than on quality alone. Firms respond to consumer demands for different levels of value by price lining and product lining [9, 31, 35], with countervailing consequences on correlations among product attributes. First, improving performance simultaneously on two or more attributes increases costs. Therefore, among brands subject to the same cost constraint, attributes tend to be correlated negatively. However, because manufacturers try to achieve different positions on price and quality, such as (low P, low Q) versus (high P, high Q), product attributes can be positively correlated if some manufacturers employ low cost materials while others use high cost materials. These two economic considerations -- supply side costs versus demand side price lining -- may push attribute correlations in either direction. Thus, theory alone cannot decide which force, if either, will predominate. However, section two of this essay reviews empirical evidence regarding the relative strength of these forces.

Design Standards

Product manufacturers face a second set of constraints due to product design tradeoffs. These constraints are similar to those in the economic category but they are a function of design potential or design standards rather than strict cost considerations. For example, upright refrigerators conform to certain standards of exterior dimension. These standards, which have evolved from traditions and housing and safety codes, require that freezer volume and refrigerator volume be traded off directly. Across competing brands of like size, therefore, levels on these two attributes will be negatively correlated. This result has been substantiated by Curry and Menasco [7] and by Curry and Faulds [4].

Other design constraints may lead to positive correlation between certain pairs of attributes. For example, if underwriter laboratories requires power levels commensurate with oven volume in microwave ovens, then levels on these two attributes will be positively correlated across competing brands. Thus, depending on the design standard, code or convention, certain pairs of product attributes may be correlated positively while others are correlated negatively. The sign of the correlation can often be predetermined by an analysis of the code specifications.

Natural Laws

A final set of manufacturing constraints results from natural physical laws that directly affect product design and manufacturing feasibility. An extreme example is the mass-by-velocity tradeoff: McDonald-Douglas Corporation can not manufacture a space shuttle capable of exceeding the speed of light. More common tradeoffs exist between fuel consumption and power in engines, between drag coefficients and exterior volume in vehicles and between softness and strength in tissues. In these cases the design engineers confront apparently impenetrable natural barriers.

Natural laws may not always create negative correlations between attributes, as some authors suppose [1, 2, 12, 15]. For example, certain physical attributes of living organisms are positively correlated. These include an organism's overall weight and height or the size of various organs and the organism's overall weight and strength. Non-biological examples of positive correlation structures are the size of a mountain's base and its height or the swiftness of a stream and the depth of its channel. As with economic tradeoffs and design standards, natural laws can influence attribute correlations positively or negatively.

The forces discussed in this section suggest that in certain cases manufacturers can achieve higher levels on one product attribute only by accepting lower levels on a second. In other cases the levels on two or more attributes covary in tandem, leading to positive rather than negative interattribute correlations. Other examples are summarized in Exhibit 3. Thus, the correlation structure among brands in a particular product category is due to the interplay of price, cost and quality considerations in a firm's manufacturing and marketing strategies as well as to certain natural or physical laws.

These conditions have been singled out because the correlation structure among brands in a product category plays a critical role in determining how sensitive a composite quality index is to the subscales that compose it. Economic tradeoffs, design standards and natural laws interact in a way that is not apparent to consumers, manufacturers and product testers. Researchers can understand and improve product testing only if they acknowledge these links.

EXHIBIT 3

LAWS INFLUENCING INTERATTRIBUTE CORRELATIONS

TRADEOFFS (NEGATIVE CORRELATION)	CONCURRENCE (POSITIVE CORRELATION)
Economic Laws	
blankets: minimum weight/maximum insulation chocolate: rich taste/resistance to melting ladies' stockings: sheerness/ durability	shoes: durability of sole/durability of uppers appliances: special features/motor performance furniture: finish/type of wood
Improved performance simultaneously on 2 or more product attributes may increase costs. (= cost).	Manufacturers explicitly try to achieve different price/quality positions (≠ cost)
Design Laws	
vehicles: power (axle ratio)/speed refrigerators: volume of freezer/ volume of refrigerator handsoaps: cleaning ability/level of irritants insecticides: effectiveness/safety	microwave ovens: power/volume electric appliances: safety features/ power requirements
Certain design standards, codes or traditions result in tradeoffs between product attributes.	Certain design standards, codes or traditions result in concurrently high or concurrently low levels of product attributes.
Natural Laws	
autos: fuel consumption/acceleration-power paper towels: absorption/strength vehicles: wind drag/interior volume toilet tissue: softness/strength light bulbs: brightness/life	structures: weight/strength vehicles: lightness/fuel economy
Certain laws of nature, physics and engineering restrict manufacturers in achieving, simultaneously, pairs of levels on product attributes.	Certain laws of nature, physics and engineering require manufacturers to achieve, simultaneously, pairs of levels on product attributes.

Consumers

Consumers influence product quality directly by purchasing and consuming products, thereby rewarding manufacturers who supply appropriate combinations of price and quality. Consumers also influence quality levels indirectly by providing feedback to manufacturers via marketing research and complaints.

Consumers also foster quality measurement efforts by using information about product prices, features and overall quality. Consumers, therefore, judge the agreement between their own assessment of product quality and published assessments. In this role, consumers monitor the correspondence between objective quality, perceived quality, and reported quality and provide the economic link-pin supporting both suppliers of products and suppliers of information.

Exhibit 4 summarizes these ideas, while Exhibit 5 is a schematic drawing that portrays the gross relationships between the three key agents in the framework.

EXHIBIT 4

MAJOR STEPS IN THE CONSUMPTION PROCESS

	STEP	LABEL(S)
1.	Decide what product classes and which varieties from each class to buy	models of buyer behavior
1.1	The pre-purchase process	attribute identification and evaluation (see 2)
1.2	The purchase process	composition rule overall evaluations utility transformations
1.3	The post-purchase and consumption process	(see 3 below)
1.4	The repurchase process	
2.	Decide what information to collect external to the consumption process	information consumption
3.	Report opinions and evaluations to both manufacturers and consumer product testing agencies	market research complaints post-purchase process economic link-pin

Exhibit 5 indicates that each agent has control over some elements influencing product quality but little control over others. Neither one agent alone nor the three together have complete control over realized levels of product quality, because there are exogenous factors at work such as natural laws. One may justifiably assume that, in most product categories and in the industries manufacturing brands for these categories, members of these three groups do not fully understand the extent of their interactions.

EXHIBIT 5

RELATIONSHIPS AMONG THE KEY AGENTS AFFECTING PRODUCT QUALITY

EXOGENOUS VARIABLES
- Economic
- Natural
- Technological

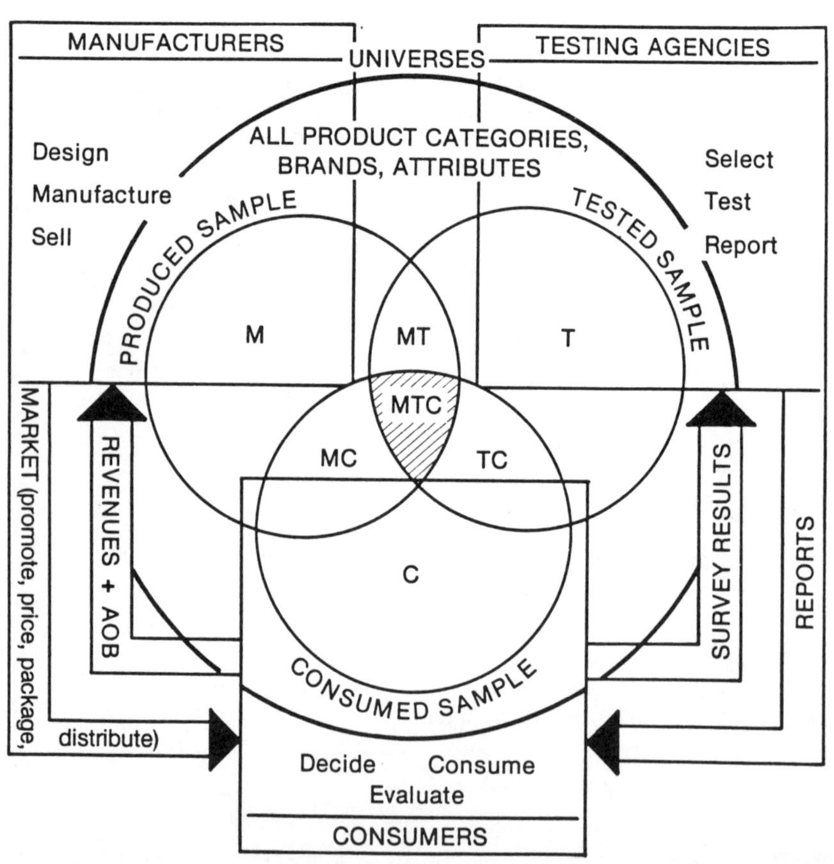

APPLICATIONS OF THE FRAMEWORK

Current Focus

The foregoing framework provides a basis for seeing where current product testing efforts are focused, for delimiting where they can be focused and for recommending where they should be focused. Currently consumer product testing agencies devote a large portion of their time and money to category definitions, variety selection and item sampling [27]. Test design and administration continues to be a high priority and the analysis and reporting of results remains each organization's raison d'être.

Within the current testing framework, one practice in particular, that of multi-attribute scoring, raises some of the most important questions.

1. How sensitive are published quality ratings to the choice of weights used in additive scoring rules?

2. In theory, how can a multi-attribute scoring process be improved?

The specific answers, derived from statistical theory, depend more basically on other aspects of the quality measurement process. The easier answers are developed first but these are followed by suggestions for research that may help solve the more complex problems.

Sensitivity to Weights

Weights make a difference when two conditions coexist. First, different assessors of quality must assign opposite or greatly differing weights to attributes. For example, assessor A assigns maximum weight to safety while assessor B gives safety his smallest weight. Second, the correlations among attributes must be predominantly negative. For example, a car may use fuel economically but accelerate slowly. Here I summarize the rationale for these conditions and account for their possible effects in the context of current practices among members of the International Organization of Consumers Unions. (For a more detailed, statistical, rationale, see Curry and Faulds [4].)

Rationale

The rationale follows from a statistical formulation of the problem as outlined in Exhibit 6. In this formulation, each of I items receives a score on each of J tested attributes.[2] These scores are weighted and added to create I overall quality scores, one for each item. Stated directly, the question is "How would the quality scores differ if a different set of weights had been used?"

EXHIBIT 6

TWO QUALITY SCALES CREATED FROM SUBSCALES

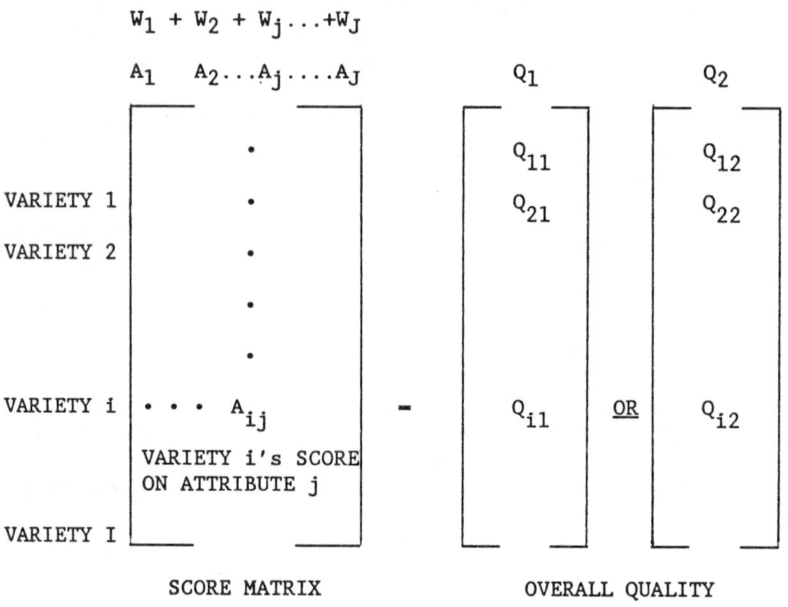

The compact answer, shown in Exhibit 7, is an expression of the product-moment correlation between quality scale Q_1 using the first set of weights and quality scale Q_2 using a second set of weights. This correlation is sensitive both to the rank order of the brands on each scale and to the spacing between the brands.

Exhibit 7 indicates that the correlation is a function of the two weight vectors and the set of pairwise interattribute

---

[2]The validity of these scores is not in question at this point in the analysis. The same scores are employed in both weighted composition rules.

correlations across the varieties tested. These pairwise correlations are summarized in the interattribute correlation matrix denoted **R**. Entries in **R** are influenced by the economic considerations, design standards and natural laws emphasized earlier. These correlations are partially under the control of manufacturers (i.e., the attributes fabricated) and partially under the control of a testing agency (i.e., the attributes tested).

EXHIBIT 7

THE PRODUCT-MOMENT CORRELATION BETWEEN TWO QUALITY INDICES CREATED AS WEIGHTED COMBINATIONS OF SUB-SCORES

$$\mathrm{COR}(Q_1,Q_2) = \frac{\mathbf{w}_1'\mathbf{R}\mathbf{w}_2}{(\mathbf{w}_1'\mathbf{R}\mathbf{w}_1)^{1/2}\,(\mathbf{w}_2'\mathbf{R}\mathbf{w}_2)^{1/2}}$$

where: first set of weights $\mathrm{w}_1' = (\mathrm{w}_{11}, \mathrm{w}_{12},\ldots,\mathrm{w}_{1J})$

second set of weights $\mathrm{w}_2' = (\mathrm{w}_{21}, \mathrm{w}_{22},\ldots,\mathrm{w}_{2J})$

$$\mathbf{R} = \begin{array}{c} \\ A_1 \\ A_2 \\ \vdots \\ \vdots \\ A_J \end{array} \begin{array}{c} \begin{array}{cccc} A_1 & A_2 & \cdots & A_J \end{array} \\ \left[\begin{array}{cccc} 1 & \rho_{12} & \cdots & \rho_{1J} \\ \rho_{21} & 1 & & \\ \rho_{31} & & \ddots & \\ \rho & & & \\ \rho_{J1} & \rho_{J2} & \cdots & 1 \end{array}\right] \end{array}$$

Implications

Exhibit 8 draws out the implications of the formula in Exhibit 7 using a hypothetical test involving three attributes. Row One is a case where these three are weighted (.5, .3, .2) to form scale Q_1 and weighted (.6, .3, .1) to form scale Q_2. Note that these two weight vectors differ little; the weights in both vectors are in the same rank order. Three possible correlation structures among varieties on these attributes are also shown. Entries in the positive structure (column one), for example, are all high and positive. The first entry in the body of Exhibit 8 is the correlation between the resulting two sets of overall quality scores--i.e., COR(Q_1, Q_2) = .999. This nearly perfect correlation indicates that, for all practical purposes, the two quality scales are the same. The different weighting vectors have not influenced the assessment of product quality in this row and column position.

Exhibit 8 illustrates the conditions necessary for two quality scales to diverge. In the worst case shown, the weights are directly counter and the product attributes are negatively correlated. In this case the two quality scales are in nearly total disagreement (COR = -.929). The brand rated first on one may very well be last on the other. This is a general result; it is not confined to these particular weight vectors nor to these three specific correlation structures.

Weights and Rank Position

Exhibit 9 provides a detailed answer to the question of how weights affect the rank position of brands in a consumer products test study. The exhibit shows how often on average a brand that is ranked in ith place on scale Q_1 will remain in the same place on scale Q_2, using four combinations of weight vectors and correlation structures. Note that if a correlation structure is positive and the weight vectors are in the same rank order, then nearly all brands remain in their original positions. This result means that, when these two conditions are simultaneously present, published quality scales are insensitive to the testing agency's choice of weights.

These results demand some empirical evidence concerning the incidence of various types of correlation structures. If such structures tend to be negative, then consumer products testing organizations must pay very careful attention to the weights they choose. On the other hand, if these structures tend to be positive, the question of specific weights is less important.

EXHIBIT 8

EXAMPLES OF THE CORRELATION BETWEEN TWO QUALITY SCALES FORMED BY USING DIFFERENT WEIGHTING VECTORS

	Weight Vectors	Correlation Structure (R): Positive	Correlation Structure (R): Orthogonal	Correlation Structure (R): Negative
		[.8 .9 / .7]	[0 0 / 0]	[−.5 −.5 / −.5]
SAME RANK ORDER	[.5 .3 .2 / .6 .3 .1]	.999	.981	.997
SAME RANK ORDER	[.5 .3 .2 / .7 .2 .1]	.997 Excellent	.949	.984
DIFFERENT RANK ORDER	[.5 .3 .2 / .2 .3 .5]	.990	Not Bad .763	Terrible −.929*
DIFFERENT RANK ORDER	[.5 .3 .2 / .1 .2 .7]	.970	Mediocre .552	Bad −.849

* This is not the theoretical minimum value. The theoretical minimum occurs when the opposing weight vectors are:

[.5 .3 .2 / 0 0 1]

EXHIBIT 9

WEIGHTING EFFECTS ON BRANDS IN DIFFERENT PLACES ON AN OVERALL QUALITY SCALE

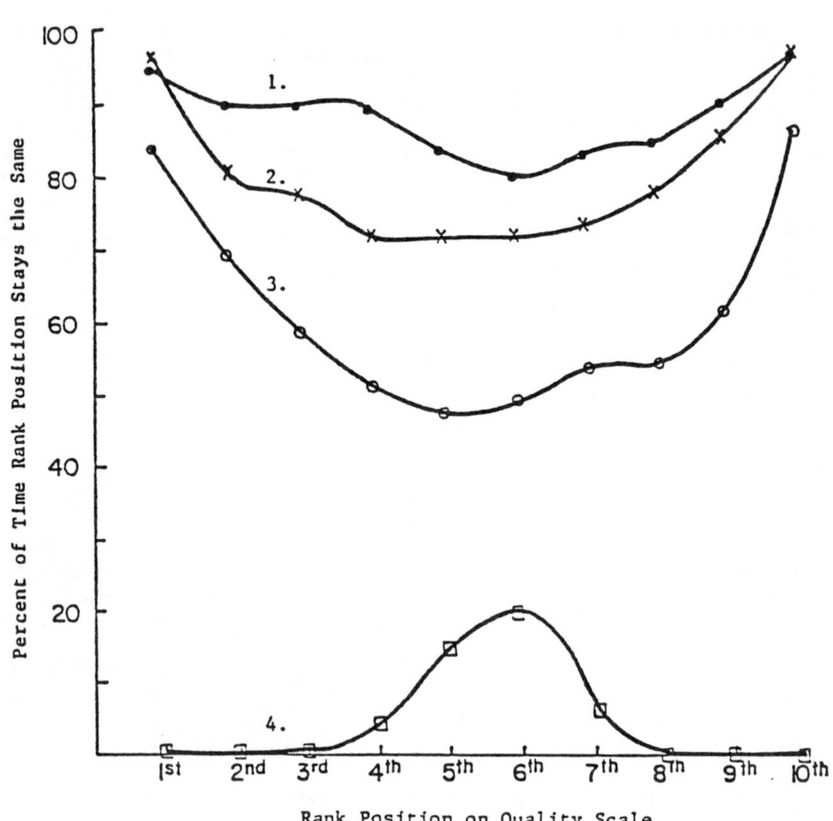

Case 1: no weight inversions/ positive covariance
Case 2: no weight inversions/ negative covariance
Case 3: weight inversions/ positive covariance
Case 4: weight inversions/ negative covariance

Correlations Among Product Attributes

To explore the implications of these theoretical findings for users of product test periodicals, we analyzed 355 non-automobile reports for the years 1978-1983 from Test, the German "Consumer Reports" published by Stiftung Warentest. Test publishes the variety-by-attribute score matrix necessary to calculate **R** within each report. Test's attribute scores are not numeric, but are provided in five categories that appear to have equal intervals (++, +, 0, -, --). Thus they permit a rough empirical test of the importance of weights.

Correlation structures were categorized as either pure or mixed, and mixed structures were further classified according to the case of most frequent occurrence. For example, in a study with five attributes there are ten pairwise correlations. If these are distributed as 7 positive, 2 negative and 1 zero, then the structure would be classified as positive dominant. If instead there had been 5 positive and 5 negative correlations, then the structure would be classified as exhibiting no dominance.

Exhibit 10 indicates that most structures (51%) are either positive (20%) or positive dominant (31%). The theory developed earlier indicates that in these studies the reported quality levels are not particularly sensitive to Test's choice of weights. On the other hand, in 42 studies (12%) the correlation structure is completely or predominantly negative. Just how sensitive are Test's results in these cases?

Reversed Weights

In the 42 cases with negative or predominantly negative correlations among attributes, Test's weights were reversed and a revised quality index was constructed from these reversed weights. For example, if the original weights were (.5, .3, .2), then the new quality scores were calculated using a (.2, .3, .5) rule.

These original and revised quality scales correlated +.65 and +.47 on average for the mixed negative dominant structures and for the purely negative structures, respectively. The average agreement between these diverse scales is, therefore, far better than the possibilities allowed by theory. In theory these (average) correlations could be negative.

EXHIBIT10

ACTUAL CORRELATION STRUCTURES FROM STIFTUNG WARENTEST

Type of Correlation Structure	Number of Studies	Percent of Total
Pure Structures	87	25%
All positive	71	20%
All zero	8	2%
All negative	8	2%
Mixed Structures	268	75%
Positive dominant	112	31%
Zero dominant	71	20%
Negative dominant	34	10%
No dominance	51	14%
Total	355	100%
Positive + Positive Dominant =	183	(51%)
Negative + Negative Dominant =	42	(12%)

These results can be explored further. For example, the effects on the quality rank of each brand where two quality scales correlate in the +.6 range are significant but not disastrous.[3] In such a case, a brand ranked first on one scale would be first on the other about 55% of the time and would rank in the top 3 on the other scale about 80% of the time.

Brands in the middle of a scale are affected most by weight reversals. For example a brand in fifth place on one scale might be first (4% of the time), second (9% of the time), third (12% of the time) or fourth (14% of the time) rather than fifth. It is likely to remain in fifth place only about 20% of the time. This brand will end up in 6th through 9th places with percentages that mirror 4th through 1st respectively, and it will be in 10th place about 2% of the time.

When the correlation structure is purely negative and the original and revised quality scales correlate in the .4 range, the situation is far worse. Furthermore, for both types of structures

[3]The reader is reminded that a correlation of 0.6 is not "high": it accounts for only 36% of the variation in the dependent variable.

these average correlations hide the fact that there were individual studies where the original and revised quality scales correlated negatively. These studies were highly sensitive to a complete reversal of weights. Whether another testing organization, the manufacturers in the industry or a large group of consumers would believe the alternative weighting scheme to be sensible is another question. However, it is clear that these particular studies and more generally any study where the correlation structure is purely or predominantly negative warrant increased attention by members of the IOCU.

Non-Additive Rules

The next question is whether the quality indexing process can be improved by using non-additive rules.

A non-additive attribute composition rule is shown below:

$$Q = w_1 A_1 + w_2 A_2 + \ldots + w_J A_J + w_{12} A_1 A_2 + \ldots + w_{ij} A_i A_j +$$

$$w_{123} A_1 A_2 A_3 + w_{ijk} A_i A_j A_k \text{ etc.}$$

The following theoretical result will help to determine the effects of introducing multiplicative components.

> Two random variables, e.g., S (sum) = $A_1 + A_2$ and P (product) = $A_1 \bullet A_2$ are correlated zero; e.g., COR (S,P) = 0 if the bivariate density for their component random variables is normal. More generally, this result holds if the bivariate density for A_1 and A_2 is symmetric; i.e., if its odd-powered moments are zero [8].

This result implies that multiplicative components in a composition rule can contribute additional information to total test scores beyond that contributed by an additive rule that uses the same raw scores. This is not evident at first glance. One might imagine that, because two scores for a variety were already weighted and added, it would be redundant to include their product in the same rule. The theory shows that a multiplicative component can add new information to a battery of overall test scores, information that is uncorrelated with the information contributed by the additive part of a scoring rule.

This theoretical result is related to the concept of orthogonal polynomials and orthogonal components in an experimental design. An example may help clarify its meaning. Exhibit 11 shows hypothetical quality scores for four varieties using a purely additive rule and a purely multiplicative rule.[4] These two scales correlate zero, as the exhibit shows algebraically. Therefore, although both rules are based on the same raw scores, they use these scores differently. The multiplicative scoring rule extracts from the raw scores a unique piece of information not extracted by the additive rule.

EXHIBIT 11

AN ADDITIVE VS. A MULTIPLICATIVE RULE
USING THE SAME ATTRIBUTE SCORES

Let:

$$Q_1 = .5A_1 + .5A_2$$

$$Q_2 = A_1 \bullet A_2$$

There are 4 varieties with the following scores:

		Attributes		Overall Quality	
		A_1	A_2	Q_1	Q_2
	1	-1	-1	-1	+1
Variety	2	-1	+1	0	-1
	3	+1	-1	0	-1
	4	+1	+1	+1	+1
Means		0	0	0	0

This result can be visualized with the help of a scatter plot. A regression line fit through the four points shown in Exhibit 12 has zero slope.

---

[4]In both rules, 100% of the weight is applied to the two attributes.

EXHIBIT 12

SCATTER PLOT OF THE SCORES FROM
TWO TYPES OF QUALITY SCORING RULES

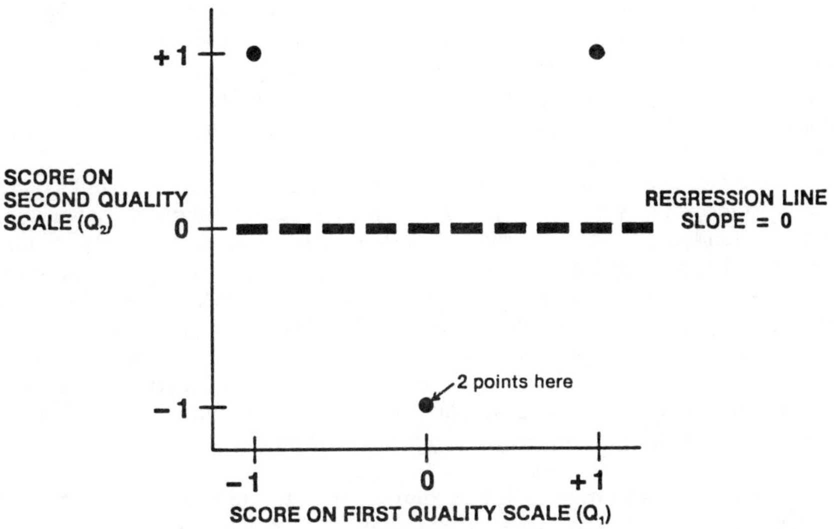

THE PRODUCT-MOMENT CORRELATION BETWEEN AN ADDITIVE QUALITY SCALE AND A MULTIPLICATIVE QUALITY SCALE IS ZERO.*

* UNDER CERTAIN CONDITIONS

Implications

Logically it might be sensible to include a multiplicative component in a product testing scoring rule. But would an agency gain from the complexity? If so how could the agency actually construct a non-additive rule in order to achieve such gains?

An answer to the first of these questions is that a multiplicative component in a scoring rule will penalize varieties that are simultaneously poor on two or more attributes and will reward varieties that are simultaneously outstanding on two or more attributes. Thus multiplicative components act to provide either a penalty or a bonus to a specific variety beyond its additive score.

Multiplicative terms behave like factor interactions, but factor interactions are supposed to be evidence of a natural law or a natural tendency between two or more attributes, a tendency that is beyond the control of the researcher. However, when constructing a scoring rule, an agency can actively decide which attributes to multiply. The agency can also decide the order of magnitude of penalties or bonuses by assigning more or less weight to a multiplicative term. Finally, an agency can employ various depths of interaction; that is, it can decide how many attributes to multiply-- two, three, or more -- to create a particular component.

These possibilities offer promise of use and misuse. Product testing agencies would have more control, yet they might have more thorny decisions to make. In certain product classes, expert arguments may suggest that high scores on two attributes must be conjointly present to achieve high levels of product quality. This possibility awaits additional discussion among those responsible for conducting product evaluations. In certain product categories, for example, a theory of engineering performance may be available that would strongly suggest the use of non-additive rules. However, it would be unwise to employ such rules in product categories where no clear rationale exists.

RECOMMENDATIONS

The recommendations that follow from the foregoing arguments are of two types: those directed at consumer product testing agencies and those directed at academic researchers. In each case, the recommendations progress from practical suggestions to more speculative ideas; some are directed at the product testing process and others at the information reporting process.

Comments Directed at Testing Agencies

1. Know the statistical properties associated with scores in each product category tested.

   1.1 For the attributes selected, what is the interattribute correlation matrix **R**?

   1.2 For the attributes selected, what is the standard deviation of scores, σ_j, on attribute j?

   1.3 How sensitive are **R** and σ_j (all j) to the varieties included in a test?

Agencies must know these properties if they are to construct reasonable indices. The interaction between the signs of the correlations in **R** and the final indice's sensitivity to an agency's choice of weights has been clearly identified. However, the final index is also sensitive to the standard deviations of scores on the various subscales. If these are different, then the subscales are doubly weighted--once explicitly by the agency-assigned weights and once implicitly by the standard deviations [6]. To avoid implicit weighting, scores on each subscale must have identical standard deviations.

This can be accomplished in two ways. First, an agency could use a z-score transformation of raw scores on each attribute before calculating the overall quality levels. Second, an agency could also systematically array the varieties tested over the same range of raw scores on each subscale. If the subscales use the integers 1-5, for example, then this second method requires that (nearly) the same number of varieties be in each category on each subscale. This method is more difficult than the first but better in the author's opinion because it forces product testers to actively and recurrently assess the implications of their scoring technique.

A related recommendation is that **R** should be an identity matrix because orthogonal attributes convey the most information to consumers. The properties of orthogonality and of equal standard deviations depend not only on scoring techniques but more importantly on which attributes and which varieties are selected for testing. Agencies must decide very carefully whether or not to keep varieties that appear to be "outliers" on one or more scales. The presence of an apparent outlier may suggest that the product category has not been defined well and that the testing agency may want to distinguish more carefully between various forms of the product.

2. The choice of weights can make a profound difference in the resulting quality index when correlations among attributes are negative. The overall quality index is also reasonably sensitive to the choice of weights when **R** is orthogonal as desired. In these cases greater care must be exercised in the choice of weights. All three of the following methods should be considered: expert judgment, consumer surveys, and theory development.

Consumer products testing agencies already employ expert judgment and consumer surveys. However, they do not to any great extent employ engineering or physical theory, even though they frequently employ engineering and physical tests. The agencies may be excused for this failure because it is expensive, time consuming and highly technical to develop theory on a category by category basis. However, theory development represents one area where the gap between academicians and staff members of consumer product testing organizations should be bridged.

Comments Directed at Academicians

1. The issue of "quatility" transformations contains a number of sub-issues that should be addressed by the academic community. These include but are not limited to the following:

   1.1 How sensitive are overall quality scores to various types of quatility transformations?

   1.2 Can general or category-specific theories be developed which describe and proscribe how various product attributes can and should be combined to affect overall quality levels?

   1.3 When should an agency use non-additive components in a scoring rule and how should such an index be constructed?

Question 1.1 is the easiest of these three to answer. It can probably be addressed via a combination of statistical theory and computer simulation. The first step would be to characterize, mathematically, the quatility transformations that agencies already use. For example, we might find that the relationship between Stiftung Warentest's (1-5) scale and certain physical characteristics -- watts, cycle times, weight, horsepower, volume, etc. -- can be described by a small family of mathematical functions. Some possibilities are shown in Exhibit 13.

EXHIBIT 13

POSSIBLE FUNCTIONS RELATING PHYSICAL AND EVALUATED LEVELS OF PRODUCT ATTRIBUTES (PARTWORTH QUALITY/QUATILITY TRANSFORMATIONS)

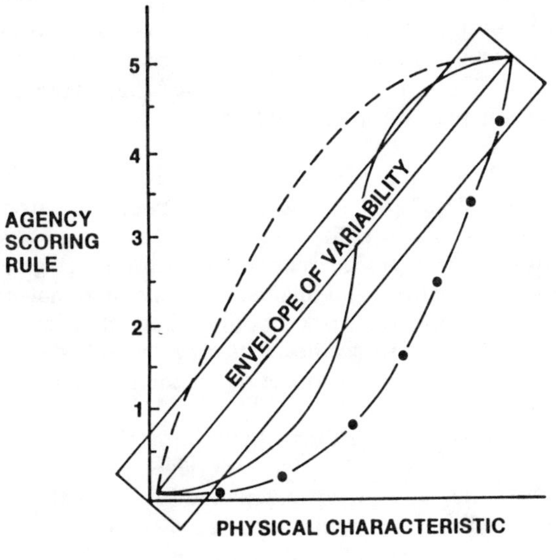

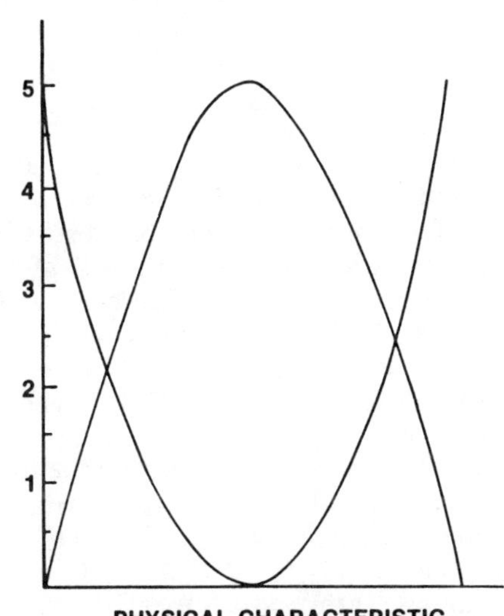

A study of sensitivity would consider logically possible and managerially relevant changes to each of these functions. The effects of these changes on an overall quality index would be documented and classified into a compact set of results and guidelines. An example of a result from this approach: "If all quatility transformations are monotone increasing, then the reported quality levels are not substantially affected by changes in their specific forms within a particular envelope of variability." (See Exhibit 13.) Details about the size and nature of the envelope of variability would have to be provided so that agencies could limit their scoring within the prescribed frontiers.

Question 1.2 asks academicians to push back the frontiers of understanding regarding the relationship between a product's physical design and its overall quality level. Academic researchers can develop theories that describe functional/utilitarian quality levels as well as aesthetic quality judgments. A functional theory would state that "this can opener works better than that one because it is designed as follows." An aesthetic theory would describe why "this can opener is prettier, more fun to use or 'classier'" than others.

Descriptive theory regarding these questions is progressing on many fronts. The subsequent step of developing normative theories of use and aesthetic appeal is much harder. Such pronouncements may well be feasible for utilitarian quality but not for aesthetic quality. Finally, the use of non-additive scoring rules must await the development of theory of the first type (utilitarian) at the very least.

Reporting

Recommendations could be offered about what should be reported, how and where the information should be reported, and when and how fast results should be disseminated. Other authors have completed or are in the process of completing large-scale studies about alternative reporting formats. These include projects regarding video text [34], educational films [20], video discs [16], on line databases [25], expert systems [13], and new print formats [29, 30]. These efforts are too comprehensive to review here.

Instead, I will present a brief schema summarizing current reporting practices and offer suggestions for additions and changes. These suggestions adhere to a general principle that more information is better. More information at greater levels of disaggregation allows information users to construct and reconstruct their own indices of quality. More published information from consumer product testing organizations thwarts criticisms of non-disclosure. More of these valuable data facilitates academic research that may resolve some of the questions posed earlier.

Of course volumes of technical facts make for poor reading. The editorial formats adopted for reporting must be chosen with care. One answer to this question is offered by the Danish testing organization, which publishes a technical brochure of test facts along with Rad Og Resultater, its consumer publication. Other equally creative responses await discovery.

Exhibit 14 displays the schema. An informal review of current publications indicates that only three -- those from Austria, Japan and Germany -- publish the weights they use in test scoring computations. None publish explicit rules or results for their quatility transformations. Only a few product testing agencies publish an easy-to-read, variety-by-attribute score matrix. Some only publish rank overall quality positions and do not publish indexed positions. Some of these publications in certain product categories appear to confuse quality levels with product value levels.

EXHIBIT 14

INFORMATION REPORTING PRACTICES

ITEM	Currently Reported By: All Agencies	Some Agencies	No Agencies
VARIETY x ATTRIBUTE SCORES	X		
WEIGHTS		X	
COMPOSITION RULE		X	
OVERALL RANKS		X	
OVERALL INDEX NUMBERS		X	
QUATILITY TRANSFORMATIONS			X
VALUE INDEX NUMBERS (P vs Q)			X
VALUE RANKS			X

This last point might serve as a basis for the systematic development of a new reporting format that explicitly includes both a quality score and a value score (e.g., an explicit price versus quality contrast) for each variety. The author has devised three different value indices, each of which uses only the rank quality position in its computation [3]. These three are currently under investigation to determine their intermeasure correlations and their sensitivity to certain assumptions. If one of these three indices emerges as clearly having properties superior to the other two, then this value index may be useful for consumers because it would simultaneously reduce consumers' information collection efforts and their computation efforts. The index would have properties highlighted by Russo [29] as being particularly appropriate in aiding consumer decision-making.

Finally, consumer products testing agencies should review their previously published studies on a category by category basis. This review would have two objectives. First, to use the same attributes over time when conducting tests in a specific category. Second, to adopt similar types of attributes across categories.

No doubt directors of these agencies feel that these objectives are currently being met. Furthermore, an audit and policy formulation session of this sort is costly. However, the audit could be carried out by a central committee of the IOCU with costs shared by all members. The benefits include improved quality in reporting. With the advent of interactive consumer information systems [24] the timing is ideal for such an audit. With modern information technology, the IOCU can automate the information reporting process and the product testing process, but only if it develops new data formats.

REFERENCES

1. BEEM, EUGENE R. (1952), "Consumer-Financed Testing and Rating Agencies," Journal of Marketing, 16 (January) 272-285.

2. BREMS, HANS (1951), Product Equilibrium Under Monopolistic Competition, Cambridge, MA.

3. CURRY, DAVID J. (1986), "Diagonal vs. Regression Based Approaches for the Construction of Value Indices," Research Note, University of Iowa (February).

4. ________ and DAVID J. FAULDS (1986), "Indexing Product Quality: Issues, Theory and Results," Journal of Consumer Research (June), 134-145.

5. ________ (1985), "The Measurement of Quality Competition in Strategic Groups," in Perceived Quality edited by Jacob Jacoby and Jerry C. Olson. Lexington, MA: Lexington Books.

6. _________ and MICHAEL MENASCO (1983), "On the Separability of Weights and Brand Scores in Consumer Decision Structures: Issues and Empirical Results," Journal of Consumer Research, 10 (June), 83-95.

7. _________ (1979), "Some Effects of Differing Information Processing Strategies on Husband-Wife Joint Decisions," Journal of Consumer Research, 6 (September), 192-203.

8. _________ and GEORGE WOODWORTH (1984), "A Structural Theory of the Effects of Product Attributes in Joint Decisions," Working Paper 84-24, University of Iowa, College of Business, Iowa City, IA 52242.

9. DIXAT, AVINASH and J.E. STIGLITZ (1977), "Monopolistic Competition and Optimum Product Diversity," American Economic Review, 67 (June) 297-308.

10. FAULDS, DAVID J. (1986), The Correspondence Between Price and Quality in Ten Nations, unpublished Ph.D. dissertation (December). The University of Iowa, Iowa City, IA.

11. GEISTFELD, LOREN V. (1986), "The Price-Quality Relationship: The Evidence We Have, The Evidence We Need," Ch. 7 in this volume.

12. GRAGG, M. and NEIL BORDEN (1938), Merchandise Testing as a Guide to Consumer Buying. Boston, MA.

13. HARMON, PAUL and DAVID KING (1985), Expert Systems: Artificial Intelligence in Business, New York: Wiley.

14. HARRIS, LOUIS and ASSOCIATES (1983), Consumerism in the Eighties. Los Angeles, CA: Atlantic Richfield Corporation.

15. HJORTH-ANDERSEN, Chr. (1985), "The Technology of Consumer Goods," paper presented to the 5th World Congress of the Econometric Society, M.I.T. (August) Boston, MA.

16. HURLY, PAUL (1986), "Boosting Sales Electronically," Industry Week (March 31), 33-35.

17. HOLBROOK, MORRIS B. and KIM P. KORFMAN (1985), "Quality and Value in the Consumption Experience: Phaedrus Rides Again," in Perceived Quality edited by Jacob Jacoby and Jerry C. Olson. Lexington, MA: Lexington Books.

18. JACOBY, JACOB and OLSON, JERRY (eds.) (1985), Perceived Quality. Lexington, MA: Lexington Books.

19. JURAN, JOSEPH M., FRANK M. GRYNA and R.S. BINGHAM, Jr. (eds.) (1974), Quality Control Handbook, New York: McGraw-Hill.

20. KNAUER, VIRGINIA (1985), "Consumers Should Know," Videotape available from Consumer Sciences and Retailing, Purdue University, West Lafayette, IN. 47907.

21. MAYNES, E. SCOTT (1976), "The Concept and Measurement of Product Quality," in Household Production and Consumption, Nestor E. Terleckyj (ed.), published by the National Bureau of Standards, Columbia University Press, New York.

22. _________ (1984), "Consumer Reports: A Consumer's Guide," Consumer Close-Ups compiled by the Department of Consumer Economics and Housing, Cornell University, Ithaca, NY 8, 1-14.

23. _________ (1976), Decision-Making For Consumers: An Introduction to Consumer Economics, New York: Macmillan.

24. _________, JAMES N. MORGAN, WESLEY VIVIAN and GREG J. DUNCAN (1977), "The Local Consumer Information System: An Institution-to-be?" Journal of Consumer Affairs, (Summer), 17-23.

25. MITCHELL, JEREMY (1986), "An Electronic Future?" Ch. 14-A of this volume.

26. MORRIS, RUBY T. (1971), Consumers Unions' Methods, Implications, Weaknesses, and Strengths. New London, CT: Litfield.

27. PITTLE, R. DAVID (1983), "Key Decisions in Evaluating Consumer Products," paper presented to the International Organization on Consumers Unions Testing Committee Workshop on Evaluation of Product Test Results; Amsterdam.

28. RIESZ, PETER C. (1978), "Price versus Quality in the Marketplace," Journal of Retailing, 54 (Winter), 15-28.

29. RUSSO, J. EDWARD (1986), "Information Processing from the Consumer's Perspective," Ch. 9 of this volume.

30. ________ (1986), "Toward Intelligent Product Information Systems for Consumers," Journal of Consumer Policy, 10 (June), 109-138.

31. SCHMALENSEE, RICHARD (1978), "A Model of Advertising and Product Quality," The Journal of Political Economy 86, 3, 485-503.

32. SILBER, NORMAN ISAAC (1983), Test and Protest, The Influence of Consumers Union, New York: Holmes and Mier.

33. SUTTON, ROBERT J. and PETER C. RIESZ (1979), "The Effect of Product Visibility upon the Relationship Between Price and Quality," Journal of Consumer Policy, 3(Spring), 145-150.

34. TALARZYK, W. WAYNE, ROBERT E. WIDING and JOEL URBANY (1984), "Videotex and the Consumer," in Thomas C. Kinnear (ed.) Advances in Consumer Research, 11 Provo, Utah: Association for Consumer Research.

35. TELLIS, GERARD (1986), "Beyond the Many Faces of Price: An Integration of Pricing Strategies," Journal of Marketing, 50 (October), 146-160.

36. THORELLI, HANS B. and SARAH V. THORELLI (1977), Consumer Information Systems and Consumer Policy. Cambridge, MA: Ballinger.

37. WARNE, COLSTON E. (1982), "CU's Contribution to the Consumer Movement," in National Consumers Committee for Research and Education, Consumer Activists, They Made a Difference, Mt. Vernon: Consumers Union Foundation; Chapter 5.

38. YOUNG, MURRAY and W. WAYNE TALARZYK (1985), "The New Electronic Media Videotape," Working paper No. 85-77, (August) Ohio State University, Marketing Department, 1775 S. College, Columbus, OH 43210.

Chapter 7

ABOUT THE AUTHOR

Loren V. Geistfeld has exercised a leadership role in his profession and at The Ohio State University. Geistfeld served the American Council on Consumer Interests (ACCI) as Treasurer (1980-82), as Chair of the ACCI Research Committee (1981-83), and as a Member of the Editorial Board of the Journal of Consumer Affairs (1979--). At the Ohio State University Geistfeld has been Chair of the Department of Family Resource Management (1978-84) and is now Associate Dean of the College of Home Economics.

Geistfeld received his Ph.D. in Agricultural and Applied Economics from the University of Minnesota in 1974. He is the author of "Consumer Decision Making: The Technical Efficiency Approach," and (with Rosemary Key), "A Decade in Perspective 1975-84: Focus and Trends in the Journal of Consumer Affairs" published in the Journal of Consumer Research and the Journal of Consumer Affairs, respectively.

THE PRICE QUALITY RELATIONSHIP: THE EVIDENCE WE HAVE, THE EVIDENCE WE NEED

Loren V. Geistfeld

SUMMARY

Price-quality studies can be classified into two categories: those using a summary measure, or indexes of quality, and those using multivariate quality measures. The literature using summary quality measures is the most extensive and can be divided into studies using ordinal and cardinal measures of quality. Studies using summary quality measures suggest that consumer markets are not working well as evidenced by weak price-quality relationships.

Multivariate studies are based on the hedonic technique or on Kelvin Lancaster's model of consumer demand. This literature suggests price and quality are reasonably well related; however, the theoretical and empirical limitations of this work are such that these conclusions must be questioned.

The paper concludes by noting seven research needs. These are: increased study of service markets; increased use of cardinal quality measures; the use of stronger analytical tools; the use of a wider variety of data sources; increased use of actual price paid; explicit recognition of seller characteristics; and the use of characteristic weighting in multivariate studies.

INTRODUCTION

The literature examining the association between price and quality is varied and interesting. There has been work in economics on the theoretical implications of incomplete information on market equilibrium conditions. Consumer behavior scholars have studied the relationship between perceived quality and price. Scientists from a variety of academic areas have studied the association between measured quality and price. It is this last body of literature that is the focus of this paper.

The price-quality relationship is studied because it provides evidence of how well the needs and wants of consumers are being met through purchase decisions in the marketplace. If the relationship between price and quality is poor, markets are not working well and consumers are not making efficient use of their resources. Efficient consumer decision making occurs when "consumers use their limited financial, material, time and human resources in a way such that the greatest bundle of goods possible is obtain through a purchase decision" [17, p. 44]. A likely cause of inefficient consumer decision making, as exemplified by poor relationship between price and quality, is that consumers do not have sufficient information to make purchase decisions or do not effectively use the information that they have. Evidence that markets work poorly may suggest the need for some type of intervention in the marketplace.

This paper does not directly address issues related to the assessment of product quality. Instead, problems related to measuring quality are noted as they affect the price-quality relationship. A discussion of quality *per se* is left to Professor Curry's paper in this volume [Ch. 6].

The lack of consistent terminology in the literature is frustrating. To facilitate the discussion of the price-quality relationship, three key terms are defined and followed consistently:

Product: "The set of goods which, for some maximum outlay, will serve the same general purpose in the judgment of the purchasing consumer" [34, p. 53].

Variety: "A particular brand-model combination of a product, e.g., Frigidaire, Model DAT, automatic clothes dryer" [15, p. 11].

Characteristic: "...any feature of a product which is intrinsic to the product and which, directly or indirectly, influences a consumer's evaluation of a specific product variety" [21, p. 303].

The remainder of this paper is divided into three major sections. The section which follows focuses on those studies of the price-quality relationship using a summary measure of quality. The second section looks at studies where multivariate measures of quality have been used. The final section summarizes what has been learned about the price-quality relationship and proposes an agenda for future research in the area.

SUMMARY MEASURES OF QUALITY

Much of the research examining the price-quality relationship utilizes a summary measure of quality. Although most of these studies have used ordinal quality measures, several studies have used cardinal measures (interval or ratio scaled). Virtually all of the research using ordinal measures of quality have employed rank order correlations, usually the Spearman rank order correlation coefficient. Those studies using cardinal quality measures have used a variety of analytical techniques. With but few exceptions, the source of quality data has been Consumer Reports (CR) or Consumers' Research Magazine (CRM). Price data were generally taken from CR or CRM. A few researchers, however, have used price data collected in local markets.

Ordinal Quality Studies

In this section more than a dozen studies that assess the price-quality relationship using an ordinal measure of quality are summarized. All but one used the Spearman rank order correlation coefficient to measure the relationship between price and quality.

Oxenfeldt was the first researcher to use rank order correlation to study the price-quality relationship [39]. He sought to answer such questions as whether there is a difference between the "Best Buys" noted in CR and the product varieties purchased by the average consumer, whether price is a reliable indicator of quality, and whether the ratings of a given brand tend to be stable over time.[1] He studied 35 products from 36 tests reported in CR between 1939 and 1949 with the price data also coming from CR. Oxenfeldt concluded that the relationship between price and quality was generally weak. In a series of footnotes, he noted several limitations intrinsic to his study. First, while the prices used were those actually paid by Consumers Union (CU) shoppers, they were averaged into a single value without regard for the type of store in which the product was purchased or the geographic location of the purchase. Second, CU does not test all products, making it possible that better (worse) products may be on the market at lower (higher) prices.

Friedman's article [13] published in 1967 was the first of a series of articles appearing over a 15-year period analyzing the price-quality relationship. His article focused on the extent to which price may reflect quality. He studied 29 products reported in CR between 1961 and 1965. The products fell into three general categories: cleaning and maintenance, clothing, and foods. In general, he found the association between price and quality to be quite low. The association between price and quality was especially low for cleaning/maintenance supplies and food, and somewhat higher for clothing. Friedman discussed the problems inherent to the use of ordinal data noting that

> "We speak of a ten-pound bag of sugar as weighing twice as much as a five-pound bag, but we would be most reluctant to make the analogous judgement on the quality dimension with regard to the relation between two ranks of ten and five... Because of the mathematical crudeness which typically characterizes the quality measure...we are usually not able to construct a meaningful measure of price per unit of quality" (p. 14).

The Morris and Bronson article [38], "The Chaos of Competition," is possibly the most frequently cited paper in this body of literature. They used price and quality data from 48 product tests reported in CR between 1958 and 1967 and found a slightly higher average level of correlation as compared with earlier studies. They expanded on previous research by studying the extent to which the price-quality relationship shifts over time for a given

---

[1]Oxenfeldt [39] provides an interesting discussion of the concept of quality and how it is measured. His paper raised issues and analysed data in ways being approached 30 years later.

product. Wide shifts in the rank correlation between price and quality were found for detergents, manual defrost-top freezer refrigerators, and vacuum cleaners. Morris and Bronson concluded that price and quality correlated at such a low level as to be meaningless and that price-quality correlations exhibit instability over time. When discussing limitations of their study, Morris and Bronson noted that the method of scoring used by CU to measure quality may not reflect consumer's preferences and that the number of market samples tested makes statistical reliability difficult to obtain.

A study, published in the Journal of Advertising, by Marquardt and McGann [31] was the first to use a large data set to analyze the relationship between price and quality. They studied 1,828 varieties from 131 tests reported in the Consumer Reports 1973 Buyers' Guide Issue. The analysis revealed that for a majority of the products, the correlation between price and quality was not statistically significant and the authors concluded that "a large and growing number of product categories are sold at retail prices which do not provide even ordinal guides to quality" (p. 31).[2]

Sproles [46] made a significant improvement with respect to analytical rigor. He used quality data from 135 tests appearing in CR and CRM between 1972 and 1974. The tests fell into five major categories and as with preceding work, price data came from CR/CRM. He found an average level of rank correlation similar to those reported in earlier research. Sports equipment exhibited a higher than average price-quality relationship while large appliances exhibited a lower than average price-quality relationship. Sproles concluded that "an objective price-quality relationship cannot be generalized across products...[and] consumers following the decision rule of price-equals-quality would perhaps make satisfactory or maximizing decisions in over half of their choices" (p. 74). An interesting analytical technique used by Sproles was the distinction between positive relation, inferentially positive relation, no well-defined relation, inferentially negative relation, and negative relation. Positive and negative relations were statistically significant at the 0.05 level; inferentially positive and inferentially negative relations were not statistically significant but were

[2]Marquardt and McGann [31] also examined the relationship between the price-quality relationship and advertising. They concluded that "heavy advertising is strongly associated with high quality products..." (p. 31). Another study examining the association between advertising and the price-quality relationship is Rotfeld and Rotzoll [43].

respectively greater than 0.30 or less than -0.20. These cutoffs were determined such that a difference of approximately 10% or more existed in mean prices of products in the top and bottom quality quartiles. Correlation coefficients not falling into one of these classifications were deemed to have no well-defined relation. In discussing limitations of the study, Sproles noted that the validity of comparative product testing as a source of objective data on product quality is a concern. He also noted that high and positive Spearman coefficients do not imply perfect markets because of the intrinsic limitations of a rank order statistic; that using CR/CRM price data does not allow for price variation within and across local markets; and that there is no assurance that reported price-quality relationships are constant over time.

In 1978 Riesz [41] reported a large sample study based on 10,162 varieties from 685 product tests reported in CR over a 15-year period from 1961-1975. He found that for 10 of the 15 years, the coefficient between price and quality was within one standard deviation of the mean correlation coefficient for the entire 15-year period, and that there was no trend in the average annual price-quality coefficient. This suggests that the relationship between price-quality is independent of economic condition.[3] He also found that the proportion of nondurable products with a negative coefficient was twice the proportion of durables with a negative coefficient. Like other authors, he raised concerns about the use of price as an indicator of quality. Riesz specifically noted that the use of rank data results in the loss of information.

Sutton and Riesz [48] used price and quality data published in CR between 1961 and 1978. They studied the price-quality relationship for toilet articles, cosmetics, and clothing, and sought to determine whether the relationship is different for socially visible products which elevate a consumer's self worth or image through the purchase of a product as opposed to products that are less visible. They found that toilet articles and cosmetics had lower mean and median coefficients than did clothing. A comparison of the price-quality relationships for visible and nonvisible clothing suggested the relationship is somewhat lower for visible clothing suggesting that elements other than quality affect the purchase decision for these products.

---

[3]Ackerman and Yamada [1] consider the effect of economic conditions on the price-quality relationship using Japanese data. Their results were inconclusive but suggested that major economic dislocations may affect the relationship.

A third article by Riesz [42] focused on packaged food products. An examination of the relationship between price and quality for 679 varieties of packaged foods from 40 product tests reported in CR between 1961 and 1975 revealed an average correlation coefficient much lower than that reported in previous studies. Riesz concluded that the "market for packaged food products, particularly convenience foods, is performing quite imperfectly" (p. 243). He noted that CR does not incorporate intrinsically subjective characteristics into their assessment of quality, a factor that might affect the price-quality relationship.

Dardis and Gieser [10] investigated what changes, if any, have occurred over time in the price-quality relationship for durable goods. They studied "white" goods, "brown" goods, other major appliances, small appliances, and cameras from 105 tests published in CR between 1970 and 1977. They concluded that higher priced goods do not necessarily have a better price-quality relationship and that the price-quality relationship for white and brown goods varies over time. Upon comparing their findings with those of Morris and Bronson [38], they found no meaningful change in the overall price-quality relationship over time.

Geistfeld's study [18] is the only one in this body of literature that used local market prices; however, he did use CR/CRM ratings between 1976 and 1979 as the measure of quality. Price data were collected through store surveys in Indianapolis and Lafayette, Indiana. Because data were collected in local markets, Geistfeld's unit of observation is varieties sold in specific stores in Indianapolis and Lafayette instead of the set of varieties tested. Geistfeld sought to ascertain (1) limitations arising from the use of price data published in CR/CRM and (2) the extent to which geographic location and seller attributes affect the price-quality relationship. Eighteen products sold in 78 stores were studied from the Lafayette market and 12 products sold in 97 stores were studied from the Indianapolis market. Geistfeld concluded that the use of prices published in CR/CRM may overstate the price-quality relationship that exists in specific, local markets. He also concluded that the price-quality relationship varies across markets and by store type. Geistfeld noted a limitation not previously identified: the need to weight data by market share. A high price, low quality item characterized by low sales will affect the price-quality relationship to the same degree as a low price, high quality item with high sales if observations are not weighted by sales or market share.

An interesting study of the price-quality relationship for running shoes was reported by Archibald, Haulman and Moody [3] in the <u>Journal of Consumer Research</u>. They used quality ratings from the October 1979 issue of Runner's World (RW); their prices were the suggested retail price published in RW and the selling price reported by the managers of several Athlete's Foot retail stores. They found that the RW prices corresponded closely with those provided by the Athlete's Foot retailers during the first four months shoes were sold. They studied 178 varieties of running shoes produced by 34 manufacturers and found a rank order correlation of 0.21 using the price data published in RW. They concluded that price and quality were positively related at a level so low as to suggest the co-existence of good and bad buys in the market. Even though a substantially different data source was used in this study, the correlation for this one product is similar to the average correlation coefficient found in the other studies.

Lesser and Masson's 1983 study [30] did not add significantly to this body of literature. It did, however, contribute to the emerging sense that markets perform poorly, as reflected in a rank order correlation between price and quality.

Studies of the price-quality relationship were limited to U.S. consumer markets until Yamada and Ackerman [51] studied the Japanese market. They used rating and price data from Monthly Consumers, a product test magazine published by the Japanese Consumer Association. Analyzing a sample of 663 varieties from 79 product tests published between January 1972 and December 1981, they uncovered something reported in no other study--a negative average price-quality correlation. This suggests the possibility that the Japanese market may be even more imperfect than the U.S. market. Bicycles were found to exhibit a relatively large and positive mean correlation while stove/heaters, microwave ovens, rice cookers and electric razors had a negative mean coefficient. Other products had near zero coefficients. Yamada and Ackerman found little consistency in coefficients over time. To a degree greater than any other study, they identified the limitations of this type of research: (1) manufacturer list prices may not reflect local market prices, (2) varieties selected for testing may not reflect the set of varieties sold in the market, (3) the quality measures may be incomplete because subjective characteristics and seller characteristics are not included, (4) informed consumers may assess quality differently than a consumer product testing organization, (5) rank order correlations do not account for the magnitude of differences between levels of quality, and (6) data should be weighted by market share.

An article by Gerstner [22] in the Journal of Marketing Research made a significant extension to the price-quality relationship literature. Gerstner focused on frequently versus infrequently purchased varieties. His sample of 1,983 varieties consisted of 86 frequently purchased and 59 infrequently purchased products. As in earlier studies, price and quality data came from CR for the years 1980 and 1982. Gerstner used the Kendall rank order coefficient. This measure yields smaller correlation coefficients than Spearman's due to differences between the computational algorithms. For this reason order of magnitude can not be compared with other studies. For 72% of the infrequently purchased items and 82% of the frequently purchased items, the rank order coefficients were not significantly different from zero. The author concluded "that for many products the relation between price and quality is weak...[and]...thus quality-price relations are product-specific, with frequently purchased items displaying weaker relations than non-frequently purchased items" (p. 214). Two reasons for the weak price-quality relationship for frequently purchased items were posited. First, it "could be attributed to the fact that non-frequently purchased items usually are more expensive and big-ticket markets are more likely to behave better because the financial commitment of consumers is substantial...[and]...Second, the weaker price-quality relationship could be caused by size variations across brands, which make price-quantity and price-quality comparisons more difficult" (p. 214). Gerstner called attention to possible limitations of this type of research not cited by earlier researchers: (1) CR ratings may not be totally unbiased because it may be in the interest of CU to show that markets work poorly, (2) CR ratings focus on the average consumer and thus do not consider market segmentation.

What has been learned from 35 years of research on the price-quality relationship using ordinal quality measures is summarized in Table 1. The low level of the mean correlation coefficient suggests that consumer markets do not work well. The mean Spearman coefficients listed for each of the 13 studies have an average value of 0.19 with a median value of 0.22. The median value of individual studies is generally larger than the corresponding mean value which suggests that the number of positive coefficients is greater than the number of negative coefficients. However, no median value approaches 0.50, reinforcing the sense that markets are not working well.

Before one accepts or rejects the conclusion reached in the preceding paragraph, the limitations of this body of research must be considered. The limitations identified by the various authors can be divided into four groups: quality measure, price measure, representativeness, and statistical analysis.

TABLE 1

A Summary of Findings From Studies Using Ordinal Measures of Quality

Author	Date	Tests	Varieties	Range	Mean	Median	Negative Coefficients	Product Type	Comments
Oxenfeldt [39]	1950	36	686	-0.81 to 0.82	0.25	0.34	25%	Primarily Non-Durables	Field study
Friedman [13]	1967	29	---	-0.59 to 0.78	0.15	0.20	31%	Non-Durables	Focused on more homogenous set of products
Morris & Bronson [38]	1968	48	636	-0.66 to 0.96	0.29	0.36	21%	Primarily Durables	Shift of relation-ship over time
Marquardt & McGann [31]	1975	131	1828	-0.90 to 0.94	0.22	0.25	31%	Mixture	Large data set
Sproles [46]	1977	135	1880	-0.66 to 0.90	0.26	0.34	23%	Primarily Durables	Large data set analyzed by product group
Riesz [41]	1978	685	10162	---	0.26		21%	Mixture	Shift in relationship over time
Riesz [42]	1979	40	675	-0.65 to 0.88	0.09	0.08	33%	Non-Durables	Studied only food
Sutton & Riesz [48]	1979	54	878	-0.71 to 0.94	0.26	0.18	33%	Non-Durables	Effect on relationship of socially visible products
Dardes & Gieser [10]	1980	105	---	-0.83 to 0.86		0.31		Durables	---
Gerstner [22]	1985	145	1983	-1.00 to 0.73[a]	0.01[a]	0.12[a]	29%	Mixture	Explain different relationship between durables and non-durables
Yamada & Ackerman [51]	1984	79	683	-0.80 to 0.87	-0.06	-0.15	56%	Durables	Japanese Data
Archibald, et al. [3]	1983	1	178		0.21	0.21		Non-Durables	Data from <u>Runner's World</u>
Geistfeld [18]	1982	17[b] 13[c] 14[d]	262 123[e] 128[e]	-0.43 to 0.69 -0.82 to 0.79 -0.75 to 0.83	0.30 0.11 0.19	0.30 0.12 0.38	12% 38% 36%	Durables	Used price data specific to markets and to store type.

a. Kendall Coefficient
b. Results using CR/CRM price data
c. Results using Lafayette price data
d. Results using Indianapolis price data
e. Actual observation was items sold in all stores surveyed

Many quality related concerns surround the use of data developed by consumer product testing organizations. These measures of quality do not include inherently subjective characteristics (styles, aesthetics), do not include seller characteristics (locational convenience, friendliness), and may use a set of characteristic weights not reflective of the fully informed consumer. The bias caused by the exclusion of various types of characteristics depends upon the type of product being studied. Almost none of the products analyzed in the 13 studies summarized in Table 1 are of the type where one would expect extensive subjectivity with respect to the assessment of quality. If the aesthetics or style were important, such as fashion clothing, this could be an issue. Seller characteristics may not be as critical as one may think at first blush. Automobiles have been excluded from the samples under study. Automobiles, unlike most of the products that have been studied, require regular service and repair. Among the products studied, the only types that approached this level of need for service and repair were white and brown goods. However, it is not uncommon for these goods to function for many years without being serviced or repaired. The products studied tend toward the type of goods where consumers focus more on the characteristics of the good, per se, than on the retailers selling the goods. Nonetheless, as noted in the next paragraph, the effect of seller characteristics needs to be studied more carefully. Recent research by Curry and Faulds [8] suggests the differences in consumer weighting for specific characteristics may not be as critical as once thought. Therefore, the problems arising from the assignment of different weights by informed consumers to different characteristics may not be too serious.

The price measures used were generally those published in product testing magazines. These prices can be criticized as not reflecting what actually happens in a specific market since they are averages of what shoppers paid when purchasing the varieties for testing or the list price. Evidence presented by Geistfeld [18] suggests that it is appropriate to collect actual local prices instead of using those supplied by CR. However, this makes a study of the effect of seller characteristics important because local market prices may include a "seller characteristics" effect.

The issue of representativeness is the extent to which the assessment of the price-quality relationship reflects what actually exists in the marketplace. The first potential problem is the extent to which the quality measure reflects the products and varieties actually being sold. CU tries to focus on the varieties which command a meaningful market share but cannot test every variety being sold. This becomes a problem only to the extent that an excluded variety commands a significant share of the market. A related issue is the need to weight the data by market share. If data are not weighted, varieties commanding a small share of the market affect the statistical results to the same extent as a variety commanding a large share of the market. The third representativeness issue relates to the fact that consumer product testing organizations often test only one specimen of a variety. This raises questions as to the reliability of the quality ratings derived from such tests. Maynes [34] discusses this and suggests that CU has developed procedures to minimize the effects of this problem.

The major statistical analysis issue is the use of rank order statistics to assess the price-quality relationship. Since the correlations listed in Table 1 are so low, one can have some confidence that the findings of a poor price-quality relationship would hold in other circumstances where parametric statistics can be used. The problems associated with rank order statistics are discussed in greater detail in the last section of this paper.

Cardinal Quality Studies

The research reported in the previous section was based on ordinal, or ranked, quality data. In this section price-quality studies (1) using cardinal measures of quality or (2) focusing on homogeneous products are discussed. This body of research, too, started with Oxenfeldt. However, this literature is not as extensive as that using ordinal measures.

Oxenfeldt [39] based his research on a cardinal measure of quality using actual CU product test scores. He divided quality scores by price to get quality points per dollar spent with the highest "quality price" denoting the optimal variety. The "quality price" of the ideal variety was divided by the median "quality price" (an indication of satisfaction per dollar spent for the typical consumer) for all varieties. This measure indicates the proportion of the potential utility the consumer actually receives. The median score for these computations across 43 products ranging from diapers to salad dressing was 0.65, suggesting that the average consumer achieved about two-thirds of potential satisfaction. In another set of computations for which rating scores were not available, Oxenfeldt studied varieties placed into the same quality rating group by CR. He divided the lowest price by the median price (an indication of the price paid by the typical consumer) in a given constant quality category to give a measure of minimum wastage. For 24 products ranging from baked beans to hair dressing, the ratio ranged from 1.00 to 0.05, with a median of 0.61 which suggests that the typical consumer paid approximately 60% more than necessary to purchase a variety of given quality. Implicit assumptions of the "quality price" analysis is that (1) the quality scores reflect the extent to which a variety confers utility on a consumer and that (2) the most quality points per dollar spent is the ideal. This does not allow decision making at the margin. However, it will become clear that this early research set the foundation for subsequent research using cardinal measures of quality.

Cardinal measures of quality were not used again until Maynes [32]. In his paper Maynes introduced the notion of "quality adjusted price" which is the price of a variety divided by its quality score--the reciprocal of Oxenfeldt's "quality price." The cardinal measures of quality were developed by students completing a class assignment to assess the quality of the varieties for a given product and to collect market prices for the various varieties. Using these data "quality adjusted prices" were found, ranging from $104 to $278 for mattresses, from $18 to $56 for food blenders, from $12 to $42 for wool carpeting, and from $198 to $348 for automobile insurance.

In a subsequent study by Maynes [33], "quality adjusted prices" for sofa beds were reported to range from $395 to $1,033. These data were also collected as part of a student project. In this paper Maynes introduced the notion of the Perfect Information Frontier (PIF) which, in price-quality space, was defined as "the set of points, and the line segments connecting them, for which a given level of quality may be purchased at the lowest price" (p. 535). The key behavioral concept underlying the PIF is that the informed, rational consumer would purchase only those products lying on the PIF. This suggests that the greater the number of observations lying off of the PIF and the greater their distance above the PIF, the greater the imperfection of the market. It should be noted that the PIF assesses the informational performance of a market. It does not deal with structural performance such as high prices caused by monopolists. A key point to note is that the construction of a PIF depends on a cardinal measure of quality since as one moves along the frontier, incremental changes occur between price and quality.

The first attempt to systematically apply the PIF to an assessment of market imperfection was reported in Maynes [35]. Using data collected in three cities, an analysis of the markets for products of uniform quality (term life insurance and film), and variable quality (pocket cameras) was conducted. Quality data came from data published in CR while price data were collected through a market survey. Term life insurance, sold by highly rated companies, was considered to be a homogeneous product since one is purchasing only protection. In a study of the Ann Arbor, Michigan market, substantial price variation was found for participating and non-participating term life insurance. For Kodachrome 126 film sold in the Ann Arbor market, a product of uniform quality, the highest price exceeded the lowest price by 60%. The product of variable quality -- pocket cameras -- was studied in three markets--Minneapolis, Ann Arbor, and Ithaca, New York. Since CR reported numerical test scores for this product, a cardinal measure of quality was readily available. It was found that the PIF for Ithaca was relatively higher than for the other two cities while for Ann Arbor it was the lowest. This suggests that fully informed consumers pay most for a pocket camera lying on the PIF in Ithaca and the least in Ann Arbor. The data also revealed the most dispersion above the PIF for Minneapolis and the least for Ithaca.

Geistfeld, Maynes, and Duncan [20] extended the analysis of market imperfections to a broader range of products. Since CR gives numerical rating scores for very few products and given the difficulty of converting the rankings reported in CR into cardinal measures, the authors examined market imperfections by holding quality constant and focusing on the price variation of a given variety within and across markets.[4] To study the degree of price variation three measures were used: the minimum price for which a variety was sold in a given market; the relative minimum which is the lowest price in a given market divided by the largest minimum price across all markets (This indicates how competitive one market is relative to another.); and relative range which is found by taking the difference between the maximum price and the minimum price in a given market and dividing this by the minimum price (This indicates the degree of informational imperfection in a given market.). Three cities, Minneapolis, Ann Arbor and Ithaca, and six products, porch/deck paint, blankets, ten-speed bicycles, dishwashers, microwave ovens, and pocket cameras, were analyzed. The relative range for each product in each city was:

	Paint	Blankets	Bicycles	Dishwashers	Microwave Ovens	Pocket Cameras
Ann Arbor	.06	.20	.03	.16	.24	.31
Ithaca	---	.09	.08	.25	.24	.14
Minneapolis	.02	.25	.06	.16	.22	.31

[4]In 1979 Jung [28] used a similar approach to study refrigerator markets. A serious flaw of his study was the implicit assumption that the three varieties of refrigerators studied were of uniform quality.

Since relative range indicates the degree of informational imperfection in a local market, the data listed suggest the degree of informational imperfection varies by product and across markets. For blankets, dishwashers, and pocket cameras, the highest price of a given variety typically exceeded the lowest price by more than 20%, while for paint and bicycles it was less than 10%. The authors noted that the relative range is indicative of informational imperfection only to the extent that search costs are small relative to product price.

Duncan [12] provided the first systematic, in-depth analysis of consumer markets using the PIF when he studied the camera market in Ann Arbor. The study examined what happened over time with respect to product availability, the availability of higher quality products, and the relationship between price and quality. The author used actual test scores for SLR cameras reported in CR in November 1974 and pocket cameras reported in CR in June 1978 as a source of quality data. Price data were obtained through in-store surveys. Duncan studied the relationship between price and quality using price-quality graphs (PIF) and correlation analysis. In an analysis of the price-quality graphs, it was found that pocket cameras tend to be more closely clustered around the PIF than SLR cameras. This was confirmed by zero-order correlation coefficient of 0.11 for SLR cameras and 0.68 for pocket cameras. Duncan noted that the price dispersion was too large to be attributed solely to search cost differences. The author also found that there was a tendency, over time, for lower quality varieties to disappear more quickly from the market than higher quality varieties. It was noted that there was a slight tendency for price dispersion to decrease and for price-quality correlations to increase over time.

Maynes and Assum [36] reported an extensive study using the PIF concept in its most rigorous application to date. They focused on the Syracuse, New York market. As with other research, the quality information came from CR and prices from a market survey. One important difference, however, was that the authors constructed a cardinal measure of quality for some products using CR ranking information, not reporting the details of the procedure in the article. The authors used price dispersion as the measure to summarize the degree to which price-quality points lie above the PIF. They defined price dispersion as the ratio of the highest price to the PIF price for a given level of quality. For products of homogeneous quality, the PIF degenerates to a point; therefore, price dispersion is found by dividing highest price by the lowest price. For products of variable quality, price dispersion was defined "as the ratio of highest price to corresponding frontier price at a constant quality level between the median and the 75th percentile"

(p. 68). The operating assumption is that the lower the degree of price dispersion, the lower the degree of market imperfection. They studied 17 products and collected price data between February and April, 1978. The authors reported that for 23% of the products, the highest price exceeded the lowest price by less than 30%. For 42% of the products studied, the highest price exceeded the lowest price by 100% or more.

Maynes, et al. [37] did not add further analysis to this body of literature, but they did pull together the work which had been previously reported. They noted that for 44% of the products previously studied, quality constant, the highest price was more than twice the lowest price, and that for 76% of the products previously studied, the highest price was at least 50% greater than the lowest price, quality constant. They concluded that, even given the limitations of this research, the differences between highest price and lowest price are so large that possible measurement errors are unlikely to reduce the meaningfulness of the findings.

What does this body of research tell us about the price-quality relationship? Oxenfeldt [39] reported that consumers realized only two-thirds of potential satisfaction; Maynes [35] noted that the highest price for film is 60% greater than the lowest price; Geistfeld, Maynes, and Duncan [20] reported that highest price exceeded lowest price by more than 20% for blankets, dishwashers, and pocket cameras; Duncan [12] reported a correlation of 0.11 for SLR cameras and 0.68 for pocket cameras; and Maynes and Assum [36] noted that for 42% of the products studied, quality constant, highest price exceeded lowest price by 100% or more. This is strong evidence of poorly working markets. However, to what extent do the assumptions and limitations of this research limit the confidence with which one can accept these findings? This is discussed in the paragraphs which follow.

The articles just summarized noted a number of assumptions/limitations implicit to this type of research. To assess the validity and usefulness of this body of research, it is important that the assumptions and limitations be considered. One set of assumptions/limitations relates to the measure of quality: Does the quality measure reflect the fully informed consumer? Is the exclusion of subjective and seller characteristics from the quality measure a "serious" problem? Is the assumption that fully informed consumers make uniform assessments of quality a serious limitation? In the light of previous discussion, the effects of these quality problems are not too serious. The most serious quality measure problem in the literature reviewed in this section is the construction of a cardinal measure of quality from CR data and the use of students to develop measures of quality through class assignments. The extent to which these constructed measures of quality are truly defensible is not clear. This issue is more fully discussed in the last section of this paper.

The second set of problems relates to the measurement of price. When price data are collected in local markets, the need to define a market becomes critical. Maynes and Assum [36] defined a market as "the set of sellers the consumer might consider if he or she possess accurate information regarding the existence of sellers and brands as well as the range of prices and qualities available" (p. 67-68). To the extent that this definition is adequately operationalized, no problems arise. A related issue is the need to carefully define the product for which variety prices are collected. Measures of price dispersion which mix BMWs and Yugos would not be very meaningful. However, to the extent that the definition of "product" noted in the introduction to this paper is followed, problems should be minimal. The problems related to price measurement do not appear to be critical in the research just summarized.

Two "external effects" merit our consideration. First, a measure of price dispersion may not reflect market imperfections if search costs are high relative to the price of the product studied. If one is studying the market for wooden pencils, a price range of 5 cents to 10 cents may not be meaningful. By contrast a price range for compact automobiles of equal relative magnitude, ranging from $8,000 to $16,000, may denote serious informational imperfections. Many of the potential problems arising from search costs can be handled through an appropriate definition of the market. The second issue in this area is the practice of price discrimination which will contribute price variation, even when quality is held constant. For example, a senior citizen discount reduces the price for an item independent of any of the characteristics of the item. Price discrimination has not been explicitly studied in the research reported in this section.

A serious limitation of the research reported above is the relatively crude way in which price dispersion was measured. If one wants to measure information imperfections over an entire market, this measure must be improved. This is discussed more fully in the closing section.

MULTIVARIATE MEASURES OF QUALITY

Multivariate measures of quality have been used to assess the price-quality relationship to a limited degree. There has been some work using the hedonic technique to examine how well markets function. Even though the Lancaster [29] model of consumer demand has implications for the assessment of the price-quality relationship, existing studies address the price-quality issue tangentially.

Hedonic Technique

The hedonic technique uses multiple regression to decompose the prices of the varieties of a product into implicit, or imputed, characteristic prices. In these analyses variety price is a dependent variable with variety characteristics being the independent variables. The estimated coefficients are interpreted as implicit prices of the characteristics.

The hedonic technique has been used extensively as a tool to correct price indexes for quality change [2, 4, 23, 26]. The intent of this research was to assess the extent to which changes in prices over time could be attributed to changes in the quality of goods rather than general inflation. This particular body of literature, while interesting, is not germane to the topic being discussed here. However, two papers have been published that attempt to assess the relationship between price and quality using the hedonic approach.

Griliches [24] first proposed that the hedonic technique could be used to assess the working of markets. He argued:

> "Given an estimated price-quality equation for a particular period, the estimated residual for a specific model or brand could be interpreted as a measure of over or under pricing relative to the quality content of this model. If, with the help of residuals, we were able to predict reasonably well the market share experience of different models or brands, i.e., 'over priced' items losing and 'under priced' items gaining, this would provide strong support for the correctness of our price-quality equation and its interpretation" (p. 109).

Cowling and Rayner [6] using data on farm tractors sold in the United Kingdom between 1948 and 1965 examined price residuals as suggested by Griliches. In a series of analyses using the residual as an independent variable to explain market share, measured both by quantity sold and value sold, they found the coefficient of the price residual variable to be consistently negative and significant as Griliches had predicted. This suggests that those products which are "overpriced" have a declining market share. Turning to automobiles in the United Kingdom, Cowling and Cubbin [5] obtained similar results. Again, market share declined as price residual increased.

This research, then, suggests that markets might be working well. Before accepting this conclusion, however, the implicit assumptions and limitations of this research must be examined.

The first factor to consider is the implicit assumptions underlying the hedonic technique. Archibald, Haulman and Moody [3] noted that the hedonic technique "is based upon the assumption that price is the best measure of product quality, an assumption equivalent to saying that on the average there is no such thing as a good buy or a bad buy" (p. 347). In other words, the hedonic technique is based on the implicit assumption that consumers "get what they pay for" or that the market works properly. This is supported by Triplett [49] who noted that the hedonic technique is based on the notion that a product of lower quality will never be purchased at the same price or at a lower price as a product of higher quality. The issue becomes whether it is reasonable to assess the workings of a market using a technique that is based on the implicit assumption that the market is already working well. Surely, the answer is no.

The second issue relates to the interpretation of the residual, per se, as a measure of over or under pricing. Adelman and Griliches [2] noted: "...this measure of 'quality change' is based only on those 'qualities' for which a price is being paid or exacted, and only to the extent of the price differential. If these price differentials are 'phony' or 'too high' or 'too low' from some omniscient point of view, the index will not take this into account" (p. 539). This suggests that market imperfections may actually be buried in the implicit prices and not absorbed in the residual. In addition residuals reflect over or under pricing only if the regression equation is completely specified and there is no sampling error. Clearly, sampling errors do exist and the specification of quality is elusive, at best. This suggests that the use of residuals is not likely to be helpful when explaining the market performance for most products.

Based on this discussion, the hedonic technique does not appear to be a viable tool to assess the price-quality relationship. This may suggest why no one since Cowling and Cubbin [5] has attempted this type of analysis.

Characteristics Approach

In 1929 Waugh [50], in a book based on his dissertation, reported on how quality affected vegetable prices. His purpose was to select several characteristics that might affect consumer or dealer purchase decisions and to assess the effects of each characteristic on price. It should be noted that Waugh's characteristics were determined independent of price and then later, related to price. Thus, Waugh did not fall into the trap implicit in the hedonic approach in which the interaction between price and characteristics was used to identify those characteristics related to quality. Waugh studied 200 lots of asparagus sold in the Boston Wholesale Market in 1927. Using multiple correlation, he ascertained the effects on price of the length of green color, average size of stalks, and uniformity of stalks within a bunch. Length of green color was found to be the most important characteristic with each additional inch of green color increasing the price per dozen bunches by 38 1/2 cents. This accounted for 40% of the variation in market price. Other things equal, the number of stalks per bunch (average stalk size) accounted for 15% of the variation in price, and uniformity of stalk size accounted for 2% of the variation in price. Together, these three characteristics accounted for 58% of the variation in market price.

Two papers using the Lancaster model as a conceptual base are of interest. The first paper focused on a consumer decision making tool called the Technical Efficiency Approach (TEA) [16]. The TEA identified relative prices such that variety A provides at least the same amount of n - 1 characteristics and more of the nth characteristic as variety B. The assumptions underlying the model include (1) the consumer accepts as relevant the set of product characteristics, (2) the decision to purchase was made prior to using the TEA, (3) the desired maximum expenditure was determined prior to using the TEA and (4) products and characteristics are continuously divisible. Geistfeld [16] noted that "...the TEA provides an upper and lower bound to the ratio of variety prices such that if this ratio is less than the lower bound or is larger than the upper bound, one variety is too costly relative to the other for what it provides" (p. 52). Using test data obtained from CU, Geistfeld computed the appropriate upper and lower bounds for product price for automatic clothes dryers. The characteristics used were: convenience and construction, machine operation on normal setting, machine operation on delicate setting, time required to dry an eight pound test load, cost of operation, and effectiveness of the cool down phase of operation. Using price data from the National Appliance and Radio-TV Dealers Association, Geistfeld [15] found that three of twenty-eight actual price ratios were outside of the range defined by the TEA.

Hjorth-Andersen [25] examined the relationship between the concept of quality and market efficiency. Deficiencies with parts of the paper have been noted by Curry and Faulds [9] and Sproles [47]. However, Hjorth-Andersen's paper does have implications for assessing the price-quality relationship by using a multivariate approach to quality. "Inefficiency" was defined as a situation in which variety A possesses the same amount of all characteristics as variety B except one for which it possesses less while having a price equal to or larger than the price of variety B. (Note the similarity to the TEA.) Hjorth-Andersen noted that one could calculate the prices at which the inefficient varieties are no longer inefficient. However, he pointed out the need to assume transitivity across varieties for this to work. Geistfeld [16] had argued much earlier that (1) transitivity is a valid assumption only if varieties are continuously divisible and that (2) one must make all pair-wise comparisons to identify inefficient varieties in this situation.

The multivariate models based on Lancaster [29] are interesting, but they assess the workings of the market from a limited perspective. In identifying inefficient varieties by examining the extent to which they possess or do not possess sufficient quantities of a set of characteristics, one is examining characteristics _per se_ and not the degree to which consumers value one characteristic over another. The TEA focuses only on the shape of the budget constraint and shows when a configuration makes a variety inefficient. Equally important is the point on the budget constraint at which an individual consumer locates. This allows individual weighting of characteristics. Consumer preferences for characteristics must be considered if market effectiveness is to be properly evaluated. To evaluate market effectiveness based only on the degree to which varieties possess characteristics is inappropriate since the critical issue is whether or not consumers are maximizing utility--something which suggests a need to incorporate satisfaction into the analysis. This pushes one toward the use of an index of quality when evaluating the price-quality relationship.

WHAT WE HAVE AND WHAT WE NEED

The Evidence We Have

The studies using summary measures (indexes) of quality suggest that consumer markets are not working well. This is indicated by a generally weak relationship between price and quality. It is likely that this conclusion would hold even if the problems, conceptual and empirical, relating to this body of literature were solved.

The studies using a multivariate assessment of quality suggest that markets may be working relatively well. This conclusion cannot be accepted with confidence given the conceptual and empirical limitations surrounding this body of research.

The Evidence We Need

There has been criticism of the use of rank order statistics when assessing the price-quality relationship. This problem has been recognized by several of the scientists using this technique. However, the ordinal quality data from CR on which all relied gave them no alternatives. Sproles [46] noted that "a highly positive rank correlation does not suggest that each increase in price will be accompanied by an equal incremental increase in quality. A consumer may have to pay a substantial premium to obtain a highly rated product...oppositely, a small increase in price could be accompanied by a large increase in quality..." (p. 75). Geistfeld [18] illustrated the loss of information concerning the order of magnitude of differences with the following example:

Examples

#1		#2	
X	Y	X	Y
1	1	1	1
2	2	2	100
3	3	3	1000
$r_s = 1.0$		$r_s = 1.0$	

Even though the Spearman coefficient is the same in both instances, the underlying data are much different--the magnitude of the incremental differences in Y has been lost. However, it is not appropriate to leap to the erroneous conclusion that rank order coefficients tell nothing. Rank order correlation coefficients do reflect the extent to which orderings differ. Geistfeld [18] provided another example to illustrate this point:

Examples

#3		#4	
X	Y	X	Y
1	1	1	3
2	3	2	2
3	2	3	1
$r_s = 0.5$		$r_s = -1.0$	

In both cases the orderings do not coincide for two observations; however, the extent to which orderings do not agree is more pronounced in the right data set. This is reflected in the Spearman coefficients. Rank order correlation has been a viable tool to get a sense of the price-quality relationship. However, if consumers are to be advised with respect to purchase decisions, or hope to get a more precise sense of the nature of the price-quality relationship, the need to pursue the use of cardinal measures of quality and to use the analytical techniques which this type of data allows becomes obvious.[5]

The literature based on the perfect information frontier generally uses a measure of price dispersion to assess the price-quality relationship. If the product is of uniform quality, this implies dividing the highest price by the lowest price. For products of variable quality, the highest price is divided by the frontier price at a given level of quality. There are two issues with respect to this measure of price dispersion which should be addressed in future research. First, Maynes and Assum [36] measured price dispersion between the median and 75th quality percentiles. This is bothersome since it implies that the price dispersion over the other three

---

[5]Siegel [44] has noted that the Spearman Coefficient is 91% as efficient as the Pearson r when used to test the existence of an association in a population and when the population has a bivariate normal distribution and is measured on, at least, an interval scale. This relates to the statistical significance of the association and not the magnitude of the association as reflected in the value of the estimated coefficient. Since size as well as statistical significance of the association is important for price-quality studies, the need to use parametric measures remains.

quartiles is not significant to the assessment of the price-quality relationship in a given market. Surely a strong assumption. Second, the dispersion of price is taken as the highest price relative to lowest price, at a given level of quality. This can be a very deceptive measure. At a given level of quality, if n - 1 of the varieties lie on the PIF with the nth variety lying substantially off of the PIF, the price-quality relationship would be considered weak; however, if n - 1 varieties were off the PIF with the nth variety being on the PIF, none of the n - 1 varieties being as far off the PIF as in the previous example, the price-quality relationship could be said to be quite good. To resolve these problems the degree of price dispersion for each of the n varieties could be averaged to reflect the price-quality relationship for a given market. For off-frontier varieties, where no variety lies on the frontier at the given quality level, the PIF could be used to estimate the appropriate price by using the line segment connecting the quality levels bracketing the variety in question. For the PIF to provide a clear picture of the price-quality relationship in a market, all varieties sold in the market must be reflected in the summary statistics and not just two varieties from the set of possibilities.

Another area that needs to be addressed in future research is the source of data used to measure quality. All studies, except two, are based on CR ratings. As long as this is done, there will be concerns with the price-quality relationship reflecting the unique aspects of quality measurement as done by CU. More individuals need to pursue the track taken by Archibald, Haulman, and Moody [3] in using other sources of quality data.[6]

To the extent that quality rankings continue to be the primary data source, techniques to recover cardinality need to be investigated. Curry [7] used the Law of Comparative Judgement to transform ordinal quality comparisons between firms into interval quality scales. To use this technique to develop interval quality scales among varieties of products is probably not feasible. However, this general line of reasoning may be worth pursuing.

The trend toward the use of price data obtained in local markets needs to be continued. The closer we get to the actual price paid for a variety by the consumer, the better will be our

[6]A possible approach is the one used by Gale and Dardis [14] in which they performed their own assessment of quality and then used this to examine the price-quality relationship for men's durable press shirts. A more recent study using a similar methodology is Dardis, Spivak and Shih [11].

measure of market imperfections. However, we do not need to treat all product varieties equally. For example, the use of "sticker prices" for automobiles would be misleading due to discounting and special financing packages. By contrast, there would be little need to survey consumers or sellers for prices of regulated telecommunications services. The key point is that prices must reflect what consumers actually pay for the variety.

When collecting market specific prices one is forced to address the issue of seller characteristics since selling price might be expected to reflect the characteristics of the seller as well as the specific product. Rather than trying to incorporate seller characteristics directly into a quality measure, it seems more appropriate to focus directly on the extent to which seller characteristics are related to price. Duncan [12] reported that in his sample sellers were not consistently "high-priced" or consistently "low-priced" across varieties. This indicates that price may be independent of seller characteristics. Since Duncan's work is suggestive and not definitive, we need more systematic evidence of the extent to which consumers are willing to pay for specific seller characteristics.

Even though multiattribute quality measures have been relatively unsuccessful, it would be imprudent to ignore them. If two quite different, but equally valid, analytical approaches come to the same conclusion, the case for or against any issue becomes much stronger. However, when using multivariate techniques, the underlying assumptions must be realistic. For example, the implicit "perfect market" assumption of the hedonic technique raises serious questions as to its viability as a tool for assessing the price-quality relationship. By the same token, the instrument used to assess the price-quality relationship cannot be used to define quality. Contrary to the principles just stated, in many applications the hedonic technique is used to identify characteristics associated with product quality. The validity of this approach rests on the assumptions that markets work perfectly and that price reflects the decisions of fully informed consumers. A better approach would be to identify quality measures independent of the market. Archibald, Haulman, and Moody [3] clearly articulated this problem when they noted that "the notion that quality can be found using attribute prices is flawed...a proper measure of quality is independent of cost considerations: quality is a utility (performance) concept and not a market equilibrium concept" (p. 349).

Perhaps the most serious deficiency of the multivariate quality measures is the inability to build characteristic weighting into the system. Ironmonger [27] outlined a model of consumer demand that may solve this problem. Ironmonger considers utility to be a function of satisfied wants and not of characteristics. Satisfying wants is a function of characteristics, but utility is achieved only when characteristics desired by the consumer are consumed. It is unfortunate that consumer researchers have been oblivious of Ironmonger. They should study the possibilities of his conceptual framework for assessing the price-quality relationship.

The research agenda items noted to this point focus on ways to improve what has been done. There remains, however, a major deficiency in the existing body of price-quality literature that should be addressed. This is the relative neglect of research on the market for services.[7] At this time there are two services which warrant special study given the rapidly changing environment in which they are sold: financial services and telecommunications services.

Geistfeld [19] has argued that deregulation of the financial and telecommunications industries poses staggering implications for consumers. He noted that "the proliferation of new products and services, and the advent of new, often forced, choices are requiring consumers to make decisions for which they are ill prepared.... This suggests the need for research to identify the extent to which consumers are making suboptimal choices..." (p. 9).

Simon [45] reported findings supporting Geistfeld's concern. She noted that only 40% of households studied purchased IRA's consistent with their preferences. While this research is not definitive, it does support the desirability of undertaking intensive studies of the markets in which services are sold.

In summary, the agenda for future research on the relationship between price and quality should focus on:

1. The market for services, especially financial services and telecommunications services.

---

[7]Maynes [35] looked at term life insurance as part of a broader study, but this could hardly be termed as study of services. The Center for the Study of Services publishes Washington Consumers' Checkbook which contains evaluations of retailers and service providers. These evaluations are collected via member surveys. This publication could be a data source for the studies of services. A similar publication is the Bay Area Consumers' Checkbook published in San Francisco.

2. The use of cardinal measures of quality. CU should be encouraged to publish cardinal quality scores in CR. To the extent that CR continues to offer rank quality data, researchers must develop ways to extract credible cardinal measures of quality.

3. The use of stronger analytical techniques. Better measures of price dispersion need to be developed. Statistics that reflect differences in all prices should be used to the extent possible.

4. The use of a variety of data bases as a source of quality measures.

5. The use of prices actually paid by consumers for varieties.

6. The extent to which seller characteristics are reflected in price.

7. The weighting of characteristics in multivariate measures of quality.

Existing research suggests that consumer markets are not working well as indicated by weak price-quality relationships. If new research following the suggestions outlined above supports the evidence we have, the argument that markets work poorly will become overwhelming. However, if additional research, based on these recommendations, indicates that markets are working well, we should be pleased.

REFERENCES

1. ACKERMAN, NORLEEN M. and YOSHIKO YAMADA (1986), "Do Economic Conditions Influence Product Price-Quality Correlations," in Karen P. Schnittgrund (Ed.), Proceedings, 32nd Annual Conference of the American Council on Consumer Interests,286-292.

2. ADELMAN, IRMA and ZVI GRILICHES (1961), "On an Index of Quality Change," Journal of American Statistical Association, 56(No. 295; September):535-548.

3. ARCHIBALD, ROBERT B., CLYDE A. HAULMAN, and CARLISLE E. MOODY, JR. (1983), "Quality, Price, Advertising, and Published Quality Ratings," Journal of Consumer Research, 9(No. 4; March):347-356.

4. CAGAN, PHILLIP (1971), "Measuring Quality Changes and the Purchasing Power of Money: An Exploratory Study of Automobiles," in Zvi Griliches (Ed.), Price Indexes and Quality Change, Cambridge: Harvard University Press, pp. 215-239.

5. COWLING, K. and J. CUBBIN (1971), "Price, Quality and Advertising Competition: An Econometric Investigation of the United Kingdom Car Market," Economica, 38(No. 152; November):378-394.

6. _________ and A.J. RAYNER (1970), "Price, Quality and Market Share," Journal of Political Economy, 78(No. 6; November-December):1292-1309.

7. CURRY, DAVID J. (1985), "Measuring Price and Quality Competition," Journal of Marketing, 49(No. 2; Spring):106-117.

8. _________ and DAVID J. FAULDS (1985), "The Measurement of Quality Competition in Strategic Groups," in Jacob Jacoby and Jerry C. Olson (Eds.), Perceived Quality, How Consumers View Stores and Merchandise, Lexington, MA: Lexington Books, pp. 269-293.

9. _________ (1986), "Indexing Product Quality: Issues, Theory and Results," Journal of Consumer Research, 13(No. 1; June): 134-145.

10. DARDIS, RACHEL and NANCY GIESER (1980), "Price and Quality of Durable Goods: Are They More Closely Related in the Seventies than in the Sixties?" Journal of Consumer Policy, 4(No. 3; September):238-248.

11. _________, STEVEN M. SPIVAK and CHI-MEI SHIH (1985), "Price and Quality Differences for Imported and Domestic Men's Dress Shirts," Home Economics Research Journal, 13(No. 4; June):391-399.

12. DUNCAN, GREG J. (1981), "The Dynamics of Local Markets: A Case Study of Cameras," Journal of Consumer Affairs, 15(No. 1; Summer):64-74.

13. FRIEDMAN, MONROE P. (1967), "Quality and Price Considerations in Rational Consumer Decision Making," Journal of Consumer Affairs, 1(No. 1; Summer):13-23.

14. GALE, ARLEE and RACHEL DARDIS (1970), "Predicting Product Performance by Price," Journal of the American Association of Textile Chemists and Colorists, 2(No. 10; May):159-163.

15. GEISTFELD, LOREN V. (1974) "A Technical Efficiency Approach to Consumer Decision Making," unpublished Ph.D. thesis, University of Minnesota.

16. _________ (1977), "Consumer Decision-Making: The Technical Efficiency Approach," Journal of Consumer Research, 4(No. 1, June):48-56.

17. _________ (1981), "Measurement of Informational Adequacies and Imperfections in Local Consumer Markets," in Carol B. Meeks (Ed.), Proceedings, 27th Annual Conference of the American Council on Consumer Interests, 44-49.

18. _________ (1982), "The Price/Quality Relationship Revisited," Journal of Consumer Affairs, 16(No. 2; Winter):334-346.

19. _________ (1985), "Effects of Utilities and Financial Institution Deregulation on Consumers," A Speech Presented to the American Home Economics Association, Working Paper 85-02, Department of Family Resource Management, The Ohio State University.

20. _________, E. SCOTT MAYNES, and GREG J. DUNCAN (1980), "Informational Imperfections in Local Consumer Markets: A Preliminary Analysis," in Jerry C. Olson (Ed.), Advances in Consumer Research, Volume 7, Ann Arbor, MI: Association of Consumer Research, pp. 180-185.

21. _________, GEORGE B. SPROLES and SUZANNE B. BADENHOP (1977), "The Concept and Measurement of a Hierarchy of Product Characteristics," in William Perreault (Ed.), Advances in Consumer Research, Volume 4, Atlanta: Association for Consumer Research, pp. 302-307.

22. GERSTNER, EITAN (1985), "Do Prices Signal Higher Quality," Journal of Marketing Research, 22(No. 2; May):209-215.

23. GRILICHES, ZVI (1964), "Notes on the Measurement of Price and Quality Changes," in Edward F. Denison and Lawrence R. Klein (Eds.) Models of Income Determination, Princeton: National Bureau of Economic Research, pp. 381-404.

24. ________ (1968), "The Hedonic Price Indexes for Automobiles," in Arnold Zellner (Ed.), Readings in Economic Statistics and Econometrics, Boston: Little Brown and Co., pp. 103-130.

25. HJORTH-ANDERSEN, CHRISTIAN (1984), "The Concept of Quality and the Efficiency of Markets for Consumer Products," Journal of Consumer Research, 11(no. 2; September):708-718.

26. HOGARTY, THOMAS F. (1975), "Price-Quality Relations for Automobiles: A New Approach," Applied Economics, 7(No. 1; March):41-51.

27. IRONMONGER, D.S. (1972), New Commodities and Consumer Behavior, Cambridge: Cambridge University Press.

28. JUNG, ALAN F. (1979), "Price Variations for Refrigerators Among Retail Store Types and Cities," Journal of Consumer Affairs, 13(No. 1; Summer):108-116.

29. LANCASTER, KELVIN (1971), Consumer Demand, New York: Columbia University Press.

30. LESSER, WILLIAM H. and ROBERT T. MASSON (1983), "Quality Signaling and Oligopolistic Overcharges," Policy Studies Review, 2(No. 3; February):484-494.

31. MARQUARDT, RAYMOND A. and ANTHONY F. MCGANN (1975), "Does Advertising Communicate Product Quality to Consumer? Some Evidence From Consumer Reports," Journal of Advertising, 4(No. 4; Fall):27-33, 48.

32. MAYNES, E. SCOTT (1973), "Consumerism: Origin and Research Implications," in Eleanor Bernert Sheldon (Ed.), Family Economic Behavior, Philadelphia: J.B. Lippencott Company, pp. 270-294.

33. ________ (1976), "The Concept and Measurement of Product Quality," in Nester E. Terleckyj (Ed.), Household Production and Consumption, New York: National Bureau of Economic Research, pp. 529-560.

34. ________ (1976), Decision-Making for Consumers, New York: Macmillian Publishing Company.

35. ________ (1978), "Informational Imperfections in Local Consumer Markets," in Andrew Mitchell (Ed.), The Effect of Information on Consumer and Market Behavior, Chicago: American Marketing Association, pp. 77-85.

36. ________ and TERJE ASSUM (1982), "Informationally Imperfect Consumer Markets: Empirical Findings and Policy Implications," Journal of Consumer Affairs, 16(No. 1; Summer):62-87.

37. ________, ROBIN A. DOUTHITT, GREG J. DUNCAN and LOREN V. GEISTFELD (1984), "Informationally Imperfect Markets: Implications for Consumers," in Seymour Sudman and Mary A. Spaeth (Eds.), The Collection and Analysis of Economic and Consumer Behavior Data, In Memory of Robert Ferber, Champaign, IL: Bureau of Economic and Business Research, University of Illinois, pp. 185-198.

38. MORRIS, RUBY TURNER and CLAIRE SEKULSKI BRONSON (1969), "The Chaos of Competition Indicated by Consumer Reports," Journal of Marketing, 33(No. 3; July):26-34.

39. OXENFELDT, ALFRED R. (1950), "Consumer Knowledge: Its Measurement and Extent," Review of Economics and Statistics, 32(No. 4; November):300-314.

40. RAYNER, A.J. (1968), "Price-Quality Relationship in a Durable Asset: Estimation of a Constant Quality Price Index for New Farm Tractors, 1948-1965," Journal of Agricultural Economics, 19(No. 2; May):231-249.

41. RIESZ, PETER C. (1978), "Price Versus Quality in the Marketplace, 1961-1975," Journal of Retailing, 54(No. 4; Winter):15-28.

42. ________ (1979), "Price-Quality Correlations for Packaged Food Products," Journal of Consumer Affairs, 13(No. 2; Winter):236-247.

43. ROTFELD, HERBERT J. and KIM B. ROTZOLL (1976), "Advertising and Product Quality: Are Heavily Advertised Products Better?" Journal of Consumer Affairs, 10(No. 1; Summer):33-47.

44. SIEGEL, SIDNEY (1956), Nonparametric Statistics for the Behavioral Sciences, New York: McGraw-Hill Book Company.

45. SIMON, ALICE (1985), "Using a Characteristic and New Commodities Approach to Explain IRA Selection," in Karen P. Schnittgrund (Ed.), Proceedings, 31st Annual Conference of the American Council on Consumer Interests, pp. 72-78.

46. SPROLES, GEORGE B. (1977), "New Evidence on Price and Product Quality," Journal of Consumer Affairs, 11(No.1; Summer):63-77.

47. ________ (1986), "The Concept of Quality and the Efficiency of Markets: Issues and Comments," Journal of Consumer Research, 13:(No. 1; June):146-148.

48. SUTTON, ROBERT J. and PETER C. RIESZ (1979), "The Effect of Product Visibility on the Relationship Between Price and Quality," Journal of Consumer Policy, 3(No. 2; June):145-150.

49. TRIPLETT, JACK E. (1971), "The Theory of Hedonic Quality Measurement and Its Use in Price Indexes," BLS Staff Paper 6, BLS, U.S. Department of Labor.

50. WAUGH, FREDERICK (1929), Quality as a Determinant of Vegetable Prices, New York: Columbia University Press.

51. YAMADA, YOSHIKO and NORLEEN ACKERMAN (1984), "Price-Quality Correlations in the Japanese Market," Journal of Consumer Affairs, 18(No. 2; Winter):251-265.

Chapter 8

ABOUT THE AUTHOR

Roland Huttenrauch has been Director and Head of the Technical Department of Stiftung Warentest, the German Consumers Union, since 1967. Dr. Ing. Huttenrauch was trained as a physicist, receiving his engineering degree and his Dr. Ing. degree from the University of Berlin in 1961. Before joining Warentest in 1965, he was a teacher at the Polytechnical High School in Berlin.

Huttenrauch has been active in the international consumer movement, serving as Chairman of the Product Testing Committee of the International Organization of Consumers Union since 1975. He was the author of the first scholarly article specifying the concept of quality [1].

ENVIRONMENTAL CONSIDERATIONS AND THE ASSESSMENT OF QUALITY

Roland Huttenrauch

In my view the primary task of a consumer product-testing organization is to provide consumers with all the information they need to make rational buying decisions. Thus, the most important criterion for judging the success of our product testing activities is not whether the information we provide reflects a reliable and defensible theoretical concept, but whether we have helped consumers in their daily purchase decisions. Naturally, this implies that we have not misled consumers because of imperfections in our comparative product testing procedures.

Ours is a mass audience--our magazine, *Test*, is bought by 700,000 out of 55 million. Hence, we do not try to evaluate the subjective characteristics of products, e.g., appearance. Such subjective characteristics may be dealt with by personal contact between a buyer and a salesperson or may be evaluated by the consumer's own experiences. Apart from these subjective characteristics, *we believe it is important to give an overall rating to every product*. Overall ratings are easy to understand. But some purchase problems arise from the differing capacities of different consumers. For example, a household appliance that most consumers find complicated to use may present no problem whatsoever for the technically talented. For others, it may be overwhelming.

Therefore it is necessary to make the assumptions lying behind our overall rating as comprehensible as possible. Then the consumer can decide for him/herself whether or not to accept these assumptions or to make his/her own. This applies most strongly to the weights assigned to each characteristic. We publish characteristic weights so that the user of our product ratings can adjust the rating to his or her own weights.

ENVIRONMENTAL CONSIDERATIONS

Recently, a special weighting problem has arisen: how much weight to assign to the environmental impact of products. What is unusual about this new "component of quality" is that it usually confers less utility to the individual consumer than to the general public. In his paper, "The Concept and Measurement of Product Quality," E. Scott Maynes [2] defines quality as "the subjectively weighted average of characteristics" where characteristics are in turn defined as "services giving rise to utility." This means that the quality of a product is high if the utility for the individual consumer is high.[1] But negative environmental impact may confer less disutility on the individual than on consumers collectively.

In many cases a product that treats the environment "favorably" will treat the individual consumer poorly, performing less well than its competitors. The extent to which the individual consumer takes this environmental impact into account in purchasing depends upon his or her own willingness to subordinate his individual needs to those of the public. This means that "quality" may possess an ideological component. In many cases a consumer will accept inferior products to advance the public interest. In some cases he will be forced to pay a higher price for lower quality, where "quality" reflects only the interests of the individual.

Laundry Detergents As An Example

A recent study of "alternative detergents" by my organization, Stiftung Warentest, showed that at present there is no detergent on the German market that combines optimal washing effectiveness with optimal environmental compatibility. Instead, one observes a negative correlation: the greater the environmental compatibility, the lower the washing effectiveness. Thus, a quality rating based solely on washing effectiveness would be highly misleading to an environmentally conscious consumer. But in the view of Stiftung

---

[1]Maynes' characteristics can reflect social considerations such as environmental impact. The issue of the extent to which they will reflect social considerations is empirical.

Warentest it would be wrong to assign a negative overall rating to a product that performed well on washing effectiveness, but which was environmentally damaging. To do so would mislead the consumer.

We had to face up to and answer the question of whether we should rate the quality of a product on the basis of its benefit (1) to the individual, or (2) to the public. We decided that it would be inexpedient to publish a summary combining both perspectives. Instead, we decided to make two separate statements, one relating to "egoistic quality," taking account only of those characteristics that are useful to the individual, and a second, supplementary statement dealing with "social quality." The final decision would be left to the individual consumer. This decision would reflect his/her commitment to the public interest.

This stance reflects our view of our role as a consumer organization. We should advise consumers, not patronize them. We should provide consumers with information they cannot obtain themselves. But final choices should be made by each consumer, relfecting his/her values and level of information.

Energy Use: A Second Example

Energy use affords a second example of our "split" quality rating. This case is somewhat more complicated because the energy consumption of a household appliance contains both egoistic and social components of quality. Egoistically, an appliance high in energy use places a burden on the consumer's pocketbook. Socially, it wastes scarce resources. In our publication, energy use is considered in two ways: first, it is reflected in egoistic quality, taking into account the level of operating costs; second, it includes a separate statement regarding the social quality component.

Separate treatment of egoistic and social components is necessary because they have different time perspectives. Assume that physicists succeeded in producing electricity by inexhaustible nuclear fusion. The considerable investment required to convert to fusion technology would take a very long time. Hence, we would expect the real price of electricity to change but slowly and egoistic quality to continue to place great weight on the amount of electricity used. Not so with social quality. As we converted to fusion, the environmental impact of electricity use would recede over time, greatly altering the assessment of electricity-using appliances from the social viewpoint.

APARTHEID AND PRODUCT TESTING

Permit me one final example that is only partly serious, but which elucidates the problem of taking social concerns into account in product testing. My example refers to South Africa and apartheid.

The illustration centers on washing machines and the materials needed for their manufacture. The drum of a washing machine can be fabricated from different materials--plastic, enameled sheet iron, stainless steel. Under existing technology, stainless steel performs best. Chromium is a critical component in the manufacture of stainless steel, accounting for 18 percent by bulk. It happens that the Republic of South Africa accounts for 20 percent of world production and 58 percent of world reserves. Further, the export of chromium is important for South Africa economically.

Now there are many consumers--not a few in Europe--who strongly oppose the apartheid policies of the South African Government and strongly support the application of economic sanctions against South Africa. In their view it would be immoral to purchase stainless steel components, manufactured from chromium produced in South Africa. Consumers holding these views would doubtless want to know both (1) the "egoistic quality" of alternative washing machines and (2) whether their manufacture involved the use of chromium produced in South Africa. For some consumers this knowledge would result in the non-purchase of a superior washing machine if it contained components from South Africa.

Summing up, it is my belief that the problem of environmental impact of consumer products will concern us more intensively in the future, posing problems both for ordinary consumers and for consumer product testing organizations. It will be interesting to see what will be the impact, if any, of negative environmental impacts on the market shares of product variants of this type. Almost certainly, environmental considerations will pose new scientific problems for product testers.

REFERENCES

1. HUTTENRAUCH, ROLAND (1973), "Probleme um Qualitat und Preis beim Warentest," Markenartikel, September, pp. 434-444.

2. MAYNES, E. SCOTT (1976), "The Concept and Measurement of Product Quality," in Nestor E. Terleckyj, ed., Household Production and Consumption, Studies in Income and Wealth, Volume 40 (New York: Columbia University Press), pp. 529-560.

ABOUT THE AUTHOR

E. Scott Maynes is Professor in the Department of Consumer Economics and Housing at Cornell University. For further background see Headnote, Chapter 1.

WEIGHTS, CARDINALITY, AND SCALING IN ASSESSING QUALITY

E. SCOTT MAYNES

My stance in these comments is that of a scholar-discussant representing consumers.

The papers by Geistfeld and Curry are exemplary. They cover their subjects completely, carefully, clearly, and provocatively. Geistfeld's verdict is that most consumer markets are informationally imperfect, i.e., characterized by substantial price variation, quality constant. His conclusion poses a challenge for consumer researchers and consumer educators that is both worthy and difficult. What shopping procedures can we recommend that will enable consumers to succeed in such markets? What policies or institutions can we propose that will make markets more informationally perfect?

Apart from its intrinsic merits, Curry's paper is significant because it represents the inauguration of a fruitful dialogue between the consumer product testing professionals and the scientific community. For too long, discussions of product evaluations have been the almost exclusive domain of the product testing fraternity. For too long, the determination of exactly what is to be published has been the outcome of a tug of war between product testers and editors. In my view this entire process needs review, criticisms, and suggestions from the scientific community. The Curry paper represents a step in this direction.

Finding no major faults in the papers, my role will be to underline four issues, called to mind by the papers of Geistfeld and Curry. They are:

1. The Weighting of Price-Quality Maps by Market Shares;
2. The Consumer's Need for Cardinal Measures of Quality;
3. Weights and the Reporting of Product Test Results;
4. Calibration and Uniform Assessments of Quality.

THE WEIGHTING OF PRICE-QUALITY MAPS BY MARKET SHARES

Price-quality maps were conceived to meet the needs of the individual consumer: they depict the price-quality possibilities located in a particular market. All that matters from the viewpoint of the individual consumer is that a seller stands ready to offer one or more units for each point depicted. To characterize the economic performance of an entire local market, however, one wants to know more. As Geistfeld points out correctly, one wants to know how many units are sold at each price-quality point. Only when each point is weighted by the number of units sold can one be sure that an entire market is informationally imperfect. Securing information regarding the numbers of units sold at each price-quality point poses a worthy research challenge.

THE CONSUMER'S NEED FOR CARDINAL MEASURES OF QUALITY

Assume that consumers wish to spend their incomes among various goods, in such a way as to maximize G_i, the quality obtained from each good, i. The mathematics of maximization readily give the first-order conditions for achieving the consumer's goal. Spend your income so that:

$$(1) \quad \frac{dG_I}{P_l} = \frac{dG_2}{P_2} = \ldots\frac{dG_i}{P_i}$$

where:

G_i = The quality of good, i

P_i = The price of good, i.

To achieve these conditions, the consumer needs to know by how much the quality of one variety of a good exceeds the quality of another. This would be supplied by a cardinal measure of quality.

The same point may be expressed in common sense terms. We recognize that money is cardinal, i.e., that a dollar is two times as much as a half-dollar. Suppose that product variant A costs 25% more than B. One "naturally" wants to know by how much A is better as compared with B. It is not enough to know that "A is better than B."

Unfortunately, most of the Consumers Unions of the world provide ordinal rather than cardinal information on quality. The following tally of product tests summarized in the 1986 Buying Guide Issue of Consumer Reports is typical:

Table 1

Type of Rating	Characterization of Measure	Number of Tests	Percentage Distribution
Ordered by Overall Quality	Ordinal	46	44%
Ordered Within Groups[a]	Ordinal	43	41%
Ordinal Total		89	85%
Numerical Quality Scores	Cardinal	9	8%
Quality Uniform: Ordered by Other Principle	Cardinal	7	7%
Cardinal Total		16	15%
TOTAL		105	100%

[a] A typical heading reads: "In order of estimated overall quality. Products judged equal are bracketed."

Thus, for 15% of tests, the reader of Consumer Reports is provided with appropriate cardinal quality scores. For the remaining 85%, he or she must seek to make do with unsatisfactory ordinal measures. For the 41% ordered by groups, the situation is even more unsatisfactory. The reader is not told whether the difference between groups is (1) a statistically significant difference, (2) a just discernible difference, (3) or what. The reader is left to "read the minds" of the testers and editors.

In the scoring of their underlying product tests, almost all the product-testing organizations actually calculate numerical quality scores that are cardinal in character. I call upon the Consumers Unions of the world to share this greater and needed information with their reader-member-purchasers.[1]

---

[1]My "call" began to be answered in 1986 by Consumers Union of the U.S. CU introduced cardinal data in charts so drawn that the reader could only distinguish significant differences. For example a difference between 90 and 91 on a 0 to 100 scale is not

WEIGHTS AND THE REPORTING OF TEST RESULTS

The possibility that different individuals will assign different weights to different product characteristics and the assumed effects of these weights on overall quality evaluations has evoked negative reactions on the parts of both scholars [4] and ordinary consumers. During my 9-year tenure as a Board Member of Consumers Union, I was the target of numerous harangues regarding CU's wrong-headed weights and their presumed deleterious effects on product ratings.

We are indebted to David Curry and David Faulds [1] for the extraordinary and perhaps unexpected finding that "weights don't matter, usually." This generalization rests on (1) a mathematical derivation and (2) an empirical analysis. The derivation revealed the two coordinate conditions under which weights matter. Somewhat simplified, they are:

1. When Assessors A and B have "opposite" weights, e.g., A assigns safety a maximum weight while B assigns safety a minimum weight, AND

2. Characteristics of products are negatively correlated with one another, e.g., varieties scoring high on safety tend to score low on comfort.

Curry and Fauld's empirical analysis rested upon a sample of 450 non-automobile product tests of Stiftung Warentest. Weights "mattered" in only 2% of tests under a "strong" interpretation of these conditions and for an additional 12% of tests under a less stringent interpretation of the Curry-Faulds conditions. Hence, my interpretation that weights don't usually matter.

For the "delegators" among users of product-testing periodicals, i.e., those who delegate by relying wholly and unquestioningly on the ratings of the product testing organizations, these results are irrelevant. But for those who wish to make their own choices, these results are highly reassuring: they imply that differing weights do not affect overall choices in most cases.

For the consumer product testing organizations these results are an enormous boon. They excuse the organization from the

---

visually distinguishable on the charts appearing in Consumer Reports. And it should not be since CR's measurements are not that precise and such a difference, even if measured perfectly, would not be "important" to the consumer.

troublesome task of fixing weights except where the structure of product characteristics contains negative correlations. Under these latter circumstances--now about one-seventh of all tests--the testing organization should fix weights and alert its readers to the implications of weights in interpreting quality ratings for this product set. One hopes that, in the future, the product testing organizations will be more candid with their readers than they have been in the past. At present (to the best of my knowledge), only three product-testing organizations publish their weights--those of West Germany, Austria, and Japan.

The papers by Geistfeld and Curry carry messages for consumer educators, too. It is imperative that consumer educators be able to understand and communicate the implications of informationally imperfect markets -- (1) that these markets pose great possibilities for gain to individual consumers, but (2) that they are badly functioning markets that serve consumers in general. Educators must also be able to understand and communicate the concept of product quality and to say when weights are or are not relevant.

CALIBRATION AND UNIFORM ASSESSMENTS OF QUALITY

In using the cardinal quality scores of product testing organizations, the reader must assume that informed consumers make uniform assessments of quality. Otherwise, CU's assessments may not be "my" assessment. Since quality is measured as the sum of weights-times-characteristic scores for each characteristic, violations of this assumption may arise from either (1) weights or (2) characteristic scores, the latter denoting the extent to which a particular product variant yields satisfaction on a particular characteristic, e.g., durability. The discussion above dealt with weights and provided reassuring new insights from Curry and Faulds. We now turn to the matter of characteristic scores.

Both Curry and Faulds [1] and Maynes [3] assert that the ordering of characteristic scores is robust. The reason: the quality ratings, whether ordinal or cardinal, are based on reproducible (1) laboratory tests, (2) controlled use tests, or (3) sample surveys. All three, when well executed, have known and generally acceptable limits of precision.

Problems arise when one seeks to assign scores that are cardinal. For example, consider two people assessing the "taste" of identical samples of Friendly's vanilla ice cream under constant conditions. They are asked to assign numbers on a 0 to 10 scale. It seems quite possible that two assessors possessing, by assumption, identical tastes, may assign different scores, for example, 8 vs. 9.

Why? This is an intrinsically subjective scale. Similarly, two survey respondents, both of whom judge President Reagan's overall performance to be "very good," may use different numerical values in reporting their assessment. By the same token, a score of 5 on a 0 to 10 scale may denote different "true" feelings when assigned by different assessors.

My hypothesis is that each individual uses a different subjective scale, just as different individuals have distinctive fingerprints. Further, I believe that the use of this scale is uniform across domains (quality assessments, political perceptions, weather) and over time.

An experiment by Maynes a decade ago [3] supports this hypothesis. A sample of 25 students were asked to assess the quality of 17 varieties of 10-speed bicycles. The students were made "fully informed" by (1) being taught the weighted average model of quality, and (2) being supplied with tabulated results of Consumer Reports' detailed tests, showing characteristic scores. Thus, an estimate was obtained of each student's assessment of the quality of each bicycle and also, by inference, of each student's subjective scale.

Each person's subjective scale has two dimensions, (1) its midpoint[2] and (2) its dispersion. In this exercise we obtained for each assessor 17 observations of (1) his/her midpoint as approximated by the mean and (2) his dispersion as measured by the standard deviation. Tabulations of the resulting overall quality scores, which had a potential range of 0 to 1,000, are revealing.[3] Table 2 shows the dispersion of mean quality scores while Table 3 shows the dispersion of standard deviations of quality scores. To say the least, the results are striking. Instead of a strong concentration of means about the 500 value that one would intuitively expect, we observe substantional variation, the highest mean exceeding the lowest by almost 2 to 1 (Table 2). The case of standard deviations (Table 3) is even more eye-catching. Here the

---

[2]The more general parameter would be the anchor point, defined as the point relative to which the other values are selected. The anchor point could be the midpoint, the lower boundary, the upper boundary, or both boundaries.

[3]The data pertain to overall quality scores that may be influenced by both weights and characteristic scores. That these effects were observable with these more complex variables suggests that they are robust.

largest standard deviation exceeds the smallest by an extraordinary 3 to 1. A scan of the percentiles in each table shows that these tendencies characterize the entire range of both distributions, not just their extreme values. The results are consistent with the hypothesis of different individuals using different subjective scales. Would these tendencies hold for (1) different domains, (2) different instructions to assessors/respondents, (3) different groups of people? The answer demands further research.

How should one "adjust" these assessments for the use of different scales? The answer: calibrate, by (l) expressing each assessor's quality score in terms of his or her own standard deviations, and (2) substituting the grand mean for each assessor's own mean quality score. This procedure, used in the 1976 study, should solve the calibration problem and thus reveal whether different fully informed assessors make different assessments of quality -- the original problem posed.

The possibility of different individuals using different subjective scales represents, I believe, a major scientific problem. Its confirmation and resolution should solve such enigmas as the "impossibility of interpersonal comparisons of marginal utility" and the problem posed here as to whether fully informed consumers would typically make uniform assessments of quality. It might also make possible the use of smaller sample sizes in survey explorations of subjective phenomenon to attain the same level of precision.

My purpose here is to lay this research question on the table. I challenge all of you to a race to see who will first solve this problem persuasively! In my judgment the race should serve us all-- scholars and consumers.

Table 2: How Means of Quality Scores Varied Over Assessors[a]

Percentile	Means of This Assessor's Scores
10th	463
25th	540
50th	588
75th	610
90th	652
Range	385 to 656

[a]The table reads: "For the lowest 10 percent of assessors, the mean quality sccore was 463 or less, for the lowest 25th, 540 or less; etc. The range in mean scores was from 385 to 656.

Table 3: How Standard Deviations of Quality Scores Varied Over Quality Assessors[a]

Percentile	Standard Deviation Of This Assessor's Scores
10th	110
25th	132
50th	165
75th	231
90th	263
Range	92 to 278

[a]The table reads: "For the lowest 10 percent of assessors (out of 25), the standard deviation of the quality scores they assigned to 17 varieties of bicycles was 110; for the lowest 25 percent, 132; etc. The range in standard deviations was from 92 to 278."

REFERENCES

1. Curry, David J. and David J. Faulds (1986), "Indexing Product Quality: Issues, Theory, and Results," Journal of Consumer Research, 13, No. 1, June, pp. 134-145.

2. Maynes, E. Scott (1978), "Attitudes, Behavior, and Economics," in Milton J. Younger and Stephen J. Cutler (eds), Major Social Issues, A Multidisciplinary View, New York: Free Press, 390-411.

3. ________ (1986), "Toward Market Transparency," pp. 61-89 in M. Goyens (ed), Price Information and Public Price Controls, Consumers and Market Performance, Proceedings of the European Workshop on Consumer Law, 1985, Louvain, Belgium: Centre de Droit de la Consommation, University of Louvain.

4. Miller, Roger LeRoy (1981), Economic Issues For Consumers, 3rd Edition, St. Paul, Minnesota: West Publishing Company.

Chapter 9

ABOUT THE AUTHOR

J. Edward Russo is Associate Professor of Marketing and Behavioral Science at Cornell University. His early career was spent in psychology, starting with a Ph.D. in psychology from the University of Michigan in 1971 and continuing in the Department of Psychology at the University of California, San Diego. He shifted into Marketing at Carnegie-Mellon, then the University of Chicago, and currently Cornell. His strongest research interests are information processing psychology, new information technologies, and decision aiding. Russo is a member of the Editorial Boards of the Journals of Consumer Policy and, Consumer Research

INFORMATION PROCESSING FROM THE CONSUMER'S PERSPECTIVE

J. Edward Russo

SUMMARY

Consumers use product information only when its perceived benefits exceed its costs. The latter include such nonmonetary considerations as processing effort and annoying or tedious experiences. Given consumers' limited knowledge and effort resources, as well as an inhospitable information environment, it may be more productive to change the environment to adapt to consumer limitations than to change consumers to adapt to the environment. Illustrations are provided of techniques that reduce information processing effort and thereby shift the cost-benefit balance in favor of information use.

This paper examines the acquisition and use of product information from the consumer's perspective. The initial focus is on a psychological description of consumers, especially their information processing limitations. This complements normative approaches from economics or education that call for rational or educated/informed consumers. The descriptive review is followed by a theoretical structure in which consumers decide whether to use product information on the basis of its perceived benefits and costs. It is argued that this is a powerful framework for explaining consumer's acceptance and use of both existing and future product information.

Once this descriptive foundation is laid, the paper turns to the more prescriptive task of facilitating consumer information processing. This can be accomplished by increasing the benefits derived from product information or by decreasing the costs of acquiring and using the information. One can also classify techniques for helping consumers with information processing as ones that either change consumers, e.g., by educating them, or change the environment, e.g., by presenting information in a more hospitable format. Also considered is how new information technologies will impact consumer information processing by altering the differential between benefits and costs.

* * * *

ENVIRONMENTAL AND CONSUMER BARRIERS TO EFFECTIVE USE OF PRODUCT INFORMATION

What prevents the use of more product information by consumers? In this section I examine the two classes of barriers to greater information usage, human and environmental. Admittedly these areas interact, often with one compensating for the other. For instance, more knowledgeable consumers can overcome an inhospitable information environment, or making the environment more "user friendly," can increase access to disadvantaged consumers. Nonetheless, the human and environmental barriers to information processing can usefully be separated.

Consumer Barriers to Effective Information Use

I consider three difficulties commonly ascribed to consumers: insufficient knowledge, inadequate effort, and information processing limitations. I shall argue that limited information processing is a false problem, while the role of effort is more important than is generally recognized. We begin, however, by considering what is probably the greatest consumer-based barrier to effective use of product information, insufficient knowledge.

Knowledge

Consumers often do not know how to use available information. For expensive but infrequent purchases like a house or automobile, consumers rarely know all of the relevant attributes. Consequently, they may not gather the right information even when it is available (e.g., ask the right questions of the seller). Even for products that are familiar and frequently purchased, consumers often do not know how to interpret information that is provided. It may be quite difficult to understand the value of some new feature of a TV or even the value of niacin[1] in a TV dinner.

A principal finding of cognitive psychology is that knowledge is domain-specific. Someone may be an expert chess player but quite ordinary at other board games like checkers or the Japanese game of go. Because consumers buy so many different products, it is impossible to be very knowledgeable about all of them. Generally speaking, the knowledge differences between experts and novices are substantial, and consumers are novices. One of the big differences between corporations and consumers as buyers is their level of expertise. When a company buys a mainframe computer, it calls upon the professional expertise of its own data processing department and, if necessary, outside consultants. Because consumers who are buying a personal computer work on a much smaller scale, they do not have access to independent experts. They must make do with whatever knowledge they can glean from friends, publications, and the self-interested salespeople at computer stores.

To understand the difficulties consumers have in dealing with the product information environment it is essential to appreciate the impediment caused by a lack of knowledge. The availability of information can do little to aid consumers if they don't have enough knowledge to understand it.

Effort

Physical and mental effort is costly. Consumers have better things to do with their time and energy than make the optimal choice of a TV set, much less of a TV dinner. Yet given limited knowledge, considerable effort is often needed to generate information that is useful to the purchase decision. The expenditure of effort is further discouraged by the increasing value of time (e.g., [24]), which is the main cost of effort.

The combination of high demand for effort and its limited supply, given more attractive uses, suggests that increasing consumers' effort is not an easy path to better purchase decisions. The topic of effort, however, is still important and may be part of a solution to the problem. We return to the role of effort in a later section.

---

[1]Niacin is a B vitamin whose deficiency in the body results in pellagra. It is one of the eight "leader" nutrients that the FDA requires on many food packages, including frozen (TV) dinners.

One further aspect of effort should be appreciated, its flexibility in compensating for failures of information or knowledge. Although in many cases information seems not to be available, we often find that it is if we expend enough effort. For example, any individual buying a TV set could, in principle, collect all the prices for all brands available by traveling to and negotiating with all local vendors. Similarly, with enough effort we could increase our own knowledge to that of an expert in TV sets. Although such action is rarely justified, it is important to appreciate how consumer effort can, in principle, overcome other barriers to the effective use of product information.

Information Processing Limitations

Although human information processing is limited, these limits are largely irrelevant to consumers' effective use of product information. Most of us know that short-term memory is limited to relatively few items. Five to seven is the maximum usually given. However, limited short-term memory (which is really limited central processing capacity), is seldom a barrier to the effective use of product information. Because this is a momentary limit on information processing capacity, consumers can usually circumvent it by devoting more time to a task. Thus, if we are confronted with a great deal of information, we simply take more time to sort through it. The fact that we can process only a limited amount of information at any moment is compensated by devoting more total time.

Note that again effort compensates for some other obstacle. Human information processing is momentarily limited, but not limited in total. By expending enough effort, the total amount of product information that can be processed is essentially unlimited.

Environmental Barriers

The information environments in which consumers must operate may be hospitable or hostile. A hospitable environment offers information in a type and amount useful to consumer decision making. For instance, many consumers rely on the movie and restaurant reviews in newspapers, books and other media. This information normally includes both an overall evaluation on a familiar scale like 0 to 4 stars or thumbs up/down and a more detailed narrative. In evaluating products, Consumer Reports magazine rates both overall quality and individual attributes in a way that allows readers to compare many different brands. There are also services that search for the lowest airfares, comparative lists of the personal loan rates available from lending institutions, and other examples of information whose type or amount match consumers' needs.

Missing Information

Unfortunately for consumers, there are more areas of information hostility than hospitality. Often there is not enough information. Consumers generally have great difficulty obtaining useful information on the quality of such services as physicians, auto repairs, and financial advisors. Similarly, information on local prices and product availability is rarely accessible in a convenient form. Other inhospitable areas include the many products that magazines like Consumer Reports do not evaluate (e.g., wristwatches).

Insufficient information occurs for several reasons. The costs of gathering and synthesizing the information may be too great, given a small market size or no market mechanism to compensate the information provider. Local prices and product availability are one example where market mechanisms do not provide valuable information to consumers (but for an exception see [42]). The problem of the costs of information provision exceeding potential revenue is exacerbated by "free riding" [12]. This occurs when the original information provider is not compensated for benefits accruing to its users. For example, a brand highly rated by Consumer Reports may advertise its high rating without compensating the magazine. Similarly, a single magazine subscription may be passed on to other readers who derive benefits without contributing to the cost of producing the information. For a discussion of this and other issues related to the "public good" nature of product information see [2]. An overview of economists' approaches to problems of imperfect information environments can be found in Ippolito [20].

Another cause of insufficient information is sellers who actively prevent information from reaching consumers. To cite just one instance, when the comparative prices of a city's major supermarket chains were published in local newspapers, some of these chains pressured publishers into ceasing publication by threatening to withdraw their advertising. This occurred in two separate studies of comparative price lists and in five different cities [4, 9].

Irrelevant Information

A second kind of information hostility is the wrong kind of information. The nutrition information on many packaged foods focuses on positive nutrients like niacin and riboflavin, which consumers care little about. In contrast, information on negative food components like cholesterol, sugar, and chemical additives is unavailable though consumers view it as more valuable [17, 31].

Closely related is the problem of too much objective, technical information where, instead, some evaluation is needed by consumers. Government publications often inundate the reader with objective details like the acoustical performance of hearing aids, that are uninterpretable by the ordinary consumer. Similarly, fact sheets presenting the physical dimensions of automobiles (wheel base, total weight, width, gas tank capacity, etc.) are usually of little use in deciding which car, model, and options are best suited to a buyer's needs.

Finally, much of the available information describes single brands only. Instead, consumers usually need help in comparing competing brands.

Biased Information

A final problem is information that is biased by the agenda of the information provider. This often characterizes information from salespersons, e.g., from those who represent single brands (like a single life insurance company or automobile nameplate) or from those who profit more from selling one brand over another. It goes without saying that most advertising touts the superiority of a brand no matter how inferior it is -- and offers little if any factual information [e.g., 39]. Biased information, however, is not confined to sellers. Other information providers may have agendas that involve persuading consumers to buy or not buy a particular product.

Unfortunately the information that is most biased is often the most accessible to consumers. The self-interest that leads to the creation of biased information often leads to its aggressive dissemination. Thus, most of the information that reaches consumers is biased information that they encounter incidentally, like advertising. The unbiased sources must usually be sought out by consumers, e.g., reports from independent testing organizations. There are noteworthy exceptions like regular media reports on health, cinema reviews, and the like. But these are exceptions. Caveat emptor applies not only to products but to product information as well.

The Consumer's Decision to Seek and Use Product Information

Given all the imperfections of the environment and of consumers themselves, how do they deal with the task of obtaining product information? I believe that the decision to seek and use information is based on a cost-benefit analysis from the consumer's perspective. For information to be sought or used the benefits anticipated by the consumer must exceed the expected costs. The consumer's cost-benefit analysis may be brief and imperfect, but it is usually performed, and it forms a very general principle of consumer information processing. Understanding this analysis enables us to predict whether new forms of product information will succeed or fail. It can also be used to guide the redesign of current information to make it more useful to consumers.

Any attempt to apply this analysis to predict whether information will be used requires that we understand the benefits and costs as the consumer perceives them. The specific benefits and costs as experienced by consumers can be subtle, even hidden. Thus, an important challenge is to formulate a full list of benefits and costs from the consumer's perspective.

Benefits of Information Use

It is useful to distinguish between concrete and intangible benefits. While the former tend to be well-recognized economic benefits, the latter are often obscure. Yet the intangible benefits play just as important a role in determining whether information will be used by consumers.

The main concrete benefit of using product information is maximizing the personal utility of the purchased product, i.e., the specific brand, model, options, accessories, price, and vendor. Other tangible benefits include optimal use of the product (e.g., its full range of uses) and the minimization of its post-purchase costs (e.g., the costs of maintenance, insurance, repair, and disposal).

Intangible benefits. The intangible benefits are more psychological and much harder to translate into monetary terms. They include an increased certainty that the best product has been selected or, conversely, a reduced risk of making a suboptimal choice. Other intangible benefits are safe use of the product and a gain in product knowledge, though this may only be valuable for future purchases.

Some intangible benefits have more to do with the decision process itself than the chosen alternative. Consumers may be more or less satisfied with the way the decision was made, e.g., the completeness of the information availed, the logic of the choice process, or the presence of convergent recommendations from different sources. This justifies to oneself that the decision was a good one. Similarly, the ability to justify a product decision to others like a spouse or friends who seek advice, may be based on a good decision process.

These intangible, psychological benefits turn into costs if they fall below some expectation or reference level. For example, satisfaction with the availed information becomes dissatisfaction if the completeness of this information falls below some subjective threshold.

A final intangible benefit is the experiential value of the process. Acquiring and using information may be enjoyable, entertaining, etc.; or it may be annoying and frustrating. In the latter case the experiential value is negative and moves into the cost column.

Experiential value is an underappreciated component of the decision to use product information. To a large extent, it explains why people watch things as non-informative as TV commercials and in-store videos. Horne [18] examined users and non-users of an electronic funds transfer system at grocery stores and other non-bank locations. The one characteristic of this service that most discriminated between potential users and non-users was "enjoyment of using." This attribute seems to capture the notion of experiential value and to support the claim that the capacity to entertain as well as inform may determine whether information is used by consumers. As an example of negative experiential value, Elton and Carey [11] report that users of a videotex system found unacceptable a delay of 6 or more seconds between an information request and its reception on the screen.

The preceding catalog of benefits is summarized in Table 1 and parallels Russo [36]. I recognize that it may not be complete and that other taxonomies are possible [e.g., 8, 29, 38]. What seems most important, however, is the recognition of non-economic benefits, including those derived from the decision process itself. These other benefits enter into the overall cost-benefit balance and are fully capable of influencing the consumer's decision to use product information.

Costs of Information Use

The costs of acquiring and using product information can also be partitioned into tangible and intangible. The former are mainly monetary. The latter are more psychological like processing effort and negative process experiences.

TABLE 1

BENEFITS AND COSTS OF USING PRODUCT INFORMATION

	Benefits	Costs
Tangible	Increased utility of the chosen alternative (adjusted for price)	Monetary costs of equipment, documents, access time, etc.
	Full use of the product	Placement on unwanted mailing lists
	Reduced post-purchase costs (maintenance, insurance, etc.)	
Intangible	Reduced risk	Effort to use the system
	Safe use of the product	Effort to learn to use the system
	Knowledge for future purchases	Dissatisfaction with completeness of information acquired
	Satisfaction with completeness of information acquired	Inability to justify the decision process to oneself and/or others
	Ability to justify the decision process to oneself and/or others	Negative use experiences: annoyance, frustration, tedium, etc.
	Entertainment value; amusement, informativeness (for its own sake), etc.	

<u>Tangible costs</u>. These refer to all direct payments. They may include a subscription to <u>Consumer Reports</u>, travel costs to a vendor, the price of videotex hardware (to the extent that this equipment is bought to provide access to product information), mailing expenses to obtain information from a government agency, and a guidebook to the restaurants and hotels of a travel destination. Monetary costs can, in principle, be very high. For example, an expert consultant could be hired to advise on the purchase of a house or the selection of a medical service provider. This is rarely done by individual consumers (as opposed to corporations), although interior designers for homes and financial advisors are frequently used by upper income consumers. Note also that some product information is free, at least in the sense of direct

monetary cost. The nutrition information on food packages is one example.

Intangible Costs. An important intangible cost is the physical and mental effort required to acquire and process product information. In some cases effort is the largest single cost in using information. In many others the effort cost is so high (relative to the benefits) that available information is never used. For example, the comparative lists of supermarkets' food prices [4, 9] could be compiled by any shopper--although only with much time and effort. Similarly the price-quality charts advocated by Maynes [26] are largely a matter of effort. The information on prices is available from vendors and the quality information is taken from Consumer Reports (although any other credible source could be used).

What exactly do we mean by mental effort? It is simplest to think of effort as the work done by our information processing apparatus. There are some situations where our momentary processing resources (or central processing capacity) are not fully occupied, e.g. driving an automobile or performing other highly automated tasks. Because their full cognitive resources are not needed, experienced drivers can simultaneously listen to the radio or converse with a rider. In contrast, using product information absorbs these thinking resources completely. When we compare unit prices in a supermarket, talk with a salesperson, or read Consumer Reports, our central processing capacity is completely absorbed.

Note that this concept of effort as work is total effort. It should be contrasted to momentary effort which is the percentage of processing capacity being used at any given moment. Momentary effort cannot be substantially increased. Indeed, this is what is meant by information processing limitations, discussed earlier. Total effort, however, is easily expandable by devoting more time to a task. The relationship between the two is straightforward: total effort is the product of momentary effort and time. That is, in any task (like processing product information) where 100% of momentary capacity is used, effort can be indexed by time. Twice the time spent comparing unit prices means twice the effort. It is essential to recognize that it is total effort that enters into the cost-benefit analysis, not momentary effort.

The value of effort, or of the time fully occupied by the acquisition and use of product information, is best measured as an opportunity cost. That is, effort cost can be measured by the value of the alternative uses for that time. For consumers with more productive alternative uses effort costs are higher than for those with less productive alternate activities. A characteristic of contemporary industrial societies is the increasing value, and the perceived scarcity, of time as the range of attractive and productive activities increases [e.g., 3, 16]. This trend raises the cost of the effort required to acquire and use product information.

Information processing effort can be partitioned into three components: collection, comprehension, and computation [35, 37]. Collection refers to the effort of acquiring or gathering the relevant product information, such as the time to telephone vendors for prices or to examine different packages for nutrition information. Comprehension effort is needed to understand and evaluate the information that has been collected. Is a "sale price" really a discount? How important is niacin to your family's diet? Finally, computation effort captures the mental work needed to derive a choice or judgment from the collected and comprehended information. It might mean comparing reliability differences, calculating unit prices, or deciding which TV dinner offers the best overall nutrition. The partitioning of effort into these three components is useful for designing strategies that lower information processing effort. These effort-reducing strategies play an important role in the next section.

Several intangible costs are simply the reverse of benefits listed above. When they fall below some reference point these benefits become costs, e.g., the completeness of the product information and the justifiability of the decision process itself. The most important of these reversible considerations, however, is <u>experiential costs</u>. These are the negative experiences associated with the process of using the product information. An example mentioned earlier is users' annoyance at the delay between the request and arrival of information in certain restricted videotex systems. Consider a one-way information system using television signals (and special equipment for decoding the signal) to transmit "pages" of information. This is a restricted form of videotex known as teletex in Great Britain [27, 28]. Users can select any page desired but they must wait until that page is transmitted before they can see it on their TV screens. The resulting delays are surprisingly annoying, with those in excess of 6 seconds judged to be unacceptable [11].

More common examples of experiential costs are the unpleasantness associated with extracting information from uncooperative salespeople (e.g., trying to obtain prices for several brands over the telephone), or the frustration ordinary consumers experience trying to understand government reports that seem overly technical. These experiential costs are often underappreciated in the design of product information formats and systems.

Experiential costs are conceptually distinct from mental effort. The cost of effort is the time lost, specifically the opportunity cost of not doing something else with the time spent using the product information. Experiential costs (or benefits) refer to the quality of the experience of information use. How much a consumer dislikes (or likes) interacting with a salesperson or reading a Consumer Reports article is entirely separate from what else they might have done with their time.

The Generality of the Cost-Benefit Analysis of Information Use

Consumers' use of a cost-benefit analysis to decide whether to use product information may be very detailed or only approximate. However, I believe that it is generally performed. Especially during their first experience with new product information, people monitor its benefits and costs and make a judgment as to whether further use is warranted. Effort costs and experiential benefits/costs are particularly transparent to the user. Other benefits may be harder to estimate (e.g., the increase in the utility of the chosen product), while still others may be underappreciated (e.g., the long-term value of increased knowledge). The analysis may also be subject to judgmental biases [e.g,. 1, 21].

Nonetheless, however imperfectly it is done, a cost-benefit calculation is usually performed. It is used by both educated and uneducated consumers, the rich and poor, ignorant and knowledgable, old and young, and those in the Third World as well as in industrialized societies. In short, the usefulness of any particular information can be understood in terms of a benefit-cost analysis from the consumer's perspective.

Adaptive Tradeoffs Among Costs and Benefits

Costs and benefits are relative and can be traded off. One can think in terms of a portfolio of costs (or benefits) that can be shifted into a configuration that is optimal for the individual consumer. For people who place a very high value on vitamins and minerals, it may be worth expending the effort to read and gather the information from the nutrition labels of competing food products. It may also be worth seeking out books on nutrition or articles on particular nutrients to increase their nutrition knowledge. Wealthier consumers with the same concern might hire a professional nutritionist to provide advice rather than educate themselves.

The point is that consumers are adaptive. We should recognize their ability to adaptively trade off costs (or benefits) in their own self-interest. Consider the challenge of increasing consumers' knowledge, and suppose there are two different kinds of consumers. Group A is characterized by low financial resources (a high cost of spending money) but considerable time (a low cost of information processing effort). Group B is the opposite, money is plentiful but time is not. Group A will trade a substantial amount of time to save money, while Group B will make the opposite trade, spending money to save time. To increase the knowledge of both groups may require different education tactics. A free pamphlet, even if long and dull, may work for the first group while the second needs a briefer communication vehicle even if it is more expensive. It is important to appreciate that the minimum total cost may be achieved in very different ways for different consumers.

AIDING CONSUMER INFORMATION PROCESSING

If consumers rely on a cost-benefit analysis, as I have claimed, then effective strategies for aiding consumer use of product information can be based on these concepts. Specifically, effective techniques should increase benefits, reduce costs, or accomplish both.

In this section I contrast these two approaches and argue for the special promise of techniques that reduce the cost of information processing effort. However, let me first address an important definitional issue. If a supermarket posts unit prices for the first time, does the value of this new information derive from a greater benefit or a lower cost? Although it may seem that this new information must, by definition, increase benefits, I propose the opposite view. In this case the information needed to compute unit prices was always available and, therefore, the benefits were always available and have not been increased. Instead, the effort cost of computing unit prices has been eliminated. The net result is a superior cost-benefit differential, but because the costs have been reduced, not because the benefits have been increased. I recognize that this distinction is somewhat arbitrary, but an emphasis on effort costs will prove useful.

Increasing Benefits

There are two ways to increase the benefits of information use as perceived by consumers. We can provide valuable new information or we can persuade consumers that currently available information has more value than they previously thought.

Genuinely new information might come from a *Consumer Reports* article on a product never previously evaluated, like wristwatches or hotel chains. It can also arise from the updating of old information like an article that evaluates the current models of automobiles or personal computers.

The new information technologies can also provide more beneficial information [36]. For example, video discs and computer graphics will eventually provide consumers with detailed information on the assembly and operation of new products. This technology is currently being used to train professionals such as automobile mechanics and sales people. We return to the potential of the new technologies for aiding consumer information processing in the next section.

An alternative to creating new, more beneficial product information is to increase the perceived benefits of existing information. In some cases consumers may undervalue information. For example, there is new knowledge on the value of calcium in diets and the skin cancer danger from suntanning. In the past consumers have been made aware of the danger from smoking cigarettes and the value of regular flossing of the teeth. Communicating new knowledge to consumers is the role of consumer education.

Consumer educators face a complex problem when consumers don't seem to want to learn or, from a different perspective, when consumers see the benefits as less valuable than professional educators do. For instance, nutritionists argue for the benefits of vitamins like niacin and specifically for using nutrition information to assure that the recommended daily allowances of vitamins and minerals are consumed. Yet many consumers ignore this information and, when asked, judge its value to be low [17, 31]. Consumers' perception of benefits can be changed via advertising and other mass persuasion techniques. However, although these techniques have proved successful in many cases, this mode of persuasion is relatively slow and expensive. It may take years to alter consumers' perceived value of information.

Reducing Costs

I shall focus mainly on the reduction of information processing effort. Monetary and experiential costs are also worthy of attention. However, the former depend on factors like technology and market mechanisms which are largely outside the scope of this paper, while experiential costs will be briefly addressed in a later section. Recalling the possibility of trading off effort to overcome barriers like availability and knowledge, let us take a broad view of effort reduction. Specifically, let us accept the challenge of finding creative ways to lower the three kinds of effort costs so as to make the available information worth processing.

Reducing Collection Effort

If the information is out there but consumers are not using it, the problem may be the effort needed to collect it into a useful form. For the past decade the Massachusetts State Banking Department has compiled lists of mortgage and auto loan rates [22]. Each list is specific to a particular region and is updated twice monthly. A sample of the mortgage rate portion from the June 1, 1986 list is shown in Figure 1. Selected from the complete set of 123 lending institutions are 23 that cover the full range of available rates. The Federal Reserve System has recently tested the effects of these loan rate schedules in three separate markets (Rochester, New York; Akron, Ohio; and Sacramento, California) over a period of one year. The Fed's focus was on the response of lending institutions rather than on the behavior of consumers that presumably causes an institutional response. Disseminating the comparative mortgage rate information resulted in significantly lower mortgage rates and less dispersion among rates from different lenders [7]. The success of at least one commercial service that reports mortgage rates is further evidence of the value of such lists to consumers [22].

Note how these lists do no more than save consumers the effort of gathering the same information for themselves. The lists do little to lower comprehension or computation effort. For example, they do not identify those institutions with the lowest rates, compute an overall average, or perform other computations that consumers need to make comparisons. An interesting challenge is how to modify the list in Figure 1 to encourage greater consumer use.

As a second example Figure 2 shows a schematic residential utility (electricity) bill that includes a comparison to the previous year's consumption. This comparison enables consumers to determine whether major energy conservation actions like adding insulation or lowering the winter thermostat were successful. When the Atlantic City Electric Co. switched to this billing format in 1974, energy consumption dropped 3% [33]. Note that the previous year's consumption was available from most consumers' own records. What Atlantic City Electric's bills did was reduce the effort to compare the old and new consumption. Other examples of reducing energy consumption via feedback are reported by Ritchie and McDougall [32] and by Winett and Kagel [46].

FIGURE 1

THE SHOPPER'S CREDIT GUIDE (ABRIDGED) ASSEMBLED AND PUBLISHED BY THE STATE BANKING DEPARTMENT OF MASSACHUSETTS

Name of Lending Institution	Phone Number	Fixed Rate Mortgages (15 yr. term)	Adjustable Mortgage Rates (1-5 yr. adjustments)	Minimum Downpayment (Percent needed)
Banks				
Beverly Savings	927-0333	10.74%	9.41%	5%
Cambridge Savings	864-8700	10.43	9.65	10%
Century B & Trust	391-4000	10.36	None	5%
Dedham Inst. Sav.	329-6700	10.18	12.62	20%
Depositors Trust Co.	826-5800	10.10	9.30	20%
East Boston Savings	567-1500	10.89	8.86	10%
East Cambridge Sav.	354-7700	11.18	9.69	20%
Framingham Trust	872-4368	None	10.37	20%
Lexington Savings	862-1775	10.65	8.61	20%
Lincoln Trust	545-4150	10.61	11.63	20%
Medway Coop.	533-8661	11.75	N/A	20%
Newton South Coop.	969-4300	11.16	None	20%
Provident Inst. Sav.	423-9600	10.62	9.20	5%
South Weymouth Sav.	337-7800	10.96	10.08	10%
Waltham Savings	894-7790	None	10.38	20%
West Newton Sav.	244-2000	10.61	9.04	10%
Winchester Coop.	729-3620	10.52	10.50	20%
Credit Unions				
Carmel C.U.	884-3967	10.43%	N/A	N/A
Metropolitan C.U.	884-7200	11.50	11.50%	20%
Saugus C.U.	233-0010	11.25	None	None
Mortgage Companies				
First Atlantic	367-7180	10.01%	10.18%	5%
Lomas & Nettleton	273-1919	10.37	10.50	5%
Malmart	738-4646	10.10	9.43	5%

FIGURE 2

A MONTHLY RESIDENTIAL ELECTRIC BILL WITH PREVIOUS YEAR'S CONSUMPTION INCLUDED FOR COMPARISON

Billing Period: November 30 to December 29		Amount Due
Consumption (Kwhr)		$238.88
Current Billing Period	Same Period Last Year	Date Due
2275	2472	Jan. 15

As a last example of reducing collection effort, a price-quality chart [26] is reproduced in Figure 3. These charts include price and quality information in a local market. Figure 3 shows the market for portable electric typewriters in Phelps, New York in April 1983 including prices for the same brand/model at different vendors. Maynes has argued that such charts, if widely available, would be used by consumers to "police" local markets. The low cost sellers would be rewarded with more business, and prices would generally move closer to the "perfect information frontier."

Reducing Comprehension Costs

The trick to reducing comprehension effort is taking advantage of existing knowledge rather than trying to increase knowledge via consumer education. The latter is a difficult and more costly approach to aiding consumers.

For one example of reduced comprehension effort we return to the perfect information frontier in Figure 3. Maynes [26] uses this device to make clear to users of his price-quality charts that only a few products should be considered for purchase. All those not on the perfect information frontier can be ignored because for each of these there is at least one other product (on the frontier) that is clearly superior. Superior means lower in price with no sacrifice of quality, or better in quality without paying a higher price. By adding the frontier to his price-quality chart, Maynes makes it easier for consumers to understand that certain products can be automatically eliminated.

FIGURE 3

PRICES AND QUALITY IN A LOCAL MARKET: SINGLE-LENS REFLECT CAMERAS IN ANN ARBOR, 1974

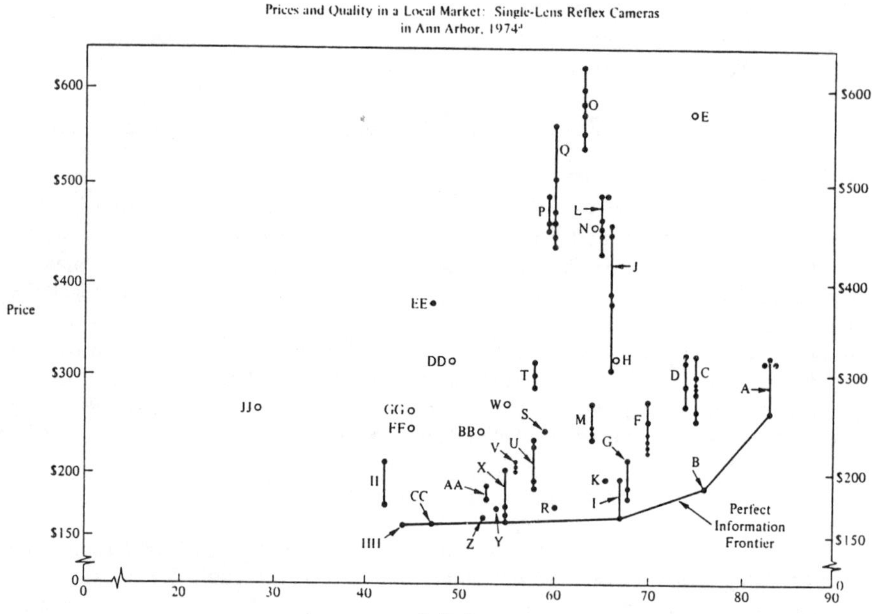

[a]Source: Quality Scores *Consumer Reports*, November, 1974
Prices-Collected by Blanche R. Maynes, November 18-26, 1974

The symbol o denotes the list prices of specimens which could not be purchased in Ann Arbor. The others points plotted represent actual prices.

Used by permission from E. Scott Maynes, Decision-Making For Consumers: An Introduction to Consumer Economics, 1976, MacMillan Publishing Co., Inc., New York.

A second example is shown in Figure 4. A new concept, the Nutrition Quotient, was introduced to describe the overall nutritional value of a food [37]. This quotient is basically a nutrient density measure, i.e., a ratio of nutrition to calories. The figure shows all TV dinners sold at a supermarket ordered by their Nutrition Quotient. To communicate this novel measure in an easy way, a "star rating" was added with more stars indicating a better nutritional value. A star symbol was used because it is both positive and familiar, often seen with ratings of films and hotels. Consumers who did not want to take the time to read the explanation of the Nutrition Quotient in the fine print could use the stars to guide their judgment.

Reducing Computation Effort

Once information has been gathered and understood it must be used to draw an inference as to which product is best or which ones are acceptable. This inference process requires computation, not in the sense of arithmetic operations, but more generally as symbol manipulation. Of course, computation can sometimes be purely numerical, as the Nutrition Quotient in Figure 4 illustrates. The quotient is calculated from a formula based on the calories and the percent of the U.S. Recommended Daily Allowance of eight nutrients contained in a standard serving of a food. Thus, this single value summarizes the information in nine other numbers. Without it as a guideline, consumers would have to come to some kind of overall judgment themselves, either expending substantial computational effort or engaging in gross simplifications that risk considerable inaccuracy (like ignoring many nutrients altogether).

Saving computational effort can be used to improve the energy feedback shown in Figure 2. Consumers who receive this information may want to know the percentage change in energy consumption from the previous year. Further, this change could usefully be translated into dollars (at the current cost per kilowatt). A monthly bill augmented by this information is shown in Figure 5. To make the year-to-year comparison more accurate, the two billing periods have been equated for weather conditions and number of days. These last two enhancements involve some information collection as well as computation. They are also quite easy for utility companies to provide while being quite effortful for all consumers (and beyond the knowledge of some).

FIGURE 4

A NUTRITION CHART WITH STAR RATINGS THAT LOWER THE EFFORT REQUIRED TO COMPREHEND THE NUTRITION QUOTIENT, A NEW MEASURE OF THE OVERALL NUTRITIONAL VALUE OF A FOOD

Add Stars to A Balanced Diet For Better Nutrition

The star rating makes it easier to see at a glance which foods provide "better nutrition" based on the NUTRITION QUOTIENT important. See detailed explanation to the right. A food gets ★★★★ if its NUTRITION QUOTIENT is above 10, ★★★ if above 4, ★★ if above 2, and ★ if above 1.

The NUTRITION QUOTIENT of each product is a way of measuring the average "nutritional return" you get for each calorie you eat. The nutritional return is based on the U.S. RDAs in a standardized serving for each of the following nutrients: protein, vitamin A, vitamin C, thiamine, riboflavin, niacin, calcium, and iron. Using the NUTRITION QUOTIENT formula, developed by J. Edward Russo, a NUTRITION QUOTIENT of 1 indicates a nutritional return equal to the calories consumed. Numbers higher than 1 mean more nutritional return per calorie, but numbers lower than 1 mean less.

This chart is part of a research project under the direction of Associate Professor J. Edward Russo, Consumer Behavior Laboratory, Graduate School of Business, University of Chicago, Chicago, Illinois 60637. Products are not included on the list if an estimate for each of the nutrients listed to the left was not available from either the manufacturer or the U.S.D.A. Handbook "Nutritive Values of American Foods." Additionally, new items or items not carried by most stores are not included. Inclusion of any product on the list does not constitute an endorsement. For more information, contact the Consumer Behavior Laboratory.

TV DINNERS
Serving Size 1 Dinner

Percentage of U.S. Recommended Daily Allowance (U.S. RDA)

Nutrition Quotient	TV Dinner	Weight in Ounces	Calories	Protein	Vitamin A	Vitamin C	Thiamine	Riboflavin	Niacin	Calcium	Iron
★ ★ 2.2	Turkey, Banquet	11.00	293	35	80	35	10	10	35	8	15
★ 1.9	Veal Parmigian, Banquet	11.00	421	30	140	20	15	15	20	20	15
★ 1.7	Turkey, Man-Pleaser, Banquet	19.00	620	60	150	25	20	20	45	15	25
★ 1.7	Turkey, Swanson	11.50	360	45	60	30	10	10	35	6	10
★ 1.6	Chicken, Fried, Banquet	11.00	530	40	100	35	10	15	35	30	25
★ 1.5	Italian, Banquet	11.00	446	30	90	15	35	15	15	6	25
★ 1.4	Sirloin, Chopped, Swanson	10.00	460	50	80	15	15	15	30	2	20
★ 1.4	Salisbury Steak, Banquet	11.00	390	30	80	10	10	10	20	10	20
★ 1.4	Beef, Banquet	11.00	312	45	4	10	8	15	30	4	30
★ 1.3	Macaroni & Cheese, Swanson	12.50	390	15	100	◊	10	20	6	20	8
★ 1.3	Beef, Chopped, Banquet	11.00	443	30	90	10	8	15	20	6	20
★ 1.3	Chicken, BBQ, Hungry-Man, Swanson	16.50	760	60	110	6	30	35	60	8	30
★ 1.2	Beef, Swanson	11.50	370	60	6	10	10	20	30	4	20
★ 1.2	Fish Dinner, Banquet	8.75	382	30	50	20	20	8	20	6	10
★ 1.2	Meat Loaf, Banquet	11.00	412	30	45	15	10	15	20	8	25
★ 1.2	Meat Loaf, Man-Pleaser, Banquet	19.00	916	60	160	25	20	20	30	15	40
★ 1.2	Turkey, Three Course, Swanson	16.00	520	60	15	30	20	15	40	10	20
★ 1.1	Turkey, Hungry-Man, Swanson	19.00	740	100	20	40	20	15	60	10	25
★ 1.1	Chicken, Hungry-Man, Swanson	19.00	730	90	15	30	20	20	70	15	20
★ 1.0	Chicken, Man-Pleaser, Banquet	17.00	1016	90	90	10	15	20	60	45	35
★ 1.0	Chicken, Swanson	11.50	570	60	40	10	10	15	45	6	15
★ 1.0	Mexican Dinner, Banquet	12.00	571	35	25	15	15	10	15	50	35
★ 1.0	Chopped Sirloin, Steak House	9.50	760	90	2	35	20	20	15	4	35
9	Salisbury Steak, Man-Pleaser, Banquet	19.00	823	60	90	15	15	15	50	4	35
.9	Chicken, Fried, Hungry-Man, Swanson	15.75	910	100	2	25	25	25	80	10	30
.9	Lasagna, Hungry-Man, Swanson	17.75	740	40	20	20	40	35	25	25	30
9	Beef, Hungry-Man, Swanson	17.00	540	60	2	4	20	30	30	4	20
.9	Salisbury Steak, Three Course, Swanson	16.00	490	35	6	20	20	15	30	8	20
.9	Beef Enchilada, Swanson	15.00	570	30	50	◊	15	10	20	20	25
9	Chicken, Three Course, Swanson	15.00	630	50	30	4	20	10	50	8	15
.8	Beef Chop Suey, Banquet	12.00	282	20	6	8	6	8	15	4	15
.8	Fish 'N Chips, Swanson	10.25	450	50	6	10	15	8	25	4	10
8	Beef, Chopped, Hungry-Man, Swanson	18.00	730	30	45	15	20	20	45	6	25
.8	Chicken, Crispy, Swanson	10.75	650	50	4	2	30	15	50	10	15
.8	Beans And Franks, Banquet	10.75	591	25	40	15	20	10	15	15	20
8	Chicken, BBQ, Swanson	11.25	530	25	20	4	10	20	40	8	15
.8	Spaghetti, Swanson	12.50	410	20	15	10	15	10	15	8	15
.8	Chicken, Western Style, Swanson	11.75	460	35	10	◊	15	20	20	6	15
.7	Rib Eye, Steak House	9.00	820	70	2	30	15	20	40	4	30
.7	Meat Loaf, Swanson	10.75	530	30	10	20	10	15	20	8	20
7	Salisbury Steak, Hungry Man, Swanson	17.00	870	70	10	6	15	25	50	10	30
7	Beef Tenderloin, Steak House	9.50	920	70	2	30	20	20	45	4	35
7	Sirloin, Steak House	9.50	920	70	2	30	20	20	45	4	35
.7	Salisbury Steak, Swanson	11.50	500	45	◊	◊	8	15	25	8	15
7	Veal Parmigiana, Hungry-Man, Swanson	20.50	910	60	10	6	20	30	30	25	30
7	Chicken, Western Style, Hungry-Man, Swanson	17.75	890	70	10	◊	25	35	40	10	15
6	Noodles And Chicken, Swanson	10.25	390	20	10	2	10	8	15	4	8

◊ contains less than 2% of the US RDA of the nutrients.

Note: The US RDAs listed here apply primarily to adults and children over 4. For children under 4, pregnant or nursing women, or other people with special health considerations this guide should be adjusted with the help of a physician and or dietitian.

PLEASE NOTE: TV dinners differ in weight. The nutrition listed depends on the weight of each dinner.

For Best Nutrition Eat a Variety of Foods, Including Those Not on This Chart.

FIGURE 5

A MONTHLY RESIDENTIAL ELECTRIC BILL
WITH LAST YEAR'S CONSUMPTION ADJUSTED FOR
WEATHER AND NUMBER OF DAYS BILLED AND
EXPRESSED IN BOTH PERCENT CHANGE AND DOLLAR TERMS

Billing Period: November 30 to December 29 | Amount Due

Consumption (Kwhr)		Change from Last Year		
Current Billing Period	Same Period Last Year*	Energy Consumed	Cost at Current Rate	$238.88
2275	2472	8% drop	$20.62 saved	Date Due
				Jan. 15

*Last year's consumption has been adjusted for differences in weather and number of billing days to make a comparison between years more accurate.

A final example of reduced computational effort involves no numerical calculation but an organization of collected information that facilitates relevant comparisons. Figure 6 shows a list of breakfast cereals ordered according to their added sugar from the least (top) to the most (bottom). When these lists were posted in a supermarket, the brands lowest in added sugar increased their market share by 2.7% (from 43.2% to 45.9% of the total cereal market). The market share of the highest brands, those with 3-4 teaspoons of added sugar per 1 oz. serving, dropped from 18.2% to 15.9% [37]. This drop represents a 13% loss in sales volume for the high sugar cereals.

The same idea of an ordered list to reduce computational effort has been applied to unit prices [34]. A supermarket chain that displayed unit prices on shelf tags also posted a list like that shown in Figure 7. The original shelf tag display of unit prices produced a 1% decrease in the price paid per unit over six different product categories. When the ordered lists were posted consumer expenditures per unit dropped an additional 2%. That is, the effort

FIGURE 6

ALPHABETICAL GUIDE TO THE NUMBER OF TEASPOONS OF ADDED SUGAR PER SERVING

Cereal Brand	Number of Teaspoons per 1 Oz.* Serving	Cereal Brand	Number of Teaspoons per 1 Oz.* Serving
All Bran	1 1/4	Lucky Charms	2 3/4
Alphabits	2 3/4	Most	1 1/2
Apple Jacks	2 1/2	Nat V Cn/Rn Granola	1 3/4
Bran Buds	2	Nat V Fr/Nut Granola	2
Bran Chex	1 1/4	Nat V Hn/Ots Granola	1 1/2
Buc Wheats	2 1/4	Nutri-Grain-Barley	0
Cap'n Crunch	3	Nutri-Grain-Rye	0
Cp. Cr. Crunchberries	3 1/4	Nutri-Grain-Corn	0
Cheerios	1/4	Nutri-Grain-Wheat	0
Cinnamon Life	1 1/2	Nutr-Grain-Wht/Rsn	1 1/2
Cocoa Krispies	3	100% Bran Cereal	1 1/2
Cocoa Pebbles	3 1/4	Post Toasties	1/2
Cocoa Puffs	2 3/4	Product 19	3/4
Cookie Crisp	3 1/4	Puffed Rice	0
Corn Bran	1 1/2	Puffed Wheat	0
Corn Chex	1/2	Quaker 100% Nat Cer	1 1/2
Corn Flakes-Kellogg's	1/2	Okr 100% Nt Cer R/D	1 1/2
Corn Flakes-W Fam	1/2	Raisin Bran - Post	2
Cracklin Bran	2	Raisin Bran - Kellogg's	3
Crispy Rice	3/4	Raisin Grape Nuts	3/4
Crsp. Whts 'n Raisins	2 1/2	Raisins, Rice & Rye	2 1/2
C.W. Post	1 3/4	Rick Chex	1/2
Dinky Donuts	2 3/4	Rice Krispies	3/4
40% Brank Flakes-Kellogg's	1 1/4	Shredded Wheat	0
40% Bran Flakes-Post	1 1/4	Special K	1/2
Froot Loops	3 1/4	Sugar Corn Pops	3
Frosted Mini-Wheats	1 3/4	Sugar Frosted Flakes	2 3/4
Frost Mini-Whts-Apl	2	Sugar Puffs	3 1/2
Fruit & Fib w/Apl/Cin	1 3/4	Sugar Smacks	4
Frt & Fib w/Dt/Rs/Wl	1 3/4	Super Sugar Crisp	3 1/2
Fruity Pebbles	3 1/4	Team	1 1/4
Golden Grahams	2 1/2	Toasted Oats	1/4
Grape Nuts	0	Toasty O's	1/4
Grape Nut Flakes	1 1/4	Total	3/4
Hon/Nut Corn Flakes	2 1/4	Trix	3
Honey Bran	1 3/4	Waffelos-Blueb Flv	3 1/4
Honey Nut Cheerios	2 1/2	Waffelos-Mpl Srp Flv	3 1/4
Honeycomb	2 3/4	Wheat Chex	1/2
Kix	1/2	Wheat & Raisins Chex	3/4
Life	1 1/2	Wheaties	3/4

*A 1 ounce serving of cereal can be as little as 1/3 cup to as much as 1 1/4 cup. Check the side panel of the cereal box for the manufacturer's recommended serving size. The natural sugars within raisins and dates have been included in the added sugar content of the listed cereals.

reduction achieved by gathering all the unit prices together and then ordering them for easy comparison tripled the value of the normal posting of unit prices on shelf tags.

FIGURE 7

A SAMPLE LIST OF UNIT PRICES

LIQUID DETERGENTS FOR DISHES

Listed in Order of Increasing Price per Quart

PAR 48 oz.	54¢	36.0¢ PER QUART
PAR 32 oz.	38¢	38.0¢ PER QUART
SWEETHEART 23 oz.	55¢	55.0¢ PER QUART
BROCADE 48 oz.	85¢	56.7¢ PER QUART
SWEETHEART 22 oz.	39¢	56.7¢ PER QUART
SUPURB 32 oz.	59¢	59.0¢ PER QUART
WHITE MAGIC 32 oz.	59¢	59.0¢ PER QUART
BROCADE 32 oz.	63¢	63.0¢ PER QUART
BROCADE 22 oz.	45¢	65.5¢ PER QUART
SUPURB 22 oz.	45¢	65.5¢ PER QUART
WHITE MAGIC 32 oz.	45¢	65.5¢ PER QUART
BROCADE 12 oz.	27¢	72.0¢ PER QUART
SUPURB 12 oz.	29¢	77.3¢ PER QUART
IVORY 32 oz.	80¢	70.0¢ PER QUART
DOVE 22 oz.	56¢	81.5¢ PER QUART
IVORY 22 oz.	56¢	81.5¢ PER QUART
LUX 22 oz.	56¢	81.5¢ PER QUART
PALMOLIVE 32 oz.	85¢	85.0¢ PER QUART
IVORY 12 oz.	32¢	85.3¢ PER QUART
PALMOLIVE 22 oz.	60¢	87.3¢ PER QUART
PALMOLIVE 12 oz.	34¢	90.7¢ PER QUART

Which Strategy to Take?

An important choice facing those who would like to aid consumer information processing is whether to follow a strategy of increasing benefits or of reducing costs. Naturally, one wants the greatest improvement in the cost-benefit differential for the resources expended. There is no single guideline that applies to all cases. Depending on the kind of information, the nature of the environment, the communication technology available and so on, either path may prove superior.

Two principles, however, have emerged from my own experience. First, if no new information is generated but instead we are dealing with existing information, I have found it more effective to reduce costs than to increase benefits. This principle applies especially when the main costs are information processing effort and the way to increase benefits is to persuade people that the benefits are higher than they currently believe. In the case of nutrition information in supermarkets, a survey of field studies revealed that not one of the four studies designed to increase the perceived benefits of nutrition information had any impact on food choices [37. These studies were sometimes quite substantial in budget, professional in their message construction, communicated via newspapers and radio, and conducted for periods up to a year. Yet in no case was there any significant impact on food purchases. In contrast, three of the four studies using an effort reduction strategy succeeded in improving the nutritional value of food shoppers purchased. At least in this situation, decreasing information processing effort has proved more productive than trying to increase the perceived benefits of information use.

A second principle deals with genuinely new information. If new information succeeds in decreasing the cost-benefit differential, it usually does so by providing benefits substantially above previous levels rather than by decreasing costs. A Consumer Reports rating of hotel chains would be one example.

Changing People or Changing Environments?

I have found it more effective to change the environment to adapt to people than to change people to adapt to the environment. The examples given above change the information environment by collecting, evaluating, and computing information to make it more accessible and useful to consumers. In a similar way the presentation of new information via video discs or computer graphics changes the environment.

Changing people is much more costly, although at times the cost is worth it. Increasing knowledge is usually costly, as consumer educators know. However, increasing knowledge about a single fact may be relatively easy. More importantly, increasing knowledge has a long-range payoff. The long-term benefit is analogous to the classic parable of self-sufficiency. "If you give people fish, they eat today. If you teach them how to fish, they can eat forever." At its most effective, increasing consumer knowledge is like teaching the skill of fishing--its benefits are reaped forever.

One limitation of this approach, however, is that knowledge can become outdated. Fishing stays fishing, but consumer goods change continually. Sometimes we are offered novel goods, like personal computers or financial advisors. Similarly, technology changes familiar products like kitchen stoves (programable timers, self-cleaning ovens, energy efficiency, etc.). Consumer knowledge of food has been enormously complicated by the development of highly processed foods over the last quarter century and by our changing understanding of nutrition and health. For instance, the emphasis in health has shifted from ingesting enough positive nutrients to avoiding negative ones. Liver was a good source of iron; it is now a dangerous source of cholesterol and unwanted chemicals. Hot dogs were as American as apple pie. Now they contain cancer-causing nitrites (and the "empty calories" in apple pie are not so good for you either). Although I exaggerate a bit with these examples, the main conclusion that product knowledge is continually being outdated has never been more valid.

There often seems to be a preference for changing people over changing environments. Maybe we believe that people ought to be capable of good decisions. When economists model individuals as utility maximizers, they place the burden of intelligent behavior on the individual, not other actors in the environment. Furthermore, some progress in changing people always seems within the reach of those who wish to improve consumer information processing. Either a little progress with nearly everyone or more substantial progress with a select few people is usually possible.

In contrast, changing the environment seems more difficult. Getting newspapers to provide comparative lists of supermarket prices is beyond the power of consumers. And even if the environment is momentarily changed, there is often uncertainty as to whether the endeavor will succeed on a steady-state basis. Think of the number of consumer information programs that have been tried and failed. Nevertheless, I believe that more improvements in consumer information processing will come from careful changes in the environment than from efforts to change consumers themselves.

Summary

Working within the cost-benefit framework, aiding consumer information processing can follow a strategy of increasing benefits or reducing costs. And either of these can be achieved by helping people adapt to the existing information environment or by changing the environment to adapt to people. Table 2 categorizes the specific actions discussed above into the four cells that result from this two-way classification.

The critical question is: Which of these four approaches is best? The answer depends on the situation. In my own experience with existing information, reducing effort costs has proved more effective than trying to persuade consumers to value information more highly. With genuinely new information a benefit strategy may generally prove superior. Finally, I suspect that in most situations changing the environment to adapt to the knowledge and effort limits of people will be more effective than changing people to adapt to a generally inhospitable information environment. This focus on changing the environment becomes more important in a world where products are continually changing and knowledge is constantly becoming outdated.

Information Processing Aids From New Technologies

One of the most promising sources of information processing aids is new information technologies. In this section I review briefly the most pertinent of these technologies and consider how they can aid the information processing of product information by consumers.

Several new technologies have the potential to improve the information that is provided to consumers. The most promising are telecommunication, video, and computer technologies. Since my goal is mainly to illustrate, I will discuss representative examples from each. More complete reviews of these new technologies, including discussions of how they may influence the marketplace as well as consumers, can be found in [6], [30], [40]. [41] considers the public policy ramifications of these technologies.

Telecommunication: Videotex

Videotex is a two-way communication system in which a signal is transmitted by telephone lines or cable to specially equipped TV monitors. Via a keypad, the at-home consumer can send signals back to a computer where the signal originates. Consumers use the keypad to select the information screens they want. Videotex holds great promise as a provider of product information to consumers [14, 44]. This promise has yet to be realized in the U.S. [43], but has in France where a national videotex system (Teletel) is operated by the country's telecommunication organization [25]. As of March 1986, over 2000 private companies use the system to provide on-line services to consumers. Many of these involve product information, including prices, availability, vendors, etc.

TABLE 2

AIDS FOR INCREASING CONSUMER USE OF PRODUCT INFORMATION CLASSIFIED BY TYPE OF STRATEGY AND LOCUS OF CHANGE

Type of Strategy	Locus of Change: Consumer	Locus of Change: Environment
Increase Benefits	Consumer education: (a) to inform consumers about product attributes they were unaware of, e.g., the danger of nitrites in hot dogs or (b) to persuade consumers to place a higher value on known attributes, e.g., the value of flossing teeth. The latter is similar to seller advertising.	New Information: (a) old format but new concept, e.g., a CR article on wristwatches or hotel chains; or (b) new format, e.g., video discs with full motion color and sound instructions on product assembly. Increasing experiential benefits via more entertaining information.
Decrease Costs	Consumer education to make existing information more easily understood (decreased comprehension effort).	Information formats that reduce processing effort. Reduction in monetary costs via market mechanism (economies of scale, competition, etc.), government subsidies, etc.

A videotex product information system offers the benefits of timely information such as all top quality restaurants that are open on a Sunday evening within a 15 minute walk of your hotel. A related benefit is continual updating of information like weather, traffic, and road conditions for someone about to make an auto trip. Businesses are using in-house videotex to provide employees with "smart" telephone directories, information on training courses and personnel benefits and, using the graphics capability of videotex, locations of hotels in a city about to be visited [5].

These business uses are good examples of information that can be seen as offering either greater benefits or reduced costs, especially effort costs. Even the hotel map could be obtained with enough effort, and certainly the other information could be found (with some difficulty) in printed documents. However, whether we view the effects of videotex as increasing benefits or reducing costs, the system has many natural advantages for communicating product information. These are summarized in Table 3.

Video: Video Discs and Computer Graphics

A video disc player with a keyboard control enables the consumer to access any part of the disc within a few seconds. The monitor then displays a full color and motion image with sound. This system might be used to communicate information that involves motion, such as showing the product in active use or illustrating repair procedures. Augmented by computer graphics, the system may display products in use better than an actual salesperson at a retail outlet. Consider, for example, lawn mowers or washing machines, products whose actual use cannot be well demonstrated in a store.

If entertainment is designed into the video material, experiential benefits may be high. Certainly the potential is there to make video discs as entertaining as television. Sellers are currently using entertainment benefits as part of what draws consumers to electronic kiosks [19, 43]. These are video disc systems connected to a central facility. They enable shoppers to order as well as view videos of products.

Computers: Expert Systems

An expert system uses "intelligent" software to capture the expertise of a human expert in a computer program. These systems maintain a <u>dialog</u> with their users [36]. They are capable of explaining much of their own reasoning and are easily modified to incorporate new information. At the moment no expert system has been constructed for consumers. The users of current systems are all professionals like physicians [10] and salespeople who configure computers [15]. The closest to a consumer system is one that advises cotton farmers on such daily decisions as irrigation and fertilization levels [23]. This system performed quite well in a small

TABLE 3

THE EFFECT OF NEW INFORMATION TECHNOLOGIES
ON THE COSTS AND BENEFITS
OF USING PRODUCT INFORMATION

Product Information	Benefit Enhancements	Cost Reductions
Videotex	Timely information, e.g. availability of theater tickets, or travel reservations.	Reduced effort costs, especially collection costs but also computation and, less often, comprehension costs.
	Updated information, e.g., vendors' current stock or the predicted weather conditions at a travel destination.	Reduced experiential costs from information delays and negative experiences with salespeople.
	City maps with hotels, restaurants and entertainment facilities shown as requested.	
Video discs and Computer Graphics	Superior new information e.g., full color, motion and sound instructions for the assembly or repair of products.	Reduced comprehension cost from the power of the technology to explain and instruct.
	Increased product knowledge via consumer education.	Reduced collection costs, depending on the contents of the disc.
	High potential for experiential value.	Fewer negative experiences with salespeople.
Expert Systems	The economic benefits of better product decisions	Fewer negative experiences with salespeople.
	Certainty of a good purchase decision	Reduced computation costs because the system performs many inferences.
	Increased product knowledge from the instructional capabilities of the system.	

field test and is being tested more widely. A similar system is being built for French farmers to aid in the diagnosis of crop diseases [13]. This latter system includes a video disc so that users can compare visually the state of their crop with pictures of prototypical disease symptoms.

The potential value of expert systems to consumers is enormous. This technology approaches the ideal source of product information, a trustworthy human expert. An expert system reduces computation cost because its job is to draw inferences. It also reduces collection and comprehension costs to the extent that it gathers information and makes it more easily understood. But its main value is an increase in benefits such as the utility of the chosen alternative, certainty that a good decision has been made, and learning for future product decisions. To get some idea of the potential of expert systems consider the task of purchasing an automobile, i.e., selecting the best make, model and options from the myriad possibilities. Contrast using all the information in Consumer Reports with access to a professional consultant with all this and more information available to him/her. An expert system is closer to the human expert than to Consumer Reports.

Combined Systems

What I hope will eventually emerge is a conjunction of the new technologies, such as an expert system that can access a video disc and is transmitted via telephone lines or cable. It may not be long before a substantial number of U.S. homes have the hardware required by such a combined system. Once it is available, a consumer can "discuss" a potential purchase with an expert who can demonstrate via the video disc important aspects of the product's construction, durability, operation, repair, etc. This can be done at 9 PM on a Sunday evening, suspended for a discussion with a spouse, and then resumed. To check the expert's recommendation another expert system could be contacted for a second opinion. Finally, the product could be ordered via videotex at a substantial discount below the retail price. And all this could be completed before 10 PM. Such a hospitable environment for consumers will not be realized for years. Nonetheless, it illustrates the environmental changes that may alter the cost-benefit balance in favor of processing product information.

REFERENCES

1. BAZERMAN, MAX H. (1986), Judgment in Managerial Decision Making, New York: Wiley.

2. BEALES, HOWARD, RICHARD CRASWELL, and STEVEN SALOP (1981), "The Efficient Regulation of Consumer Information, Journal of Law and Economics, 18, 421-447.

3. BERRY, LEONARD L. (1979), "The Time-Buying Consumer," Journal of Retailing, 55, 58-69.

4. BOYNTON, R.D., B.F. BLAKE, and JOSEPH N. UHL (1983), "Retail Price Reporting Effects in Local Food Markets," Journal of Agricultural Economics, 65, 20-29.

5. BURSTYN, H. PARIS (1985), "Videotex Enters Corporate Channels," High Technology, December, 64-65.

6. BUTLER COX (1984), Information Technology: Its Impact on Marketing and Selling. The Butler Cox Report Series, 12 Bloomsburg Square, London.

7. CANNER, GLENN B. and GREGORY E. ELLIEHAUSEN (1986), An Analysis of the Effects of a Comparative Price Program on Competition in Consumer Credit Markets. Paper presented at the Financial Management Association Meetings, New York, New York, 16 October.

8. CAPON, NOEL and RICHARD J. LUTZ (1979), "A Model and Methodology for the Development of Consumer Information Programs," Journal of Marketing, 43, 58-67.

9. DEVINE, D. GRANT and BRUCE W. MARION (1979), "The Influence of Consumer Price Information on Retail Pricing and Consumer Behavior," American Journal of Agricultural Economics, 228-237.

10. DUDA, RICHARD O. and EDWARD H. SHORTLIFFE (1983), "Expert Systems Research," Science, 220 (4594), 15 April, 261-268.

11. ELTON, MARTIN and JOHN CAREY. "Teletext For Public Information: Laboratory and Field Studies," In Jerome Johnston (ed.), Evaluating the New Information Technologies. New Directions for Program Evaluation, no. 23. San Francisco: Jossey-Bass.

12. EOVALDI, THOMAS L. (1985), "The Market for Consumer Product Evaluations: An Analysis and a Proposal," Northwestern University Law Review, 79, 1235-1268.

13. GALLAGHER, ROBERT T. (1985), "French Farmers to Diagnose Crop Diseases with AI," Electronics (renamed from Electronics Week), 27 May, 25.

14. GRUNERT, KLAUS G. (1984), "Consumer Information Systems in Videotex: Design and Acceptance," Journal of Consumer Studies and Home Economics, 8, 183-198.

15. HARMON, PAUL and DAVID KING (1985), Expert Systems: Artificial Intelligence in Business, New York: Wiley.

16. HAWES, DOUGLASS K. (1979), "Time and Behavior," in O.C. Ferrell, Stephen W. Brown and Charles W. Lamb, Jr. (Eds.), Conceptual and Theoretical Developments in Marketing. Chicago: American Marketing Association.

17. HEIMBACH, JAMES T. (1981), "Defining the Problem: The Scope of Consumer Concern with Food Labeling," in Kent B. Monroe (Ed.), Advances in Consumer Research, 8 (474-476). Ann Arbor, MI: Association for Consumer Research.

18. HORNE, DAVID ANDREW (1982), Consumer reaction to a financial service innovation: Electronic funds transfer - point of sale devices. Unpublished doctoral dissertation, University of Michigan.

19. HURLY, PAUL (1986), "Boosting Sales Electronically," Industry Week, March 31, 33-35.

20. IPPOLITO, PAULINE M. (1986), "Consumer Protection Economics: A Selective Survey," in Pauline M. Ippolito and David F. Scheffman (Eds.), Empirical Approaches to Consumer Protection Economics (pp. 1-33). Washington, D.C.: Federal Trade Commission.

21. KAHNEMAN, DANIEL, PAUL SLOVIC and AMOS TVERSKY (1982) Judgment Under Uncertainty: Heuristics and Biases. Cambridge, England: Cambridge University Press.

22. LANGLEY, MONICA (1985), "Federal Reserve Experiment Could Make Shopping for Personal Loans Much Easier," Wall Street Journal, July 26, 1985, 23.

23. LEMMON, HAL (1986), "Comax: An Expert System for Cotton Crop Management," Science, 233, 4 July 1986, 29-31.

24. LINDER, STAFFAN B. (1970), The Harried Leisure Class. New York: Columbia University Press.

25. MAYER, ROBERT N. (1986), Videotex in France: The Other French Revolution. Salt Lake City, UT: University of Utah, Department of Family and Consumer Studies. Working Paper No. 86-5.

26. MAYNES, E. SCOTT (1978), "Information Imperfections in Local Consumer Markets," in Andrew A. Mitchell (Ed.), The Effect of Information on Consumer and Market Behavior (77-85). Chicago: American Marketing Association.

27. ________ (1982), Prestel in Use: A Consumer View. National Consumer Council (Great Britain).

28. ________ (1984), "Prestel's Lessons for Americans," in Thomas C. Kinnear (Ed.), Advances in Consumer Research, 11 (520-524). Provo, UT: Association for Consumer Research.

29. ________ (1986), "Towards Market Transparency," in M. Goyens (ed.), Price Information and Public Price Controls, Consumers and Market Performance. Louvain, Belgium: Centre de droit de la consommation, University of Louvain.

30. MITCHELL, JEREMY and LOVEDAY MURLEY (1985), The Information Society: A Strategy for Consumers (second edition). London: U.K. National Consumer Council.

31. PUTNAM, JUDY JONES and JON WEIMER (1981), "Household Diet Changes Linked to Nutritional Concerns," Staff paper, Economics and Statistical Service, U.S. Department of Agriculture, Washington, D.C., 20250.

32. RITCHIE, J.R. BRENT and GORDON H.G. MCDOUGALL (1985), "Designing and Marketing Consumer Energy Conservation Policies and Programs: Implications from a Decade of Research," Journal of Public Policy and Marketing, 4, 14-32.

33. RUSSO, J. EDWARD (1977), "A Proposal To Increase Energy Conservation Through Provision Of Consumption And Cost Information To Consumers," in Barnett A. Greenberg and Danny N. Bellenger (Eds.). Contemporary Marketing Thought: 1977 Educator's Proceedings. Chicago: American Marketing Association, 437-442.

34. ________ (1977), "The Value of Unit Price Information," Journal of Marketing Research, 14, 193-201.

35. ________ (1981), "The Decision to Use Product Information at the Point of Purchase," in Ron Stampfl and Elizabeth Hirschman (ed.), Theory in Retailing: Traditional and Nontraditional Sources. Chicago: American Marketing Association.

36. _________ (1987), "Toward Intelligent Product Information Systems for Consumers," Journal of Consumer Policy, 10, 109-138.

37. _________, RICHARD STAELIN, CATHERINE A. NOLAN, GARY RUSSELL and BARBARA L. METCALF (1986), "Nutrition Information in the Supermarket," Journal of Consumer Research, 13, 48-70.

38. SEPSTRUP, PREBEN (1980), "Consumption of Mass Communication: On Construction of a Model on Information Consumption Behavior," in Jagdish Sheth (ed.), Research in Marketing, 3, 105-142.

39. _________ (1985), "Information Content in TV Advertising," Journal of Consumer Policy, 8, 239-265.

40. SEPSTRUP, PREBEN and FOLKE OLANDER (1986), Consumer Information in the Electronic Media. Aarhus: Aarhus School of Business Administration and Economics, Department of Marketing. Working Paper No. 4.

41. SHAPIRO, STANLEY J. (1986), "Home As An Electronic Marketplace: The Consumer Protection and Public Policy Issues," Journal of Public Policy and Marketing, 5, 212-226.

42. SMITH, RUSSELL L. (1980), "Staying Alive While Providing Consumer Information: The Vector Enterprises Solution," in Jerry C. Olson (Ed.), Advances in Consumer Research, 7 (246-249). Ann Arbor, MI: Association for Consumer Research.

43. TALARZYK, W. WAYNE (1986), Electronic Retailing in the United States: Trends and Potentials. Columbus, Ohio: Ohio State University. Working Paper Series No. 86-90.

44. TALARZYK, W. WAYNE, ROBERT E. WIDING and JOEL E. URBANY (1984), "Videotex and the Consumer," in Thomas C. Kinnear (ed.) Advances in Consumer Research, 11, Provo, Utah: Association for Consumer Research.

45. VLOYANETES, PETER and MARK MAGEL (1986), "Electronic Retailing," Marketing Communications, May, 31-34, 37, 79.

46. WINETT, RICHARD A. and JOHN H. KAGEL (1984), "Effects of Information Presentation Format on Resource Use in Field Studies," Journal of Consumer Research, 11, 655-667.

Chapter 10

ABOUT THE AUTHOR

Klaus G. Grunert is Professor of Marketing at the Aarhus School of Business Administration, Denmark. A consumer economist with a psychological orientation, Grunert has spent most of his career at the University of Hohenheim, earning his Ph.D. at Hohenheim and as a member of the faculty. Widely published in consumer journals, Grunert's strongest research interests have been the establishment and evaluation of consumer information sources and systems with a special focus on Bildschirmtext, the German videotex system.

COMMENTS ON J. EDWARD RUSSO

Klaus G. Grunert

Information processing has been one of the major concerns of consumer research within the past ten years or so. Russo has done a fine job of integrating much of this research from a consumer viewpoint, arriving at some clear-cut conclusions. There are few things in the paper with which I do not agree. What I will do then is trace Russo's main argument, and pose four questions that I think warrant additional comments.

The author's main argument runs as follows. Whether a consumer will process a given piece of information or not is determined by the perceived benefits and costs of doing so. The major cost factors are monetary costs and effort, the latter being the product of time used and central processing capacity allocated to the task. If the aim is to increase consumer information processing, reducing effort is regarded as a generally better strategy than increasing benefits. Finally, new information technologies will be useful in helping to reduce effort (and also to increase benefits).

Is Cost-Benefit Analysis Ubiquitous?

Russo maintains that a cost-benefit analysis always occurs when people decide to use or not to use a piece of information. The assertion that cost-benefit analysis is ubiquitous is a very old one indeed. In fact, it is one of the cornerstones of economic theory. However, economic theory also has shown that this assertion may be tautological, i.e., cannot be subjected to empirical test. This is when costs and benefits are not independently measured, but are inferred from actual behavior. Russo goes beyond this tautological approach to specify certain types of costs and benefits that are amenable to empirical measurement. Still, if a consumer would be found to act inconsistently with predictions from a cost-benefit analysis using the variables ascertained, we would probably rather look for omitted costs or benefits than abandon the idea of cost-benefit analysis altogether.

There is nothing wrong with this. The cost-benefit approach is a useful and fruitful way to view a certain phenomenon. It is fruitful, because it leads to concrete proposals for improvements in consumers' information environment--proposals that can be evaluated empirically. It is the fruitfulness of the approach that commends it, not whether we can show empirically that people usually weigh costs and benefits.

IS INFORMATION PROCESSING ALWAYS EFFORTFUL?

It seems trivial to say that information processing involves the use of time and central processing capacity. Still, it assumes that information processing is conscious and serial. To use a distinction going back to Schneider and Shiffrin [6], Russo is concerned with controlled, or strategic, information processing. In addition to controlled information processing, there exists automatic information processing. This type of information processing is unconscious or semiconscious, is characterized by parallel rather than serial processing, and uses little or no central processing capacity.

The subject of automatic processes in consumer information processing is underresearched. Research in this area might address the following questions: How, controlling for differences in effort, do consumer decisions differ due to automatic processes? How do people differ in allocating total information processing to automatic and controlled processes for different types of decision? To what extent does the amount of information processed differ when effort is held constant? Lacking answers to these questions, I shall use Russo's threefold distinction of collection, comprehension, and computation to delineate possible effects of automatic processes.

Collection

In unintentional information collection, automatic processes determine which information is attended to and possibly stored, and which is not. In intentional information collection, automatic processes determine which targets of information search come to the mind of the consumer.

Comprehension

Automatic processes largely determine how new information is linked to stored knowledge. This in turn determines how new information is interpreted and understood.

Computation

Some information integration, i.e., the combination of pieces of information to form an overall evaluation, may occur automatically. It turns out that one of the more prominent models of automatic cognitive processes, the model of spreading activation in a semantic network, accounts for evaluations that are structurally similar to the linear judgement model [2].

Thus, automatic processes may set the limits within which controlled processes can operate. Indeed, in low value purchases, where there is very little controlled processing, these limits may be very narrow. Policy measures aimed at reducing the effort of information processing hence can operate only within these limits. They have to take the outcomes of automatic processes as given. This considerably limits what can be done.

-- Even if collection effort is reduced, only information already salient in a consumer's cognitive structure will be collected. This principle might rule out the "collection" of a cigarette health warning.

-- Ordinarily, achieving change in comprehension requires information that will activate relevant parts of the cognitive structure to which the new information can be related. Russo's interpretation of "reducing comprehension effort" is not clear to me. It seems to me that the examples he gives focus more on reducing computation effort than on reducing comprehension effort. The two are related, but different.

-- Computation can take place only on the basis of evaluations that have already been established automatically.

If the outcomes of automatic processes limit what can be done by reducing the effort associated with controlled processes, can automatic processes be changed? It is probably difficult to change the processes themselves. After all, they are unconscious! But the outcomes can be altered by changing the cognitive structure on which these processes operate. This, however, means learning: It means changing people, not just the environment. The limitations of what can be achieved by changing the environment should be kept in mind. In a sense, emphasizing changes in environment represents a conservative approach because it takes people's cognitive structure as given. To help people make better decisions, better from both individual and societal points of view, we need to both: (1) create a hospitable information environment and (2) a receptive cognitive structure.

WHAT IS THE COST OF REDUCING EFFORT?

I tried to show that automatic processes set limits within which controlled processes operate. Within these limits, the attempts to reduce effort described by Russo can represent meaningful strategies. Russo deals with two such strategies (1) reducing collection effort and (2) reducing computation effort. Reducing collection effort is unproblematic. But one should note, given scarce resources, the decision to make one type of information easier to collect implies that a different type of information cannot be made easier to collect. Policymakers will have to choose among different frameworks for reducing collection effort.

Attempts to reduce computation effort can create new costs for the consumer. These are costs that he/she might not even perceive, at least not before the purchase. If such measures entail, as Russo writes, shifting "the burden of intelligent behavior" from the individual to the environment, someone else obviously has to do the thinking. Further, it has to be done in a uniform way, ignoring individual differences among consumers. This does not pose a problem in cases where individual differences are small, or where individual differences exist but are more than outweighed by a considerable knowledge differential between the information creating expert and the average consumer. In other cases, the provision of "pre-processed" information may lead some consumers to make choices based on the preferences of others, thus thwarting consumer sovereignty. Putting it another way someone has provided data that might lead a consumer to a choice different from what he would have arrived at on his own. This could be a problem in all the examples given: overall ratings of comparative product tests, nutrition stars, perfect information frontiers, they are all devices based on the hypothetical demands of an average consumer. If individual differences in demand are great, the decrease in processing effort resulting from the use of these measures may be partly offset by a <u>decrease in utility</u> from the purchase of the "wrong" product variant.

HOW HELPFUL ARE THE NEW MEDIA?

Russo lists ways in which new information media like videotex, videodiscs or expert systems might enhance benefits and reduce costs of information processing. That the potential is there I agree. But our experience to date, especially with videotex, should give rise to some doubts. First of all, the technical feasibility of the medium says nothing about which information will be provided. Usually this is left to market forces to which all the usual problems apply, e.g., the "free-rider" problem mentioned by Russo. It may not be profitable for a supplier to assemble a list of "good" restaurants within fifteen minutes' walking distance from your hotel, no matter how desirable such a list may be to you! In the German videotex system -- one of the largest in existence -- there is no list of this type. So far information providers have underutilized the information updating possibilities of videotex [4]. Only with strong governmental support -- for consumer information -- both financial and otherwise -- will we see videotex emerging as a major source of consumer information.

The videotex technology confronts other problems as well. For certain tasks the effort encountered in using videotex is higher than that required by the traditional media [1, 7]. While first-time users seem to achieve considerable "experiential benefits" [3], this may be offset in the long run by experiential costs due to delays in information retrieval and frustrations due to information not found [5]. Finally, consumer acceptance of all videotex systems operating today--with the exception of France, where the equipment is free--is rather low. This is completely consistent with Russo's cost-benefit framework: the costs of buying and using videotex are high while benefits are uncertain.

REFERENCES

1. ERNST, MATHIAS (1985), Bildschirmtext-Informationen fur Konsumguter-Kaufentscheidungen, Heidelberg: Physica.

2. GRUNERT, KLAUS G. (1982), "Linear Processing in a Semantic Network: An Alternative View of Consumer Product Evaluation," Journal of Business Research, 10:31-42.

3. _________ (1984), "Consumer Information Systems in Videotex: Design and Acceptance," Journal of Consumer Studies and Home Economics, 8:183-198.

4. KAPS, RALPH ULRICH (1983), Die Wirkung von Bildschirmtext auf das Informationsverhalten der Konsumenten, Munich: Fischer.

5. KUHLMANN, EBERHARD and BALDERJAHN, INGO (1984), Verbraucherinformation fur Jugendliche uber Bildschirmtext, Munich: Fischer.

6. SCHNEIDER, WALTER and SHIFFRIN, RICHARD M. (1977), "Controlled and Automatic Human Information Processing: I. Detection, Search, and Attention," Psychological Review, 84:1-66.

7. SHARMA, SUBHASH, BEARDEN, WILLIAM O. and TEEL, JESSE E. (1983), "Differential Effects of In-Home Shopping Methods," Journal of Retailing, 59(No. 4):29-51.

ABOUT THE AUTHOR

Michael B. Mazis is Professor and Chairman of the Department of Marketing at the American University. Mazis received his Ph.D. in Marketing from Pennsylvania State University in 1971. His career has included both academic and government policy positions. He served on the faculties of the University of Florida and American University. From 1977 to 1979 he was Chief, Marketing and Consumer Research, at the Federal Trade Commission. Not surprisingly, his research interests focus on the intersection between consumer policy and marketing. His publications have appeared in the Journal of Marketing, Journal of Marketing Research, and Journal of Consumer Research.

OVERLOOKED MECHANISMS FOR CONVEYING INFORMATION TO CONSUMERS

Michael B. Mazis

Are consumers confronted with a "hostile" information environment when they are about to make purchase decisions? In his paper, "Information Processing from the Consumer's Perspective," Russo argues that consumers face a "hostile" environment because needed information is lacking altogether or is unavailable in a useful form [12]. To remedy this "hostile" environment, Russo suggests that information providers focus on the consumer's information search process.

Russo also believes that consumers engage in a reasoned cost-benefit calculation to determine whether more information is needed for a purchase decision. According to Russo, an understanding of the cost-benefit calculation can lead to "the redesign of current information to make it more useful to consumers."

Russo's analysis is incomplete in three ways. First, there is ample evidence that consumers face an environment of abundant information. This environment is imperfect; consumers frequently do not have all the information necessary to make ideal decisions. However, with a modest amount of effort, consumers can make satisfactory decisions with available information.

Second, consumers often do not engage in the deliberative cost-benefit calculations implied in Russo's framework. Consumers acquire information through a variety of means. Much of the information used in decision making is acquired passively as part of the consumer's daily routine. This passively acquired information has a major impact on consumer decisions and reduces the need in many cases for extensive information search.

Finally, optimal results will not usually be achieved solely by redesigning the information environment based on Russo's cost-benefit framework. Labeling, point-of-purchase signs, and other consumer information have had only a modest impact on changing consumer behavior. Maximum results will be achieved by creating an information environment that is compatible with marketplace incentives.

ABUNDANT INFORMATION ENVIRONMENT

Despite claims to the contrary, consumers face an environment of abundant information. In recent years, nutrition and ingredient information has been added to food product labels. Fiber content and care instruction labels are now mandatory on clothing. Cigarette packages contain both tar and nicotine levels and health warnings. Even life and luminesence information is marked on light bulb packages.

In addition, Consumer Reports and specialized magazines in the athletics, home electronics, computer, and automobile industries provide detailed product performance ratings. Ratings on service providers are now increasingly available on a local level by Washington Consumers' Checkbook and other magazines. Newspaper advertising continues to be an important source for price and product availability information.

There is evidence, however, that many consumers do not actively search for information when they are about to make a purchase decision [16]. Russo argues that consumers fail to search because information acquisition is too costly due to the effort required. However, going to the library to read a copy of Consumer Reports is not especially burdensome. Therefore, the cost of search is not a relevant deterrent to much information acquisition.

Russo neglects to mention three factors that have an important impact on the amount of information search. First, many consumers simply lack the basic shopping skills that should be provided in the home or in school. For example, few consumers understand how to search for the lowest priced automobile and how to use unit price information in supermarkets.

Secondly, consumers have learned to rely on certain misleading signals as a simple way to obtain product information. For example, price is one such signal, although considerable evidence suggests that there is little relationship between price and quality for many products [2]. Yet another unreliable signal is advertising.

Advertising is used as a simplifying cue also. Consumers may reason that any firm with a large advertising budget must have many customers satisfied with the high quality of the firm's offerings [9]. Again, the correlation between extensive advertising and quality is questionable.

Finally, consumers may not engage in deliberative information search because the desired information is already known. Consumers may already have a good idea about product availability or quality through previous experience or through information acquired while engaged some other activity, such as watching a television commercials.

NON-DELIBERATE INFORMATION ACQUISITION

There is considerable evidence that consumers acquire much information through non-deliberative or passive information acquisition [1]. As a result, many consumers simply do not engage in the planned cost-benefit analysis that Russo claims "almost always" takes place.

Consumers notice and remember information even though they are not actively looking for it. Research indicates that this unplanned information acquisition often has a greater impact on consumer decision making than in-store information displays designed by Russo and others that rely heavily on planned information search.

Several major studies that have provided in-store nutritional health information to consumers have shown that these displays do not affect consumer purchase behavior [3, 8, 10, 13, 15]. Studies that have reported an impact resulting from in-store information have tended to show only modest (3% to 8%) changes in purchases of targeted food products [4, 11, 13].

In contrast, publicity through the news media has been found to have a massive impact on consumer purchase patterns. For example, total prescriptions for Premarin, the largest brand of estrogens, fell by nearly 500,000 per month (about 50%) after studies were reported in the press linking the drug to cancer [6]. Moreover, the annual increase in the sale of diet soft drinks fell from 17% to 2% following the release of a study that showed malignant bladder tumors in rats fed saccharin [14]. In contrast, only small changes in sales of estrogens and saccharin resulted from warning labels that appeared one to two years after the initial news reports.

Recently, there has been a substantial increase in the awareness of aspirin as a cause of Rye's Syndrome in children with flu or chicken pox; this gain in knowledge was due almost entirely to accounts in the media rather than to labeling [7]. Also, there has been a major increase in the sale of calcium supplements, of products containing bran, and of low sodium products as a result of substantial publicity.

These findings do not mean that warning labels or point-of-purchase information cannot affect consumer behavior. In many cases, however, this impact is limited since consumers do not engage in deliberative information search prior to purchase and, therefore, ignore posters or labels. As a result, less emphasis is needed on the precise design of information disclosures. Information providers should focus their efforts primarily on developing multiple sources of information (including publicity) to enhance message impact.

STRATEGIES FOR ENHANCING THE USE OF MARKETPLACE INFORMATION

Since consumers often do not follow a cost-benefit rule in acquiring information, information providers should not concentrate their efforts exclusively on the "redesign of current information to make it more useful to consumers" as Russo has claimed. In many cases, reliance on marketplace incentives rather than changes in the information environment will be a more productive approach [5].

Marketplace incentives can take several forms. For example, restrictions against advertising can be lifted in some cases, which can give suppliers additional incentives to provide information. This has been accomplished for eyeglasses and for legal and medical services. Also, a standard "metric" or grading system can be developed to make it easier for sellers to promote their products on important dimensions. This approach has been successful in the case of automobiles (milage ratings), cigarettes (tar and nicotine ratings), and suntan lotion (sunblocking protection ratings). In each of these cases, the environment was altered to make it easier for the market to develop effective ways of communicating information to consumers.

Consideration should be given also to removing disincentives to information provision. The F.D.A. currently requires "full disclosure" of all side effects and precautions in prescription drug advertising both to physicians and to consumers. This regulation increases the cost of providing marketplace information by raising the price of advertising. Also, extensive disclosures are required when automobile dealers advertise monthly consumer loan payments (e.g., $149 per month). This disclosure requirement discourages the provision of important price information.

Regulations that encourage accurate marketplace signalling should be adopted as well. For example, the 1975 Magnuson-Moss Warranty-FTC Improvement Act appears to have been successful in making warranty coverage an accurate signal for major appliance and automobile product quality [16].

Finally, marketplace incentives should be considered in the development of data collection and reporting systems. Newspapers, television stations, consumer groups, nonprofit organizations, industry associations and others who might find it "profitable" to conduct market surveys about product availability, retail prices, and effectiveness of service providers should be strongly encouraged.

This paper has argued that the information processing framework developed by Russo [13] is helpful in understanding consumers' information acquisition decisions. Cost-benefit analysis is used by some consumers some of the time in deciding whether to acquire additional information. However, consumers acquire information through a variety of sources. The cost-benefit model accounts for only a small portion of information used to make purchase decisions. Therefore, information providers must consider information acquisition more broadly. Publicity, through accounts in broadcast and print media, have a substantial impact on consumer decisions. This channel must be taken into account by those interested in expanding the amount of information available to consumers.

Sellers should also be given incentives to provide information to consumers. Focus on increasing incentives for sellers to provide needed information is likely to yield greater benefits to consumers than reliance on information processing techniques that redesign existing information. Repetition of information through "powerful" and dramatic techniques will have the greatest impact on consumers.

REFERENCES

1. BEALES, HOWARD, MICHAEL B. MAZIS, STEVEN C. SALOP and RICHARD STAELIN (1981), "Consumer Search and Public Policy," Journal of Consumer Research, 8 (June): 11-22.

2. GEISTFELD, LOREN V. (1986), "The Price-Quality Relationship: The Evidence We Have, The Evidence We Need," Ch. 7 in this volume.

3. JEFFERY, ROBERT W. , PHYLLIS L. PIRIE, BARBARA S. ROSENTHAL, WENDY M. GERBER and DAVID S. MURRAY (1982), "Nutrition Education in Supermarkets: An Unsuccessful Attempt to Influence Knowledge and Sales," Journal of Behavioral Medicine, 5: 139-200.

4. LEVEY, ALAN S., ODONNA MATHEWS, MARILYN STEPHENSON, JANET E. TENNEY and RAYMOND E. SCHUCKER (1985), "The Impact of a Nutrition Information Program on Food Purchases," Journal of Public Policy and Marketing, 4: 1-13.

5. MAZIS, MICHAEL B., RICHARD STAELIN, HOWARD BEALES and STEVEN SALOP (1981), "A Framework For Evaluating Consumer Information Regulation," Journal of Marketing, 45 (Winter): 11-21.

6. MORRIS, LOUIS A. (1980), "Estrogenic Drugs-Patient Package Inserts" in Product Labeling and Health Risks, eds., Louis Morris, Michael B. Mazis, and Ivan Barofsky. Cold Spring Harbor, NY: Barbury Center, Cold Spring Harbor Laboratory.

7. MORRIS, LOUIS A., RONALD KLIMBERG, EVELYN GORDON and JANET ARROWSMITH (1985), A Survey of Aspirin Use and Rye's Syndrome Among Parents. Springfield, VA: NTIS, August.

8. NATIONAL HEART, LUNG and BLOOD INSTITUTE (1983), "Foods for Health: Report of the Pilot Program," National Insitutes of Health Publication No. 83-2036.

9. NELSON, PHILLIP (1970), "Information and Consumer Behavior," Journal of Political Economy, 78: 311-29.

10. OLSON, CHRISTINE, CAROL A. BISOGINI and PATRICIA F. THONNEY (1982), "Evaluation of a Supermarket Nutrition Education Program," Journal of Nutrition Education, 14: 141-45.

11. RUSSO, J. EDWARD (1977), "The Value of Unit Price Information," Journal of Marketing Research, 14: 193-201.

12. ________ (1986), "Information Processing from the Consumer's Perspective," Ch. 9 in this volume.

13. RUSSO, J. EDWARD, RICHARD STAELIN, CATHERINE A. NOLAN, GARY RUSSELL and BARBARA METCALF (1986), "Nutrition Information in the Supermarket," Journal of Consumer Research, 13 (June): 48-70.

14. SCHUCKER, RAYMOND E., RAYMOND C. STOKES, MICHAEL STEWART and DOUGLAS P. HENDERSON (1983), "The Impact of the Saccharin Warning Label on Sales of Diet Soft Drinks in Supermarkets," Journal of Public Policy and Marketing, 2: 46-56.

15. SORIANO, ESTEBAN and DAVID M. DOZIER (1978), "Selling Nutrition and Heart-Healthy Diet Behavior at the Point-of-Purchase," Journal of Applied Nutrition, 30: 56-65.

16. WEINER, JOSHUA LYLE (1985), "Are Warranties Accurate Signals of Product Reliability," Journal of Consumer Research, 12 (September): 245-50.

17. WILKIE, WILLIAM L. and PETER R. DICKSON (1985), Shopping for Appliances: Consumers' Strategies and Patterns of Information Search. Cambridge, MA: Marketing Science Institute.

ABOUT THE AUTHOR

Richard W. Olshavsky is Professor of Marketing at Indiana University. A psychologist, Olshavsky received his Ph.D. in Psychology from Carnegie-Mellon in 1967. He is a prolific author whose articles, focusing mainly on the psychology of consumer decision-making, embrace a broad range of applications. Olshavsky is a member of the Editorial Boards of the Journal of Consumer Research and Psychology and Marketing.

DETERMINANTS OF INFORMATION USE: BEYOND THE SIMPLE COST-BENEFIT MODEL

Richard W. Olshavsky

Russo's recommendations for effective techniques for aiding consumers in their use of product information are based upon the traditional cost-benefit model of information search/use. Russo states, "If consumers rely on a cost-benefit analysis, as I have claimed, then strategies for aiding consumers in their use of product information should be based on this analysis. Specifically, effective techniques should increase benefits, reduce costs, or accomplish both." Russo then argues that attempts to increase the benefits are "relatively expensive and slow." Hence the more productive approach is to reduce information processing efforts (costs), thereby shifting the cost-benefit balance in favor of information use.

My own work on information processing behavior suggests that the cost-benefit model of information use is overly simplistic [1, 2, 3]. Consequently, the techniques being suggested by Russo may have appropriate but only limited applications. Indeed, in some situations they may even be dysfunctional.

There are at least four major weaknesses with the cost-benefit model and hence with Russo's suggestions. I will address each in turn, citing my own theoretical views where appropriate.

WEAKNESSES IN THE COST-BENEFIT MODEL

Weakness 1: Relatively Fixed Pre-Existing Desires/Preferences

A consumer's desire for information is assumed to originate at the level of "desire formation" for the basic product/service, associated services, or methods/strategies employed. Hence, if the consumer already knows that he/she has no desire for a particular good, then no desire is likely to exist for information relating to that good. Similarly, if a consumer has already formed a desire for a good, he/she may no longer desire any further information about that good.

For the reasons just stated the notion that the consumer is always "in the market" for information regarding a good is invalid for many consumers and for many goods at a particular point in time.

Weakness 2: "Other-Based" Desire or Preference Formation Strategies

Even if consumers are "in the market" for a good and have not yet established a desire for a good or a preference for a brand, they still may not desire any information. The reason: Consumers do not have to form desires or form preferences "on their own." There are at least two "other-based" strategies by which desires and/or preferences can be formed: (1) following a recommendation from a friend, a salesperson, or a product-testing organization, and (2) imitation of another consumer [4, 6]. In effect, the consumer can "delegate" the choice to someone else.

Weakness 3: Pre-Existing Knowledge Viewed As Sufficient

A consumer may have no desire for further information to make a choice about a particular good or brand because he/she believes that "enough" information is already available in his/her long term memory, thus rendering the benefits of additional information very small or zero.

Weakness 4: "Erroneous" Pre-Existing Knowledge

Similarly a consumer who "believes" <u>erroneously</u> that he/she is knowledgeable regarding his/her requirements and the product may not desire any further information.

IMPLICATIONS FOR RUSSO'S SUGGESTIONS

The first two cases make the traditional cost-benefit model irrelevant for a significant number of consumer purchase situations. Ordinarily, efforts to facilitate consumers' use of information will be futile. But Russo's devices could work <u>indirectly</u>, not through their effects on consumers, but instead through their effects on advisors to the consumer. Following Russo, consider the provision of information of mortgage rates. This might influence real estate agents who <u>then</u> influence home-buying consumers, thus increasing the number of applicants to institutions with the lowest rates.

An undesirable by-product of Russo's suggestions might be its encouragement of consumers planning to use an "own-based" choice strategy to switch to an "other-based" choice strategy. As Olshavsky and Rosen [5] have argued with respect to the type of information presented by product-testing organizations (i.e., recommendations or detailed descriptions of alternatives), the presentation of recommendations could encourage consumers to depend exclusively on others' recommendations, thereby undermining consumer sovereignty.

Weakness 3 -- Present Knowledge Viewed As Satisfactory-- implies that a reduction in the cost of information as suggested by Russo, will not stimulate information use among these consumers. They view their present, although limited, level of knowledge as satisfactory and perceive the benefits of further information to be zero or very small.

Similarly, Weakness 4 -- consumers who view their erroneous stock of information as satisfactory -- implies that a reduction in the cost of information will not further information use since these "naive" consumers also perceive the benefits of further information to be very small or zero.

These last two implications are the most serious for Russo's suggestions concerning cost reduction. It may well be that the most important consumer information problems (i.e., nutrition, health, safety, and energy use) arise from consumers' beliefs that they have either enough information (<u>when in fact they do not!</u>) or that they have accurate information (<u>when in fact they have many misconceptions!</u>).

The basic issue therefore is not simply whether perceived benefits exceed perceived cost, as argued by Russo, <u>but whether the benefits of additional information are accurately perceived</u>. Hence Russo may be skirting the really difficult and important information problems of consumers. The studies showing a reduction in cost results in a significant increase in information use in some settings are not under dispute here. But it is argued that these results could only have been observed because the consumers involved in these studies had already been persuaded (by the earlier efforts of other change agents) of the benefits of additional information. (This would have occurred prior to Russo's experiments for the types of products and issues involved, i.e., energy, nutrition, and thrift.)

CONCLUSIONS

Russo's suggestion that a reduction in the cost of information is a more productive approach to aid consumer use of information may only apply in those situations where the perceived benefits of that information have already been established by the prior efforts of some other change agent(s). Cost reduction approaches per se are expected to be ineffective in those areas where (1) consumers either do not desire any further information (i.e., consumers are "not in the market" for the good or the consumer "delegates" the choice to others) or (2) where consumers do not perceive the benefits of additional information to be much greater than zero (in some cases, due to an insufficient amount of information or due to erroneous information). It seems therefore that the really difficult issues regarding the stimulation of consumer use of information must still be addressed by establishing an accurate perception of the benefits of such information.

REFERENCES

1. OLSHAVSKY, RICHARD W. (1985), "Toward a More Comprehensive Theory of Choice," Advances in Consumer Research, Elizabeth C. Hirschman and Morris Holbrook (eds.), Vol. XII, Provo, Utah: Association for Consumer Research, 465-470.

2. _________ (1985), "Perceived Quality in Consumer Decision Making: An Integrated Theoretical Perspective," in Perceived Quality -- How Consumers View Stores and Merchandise, Jacob Jacoby and Jerry Olson (eds.), Lexington Books, Lexington, MA, 3-29.

3. _________ (1987), "Toward a Unified Theory of Consumer Behavior," forthcoming in Marketing Theory, (eds.) Russell Belk and Gerald Zaltman, Proceedings of the 1987 AMA Winter Educators' Conference, 280-283.

4. _________ and DONALD GRANBOIS (1979), "Consumer Decision Making -- Fact or Fiction?", Journal of Consumer Research, 6 (September), 93-100.

5. _________ and DENNIS L. ROSEN (1985), "Use of Product-Testing Organizations' Recommendations as a Strategy for Choice Simplification," The Journal of Consumer Affairs, 19, Summer, 118-139.

6. ROSEN, DENNIS L. and RICHARD W. OLSHAVSKY (1987), "A Protocol Analysis of Brand Choice Strategies Involving Recommendations," Journal of Consumer Research, 14, December.

Chapter 11

ABOUT THE AUTHOR

Pauline M. Ippolito is an economist in the Bureau of Economics at the Federal Trade Commission. Trained in Mathematics with a Ph.D from Northwestern University in 1976, Ippolito "did Mathematics" with George Mason University and the Economic Research Section of the U.S. Department of Agriculture before migrating into Economics and Consumer Protection policy. She has been with the FTC in a variety of managerial and staff positions since 1979. Of special interest to readers of this volume, Ippolito edited, with David Scheffman, Empirical Approaches to Consumer Protection Economics, a book based on a conference of mainstream economists from government and academia [31].

THE ECONOMICS OF INFORMATION IN CONSUMER MARKETS: WHAT DO WE KNOW? WHAT DO WE NEED TO KNOW?[1]

Pauline M. Ippolito

SUMMARY

This paper reviews major developments in the economics of information literature as it applies to consumer markets. The idea that information deficiencies or asymmetries can have profound effects on markets is now well established in a substantial body of literature. The view that many market institutions and many government policies may be beneficial responses to these information problems is equally well established. But many important questions remain.

In particular, this review highlights the need for empirical testing of the information developments of the last 20 years. Currently there is little evidence to indicate which of the potential market responses to information problems are actually used and under what circumstances. Moreover, the fact that potential policy solutions are available does not indicate that those solutions will be adopted without distortion. The small empirical literature measuring the effects of consumer protection regulation suggests that the regulatory process may often lead to policies that deviate significantly from the theoretically optimal policies. A better

---

[1]The opinions expressed in this paper are those of the author and do not necessarily reflect those of the Federal Trade Commission. I am indebted to John Calfee and Richard Ippolito for helpful comments on an earlier draft.

understanding of the process and its results over time are also suggested as important research priorities.

* * * *

INTRODUCTION

In the last twenty years, the role of information in markets has become a major topic of research for economists.[2] This is particularly true for those interested in consumer markets and in the effects of consumer protection law and regulation.

In this paper I will review some of the major developments in the economics of information as they relate to our understanding of consumer markets. My review will be limited to developments in the core economic areas of this research. In particular, I will touch only tangentially (or not at all) on the interesting, related work in the fields of law and economics, marketing, and regulatory theory.

Twenty years ago economists simply ignored consumer protection policy. In many ways, this is not surprising. The economics of consumer protection regulation is essentially contained in the economics of information. Twenty years ago there was no "economics of information." This is not to imply that economists did not recognize the importance of information in markets. However, with few exceptions,[3] this recognition did not lead to any serious analysis of the effects of asymmetric information on individual behavior or on market performance.

Today the situation has changed dramatically. Among economists there is a growing recognition that the information environment can have profound effects on market outcomes. Many market institutions and many government policies are now seen to be shaped fundamentally by asymmetries in the information available in transactions. This recognition stems in part from a renewed

---

[2]Portions of this paper are drawn from the closely related but more policy oriented paper, Ippolito [31].

[3]In the Wealth of Nations (1776), for instance, Adam Smith [68] noted that wages would have to vary with the amount of trust placed in workmen -- reflecting his recognition of the special market response needed to deal with this type of information problem. Stigler's (1961) paper [71] is certainly very unusual for its time as is the earlier paper by Scitovsky (1950) [66], both of which attempted to analyze the implications of information asymmetries.

awareness of the most basic of economic principles -- the costs and "ownership" of information are just as real as those of any other commodity -- and this fact leads to predictable implications for behavior.

Despite substantial progress, our understanding of efficient consumer protection policy is still very limited. While there is no doubt that information asymmetries can have substantial effects on markets, it is also true that markets have a variety of methods for alleviating these problems. Government policies usually vie directly with these market solutions.

The literature to date is inconclusive on when and what type of government policies will in fact lead to superior market performance. There is currently very little empirical research that adequately tests the effects of various consumer protection laws. Moreover, there is growing evidence that government policymaking is itself subject to a variety of strong pressures having little to do with consumer welfare. This suggests that imperfect market solutions should not be compared to ideal government policies, but to the policies that will actually be implemented and evolved over time.

With these broad themes in mind, this paper is organized with two primary goals:

(1) To highlight the major developments in the economics of information and the research agenda these developments suggest for those interested in consumer markets and consumer protection policy;

(2) To demonstrate that an economic perspective can contribute greatly to our understanding of the interesting but difficult questions raised by these issues.

INFORMATION ABOUT PRICES

The early economics of information literature focused on the lack of information about prices. Stigler's seminal 1961 article [71] observed that if consumers did not have costless information about prices, some degree of price dispersion would remain even in otherwise competitively-structured markets. The intuition behind this result is quite simple: consumers will search for the lowest price in the market until the cost of searching further exceeds the expected gain from more search. This search process limits sellers' ability to charge high prices, but the discipline is clearly weaker when search costs are high.

Much work has followed the Stigler paper refining various aspects of this simple model,[4] but the fundamental result of this literature has remained: if price information is costly to acquire, prices will be higher than competitive levels and some price dispersion will remain in the market. The magnitudes of these effects vary directly with the cost of price information for consumers.

Related work[5] shows that individual sellers have an incentive to reduce consumers' search costs, e.g., through price advertising. If sellers can efficiently reduce search costs, competitive pressures on sellers should result in an equilibrium with lower search costs, lower prices and less price dispersion. Collectively, of course, sellers would prefer that search costs be kept high, but without some mechanism to effect this collective action, competition should work to alleviate the problem.

This line of literature has had a direct impact on policy. Government regulations or private rules (like professional codes of conduct) that restrict the flow of price information are now subject to increased legal scrutiny. This impact has been greatest in the occupational regulation area, where restrictions on advertising are being removed gradually. For instance, in 1978 the FTC passed a trade regulation rule prohibiting states and trade organizations from restricting advertising for eyeglasses and related services. The published basis for this rule[6] was essentially the conclusion of this literature: that restricted price advertising increased the consumer's cost of acquiring price information and thus increased the average and the dispersion of prices in the market. Removal of regulatory prohibitions on advertising by drug stores, lawyers, dentists and

---

[4]See, for instance, Butters [12], Rothschild [61], Salop [63], and Stiglitz [72].

[5]See Grossman and Shapiro [25] and Butters [13] for models of advertising that serves a similar information function in helping consumers find preferred products. In these cases, sellers voluntarily advertise to improve the consumer's search process.

[6]See Statement of Basis and Purpose and Final Trade Regulation Rule for the Advertising of Opthalmic Goods and Services, FTC, 16 CFR Part 456, <u>Federal Register</u>, June 2, 1978, Volume 43, No. 107. This portion of the rule was eventually remanded to the Commission by the review courts for evidentiary reasons. In the meantime, however, many state legislatures had enacted the essence of the rule.

other medical professionals are other recent examples of this movement.

More subtly, this line of literature has increased the general awareness that information flows are as important to efficient markets as other more traditionally-recognized features, like the number of firms. This realization is partially responsible for the current more skeptical view of the classic structure-conduct-performance model of markets that was the economic foundation for much of antitrust policy.

If large firms can reduce search costs more effectively, through price advertising or reputation, for instance, then a growth in concentration may benefit consumers and increase competition in markets where information is costly. This would explain the often-observed reality that some markets with few sellers seem very competitive, while some markets characterized by many sellers frequently seem quite uncompetitive (see [72], for example). One of the primary changes in the eyeglass market since the removal of restrictions on price advertising has been a substantial growth in chain retailers -- who advertise regularly and who appear to have been a substantial force in reducing prices.[7]

Related to these developments is the move away from the negative and almost universally hostile view of advertising that had dominated the earlier economics literature (see [66], for instance). Before these recent developments, economic analysis of advertising had been generally limited to discussions of its potential as a barrier to entry (thus, limiting competition) or of its use as a persuasive device to increase consumer demand. Studies of the price effects of regulations prohibiting advertising[8] provided the first direct evidence of advertising's information effects. Together with later work on advertising's potential as a quality-assuring device (reviewed below), this literature has contributed to a more tempered view of advertising's economic function -- a function that we are only beginning to understand.

---

[7]In some states other restrictions on chains were also removed, coloring the assessment of causality. In November 1984 the FTC opened a new rulemaking that would override remaining state laws that continue to restrict some commercial practices of opticians.

[8]See Benham and Benham [6], Bond et al. [9], Cady [14], and Jacobs et al. [34].

Despite these advances, there are still important research questions dealing with costly price information. In the literature to date, price is taken to be immediately verifiable and there is no uncertainty about the quality of the good itself.[9]

In some markets, like the automobile market, products occur in great variety. This may make it more difficult for firms to reduce consumer search costs through price advertising. The wide range of product variants allows competing sellers more opportunity to advertise selective low prices which may not be indicative of the seller's prices overall. Consumers would presumably learn to discount advertising in such a market, but advertising's ability to lower search costs would nevertheless be limited.

If these information problems are important for this type of market, prices should be higher than competitive levels and price dispersion should remain. However, there may also be other implications. For instance, high levels of search costs for many consumers may suggest a rationale for the persistence of "negotiated" prices in these markets long after they have been replaced by posted prices in most consumer markets.

The availability of a price "index" that is related to product variety might be an important catalyst for reducing search costs in these markets. It might be beneficial as a policy matter, for instance, to allow auto retailers to use "invoice prices" in their advertising[10] if those "prices" have a sufficiently high correlation with the underlying cost -- even if it is known that these prices overstate true manufacturer prices to the seller. "Invoice prices" in this case might provide an index around which retail sellers could inform consumers of their <u>relative</u> prices. This may be all that is needed to encourage price competition. Manufacturers' list prices may play the same role.

The question of price information for products that occur in great variety is similar to the issue of price information for multi-product sellers, like grocery retailers. The number of products of interest to the average consumer and the variation in his

---

[9]In this sense these results also apply to any quality dimension that is verifiable on inspection, that is any "inspection characteristic" in Nelson's terminology [53].

[10]Here I have in mind advertising by auto retailers with claims like "prices only $50 over invoice price" or "the sale of the year -- all models slashed to $50 below invoice price."

purchases from week to week makes price information difficult to collect. The ease with which prices can be changed by the seller and the large number of dimensions involved also make this market distinctive. It responds to this information problem by providing large amounts of price advertising.

Some study of information in grocery markets has been done (see [42, 11], for instance). Yet there is much that we do not understand about this type of price information problem. For instance, does the nature of the information problem lead to the large amount of price variability observed in these markets? Do some well-known brands take on an information role in these markets, because they are a convenient "index" on which to compare different sellers' prices? At a minimum, analysis of pricing information in these settings defies the conventional wisdom that pricing issues are simpler to analyze than quality information issues.[11]

The use of uncertain prices, that is, prices that are not fixed and known at the point of sale, also raises unexplored issues. It is traditional in the purchase of "participating" life insurance policies, for instance, that the buyer pays a nominal price at the point of purchase but that part of this price is later refunded as a "dividend" at the discretion of the seller. Similarly, the purchase of durable goods often requires the subsequent purchase of replacement parts at prices that are set by the seller. The fact that these institutions survive and are not replaced by full pricing contracts at the point of sale suggests that some type of reputation mechanism operates to discipline sellers. Yet there has been very little study of this issue, and there is some evidence that information affects these markets. (See [45] on the life insurance market, for instance.)

---

[11]At the FTC, for instance, issues involving this type of market are repeatedly addressed: what deception standard should be applied to grocery stores attempting to claim "lowest prices"? how significant is it if too strict a policy is adopted? what merger policy should be adopted for grocery chains? are the information issues here significant and how should they enter the analysis? should firms be allowed to restrict access to "price checkers" who wish to publish the data? how important is it that private property concerns be balanced against the value of improved information in these markets? do grocery stores have appropriate incentives to stock sufficient merchandise when they advertise price "specials"? (The FTC Unavailability of Advertised Specials Rule that regulated stock levels in such cases is currently being reconsidered.)

These more complex pricing issues seem the most fertile areas for future research on the economics of costly price information. There is currently little work on the market's attempts to deal with these issues or on the resulting equilibria. Moreover, advances in technology, like the extensive use of computers in retail sales, are generating potential data sources that create exciting new research opportunities at a level of detail never before possible. Data generated by grocery scanning equipment, expecially when tied to individuals' purchase behavior, are a good example of these data developments. (See [38] for a recent example of the use of these data.)

Some of these new data sources may even allow study of differences in search behavior across types of individuals. For instance, search theories that predict that all consumers do not have to be informed for the market to work well might be tested [63]. Also the empirical importance for search behavior of individuals' value of time (as proxied by wage rate, for instance) versus their efficiency of search (proxied by education, for instance) might be measured directly in particular markets.

This type of research might have direct implications for policy. Evidence of deception is often drawn from consumer surveys where consumers are asked the meaning of suspect claims. If a significant number of consumers appear to be misinformed after exposure to the claim, a deception case might be pursued. Yet if research shows that the market is well disciplined when only a portion (maybe a particular portion) of the public understands the issue, the damage from such misinformation might be minimal. From an economic perspective, there is little consumer benefit to pursuing deception in such cases. In this view the effect of a claim on the market equilibrium is most important, not whether all consumers in the market understand enough to independently generate the result.

INFORMATION ABOUT QUALITY

Overview

The market's ability to deal with imperfect information about the quality characteristics of goods has been the focus of much of the recent information literature. Early work explored the potential quality problem in its simplest form. In a static setting, if consumers cannot judge quality prior to purchase, sellers have an incentive to promise high quality goods, but deliver low quality goods. As is typified by the now-classic Akerlof's [1] "lemons" model, this is true even if consumers can judge average quality in the market. This simple static model has been generalized in several ways, but the quality degradation result has remained the basic finding.

More recent work on the quality information issue has focused on two broad issues: the extent to which market mechanisms exist to correct the simple "lemons" incentive and the potential role for policy solutions to quality problems. As described below, many of the market mechanisms are tied to dynamic considerations that the simple static model did not capture. For instance, a firm will not cheat consumers today if this sufficiently reduces future profitability. It turns out that there are a wide variety of ways in which this type of mechanism can serve to counter the "lemons" incentive. Other static mechanisms have also been identified. This literature is relatively recent and still developing.

Policy solutions to quality information problems have also been explored, but usually in the context of the simple Akerlof-type models. In this simple setting there are policies that can clearly improve market performance. In contrast, there is very little work to date that investigates policy alternatives in settings where there are market mechanisms that ameliorate quality information problems. Here policy solutions to quality questions often vie directly with market solutions. We understand little about when such policy responses would be more efficient than the market solutions they would displace. This question is especially important in light of the recent regulation literature suggesting that the political economy problems inherent in the legislative process often lead to policy that is predictably different from optimal policy.

Overall, recent research progress in these areas has injected more caution into policy recommendations on quality issues: we have only limited understanding of the underlying information issues themselves; we are only beginning to understand the extent and limits of the market's ability to address these issues; and we are increasingly aware of the strong forces other than consumer welfare that drive the regulatory process.

In reviewing the quality information literature, my discussion will be organized in terms of the source of the potential solution to the information asymmetry. The first two sections review purely private remedies: from producers themselves and from other parties. The third section briefly reviews contracting solutions, which can be purely private or which can rely on judicial enforcement. Finally, policy approaches are briefly discussed.

Information Provided By Producers

Signals, Bonds and Reputations

Producers often have information about the quality of the goods they sell. Unfortunately, claims by sellers are suspect. A primary focus of the literature in this area has been the identification of conditions which lead to credible producer claims. In the literature these issues are discussed under the overlapping topics of "signals," "bonds" and "reputation."

In information theory, a **signal** is any bit of information that can improve the predictability of a second bit of information. In an economic setting, this predictability is derived from economic forces. For an activity to serve as an economic signal of quality, it must be less costly (or more productive) for high quality sellers to undertake the activity than for low quality sellers to do so.

Spence [69] first introduced this idea in a labor market setting where higher quality workers were able to reveal this fact through an investment in education, because for them education was less costly to acquire than it was for lower quality workers. The idea has broad potential applicability: the use of warranties by sellers of high quality goods who would expect to pay less under the warranty; the amount of advertising used to attract new customers by sellers who depend on repeat purchase or referrals by satisfied customers [53]; and the higher deductible amount chosen by low risk insurance buyers who expect to lose least from this choice [62] are examples of economic signals.

Bonding devices, or **bonds**, are capital assets or secured monies that are forfeited if the bonded party does not perform as promised. In many markets, voluntary bonding devices can act as signals of quality: the loss of the bond value once the low quality is discovered is sufficient to make cheating uneconomic. Viewed in this way, quality-specific investments become information devices [40]. For example, designing and furnishing retail establishments so that they cannot easily be transferred to other uses acts as an assurance to customers that the firm will provide the promised quality (because the investment will be worthless if the firm is discovered to be cheating). Investment in durable brand name recognition, through advertising or other means, can have the same effect [39, 51].

In general, quality bonds are signals of quality, but signals are not necessarily bonds. To see this, it is important to make a distinction between two different types of quality issues: those where cheating can be (partially) detected ex post and those where it cannot. Since bonds depend fundamentally on the "punishment" inherent in the loss of the bond value, bonding devices can be used only in the first case where cheating is at least somewhat detectable.

In contrast, non-bonding signals can arise even if low quality can never be detected in individual units as long as there is some cost or productivity advantage in acquiring the signal for high quality goods or sellers. In the Spence labor example, for instance, education is a non-bonding signal that screens higher ability workers on the basis of a cost advantage in acquiring education; it has no bonding effect to prevent shirking by any type of worker once employed.[12] Other things equal, bonding signals are more efficient and can be used under a broader set of market conditions than non-bonding signals since they impose most of their cost only if the firm cheats [31].

In economic usage, a firm's **reputation** is a particular type of bond. The stock of goodwill inherent in the firm's reputation can be lost if cheating is detected. For reputation to induce a firm to continually provide high quality goods, the firm must be subject to a stream of penalties--if it cheats [40, 67]. For example, the firm might lose its ability to charge high "premium" prices. The penalty must be greater than the short-term gain from cheating. The premiums are the market return to the reputation. In a competitive setting, the premiums are secured at the margin by sunk costs sufficient to justify this higher return.

The idea that sellers can affect the credibility of their claims through signalling and bonding mechanisms is well established theoretically. What is lacking currently is a better understanding of the characteristics of markets where these forces will be sufficiently strong to actually discipline sellers.

Moreover, there is little evidence or insight on the choice of mechanisms for use as a quality signal. For instance, there are theoretical arguments suggesting that introductory and other pricing policies will dominate advertising, unless advertising is more noticeable or more durable than a similarly expensive pricing program [31]. Similarly, despite its theoretical plausibility, a recent

---

[12]Under different economic assumptions, of course, educational expenses could serve a bonding function; for instance, this might be the case where education is specific to an occupation and where poor performance or ability is at least somewhat detectable.

study by Lacko [41] suggests that warranties do not serve a signalling function in the used car market. However, more general dealer reputations do seem to play a quality assurance role. These issues of the choice of quality signal and the empirical testing of these theories in actual markets are prime areas for further research in consumer markets.

A related topic that deserves more attention is how the nature of the product and of the information flows in a market affect the choice and size of the quality bond necessary to assure performance. An essential feature of any quality bond, like reputation, is that cheating must be sufficiently discoverable. Because the ability to punish the firm is distributed among individual consumers, it is the accumulation of individual reactions that is ultimately important in disciplining cheating.[13] The ease with which cheating is detected and the speed with which this information spreads to future consumers should influence the size of the bond (and therefore the price premium) necessary to secure performance.

The particular type of quality involved is relevant to this information spread issue. For instance, for stochastic quality issues involving differences in a low rate of defect, only a small percentage of consumers will actually purchase a defective good, and they will not be able to determine easily whether their breakdown is symptomatic of a higher breakdown overall. In contrast, a quality issue involving the use of inferior materials and a shorter useful life for all units of a good should be more easily diagnosed by a much larger segment of the market. To achieve the appropriate incentives in both cases, the bond and the premium would have to be much larger in the first case than in the second (assuming the same total reduction in value from cheating).

More generally, reputation or other bonding devices will be less costly in cases where information about cheating will spread broadly and clearly. This would be the case where (1) the quality degradation is widespread among consumers, (2) its cause is easily diagnosed, or (3) ex post information from other sources is widely available. This is the reason that the literature has so consistently focused on the frequency of repeat purchase as an important determinant of effective reputations. Should cheating occur, more frequent purchases by all consumers improves the development and

---

[13]On this count, Klein and Leffler [40] assume that any cheating is immediately known by all consumers. Shapiro [67] allows for a lag in discovery and some averaging over time, but again the knowledge is held by all consumers.

spread of information. However, it is important to an understanding of reputation and other quality bonds that the focus be kept on the relevant issue -- the spread of accurate information if the firm cheats -- rather than on one particular way in which that information will spread.

These arguments suggest, for instance, that in some cases consumer information publications may do more to improve the functioning of markets by providing ex post information on product performance than they do through efforts to evaluate quality ex ante. These arguments may also help to explain the surprisingly large stock market reactions to drug product recalls [37]. Because consumers know it is difficult to get information if a firm lowers its quality, they might react very strongly to any negative information they do receive, dramatically lowering their assessments of the firm's reputation and thus affecting stock value.

Overall, this literature demonstrates that the market is not powerless in dealing with asymmetric information. There are a variety of signalling mechanisms -- reputations, advertising, warranties, and firm-specific investments -- that are potentially capable of compensating for these information problems. Moreover, competitive pressures will induce producers to adopt these quality-assurance devices in many situations.

From a research perspective, what we need is better empirical evidence on the strength of these forces and the situations in which they will effectively correct underlying information asymmetries. The difficulty of getting data on product quality is one of the major problems for empirical work on these issues. However, it is a problem that must be faced if we are to make progress in understanding the market's ability to respond to quality information problems.

PRODUCERS' INCENTIVES TO PROVIDE INFORMATION

There is a large literature discussing the special properties of information -- most notably, the public good characteristics of information and the free-rider possibilities. The primary result of this general information literature is that information will often be underprovided. I will not review this work here, since it is discussed in many places (see, [5, 30], for instance). Instead I would like to focus briefly on producers' incentives to provide information.

Producers have some advantages as information providers. In some cases producers can bundle (positive) information with the good itself and cover the full cost of providing it, (for instance, when the information relates directly to the product, so that it is of use only if the product is purchased). In these cases, there are no incentive problems and information is provided subject only to the cost and benefit of providing it. The important question is what are the characteristics of markets where this bundling can be done and where producer incentives are correct (see Maynes [48] for a related discussion).

The signalling literature discussed in the previous section illustrates one of these sets of market characteristics. Implicit in the signalling analyses are two assumptions: (1) consumers understand the quality dimension; (2) consumers are skeptical of claims because they know that low quality sellers could profit by claiming to be high quality. In this case high quality sellers have the incentive to inform consumers that their goods are high quality, subject only to the cost of conveying that information credibly and the value that consumers attach to the information.

The information at issue in this case relates to a particular firm's product (whether it is high quality or not). This allows a complete bundling of the information with the product: consumers cannot get the benefit of the information unless they buy the product. For example, if an electrical product has Underwriters Laboratory approval, this information is of no use unless the consumer buys the product. Thus, as long as the benefit of high quality products exceeds the cost of providing the (credible) information on high quality products, the producer will raise the price of the product and provide the information. There are no public good problems and no free-rider concerns to distort producer incentives in this case.

This situation illustrates several important principles. First, it is the producer with positive information, relative to the other products in the market, who has the incentive to inform the market. This has often led to the policy recommendation that information must be required of low quality sellers. However, it is easy to show[14] that if consumers can judge the average quality of goods

---

[14]See Grossman [26] and Milgrom and Roberts [51] for the case where information is costless and truthful (because of legal punishment for deception, for instance). Generalization to the case where it is costly to provide credible information (through signalling, for instance) is straightforward though disclosure is then limited to cases where the benefits exceed the cost of the (credible)

that are "unlabelled" or are skeptical of them, there is an incentive for sellers with higher than average products to credibly inform the market of their quality whenever it is worthwhile. This reduces the average quality of unlabeled goods in the market, creating an incentive for the better unlabeled sellers remaining to provide information. Theoretically, this process is simply the "lemons" process in reverse; it leads all sellers to provide quality information except those with low quality goods. Thus, consumers in this case have all the information they need to sort quality.

Similarly, even when the information at issue is apparently negative -- like the health hazards of smoking -- producer incentives may not be as limited as has been suggested. Sellers who have a safer, substitute product should be able to draw consumers away from sellers of existing products[15] -- for the sellers with the safer product the information is positive. In the cigarette market, for instance, advertising expenditures promoting low tar/low nicotine cigarettes have been far greater than for high tar brands, and the effects on consumption have been substantial (FTC various years) [22]. Among those who smoke, virtually no one today smokes the type of cigarette that dominated the market for 25 years prior to the first cigarette health articles in the early 1950s [33]. Moreover, there is considerable evidence that in the 1950s, health-related advertising by cigarette producers was changing the market prior to any explicit government information provision and before FTC action prohibited such advertising [15].

A second principle inherent in the signalling analysis is that producers judge the value of information in terms of sales of <u>their</u> products. In the signalling analyses, for instance, consumers were assumed to understand the quality dimension. If this is not the case, a high quality producer must educate consumers on the importance of the quality dimension as well as credibly convey his high quality. The education portion of the information is certainly subject to free-rider problems -- once consumers are educated, other high quality sellers face a lower cost of informing consumers that they too are high quality and worth a higher price. This is the

---

information.

[15]Note that in this type of situation, new sellers or small existing sellers may have a greater incentive to develop new products and inform the market Posner [59]. See Calfee [15] for evidence of this in the cigarette market. Also, see Finn [23] and Liefeld and Heslop [43] for research showing that consumers are skeptical of producers' claims.

standard argument for why there may be too little information on this type of quality issue. These free-rider problems create a type of "first-mover" disadvantage.

However, there may be economic forces that directly counter this under-provision in some cases. There is a small literature suggesting that innovators sometimes have a "first-mover" advantage, that is, that they can collect a price premium by being the first to produce and promote a new product.[16] This offsets the free-riding disincentive for first movers. Empirical research in markets where new information has been important thus becomes a more pressing research priority. Certainly casual evidence from markets where sodium, fiber, calcium and cholesterol have become recent issues suggests that producer information incentives are not trivial. Better evidence on the strength of these market forces and the factors that affect them would be of significant interest for policy purposes.

Third and finally, there are cases where private incentives to provide information may lead to too much information [30]. In oligopolistic markets, for instance, a producer who has a product that is only slightly better than the existing product may be willing to bear the cost of informing the market about his product. The gain to him may include part of the profit currently going to existing firms and thus may be sufficient to cover these costs, even when the consumer benefits from the improvement would not justify the costs.

There are several implications for policy from our current understanding of producer incentives. Information is less likely to be optimal when it relates to new quality issues that are not understood by consumers, but the direction of the bias is unclear. This suggests, for instance, that policies focused on providing general information on the issue and limited to the initial education period might be more beneficial than on-going labeling of quality itself. Similarly, since producers have more incentive to provide information that has a smaller spillover effect, policy should be cautious about prohibiting claims designed to privatize general information. For example, a margarine producer has far greater incentive to advertise that "(his) Brand X has no cholesterol" than he would "All margarine -- including Brand X -- has no cholesterol."

---

[16]There are some direct information arguments for why this might be so, but even the temporary disequilibrium while competitors prepare to respond with products of their own might be sufficient in some cases. See Schmalensee [65] and Bond and Lean [10] for some evidence of lasting effects from successful early entry.

Information From Others

Private parties other than producers can also be sources of information about quality. Private standard setters and certifiers, independent information sellers and retailers are the primary examples in this class.

Selling information directly raises all of the free-rider issues traditionally discussed in the context of information problems. It is difficult to prevent the "resale" of information that is sold independently. This leads to too little production of information by independent agents. Despite these problems, a number of independent information providers exist. Consumers' Union has provided independent product quality information since 1936; its Consumers Reports magazine now has a circulation of 3.8 million. Good Housekeeping's "seal of approval" and testing lab are similarly long-lived. Other more recent entires such as Washington Consumers' Checkbook and the Bay Area Consumers' Checkbook have gone a step further by providing local price information to pair with their product quality information.

Possibly because of the problems with independent information provision, product standards that specify quality, sizing or compatibility are often developed by industry groups or by professional associations with support from industry.[17] Despite the widespread use of standards, there is little economic research in the product standards area. There are currently few theories telling us when industry agreements will lead to product standards and when such standards will be efficient. (See [20] for a recent exception.)

Certification is somewhat better understood. Independent testing laboratories test and certify that products meet specified quality standards. In most cases, certifiers do not sell their services directly to consumers. Usually it is either the producer or the retailer who has the product certified as a assurance of quality to the customer. In this sense, independent certification is a substitute for the private signalling discussed in the earlier section. Effective certification depends fundamentally on the reputation of the certifier rather than on the reputation of the producer or the retailer.

Multi-product retailers can also provide quality information directly by effectively selecting the products they offer for sale. Here all of the issues discussed under signalling and reputation

---

[17]See Hemenway [27] and FTC [21] for descriptions of standard setting organizations in the U.S.

would also be relevant but as applied to the retailer rather than the producer.

Retailers have both advantages and disadvantages as sources of information. To some extent, retailers can bundle quality information with the product. This allows them to provide more information than independent information sellers, but not as much as producers.[18] Also, multi-product retailers deal with consumers more frequently than any given producer, so any quality cheating is more likely to be discovered quickly. This gives retailers an information advantage, since the speed with which cheating is discovered is a primary factor in the determination of effective reputations or other bonding devices.

One of the relatively unexplored economic topics raised by these issues is the allocation of the quality assurance role between the producer and the seller, and the effect this allocation has on empirical work done in consumer product industries. For instance, the retail margin on the generic (or non-leading brand) version of a good is often larger than the margin on the leading brand.[19]

If this difference is determined by the differential quality-assurance roles played by the retailer and the producer in the two cases, welfare implications related to the determinants of manufacturer or retailer returns would have to be carefully considered. Much of the advertising-price literature that demonstrates that manufacturers' prices are increased by advertising, as summarized in Comanor and Wilson [16], for instance, could be subject to reinterpretation: higher advertising levels by manufacturers could simply reflect a shifting of the quality assurance role to the manufacturer, requiring a corresponding shift

---

[18]See Telser [73] or Overstreet [55] for discussions of the free-rider problems faced by the retailer. If it is costly for the retailer to provide quality certification, consumers can find out which products are high quality from the higher cost retailer but then purchase from a low overhead retailer who simply free-rides on the information. Retailers will be unable to provide as much information in this setting. These issues raise direct concerns with both the _per se_ law against manufacturers influencing the retail price through resale price maintenance and the Robinson-Patman law against differential pricing by manufacturers.

[19]See Masson and Steiner [46] for ample evidence of this margin difference in the case of prescription drugs and Albion [2] for evidence on grocery products.

in the price premiums that guarantee quality. Welfare conclusions from other branches of the advertising literature would be similarly affected.

Contracts as a Solution to Information Asymmetries

Contracts are one of the long-standing approaches for dealing with situations where the quality of the good or service is not apparent at the point of sale. In some cases, contracts are strictly private devices, but in other cases they rely on government institutions to enforce the contract. The law, and more recently the economics literature, make a distinction between explicit and implicit contracts.

Explicit contracts are usually written promises that specify the quality of the product or the parties' responsibilities in such events as product failure or late delivery. In consumer goods markets, explicit contracts are generally warranties, although in the services area contracts specifying the good itself do arise. Credit contracts and health club agreements are examples of the latter. Explicit contracts are usually taken to be legally enforceable in the sense that if disputes arise about performance under the contract, the injured party can appeal to the courts to enforce the contract.

In the economics literature, **implicit contracts** are usually contrasted with explicit contracts in two important ways: implicit contracts are not written or legally enforceable. The development of the implicit contract idea in economics has taken place primarily in the labor literature in an effort to understand employment relationships,[20] but the ideas and fundamental issues are directly applicable to product quality problems. It is usually argued that implicit contracts are used in cases where the conditions and responsibilities under the contract are too difficult or too costly to specify for inclusion in an explicit contract.[21] Because the parties to an implicit contract do not have legal recourse in the event of breach, implicit contracts must be self-enforcing, through reputations

---

[20]See Azariadis and Stiglitz [3] and the other articles in that volume for recent developments in the labor area.

[21]While plausible, this argument does raise issues, since the enforceability of contracts often depends on a reputation mechanism, which in turn depends on consumer reaction to cheating. If contract terms are complex, cheating may be difficult to detect and consumer reactions weak or haphazard. See Newbery and Stiglitz [54] for further discussion of this point.

or other bonding devices, for instance. The ease with which the breach is discovered and that information spread to future customers again becomes a critical issue.

The distinction between explicit and implicit contracts is more apparent than real in consumer product markets. Some implicit contracts can be legally enforced, for instance, under the implied warranty of merchantability of the Uniform Commercial Code. More important is the "implicit" nature of most explicit contracts for consumer products. Most of these explicit contracts are not worth enforcing should a breach occur: the cost of raising the issue legally is much larger than the injury from the breach (as with toaster and coffee pot warranties).[22] In these cases, few consumers would be expected to exercise their legal rights if the contract is not honored. This makes it difficult to argue that legal enforcement is a significant disciplining mechanism in these markets or an important explanation for the explicit contract.[23]

The widespread prevalence of explicit warranties and other consumer contracts in these situations is thus somewhat puzzling in light of the standard theories of third party enforcement of explicit contracts. Possibly these explicit contracts are offered not because they are legally enforceable, but because they are superior information devices for the development and efficacy of reputations. A written warranty, for instance, is a more specific articulation of a minimum that the manufacturer is willing to promise the purchaser. If the producer does not honor the contract, all consumers who experience the problem will be more certain that a breach has actually occurred. This improves the clarity and diffusion of

---

[22]Warranties on toasters and coffee pots illustrate this point dramatically, but even most automobile defects would fall short of covering the legal and time costs of actually enforcing the warranty on an unwilling manufacturer. See Priest [60] for an interesting discussion of consumer warranties.

[23]The economics literature on warranties generally assumes that all warranties are costlessly enforced. The extension of these analyses to costly enforcement is straightforward, and in cases where the cost of enforcement is large relative to the loss, the extension would completely undermine the value of warranties in these models. See, for instance, Courville and Hausman [17], Grossman [26] and Palfrey and Romer [56].

information about cheating and increases the effectiveness of reputations as a disciplining device in the market.[24]

Government Policy Dealing With Quality Issues

There are a number of direct government policy options that can affect the quality of goods and services in a market. Chief among these are liability rules, policies towards deception and fraud, and direct regulation through minimum quality standards or mandatory information requirements. I will not review the economic work on each of these specific policy options here. (See [31] for such a review.) Instead I would like to focus briefly on a few of the broad issues that affect research on any of these particular policy choices.

Most of the theoretical economic literature on government policies on these issues assumes that an information asymmetry exists and that the market has not responded to it in any way. However, the recent research on the variety of ways in which the market itself can sometimes address information asymmetries complicates the policy question. In cases where the market has responded (even imperfectly), policy solutions will usually replace the market-based solution.

The theoretical literature also assumes that a particular policy solution will be implemented without distortion. However, as described below, there is a growing body of economic research suggesting that this is usually not the case. Together these developments imply that the question is not whether a particular policy could have an effect on an underlying information problem, but whether a policy that will be implemented will be better on balance than the market's response.

There are certainly situations where these issues can be resolved at a theoretical level. However, in most cases the issues are essentially empirical. Does the market respond to information asymmetries as predicted by theory? How well? At what cost? Would a particular government policy go further in correcting the problem? Would it do so more cheaply? Would it be responsive to changes in market conditions and to different preferences across consumers? Can it be sucessfully implemented given the forces that govern the regulatory process?

---

[24]For a discussion of policy issues related to contracts, see [31] (1986a).

At present there has been only a limited amount of empirical economic research on the effects of past regulation in consumer markets. One of the earliest studies of consumer protection regulation was Peltzman's 1973 study of the effects of the 1962 drug amendments regulating prescription drugs [57]. Peltzman found that on balance these minimum quality regulations had deleterious effects on consumers. The slowing of drug innovation more than offset the gains from preventing inadequate drugs from reaching the market. This study has been followed by a number of other regulation studies, a few of which deal with consumer goods markets. These studies often find that the effects of consumer protection type regulations are not beneficial on balance. In fact, in many cases the studies find no more than minimal effects on safety or quality, independent of the assessment of the costs of the regulation.[25]

Much additional work needs to be done to measure the effects of these regulations. Nonetheless the findings to date suggest that progress in the regulation area requires that we be increasingly mindful of the variety of explanations that could lead to various results. Tests that go beyond simple measurement to attempt to discriminate between alternative explanations will be increasingly important to research progress.

For instance, the cited studies that find little or no beneficial effects of regulation are consistent with several hypotheses: (1) the market is often able to resolve information problems as well as regulatory solutions do, thus producing little change when regulation replaces the market solution; (2) there was no significant information asymmetry to begin with; (3) in theory government policy could do better than the market in some cases, but the regulations actually produced by the political process do not do better; and (4) the restrictions inherent in government's ability to

---

[25]See, for instance, Linneman [44] and Viscusi [75] on the Consumer Product Safety Commission; Bartel and Thomas [4], and Viscusi [74] on workplace safety regulation; Jarrell [36,37] and Hilke [28] on securities regulation; Peltzman [58] and Crandall et al. [18] on auto safety regulation; Lacko [41] on state laws governing used car markets; and Benham and Benham [6] and Bond et al. [9] on the regulation of professional services.

structure solutions to information problems limit it to relatively ineffective responses.[26]

Understanding which of these (or other) hypotheses is correct and under what circumstances is important to consumer protection policy. If there is no significant information asymmetry in a market, regulatory solutions will be futile at best.[27] If the market has responded to an underlying information asymmetry, the effectiveness of regulation relative to the market solution becomes critical.[28] Finally, the idea that a desired government policy will be implemented without distortion is being treated with growing skepticism. Evidence suggests that the political support for regulation may have as much to do with the transfers between groups as with improvements in social welfare.[29]

---

[26]For instance, the due process requirements of most rulemaking procedures make government regulations costly to produce and costly to change as markets evolve. This tends to produce very broad, unchanging regulatory solutions to information problems. The contrast between government disclosure programs and firm advertising campaigns illustrates this point dramatically.

[27]For instance, Lacko [41] found this to be the case in the market for newer used cars (those under 7 years old) -- despite the used car market's almost cliched use as an example of a market with asymmetric information. For older used cars, Lacko did find evidence of an information asymmetry.

[28]For example, several recent studies have attributed their findings of no lemons equilibrium to significant market responses. Weicher [76] found no evidence of a lemons equilibrium in the market for new homes, a finding he hypothesized was due to builder reputation effects or the role of banking intermediaries. Similarly, Bond [7, 8] found no lemons equilibrium in the used market for trucks less than ten years old, which he also attributed to market forces. Lacko ([41] found direct evidence of information asymmetries in the older (more than 7 year old) used car market, but these asymmetries were eliminated by market forces that disciplined dealers. This was not the case for the submarket of private sales through newspaper ads, where reputation and other market mechanisms could not work.

[29]See Friedman [24] for a particularly readable discussion of this general view and McCormick [49] for a review of the related economic literature. The Bartel and Thomas [44] study of OSHA

CONCLUSION

In the last twenty years, economic research has focused increasingly on the importance of information asymmetries in markets, and in particular, on their importance in consumer markets. The potential for information to affect market performance has been amply demonstrated. In recent years, the focus has turned to efforts to understand better the market's ability to respond to these information problems and the forms these responses will take.

Empirical work on the economics of information in consumer markets is just beginning, but it presents an exciting agenda of research issues. There are currently many economic models specifying the effects of asymmetric information and the nature of market responses to them, models that merit empirical testing in different markets. Moreover, the availability of new computer-generated retail data presents opportunities to examine these issues in actual markets, rather than in the potentially limiting experimental settings of the past.

There is also a broad agenda of research topics dealing with the role and effectiveness of regulatory solutions to consumer information problems. Measuring the effects of past consumer protection activities is a pressing research priority. Equally important are the more recent efforts to identify the reasons why past efforts had the effects they did. Empirical research designed to test the extent to which regulation merely replaces market solutions and the current theories about the regulatory process itself are of special interest at this point.

What do we know about the economics of information in consumer markets? Much more than we knew twenty, or even ten, years ago. Information can matter not only in how well the market performs, but in how the market organizes itself to adjust to information issues. What do we need to know? First and foremost, we need to understand which theoretical approaches are empirically most useful in understanding consumer markets. Which information issues are important and which are not? Where can the market deal effectively with these issues and where will it have most difficulty? And if government policy is contemplated as a solution, we need to

---

safety regulation is a recent example of a study in this vein. They find only small effects on worker safety, significant costs of the regulation, and substantial effects in eliminating competition from small firms and nonunionized labor.

understand what will actually come out of the regulatory process and how that policy will be influenced over time.

REFERENCES

1. AKERLOF, GEORGE A. (1970), "The Market for 'Lemons': Quality Uncertainty and the Market Mechanism," Quarterly Journal of Economics, August, 84, 488-500.

2. ALBION, MARK S. (1983), Advertising's Hidden Effects, Auburn House, Boston.

3. AZARIADIS, COSTAS, and STIGLITZ, JOSEPH E. (1983), "Implicit Contracts and Fixed Price Equilibria," Quarterly Journal of Economics, Supplement 98, 1-22.

4. BARTEL, ANN P. and THOMAS, LACY GLENN (1985), "Direct and Indirect Effects of Regulation: A New Look at OSHA's Impact," Journal of Law and Economics, April, 28, 1-25.

5. BEALES, HOWARD, CRASWELL, RICHARD, and SALOP, STEVEN (1981), "The Efficient Regulation of Consumer Information," Journal of Law and Economics, December, 24, 491-539.

6. BENHAM, LEE, and BENHAM, ALEXANDRA (1975), "Regulating Through the Professions: A Perspective on Information Control," Journal of Law and Economics, October, 18, 421-447.

7. BOND, ERIC W. (1982), "A Direct Test of the 'Lemons' Model: The Market for Used Pickup Trucks," American Economic Review, September, 72, 836-840.

8. _________ (1984), "Test of the Lemons Model: Reply," American Economic Review, September, 74, 801-804.

9. BOND, RONALD S., ET AL. (1980), Effects of Restrictions On Advertising and Commercial Practices In the Professions: The Case of Optometry, Staff Report to the Federal Trade Commission, Washington, D. C., September.

10. _________ and LEAN, DAVID F. (1979), "Consumer Preferences, Advertising and Sales: On the Advantage From Early Entry," FTC Working Paper No. 14, October.

11. BOYNTON, ROBERT D., BRIAN F. BLAKE and JOE E. UHL (1983), "Retail Price Reporting Effects in Local Food Markets," American Journal of Agricultural Economics 65:1, February, 20-29.

12. BUTTERS, GERARD R. (1977), "Equilibrium Distribution of Sales and Advertising Prices," Review of Economic Studies, October, 44, 465-491.

13. _________ (1977), "Equilibrium Advertising and Search for a Heterogeneous Good," Mimeo.

14. CADY, JOHN (1976), Restricted Advertising and Competition: The Case of Retail Drugs, American Enterprise Institute, Washington, D.C., March.

15. CALFEE, JOHN E. (1985), "Cigarette Advertising, Health Information and Regulation Before 1970," FTC Working Paper #134, December.

16. COMANOR, WILLIAM S., and WILSON, THOMAS A. (1979), "Advertising and Competition: A Survey," Journal of Economic Literature, June, 17, 453-476.

17. COURVILLE, LEON, and HAUSMAN, WARREN H. (1979), "Warranty Scope and Reliability Under Imperfect Information and Alternative Market Structures," Journal of Business, July, 52, 361-378.

18. CRANDALL, ROBERT W. ET AL. (1986), Regulating the Automobile, The Brookings Institution, Washington, D.C.

19. DEVINE, D. GRANT and BRUCE W. MARION (1979), "The Influence of Consumer Price Information on Retail Pricing and Consumer Behavior," American Journal of Agricultural Economics 61:2, May, 228-237.

20. FARRELL, JOSEPH and SALONER, GARTH (1985), "Standardization, Compatibility, and Innovation," Rand Journal of Economics, Spring, 16, 70-83.

21. FEDERAL TRADE COMMISSION (1978), Standards and Certification Proposed Rule and Staff Report, Bureau of Consumer Protection, Washington, D.C.

22. _________, Report of Tar and Nicotine Content, Washington, D.C., various years.

23. FINN, DAVID W. (1980), "Inferential Belief Formation Through the Use of Non-information: An Example," in Advances in Consumer Research, 8, Kent B. Monroe (Editor), Association for Consumer Research, Ann Arbor, Michigan, October, 344-348.

24. FRIEDMAN, MILTON (1986), "Economists and Economic Policy," Economic Inquiry, January, 24, 1-10.

25. GROSSMAN, GENE M. and SHAPIRO, CARL (1984), "Informative Advertising with Differentiated Products," Review of Economic Studies, January, 51, 63-81.

26. GROSSMAN, SANFORD J. (1981), "The Informational Role of Warranties and Private Disclosure About Product Quality," Journal of Law and Economics, December, 24, 461-483.

27. HEMENWAY, DAVID (1975), Industrywide Voluntary Product Standards, Ballinger, Cambridge, MA.

28. HILKE, JOHN C. (forthcoming), Minimum Quality Versus Disclosure Regulations: State Regulation of Opened-Ended Investment Company Issues and Common Stock Issues, Staff Report, Federal Trade Commission, Washington, D.C.

29. HIRSHLEIFER, JACK (1973), "Where Are We in the Theory of Information," American Economic Review, May, 63, 31-39.

30. _________ (1973), "The Private and Social Value of Information and the Reward to Inventive Activity," American Economic Review, 61, 561-574.

31. IPPOLITO, PAULINE M. (1986), "Consumer Protection Economics: A Selective Survey," in Empirical Approaches to Consumer Protection Economics, Pauline M. Ippolito and David T. Scheffman, Editors, Federal Trade Commission, Washington, D.C.

32. _________ (1986), "Advertising and Product Quality: The Role of the Bonding Characteristics of Advertising," FTC Working Paper No. 148, December.

33. _________ and IPPOLITO, RICHARD A. (1984), "Measuring the Value of Life from Consumer Reaction to New Information," Journal of Public Economics, November, 25, 53-81.

34. JACOBS, WILLIAM W., ET AL. (1984), Improving Consumer Access to Legal Services: The Case for Removing Restrictions of Truthful Advertising, Staff Report, Federal Trade Commission, Washington, D.C., November.

35. JARRELL, GREGG A. (1981), "The Economic Effects of Federal Regulation of the Market for New Security Issues," Journal of Law and Economics, December, 24, 613-675.

36. _________ (1984), "Change at the Exchange: The Causes and Effects of Deregulation," Journal of Law and Economics, October, 27, 273-312.

37. _________ and PELTZMAN, SAM (1985), "The Impact of Product Recalls on the Wealth of Sellers," Journal of Political Economy, June, 512-536.

38. KATZ, MICHAEL L. and SHAPIRO, CARL (1986), "Consumer Shopping Behavior in the Retail Coffee Market," in Empirical Approaches to Consumer Protection Economics, Pauline M. Ippolito and David T. Scheffman, Editors, Federal Trade Commission, Washington, D.C.

39. KIHLSTROM, RICHARD E., and RIORDAN, MICHAEL H. (1984), "Advertising as a Signal," Journal of Political Economy, June, 92, 427-450.

40. KLEIN, BENJAMIN, and LEFFLER, KEITH B. (1981), "The Role of Market Forces in Assuring Contractual Performance," Journal of Political Economy, August, 89, 615-641.

41. LACKO, JAMES M. (1986), Product Quality and Information in the Used Car Market, Staff Report, Federal Trade Commission, Washington, D.C.

42. LESSER, W.H. and W.K. BRYANT (1982), "Predicting the Direct Benefits of a Food Price-Reporting or Preference-Changing Program," American Journal of Agricultural Economics 64:1, February, 129-133.

43. LIEFELD, JOHN and HESLOP, LOUISE A. (1985), "Reference Prices and Deception in Newspaper Advertising," Journal of Consumer Research, March, 11, 868-876.

44. LINNEMAN, PETER (1980), "The Effects of Consumer Safety Standards: The 1973 Mattress Flammability Standard," Journal of Law and Economics, October, 23, 461-479.

45. LYNCH, MICHAEL P. and MACKAY, ROBERT J. (1985), Life Insurance and Consumer Information, Staff Report, Federal Trade Commission.

46. MASSON, ALISON, and STEINER, ROBERT (1985), The Effects of State Drug Product Selection Laws, Staff Report to the Federal Trade Commission, Washington, D.C.

47. MATTHEWS, STEVEN, and MOORE, JOHN (1983), "Monopoly Provision of Product Quality and Warranties," Unpublished paper, September.

48. MAYNES, E. SCOTT (1979), "Consumer Protection: The Issues," Journal of Consumer Policy, 3, 97-109.

49. MCCORMICK, ROBERT E. (1984), "The Strategic Use of Regulation: A Review of the Literature," in The Political Economy of Regulation: Private Interests in the Regulatory Process, R. Rogowsky and B. Yandle, Editors, Federal Trade Commission, Washington, D.C., March.

50. MCCRACKEN, VICKI A., ROBERT D. BOYNTON and BRIAN F. BLAKE (1982), "The Impact of Comparative Food Price Information on Consumers and Grocery Retailers," Journal of Consumer Affairs, 16:2, 224-240.

51. MILGROM, PAUL and ROBERTS, JOHN (1986), "Price and Advertising Signals of New Product Quality," Journal of Political Economy. August, 94, 796-821.

52. _________ (1986), "Relying on the Information of Interested Parties," Rand Journal of Economics, Spring, 17, 18-32.

53. NELSON, PHILLIP (1974), "Advertising As Information," Journal of Political Economy, July-August, 81, 729-754.

54. NEWBERY, DAVID M., and STIGLITZ, JOSEPH E. (1983), "Wage Rigidity, Implicit Contracts, Unemployment and Economic Efficiency," The Economic Journal, June 1987, Vol. 83, No. 381, pp. 416-430.

55. OVERSTREET, THOMAS R. (1983), Resale Price Maintenance: Economic Theories and Empirical Evidence, Staff Report, Federal Trade Commission, November.

56. PALFREY, THOMAS, and ROMER, THOMAS (1983), "Warranties, Performance, and the Resolution of Buyer-Seller Disputes," Bell Journal of Economics, Spring, 14, 97-117.

57. PELTZMAN, SAM (1973), "An Evaluation of Consumer Protection Legislation: The 1962 Drug Amendments," Journal of Political Economy, September/October, 81, 1049-1091.

58. ________ (1975), "The Effects of Automobile Safety Regulation," Journal of Political Economy, August/December, 83, 677-725.

59. POSNER, RICHARD A. (1977), Economic Analysis of Law, Little, Brown and Co., Boston.

60. PRIEST, GEORGE L. (1981), "A Theory of Consumer Product Warranty," Yale Law Journal, May, 90, 1297-1351.

61. ROTHSCHILD, MICHAEL (1973), "Models of Market Organization with Imperfect Information: A Survey," Journal of Political Economy, November/December, 81, 1283-1308.

62. ________ and STIGLITZ, JOSEPH (1976), "Equilibrium in Competitive Insurance Markets: An Essay on the Economics of Imperfect Information," Quarterly Journal of Economics, November, 90, 629-650.

63. SALOP, STEVEN (1976), "Information and Monopolistic Competition," American Economic Review, May, 66, 240-245.

64. ________ (1978), "Parables of Information Transmission in Markets," in The Effects of Information on Consumer and Market Behavior, Andrew W. Mitchell (Ed.), American Marketing Association, Chicago.

65. SCHMALENSEE, RICHARD (1982), "Product Differentiation Advantages of Pioneering Brands," American Economic Review, June, 72, 349-365.

66. SCITOVSKY, TIBOR (1950), "Ignorance as a Source of Oligopoly Power," American Economic Review, May, 40, 48-53.

67. SHAPIRO, CARL (1983), "Premiums for High Quality Products as Returns to Reputation," Quarterly Journal of Economics, November, 98, 659-679.

68. SMITH, ADAM (1776), An Inquiry into the Nature and Causes of the Wealth of Nations, The Modern Library, New York, 1937 printing.

69. SPENCE, MICHAEL (1974), "Competitive and Optimal Responses to Signals: An Analysis of Efficiency and Distribution," Journal of Economic Theory, March, 7, 296-332.

70. ________ (1976), "Informational Aspects of Market Structures: An Introduction," Quarterly Journal of Economics, November, 90, 591-597.

71. STIGLER, GEORGE J. (1961), "The Economics of Information," Journal of Political Economy, June, 69, 213-225.

72. STIGLITZ, J. E. (1979), "Equilibrium in Product Markets with Imperfect Information," American Economic Review, May, 69, 339-345.

73. TELSER, LESTER G. (1960), "Why Should Manufacturers Want Fair Trade?", Journal of Law and Economics, October, 3, 86-105.

74. VISCUSI, W. KIP (1979), "The Impact of Occupational Safety and Health Regulation," Bell Journal of Economics, Spring, 10, 117-140.

75. ________ (1985), "Consumer Behavior and the Safety Effects of Product Safety Regulation," Journal of Law and Economics, October, 28, 527-553.

76. WEICHER, JOHN C. (1986), "The Market For Housing Quality," in Empirical Approaches to Consumer Protection Economics, Pauline M. Ippolito and David T. Scheffman, Editors, Federal Trade Commission, Washington, D.C.

Chapter 12

ABOUT THE AUTHOR

Brian T. Ratchford is Professor of Marketing at the State University of New York at Buffalo. A marketer trained in Economics with a Ph.D. from the University of Rochester in 1972, Ratchford has spent his entire career at SUNY-Buffalo except for 1977-78 when he was a Fellow at the European Institute for Advanced Studies in Management in Brussels. A prolific researcher, Ratchford's publications reflect his abiding interest in applying both economic and marketing concepts to marketing problems in a rigorous fashion. Ratchford is on the Editorial Boards of Journals of Consumer Research, Marketing Science, Economic Psychology, and Marketing.

THE ECONOMICS OF INFORMATION: THE VIEWS OF A MARKETING ECONOMIST

Brian T. Ratchford

The paper by Ippolito presents an admirably well organized and thoughtful summary of a vast literature that touches on a wide variety of issues. Moreover this paper does an excellent job of presenting issues which require further research. Anyone interested in finding problems to work on in this area would do well to read the Ippolito paper, carefully.

SOME MISSED LITERATURE

As usual there are a few quibbles. While the paper does a superb job of dealing with the literature on quality and associated issues of signalling and information provision, there seem to be gaps in its treatment of consumer search behavior. In particular, Ippolito states that "In the literature to date, price is taken to be immediately verifiable and there is no uncertainty about the quality of the good itself (p. 5)." Wilde [10] is a conspicuous exception to this statement. He considers as an example search for a good whose quality can only be verified on consumption, an "experience good." Another potentially useful and unreferenced article is Weitzman [11]. This interesting article relaxes the restrictive assumption of equal priors across brands that is normally incorporated into economic models dealing with search. A third article that is worthy of attention is Carlson and McAfee [1]. While the authors make a number of restrictive assumptions about the nature of search behavior and deals only with a homogeneous good, this article is important because it provides a framework for empirical analysis, deriving a number of testable propositions. Therefore it is a potential catalyst for the empirical work for which Ippolito calls so often. An empirical test of the Carlson-McAfee model is provided by Dahlby and West [2]. While The Carlson-McAfee model is probably not satisfactory in its present state, those interested in pursuing empirical work may find it a useful starting point.

GAINS IN THE ECONOMICS OF INFORMATION LITERATURE

Perhaps the best conclusion that can be drawn from the literature reviewed by Ippolito is: "It depends." While this may seem very unsatisfactory, it is infinitely preferable to an acrimonious debate between those who view firms as nasty exploiters of consumers through advertising and other tricks, and those who reject even the possibility that a market might not be perfectly competitive. These extremes seemed to characterize the state of thinking about market performance twenty years ago. Now we have arrived at a somewhat realistic notion of what the possibilities are.

Perhaps the major advance of this literature has been its focus on the consumer's role in determining market behavior. It is now clear that consumers can exert considerable control over market behavior, but that it might be costly for them to do so. It is now recognized that advertising can be a cheap source of information, that consumers can discount if they believe it to be somewhat misleading. It is now acknowledged that the opportunity to make repeat purchases can exert a powerful disciplining force on a market. It is now understood that only a fraction of consumers need to be knowledgeable for a market to function almost competitively. While these views may have always been obvious to marketing practitioners, they were certainly not understood by economists until recently.

THE LITERATURE BEYOND ECONOMICS

At virtually every section of her paper, Ippolito concludes that empirical study of an issue is required. While it was understandably not her purpose to review literatures beyond economics, there has been work in other areas which provides relevant empirical results. In particular, there is a vast literature on consumer search behavior in marketing and related disciplines. There is also a very large literature on empirical price-quality relations and price distributions, which is in fact the focus of another session of this Conference.

Lessons From The Marketing Literature on Search

Though the marketing literature is subject to limitations created by the need to collect information on behavior through surveys that often take place months after purchase, the empirical research on consumer search appears to answer some of the questions raised by Ippolito (to be dealt with later -- p. 8). The amount of search seems positively related to education (a plausible proxy for "efficiency" in search), to have a curvilinear relation with income (a proxy for time costs) with middle income consumers searching the most. It seems plausible that low income consumers have fewer alternatives while higher income consumers find it too expensive to search. (See [7] for a review of this evidence.)

But the most striking result from this empirical literature is that consumers search little, even for expensive items such as cars [7]. Alternatively (1) they can gather a great deal of information from one source, (2) they have strong prior beliefs about which brand is best, (3) they have high search costs, or (4) their search behavior is in some sense nonoptimal. Since consumers tend to buy the same brand when satisfied with their last purchase and tend to search less as their experience increases, prior beliefs undoubtedly do play a role [7]. Empirical estimates of search costs, inferred from observed market behavior, suggest that these costs are rather high for consumers who shop optimally. Dahlby and West [2] estimate that search costs may be around $30 (Canadian) per brand of auto insurance examined; Ratchford and Gupta [8] obtain tentative estimates for various appliances which are similar. The empirical phenomenon of little search should be kept in mind by economists and policy makers who sre studying the economics of information.

As documented in other sessions at this Conference, the empirical price-quality literature reveals price-quality correlations that tend to be low. Thus, contrary to some theoretical results, price does not generally appear to be a particularly good signal of quality. (It should, however, be kept in mind that there are potentially serious measurement problems with both variables.) A serious drawback of this empirical price-quality literature is that it lacks an explicit theoretical framework, making it hard to draw any firm conclusions about market behavior on the basis of the observed correlations (Ratchford and Gupta [8] elaborate on this point). An interesting recent exception is Tellis and Wernerfelt [9], who derive an explicit relation between price-quality correlations in market equilibrium and the level of consumer information. They show that, if the information level is sufficiently small, the observed price-quality correlation could be negative! More such attempts to link models of market equilibrium with empirical approaches are needed.

Ippolito identifies repeat purchases as a device that enables consumers to discipline markets and that these repeat purchases will be an important determinant of effective "reputations." Evidence from marketing practitioners and scholars verifies this conjecture. In my judgment most accept the view that advertising or other promotional efforts can induce trial of a new brand, but that repeat purchasing is determined mainly by product performance. Thus forecasting models for new frequently purchased brands routinely separate trial and repeat purchases, routinely modelling trial, but not repeat purchases, as a function of advertising and promotions [5].

In sum, there is a fair amount of empirical evidence in the marketing and related literatures bearing on the issues raised by Ippolito. Search by consumers conforms fairly well to the predictions of a cost-benefit model. However, consumers do not appear to search much. Moreover, observed price-quality correlations tend to be low, calling into question models positing that price as an accurate signal of quality. On the other hand, consumers avoid repeat purchases of unsatisfactory new brands, suggesting that this mechanism for disciplining markets generally works.

WHAT MARKETING CAN DO FOR ECONOMICS AND VISE VERSA

In addition to providing germane empirical evidence, the marketing literature can help economists in theory building. The marketing literature is replete with many potentially useful descriptive models of consumer decision making processes. In particular, the literature on pricing might provide some useful insights into modeling consumer reactions to information when a variety of products are available from a given seller [3, p. 240]. Relevant references are Monroe [4] and Rao [6].

In my view there is a need to integrate the highly theoretical approaches of economists with the highly empirical approaches of marketers. The economists should construct models that are amenable to testing. Marketers need to develop theories which will facilitate the interpretation of their findings.

THE FUNDAMENTAL QUESTION: ARE INFORMATIONALLY IMPERFECT MARKETS HARMFUL?

The most fundamental issue to be addressed is: "How much does it cost?" At the present time there exists precious little reliable evidence regarding the costs that imperfect information imposes on consumers and producers, let along whether these costs could be lowered by the adoption of particular policies. The literature on price-quality relations and price dispersion is of little help because it does not document the frequency with which consumers purchase "bad buys," i.e., pay "high" prices for a given quality. Investigation of this issue should take precedence over others. If imperfections are small, the other issues may be of little practical importance.

REFERENCES

1. CARLSON, J. and R. MCAFEE (1983), "Discrete Equilibrium Price Dispersion," Journal of Political Economy, 91(3), 480-493.

2. DAHLBY, BEV and DOUGLAS S. WEST (1986), "Price Dispersion in an Automobile Insurance Market," Journal of Political Economy, 94, 418-438.

3. IPPOLITO, PAULINE (1986), "The Economics of Information in Consumer Markets: What Do We Know? What So We Need To Know," Ch. 11 of this volume.

4. MONROE, KENT (1979), Pricing: Making Profitable Decisions, New York: McGraw-Hill Book Company.

5. NARASIMHAN, CHAKRAVARTI and SUBRATA K. SEN (1984), "New Product Models for Test Market Data," Journal of Marketing, 47(1), 11-24.

6. RAO, VITHALA (1984), "Pricing Research in Marketing: the State of the Art," Journal of Business, 57, S39-S60.

7. RATCHFORD, BRIAN T. (1982), "Cost-Benefit Models for Measuring Consumer Choice and Information Seeking Behavior," Management Science, 28(2), 197-212.

8. _________ and P. GUPTA (1986), "On Measuring the Informational Efficiency of Consumer Markets," unpublished paper, State University of New York at Buffalo.

9. TELLIS, G. and B. WERNERFELT (1986), "The Price of Quality," unpublished paper, University of Iowa.

10. WILDE, LOUIS L. (1980), "The Formal Theory of Inspection and Evaluation in Product Markets," Econometrica, 48, 1265-1279.

11. WEITZMAN, MARTIN L. (1979), "Optimal Search for the Best Alternative," Econometrica, 47, 641-654.

ABOUT THE AUTHOR

Terry L. Roe is Professor of Agricultural Economics and Co-Director of the Economic Development Center at the University of Minnesota. After receiving his Ph.D. in Agricultural Economics from Purdue University, Roe has spent most of his career at the University of Minnesota. His main interests have been the economics of information and economic development. His interest in economic development has resulted in major stays in Tunisia and the Yale Economic Growth Center (1984-85) and shorter visits to such diverse points as Malaysia, Morocco and Egypt. His publications have appeared in the Review of Economics and Statistics, the American Journal of Agricultural Economics, and the Journal of Consumer Affairs.

IPPOLITO EXTENDED

Terry L. Roe

My compliments to the author for providing a well balanced and non-technical presentation of the key issues. In my view, the section on information provided by producers was particularly well done. My remarks may be viewed mainly as an extension of Ippolito's paper.

The economics of information to an individual can be depicted as a situation where individual choices are made conditional on unknown events. The realization of these events affects the utility the individual ultimately realizes from choices. In the case of search, the possibility exists that an additional observation may in fact yield higher expected utility. In either case, rational agents can make mistakes, or in more appropriate parlance, problems of moral hazard and adverse selection can arise. Thus the mere possibility of mistakes, i.e., that outcomes of choices are not known with certainty, may give rise to uncertainty which by itself can alter consumers' choices and increase the demand for risk diversification instruments such as insurance and warranties.

SOME IMPLICATIONS OF PRICE UNCERTAINTY

In this context, information about prices merits more attention than it has received. Most of the literature has viewed information about prices as a problem of search where the consumer ultimately knows the price of a good when possession is taken. In this case, the consumer's choice depends on the amount of search but otherwise, the consumer does not face uncertainty with respect to prices. The problem of price uncertainty is most apparent in the case of durable goods whose service flows are consumed over the life of the good. The discounted present value of a durable good includes expected maintenance costs, variable operating expenses and expected obsolescence. These components of price are unlikely to be known when the consumer accepts possession of the good. Hence, the consumer faces price uncertainty.

Price uncertainty is more pervasive than this example suggests. If consumers' behavior is viewed in a dynamic context where, for example, choices are made today contingent on future levels of planned consumption, then prices of goods and services beyond the current consumption period are also unknown. It can be shown that future price uncertainty affects current period choices in direct proportion to the consumer's aversion to risk. Depending on a consumer's attitude toward risk [8], uncertainty in prices can lead to an increase in storage and a decrease in the level of consumption. Furthermore, price uncertainty can induce repeat purchases of familiar goods. Their frequency of repair and other elements of price are better known than are the same price variables of close substitutes whose attributes, at the margin, might be even more preferred.

Uncertainty in prices adds still another dimension to the consumer's problem that is not as apparent as uncertainty in quality or commodity attributes. Namely, after possession of the good is taken, if a price is realized that differs from the expected price, then it follows from the budget constraint that other goods in the consumption bundle must be adjusted. Hence, error in the consumer's forecast of the price of an important good can induce otherwise unpreferred levels of consumption of other goods. In economies where consumers have access to capital markets, a significant portion of this adjustment might be accommodated by saving or borrowing. However, access to these markets is often limited by the nature and extent of consumers' assets so that low income households are likely to be more adversely affected by price uncertainty than are higher income households.

While the inferences from these conceptual models await empirical verification, they clearly have implications for product labeling, price forecasting and instruments for risk diversification. Furthermore, research in this area may provide other unexpected insights: for example, it might help explain how consumers' reactions to the expectation of unstable prices might contribute to business cycles.

QUALITY UNCERTAINTY AND BRAND LOYALTY

Consumers' attitudes towards risk and the importance of uncertainty with respect to product attributes have received more attention than has price uncertainty. Pope [12] has made an important conceptual contribution by extending Kihlstrom's model [11] to investigate the effect of risk attitudes over uncertain commodity attributes. Pope shows how information that serves to increase consumers' certainty about a commodity's attributes will increase its consumption relative to close substitutes. His result depends critically, however, on (1) how information interacts with the perceived transformation of goods into attributes and (2) on the extent of the consumer's aversion to risk. In his model, the _ex ante_ value of information is in direct proportion to the extent of the consumer's aversion to risk. Pope's model appears relatively tractable to empirical application.

The main section of Ippolito's paper focuses on information about quality. The literature reviewed discusses the incentives for producing, conveying and processing information in the market. As Stiglitz [15, p. 23] suggests, insights into the process of producing and conveying information are critically important to understanding the extent and nature of market failure. However, this process is complex and it varies across commodities depending on such factors as the structure of the industry, complexity of the product, nature of close substitutes and frequency of purchase. Analysis of this process suggests that the notions of market equilibrium embodied in the traditional paradigm are indeed special and that prices are only one of the mechanisms by which information is conveyed in an economy.

This dimension of the information problem gives rise to what Stiglitz [15, p. 27] refers to as the Fundamental Non-Decentralisability Theorem which contradicts traditional views. In essence, the theorem states that Adam Smith's invisible hand does _not_ work. Choices of individuals acting in their own self interest and lacking discernible market power do _not_ necessarily bring about a social welfare maximization. Hence, in principal, interventions by government or groups of consumers and/or producers can lead to a more socially optimal allocation of resources than would otherwise occur. However, as voluminous literature in industrial organization suggests, we are dealing with an indeterminant environment where reaction functions are almost surely unstable. Even with recent advances in game theory, it is unclear whether we will be able to construct theories of behavior that have universal application. Hence, in my judgment, descriptive and interpretative commodity- or situation-specific studies of the information producing and conveying process will remain an important input into judgments of market failure, i.e., the degree to which markets succeed in allocating resources such that any alternative to feasible allocation cannot make any individual better off without making another individual worse off.

INFORMATION ON QUALITY

I now turn to the demand side of the information on quality problem. The process by which information is sought, signals decoded and the consumer characteristics associated with the efficiency of this process have important policy implications. Recent studies suggest that information seekers tend to be high income, educated and mostly professional or managerial persons. Thorelli and Engledow [16] estimate that this group accounts for 10 to 20 percent of consumers. Grossman and Stiglitz's markets [6] suggests conceptual articles on the informational efficiency of markets suggests that for price signals to be informationally efficient, it is not necessary for all agents in the market to be fully informed. Price signals will convey the information held by informed agents thus reducing the need for the uninformed to expend resources to become informed, provided prices are known at the time possession of the good is taken. Empirical verification of these hypotheses should provide insights into whether goods consumed by lower income households and whether local or regional markets frequented by low income households are more prone to market failure. A positive verification should provide an important guide to the targeting of policy interventions to improve market performance.

Numerous studies (e.g., [11]) have shown that data are not "information." For instance, Bettman [3] found that consumers tend to select between brands on the basis of attributes where the attributes are evaluated relative to a previously experienced norm associated with a close product substitute rather than an external norm such as the Recommended Daily Allowance. Hence, data on product attributes tends to undergo some processing which casts the information in terms that are more easily interpreted by the consumer.

It should also be recognized that even the quantifiable attributes of most products are not exact. This means that the level of an attribute is a random variable describable by some probability density function. For instance, the likelihood of mechanical failure might be expressed by its mean and standard deviation. Consumers should be interested in the probability distribution of attributes associated with a good. This information could be cast in terms relative to an industry standard or to close substitute goods. Yet, caution must be exercised to prevent information overload. The key is to determine what information remedies are most important in confronting market failure. In providing information, priority should be accorded to product attributes (1) whose misperception is costly in terms of consumer welfare foregone and (2) whose correct assessment requires extensive search, experience or education.

THREE CONCERNS REGARDING INFORMATION POLICY

In closing, let me voice three concerns regarding information policies. My first concern is whether interventions designed to address market failure are warranted by savings in net social value. This is primarily an empirical question. While some conceptual advances toward the derivation of money measures of the value of information have been made [1, 2, 12, 13, 14], the data required and the calculations to achieve such measurements are complex. This arises in part because the conceptually appropriate measure of the value of information is an ex ante concept. Additional research is needed to simplify these measurements.

The political economy of intervention is also fraught with numerous uncertainties, as much of the literature on rent seeking suggests. (As examples, see [4] and [5].) Principal among these concerns are interventions that purport to increase informational efficiency of a particular market while in reality they impose tariffs or other barriers to entry. This is a particular concern in the case of processed foods [9]. At a time when the world economy is becoming increasingly integrated, caution must be exercised so that interventions do not result in a restraint of trade.

Finally, most of the literature in this area has not been forward looking. Changes in demographic profile, changes in educational levels, increased computer literacy, increasing incomes (and hence increases in the opportunity cost of leisure and the demand for services) and increased complexity of many products have strong implications for the extent and nature of future informational requirements of efficient markets. It would seem that more exploration into the implications of these trends would be important for guiding future inquiry and economic policy.

REFERENCES

1. ANTONOVITZ, FRANCES and TERRY ROE (1986), "Economic Efficiency and Market Information." Forthcoming in Economic Efficiency in Agricultural and Food Marketing, Iowa State University Press.

2. _________ (1986), "A Theoretical and Empirical Approach to the Value of Information in Risky Markets." The Review of Economics and Statistics, LXVIII:105-144.

3. BETTMAN, JAMES R. (1975), "Issues in Designing Consumer Information Environments." Journal of Consumer Research, 2:169-177.

4. BHAGWATI, J. N. and T. N. SRINIVASAN (1984), "DUP Activities and Economic Theory." in D. Colander, ed. Neo-Classical Political Economy, Cambridge: Ballinger Publishing Co.

5. BUCHANAN J. M. (1980), "Rent Seeking and Profit Seeking." in J. M. Buchanan, R. D. Tollison and G. Tullock, eds. Toward a Theory of Rent Seeking Society, College Station: Texas A&M University Press.

6. GROSSMAN, S. and JOSEPH E. STIGLITZ (1976), "Information and Competitive Price Systems." American Economic Review, 66:246-253.

7. _________ (1980), "On The Impossibility of Informationally Efficient Markets." American Economic Review, 70:393-408.

8. HANOCH, GLORIA (1977), "Risk Aversion and Consumer Preferences." Econometrica, 45:413-326.

9. HILLMAN, JIMMYE (1978), Non Tariff Agricultural Trade Barriers, University of Nebraska Press.

10. JACOBY, JACOB (1984), "Perspectives on Information Overload." Journal of Consumer Research, 10:432-435.

11. KIHLSTROM, R. (1974), "A General Theory of Demand for Information About Product Quality." Journal of Economic Theory, 8:413-439.

12. POPE, RULON D. (1985), "The Impact of Information on Consumer Preferences." published in Proceedings from Research on Effectiveness of Agricultural Commodity Promotion Seminar, Washington D.C.: USDA, Economic Research Service.

13. SENAUER, BENJAMIN, JEAN KINSEY, and TERRY ROE (1986), "Imperfect Mileage Information and Changing Utilities: A Model and Survey Results," The Journal of Consumer Affairs, 20:155-172.

14. _________ (1984), "The Cost of Inaccurate Consumer Information: The Case of the EPA Mileage Figures," The Journal of Consumer Affairs, 18:192-212.

15. STIGLITZ, JOSEPH E. (1985), "Information and Economic Analysis: A Perspective." Economic Journal, 95(Supplement):21-41.

16. THORELLI, HANS B. and J. L. ENGLEDOW (1980), "Information Seekers and Information Systems: A Policy Perspective." Journal of Marketing Research, 44:9-27.

Chapter 13

ABOUT THE AUTHOR

James N. Morgan is Professor of Economics and Program Director at the Survey Research Center of the University of Michigan. Morgan received his Ph.D. in Economics from Harvard University in 1947. This was followed by a distinguished career at the University of Michigan in consumer economics, survey research and statistical methodology, and in the consumer movement. Morgan's books include Income and Welfare in the United States, Productive Americans, Multiplication Classification Analysis, and the Five Thousand American Families series, the outlet for the results of the Panel Study of Income Dynamics which Morgan has directed since 1968 in collaboration with Greg J. Duncan. Active in the consumer movement, Morgan served on the Board of Consumers Union for 28 years. He is the author of Economics of Personal Choice (with Duncan). Morgan is one of the few social scientists elected to the National Academy of Sciences. Morgan is one of the most eclectic and discriminating of bibliographers. The Editor commends the list of references at the end of Morgan's paper to anyone interested in an exploration in depth of the literature on consumer choice.

CONSUMER CHOICE IS MORE THAN SEARCH

James N. Morgan

SUMMARY

We have two issues, not just one: (1) Consumer search for information, and (2) consumer insight -- as to what information is needed and how to interpret and use it. Furthermore, there are six crucial economic insights all of which must be engaged if decisions are not to be potentially regrettable. We know a lot about consumer information getting in simple situations where price and attributes are the only question. We know something about consumer problems with uncertainty and expected values. (An extensive bibliography is appended.) But we need to tackle the tough problem of what it would take to help consumers use all the insights simultaneously, and get the facts to implement them.

We suggest laboratory experiments followed by field trials with representative samples of adults that might lead to computerized teaching systems usable by adults or schools. It might seem cheaper to do it all in school, but we may not want to wait for the next generation to start tackling these problems. A complex modern society demands sophistication on the part of its members if the promise of effectively functioning markets is to be fulfilled. Government regulation and attempts to protect consumers may also be necessary, but are often a second-best answer. The best part is that a relatively small number of competent consumers may so improve markets that the rest benefit too.

INTRODUCTION

Exercising author sovereignty, I have expanded my assigned topic of consumer information search and processing to cover also the issues of (1) how consumers can know what information they should seek, and (2) what sort of processing they should put it through when they have it. The main message will be that the most important consumer problems go far beyond searching for the best buy, or finding facts about dimensions of quality. We probably waste more resources, and expose ourselves to more regret by buying the wrong kind or wrong amount of insurance or trading a car in too soon or too late, than by not finding the best quality for the price. It may be possible for markets to become more efficient so that most prices accurately reflect quality. But the task of tailoring choice to the individual's situation and needs will remain difficult and rewarding where the decision is more complex, as with insurance or annuities or investments, the benefits from a wise choice can be substantial.

RESEARCH ON CONSUMER CHOICE

Shopping and Search

There is a great deal of research on consumer shopping and information getting. It started with the pioneer work of George Katona and Eva Mueller [124] in 1954, and their findings were reconfirmed in a recent study by Wilkie and Dickson in 1985 [243]. Briefly put, there was, even in major purchases, a startling lack of deliberation, of specification of qualities, of consideration of brands, or of visiting of stores, and not even a substantial span of time from thinking of buying to purchase. Indeed, people seemed to invest more care in buying a sport shirt than in purchasing a major appliance.

Of course some choose more carefully: those with less previous experience, less satisfaction with the last purchase, more education, more time, or enough income (but not too much of it!). But the overwhelming finding in search of an explanation is the casual purchase-without-choice, even for cars. Of course, some people buy in desperation; the old washing machine broke and the laundry is piling up, or they were moving to a new residence where the appliances were not furnished. Or perhaps they had realized for some time that such a purchase was possible and had accumulated a lot of information casually without thinking of it as shopping or as explicit search for information. A lifetime of direct experience and of observing friends leaves most of us with an accumulation of wisdom on which we can call.

On the other hand, some of us have also discovered that, in a rapidly changing world, it is dangerous to rely on the past. We all need a bumper sticker which says, "PRESUME YE NOT," to alert us to the fact that the store that used to advertise that it met all other bargain prices has stopped doing it. Or, that the "bargain" week-end car rental rates now allow only 150 miles free per day. Psychologists have discovered that rats have a curious habit of occasionally pushing the wrong button even after learning that it produces a shock and the other button provides food. Ironically, this kind of curiosity may explain why rats survive so well.

Others may desire so special a set of attributes that only one specimen on the market meets their requirements. In an early study of house buying, buyers reported considering an average of one house before purchasing, i.e., had no real alternative. The fact remains, as Scott Maynes and Greg Duncan and others have demonstrated, that persistent and large price differences unrelated to quality differences remain [70, 142]. Whatever the reason, many people are not buying on the "perfect information frontier." Similar findings exist about employees' knowledge of wage differences in the same vicinity and for similar jobs that are not justified by differences in the fringe benefits or the difficulty of the work.

A large bibliography at the end of this paper shows how extensive the literature on shopping and consumer information search is. Much of it focuses on the number of brands considered, the number of stores shopped, the number of information sources used, and the lapse of time from first serious consideration to purchase. Given the advantages of quantification for testing competing hypotheses, the limited scope of data sought is understandable. Given the problem of memory, attempting to use survey questions to obtain the actual time invested in information search and choice might be futile.

Joint Deciders and Joint Decisions

Another stream of research focuses on joint decision making, usually between husband and wife. It starts with simple questions about who decides, and leads to more detailed inquiries about initiation of the issue, shopping, choosing, and implementing. Here the overwhelming finding is a perhaps exaggerated emphasis on joint decisions mutually agreed upon [177]. Of course, there is also a tendency for each spouse to take more credit than he/she gives. For some reason, wives predict family purchases better than husbands, even in areas where both say the husband decides [246]. Far less has been done on joint or related decisions, such as changing jobs and residences, or residence and commuting mode. We tend to study single decisions, treating the related ones as given (exogenous) or part of the explanation. A few studies ask whether movers optimize a function that contains both the husband and the wife's earnings and/or commuting costs.

Acceptance of Innovation

A third stream of research focuses on acceptance of innovation and delight in the new [192]. Sometimes the new is a producer product like hybrid seed or fertilizer. Often it is a consumer product like family planning devices, electric rice cookers, television, digital recordings, video cassette recorders, or home computers. Here there has been more attention to studying the process, not just outcomes. Particularly with family planning, researchers are reluctant to wait nine months after some period to see whether people have indeed succeeded in managing their fertility. Hence, they investigate knowledge, attitudes, and practice of contraception. This postpones an assessment of how well people follow the routines.

Credibility and Persuasion

There is also a vast literature on persuasion, and on the effects of the degree of credibility of a source of information or of persuasion. Much of this literature deals with non-economic choices or attitudes. In so far as consumers rely on "expert advice," we need to know more about <u>how</u> they decide <u>where</u> to get it. In a study of wealthy individuals some years ago a Survey Research Center study asked about their use of experts. Respondents generally reported getting information from a number of places, but making "their own" investment decisions [13]. But less wealthy people may be relying far more on specific advice from experts or friends. They may even treat the behavior of people they believe to be informed as a kind of model or source of "implicit" advice.

ALTERNATIVE RESEARCH APPROACHES

Experiments

Field trials, often called experiments, compete with surveys as a research technique in a number of these areas. The unheralded finding here is vast differences among the different experimental sites. These differences are often larger than the difference between the experimental sites and the control sites which constitute the focus of the experiment. As examples, change-agents designed to introduce family planning or hybrid seeds were far more successful in some places than others. In the negative income tax experiments of the 1970's the site effect was hidden since only a single experimental site was used for each experiment. Even with manpower training programs and youth employment programs, the evaluators, focusing on the presumably identical experimental inputs, paid little attention to the vast differences among sites in the outcomes. What is needed here is more attention to and more measurement of the dynamic process, the problems that arise, and what there is about some "change agents" problem solving and other procedures that makes them so much more successful.

We are the victims in this of our own scientific standards. To achieve valid statistical inference, we have borrowed from R.A. Fisher's Design of Experiments for agricultural research, the elegant procedures that allow separate estimation of each factor, and each combination of factors in case there are interaction effects. In Fisher's approach factorial or more sophisticated designs assure that the various explanatory factors being manipulated are perfectly uncorrelated with one another. This avoids the bane of most non-experimental research, the confounding of factors through their intercorrelations, a problem only partially solved by multiple regression. The experiments also promise to handle non-additive effects such as money incentives that work better when counseling takes place. But, in borrowing from Fisher and agricultural research, we are insufficiently aware of pitfalls encountered in shifting experimental designs from agriculture to social science.

A very real and central problem is the uncontrollable factors that change and intervene while experiments are being carried out. I once ran a set of experimental runoff-and-erosion plots, designed to ascertain the effect of top soil and other surface factors on erosion. The experimental plots were all sited on tiled sand bases. Ironically, we discovered that the amount of erosion was almost totally a function of the percentage of the soil surface that was bare, a factor only partially related to the soil type, planting method, crop or amount of fertilizer -- the factors whose effects the experiment was designed to measure. With human beings, far more complex events can mess up experiments. The negative income tax experiments were contaminated by uncontrollable factors during the experiment: in New Jersey by a change in the welfare law; in Seattle by a Boeing strike; in Gary, Indiana by race riots!! And if success, which usually means changing human behavior, requires that almost all of several positive things be present, and almost none of a set of possible barriers, then the attempt to isolate separate effects, combined with a rigid set of experimental procedures, is a formula for failure, for showing that something will not work. The poor current reputation of social experiments is more than just the conservatism of our day, it results from a sense that none of them was sufficiently conclusive. Yes, one could show a positive net benefit or rate of return, though even that was highly variable dependent on the particular model used and the particular methods for dealing with selection bias. (The random original assignment was contaminated by attrition bias.)

What is needed, particularly for information systems, is a new kind of field trial that is a kind of "meta-experiment." It should have controls, criteria, and measurement but the changes or inputs should include procedures for problem solving and adaptation. This suggestion would require systematic procedures for recording problems and their solutions as well as "experimental" outcomes. One would end up with evidence not on what pattern of inputs worked for one historical and geographic situation, but what degree of flexibility, what methods of problem solving, and what methods of persuasion by the change agents produced the best results. If some experimental sites do better than others, we should be pleased. It means there is something to be learned about how to produce change better. So, somewhere between the rigid experiment-- unsuitable for a changing and complex environment -- and the sloppy "demonstration project" -- lacking controls, good measurement, or criteria in advance -- there must be a middle ground that will satisfy our scientific curiosity and also produce evidence that is useful for improving society. I shall return to this issue as it relates to research on consumer choices. To reiterate: it is not enough to try a variety of rigid approaches, nor even to document the "implementation". It is the design and testing of flexible, adjustable, problem-solving approaches that is required. How does one convey economic insights in a way that responds to the individual's particular concerns (and hang-ups), preferences, and that focuses on applications of interest so as to stimulate responsiveness?

Natural "Experiments"

There continue to be events or interventions that tell us something. An example is the use of modern electronic communication. An exciting current case for study is Videotext in France. In striking contrast with the lack of success in this country and in England, the latter described by Scott Maynes [141], there appears to be a rapid explosion of use of Videotext in France.

According to Robert Mayer [140], it is used first as a substitute for the yellow pages, then for real-time dialogues (electronic "dating"!) and forums, substituting not for newspapers but for the telephone. Perhaps this means that trying to use it as a merchandising device, where the wares of one merchant at a time are displayed, fails as it should, since consumers usually want to compare a brief list of criteria across alternative vendors or products. Videotext succeeded, but not as a source of consumer information on products. Research on search shows that most of us sweep through alternatives using one or two criteria at a time to eliminate some alternatives [15]. Since merchants usually submit their information in another form, the problem may be the lack of a computer program that will simply transform it into usable arrangements. This may require some common standards of information that will allow such re-sorting.

RISK PERCEPTION AND BEHAVIOR

Another stream of research has focused on people's ability to deal with risk and uncertainty. As economists we teach that whenever there is an estimable risk with a probability attached, it makes sense to convert good or bad outcomes, benefits or costs, to "expected values" by multiplying these average benefits or costs by their probability of occurrence. We also know that when a choice has had several different outcomes the expected value of that choice is the sum of the expected values of the alternatives, even though only one of them is possible. This statement/insight is counter-intuitive. Though true, it is neither understood nor accepted by most consumers, a finding substantiated by an impressive stream of laboratory and other research by both psychologists and economists [120, 95]. According to this research, people distort their perceptions of risks in substantial and even asymmetric ways. Various theories are being advanced to explain this, but the field is in flux.

As I see it, our research has dealt with some interesting and manageable elements of consumer choice, but has almost totally neglected other important areas. Let me spell out the full range of consumer choice problems.

THE MANY DIMENSIONS OF CONSUMER CHOICE

The ordinary citizen/consumer is beset by ignorance, uncertainty, constraints, compulsions, and confusion. Let us consider each in turn:

Ignorance of the facts has been the best studied, though most attention has been paid to ignorance of prices and attributes, and perhaps qualities such as durability, energy saving, efficiency, and the like. There is also ignorance about causation -- what leads to what. For example, most citizens/consumers do not know even approximately how much of the money bet on the state lottery is taken in expenses, how much is taken by the state for schools and other useful purposes, and how much is paid out in prizes.

Ignorance of alternatives is crucial. All our theories speak of choices and the costs of foregone alternative opportunities. Unhappily, there is almost no research documenting the alternatives people have and know about. In the case of brand choice, we think we know. But even here, consumers may face limited selection availability, particularly in rural areas. Instead of exploring alternatives directly, we invest vast ingenuity in attempting to infer what the foregone alternatives might have been. In so doing we use clever, if always inadequate, methods to deal with selection bias. Such bias threatens, for example, when we infer what not-employed mothers might have earned, had they chosen to work. Direct measurement has its own problems. For instance, people's memories might be biased if we tried to uncover these facts afterward. Further, studying the process of choice before and after is expensive. But, for consumer researchers, the sheer lack of attention to the alternatives people face is appalling, and should be embarassing.

So much for ignorance, what about uncertainty? People often do not know what the future will bring. Will housing prices continue to increase? Will reductions in marginal tax rates come, reducing the subsidy to the affluent home-owners and to holders of tax-exempt bonds? Which section of town will be the favored area with the best schools and high demands for homes? Much of what we attribute to carelessness in consumer choice may simply reflect the fact that the overwhelming uncertainty of future events, or the variety of potential results from any one action. With the potential results of any given choice so variable, consumers may feel that rational calculation is not worth the trouble.

There are also constraints on our freedom to choose. In our research, we must learn how to identify those who are free to make real choices, not constrained by an absence of alternatives nor dominated by some overwhelming consideration. The reason: our economic theories of rational choice would fare better among those who genuinely make decisions "at the margin", unconstrained by outside forces.

Recent research on the lack of shopping has focused on situations that might well have constrained both shopping and choices. Some constraints are social: A famous remark by James Duesenberry at a conference of sociologists and economists is insightful [68]: "Economics is all about how people make choices. Sociology is all about why they don't have any choices to make."

Constraints can arise from (1) society, (2) the jointness of decisions made with spouse and family and (3) lack of awareness of alternatives. For example, a decision to make a major trip may trigger a lot of other dependent purchases, e.g., new clothes and equipment. The total cost, including these additional items, may be offputting. In researching such situations, the scientific paradigm of isolating factors and studying each separately may do more harm than good. We may never discover the fact that these are joint deciders and joint decisions. Treating them as constraints on a single person's decision in one area is really not adequate. However, for many purposes, including simulation of system effects, we do not need to untangle joint decisions, but merely to model what affects the set of choices. Statistically one can account for a joint decision sequentially-- accounting for one choice, then conditional on that choice accounting for the other-- in either order, with the same final predictions. Short of that, the only way to deal with constraints and overwhelming considerations is to restrict our study of choice to consumers "at the margin," i.e., those unconstrained persons who are in a position to choose among real alternatives. The proportion of consumers who can make real choices is itself interesting and important.

THE CRUCIAL PART: UNDERSTANDING ECONOMICS

Finally, and most important, we come to what I call confusion, by which I mean the failure to understand and to use crucial economic insights. Most of these are clustered around the topic of benefit-cost analysis. I have already alluded to one of them -- the use of expected values to discount risky outcomes. We can organize the elements of benefit-cost analysis around the various translations that convert things into comparable, additive, elements.

My list of crucial concepts for consumers starts with the "sunk-cost" argument:

(1) Only the Future Matters. For those who relish it, this principle can claim the authority of scripture: "Remember not the former things, nor consider the things of old." (Isaiah 43:18)

-- The implication of Concept #1 is that each potential future benefit or cost must be converted or translated into:

(2) Expected Values. This concept calls for multiplying the value or cost of an outcome by the probability that it will actually occur. To obtain the expected value of a single choice with multiple outcomes -- the typical situation -- one must sum the expected values of each alternative outcome.

(3) After-Tax Values: We benefit from after tax income. This concept calls for the subtraction of taxes and the addition of tax deductibles, always using the marginal tax rate, not the average tax rate.

(4) The Imputation of Money Values. Some benefits and costs are "implicit": you "receive" them or "pay" them without any money changing hands. Examples include (1) the net rent you "earn" as owner of your home, (2) the foregone interest on the equity in your home, and (3) the depreciation in the sale value of the home. You deal with these by imputing, or estimating, respectively (1) the net rent in dollars you would have earned renting your home to others, (2) the net interest or other income you would have earned on your home equity had it been otherwise invested, and (3) the depreciation, which may be negative when inflation is also making foregone interest very high.

(5) Real Values in Current Dollars. This concept calls for deflating future values downward, reflecting possible future inflation.

(6) Present Values. This concept requires "discounting" future benefits or costs by the estimated rate of interest you would have earned on this money. The need for discounting arises from the fact that current assets can be invested and thus increase in value over time. Much of the confusion about the cost of life insurance comes from ignoring the fact that a large future amount is equivalent to a much smaller current amount. (The term "discounting" causes confusion. It originated from the manner in which bank loans used to be made. You borrowed $100 to be repaid at the end of the year when the crops were in. The bank actually gave you $90, "discounting" the loan in advance. The $10 differences was "interest.")

The last two concepts, inflation and interest discounting, may be combined by accepting the generalization that the real rate of interest has for many years tended to be about 2% or 3%. Money or nominal interest rates tend to center around the sum of that level plus the rate of inflation. Discounting all future costs and benefits at 2 or 3% (your choice) handles both inflation and present value adjustments on the assumption that future murket interest rates will conform roughly to the long run generalization. But if future costs or benefits (but not both) are fixed in dollars, you have to forecast future inflation in order to decide.

A similar insight occurs with inflation and depreciation. People often argue that you need not consider depreciation on your house, since they actually appreciate. But in any period when things appreciate in value, market interest rates are also higher. The foregone or actual interest plus the depreciation, tend to be constant whether on a house or car. With no inflation, a car costs 25% a year in depreciation plus 2% interest (paid or foregone), while with 10% inflation the depreciation seems to be only 15%, but the interest cost is 12% for the same total of 27%. Of course, you may note that in recent years house prices rose faster than the rate of inflation while interest rate on saving accounts fell far behind the rate of inflation. Now we see interest rates on various types of saving accounts that greatly exceed "inflation plus 3%". Most economists would view both as aberrations from long term trends, neither to be counted on in the future.

Finally, since comparing the present net benefits of alternative choices may involve comparing decisions of different sizes, economists argue for making one final calculation to estimate what is called an "internal rate of return", the discount rate that makes the present net benefit zero. This is seen as the pure rate of return on that investment. Of course it only applies when there are measurable benefits AND costs, not to purchases where only the costs are measurable. But where it is applicable, it provides a pure number that can be compared across alternatives, including holding the funds in a savings account for a time. Unfortunately, its estimation requires an iterative computer program not easily available. (Indeed, my recent scanning of all the computer software designed to aid consumers found very few with a program for this calculation!) For constant single streams of benefits to compare with a present cost, or vice versa, one has a simple mortgage or annuity problem. A few inexpensive hand calculators, such as the Texas Instruments Financial Analyst, will handle that.

This discussion should be sufficient to reveal the complexity of optimal choice as economists define it and the insights required to implement it. Are there rules of thumb which approximate the optimum? My experience is that rules of thumb are dangerous, particularly in a changing world. Formerly people were told that they should never spend more than twice their annual income on a house. Or, that the stock market would protect the investor against inflation. Recent experience has invalidated both of these rules of thumb. I may even be wrong in suggesting that the market interest rate will tend to be the rate of inflation plus 2 - 3%.

Consider another example of the complexity of consumer problems. It seems possible that in shopping for a better bargain people revise their notions on the desirability of further search as they discover how much price variation, relative to quality, seems to exist. If they find wide variations, they are more likely to continue searching. Converting this idea to a computer calculation is extremely difficult. Indeed, no computer program exists for this problem (that I know of). (However, there exists a formula for the expected lower bound of a distribution once you know its variance and the number of price offers so far obtained.)

The above discussion should convince us that it is quite possible that mistakes of cognition in deciding what to buy may cost consumers more in foregone satisfaction or later regret than failures to find the best buy from a given product/market set. Think of the magnitude of the non-optimal decisions that are possible in buying a house or a car or life insurance!!

RESEARCH POSSIBILITIES

What is the best approach to research on cognitive insights and information processing? A first move might be to study consumers' present level of insight and understanding. One could "test" their insights in general, or in the context of illustrative problems. Alternatively, one could concentrate on recent major decisions. One could explore whether people considered (1) the benefits and costs of what they did and (2) some competitive alternatives, instead of simply collecting data on the amount of search.

The discovery of conceptual deficiencies on the part of consumers may be both difficult from a research viewpoint and irritating to respondents. It may also exaggerate the problem. After all, advice from experts may be a fair substitute for "own" expertise. (Consumers should be aware that most "experts" have more to sell than insights or solutions: their advice may be biased by monetary interests or their egos.)

Perhaps people learn faster and better when faced with an "important" problem. Or, perhaps they could learn with a little help. In my view, the research problem of the day is to ascertain how and under what circumstances and with what interactive approaches people are capable of understanding and using the insights of economics. Most important, we want to learn to what extent they are capable of transferring insights from the solution of one problem to a different problem.

Why is it that years of trying to teach consumer economics has not provided answers to these questions? Perhaps, because college students are more interested in getting a grade than in using the insights we convey. Perhaps, because we have not really taught the insights very well. It is true that much of consumer economics has been hortatory: Be careful; Shop well; They are "out to get you!" "They're ought to be a law!" Perhaps, because we have despaired of the ordinary consumer's intellectural capacity and hence have preferred to rely on government protection or competition to save him/her from regrettable decisions. Perhaps also, because the classroom is neither interactive enough, nor individually adaptive enough for such complex learning. And, in the elementary and secondary school, perhaps few teachers have themselves mastered the economic insights.

There exist some computer programs that play economic games at a simple level, challenging you to find the best buy. Lewis Mandel has developed a programmed teaching unit for instructing bank employees how to give financial advice to customers. Perhaps we can push such programs to a higher level of sophistication and flexibility.

I would propose, then, the following research and development program on economic insights. First we need some intensive investigations in which individuals and small groups are introduced via interactive games to economic insights in invented, but relevant and realistic choice situations. We need to record systematically the problems that arise: failure to understand, unwillingness to accept the insight, inability to apply it to the situation, lack of capacity to handle the algebra, focus on non-economic considerations, or even economic considerations whose quantification is difficult or impossible.

Out of this we would hope to develop computer programs that would then be used and developed further with probability samples of ordinary consumers. We could borrow from the technology of computer-assisted telephone interviews in survey research. Here the computer assures that answers to key questions lead to the appropriate subsequent question sequences. For the investigation of economic insights, we are proposing something more complex and sophisticated by an order of magnitude, but something easily handled by the computer. These Socratic dialogues in the guise of interviews would provide nationally descriptive measures of behavior patterns and estimates of people's capabilities for mastering economic insights.

After this, further refinements might lead to computer programs that could be used to teach consumer economics, even where the teacher did not fully understand everything at the beginning. The program would instruct both teacher and students, and would be flexible in adapting to individual preferences, interests, and idiosyncracies.

At worst, such a program would help us answer some questions about the possibilities of educating consumers and hence on the optimal relative emphasis on consumer protection, competition and anti-monopoly activities, and on consumer education as a means for improving the efficiency of a free market system. At best, it might help consumers to deal more effectively with the complex economic problems they face. It may seem easier to teach this in the public schools, but adults need the help now, and may be better motivated to put it to use.

Herbert Simon puts the usefulness of information into perspective:

> "In a world where information is relatively scarce, and where problems for decision are few and simple, information is almost always a positive good. In a world where attention is a major scarce resource, information may be an expensive luxury, diverting our attention from what is important to what is unimportant" [220, p. 13].

Consumers need to know which facts they need and what to do with them.

To begin, we would have to start with games or examples that illustrated one or two principles. My colleague, Dick Nisbett, has run some neat experiments of this sort. One involved a sample of holders of tickets to basketball games, a random half of whom were told all about how "sunk costs" should be ignored. After a one-sided game they were asked whether they left early to save a half-hour wait getting out of the parking lot. (The rationale is that the price of the ticket was a sunk cost. The spectator "gained" nothing by staying through a dull finish, except irritation and wasted time and gas.) Sure enough, more of those recently "educated" left the game early. Randomization neutralized the effects of other differences among them.

It is difficult to identify choice situations where only one or two of our six principles are involved. It would be particularly difficult, were we to rely on respondents' accounts of actual recent decisions. Hence, at least at the pilot stage, we expect to talk about gamelike choices in simplified examples. Here the respondent actually makes "decisions", is then given (stochastic) outcomes, further insights, more information, and then asked to make the next decision. Quantification of the extent of inability or unwillingness to use the data and do the calculations, and of inability to carry the logic and procedure on to the next problem, would occur. But we could also elicit complementary information in the form of proffered explanations for choices actually made. (The latter might need translation, or adjustment for rationalization.) On the other hand, only discussions of actual choices would elicit all the constraints, the non-economic considerations, and the non-measurable semi-economic dimensions that real choices involve.

Recent dramatic changes in interest rates, taxes, asset values, laws and institutions may well make people more receptive both to information and to insights. Under these conditions they may at last notice that seller-provided information is mostly biased by omission, leaving the consumer the critical task of knowing what additional information or insight is required. Serious marketers-- by providing more complex information, such as the internal rate of return on an energy-efficient appliance -- might succeed better in serving both their seller/client and the social interest. Economic insights are crucial, however important other forces may be in people's use of information and in their choices.

CONCLUSION

We can always use more studies of consumer deliberation and search, and of consumers' understanding and use of each relevant fact or principle. But a more comprehensive and dynamic interactive experimental procedure might speed progress, showing why people do <u>not</u> use economic information effectively and how we might improve things. If wise decisions require applying all six of our economic insights, in spite of various constraints and social pressures, then it is not useful to study them one at a time, nor to focus on information-getting to implement them. We must find out how to help consumers do everything right at once. And if we are unwilling to wait for the next generation, we must discover how to help adults when pressing decisions face them.

REFERENCES

1. AKERLOF, G. A. (1984), An Economic Theorist's Book of Tales: Essays That Entertain the Consequences of New Assumptions in Economic Theory. New York and Sydney: Cambridge Univ. Press.

2. _________ (1970), "The Market for "Lemons": Quality, Uncertainty and the Market Mechanism," Quarterly Journal of Economics 84, 488-500.

3. ALBA, JOSEPH W. (1985), "The Learning of Frequency Information and Its Use as a Decision Heuristic," working paper, University of Florida, Gainseville, 1985.

4. ALBA, JOSEPH W. (1983), "The Effects of Product Knowledge on the Comprehension, Retention, and Evaluation of Product Information," in Richard P. Bagozzi and Alice M. Tybout, eds., Advances in Consumer Research, Volume X, Chicago: Association for Consumer Research, 577-580.

5. ALBA, JOSEPH W. and HUTCHINSON, J. WESLEY. "A Framework for Understanding Consumer Knowledge," working paper, University of Florida, Gainesville.

6. ALBA, JOSEPH; CHROMIAK, WALTER; HASHER, LYNN and ATTIG, MARY S. (1980), "Automatic Encoding of Category Size Information," Journal of Experimental Psychology: Human Learning and Memory, 6 (July): 370-378.

7. ANDERSON, JOHN R. (1983), The Architecture of Cognition, Cambridge, MA, Harvard University Press.

8. ANDERSON, NORMAN H. (1981), Foundations of Information Integration Theory, New York: Academic Press.

9. ARNDT, JOHAN (1967), "Word of Mouth Advertising and Information Communication," in Risk Taking and Information Handling in Consumer Behavior, ed. Donald F. Cox, Boston: Harvard University Press, 188-239.

10. ASAM, EDWARD H. and BUCKLIN, LOUIS P. (1973), "Nutrition Labeling for Canned Goods: A Study of Consumer Response," Journal of Marketing. 37 (April): 32-37.

11. ATKINSON, RICHARD C. and J.F. JUOLA (1974), "Search and Decision Processes in Recognition Memory," in Contemporary Developments in Mathematical Psychology, eds. D.H. Krantz, R.C. Atkinson, R.D. Luce and P. Suppes, 1, San Francisco, 242-293.

12. AXELL, B. (1977), "Search Market Equilibrium," Scandinavian Journal of Economics, 79, 32-37.

13. BARLOW, ROBIN, BRAZER HARVEY E. and MORGAN, JAMES N. (1966), Economic Behavior of the Affluent, Washington D.C.; Brookings.

14. BEACH, LEE ROY and TERRENCE R. MITCHELL (1978), "A Contingency Model for the Selection of Decision Strategies," Academy of Management Review, 3 (July): 439-449.

15. BEALES, HOWARD; CRASWELL, RICHARD and SALOP, STEVEN (1981), "The Efficient Regulation of Consumer Information," Journal of Law and Economics 24 (December): 491-539.

16. BEALES, HOWARD; MAZIS, MICHAEL; SALOP, STEVEN and STAELIN, RICHARD (1981), "Consumer Search and Public Policy," Journal of Consumer Research 8 (June): 11-22.

17. BENHABIB, J. and BULL, C. (1983), "Job Search: The Choice of Intensity," Journal of Political Economy, 91, 747-764.

18. BENNETT, PETER D. and MANDELL, ROBERT M. (1969), "Prepurchase Information Seeking Behavior of New Car Purchasers - The Learning Hypothesis," Journal of Marketing Research, 6 (November): 430-433.

19. BERNING, CAROL; KOHN, A. and JACOBY, JACOB (1974), "Patterns of Information Acquisition in New Product Purchases," Journal of Consumer Research, 1 (September): 18-22.

20. BETTMAN, JAMES R. and PARK, C. WHAN (1980), "Effects of Prior Knowledge and Experience and Phase of the Choice Process on Consumer Decision Processes: A Protocol Analysis," Journal of Consumer Research, 7 (December): 234-248.

21. BETTMAN, JAMES R. (1979), An Information Processing Theory of Consumer Choice, Reading, Mass.: Addison-Wesley Publishing Company.

22. BETTMAN, JAMES R. and KAKKAR, PRADEEP (1977), "Effects of Information Presentation Format on Consumer Information Acquisition Strategies," Journal of Consumer Research, 3, 233-240.

23. BETTMAN, JAMES R. (1970), "Information Processing Models of Consumer Behavior," Journal of Marketing Research, 7, 370-76.

24. BIEHAL, GABRIEL and CHAKRAVARTI, DIPANKAR (1986), "Consumers' Use of Memory and External Information in Choice: Macro and Micro Perspectives," Journal of Consumer Research, 12 (March): 382-405.

25. BRANDT, W.K. and DAY, G.S. (1971), "Decision Process for Major Durables: An Empirical View," American Marketing Association Conference Proceedings, 381-385.

26. BRAVERMAN, A. (1980), "Consumer Search and Alternative Market Equilibria, Review of Economic Studies 47, 487-502.

27. BROOKER, GEORGE; WHEATLEY, JOHN J. and CHIU, JOHN S.Y. (1985), "The Effects of Sampling and Information on Brand Choice When Beliefs in Quality Differences are Ambiguous," given at ACR meeting Oct. 1985.

28. BRUCKS, MERRIE (1986), "A Typology of Consumer Knowledge Content," to appear in Advances in Consumer Research, Vol. XIII, Richard J. Lutz, ed., 1986.

29. BRUCKS, MERRIE (1985), "The Effects of Product Class Knowledge on Information Search Behavior," Journal of Consumer Research, 12 (June): 1-16.

30. _________ (1984), "The Effects of Product Class Knowledge on Information Search Behavior," Journal of Consumer Research, 12 (June): 1-16.

31. BRUCKS, MERRIE; MITCHELL, ANDREW A. and STAELIN, RICHARD (1948), "The Effect of Nutritional Information Disclosure in Advertising: An Information Processing Approach," Journal of Public Policy and Marketing, 3, 1-25.

32. BUCKLIN, LOUIS, P. (1966), "Testing Propensities to Shop," Journal of Marketing, 30, 22-27.

33. BURDETT, KENNETH and MALUEG, DAVID A. (1966), "The Theory of Search for Several Goods," Journal of Economic Theory, 24 (June): 362-376.

34. BURNS, A. C. and GRANBOIS, D.H. (1979), "Advancing the Study of Family Purchase Decision Making," Advances in Consumer Research, 6, 221-226.

35. BURNS, A. C. (1977), "Husband and Wife Purchase Decision Making Roles: Agreed, Presumed, Conceded, and Disputed," Advances in Consumer Research, 4, 50-55.

36. BURNS, ALVIN C. and HOPPER, JO ANNE (1986), "An Analysis of the Presence, Stability, and Antecedents of Husband and Wife Purchase Decision Making Influence Assessment Agreement and Disagreement."

37. CAPON, NOEL and DAVIS ROGIN (1984), "Basic Cognitive Ability Measures As Predictors of Consumer Information Processing Strategies," Journal of Consumer Research, (June): 551-567.

38. ________ and KUHN, DEANNA (1982), "Can Consumers Calculate Best Buys?" Journal of Consumer Research, 8 (March): 449-453.

39. CARLSON, JOHN A. and GIESEKE, ROBERT J. (1984), "Price Search in a Product Market," Journal of Economic Theory, 32, 337-345.

40. CARLSON, JOHN A. and GIESEKE, ROBERT J. (1983), "Price Search in a Product Market," Journal of Consumer Research, 9 (March): 357-365.

41. CARLSON, JOHN A. and MCAFEE, R. PRESTON (1984), "Joint Search for Several Goods," Journal of Economic Theory, 32, 337-345.

42. CELEC, STEPHEN E. (1981), "Is the Truth in Lending Being Told with the Annual Percentage Rate as the Measure of the Cost of Credit?" Journal of Consumer Affairs, 15 (Summer): 128-135.

43. CHAIKEN, SHELLEY E. (1980), "Heuristic Versus Systematic Information Processing and the Use of Source Versus Message Cues in Persuasion," Journal of Personality and Social Psychology, 39 (no. 5): 752-766.

44. CHESTNUT, ROBERT W. and JACOBY, JACOB (1977), "Consumer Information Processing: Emerging Theory and Findings," in A.G. Woodside, J.N. Sheth and P.D. Bennett, eds. Consumer and Industrial Buying Behavior, New York: Elsevier North Holland.

45. CHIESI, H., SPILICH, G. and VOSS, J.T. (1979), "Acquisition of Domain Related Information in Relation to High and Low Domain Knowledge," Journal of Verbal Learning and Verbal Behavior, 18, 257-273.

46. CHRISTENSEN-SZALANSKI, JAY J. J. (1980), "A Further Examination of the Selection of Problem-Solving Strategies: The Effects of Deadlines and Analytic Aptitudes," Organizational Behavior and Human Performance, 25 (February): 107-122.

47. CLARKE, YVONNE and GEOFFREY N. SOUTAR (1982), "Consumer Acquisition Patterns for Durable Goods: Australian Evidence," Journal of Consumer Research, 8 (March): 456-460.

48. CLAXTON, JOHN D., FRY, JOSEPH N. and PORTIS, BERNARD (1974), "A Taxonomy of Prepurchase Information Gathering Patterns," Journal of Consumer Research, 1 (December): 35-42.

49. CONOVER, JERRY N. (1985), "The Accuracy of Price Knowledge: Issues in Research Methodology," paper presented at annual conference of the Association for Consumer Research, Las Vegas, Nev., October.

50. COX, ANTHONY, GRANBOIS, DONALD and SUMMERS, JOHN (1983), "Planning, Search, Certainty and Satisfaction among Durable Buyers: A Longitudinal Study," in Richard P. Bagozzi and Alice M. Tybout, (eds.), Advances in Consumer Research, Vol. X, The Association for Consumer Research, 394-399.

51. COX, DONALD F. (1962), "The Measurement of Information Value: A Study of Consumer Decision Making," in Proceedings, Winter Conference, Chicago: American Marketing Association, 413-21.

52. ________ (1972), (Ed.) Risk Taking and Information Handling in Consumer Behavior, Harvard Business School, Division of Research.

53. COURVILLE, L. and HAUSMAN, W.I (1979), "Warranty Scope and Reliability Under Imperfect Information and Alternative Market Structures," Journal of Business, 361.

54. CRAIK, F. I. M. and R. S. LOCKHART (1972), "Levels of Processing: A Framework for Memory Research," Journal of Verbal Learning and Verbal Behavior, II, 671-684.

55. DARDIS, RACHEL (1980), "The Economics of Consumer Product Information," Washington, D.C.: National Bureau of Standards.

56. DASH, J.F., SCHIFFMAN, L.G. and BERENSON, C. (1976), "Information Search and Store Choice," Journal of Advertising Research, 16, 35-40.

57. DAVIS, HARRY (1976), "Decision Making Within the Household," Journal of Consumer Research, 2 (March): 241-260.

58. DAVIS, H. L. and RIGAUX, B. P. (1974), "Perceptions of Marital Roles in Decision Processes," Journal of Consumer Research, 1 (2): 51-62.

59. DAY, GEORGE S. and TERRY DEUTSCHER (1982), "Attitudinal Predictions of Choices of Major Appliance Brands," Journal of Marketing Research, 19 (May): 192-198.

60. DAY, RALPH L. and LANDON, E. LAIRD (1977), "Toward a Theory of Consumer Complaining Behavior," in Woodside, Sheck and Bennett, eds., Consumer and Industrial Buying Behavior, Elsevier North Holland, NY.

61. DHOLAKIA, R. and STERNTHAL, B. (1977), "Highly Credible Sources: Persuasive Facilitators or Persuasive Liabilities?" Journal of Consumer Research, 3, 223-232.

62. DICKERSON, MARY D. and GENTRY, JAMES W. (1983), "Characteristics of Adopters and Non-Adopters of Home Computers," Journal of Consumer Research, 10 (September): 225-235.

63. DICKSON, PETER R. and SAWYER, A.G. (1986), "Price Perceptions of Supermarket Shoppers at the Point of Purchase," Advances in Consumer Research, R. Lutz (ed.) Vol. 13.

64. DICKSON, PETER R. and WILKIE, WILLIAM L. (1979), The Consumption of Household Durables: A Behavioral Review, Cambridge, Mass., Marketing Science Institute.

65. DICKSON, PETER R.; ROBERT F. LUSCH and WILLIAM L. WILKIE (1983), "Consumer Acquisition Priorities for Home Appliances: A Replication and Re-Evaluation," Journal of Consumer Research, 9, (March): 432-435.

66. DIONNE, GEORGES (1984), "Search and Insurance," International Economic Review, 25 (June): 357-367.

67. DOMMERMUTH, WILLIAM P. (1965), "The Shopping Matrix and Marketing Strategy," Journal of Marketing Research, 2 (May): 129-132.

68. DUESENBERRY, JAMES (1960), "Comment," in Demographic and Economic Change in Developed Countries (NBER), Princeton, NJ.: Princeton U Press.

69. DUNCAN, CALVIN. P. and OLSHAVSKY, RICHARD W. (1982), "External Search: The Role of Consumer Beliefs," Journal of Marketing Research, 19 (February): 32-43.

70. DUNCAN GREG J. (1981), "The Dynamics of Local Markets: A Case Study of Cameras," Journal of Consumer Affairs, 15 (Summer): 64-74.

71. DUNCAN, G. J., MITCHELL, O.S. and MORGAN, J. N. (1984), "A Framework for Setting Retirement Savings Goals," Journal of Consumer Affairs, 18, 22-46.

72. EBBESON, E., AND KONECNI, V. (1980), "On the External Validity of Decision Making Research: What Do We Know About Decisions in the Real World?" in Cognitive Processes in Choice and Decision Behavior, T. Wallsten (ed.), Hillsdale, N.J.: Erlbaum.

73. EDELL, JULIE A. and STAELIN, RICHARD (1983), "The Information Processing of Pictures in Print Advertising," Journal of Consumer Research, 10 (June): 45-61.

74. EINHORN;, H. J. and R. M. HOGARTH (1981), "Behavioral Decision Theory: Processes of Judgment and Choice." Annual Review of Psychology, 32, 53-88.

75. ETTENSON, RICHARD; and WAGNER, JANET (1986 forthcoming), "Retail Buyers; Saleability Judgments: a Comparison of Information Use Across Three Levels of Experience," Journal of Retailing.

76. FISKE, SUSAN T.; KINDER, DONALD R. and LARTER, W. MICHAEL (1983), "The Novice and the Expert: Knowledge Based Strategies in Political Cognition," Journal of Experimental and Social Psychology, 19, 381-400.

77. FONG, G. T., KRANTZ, D. H., and NISBETT, R. E. (1986), "The Effects of Statistical Training on Thinking About Everyday Problems," Cognitive Psychology, 18, 253-292.

78. FONG, G. T., and NISBETT, R. E. (1986), "Delayed Domain-Specificity Effects in Teaching Statistical Heuristics," Manuscript in preparation, Northwestern University.

79. FOX, KAREN, and KOTLER, PHILLIP (1980), "The Marketing of Social Causes: The First 10 Years," Journal of Marketing, 44 (Fall): 24-33.

80. FRAISSE, PAUL (1984), "Perception and Estimation of Time," Annual Review of Psychology, 35, 1-36.

81. FRIED, L.S., and HOLYOAK, K. J. (1984), "Induction of Category Distributions: A framwork for Classification Learning," Journal of Experimental Psychology: Learning, Memory, and Cognition, 10, 234-257.

82. FROST, FREDERICK A. (1985), "The Role of Standards Authorities in Consumer Decision Making in Western Australia," Historical Perspective in Consumer Research: National and International Perspectives; Proceeding of the Association for Consumer Research International Meeting in Singapore, Western Australian Institute of Technology.

83. FURSE, DAVID H.; PUNJ, GIRISH N. and STEWART, DAVID W. (1984), "A Typology of Individual Search Strategies Among Purchasers of New Automobiles," Journal of Consumer Research, 10, 417-431.

84. GAETH, GARY J. and COLE, CATHERINE A. (1985), "Experience as a Mediator in Recall and Use of Information in Consumer Decision Processes," Preliminary draft of a presentation for Advances in Consumer Research Conference, October.

85. GAETH, GARY J. and SHANTEAU, J. (1984), "Reducing the Influence of Irrelevant Information on Experienced Decision Makers," Organizational Behavior and Human Performance, 33, 263-282.

86. ________ (1984), "Training Expert Makers to Ignore Irrelevant Information." Organizational Behavior and Human Performance, 33, 263-292.

87. GAL, S., LANDSBERGER, N. and LEVYKSON, B. (1981) "A Compound Strategy for Search in the Labour Market," International Economic Review, 22, 597-608.

88. GATIGNON, HUBERT and ROBERTSON, THOMAS S. (1985), "A Propositional Inventory for New Diffusion Research," Journal of Consumer Research, 11, (March): 849-887.

89. GELLER, WALTER H. (1974), "What Shoppers Know--and Don't Know--About Prices," Progressive Grocer, (November): 39-41.

90. GERSTNER, EITAN (1985), "Do Higher Prices Signal Higher Quality." Journal of Marketing Research, 2l (May): 209-215.

91. GRANBOIS, D. H. (1976), "Shopping Behavior and Preferences," Chapter 13 in Selected Aspects of Consumer Behavior, Prepared for the National Science Foundation, Washington, DC: U.S. Government Printing Office.

92. GRANBOIS, DONALD H. and BRADEN, PATRICIA L. (1970), "Good Consumership in Household Appliance Purchasing," Journal of Business Research, 4 103-116.

93. GRANBOIS, D. H. and WILLETT, P. R. (1970), "Equivalence of Family Role Measures Based on Husband and Wife Data," Journal of Marriage and the Family, 32, 68-72.

94. GREENWALD, A.G. (1968), "Cognitive Learning, Cognitive Response to Persuasion, and Attitude Change," in (eds.) A.G. Greenwald, T.C. Brock, and T.M. Ostrom, Psychological Foundations of Attitudes," Academic Press.

95. GRETHER, DAVID M. (1980), "Bayes Rule as a Descriptive Model: The Representativeness Heuristics," Quarterly Journal of Economics, 95:537-558.

96. GROSSBARD-SHECHTMAN, AMYRA (1984), "A Theory of Allocation of Time in Markets for Labor and Marriage," The Economic Journal, 94 (December): 863-882.

97. GROSSMAN, S. (1981), "The Informational Role of Warranties and Private Disclosure About Product Quality," Journal of Law and Economics, (December): 461.

98. HAGERTY, MICHAEL and AAKER, DAVID (1984), "A Normative Model of Consumer Information Processing," Marketing Science, 3, 227-246.

99. HANSEN, F. (1972), Consumer Choice Behavior: A Cognitive Theory, New York, NY: The Free Press.

100. HARMON, R. and CONEY, H. (1982), "The Persuasive Effects of Source Credibility in Buy and Lease Situations," Journal of Marketing Research, 19, 255-260.

101. HAYES-ROTH, BARBARA (1977), "Evolution of Cognitive Structures and Processes," Psychological Review, 84, 260-278.

102. HEBDEN, J.J., and J.F. PICKERING (1974), "Patterns of Acquisition of Consumer Durables," Oxford Bulletin of Economics and Statistics, 36, No. 2 (May): 67-94.

103. HEER, D. M. (1962), "Husband and Wife Perceptions of Family Power Structure," Marriage and Family Living, 24, 65-67.

104. HENDRICK, C. and SHAFFER, D. (1974), "The Effects of Arousal and Credibility on Learning and Persuasion," Psychometric Science, 20, 241-243.

105. HESS, J. (1982), "Risk and the Gain from Information," Journal of Economic Theory, 15, 231-238.

106. HINTZMAN, DOUGLAS L.; NOZAWA, GEORGIE and IRMSCHER, MARK (1982), "Frequency as a Nonpropropositional Attribute of Memory," Journal of Verbal Learning and Verbal Behavior, 21 (April): 127-14.

107. HOLBROOK, MORRIS B. (1978), "Beyond Attitude Structure: Toward the Informational Determinants of Attitude," Journal of Marketing Research, 15, 546-556.

108. HOVLAND, C. and MANDELL, W. (1952), "An Experimental Comparison of Conclusion-Drawing by the Communicator and by the Audience," Journal of Abnormal and Social Psychology, 47, 581-588.

109. HOVLAND, C. and WEISS, W. (1959), "The Influence of Source Credibility on Communication Effectiveness," Public Opinion Quarterly, 15, 635-650.

110. HUBERT, HENRI and MAUSS, MARCEL (1964), Sacrifice; Its Nature and Function, Chicago: Univerity of Chicago Press.

111. JACOBY, JACOB (1984), "Perspectives on Information Overload," Journal of Consumer Research, 10 (March): 432-435.

112. JACOBY, JACOB; SPELLER, DONALD E. and KOHN, CAROL A. (1974), "Brand Choice Behaviors as a Function of Information Load," Journal of Marketing Research, 11, 63-69.

113. ________ (1974), "Brand Choice Behaviors as A Function of Information Load: Replication and Extension," Journal of Consumer Research, 1 33-42.

114. JACOBY, JACOB and OLSON, J. C. (1977), "Consumer Response to Price: An Attitudinal, Information-Processing Perspective," in Moving Ahead with Attitude Research, Y. Wind and M. Greenberg (eds.), Chicago: American Marketing Association.

115. JACOBY, JACOB; SZYBILLO, GEORGE and SCHACK, JACQUILINE B. (1977), "Information Acquisition Behavior in Brand Choice Situations," Journal of Consumer Research, 3, 209-216.

116. JEPSON, C., KRANTZ, D. H. and NISBETT, R. E. (1983), "Inductive Reasoning: Competence or Skill?" Behavioral and Brain Sciences, 6, 494-501.

117. JOHNSON, MICHAEL D. (1984), "Consumer Choice Strategies for Comparing Noncomparable Alternatives," Journal of Consumer Research, 11 (December):41-753.

118. JOHNSON, ERIC J. and RUSSO, J. EDWARD (1984), "Product Familiarity and Learning New Information," Journal of Consumer Research, 11 (June): 542-550.

119. JOHNSON, H.; TORCIVIA, J. and POPRICK, M. (1968), "Effects of Source Credibility on the Relationship between Authoritarianism and Attitude Change," Journal of Personality and Social Psychology, 9, 179-183.

120. KAHNEMAN, D. and TVERSKY, A. (1981), "The Framing of Decisions and the Psychology of Choice," Science, 211, 453-458.

121. ________ (1979), "Prospect Theory: An Analysis of Decision Under Risk," Econometrica, 47, 263-291.

122. ________ (1973), "On the Psychology of Prediction," Psychological Review, 80, 237-251.

123. ________ (1972), "Subjective Probability: A Judgment of Representativeness," Cognitve Psychology, 3, 430-454.

124. KATONA, GEORGE and MUELLER, EVA (1954), "A Study of Purchasing Decisions," in The Dynamics of Consumer Reaction. Consumer Behavior, Vol 1, Lincoln Clark, (ed.) New York, NY: New York University Press.

125. KIEL, GOEFFREY C. and LAYTON, ROGER A. (1981), "Dimensions of Consumer Information Seeking Behavior," Journal of Marketing Research, 18 233-239.

126. KOHN, MEYER and SHAVELL, STEVEN (1974), "The Theory of Search," Journal of Economic Theory, 9, 93-123.

127. KREBS, DENNIS (1970), "Altruism: An Examination of the Concept and a Review of the Literature," Psychological Bulletin, 73 (April): 258-302.

128. KUNDA, Z. and NISBETT, R. E. (1986, in press), "The Psychometrics of Everyday Life." Cognitive Psychology.

129. LAMBERT, Z.V. (1963), "Price and Choice Behavior," 9 (October): 229-239.

130. LEEDS, RUTH (1963), "Altruism and the Form of Giving???," Merrill-Palmer Quarterly 9 (October): 229-239.

131. LEHMANN, DONALD R. and MOORE, WILLIAM L. (1980), "Validation of Information Display Boards: An Assessment Using Longitudinal Data," Journal of Marketing Research, 17 (November): 450-459.

132. LIPPMAN, STEVEN A. and MCCALL, JOHN J. (1976), "Job Search in a Dynamic Economy," Journal of Economic Theory, 12, 365-290.

133. LUSSIER, DENIS and OLSHAVSKY, RICHARD W. (1979), "Task Complexity and Contingent Processing in Brand Choice," Journal of Consumer Research, 6, 154-165.

134. MACMINN, R. (1980), "Job Search and the Labour Dropout Problem Reconsidered," Quarterly Journal of Economics, 95, 69-87.

135. MALHOTRA, NARESH K., "Information Load and Consumer Decision Making," Journal of Consumer Research, 8 (March): 419-430.

136. MANNING, R. and MORGAN, P. (1982), "Search and Consumer Theory," Review of Economic Studies, 49, 203-216.

137. MANSER, MARILYN and BROWN, MURRAY (1980), "Marriage and Household Decision-Making: a Bargaining Analysis," International Economic Review, 21 (Feb.): 31-44.

138. MARVEL, HOWARD P. (1976), "The Economics of Information and Retail Gasoline Price Behavior: An Empirical Analysis," Journal of Political Economy, 84, 1033-1060.

139. MASSY, WILLIAM F.; FRANK, RONALD E. and LODAHL, THOMAS (1968), Purchasing Behavior and Personal Attributes, Philadelphia: University of Pennsylvania Press.

140. MAYER, ROBERT N. (1986), Videotext in France: The Other Foreign Revolution, Division of Social Science Research, University of Utah, Working Paper #86-5.

141. MAYNES, E. SCOTT, (1982), Prestel In Use: A Consumer View, London: National Consumer Council.

142. ________ and ASSUM, TERJE (1982), "Informational Imperfect Consumer Markets: Empirical Findings and Policy Implications," Journal of Consumer Affairs, 16 (Summer): 62-87.

143. MCAFEE, P. (1984), "Risk, Income, Search and Price Stabilization," Research Report 8402, Department of Economics, University of Western Ontario.

144. MCCALL, J.J. (1970), "Economics of Information and Job Search," Quarterly Journal of Economics, 84, 113-116.

145. MCELROY, MARJORIE and HORNEY, MARY J. (1981), "Nash-Bargained Household Decisions: Toward a Generalization of the Theory of Demand," International Economic Review, 22 (June): 333-349.

146. MCMILLAN, J. and MORGAN, P. (1983). "Price Dispersion, Price Flexibility and Consumer Search," Research Report 8303, Department of Economics, University of Western Ontario.

147. MCGINNES, E. and WARD, C. (1980), "Better Liked than Right Trustworthiness and Expertise in Credibility," Personality and Social Psychology Bulletin, 6, 467-472.

148. MEYER, ROBERT J. (1982), "A Descriptive Model of Consumer Information Search Behavior," Marketing Science, 1, 41-61.

149. MILLER, G. and BASEHART, J. (1969), "Source Trustworthiness, Opinionated Statements and Response to Persuasive Communication," Speech Monographs, 36, 1-7.

150. MONROE, KENT B. (1976), "The Influence of Price Differences and Brand Familiarity on Brand Preferences," Journal of Consumer Research, 3, 42-49.

151. MOORE, WILLIAM L. and LEHMANN, DONALD R. (1980), "Individual Differences in Search Behavior for a Nondurable," Journal of Consumer Research 7, 296-307.

152. MORGAN, J. (1986), "Research on Choices with Alternatives, Related Choices, Related Choosers, and Use of Economic Insights: in Handbook of Behavioral Economics, Kaish and Gilad, eds. JAI Press, Greenwich, Conn.

153. MORGAN, J. (1980), "A Realistic Economics of the Consumer Requires Some Psychology," In Essays on Behavioral Economics, by G. Katona, Institute for Social Research, University of Michigan, Ann Arbor, MI.

154. MORGAN, J. and DUNCAN, G. (1981), The Economics of Personal Choice. Ann Arbor: University of Michigan Press.

155. MORGAN, PETER G. (1985), "Distributions of the Duration and Value of Job Search with Learning," Econometrica, 52 (September): 1199-1232.

156. MORGAN, PETER and MANNING, R.(1985), "Optimal Search," Econometrica, 53, 923-944.

157. MORGAN, PETER (1985), "Search and Optimal Sample Sizes," Review of Economic Studies, 50, 659-675.

158. NELSON, PHILLIP (1970), "Information and Consumer Behavior," Journal of Political Economy, 78, 311-329.

159. NEWELL, ALLEN and SIMON, HERBERT A. (1972), Human Problem Solving, New Jersey: Prentice Hall.

160. NEWMAN, JOSEPH (1975), "Consumer External Search: Amount and Determinants," in Arch G. Woodside, Jagdish W. Sheth and Peter D. Bennett, (eds.), Consumer and Industrial Buying Behavior, Amsterdam: North Holland 79-94.

161. NEWMAN, JOSEPH and LOCKERMAN, BRADLEY D. (1975), "Measuring Prepurchase Information Seeking," Journal of Consumer Research, 2, 216-222.

162. NEWMAN, JOSEPH W. and STAELIN, RICHARD (1973), "Information Sources of Durable Goods," Journal of Advertising Research, 13, 19-29.

163. NEWMAN, JOSEPH and STAELIN, RICHARD (1972), "Prepurchase Information Seeking for New Cars and Major Household Appliances," Journal of Marketing Research, 9 (August): 249-257.

164. NISBETT, RICHARD E. and WILSON, TIMOTHY D. (1977), "Telling More Than We Can Know: Verbal Reports on Mental Processes," Psychological Review, 84:3 (May): 231-259.

165. NISBETT, R. E. and BORGIDA, E. (1975), "Attribution and the Psychology of Prediction," Journal of Personality and Social Psychology, 32, 932-943.

166. NISBETT, R. E., KRANTZ, D. H., JEPSON, D. and KUNDA, Z. (1983), "The Use of Statistical Heuristics in Everyday Inductive Reasoning," Psychological Review, 90, 339-363.

167. NISBETT, R. E. and KUNDA, Z. (1985), "Perception of Social Distributions," Journal of Personality and Social Psychology, 48, 297-311.

168. NISBETT, R. E. and ROSS, L. (1980), Human Inference: Strategies and Shortcomings of Social Judgment. Englewood Cliffs, NJ: Prentice-Hall.

169. OBERMILLER, C. and WHEATLEY, J.J. (1985), "Beliefs in Quality Differences and Brand Choice," Advances in Consumer Research, 12, 75-78.

170. OLSHAVSKY, RICHARD W. and GRANBOIS, DONALD H. (1979), "Consumer Decision Making-Fact or Fiction?" Journal of Consumer Research, 6 (September): 93-100.

171. OLSHAVSKY, RICHARD W. and ROSEN, DENNIS L. (1985), "Use of Product-Testing Organizations' Recommendations as a Strategy for Choice Simplifications," Journal of Consumer Affairs, 19 (Summer): 118-139.

172. OLSON, JERRY C. (1980), "Implications of an Information Processing Approach to Pricing Research," in C.W. Lamb and P. Dunne (Eds.), Theoretical Developments in Marketing, Chicago: American Marketing Association, 13-16.

173. ________ (1977), "Price as an Information Cue: Effects on Product Evaluations," in Arch G. Woodside, Jagdish N. Sheth and Peter D. Bennett (Eds.), Consumer and Industrial Buying Behaviors, New York: North-Holland, 267-286.

174. OLSON, JERRY G. and JACOBY, JACOB (1972), "Cue Utilization in the Quality Perception Process," in M. Venkatesan (ed.), Proceedings of the Third Annual Conference, Iowa City: Association for Consumer Research, 167-179.

175. PAINTON, SCOTT and GENTRY, JAMES W. (1985), "Another Look at the Impact of Information Presentation Forms," Journal of Consumer Research, 12 (September): 240-244.

176. PARK, C. WHAN (1982), "Joint Decisions in Home Purchasing; A Muddling-Through Process," Journal of Consumer Research, 9 (September): 151-162.

177. PARK C. WHAN and LESSIG, V. (1981), "Familiarity and Its Impact on Consumer Decision Biases and Heuristics," Journal of Consumer Research, 8, 223-230.

178. PAYNE, JOHN W., BRAUNSTEIN; MYRON L. and CARROL, JOHN S. (1978), "Exploring Predecisional Behaviors: An Alternative Approach to Decision Research," Organizational Behavior and Human Performance, 22, 17-44.

179. PAYNE, JOHN W. (1975), "Task Complexity and Contingent Processing in Decision Making: An Information Search and Protocol Analysis," Organizational Behavior and Human Performance, 6, 366-387.

180. ________ (1982), "Contingent Decision Behaviors," Psychological Bulletin, 92, 382-402.

181. POLLAK, ROBERT A. (1985), "A Transaction Cost Approach to Families and Households," Journal of Economic Literature, 23 (June): 581-608.

182. PUNJ, GIRISH N. and STAELIN, RICHARD (1983), "A Model of Consumer Information Search Behavior for New Automobiles," Journal of Consumer Research, 9 (March): 336-380.

183. ________ (1980), "A Model of Consumer Search Among Stores and Brands," Working Paper #574, State University of New York at Buffalo 1983.

184. ________, "The Value of Information for Selected Appliances," Journal of Marketing Research, 17, 14-25.

185. PUNJ, GIRISH N. and DAVID W. STEWART (1983), "An Interaction Framework of Consumer Decision Making," Journal of Consumer Research, 10 (September):181-196.

186. RATCHFORD, BRIAN T. (1982), "Cost-Benefit Models for Explaining Consumer Choice and Information Seeking Behavior," Management Science, 18, 197-212.

187. RATCHFORD, BRIAN T. and VAN RAAIJ, W. FRED (1980), "The Relation Between Information Acquisition Strategy and Monetary Losses Due to Incorrect Choices," in Richard P. Bagozzi, et al, eds., Marketing in the 80's: Challenges and Changes, Chicago: American Marketing Association, 168-171.

188. RATCHFORD, BRIAN T. and AGARWAL, MANOJ K. (1979), "The Value of Information on Automobile Characteristics" in Neil Beckwith, et al., eds., 1979 Educations' Conference Proceedings, Chicago: American Marketing Association, 200-204.

189. REINGANUM, J. (1979), "A Simple Model of Equilibrium Price Dispersion," Journal of Political Economy, 87, 851-858.

190. ________ (1983), "Nash Equilibrium Search for the Best Alternative," Journal of Economic Theory, 30, 139-152.

191. RILEY, JOHN G. (1985), "Competition with Hidden Knowledge," Journal of Political Economy, 93, 958-976.

192. ROGERS, EVERETT M. (1983), Diffusion of Innovations, 3rd Edition, New York: Free Press.

193. RIVAS, JAVIER ALONSO; ROCHE, I.C. and MUGICA, J.M. (1985), "General Consumer Behaviour and Research in Spain: Past, Present and Future," Historical Perspective in Consumer Research: National and International Perspectives; Proceedings of the Association for Consumer Research International Meeting in Singapore.

194. ROSENFIELD, D. and SHAPIRO, R. (1981). "Optimal Adaptive Price Search," Journal of Economic Theory, 25, 1-20.

195. ROSS, L. (1977), "The Intuitive Psychologist and His Shortcomings," In L. Berkowitz (Ed.) Advances in Experimental Social Psychology 10, New York: Academic Press.

196. ROTHSCHILD, M. (1974). "Searching for the Lowest Price When the Distribution of Prices is Unknown," Journal of Political Economy, 82, 689-711.

197. ROTHE, J.T. and LAMONT, L.M. (1973), "Purchase Behavior and Brand Choice Determinants for National and Private Brand Major Appliances," Journal of Retailing, 49, 19-33.

198. RUSSO, J. EDWARD (1974), "More Information is Better: A Reevaluation of Jacoby, Speller and Kohn," Journal of Consumer Research, 1, 68-73.

199. RUSSO, J. EDWARD, KRIESER, GENE and MIJASHITA, SALLY (1975) "An Effective Display of Unit Price Information," Journal of Marketing, 39, 11-19.

200. RUSSO, J. EDWARD and JOHNSON, E. (1980), "What Do Consumers Know About Familiar Products?" in Jerry C. Olson (Ed), Advances in Consumer Research, 7, Ann Arbor: Association for consumer Research, 417-423.

201. RYANS, ADRIAN B. and WEINBERG, CHARLES B. (1978), "Consumer Dynamics in Nonprofit Organizations," Journal of Consumer Research, 5, 89-95.

202. SADANAND, A. and WILDE, L. (1982), "A Generalized Model of Pricing for Homogeneous Goods Under Imperfect Information," Review of Economic Studies, 49, 229-240.

203. SALOP, S. (1973), "Systematic Job Search and Unemployment," Review of Economic Studies, 40, 191-201.

204. SATTERTHWAITE, M. (1979), "Consumer Information, Equilibrium Industry Price, and the Number of Sellers," Bell Journal of Economics, 1979.

205. SCHANINGER, CHARLES M. and SCIGLIMPAGLIA, DONALD (1981), "The Influence of Cognitive Personality Traits and Demographics on Consumer Information Acquisition," Journal of Consumer Research, 8, 208-216.

206. SCHOTTER, ANDREW and BRAUNSTEIN, YALE M. (1981), "Economic Search: An Experimental Study," Economic Inquiry. 19, 1-25.

207. SCHWARTZ, A. and WILDE, L. (1982), "Imperfect Information, Monopolistic Competition, and Public Policy," American Economic Review, 72, 18-23.

208. SCHWARTZ, BARRY, (1967), "The Social Psychology of the Gift," The American Journal of Sociology, 73, 1-11.

209. SCHULMAN, G. and WORRALL, C., (1970), "Salience Patterns, Source Credibility, and the Sleeper Effect, Opinion Quarterly, 34, 371-382.

210. SCHURR, PAUL H. (1985), "Role, Situation, and Information Effects On Organizational Buyers and Sellers," Working Paper, SUNY Albany.

211. SHAPIRO, BENSON P., (1973), "Marketing for Nonprofit Organizations," Harvard Business Review, 123-132.

212. SHELUGA, DAVID A., JACCARD, JAMES and JACOBY, JACOB (1979), "Preference, Search and Choice: An Integrative Approach," Journal of Consumer Research, 6, 166-176.

213. SCHOEMAKER, ROBERT W. and SHOAF, ROBERT F. (1975) "Behavioral Changes in the Trial of New Products," Journal of Consumer Research, 2, 104-109.

214. SHERRY, JOHN F., JR. (1985), "The Cultural Perspective in Consumer Research", Prepared for the 1985 Annual Conference of the Association for Consumer Research. Las Vegas, Nevada.

215. ________ (1983), "Gift-Giving in Anthropological Perspective," Journal of Consumer Research, 10, 157-168.

216. SHERMAN, STEVEN J. and ERIC CORTY (1984), "Cognitive Heuristics," in Handbook of Social Cognition, Vol 1, R. S. Wyer and T. K. Srull, eds., Hillsdale, NJ: Eribaum, 189-286.

217. SHIFFRIN, R. M. and W. SCHNEIDER (1977), "Controlled and Automatic Human Information Processing: II. Perceptual Learning, Automatic Attending, and a General Theory," Psychological Review, 84, 127-190.

218. SHUGAN, STEVEN (1980), "The Cost of Thinking," Journal of Consumer Research, 7 (September): 99-111.

219. SIMON, M. (1979), "Imperfect Information, Costly Litigation, and Product Quality," Bell Journal of Economics.

220. SIMON, HERBERT A. (1978), "Rationality as Process and as Product of Thought," American Economic Review, 68 (May): 1-16.

221. SIMON, H.A. (1963), "Economics and Psychology," in S. Koch (ed), Psychology: A Study of a Science, Vol. 6, New York, NY: McGraw-Hill, 685-723.

222. SIMON, H. A. (1956), "Rational Choice and the Structure of the Environment," Psychological Review, 63, 129-138.

223. SINGH, SURENDRA N. and ROTHSCHILD, MICHAEL L. (1983), "Recognition As a Measure of Learning from Television Commercials," Journal of Marketing Research, 235-248.

224. SMITH, SCOTT M. (1980), "Giving to Charitable Organizations: A Behavioral Review and a Framework for Increasing Commitment," in Advances in Consumer Research, Jerry Olson (ed.). Ann Arbor: Association for Consumer Research, 753-743.

225. SPENCE, M. (1977), "Consumer Misperceptions, Product Failure and Producer Liability," Review of Economic Studies.

226. SRULL, THOMAS K. (1983), "The Role of Prior Knowledge in the Acquisition, Retention, and Use of New Information," in Richard P. Bagozzi and Alice M. Tybout, eds., Advances in Consumer Research, Chicago: Association for Consumer Research, 572-576.

227. STAELIN, R. (1978), "The Effects of Consumer Education on Consumer Product Safety Behavior," Journal of Consumer Research, 5, 30-40.

228. STERNTHAL, BRIAN and SAMUAL S. CRAIG (1982), Consumer Behavior: An Information Processing Perspective, Englewood Cliffs, NJ: Prentice-Hall.

229. STERNTHAL, B., PHILLIPS, L. and DHOLAKIA, E. (1978), "The Persuasive Effects of Source Credibility: A Situational Analysis," Public Opinion Quarterly, 285-314.

230. STIGLER, GEORGE (1961), "The Economics of Information," Journal of Political Economy, 69, 213-225.

231. SUJAN, MITA (1985), "Consumer Knowledge: Effects on Evaluation Strategies Mediating Consumer Judgments," Journal of Consumer Research, 12 (June):31-46.

232. SUMMERS, JOHN O. (1974), "Less Information is Better?", Journal of Marketing Research, 11 467-468.

233. TROUTMAN, MICHAEL C. and SHANTEAU, JAMES (1976), "Do Consumers Evaluate Products by Adding or Averaging Attribute Information?" Journal of Consumer Research, 3 (Sept.): 101-106.

234. TVERSKY, AMOS and KAHNEMAN, D. (1981), "The Framing of Decisions and the Psychology of Choice," Science, 211, 453-458.

235. TVERSKY, A., and KAHNEMAN, D. (1974), "Judgment Under Uncertainty: Heuristics and Biases," Science, 185, 1124-1131.

236. UDELL, JON G. (1966), "Prepurchase Behavior of Buyers of Small Electrical Appliances," Journal of Marketing, 30 (October): 50-52.

237. VAN RAAIJ, FRED W. (1977), "Consumer Information Processing for Different Information Structures and Formats," in William D. Perreault, (Ed.), Advances in Consumer Research, 4 (Atlanta: Association for Consumer Research): 176-184.

238. WARREN, I. (1969), "The Effects of Credibility in Sources of Testimony on Audience Attitudes Toward Speaker and Message," Speech Monographs, 36, 456-458.

239. WEITZMAN, MARTIN (1979), "Optimal Search for the Best Alternative," Econometrica, 47, 641-659.

240. WEINER, JOSHUA LYLE (1985), "Are Warranties Accurate Signals of Product Reliablity?", Journal of Consumer Research 12, 245-250.

241. WESTBROOK, ROBERT A. and FORNELL, CLAES (1979), "Patterns of Information Source Usage Among Durable Goods Buyers," Journal of Marketing Research, 16, 303-312.

242. WILKIE, WILLIAM L. (1975), "How Consumers Use Product Information: An Assessment of Research in Relation to Public Policy Needs," Washington, D.C.: U.S. Government Printing Office.

243. WILKIE, WILLIAM L. and DICKSON, PETER R. (1985), Shopping for Appliances: Consumers' Strategies and Patterns of Information Search. Cambridge, MA; Marketing Science Institute.

244. WHITTAKER, J. and MEADE, R. (1968), "Retention of Opinion Change as a Function of Differential Source Credibility," International Journal of Psychology, 3, 103-108.

245. WILTON, PETER C. and MYERS, JOHN G. (1986), "Task, Expectancy, and Information Assessment Effects in Information Utilization Processes," Journal of Consumer Research, 12 (March): 469-486.

246. WOLGAST, ELIZABETH (1958), "Economic Decisions in the Family," Journal of Marketing, 23 (Oct.): 151-158.

247. WRIGHT, PETER L. (1976), "An Adaptive Consumer's View of Attitude and Choice Mechanisms., As Viewed by an Equally Adaptive Advertiser," in Attitude Research at Bay, William D. Wells (Ed.), American Marketing Association, 113-131.

248. _________ (1975), "Consumer Choice Strategies: Simplifying vs. Optimizing," Journal of Marketing Research, 11, 60-67.

249. _________ (1974), "The Harassed Decision Maker: Time Pressures, Distractions, and the Use of Evidence," Journal of Applied Psycholgy, 59, 555-561.

250. ZAJONC, ROBERT B. and MARKUS, HAZEL (1982), "Affective and Cognitive Factors in Preferences," Journal of Consumer Research, 9, 123-131.

251. ZBYTNIEWSKI, JO-ANN (1980), "Shoppers Cry Remember the Price -- But Do They Practice What They Screech?", 119-122.

252. ZEITHAML, VALARIE A. (1982), "Consumer Responses to In-Store Price Information Environments," Journal of Consumer Research, 8, 357-369.

Chapter 14

ABOUT THE AUTHOR

Jeremy Mitchell was from 1977 to 1986 Undersecretary and Director of the National Consumer Council, London. Trained in Economics at Oxford University, Mitchell's career has centered on consumer affairs, first in Consumers' Association and later as Director of Consumer Affairs with the Office of Fair Trading. Mitchell has been deeply involved in research, first with the National Economic Development Office and then as Secretary of the Social Science Research Council from 1966 to 1974. Mitchell is the author of Marketing and the Consumer Movement (McGraw-Hill, 1978).

AN ELECTRONIC FUTURE?

Jeremy Mitchell

A ferment of experiment with electronic systems for consumer information, purchasing and payment throughout the developed countries seems to have yielded widely differing results. Morgan contrasts the "...rapid explosion of use" of videotex in France with its lack of success in the UK. However, it is important to bear in mind that in France the promotion of videotex (and the associated Minitel hardware) has been an important component of the French Government's "industrial strategy." As such, it has benefited from substantial Government subsidies. The situation in France cannot therefore necessarily by replicated in other countries. Developments in the United Kingdom videotex-based Prestel service[1] may give a more realistic idea of the potential advantages and disadvantages that electronic systems have in store for consumers.

WHERE PRESTEL STANDS

Prestel was developed and is run by British Telecom, until 1984 a state owned utility but now a public limited company operating with a Government license and subject to light regulatory control. At present, there are about 64,000 Prestel subscribers, divided almost equally between business and individual consumers. The number of subscribers has never met original expectations which were wildly optimistic. But now there is steady, though still slow, growth.

---

[1]Videotex is the generic name for the technology. Prestel is the proprietary name of the British version of videotex.

For the individual consumer, the costs of using Prestel are:

- Capital cost of about 200 for a Prestel adaptor/keyboard (though there has been a recent press report that British Telecom is thinking of providing free adaptors/keyboards).
- Prestel service subscription of £6.50 (≃ ($10.70) each quarter.
- Prestel time charge of 6 pence (≃ $0.10) per minute for use between 8 a.m. and 6 p.m. on weekdays, and between 8 a.m. and 1 p.m. on Saturdays. Use at other times carries no time charge.
- British Telecom telephone charges, usually at local rates.
- Frame charges are zero for most information providers, but range up to 50 pence (≃$0.83) per frame for some.

Most of the frames on Prestel are information frames, provided by commercial information providers. The UK National Consumer Council, Consumers' Association and other public and voluntary organizations were among the early Information Providers on Prestel. However, the high costs of maintaining an up-to-date database and the low number of individual consumers who subscribed to Prestel made it uneconomic for these organizations to continue.

The current inadequacies of Prestel as a consumer-oriented information system have been exposed by Scott Maynes [2] and <u>Prestel for People</u> [4]. From these analyses it has become increasingly clear that it is unrealistic to expect that any new mass electronic medium can be developed primarily on the basis of meeting consumers' information needs. Even when consumers perceive that they have information needs, they may think these are at present adequately met by print media, by the telephone or by word of mouth. Also, most consumers are unaccustomed to paying explicitly for information, whatever the rate of return they get.

NEW DEVELOPMENTS IN PRESTEL

The emphasis of Prestel is now beginning to shift toward interactive consumer services, such as home banking and home purchasing [3]. The Bank of Scotland has developed a Home and Office Banking Service (HOBS) which enables the consumer to scrutinise his or her account, pay bills, transfer money between accounts, and order check books and printed account statements. A simplified adaptor/keyboard costs £95, compared with the normal £200. My own estimate is that it costs the consumer around £120-

£150 per year to run a HOBS account. The Nottingham Building Society also operates a roughly similar home banking scheme on Prestel. Both financial institutions have a small branch network and clearly see home banking on Prestel as a way of expanding their consumer base without building or buying branches.

A new home purchasing service on Prestel is Telecard Supershop in West London. This offers a range of goods roughly comparable with a medium-sized supermarket - groceries, fresh food, frozen food, drink, tobacco and magazines. The consumer can place regular as well as one-off orders, and order up to 28 days in advance. The goods are delivered to the door the day after ordering by Prestel. The appeal of Telecard Supershop is clearly directed at those consumers who lead very busy lives and/or find it burdensome to go shopping for groceries. It involves a resurrection of the personal delivery service which disappeared so rapidly in the post-1945 years. Its appeal fits closely with a finding from some unpublished UK National Consumer Council research, showing that many consumers begrudge the time and effort spent on the weekly grocery shop.

Another home shopping innovation on Prestel has been introduced by a major catalogue mail order retailer, Littlewoods. A big part of the Littlewoods conventional mail order catalogue-- some 3,500 products, but significantly excluding clothing -- is now on Prestel.

None of these consumer services is in itself likely to transform Prestel into a mass consumer system. However, British Telecom will follow the French example by launching an electronic version of the classified telephone directory on Prestel in late 1986. It remains to be seen what effect this will have on the number of subscribers.

Prestel's difficulties could readily mislead people into thinking that electronic information and buying systems will never involve more than a small minority of wealthy, technologically minded consumers. However, a number of indicators that point the other way.

-- Electronic payment systems are well established and spreading rapidly. ATM's (Automated Teller Machines) have become an accepted part of the lives of consumers in developed countries. EFTPOS (Electronic Funds Transfer at Point of Sale) is beginning to take hold, if somewhat fitfully, in France, Australia, the UK and the USA. Home banking is beginning to come out of the experimental phase in France, the UK, the USA and West Germany.

-- While the examples I have given relate to videotex, videotex is only one of the possible technological modes for delivering electronic services and information to consumers. Cable and ISDN are others. We should not, as consumers, become obsessed with which particular mode, if any, will win out. Fully interactive consumer services and massive information databases are possible with various delivery modes.

-- The present inadequacies of electronically based consumer information systems can be overcome. For example, Grunert [1] carried out an experiment on the German videotex system, Bildschirmtext, to explore its potential as a medium for presenting very complex consumer information. A sophisticated database was put together on 11 compact cars, with 45 attributes for each car. Consumers could search the database by car (e.g., all about the VW Golf) or by attribute (e.g., petrol consumption for each car). Consumers' overall evaluation of the database was very high. This seems to have been at least partly due to the care with which it had been designed to meet consumers' information needs.

-- Improved consumer information will never be the primary reason for developing an electronic delivery system. However, it can be achieved within the framework of a system whose main function is to provide entertainment (e.g., cable) or provide services.

THE ADVANTAGES AND DISADVANTAGES FOR CONSUMERS

Taking together developments in electronic information, electronic purchasing and electronic payments, what are the likely consequences for the way consumers take decisions?

-- The three functions of information search, purchasing and payment can all be carried out in a short space of time -- and at a time decided by the consumer. The consumer is no longer constrained by limited shop opening or banking hours.

-- The consumer can save time on those purchases (e.g., buying groceries) where she or he begrudges spending time. The time saved can be reallocated to other, more pleasurable kinds of purchasing -- or to other activities altogether.

-- The consumer is freed from constraints of place. She or he does not have to visit the shop or the bank. The consumer controls the location at which the transaction takes place.

-- The consumer has a much more extensive and sophisticated database available before taking a decision. This is especially true for financial services, which current information inadequacies have in a number of instances (e.g., life assurance) led to very imperfect markets.

These are some of the potential gains for consumers. There are, though, potential losses, or major obstacles to be overcome.

-- The threshold costs of gaining access to electronic systems or the operating costs of participating in them may be so high that they effectively disbar the majority of consumers, leading to a divide between the haves and the have-nots. This is certainly true of many current videotex-based systems.

-- The legislative framework for consumer protection in relation to electronic systems is at present inadequate or non-existent.

-- Consumer organizations are short of the money and skills needed to ensure that independently provided information is available on electronic databases.

CONCLUSION

It would be foolish to try to predict the pace at which electronic systems will displace conventional systems for consumer information, purchasing and payment, or the exact nature of the systems that will prove themselves successfully. However, there have already been enough successful experiments and developments-- in Europe, if not in the USA -- to make it clear that they will occupy a significant place in the lives of many consumers. Consumer protagonists and consumer educators should learn to live with electronic systems and should work to optimize their development in the consumers' interests.

REFERENCES

1. GRUNERT, K.G. (1984), "Consumer Information Systems in Videotex: Design and Acceptance," Journal of Consumer Studies and Home Economics, Vol. 8, No. 3, Oxford.

2. MAYNES, E. SCOTT. (1982), Prestel in Use. National Consumer Council, London.

3. MITCHELL, JEREMY (1986), "Electronic Shopping - The Consumer Viewpoint," Trading Law, London, (in press).

4. PRESTEL FOR PEOPLE (1983), Council for Educational Technology, London.

ABOUT THE AUTHOR

W. Wayne Talarzyk is Professor and Chairman of the Academic Faculty of Marketing at Ohio State University. Trained initially as an engineer and later receiving a Ph.D. in Industrial Administration from Purdue University, Talarzyk has spent most of his academic career at Ohio State University. His research interests include consumer attitudes, lifestyles, and the new information technologies, particularly videotex. His recent books include Contemporary Cases in Consumer Behavior, Second Edition (1985), Cases for Analysis in Marketing, Third Edition (1985), and Cases and Exercises in Marketing (1987).

NEW TECHNOLOGIES IN CONSUMER INFORMATION

W. Wayne Talarzyk

It is a pleasure to be part of a program where discussants are informed that it is "appropriate to advance his/her own views." I would like to take advantage of that opportunity and build on a couple of ideas introduced by James N. Morgan in his paper, "Consumer Choice is More Than Search."

First, I agree with Morgan's basic premise: most important consumer problems go beyond searching for the best buy and finding facts about product characteristics. I also agree with his call for a "dynamic, interactive experimental procedure" which will give us a more comprehensive understanding as to how consumers use or do not use economic information effectively and how we might improve the situation.

At one point, Morgan states that the ordinary citizen-consumer faced with choices is beset by "ignorance, uncertainty, constraints, compulsions and confusion." He does not clarify what he means by "compulsions." I think he should add another difficulty not implied in other parts of his paper: indifference. In the final analysis, many citizen-consumers may be just indifferent regarding both decisions and outcomes. Other facets of their lives appear to be more important to them.

VIDEOTEX AND RELATED TECHNOLOGIES

Morgan briefly introduces the topic of videotex as a example of ways in which modern electronic communication can be used to present information to consumers. In the following I focus my discussion on videotex's potential as a consumer information vehicle.

Videotex is the generic name for a developing, interactive, mass medium that delivers text and graphic information directly to consumers. The user interacts with the system via a handheld keypad, push button console, or full alpha-numeric keyboard. Desired information is retrieved interactively with a dedicated terminal or personal computer, typically connected by telephone lines to a videotex center or "gateway" to other information bases. The retrieved information, in the form of text or graphics, is displayed on a television screen or other video device [4].

Most videotex systems offer consumers a variety of services and information bases. These include in-home shopping and banking, electronic encyclopedias, consumer information bases, news, weather and sports, classified advertising, financial and investment data, travel, entertainment and education information, electronic mail and bulletin boards, agriculturally oriented data and other information for special interest groups.

A related development is touch screen technology. To register responses to questions or cues which appear on what resembles a regular television set typically placed in some public access kiosk, consumers simply touch the appropriate area on the screen. The "touch" point delivers the desired information from a computer or videodisc machine in the kiosk. It is possible to link an on-line videotex system with the touch screen unit to provide off premise data bases.

These touch screen kiosks have been placed in shopping malls, transportation terminals, hotels, individual retail businesses and other public places. They usually provide information about businesses, products and services, community activities, locations of restaurants and theatres, public transportation schedules, and so forth. Many are equipped with printers to dispense on demand: maps, coupons and other desired printed information.

Consumer Information Applications

One of the obvious advantages of these new technologies is that consumers have more control over the types of information they receive and the manner in which they receive it. Beales, et al. [1] described the potential of these technologies by stating, "There is a need for efficient systems that deliver information that is tailor-made to specific consumers, and viewed as reducing rather than increasing the consumer's cognitive efforts."

Widing [6] describes the ways in which videotex as a medium can help achieve the four relevant objectives in designing information systems called for by Maynes, et al. [2]. "First, the information technology can be made available when the consumer wants it - at home or at the point of purchase. Second, the information can be provided speedily and on demand. Third, the computer-assisted processing potential of videotex systems can enable consumers to lower processing demands and/or obtain only as much or as little information as is desired. Fourth, the system can provide perishable information that can be quickly updated by the information provider which avoids the provision of obsolete information."

Videotex and related technologies provide tremendous opportunities to put the latest product information as well as more stable data bases at consumers' finger tips. The interactive capabilities allow consumers to choose the types of information received and the order in which it is presented. Specially developed software allows the consumer to do initial screening or processing of data based on the relative importance of product attributes or other information provided by the consumer. Again, because of the interactive capabilities, consumers can feed information back to sponsoring organizations via market research types of questions. But, are consumers willing to use these new technologies?

Current Systems Status

Videotex and touch screen technologies are meeting with mixed success throughout Europe and North America. In France videotex seems to be quite successful. French consumers are treating videotex as a kind of telephone rather than a kind of computer [5]. Prestel in Great Britain (achieving minimal success) and several of the regional videotex systems in the U.S. (Viewtron and Gateway now out of business) built large collections of data bases in central computer banks. By contrast, the French developed a centralized network, much like a telephone network, connecting many users to many independent services. The French approach cuts out several levels of menus and access problems, letting consumers connect directly to a service by dialing a standard telephone number and keying in the name of the desired service.

Among national videotex services in the U.S., CompuServe (approximately 360,000 subscribers with 10,000 additions each month) appears to be doing quite well, Dow Jones News Retrieval remains very viable; rumors abound regarding the future of The Source (recently sold to a venture capital group). Several local touch screen operations have closed while other systems report acceptable levels of consumer use but less than desired levels of advertiser support.

As Russo [3] points out, "The success of any information system for consumers depends upon consumer acceptance and use. The decision to use a system depends, in turn, upon a cost-benefit analysis from the consumer's perspective. That is, the anticipated benefits to the consumer, both tangible and intangible, must exceed the expected costs."

At the present time, most consumers are unaware that videotex exists. Most of the aware see few personal benefits from using videotex compared with alternative sources of information. Those who see value in videotex are insufficient in number to support a local or regional system. Most of their needs are met through one of the national systems.

Perhaps videotex is simply ahead of its time. Most consumers are still apprehensive about computers and "new ways" of doing things. But times will change, applications and software will improve and the economic advantages of using the new technologies will evolve.

Research Opportunities

Let me conclude by outlining several research opportunities with respect to these new technologies that may speed their adoption.

Consumer Needs -- What types of information do consumers want and how should that information be structured? Perhaps more research on the lack of acceptance of the new technologies to date can identify some unmet needs.

Product Development -- Can we develop computing packages to aid consumer decision making? Widing [6] examined ways of letting research subjects use videotex to assign their own weights to product attributes, thus enabling them to obtain "their own" assessments of quality.

Consumer Behavior Theories -- How do our theories of consumer behavior apply to data received via the new technologies compared to traditional media? For example, how does source credibility come into play over a videotex service?

Consumer Decision Making -- Does decision making improve when data is obtained interactively via a videotex system? Does the format enhance decision making?

Use of Graphics -- Are graphics an important component of information received over a videotex service or is text sufficient by itself? Do graphics become more or less important as consumers become more familiar with videotex systems?

Price Strategies -- What approach to pricing of videotex services will best meet both consumer needs and the return-on-investment requirements of videotex system operators and information providers? What role will marketers and public service organizations play in supporting the costs of these new technologies?

Privacy Issues -- Will consumers be wary of receiving or supplying certain types of information in connection with using these new technologies? Are consumers afraid that their privacy will be invaded?

Videotex and touch screen technologies have gotten off to a bad start. They have not lived up to most of their advanced press clippings. They appear to offer exciting opportunities for varied consumer applications including the delivery of consumer information. Videotex deserves continued monitoring and research activities that will help us better understand its potential.

REFERENCES

1. BEALES, HOWARD, MICHAEL B. MAZIS, STEVEN C. SALOP and RICHARD STAELIN (1981), "Consumer Search and Public Policy," Journal of Consumer Research, 8, 11-22.

2. MAYNES, E. SCOTT, JAMES N. MORGAN, VIVIAN WESTON and GREG J. DUNCAN (1977), "The Local Consumer Information System: An Institution-To-Be?" The Journal of Consumer Affairs, 11, 17-33.

3. RUSSO, J. EDWARD (1986), "From Passive to Active Information Systems for Consumers," paper prepared for the symposium, "New Challenges for European Consumer Policy," University of Hohenheim, Stuttgart, March 17-20, 1986.

4. TALARZYK, W. WAYNE and MURRAY YOUNG (1985), "The New Electronic Media 'Videotex'," Ohio State University Working Paper Series (WPS 85-77), August 1985.

5. VIDEOPRINT (1986), "French Banks Race Ahead," 7, No. 12, (June 23), 3-4.

6. WIDING, ROBERT E., II (1986), "Computer-Assisted and Static Information Provision Formats: Comparisons on Reactions, Time and Accuracy," Unpublished Doctoral Dissertation, The Ohio State University.

ABOUT THE AUTHOR

William L. Wilkie is the Aloysius and Eleanor Nathe Professor of Marketing at the University of Notre Dame. Wilkie received his Ph.D in Marketing from Stanford University in 1971. During his career he has been on marketing faculties at Harvard University, Purdue University, the University of Florida, and -- starting in 1987 -- the University of Notre Dame. A leading marketing scholar, Wilkie was President of the Association for Consumer Research in 1979-80, and has served as a member of the Editorial Boards of the Journals of Consumer Research, Marketing, Marketing Research, and Marketing and Public Policy. His textbook, Consumer Behavior, was published by John Wiley and Sons in 1986. As the representative of the Association for Consumer Research on the ACCI Research Committee, Wilkie helped plan the International Conference on Research in the Consumer Interest.

THE MARKETING CONTEXT OF CONSUMER CHOICE

William L. Wilkie

In "Consumer Choice Is More Than Search," James Morgan has identified a number of key issues. In commenting on his find and stimulating paper, I have two quite distinct alternatives. The first is to take each section and raise appropriate questions, caveats, and extensions. This might be valuable, for Morgan has raised many issues in his quest to provoke us to thought and action. Most deserve further discussion.

My second option -- the one I have adopted -- is to pose an entirely different set of issues. My issues center on the impact of marketers' actions on consumer information and choice. I believe it is crucial for consumer economists and consumer educators to consider marketing as they deal with consumer behavior, consumer policy, and research in the consumer interest.

POINT 1: THE MARKETING CONTEXT IS A POWERFUL FORCE ON CONSUMERS

In my view Morgan, while raising many other important issues, underplays marketing's role within the overall consumer system. To make this point briefly, consider the following:

-- The Staggering Quantity of Consumer Information. Whatever one's view of the character of marketer-produced information, the fact is that marketers do produce most of available consumer information. In the United States alone, over $100 billion is spent on advertising each year; a much larger amount is spent on sales promotion; over 11 million salespersons are at work at the retail level, all imparting information. When one also considers labels, inserts, and other forms of passive stimuli, it is clear that marketers are offering consumers a staggering amount of information. Moveover, some of this information is repeated frequently; some is available continuously.

-- Impacts and Effectiveness. It is also true that marketers are extremely influential sources of information. A study by Wilkie and Dickson [14] of consumers' information search activities for major appliances, showed that 41% of recent purchasers rated "the salesperson" as their "most useful information source." Surprising to us, salespersons "out influenced" the next most important sources--newspaper ads, and friend/relatives -- by three-to-one (41% vs. 14%). Consumer Reports, was listed as "most useful" by only 9% of recent purchasers. (Moreover, these results are only partially attributable to incidence of source exposure. After correction for the amount of exposure, the salesperson still emerged as the consumers' "most useful" information source. The interested reader should consult [13, pp. 505-508] for a summary and [14] for the complete report.)

MARKETING AND CONSUMER PERSPECTIVES ARE DIFFERENT

When considering the impact of marketing information on consumer choice, it is useful to recognize explicitly that perspectives of marketers differ significantly from those of consumers. Table 1 presents a simplified look at crucial areas of difference. (For detailed discussions the reader should consult [13, pp. 50-59, 586-603].) As Table 1 shows, consumers' interests are dispersed across many products and services. In each instance we search for some "best alternative" solution, driven by utility considerations. Finally -- and quite significantly with respect to Morgan's arguments -- as consumers, we need to somehow "handle" a large number of attempts by marketers to influence our choices.

The right-hand column of Table 1 presents the marketer's perspective. Marketers view consumers "externally" as "buyers." This means that a marketer does not take the consumer viewpoint, even though he himself is a consumer with respect to other products. For efficiency reasons, marketers view consumers in the aggregate -- "market" -- not as individuals to be dealt with personally. Further, each marketer thinks in very product-specific terms, concerned only with those products or services that he or she sells. The marketer is relatively unconcerned about the overall functioning of the market or the entire market economy! A consequence of this difference in focus between consumers and marketers is disparity between marketers and consumers in the expertise and resources they can apply to a given product category. As to the "correct" choice, the consumer has a relatively open mind while the marketer has an institutionally pre-determined answer to this key question. Finally, with respect to influence, the marketer's role is do everything he can to assure that the consumer's "best choices" will be a product variant offered by his firm, preferably the most profitable item.

Table 2 completes this analysis by introducing the public policymaker's perspective. Here we find an interesting mixture of consumer and marketer orientations. Public policy adopts an external perspective, but examines both buyers and sellers. Like marketers, public policymakers focus mainly on the aggregate though both policymakers and marketers are often interested in particular subgroups, or segments, within a market. Necessarily the public policymaker is concerned with a wide variety of products and services.

As we move to the last two dimensions in Table 2, we encounter important and difficult distinctions. With respect to "correct choice," public policymakers are often forced to adopt a neutral position that minimizes "normative" directions. As an example, consider the position of government policymakers toward tobacco and cigarette smoking! The same is true of "influence." Again, public policymakers may be forced to adopt neutral postures. It is difficult for policymakers to assert that influence attempts are per se good or bad, or to either encourage or to discourage influence efforts. Instead, public policy has to adopt the role of a neutral referee, assuring that the "rules of the game" are observed and asserting that the marketing/consumer environment must be fair and efficient.

Neutrality does not come easily to marketers. Almost all of the body of knowledge in marketing focuses on directional influence or persuasion. Thus our very base of knowledge is geared away from some of the key public policy considerations of the consumer interest. The challenge of utilizing, or adapting, our concepts is indeed massive. As a marketer, I am unable to clearly "position" the field of consumer economics with respect to "neutrality." But I express my concern that perhaps this discipline, too, has not yet come to grips with the question.

Table 1

Comparing Consumer and Marketer Perspectives

Characteristic	Consumers's Perspective	Marketer's Perspective
A. Point of view	Internal ("me")	External ("buyers")
B. Level of analysis	Individual ("myself")	Aggregate ("market")
C. Scope of interest	Across products ("what I buy")	Specific product ("what I sell")
D. "Correct" choice	Best alternative ("best brand for me")	Specific brand ("what I sell")
E. Role of influence	Handling influence attempts	Making influence attempts

Source: Adapted from Table 3-1 in [13, p. 52].

Table 2

The Public Policy Perspective

Characteristic	Policy Perspective
A. Point of view	External ("buyers and sellers")
B. Level of analysis	Aggregate ("affected groups")
C. Scope of interest	Across products ("all products and services")
D. "Correct choice"	Neutral ("maximize utility")
E. Role of influence	Neutral ("must be fair and not deceptive")

Source: Adapted from Table 21-1 in [13, p. 587].

A PARADOX IN THE MARKETING SYSTEM'S CONSUMER INFORMATION

Earlier I alluded to the fact that the marketing system, is "micro-based" -- that individual companies competing with each other produce a particular form of dynamic system. Perhaps because of the fact that competing firms are independent, secretive, and that adversarial relations frequently overwhelm cooperative activities, it is difficult for many marketers and consumers to think about a "marketing system" as such. This is particularly difficult if we approach issues from a managerial perspective (asking, for example, "What shall I do to increase market share in this situation?"), which has been the dominant perspective within the academic marketing field for the past twenty-five years. Very briefly, however, this is what I would like to do, in order to gain some new insights into the nature of this system.

Figure 1 introduces the key. Our micro-based marketing system calls for each seller to attempt to maximize his or her own performance, as illustrated by Budweiser beer in Figure 1. Budweiser creates its promotional/informational program and sends it out to consumers. The net message is clear: "Buy Beer, Buy Now and Buy Often, and Buy Bud Specifically!"

The right side of Figure 1 depicts the situation from the viewpoint of the consumer receiving Budweiser's message. Notice that this consumer is also receiving similar messages from many other sellers as well, including multitudinous makers of other beers (not shown for lack of space). Ironically the marketing system is sending some arresting unintended messages, messages that were not designed: "Buy All Products and Services, Buy Now and Buy Often, and Buy Every Brand!:

Simply put, our marketing system in total proposes too much consumption for every consumer. The "system" does not recognize that all consumers face a budget constraint imposed (approximately) by the amount of income they receive.

Quantity aside, the "system" is sending a message regarding the quality of products offered. Since each brand seeks to sell itself, the overall message to consumers is: "Every Brand is the Best Brand..."

These system messages and practices lead to a curious but necessary adaptation on the part of consumers: in order to effectively operate within the marketplace, they learn to ignore messages that seem irrelevant to their current interests, they learn to be skeptical of marketing chains, and they learn not to simply accept and act on all of the information provided by the marketing system. The phenomenon of consumer "low involvement" may in part stem from this system characteristic. (Of course, this adaptation by consumers then causes great problems for marketers. Marketers must now strive to overcome lowered attention and reservations on the part of the consumers with whom they are striving to communicate!)

These system characteristics also bring difficulties for consumer education, information, and choice. First, consumers have already learned to interact with the marketing system in a somewhat closed way, often with low involvement, and often with partial knowledge. Second, they have learned that often there is no obvious "best buy," given the amount of information available. While more expertise will often lead to a better or more confident choice, it could also lead to a state of higher confusion! Hence, the costs of becoming "better educated" on a particular choice may appear to be quite high. In fact, the perceived extrinsic benefits may not be high enough to overcome these costs. Thus, while we as students of the system may wish to see highly cognitive consumers searching more in their own self interest, it may turn out that the operations of the marketing system do not support this strategy. It would be interesting and instructive to attempt to work out those real life conditions under which various forms of consumer choice rules would be most advantageous.

SOME RESEARCH INSIGHTS FROM MARKETING

In closing, I would like to indicate some areas of research within marketing that seem relevant to Professor Morgan's recommendations. First, research on consumer motivation appears to offer a pessimistic forecast for his proposals on the furtherance of consumer education. We must recall the mounting evidence that many purchases are "low involvement" in nature. However, it may be worthwhile to examine further the intangible benefits that consumers receive from purchase processes that have little to do with the benefits from the products themselves. For example, for some people the act of spending money may yield psychological pleasure, involving feelings of achievement, status, control, authority, and even play. To the extent that these factors operate, our emphasis on dollar expenditure versus product performance is incomplete. Unfortunately, this factor does not support education further directed to better choices. In addition, in considering Morgan's goals, it is chastening to recall from several studies in supermarkets [8] that almost half of all purchases made there unplanned!!

Figure 1

THE HUGE NUMBER OF CONSUMER INFLUENCE ATTEMPTS FROM THE MARKETING SYSTEM

Influence attempts as seen by the marketer

"Buy Budweiser!"

Millions of Consumers

The Net Message

1. Buy beer!
2. Buy now and buy often!
3. Buy Bud specifically!

Influence attempts as seen by the consumer

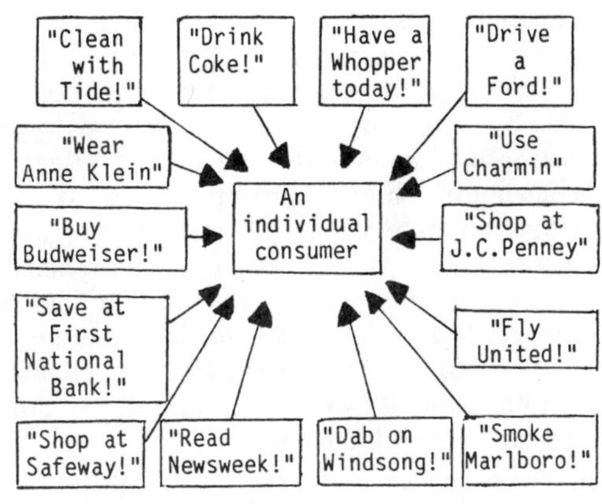

The Net Message

1. Buy all types of products and services!
2. Buy now and buy often!
3. Buy every brand!

Source: Adapted from Figure 3-1 in [13].

A second research area worthy of attention involves the degree of consumer responsiveness to marketing stimuli. This has been found to be quite high. One study of in-store supermarket displays [1], for example, found that the average display led to an increase in sales of 570%!! A second example comes from the Wilkie-Dickson study [14] and centers on how the direction and timing of the search process was influenced by the information source consulted first. Of consumers who started their search process with Consumer Reports, 81% went on to buy at a specialty appliance store. Conversely, of those who started with newspaper ads, 61% went on to buy at Sears. It is important to recognize that marketing stimuli (and Consumers Union!) can exert strong influences on the consumer choice process.

A third relevant topic involves the recent research by Jacob Jacoby and his associates [5] on consumer miscomprehension. This research compared different types of broadcast forms as to consumers' understanding of what was being said. The research team emerged with a startling result: regardless of the form (ad, news clip, public service announcement, program clip), consumers miscomprehend about 30% of the material! As you might expect, this report has generated considerable interest and controversy [3, 4, 6, 7, 9, 10]. As for consumer education, this report reinforces the notion that it will be difficult to substantially improve the cognitive performance of consumers.

The message from marketing is not completely negative regarding Morgan's proposals. A recent study by Duncan and Olshavsky [2], found that a consumers' generalized "beliefs about the marketplace" affect the search processes they employ when shopping. Consumers who believe that "Most store salespersons are well informed about the products they sell," or "The best brands...sell the most," or "Extensive shopping makes (choice) harder...," etc.) were found to be in fact search less before buying. Duncan-Olshavsky's findings suggest that interventions to modify consumers' beliefs regarding the nature of the marketplace might lead to alterations in shopping patterns and choice behaviors that would benefit these consumers.

Finally, there exists a reasonably well-developed body of work on consumer segmentation that is quite germane to the implementation of consumer education efforts. Hans Thorelli and his associates [11], have identified "information seekers" in several nations, Thorelli's information seekers tend to have similar demographic characteristics: high income, high education, high product ownership, etc.) and similar beliefs, i.e., to view advertising less favorably, to be confident of product testing, not to be innovators, etc.

Robert Westbrook and Claes Fornell [12] have employed advanced statistical analyses to distinguish four types of shoppers by their approach to information search. These include (1) those who rely on personal advice (20% of their sample), (2) those who rely primarily on store visits (30%), (3) those who combine objective information and store visits (20%), and (4) those who use information sources of any type sparingly (30%). Morgan's proposed lessons are likely to be different for each of these groups. Consideration should be given to distinct targeting efforts within the design of research in this area.

REFERENCES

1. CHEVALIER, MICHAEL (1975), "Increase in Sales Due to In-Store Display," Journal of Marketing Research, November, 426-431.

2. DUNCAN, CALVIN P. and OLSHAVSKY, RICHARD W. (1982), "External Search: The Role of Consumer Beliefs," Journal of Marketing Research, February, 32-43.

3. FORD, GARY T. and YALCH, RICHARD (1982), "Viewer Miscomprehension of Televised Communication - A Comment," Journal of Marketing, Fall, 27-31.

4. GATES, FLIECE, R. and HOYER, WAYNE, D. (1986), "Measuring Miscomprehension: A Comparison of Alternative Formats," in R.J. Lutz (ed.), Advances in Consumer Research, Vol. 13, Provo, Utah: Association for Consumer Research.

5. JACOBY, JACOB and HOYER, WAYNE, D. (1982), "Viewer Miscomprehension of Televised Communication: Selected Findings," Journal of Marketing, Fall, 12-26.

6. ________ (1982), "On Miscomprehension of Televised Communication: A Rejoinder," Journal of Marketing, Fall, 35-43.

7. MIZERSKI, RICHARD (1982), "Viewer Miscomprehension Findings Are Measurement Bound," Journal of Marketing, Fall, 32-34.

8. POINT OF PURCHASE ADVERTISING INSTITUTE (1978), Consumer Buying Habits Study: Special Report. New York: Point of Purchasing Advertising Institute.

9. PRESTON, IVAN L. and RICHARDS, JEF I. (1986), "The Relationship of Miscomprehension to Deceptiveness in FTC Cases," in R.J. Lutz (ed.), Advances in Consumer Research, Vol. 13, Provo, Utah: Association for Consumer Research.

10. SCHMITTLEIN, DAVID C. and MORRISON, DONALD G. (1983), "Measuring Miscomprehension for Televised Communications Using True-False Questions," Journal of Consumer Research, Vol. 10, 147-156.

11. THORELLI, HANS G. and ENGLEDOW, JACK L. (1980), "Information Seekers and Information Systems: A Policy Perspective," Journal of Marketing, Spring, 9-27.

12. WESTBROOK, ROBERT A. and FORNELL, CLAES (1979), "Patterns of Information Source Usage Among Durable Goods Buyers," Journal of Marketing Research, August, 303-312.

13. WILKIE, WILLIAM L. (1986), Consumer Behavior. New York: John Wiley & Sons, Inc.

14. ________ and DICKSON, PETER R. (1985), Consumer Information Search and Shopping Behavior, Cambridge, MA: Marketing Science Institute.

THE RIGHT

TO

CHOOSE

Chapter 15

ABOUT THE AUTHOR

Rachel Dardis is Professor in the Department of Textiles and Consumer Economics at the University of Maryland. Dardis received her Ph.D. in Economics from the University of Minnesota in 1965. After spending five years on the faculty of Cornell University where she attained the rank of Associate Professor, Dardis moved to the University of Maryland in 1970. Her research interests include textile economics and marketing, consumer policy analysis and international trade. She is widely published with more than 90 articles in the areas of textiles and consumer economics. She is Program Chairman for the 1988 Annual Conference of ACCI.

INTERNATIONAL TRADE: THE CONSUMER'S STAKE[1]

Rachel Dardis

SUMMARY

This paper examines the growth of trade restrictions in developed countries and the impact of such changes on consumer welfare. Analysis shows that trade protection imposes high costs on the consumer and the domestic economy. Costs include higher prices, less consumer choice and reduced incentives for the domestic industry to modernize or innovate due to the absence of competition. In many instances trade restraints mean that domestic consumers are subsidizing both domestic and foreign producers. Trade protection is regressive, imposing hardship on low-income consumers. Perversely, trade protection often fails to achieve its twin objectives of job preservation and industry modernization. Employment gains in one sector may be offset by employment losses in another sector, in particular the export sector. Trade diversion and product upgrading also reduce the efficacy of trade barriers. The growth of trade protection in recent years testifies to the continued dominance of producer/worker interest in matters of trade policy and highlights the importance of consumer education and consumer representation and influence in trade policy decisions.

---

[1]This paper is an expanded version of Dardis' earlier paper, "Government Intervention and Consumer Welfare: The Impact of International Trade Restrictions," Journal of Consumer Policy, 9 (3), September, 1986, pp. 243-260.

INTRODUCTION

The establishment of the General Agreement on Tariffs and Trade (GATT) in 1948 was designed to liberalize trade between countries and to increase the growth and prosperity of market-oriented economies. GATT was successful in the 1950s and 1960s in promoting trade liberalization, particularly with respect to tariff rates. Unfortunately, the reduction in tariff rates was offset to a considerable extent by the growth of non-tariff barriers to trade in the developed countries. These included sector agreements for commodities, effectively removing them from the GATT rules of international trade, and quantitative restraints such as Orderly Marketing Agreements (OMAs) and Voluntary Export Restraints (VERs).[2] The growth of import protection in the developed countries has imposed high costs on consumers. It has also harmed them indirectly by insulating major sectors of the domestic economy from international competition.

The objectives of this paper are to examine the growth of trade restraints in the developed countries and the impact of such changes on consumer welfare. The paper has four sections. The first section examines the principles underlying the GATT system and the successes and failures of the GATT in achieving trade liberalization. The second part focuses on the producer interest in trade restraints and the degree to which protectionist trade policies can achieve their objectives. The third part considers consumer gains from trade and the impact of trade restraints on the consumer and the economy. The effects of protection are examined for a variety of trade restrictions and for homogeneous and differentiated import products. The fourth part draws on the models discussed in the preceding section and provides empirical estimates of the costs of U.S. trade restraints for five commodities. The commodities are apparel, automobiles, color TVs, footwear and sugar. Consideration is also given to the impact of trade restraints on domestic firms and workers in the protected industries.

---

[2]Under voluntary export restraints (VERs) or Orderly Marketing Agreements (OMAs) the exporting country controls or limits its exports. The quantity restrictions or quotas are thus voluntary. In contrast mandatory quotas are implemented and administered by the imported country and are authorized by specific legislation in that country. Fear of mandatory quotas by importing countries may be one reason for the use of voluntary quotas by exporting countries. For a more complete discussion of the various types of quantitative restrictions see Morkre and Tarr [30, pp. 35-40].

THE INTERNATIONAL TRADE SYSTEM AFTER WORLD WAR II

Establishment of General Agreement on Tariffs and Trade (GATT)

The GATT system was founded in 1948 in order to restore order to an international trading system which had fallen into disarray during the 1930s [15]. Under GATT it was agreed that the trade policies of signatory countries should be governed by certain principles. The principles were: liberalism, transparency, stability, and non-discrimination.

Liberalism meant relying on markets to allocate resources as opposed to discretionary government intervention and the expansion of world trade through liberalization of import restrictions. Tariffs were selected as instruments of protection because they were transparent, easy to negotiate and compatible with the price mechanisms of the market. Stability and transparency were ensured by placing conditions on the ways in which protection could be increased. Finally, the principle of non-discrimination meant that the benefits of trade liberalization would accrue to all exporting countries.

Golt noted that the above rules were of particular importance for smaller, politically weaker countries.

> '[A] significant element [in the GATT design] was the view of the body of international rules, customs and practices not only as governing the relationships of the strong countries toward each other but also as safeguards for the weaker partners in the international system... There was to be no repetition of what was seen as a particular evil of the 1930s -- the operation of bilateral bargaining through which a strong country, by the sheer use of its commercial power and, even more objectionably, its political power, imposed its own desired patterns of trade upon a weaker trading partner... [18, p. 10].

Successes and Failures of the GATT System

Dunn, et al. commented that the GATT system was an agreement among diverse countries which "lacked full confidence both in one another and the advisability of liberal trade and consequently insisted both on the right to maintain protection and on the preservation of several means of escape from their commitments" [15, p. 112]. As a result, the principles of GATT were weakened by several articles. Thus GATT permitted the re-negotiation of tariffs (Article XXVIII), the imposition of non-discriminatory protection against imports of a particular product in an emergency (Article XIX), the introduction of general restrictions for balance of payments purposes (Article XII), and the imposition of quantitative restrictions for agricultural imports (Article XI).

GATT's greatest success was with tariffs which were reduced in seven rounds of multilateral negotiations. It is estimated that the average most favored nation tariff of developed countries on industrial products will be less than 5 percent when the Tokyo Round cuts are completed in 1988 [15]. However, the decline in tariff rates has been offset by two major developments. These developments were a response to pressures for protection which might have otherwise threatened the trade liberalization achievements of the 1950s and 1960s.

The first development was the exemption of entire industries from the trade liberalization process. Temperate-zone agricultural products were the first exemption and trade in these products was removed from all GATT governance in the early 1950s [22]. This was followed by discriminatory restraints against exports of textiles and apparel from developing countries which culminated in the Multi-Fiber Arrangement of 1974 [23]. There are indications that similar systems of protection are emerging for other industries such as steel and automobiles [15].

The second development was the weakening of the non-discrimination principle due to preferential trading arrangements between countries and the use of voluntary quantitative restraints by Japan and advanced developing countries in response to protectionist pressures from the developed countries.

Morkre and Tarr attributed the popularity of quantitative restraints (QR's) to political considerations.

> "Despite the fact the QR's impose the additional costs on the domestic economy of expropriated profits by exporters and the potential for creating domestic monopoly power, they have become increasingly popular in the 1970's. Ironically, it is precisely the feature of OMA's that makes them more costly to the domestic economy that makes them politically attractive. In general the exporting nation can be expected to be a major political obstacle in a

> protectionist effort. In offering an OMA, however, the exporting nation may be "bought off" by the possibility of expropriating the scarcity rents; this considerably reduces the possibility of retaliatory trade actions" [30, p. 169].

The growth of discriminatory quantitative restraints has been associated with the failure of Article XIX which permits emergency protection but only on a non-discriminatory basis. Dunn et al. note that "governments have found 'informal' discriminatory arrangements, namely Voluntary Export Restraints (VERs), negotiated outside the GATT system a more attractive alternative" than Article XIX [15, p. 112]. There has been debate recently concerning a revision of Article XIX which would permit the use of discriminatory protection for a particular product. This revision, which would legalize the existing unofficial VERs and OMAs, was proposed by the European Economic Community during the 1973-1979 Tokyo Round. It was opposed by small countries for the reasons given below.

> "Since Article XIX does not allow selective protection, the Commission of the European Community, if it wants to take action against one exporting country among several, must move out of the bounds of the GATT and negotiate a VER with the country against which it wants to act. Hence that country retains some control over the form and scope of the action. The result is that a country accepting a VER typically obtains something in return. The most obvious return is that although the physical volume of its exports to the Community is reduced by a VER, the per unit price it obtains for them is usually increased. The supplier in the exporting country, not the importer, collects the rent associated with the restriction. The supplying country may earn more from its smaller volume of sales to the Community than it would if there were no restriction on the level of its exports.
>
> The European Community's proposed revision of Article XIX would remove the ability of a developing country to obtain this quid pro quo. Were that revision incorporated in GATT, the Community - and of course other troubled giants - could legally apply selective, which is

> to say discriminatory, protection against one, two or three countries" [3, pp. 61-62].

Dunn, et al. also warned that "the official sanction of discrimination might result in the proliferation of comprehensive global systems of bilateral restraints as in the Multi-Fiber Arrangement" [15, p. 121]. These official quantitative restraints might undermine the international trading system far more than unofficial quantitative restraints.

TRADE RESTRAINTS: THE PRODUCER' PERSPECTIVE

Factors Influencing Trade Policy Changes

The growth of trade restraints by the developed countries has been attributed to three major factors [33]. The first factor is the slow rate of economic growth in the United States and other developed countries, resulting in recessions and rising levels of unemployment. In many instances these conditions have been aggravated by the growth of imports which have reduced the demand for domestically produced goods. International competition has always been severe for labor intensive industries such as clothing and footwear since productivity improvements are insufficient to compensate for wage differences between developing and developed countries. More recently, international competition has increased for mature industries such as automobiles, steel and consumer electronics reflecting the expansion of world production and in some cases excess capacity. As a result, there has been pressure for protection from workers and labor unions. Import impacted industries have also pleaded for protection citing the need for a stable trading environment if they are to plan effectively [3].

> "First, governments must deal with increasingly articulate, narrowly-defined pressure groups unconcerned by the macro-economic impact of their behavior. This is partly because the growing scope of public involvement in the economy has itself encouraged more sectional interests to become politically organized, as the frequency and density of their contact with governments rises. Second, the range of policy instruments governments can use for responding to these pressures has diminished. Increasing economic interdependence constrains individual government's choices. Because of the inefficacy of macro-economic policy in maintaining full

employment and budgetary constraints on social welfare programmes, consensus maintenance has become more difficult. The attractiveness of import protection - which is off-budget, highly visible to the protected group, but much less visible to others in terms of its costs - has consequently increased" [33, p. 20].

LIMITATIONS OF PROTECTIONIST TRADE MEASURES

The major goals of protectionist measures are to preserve jobs and to provide time for modernization by import impacted industries. Protectionist measures will increase prices and output of domestic firms and the ensuing profits may be used for industry restructuring. However, the OECD study cautions that modernization need not necessarily occur. Thus "by reducing pressures for adjustment to occur and, given the substantial costs adjustment entails, protection can perpetuate technical and economic inefficiency" [33, p. 16]. The report also points out that "protection itself becomes less effective in promoting adjustment when -- as a result of the repeated renewal of protectionist measures -- the firms being protected have no reason to expect that they will ever be exposed to the full challenge of international competition" [33, p. 22]. In addition the two objectives are frequently incompatible. Modernization will increase job losses while attempts to preserve jobs will delay modernization.

The ability of trade restraints to assist domestic firms and workers may also be limited by the following: (1) response of foreign suppliers, (2) diversion of benefits to foreign suppliers, (3) impact of protection on export industries and (4) domestic macroeconomic policies. Each of these factors is discussed in the following sections.

Response of Foreign Suppliers

Trade restraints have frequently resulted in changes in the country and product composition of trade which have undermined their effectiveness. Changes in country composition or trade diversion occurs in the case of discriminatory restrictions against imports from certain countries. An example is the OMA for color TVs between the United States and Japan which was initiated in 1977. At the time of the agreement Japan accounted for 90 percent of U.S. imports. Two years later, Japan's share had declined to 50 percent while the share of other Asian countries had increased from 15 percent to 50 percent. Morkre and Tarr [30] concluded that the impact of the OMA in the 1977/78 period had been negligible due to such trade diversion. Trade diversion has also occurred for textiles and apparel, footwear and steel [33, 44].

Changes in product composition occur most frequently in the case of quantitative restraints as exporters seek to compensate for quantity reductions by selling more expensive products. An example of product upgrading is given by the U.S. Voluntary Export Restraint (VER) for Japanese automobiles which lasted from April 1981 to March 1985. Quality changes occurred in the case of 60 percent of exports and resulted in a 12 percent price increase. The remainder of the price increase (16 percent) was due to profit-taking by Japanese manufacturers in response to the demand/supply imbalance [12]. By the time the VER was discontinued Japanese manufacturers had increased their market share of luxury and sports cars and had used the profits from the VER to expand their product line [14, 27, 33]. This meant increased competition, but of different form, for U.S. manufacturers.

Diversion of Benefits to Foreign Suppliers

As noted earlier, quantitative restrictions such as OMAs and VERs are implemented by exporting countries who increase prices to compensate for quantity reductions. The retention of this scarcity rent by the foreign supplier means that part of the benefits of protection are diverted from domestic suppliers to foreign suppliers. If tariffs were used or quotas auctioned by the importing country then the tariff revenue or scarcity rent could be used to provide adjustment assistance to domestic firms and workers. In addition, the higher profits accruing to exporting countries under quantitative restraints may be used to strengthen their industrial capabilities and to expand their production lines. This increases international competition for the domestic economy.

Impact on Export Industries

In this instance, protectionism is a two-edged sword in that some jobs in import impacted industries may be saved at the expense of jobs in export oriented industries. This loss of jobs is due to rising costs in the export sector from high input prices and the adoption of retaliatory measures by foreign suppliers. The European Task Force on Trade Policy concluded that protection was more likely to redistribute employment than to increase it.

> Rather than increasing the overall level of employment, protection is likely merely to redistribute it among industries: increasing

> employment, perhaps, in enterprises in protected industries, but reducing employment in exporting industries and enterprises. Since the latter are likely to be among a country's most efficient, relative to the rest of the world, and industries and enterprises needing protection are likely to be among its least efficient, this is an especially bad effect. It retards the transfer of labour, capital and skills into those efficient industries and enterprises on which the future prosperity of the country is likely to depend and instead artificially retains labour, capital and skills in industries and enterprises that have difficulty in maintaining themselves without a governmental crutch - without public assistance of some kind. But to accept these costs is not to guarantee any corresponding benefit to the community at large. To repeat, protection is unlikely to have any substantial effect on the overall level of employment and, in many circumstances, what effect it does have, especially in the longer run, will be negative. To translate concern for the unemployed into support for protection is dangerously facile [3, pp. 5-6].

Similar concerns have been expressed by Dunn, et al. [15], Minard [28] and the OECD Economic Policy Committee [33].

Impact of Macroeconomic Policies

Trade protection by changing price and wage behavior may also stimulate inflation and in turn macroeconomic policies aimed at reducing inflation. This may result in a fall in employment for the economy as a whole even though some jobs in import impacted industries are saved. This result has been reported by both Cable [5] and Aislabie [1].

TRADE RESTRAINTS: THE CONSUMER'S PERSPECTIVE

Consumer Gains From Trade

Consumer gains are based on the increase in consumption possibilities due to trade. Trade encourages countries to specialize in the production of goods and services where they have a comparative advantage and also means that the cost savings from such specialization are passed on to consumers. In addition trade enables consumers to purchase goods and services from an international rather than national marketplace and to take advantages of production possibilities in different countries.

The dynamic gains from trade are even more significant. First, trade provides a stimulus to domestic producers to respond to changes in production technologies and to adopt the lowest cost methods of production. The U.S. steel and automobile industries are examples of industries that have adopted new production technologies from abroad due to the pressures of international competition [4, 43, 46].

Second, trade encourages process and product innovation as producers seek to maintain their competitive position on international markets. Finally, trade creates an environment in which producers are responsive to consumer needs. Thus, automobile imports permitted consumers to signal their interest in small fuel efficient cars at a time when Detroit was concentrating on the production of large cars which were more profitable [46].

Impact of Trade Restraints on Consumers

The direct consumer losses from trade restraints have been summarized by Bergsten as follows.

> "Consumers suffer from restriction on international trade in several ways. Tariffs raise the price of imported goods. Quotas and 'voluntary' export restraint agreements reduce the quantity of foreign goods available. Thus they also raise prices. They also limit significantly the range of consumer choice by making some goods totally unavailable, both because of the low levels set by the quotas themselves and because foreign sellers can often reduce their losses from the imposition of quantitative controls by discontinuing lower priced items in favor of those with higher unit prices. Low-income consumers generally suffer most because low-price goods from abroad are the primary targets of U.S. import restrictions" [4, p. 2].

Product upgrading and its detrimental effects on consumers was also noted by Mintz [29] and the OECD Economic Policy Committee [33].

The indirect losses from trade restrictions include reduced competition and innovation on the part of the protected domestic industries due to the reduction in international competition. Bergsten [4] noted that international competition is of particular importance for industries that are dominated by a few large firms since they tend to be less responsive to market pressures. Protection also reduces the incentive for domestic firms to accept foreign innovations, to develop innovations of their own or to improve product quality and design in order to compete with imports. All of these strategies would increase consumer welfare.

The OECD Economic Policy Committee [33] also noted the cumulative effect of protectionist measures on overall economic performance. According to the report "poorer economic performance as a result of protection is aggravated by a deteriorating environment for policy making. Macro-economic policy is more difficult to implement when a large part of the domestic economy expects to be shielded from the competitive discipline of product and labor markets" [33, p. 22]. The same sentiment was echoed by Benard, et al. who stated that "competition is a spur to progress" and that it was "difficult to believe that enterprises would be at their best if they were carefully guarded from the best performance of others" [3, p. 8].

WELFARE LOSS MODELS

Models for estimating consumer and welfare losses from trade restraints are discussed in the next section. Partial equilibrium analysis is used in all instances under the assumption that the major impact of trade restraints is confined to the protected industry. The first two models examine the losses from tariffs and quotas on products which are homogeneous with domestic products. The third model examines the losses from quotas for a differentiated import product while the final model examines the losses from product standards.

Welfare Loss from Tariffs or Quotas

Either tariffs or quotas may be used to increase prices in the importing country. There are two kinds of quotas -- mandatory quotas and voluntary quotas. The latter are called orderly marketing agreements or voluntary export restraints and differ from mandatory quotas in that they are established with the consent of the exporting country and are administered by the exporting country. While a voluntary quota is more desirable than a mandatory quota in that trade reprisals from other countries are minimized, its effect on competition, prices and quality is the same.

Voluntary quotas also generate a higher welfare loss since they permit retention of the scarcity rent by foreign suppliers.

A comparison of the impact of tariffs and quotas is shown in Figure 1. The domestic demand and supply curves are given by DD and SS respectively. The world supply curve, P_1P_1 is horizontal indicating that the world supply is perfectly elastic as far as imports for this particular country are concerned. In the initial situation the domestic price is P_1 with imports accounting for Q_E - Q_A units and domestic production accounting for Q_A units. Imposition of a tariff shifts the world supply price from P_1 to P_2 with a resulting decline in imports to Q_F - Q_B. The loss in consumer surplus from the price increase is equal to the area P_1P_2FE.[3] Part of the loss, however, is returned to the government in the form of tariff revenue -area CBFG. In addition there is a gain in producer surplus from the higher prices which is equal to the area P_1P_2BA. The welfare loss from the tariff is equal to the two areas, ABC and EFG. The first area represents a production efficiency loss when domestic production replaces lower cost imports. The second area represent a consumption efficiency loss as some consumers who are willing to buy low cost imports are forced out of the market due to higher prices. These areas are often called the deadweight production and consumption losses.

Imposition of a quota limiting imports to Q_F - Q_B, could achieve the same price increase from P_1 to P_2 and entail similar gains and losses to producers and consumers respectively. However, the area CBFG, which is called the scarcity rent, may go to either the importing or exporting country. If the importing country auctions quotas, then the scarcity rent will accrue to the government in the same manner as tariff revenue. If the importer is free to select his source of supply among exporters, then the importer as opposed to the government will gain the scarcity rent. Mintz comments, however, than both these developments are unlikely and notes that "when quotas are assigned to specific countries, the exporters in these countries typically control the allocation of the quota and pocket the profit. This is always true of voluntary quotas which means high profits for selected foreign exporters --

---

[3]The welfare loss to consumers from a price increase is measured by the compensating variation in income which is the area under the compensated demand curve. However, if the income effect of a price change is small, then the ordinary demand curve and the compensated demand curves are similar and the area under the ordinary demand curve (consumer surplus) may be used to measure the welfare loss [9].

FIGURE 1

WELFARE LOSS FROM TARIFFS OR QUOTAS:
HOMOGENEOUS PRODUCT

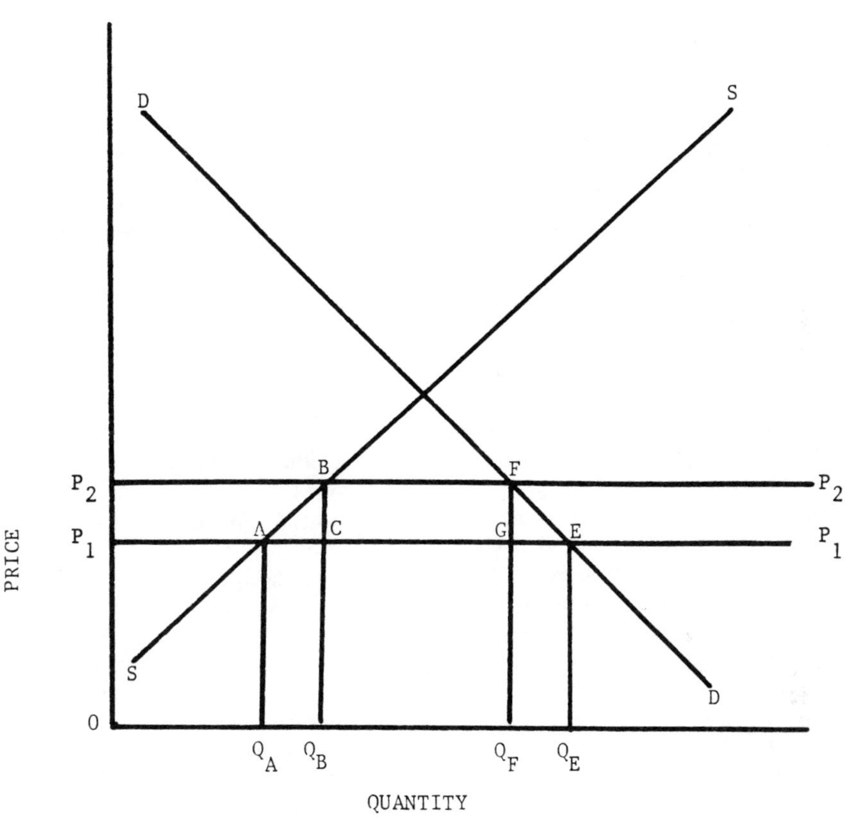

profits which are, of course, a pure burden on the importer's economy" [29, p. 17]. Voluntary quotas will thus result in a higher welfare loss then tariffs due to the loss of scarcity rent.

A final comparison between tariffs and quotas relates to the degree of protection provided by the trade regulation. Most authorities agree that a tariff does not provide the same degree of protection to the domestic manufacturer as a quota since a reduction in world market prices will weaken the protective effect of a tariff. In addition, the foreign manufacturer may reduce prices in order to offset the price increase from a tariff. In contrast, a quota limits the quantity of foreign goods that may be imported irrespective of price changes. If the voluntary marketing agreement is limited to a few countries, however, its effectiveness is likewise limited since non-participating countries may respond to the export opportunity created by such agreements.

Welfare Loss from Tariffs and Quotas

The welfare loss from a combined system of protection (tariffs and quotas) is given in Figure 2. Again P_1 represents a world price in the absence of trade restrictions while P_2 is the price once the tariff is imposed. Imposition of a quota limits the quantity that may be imported to Q_F - Q_b. As a result, the price increases to P_3. The loss in consumer surplus from the total change in prices from P_1 to P_3 is equal to P_1P_3FE while the gain in producer surplus from the price increase is equal to P_1P_3BA. In addition, there is a gain in tariff revenue (area h). The welfare loss due to the tariff and quota is then given by the areas a, b, c, e, f, g, and i. The areas a and e represent the cost of the tariff while the areas b, c, f, g, and i represent the additional cost of the quota once a tariff is in effect. The quota cost has three components. The first component is the loss in tariff revenue due to the reduction in imports (areas b and f). The second component is the loss due to increased domestic production and reduced domestic consumption (area c and g) while the third component is the loss in scarcity rent (area i). As noted earlier, this scarcity rent is likely to be retained by exporting countries in the case of voluntary quotas.

Welfare Loss from Quotas on a Differentiated Product

The above discussion is based on the assumption that imports and domestic products are perfect substitutes. In many instances trade restrictions may be imposed on products that are not perfect substitutes, such as automobiles. The welfare loss estimation under these circumstances is shown in Figure 3. The demand and supply curves for the imported good, which are given in the top diagram,

FIGURE 2

WELFARE LOSS FROM TARRIFFS AND QUOTAS:
HOMOGENEOUS PRODUCT

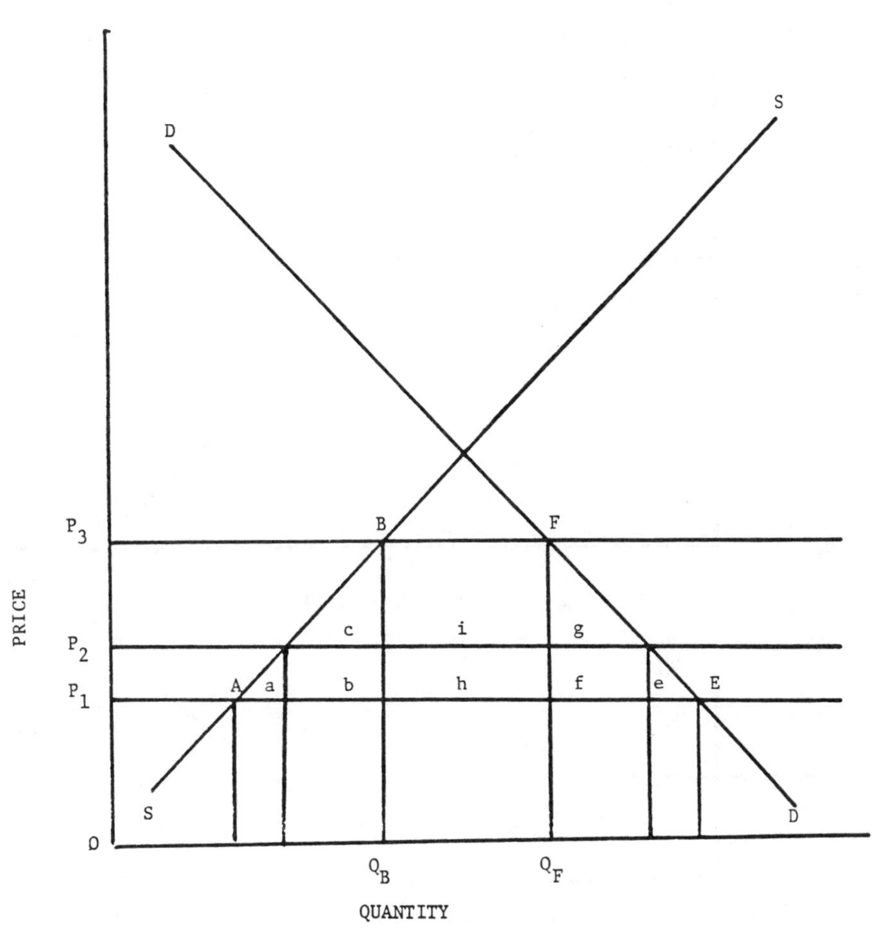

FIGURE 3

WELFARE LOSS FROM QUOTAS ON A DIFFERENTIATED PRODUCT

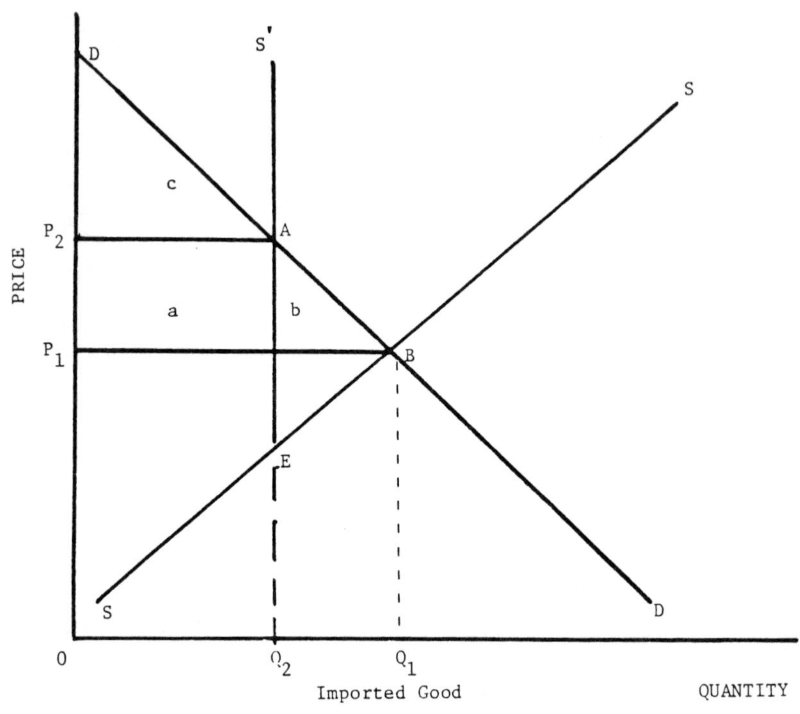

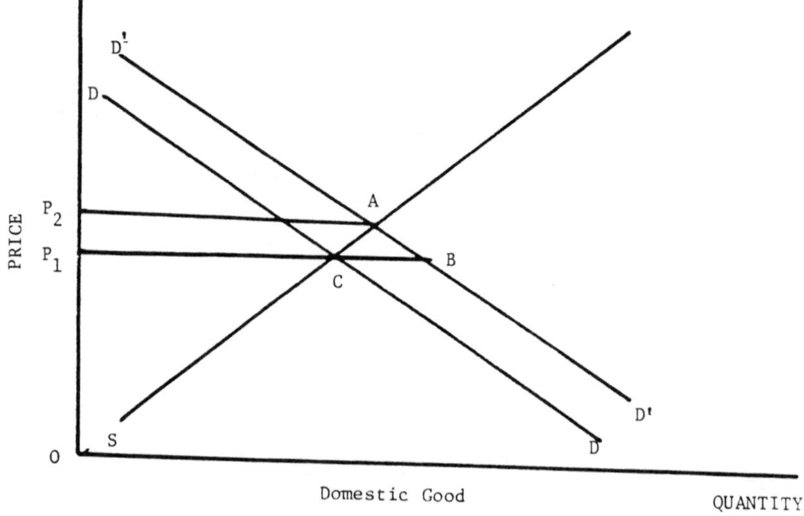

result in a price and quantity of P_1,Q_1 under free trade. Imposition of a quota results in a new price and quantity of P_2,Q_2. The welfare loss and consumer loss is given by the area P_1P_2AB. It includes the scarcity rent retained by the foreign supplier (area a) and the loss to consumers who leave the market due to higher prices (area b). Provision may also be made in this model for improvements in product quality. Thus, if 30 percent of the price increase from P_1 to P_2 is due to product upgrading, then 30 percent of area a must be deducted from the welfare loss and the consumer loss since higher prices mean higher quality. Area b is unaffected by quality changes.

Imposition of the quota also shifts the demand curve for the domestic good which is shown in the lower diagram. The resulting price increase from P_1 to P_2 entails a consumer loss equal to the area P_1P_2AB from which must be deducted the gain to domestic producers (area P_1P_2AC). The net welfare loss is the area ABC. The loss in the domestic market is considerably smaller than the loss in the import market reflecting the fact that consumer losses in the domestic market are offset by domestic producer gains.

Welfare Loss from Product Standards

Mandatory standards e.g., health and safety standards, may also be used to protect domestic firms and workers though their ostensible purpose is to protect consumers.[4] The cost of such standards may be estimated using the differentiated import product model (Figure 3). There are two possibilities when the standard is imposed. First, the imported product cannot meet the standard. In this instance the consumer loss in the import market is equal to the areas a, b and c in Figure 3. Second, the imported product may comply with the standard but its price increases from P_1 to P_2. This reflects a shift in the foreign supply curve which now intersects the domestic demand curve at point A rather than at point B. The consumer loss in the import market is now given by the areas a and b.

In both instances consumer losses in the domestic market may be estimated in the manner previously described.

---

[4]One of the most famous cases in Europe is the "Cassis de Dijon" case [3, p. 20]. The European Court of Justice, Luxemburg found that a German regulation which had prevented the sale of a French liqueur in the Federal Republic of Germany could not be justified on health or consumer protection grounds.

CASE STUDIES IN U.S. TRADE RESTRAINTS

Five consumer commodities were identified for analysis based on differences in trade restraints and number of countries involved. The commodities were apparel, automobiles, color TV's, nonrubber footwear and sugar. Domestic and imported goods were considered as homogeneous in the case of apparel, color TVs and sugar while automobiles and footwear were treated as differentiated import products. The costs of protection for consumers and the economy are first considered followed by a discussion of the impact of import protection on firms and workers in the protected industries.

Costs of Protection: Procedure

Apparel

The U.S. apparel industry has been protected by a comprehensive system of tariffs and quotas since 1974 when the first Multi-Fiber Arrangement (MFA) was enacted [45]. Under the MFA bilateral agreements were made between the United States and major textile and apparel exporting countries for specific products. Losses were estimated for 1980 using the tariff/quota model shown in Figure 2 [10].

It was assumed that an item entering the United States for a price of one dollar would incur transportation costs and distribution costs of 30 cents and tariff costs of 27 cents. The price impact of the quota was 16 cents based on a 10 percent price difference between domestic and imported apparel at the same U.S. distribution level [25]. Price elasticities of demand and supply were based on the price elasticity of demand for imports [35, 40] and the relationship between this elasticity and domestic price elasticities.

There was one important exception to the tariff/quota model shown in Figure 2. It was assumed that competitive conditions in the world export market would place pressure on foreign suppliers so that they could not gain the scarcity rent from the quota.[5] This assumption was based on the fact that the MFA was confined to major exporting countries and major product categories so that some U.S. imports were not covered by the MFA. In addition, some exporting countries did not fill their quotas each year [44]. In the

---

[5]Recent research by Tarr and Morkre [42] suggests that quota premiums have been charged by some exporting countries who were in a favorable demand/supply situation. Neglect of this effect means that losses will have been underestimated.

short-run the scarcity rent from the quota could be captured by U.S. distributors. However, in the long-run it was assumed that competitive conditions in retailing would result in the return of the scarcity rent to consumers. This could occur through price differences for domestic and imported products at the retail level or through the use of higher mark-ups on imported goods to offset lower mark-ups on domestic goods.

Automobiles

A VER for Japanese automobiles was initiated in 1981/82 and was extended for four years. Losses were estimated for the third year of the VER (1983/84) using the differentiated product model shown in Figure 3 [12]. Losses for Japanese cars were based on profit-taking, i.e. retention of the scarcity rent, as well as product up-grading. Price increases ranged from 16 percent (no quality changes) to 28 percent (quality changes). In addition, provision was made for the response of U.S. dealers of Japanese cars to a demand/supply imbalance in the third year of the VER. It was assumed that dealers would increase prices by $1,000 over list price [16, 26]. In the case of small domestic cars the sales weighted price increase was $466 which is similar to other estimates [8, 38]. A unitary price elasticity of demand was used for both Japanese and U.S. automobiles based on studies by Carlson [6] and Chase Econometrics [7].

Color TVs

An OMA was initiated with Japan for color TVs for a three year period commencing July 1, 1977. The analysis was confined to the first year of the OMA (1977/78) since the OMA was extended to Taiwan and South Korea in 1979 [30].

Nonrubber Footwear

Two OMAs were initiated with Taiwan and South Korea in 1977/78 and lasted four years. Losses were estimated for the fourth year of the OMA (1980/81) and imported and domestic footwear were treated as imperfect substitutes based on considerable price/quality differences between the two categories. Losses were confined to Taiwanese and South Korean footwear since imports from other countries and excess capacity in the domestic footwear industry continued to exercise competitive pressure on the domestic footwear industry [11].

The welfare loss from the OMAs was based on the retention of the scarcity rent by Taiwan and South Korea, the consumption loss due to higher prices and the loss in tariff revenue from the reduction in imports from Taiwan and South Korea, a loss which was not offset by an increase in imports from other countries. Provision was also made for product up-grading in estimating the scarcity rent loss. The price elasticity of demand for imports was equal to 1.5 based on a study by Szenberg, Lombardi and Lee [41].

Sugar

Import quotas were imposed by the United States in 1982 on all exporting countries when falling world prices meant that the existing system of protection was inadequate to achieve the desired U.S. price levels. Losses were estimated for 1982/83 using the tariff/quota model shown in Figure 2 [13]. It was assumed that there would be no change in the world price of sugar from changes in U.S. trade restrictions due to excess world sugar stocks. The price elasticity of demand was 0.2 based on work by Johnson [21] and Morkre and Tarr [30]. The price elasticity of supply was 1.66 based on a study by Gemill [17] who estimated separate price elasticities of 1.57 and 1.75 for sugar and sugar beet respectively.

Costs of Protection: Results

No price increases were observed for color TVs in the United States during the first year of the OMA with Japan. Morkre and Tarr [30] concluded that this was due to the significant increase in supply from Taiwan, South Korea and Mexico and the appreciation of the yen. As a result "the welfare costs to consumers and the inefficiency losses to the U.S. economy have been marginal" [30, p. 87]. The quotas in this instance were non binding in contrast to quotas for the other four commodities.

The cost of protection for the other four commodities are given in Table 1. All costs are expressed in 1984 dollars for purposes of comparison. The various demand and supply elasticities as well as assumptions concerning producer response and world prices are given in footnotes. High and low estimates were obtained for apparel, automobiles, and footwear.

The U.S. consumer loss is given in the first column followed by the U.S. producer/distributor gain and the tariff revenue gain. Deduction of these gains from the consumer loss yields the welfare loss which is given in the last column. Foreign producer gain (or scarcity rent) is given in the fourth column to show the transfer which occurs from U.S. consumers to foreign producers under quantitative restrictions.

Table 1

Costs of U.S. Trade Restrictions in 1984 Dollars ($ Billion)

Commodity (Year)	Estimate	U.S. Consumer Loss (1)	U.S. Producer/ Distributor Gain (2)	U.S. Tariff Revenue Gain (3)	Foreign Producer Gain (4)	U.S. Welfare Loss (5)
Apparel[a] (1980)	Low	13.113	10.374	2.003	0	0.736
	High	13.527	10.374	2.003	0	1.150
Automobiles[b] (1983/84)	Low	3.210	0.847	0	1.938	2.363
	High	5.457	2.577	0	1.938	2.880
Sugar[c] (1982/83)	--	2.534	0.931	0.129	0.685	1.474
Footwear[d] (1980/81)	Low	0.370	0	0.087	0.069	0.283
	High	0.651	0	0.087	0.328	0.564

[a] $n_s = 0.25$; $n_d = 0.25$, 0.50 for low and high estimates respectively.

[b] $n_s = n_d = 1.00$; high estimates reflect profit-taking by U.S. distributors of Japanese cars.

[c] $n_s = 1.66$; $n_d = 0.20$; unchanged world price when tariffs/quotas are removed.

[d] $n_s = 1.5$; low estimates reflect provision for product upgrading.

The consumer loss for apparel is considerably higher than the losses for automobiles or sugar. However, the welfare loss is smaller. This reflects the deduction of producer/tariff revenue gains and the absence of foreign gains in the case of apparel. Thus the welfare loss for apparel only includes the inefficiency losses from expanded domestic production and reduced domestic consumption. In contrast the welfare losses for automobiles and sugar include both inefficiency losses as well as transfers to foreign producers. These transfer losses could have been avoided if quotas had been auctioned by the U.S. government or if tariffs had been used in place of voluntary quotas.

Footwear has the smallest consumer loss reflecting the fact that only two exporting countries are involved -- Taiwan and South Korea. In contrast to the other three commodities there are no domestic producer gains since conditions remained competitive in this industry in spite of trade restrictions.

Impact of Trade Restrictions on Different Income Groups

The impact of U.S. trade restrictions on different income groups was investigated by Hickok [19]. The commodities examined were apparel, automobiles and sugar. Consumer losses were confined to changes in consumer expenditures in 1984, due to trade restrictions. In spite of this, the losses reported by Hickok were similar to those reported in Table 1. They are given below.

Apparel: $8.5 to $12 billion

Automobiles: $4.5 billion

Sugar: $3 billion

The results for different income groups are given in Table 2. The cost of protection as a percent of income ranges from 1.11 percent for the highest income group to 1.56 percent for the lowest income group. A comparison of this rate with the Federal income tax rate which is given in the next column yields an income tax surcharge which is equivalent to the cost of protection. This surcharge ranges from 5 percent for the highest income group to 23 percent for the lowest income group. These data clearly indicate the regressive nature of trade restrictions which penalize the lowest income consumers most severely.

Table 2

Tax Effect of U.S. Trade Restrictions for Apparel, Automobiles, and Sugar in 1984

Income Group ($)	Cost of Protection as a Percent of Income[a] (%)	Federal Income Tax Rate (%)	Income Tax Surcharge Equivalent to Cost of Protection[b] (%)
7,000- 9,350	1.56	6.90	23
9,350-11,700	1.44	8.48	17
16,400-18,700	1.36	11.49	12
28,050-35,100	1.20	16.66	7
46,800-58,500	1.11	23.50	5

[a]The percent increase in price multiplied by the percentage of income spent on each product in 1972-1973.

[b]Cost of protection divided by the Federal income tax rate.

Source: Hickok (1985).

Impact of Alternative Systems of Protection

The impact of alternative systems of protection was examined using data for sugar [13]. The three systems of protection for sugar are given in Table 3. The first system (tariff/quota system) was already presented in Table 1. In addition to U.S. consumer losses and U.S. producer gains the absolute and relative welfare losses and cost to the U.S. government are given. The absolute welfare loss was obtained in the manner previously described while the relative welfare loss is the absolute welfare loss divided by U.S. producer gain.

The tariff/quota system has an absolute welfare loss of $1.474 billion and a relative welfare loss of 158 percent. This means that every $100 transferred to U.S. sugar growers has a transfer cost of $158, which is extremely high. The second system is a tariff system. There is no change in U.S. consumer loss or U.S. producer gain. However, the absolute and relative welfare losses decline since the scarcity rent loss (0.685 billion) is replaced by a tariff revenue gain. Only the deadweight production and consumption losses are incurred under this system.

The third system is a deficiency payment system under which U.S. producers receive payments from the U.S. government equal to $1.537 billion ($0.931 + $0.606 billion). There is no consumer loss and only the deadweight production loss remains ($0.606 billion). This system is more efficient than the other two systems since it has a relative welfare loss of 65 percent. It only costs the economy $165 to transfer $100 to sugar growers as opposed to $258 and $185 for the first and second systems respectively. It is also more equitable in that tax revenues are used to defray the costs of such a program rather than the U.S. sugar consumer.

While the third system of protection is more favorable to consumers and the economy, it is the only system which imposes direct costs on the U.S. Government. This may explain why deficiency payments have not been used. Increased government expenditures under a deficiency payments system will result in higher deficits or higher taxes, both of which are likely to be opposed by the President and/or Congress. Thus a more efficient and equitable system of protection is rejected.

Table 3

Impact of Alternative Systems of Protection for Sugar in 1984 Dollars

System of Protection	U.S. Consumer Loss ($ Billion)	U.S. Producer Gain ($ Billion)	Absolute Welfare Loss ($ Billion)	Relative Welfare Loss[a] (%)	Cost to U.S. Government ($ Billion)
Tariff/Quota	2.534	0.931	1.474	158	0
Tariff	2.534	0.931	0.789	85	0
Deficiency Payments	0	0.931	0.606	65	1.537

[a]Absolute welfare loss divided by U.S. producer gain.

DISCUSSION

Several conclusions may be drawn concerning the costs of trade restraints. First, alternative systems of supply play a major role in determining the impact of trade restraints on consumers and the economy. Thus, high costs are incurred when all countries are included in the trade restraint (sugar) or when substitutes for the dominant exporter are lacking (automobiles). Costs are high for apparel since tariffs are applied to all imports. However, costs might be even higher if global quotas were used instead of the existing specific product/country quotas based on bilateral agreements. Thus, the scarcity rent could be retained in the United States. No costs were observed for color TV's due to import substitution, i.e., the quotas were non-binding.

Second, trade restraints result in income transfers from consumers to producers. In the case of quantitative restrictions transfers may occur to foreign as well as to domestic producers. Trade restrictions are also regressive. Lower income consumers pay proportionately more than upper income consumers when prices increase due to trade restraints. In addition, quantitative restrictions stimulate product up-grading which means that lower cost imports are discouraged. A classic example of product up-grading occurred during the VER with Japanese automobiles when the small "economy" Japanese car disappeared [14, 27].

Finally, the welfare loss is influenced by the specific protectionist measures used. Voluntary quotas, which permit retention of the scarcity rent by exporters, impose higher welfare losses than tariffs which impose higher welfare losses than deficiency payments for the same level of domestic producer protection.

Benefits from Protection: Impact on Domestic Firms and Workers

Apparel

The U.S. International Trade Commission [44] noted that textiles and apparel imports had continued to grow in spite of the MFA. This was due to the fact that bilateral agreements were only negotiated with major exporting countries and for major product categories. As a result, imports of fabrics and apparel doubled between 1976 and 1984. Imported apparel accounted for 33 percent of the U.S. market in 1984 compared to 22 percent in 1979 [37]. Dissatisfaction with the MFA led to a proposal for global quotas on all textiles and apparel which was vetoed by President Reagan in December, 1985. However, the industry continues to press for tighter import controls. Apparel workers remain among the lowest paid workers in manufacturing in the United States. Employment is likely to decline in the future due to import competition, industry modernization and increased reliance on off-shore production by domestic firms.

Automobiles

The two objectives of the VER were to save the jobs of American workers and to make the industry more competitive with imports by providing time for modernization and adjustment. According to most industry analysts, neither of these objectives had been realized when the VER ended [8, 24, 38, 43]. The VER had a small impact on employment due to increased automation by American firms and reliance on off-shore production. As a result, Crandall [8] estimated that the cost per job saved was $160,000. He also noted that import quotas did not appear to have advanced the competitiveness of the U.S. automobile industry and that "their desirability turns on whether Americans wish to pay large premiums on their cars in order to increase the employment of automobile workers at wages far above the manufacturing average" [8, p. 16].

Color TVs

As noted earlier the OMA had a marginal impact on prices in its first year due to the growth of imports from other countries.

As a result the OMA was extended to include South Korea and Taiwan. Prices increased and some jobs were saved. However, the principal gainer from the extended MFA was Japan which had set up production facilities in the United States [33, p. 164]. Few benefits accrued to the domestically owned firms.

Nonrubber Footwear

Yoffie [47] examined the impact of the OMAs on the domestic footwear industry and concluded that they had been ineffective in assisting the industry. The number of firms and workers continued to decline during the OMAs while the market share of imported footwear increased from 45 percent in 1975 to 50 percent in 1981 [11]. The cessation of the OMAs increased the problems of the domestic footwear industry and led to a recommendation by the U.S. International Trade Commission, in June 1985, to impose quotas on all imports [20]. This recommendation was rejected by President Reagan due to the high cost involved. It was estimated that the cost per job saved would have been $30,000 in an industry whose annual wages were $14,000 [20, 36].

Sugar

World sugar prices have continued to remain depressed. So there is little doubt that the new sugar program has benefitted domestic sugar growers. However, the high transfer costs raise questions concerning the efficiency of the existing system and suggest that once again we may be faced with a problem characterized by "large costs and small benefits" [21].

CONCLUSIONS

The preceding analysis indicates that trade restraints impose high costs on consumers and the economy. The direct costs are higher prices paid by consumers and the reduction in consumer choice due to product upgrading. The indirect costs include the lack of incentive for the domestic industry to respond to changes in production and consumption and the pervasive effects of protectionist measures on economic efficiency and economic growth.

The high costs of trade restraints may yield few, if any, benefits. Thus trade restraints face severe limitations in achieving their twin objectives of job preservation and industry modernization. Employment gains in one sector may be offset by employment losses in another sector, notably the export sector. Trade diversion and product upgrading also reduce the efficacy of trade restraints as new sources of supply and new products continue to exert competitive pressures on domestic industries. In addition, the necessary long term adjustment and modernization of the domestic industry may never occur as the need for job preservation dominates industry modernization. Thus the potential benefits from import protection may never be realized.

The imbalance between the costs and benefits of import protection was acknowledged in a recent report on protectionism and the European Community [3]. The authors of this report stated that the economies of the Community are not underprotected and the real "danger is that they will be over-protected." "The balance has shifted too far in the direction of protectionism and the present problem is that the gains from trade and competition are being grossly neglected" [3, p. 8]. Protectionism for products such as textiles and apparel also threatens the extension of GATT trading rules to new areas such as services and high technology where trade restrictions have been widespread. Many Third World countries fear that they will be at a trade disadvantage in high technology and services while continuing trade restraints will prevent them from expanding production and exports in the labor-intensive sectors where they have an advantage.

Finally, trade policies in the 1970s and 1980s reflect the dominance of special interest groups and provide support for Stigler's theory of regulation. Stigler argues that the state's power to coerce provides opportunities for the "utilization of the state by an industry to increase its profitability" [39, p. 4]. As a result, industries with sufficient political power will seek to limit or control entry through regulatory agencies such as the Civil Aeronautics Board or by means of trade regulation. Peltzman noted that the resulting product protection "represents the dominance of a small group with a large per-capita stake over a larger group (consumers) with more diffused interests" [34, p. 212]. Stigler's theory has been called the "capture" theory of regulation in that regulation is supplied in response to the demand of interest groups who are attempting to maximize the income of their members. Dunn et al. commented on the power of special interest groups in matters of trade policy and noted that they tended to be "focused and highly organized whereas the interest in liberal trade is widespread and harder to organize" [15, p. 4]. Olson [31] attributed part of the problems of mature economics to special interest groups and advocated free trade as one method for curbing their political power.

The capture theory of regulation indicates the importance of consumer input in trade policy decisions. This was recognized in a recent symposium on consumer policy and international trade [32].

The authors also noted the need for consumer information and education if consumers are to play an effective role in trade policy formulation.

> "Consumers and consumer representatives are often at a disadvantage in terms of influencing trade policy decisions. Consumer interests are generally more diffuse geographically and in terms of product coverage than those of domestic producers of a particular commodity. Further, having focused to date their efforts on the implementation of consumer protection laws, for lack of resources or other reasons, consumer representatives may not always have been aware of the consumer impact of trade policy measures and thus may not have taken full advantage of existing possibilities to exert influence on trade policy decisions. Indeed, they may not always have been aware of the consumer impact of trade policy measures" [32, p. 288].

A study of consumer activists in the United States indicated a similar lack of awareness and concern by consumer advocates [2].

This lack of awareness may explain consumer apathy in the past to trade policies which are detrimental to their interests. The challenge for consumer educators is to alert consumers and consumer representatives to the consequences of various trade policies so that they may become effective in advocating for policies which promote their interests.

REFERENCES

1. AISLABIE, E. J. (1983), "The Australian Tariff as a Selected Employment Policy Investment: An Empirical Study," Australian Economic Papers, 22 (Summer): 119-131.

2. ANGEVINE, I. (Editor) (1982), "Consumer Activists: They Made a Difference," New York: Consumers Union Foundation.

3. BENARD, A., ET AL. (1984), A Europe Open to the World, London Trade Policy Research Center.

4. BERGSTEN, C. F. (1972), "The Cost of Import Restrictions to American Consumers," New York: American Importers Association.

5. CABLE, V. (1983), Protectionism and Industrial Decline, London: Hodder and Stoughton.

6. CARLSON, R. L. (1978), "Seemingly Unrelated Regression and the Demand for Automobiles of Different Sizes, 1965-1975: A Disaggregate Approach," Journal of Business, 51 (April): 243-262.

7. CHASE ECONOMETRICS (1981), Short-Run Passenger Car Forecast (Executive Summary), May 15.

8. CRANDALL, R. W. (1984), "Import Quotas and the Automobile Industry: The Costs of Protectionism," Brookings Review, 2 (Summer): 8-16.

9. CURRIE, J. M., J. A. MURPHY and A. SCHMITZ (1971), "The Concept of Economic Supplies and Its Use in Economic Analysis," Economic Journal, 81 (December): 741-99.

10. DARDIS, R. and K. COOKE (1984), "The Impact of Trade Restrictions on U.S. Apparel Consumers," Journal of Consumer Policy, 7 (January): 1-12.

11. _________ and J-Y LIN (1986), "The Welfare Impact of Orderly Marketing Agreements for Nonrubber Footwear," Home Economics Research Journal, 15 (September): 64-72.

12. _________ (1985), "Automobile Quotas Revisited: The Costs of Continued Protection," Journal of Consumer Affairs, 17 (Winter): 277-292.

13. DARDIS, R. and C. YOUNG (1985), "The Welfare Loss from the New Sugar Program," Journal of Consumer Affairs, 19 (Summer): 163-176.

14. DELORENZO, M. (1982), "With Limits on U.S. Imports, Japanese Makers Shift Effort to Higher Price Luxury Lines," Automotive News, October: E-14.

15. DUNN, L., ET AL. (1983), In the Kingdom of the Blind, London: Trade Policy Research Center.

16. FISHER, A. (1984), "Can Detroit Live Without Quotas," Fortune, 109 (June 25): 20-25.

17. GEMILL, G. (1977), "An Equilibrium Analysis of U.S. Sugar Policy," American Journal of Agricultural Economics, 59 (November): 609-612.

18. GOLT, S. (1978), Developing Countries in the GATT Systems, London: Trade Policy Research Center.

19. HICKOK, S. (1985), "The Consumer Cost of U.S. Trade Restraints," Federal Reserve Bank of New York Quarterly Review, Summer: 1-12.

20. HUFBAUER, G. (1985), "But the Footwear Industry Could Use a Little Relief," Washington Post, August 13: A17.

21. JOHNSON, D. G. (1974), The Sugar Program: Large Costs and Small Benefits, Washington, D.C.: American Enterprise Institute for Public Policy Research.

22. _________ (1973), World Agriculture in Disarray, London: Trade Policy Research Center.

23. KEESING, D. B. and M. WOLF (1980), Textile Quotas Against Developing Countries, London: Trade Policy Research Center.

24. KNIGHT, J. (1984), "Import Quotas Put Cars Out of Reach," Washington Post, Feb. 27: 1-17.

25. KURT SALMON ASSOCIATES (1981), "The Impact of Technology on the Apparel Manufacturer," Bobbin, 22 (6): 39-44.

26. MCGRATH, A. (1983), "Import Quotas: The Honda Dealer's Best Friend," Forbes, 132 (December 5): 43-44.

27. MINARD, L. (1984), "Cover Story: Japan Moves Up," Forbes, 134 (September): 41-48.

28. ________ (1985), "Noah's Ark, Anyone?" Forbes, 136 (August): 76-81.

29. MINTZ, I. (1972), U.S. Import Quotas: Costs and Consequences, Washington, D.C.: American Enterprise Institute for Public Policy Research.

30. MORKRE, M. E. and D. G. TARR (1980), Federal Trade Commission, Bureau of Economics, Staff Report on Effects of Restrictions on United States Imports: Five Case Studies and Theory, Washington, D.C.: U.S. Government Printing Office.

31. OLSON, M. (1982), The Rise and Decline of Nations, New Haven: Yale University Press.

32. OECD (1985), Committee on Consumer Policy, Consumer Policy and International Trade, Paris: OECD.

33. ________ (1985), Economic Policy Committee, Cost and Benefits of Protection, Paris: OECD.

34. PELTZMAN, S. (1976), "Toward a More General Theory of Regulation," Journal of Law and Economics, 19 (August): 211-240.

35. PELZMAN, J. and C. E. BRADBERRY (1980), "The Welfare Effects of Reduced U.S. Tariff Restrictions on Imported Textile Products," Applied Economics, 12 (December): 455-465.

36. PERL, P. (1985), "Displaced Shoe Workers to be Aided," Washington Post, September 14: A4.

37. PRATT, R. A., JR. (1985), "Protest Over Imports Changing Course of U.S. Trade Policy," Washington Post, October 13: D1-D2.

38. SAMUELSON, R. J. (1984), "Auto Makers Find Quotas Addicting," Washington Post, June 13: F1-F2.

39. STIGLER, G. (1971), "The Theory of Economic Regulation," Bell Journal of Economic and Management Sciences, 2: 3-21.

40. STONE, J. A. (1979), "Price Elasticities of Demand for Imports and Exports: Industry Estimates for the U.S., the E.E.C., and Japan," Review of Economics and Statistics 62: 306-312.

41. SZENBERG, M., LOMBARDI, J. W. and E. Y. LEE (1977), Welfare Effects of Trade Restrictions: A Case Study of the U.S. Footwear Industry, New Jersey: Academic Press.

42. TARR, D. G. and M. E. MORKRE (1984), Aggregate Costs to the United States of Tariffs and Quotas on Imports, Federal Trade Commission, Bureau of Economics, Washington, D.C.: U.S. Government Printing Office.

43. U.S. INTERNATIONAL TRADE COMMISSION (1985), A Review of Recent Developments in the U.S. Automobile Industry Including an Assessment of the Japanese Voluntary Restraint Agreements, USITC Publication 1648, Washington, D.C.

44. ________ (1985), Emerging Textile-Exporting Countries, 1984, USITC Publication 1716, Washington, D.C.

45. ________ (1981), The Multi-Fiber Arrangement, 1973-1980, USITC Publication 1131, Washington, D.C.

46. YATES, B. (1984), The Decline and Fall of the American Automobile Industry, New York: Vintage House.

47. YOFFIE, D. B. (1981), "Orderly Marketing Agreements as an Industrial Policy: The Case of the Footwear Industry," Public Policy, 29 (Winter): 93-119.

Chapter 16

ABOUT THE AUTHOR

Robert W. Crandall is Senior Fellow at The Brookings Institution. For further background, see the Headnote to Chapter 4.

THE DARDIS PAPER: SOME SUGGESTIONS

Robert W. Crandall

Dardis' paper represents a commendable effort to summarize the extensive literature on trade protection. It distinguishes between tariffs and quotas. It is appropriately skeptical of the value of "temporary" trade protection in generating industry modernization and rejuvenation. It even discusses briefly the role of product standards as trade barriers.

My criticisms of the paper are, therefore, more of a plea for some extensions and amplifications, rather than quibbles with the paper's methodology or substantive conclusions.

Producers Versus Consumers

From the outset, the paper sets up trade protection as a struggle between producers and consumers. It then points out why trade protection may not work to the long-run benefit of the protected industry. This discussion could be improved if it referred to Robert Lawrence's detailed studies of those industries receiving "escape clause" protection in the United States [3, 4]. As Lawrence shows, trade protection is very rarely effective in providing incentives or opportunities for industry adjustment.

In addition, Dardis should comment on the ability of owners of productive factors to appropriate the rents from protection. Have steelworkers and autoworkers not earned large rents from trade protection? How has this appropriation of rents affected the long-run health of these industries?

Domestic Concentration and the Choice of Tariffs or Quotas

There is a rather pervasive belief that tariffs are superior to quotas or orderly marketing agreements because the latter transfer rents to foreign producers. In fact, tariffs are also superior for another reason: they limit the ability of concentrated domestic industries to exert monopoly (or oligopoly) pricing power. Dardis should refer to the recent work by Dixit [1] and Krishna [2] that has focused on the important relationship between market power and the welfare loss due to quotas. This suggests that the simple, competitive analysis used in Table 1 may not be valid for the automobile industry, for example.

The superiority of tariffs over quotas, however, should not lead one to believe that a government has a free choice between them. Since import quotas confer a share of the monopoly rents of protection upon foreign producers, it is likely to be much easier to implement without retaliation from foreign governments. This explains part of their current allure to U.S. policymakers. Thus, if protection cannot be avoided due to domestic political considerations, a quota may be better than a tariff, particularly in a competitive industry.

The Quantitative Effects of Trade Restrictions

Dardis estimates the quantitative impacts of trade restrictions in four industries -- apparel, automobiles, footwear, and sugar. These calculations are summarized in Table 1 but are not explained. There is a tabulation of assumed elasticities, but how do we know whether the quotas are binding in each case? Moreover, is the competitive assumption the correct one (see above)?

In Table 1, Dardis provides an estimate of the producer gains, consumer losses, and welfare losses from protection in each of the four industries surveyed. It would be interesting to allocate the "producer" gains between owners of capital and labor, but perhaps this is asking too much of a survey paper.

The Political Economy of Protection

In closing, Dardis gives us a few thoughts on the public choice issues involved. Why do we find protection enduring and proliferating when the costs are so high and the benefits so low? This section is somewhat unsatisfying, for it simply invokes the concentrated benefits-dispersed costs argument as well as consumer ignorance.

She concludes with a plea for greater consumer education on these issues, suggesting that consumer knowledge might overcome the unfavorable balance of political forces that drives protectionist policy. I only wish that I could be that optimistic!

REFERENCES

1. DIXIT, A. (1984), "International Trade Policy for Oligopolistic Industries," The Economic Journal, (Vol. 94; Suppl.): 1-16.

2. KRISHNA, K. (1984), "Trade Restrictions as Facilitating Practices," manuscript, Princeton University.

3. LAWRENCE, R.Z. and P. DEMASI (forthcoming), "Do Industries with a Self-Identified Loss in Comparative Advantage Ever Adjust?" in Domestic Adjustment and International Trade, Gary C. Hufbauer and Howard F. Rosen, eds., Washington, DC: Institute for International Economics.

4. _________ and R.E. LITAN (1986), Saving Free Trade, Washington, DC: The Brookings Institution.

ABOUT THE AUTHOR

Erich Linke is Principal Administrator in the Enterprise and Consumer Affairs Division of O.E.C.D., the Paris-based Organization for Economic Cooperation and Development. An Austrian by nationality, Linke received his Doctorate in Economics from Wirtschaftsuniversitaet in Vienna in 1967. For ten years, starting in 1962, Linke was the representative of the Austrian Chamber of Commerce in the Austrian consumer organization, the Verein fuer Konsumenteninformation. With OECD since 1972, Linke is in charge of the OECD Committee on Consumer Policy. He has authored and co-authored many OECD Reports on consumer policy issues covering such topics as deceptive packaging, consumer credit, mail order trading, product safety, and videotex.

INTERNATIONAL TRADE AND THE CONSUMER: REPORT ON AN OECD SYMPOSIUM[1]

Erich Linke

Dardis' case studies and her general conclusions agree with similar work carried out in OECD and by several national and international consumer organizations, particularly, the United Kingdom Consumers Association and by BEUC (the Bureau Europèen des Unions des Consommateurs). All have examined the linkages between consumer policy and international trade. Since Rachel Dardis's study ends with a reference to the International Symposium on Consumer Policy and International Trade organized by the OECD Committee on Consumer Policy in November 1984, I should like to comment on the discussions at the Symposium and follow-ups to these discussions.

THE NATURE OF THE OECD SYMPOSIUM

The symposium brought together some 150 representatives from governments, international organizations, trade and industry, trade unions and national and international consumer organizations to

---

[1]OECD is the Organization for Economic Cooperation and Development. It serves as an economic planning group for the member countries of OECD. The member nations include: Australia, Austria, Belgium, Canada, Denmark, Finland, France, Germany, Greece, Iceland, Ireland, Italy, Japan, Luxembourg, Netherlands, New Zealand, Norway, Portugal, Spain, Sweden, Switzenland, Turkey, United Kingdom and United States. The papers and proceedings of the Symposium were published in 1986 under the title "International Trade and the Consumer."

discuss the consumer interest in international trade, until then a somewhat neglected topic. The symposium centered on three main themes: (1) the effect of trade policy on the consumer interest; (2) the impact of consumer policy on international trade; and, (3) the consideration of consumer interests in formulating and implementing trade policy. In organizing the Symposium the Committee had the following goals:

-- To test and to deepen the analysis of trade and consumer policy issues contained in the Committee's background report to the Conference and to assist the Committee in developing its future activities on these issues;

-- To identify the consumer interest in international trade by showing how the impact of trade policy measures on consumers can best be assessed;

-- To consider how the consumer interest can be given proper weight in the assessment of trade policy measures at the national and international levels;

-- To contribute to an increase in the general awareness of the link between consumer policy considerations and international trade.

A report to the OECD Council summarized the results of the Symposium, concluding with a number of suggestions for national and OECD actions. These recommendations were approved by the Council. They included measures to improve information for decision-making and to improve the institutional framework in member countries. Specifically, the recommendations stressed that:

-- "Trade officials should take into account the consumer policy implications and in general seek the advice of consumer policy officials before making decisions likely to have a significant impact on consumer interests. There are various options for organizing such participation, e.g., informal but regular contacts, establishment of standing interdepartmental committees or task forces, and arrangements providing the possibility for authorities responsible for consumer and competition policies to make written or oral presentations in public hearings."

Moreover, the Council approved a "Checklist for the Assessment of Trade Policy Measures" which had been jointly developed with the OECD Committee of Experts on Restrictive Business Practices, the

Committee that deals with competition policy in OECD countries. See Appendix at the end of this chapter for the Checklist.

After this account of OECD's work, it is natural to turn to what was actually discussed and what might be done in furtherance of these recommendations. In responding to this, I come back to the three main themes of the Symposium, i.e., the consumer interest in international trade, the impact of consumer policy on the latter, and the potential for consumers' influence on policy decisions in the area of international trade.

THE CONSUMER INTEREST IN INTERNATIONAL TRADE

As to the consumer interest in international trade, we have to be realistic lest the "consumer interest" degenerate into a reference as artificial as the "Economic Man" of pure theory, and nothing more. The consumer is certainly interested in international trade. But, to say the least, this interest has been hardly articulate and resolute. Can consumer organizations give voice to this vague discontent with trade measures in a way that gives consumers some weight in the decision-making process? We must first acknowledge that, until now, trade issues have not been among the main preoccupations of consumer organizations in most countries. This is the case for three main reasons: (1) first and foremost, the organizations' lack of financial and human resources; (2) the structure of consumer organizations, meaning their "ideological" background and dependence on their constituent national bodies, and, (3) the "marketing" aspect of the issue, meaning the difficulty of arousing interest in an abstract principle like free trade as contrasted with a spectacular product safety issue or an "unfair" marketing practice.

Does economic chauvinism affect the position of consumer organizations in particular countries? Traces of it certainly exist, but it probably should not be overrated. In one European country opinion polls have shown that survey responses to the crucial question "Do you prefer domestic or imported goods?" seem to be dominated by a "social desirability" attitude that is protectionist. The actual buying decision, on the other hand, is a purely economic consideration, or, occasionally, even a long standing prejudice in favor of foreign goods. In the only country --Japan-- where consumer organizations have publicly approved protectionism, the situation seems to be more complex. The very interesting contribution by Professor Hamada of Tokyo University at the OECD Symposium showed that, apart from certain attitudes attributable to the specific socio-cultural background, the firm views of consumer organizations on this issue do not always correctly reflect the ideas consumers have about the prices of agricultural products, for example, and protectionism in this field. A first task for consumer organizations should be to stimulate consumer interest in trade matters. This might be accomplished by providing very concrete information on unexplained price differences between countries for certain products, brands or services. The UK Consumers' Association goes much further, providing readers of its publications with concrete advice on how to obtain the cheaper products, e.g. cars from abroad! Even if such an action does not yield substantial and immediate gains for consumers as a whole, it might create the basis and the climate for more efficient policy action. The BEUC (European Bureau of Consumer Unions) is just starting a large scale publication, "Consumers Without Frontiers," which includes an "Action Guide" on trade issues addressed to national consumer groups.

PROTECTIONISM AS A WOLF IN SHEEP'S CLOTHING

The Symposium provided some amusing examples of how <u>consumer</u> protection can discreetly be converted into a convenient <u>protectionist</u> device. While manufacturers usually denounce consumer protection measures, they often "discover" the virtues of such measures if they help exclude imports of substitute products from abroad! The illustrations from OECD experience, with the "Cassis de Dijon" case as the most publicized example, suggest that consumers should beware of their would-be "protectors" especially when the protector is their government intervening to keep out imports. On the other hand, consumers should, of course, vigorously react wherever their legitimate interest in safe goods and fair marketing practices is threatened.

This also means that national and international consumer organizations should scrutinize closely their own suggestions for new safety requirements. The OECD Committee on Consumer Policy has taken up this issue in a project which was launched in September, 1986. This project will examine the procedures governing the development of product standards at national and international levels. The project deals with the issues of consumer involvement in the development of standards, the relationship between standards and mandatory safety requirements, the necessity for standardization and harmonization, the potential for "overstandardization," and the search for other options facilitating cross-border flows of goods and services.

THE REPRESENTATION OF CONSUMER INTERESTS

The final major topic at the Symposium, the consideration of consumer interests in the formulation and implementation of trade policy, is now continually reviewed by the Committee. It would be unrealistic to assume that, because of the Symposium and its approval of the related recommendations, the situation will change much sooner. Only a few countries have established procedures and institutions dealing in a systematic way with the scrutiny of restrictive trade measures, e.g., the United States and Australia. But the important result is that consumer policy officials in OECD countries have begun to assume their proper role in possibly influencing the decision-making of their countries in the trade field. Now they have a firmer solid basis for speaking up on behalf of the consumers.

One of OECD's major advantages is that it constitutes a forum where a very open exchange of views on various policy issues can take place. In this sense, the exchange of views on the ways and means of achieving a better integration of consumer policy interests in the discussion of trade policy matters will continue. In the long run, the existence of this forum strengthens genuine consumer representation in the fomulation of trade policies.

Given the limited resources of both consumer organizations and consumer authorities, international trade policies represents an arena where the academic community, with its expert knowledge, can play a particularly important and useful role.

APPENDIX

INDICATIVE CHECKLIST FOR THE ASSESSMENT OF TRADE POLICY MEASURES[2]

1) Is the measure in conformity with the country's international obligations and commitments?

2) What is the expected effect of the measure on the domestic prices of the goods or services concerned and on the general price level?

3) What are the expected direct economic gains to the domestic

[2]This checklist applies to all trade policy measures other than laws relating to unfair trade practices.

sector, industry or firms in question (technically, the increase in producers' surplus)?

4) What types of jobs are expected to be affected by the measure? What are the net employment effects of the measure in the short and long term?

5) What are the expected (direct) gains to government revenues (e.g., from tariffs, import licenses, tax receipts) and/or increased government costs (e.g., export promotion, government subsidies, lost tax revenues)?

6) What are the direct costs of the measure to consumers due to the resulting higher prices they must pay for the product in question and the reduction in the level of consumption of the product (technically, the reduction in consumers' surplus)? Are there specific groups of consumers which are particularly affected by the measure?

7) What is the likely impact of the measure on the availability, choice, quality and safety of goods and services?

8) What is the likely impact of the measure on the structure of the relevant markets and the competitive process within those markets?

9) In the medium and longer term perspective, will the measure, on balance, encourage or permit structural adaptation of domestic industry leading over time to increased productivity and international competitiveness. Or will it further weaken and delay pressures for such adaptation? Is the measure of a temporary nature? Is it contingent on, or linked to, other policy measures designed to bring about the desired structural adjustment?

10) What will be the expected effect on investment by domestic firms in the affected sector, by potential new entrants and by foreign investors?

11) What could be the expected economic effects of the measure on other sectors of the economy, in particular, on firms purchasing products from, and selling products to, the industry in question?

12) What are the likely effects of the measure on other countries? How can prejudice to trading partners be minimized?

13) How are other governments and foreign firms likely to react to the measure and what would be the expected effect on the economy of such actions? Is the measure a response to unfair practices in other countries?

A FOLLOW-UP TO CRANDALL'S COMMENTS

Rachel Dardis

The comments by Crandall are insightful and provide an additional perspective on the impact of trade restrictions. I respond to three issues raised by Crandall. They are (1) the "success" of trade protection measures, (2) domestic concentration and the choice of tariffs or quotas, and (3) estimating the costs of U.S. trade restrictions.

The political economy of protection is a critical area for consumer researchers where I fear I have no new insights. It is possible that trade restrictions represent a type of market failure that will remain uncorrected due to transaction costs, free riders, and information costs.

SUCCESS OF TRADE PROTECTION MEASURES

The recent book by Lawrence and Litan [4] provides a comprehensive account of U.S. trade policy and trade adjustment assistance programs in the Postwar Era. The authors conclude that trade protection has been ineffective in increasing employment or restoring competitiveness for many American industries. They also point out that unions may be encouraged to seek higher wages for their members under long-term protection and that such wage increases will further reduce the competitiveness of domestic industries. As Crandall points out, this type of rent seeking should have been discussed in the paper since it affects the competitive positions of protected industries as well as the gains of owners of labor from protectionist measures.

Crandall's comments about the <u>in</u>effectiveness of "escape clause" protection in the United States is somewhat surprising since the analysis of Lawrence and Litan indicates that this program has been relatively successful. This stands in contrast to the trade adjustment assistance program which has neither encouraged adjustment nor provided adequate compensation for domestic firms and workers. The authors did note, however, several problems with the "escape clause" programs. First, it is very costly to consumers, in particular when quotas are used rather than tariffs. Second, the uncertainty that relief will be granted has encouraged domestic industries to seek alternative protectionist measures which are generally costly and last longer than escape clause relief [4, pp. 48-51].

DOMESTIC CONCENTRATION AND THE CHOICE OF TARIFFS OR QUOTAS

This topic was not addressed in my paper and is important in view of the growth of protectionist measures for many oligopolistic industries in the United States such as automobiles and steel. The ability of quotas to increase the market power of domestic firms is noted by Lawrence and Litan [4]. Thus, quotas limit the quantity of foreign goods that may be imported irrespective of prices in contrast to tariffs and strengthen the market power of domestic producers. This, in turn, reinforces "oligopolistic pricing patterns in imperfectly competitive industries, and, relative to tariffs, can delay the transfer of resources out of protected industries" [4, p. 49]. For all industries, quotas are inferior to tariffs since they provide no revenue and increase the profits of foreign manufacturers which may mean increased competition for domestic manufacturers.

While the competitive model is not appropriate for the automobile industry, the analysis remains valid in that quotas increase prices for both domestic and foreign automobiles. Krishna [2] discusses this type of development in a duopoly situation where there is no collusion before trade protection. Once import quotas are increased, both domestic and foreign firms can increase prices and profits. The losers are the domestic consumers who pay higher prices for both products.

Finally, there is an interesting analysis by Krugman [3] of import protection as export promotion. In this analysis the domestic and foreign markets are oligopolistic and segmented. There are static and dynamic economics of scale. Import protection gives the domestic firm the opportunity to obtain scale advantages over foreign rivals which results in lower marginal costs. Thus, the firm is competitive in the export market. However, this advantage is unlikely to be maintained since the other country also has an incentive to protect its domestic market and to export. As Dixit points out, the pursuit of such policies by both countries will be "mutually destructive" [1, p. 14].

ESTIMATING THE COSTS OF U.S. TRADE RESTRICTIONS

My paper as published (in contrast to the paper presented at Wingspread) includes more information on the procedures used to obtain the costs of U.S. trade restrictions for four industries. The quotas were not binding for color TV and were binding for automobiles, sugar and non-rubber footwear. In the case of sugar, all exporters were covered. In the other two cases, alternative sources of supply did not compensate for quantity reductions from major exporters. Quotas for apparel are more complex since not all countries and products are covered under the MFA. Thus, the retention of the scarcity rent by foreign exporters was viewed as unlikely since price increases would have created export opportunities for countries and products not covered under the MFA. The ability of major exporters such as Hong Kong, South Korea and Taiwan to retain part of the scarcity rent is acknowledged in the paper.

REFERENCES

1. DIXIT, A. (1984), "International Trade Policy for Oligopolistic Industries," Economic Journal (Supplement), 84: 1-16.

2. KRISHNA, K. (1983), "Trade Restrictions as Facilitating Practices," Manuscript, Princeton University, cited in [1].

3. KRUGMAN, P. (1984), "Import Protection as Export Promotion: International Competition in the Presence of Oligopoly and Economies of Scale," in Monopolistic Competition and International Trade, K. Kierzkowski (ed.), Oxford: Clarendon Press.

4. LAWRENCE, R.F. and R.E. LITAN (1986), Saving Free Trade: A Pragmatic Approach, Washington, D.C.: The Brookings Institution.

Chapter 17

ABOUT THE AUTHOR

Michael R. Reich is Associate Professor in the Harvard School of Public Health and Executive Director of the Takemi Program in International Health. Reich started his career on a "hard science" course, taking his undergraduate degree from Yale University in Molecular Biophysics and Biochemistry; he then moved to the social sciences with a Master's in East Asian Studies in 1975 and a Ph.D. in Political Science in 1981 from Yale. Reich spent the years 1971-74 and six months of 1978-79 in Japan before going to Harvard University where he was associated with various institutes dealing with international affairs. His publications reflect a continuing interest in international health problems, e.g., Health, Nutrition and Economic Crises: Approaches to Policy in the Third World (co-editor, 1987) and Island of Dreams: Environmental Crisis in Japan (co-author, 1975).

INTERNATIONAL TRADE AND TRADE-OFFS FOR THIRD WORLD CONSUMERS [1]

Michael R. Reich

SUMMARY

International trade creates important trade-offs for Third World consumers, resulting from problems in the processes of information flow, choice, and redress. The conventional view of international trade does not adequately address the special difficulties confronted by Third World consumers. This paper focuses on health and safety problems associated with international trade. Information flow is obstructed by great distances between producer and consumer, so that Third World consumers tend to lack adequate information, especially on health and safety issues, on products arriving through international trade. Consumer choice is limited by the constraints on information flow and by corporate and government policies. Redress is difficult to obtain due to the complexities of international

---

[1]The author especially thanks two friends, economists C. Peter Timmer and Guy Carrin, for their thoughtful comments and valiant efforts to instruct a political scientist about issues of trade and consumers. Revision of the paper was greatly assisted by comments from participants at the International Conference, from members of the research seminar of the Takemi Program in International Health at the Harvard School of Public Health, and from Ann Gardner and David Hemenway.

trade and the undeveloped systems of tort law or other systems to seek compensation in most poor countries. The problems with these three processes reflect broader issues with the market model of trade between rich and poor countries. The analysis suggests policy approaches for national and international organizations and indicates additional areas and questions for research.

INTRODUCTION

International trade creates real trade-offs for consumers. These trade-offs are especially important in Third World countries, where consumers are subject to more pressing constraints than in rich countries. Yet the trade-offs from international trade are rarely explicit, and consumers are often not aware of consequences until long after choices have been made.

This paper analyzes the trade-offs of international trade for Third World consumers by exploring the problems that occur in three important processes: information flow, choice, and redress. Problems related to health and safety receive special attention from a perspective that stresses politics as well as economics. The analysis does not argue against trade _per se_ (since trade can benefit Third World consumers), but rather that the problems of trade must be recognized and dealt with appropriately by all parties involved.

The three processes provide a conceptual structure for examining the trade-offs and policy options for Third World consumers. Great distances between producer and consumer create obstacles to information flow, especially on safety and health issues, so that Third World consumers tend to lack information on products arriving through international trade. The constraints on information flow, along with corporate and government policies, result in limitations on consumer choice. When injury occurs, the complexities of international trade and the undeveloped systems of redress in most poor countries pose formidable barriers to Third World consumers who might seek damages. These three consumer processes raise broader problems, briefly reviewed below, with the market model of trade between rich and poor countries. The conclusion presents efforts by national and international organizations to deal with the trade-offs of international trade for Third World consumers and indicates additional areas and questions for research.

THE CONVENTIONAL VIEW

In the early 1800s, David Ricardo developed the theory of comparative advantage, which ever since has provided a central support for the free market view of international trade [26]. Ricardo used a two-country, two-commodity model to demonstrate that each country would be better off if it produced the good that it could make relatively more cheaply and then traded it to the other country. By this prescription, England should produce textiles, Portugal should make wine, and each sell to the other. The model recommends this result, despite the fact that England had an absolute advantage in both, meaning that it could produce both more cheaply than Portugal. Portugal had a relative advantage in producing wine (measured in hours of labor), meaning that it could produce wine more cheaply than textiles. According to this theory, if each country specializes in products made with the greatest relative efficiency within its borders, then trade will benefit both partners. Derived from a much simplified model of the real world, this principle states a basic, universally accepted, driving force of international trade.

The notion of gains from free trade has remained a powerful image in modern society. As recently as May 1986, following the economic summit conference in Tokyo, President Ronald Reagan declared that the "rising tide of prosperity in the industrial democracies was demonstrating the wisdom of the free market policies we've pursued." Poor countries, he said, should apply similar policies. "For developing countries as well. . . the principles of the free market are more important to progress than any level of economic aid" [23].

Democrats have also proclaimed free trade as the solution to multiple problems. As an example, President John F. Kennedy in 1962 appealed to Congress to pass the Trade Expansion Act, citing benefits at home and abroad from expanded trade [16]. He argued that the law would contribute to efforts to "promote the strength and unity of the West," "prove the superiority of free choice," "aid the developing nations of the world and other friends," and "maintain the leadership of the free world." Of particular concern in this essay, Kennedy predicted the benefits for consumers:

> The American consumer benefits most of all from an increase in foreign trade. Imports give him a wider choice of products at competitive prices. They introduce new ideas and new tastes which often lead to new demands for American production.
>
> Increased imports stimulate our own efforts to increase efficiency, and supplement anti-trust and other efforts to assure competition. Many

> industries of importance to the American consumer and economy are dependent upon imports for raw materials and other supplies. Thus American-made goods can also be made much less expensively for American consumers if we lower the tariff on the materials that are necessary to their production.

In addition to competitive benefits, Kennedy noted that most imports (60 percent, he said) did not directly compete with American products and also provided goods that the United States did not produce at all or in significant quantity. Imports were estimated as competing with only one or one and one-half percent of total U.S. production, and "even these imports create jobs" directly or indirectly. Although imports today compete with a much larger portion of U.S. production, the calls for free trade from the Reagan administration remain loud and clear.

Throughout history, however, the calls for free trade have been accompanied by concern about adverse consequences. Even Adam Smith, considered the father of laissez faire, warned in an oft-cited passage of 1776 that not all parties would benefit equally from trading [34]:

> The discovery of America, and that of a passage to the East Indies by the Cape of Good Hope, are the two greatest and most important events recorded in the history of mankind. . . What benefits, or what misfortunes to mankind may hereafter result from those great events no human wisdom can foresee. By uniting, in some measure, the most distant parts of the world, by enabling them to relieve one another's wants, to increase one another's enjoyments, and to encourage one another's industry, their general tendency would seem to be beneficial. To the natives, however, both of the East and West Indies, all the commercial benefits which can have resulted from those events have been sunk and lost in the dreadful misfortunes which they have occasioned.

In the nineteenth century, European imperialism continued to introduce poor countries to the "commercial benefits" and "dreadful misfortunes" of joining the world economy. At the same time, however, latecomers to industrial development in Europe, as well as Japan and the United States, questioned the advantages of a fully open economy and restricted imports to protect recently established infant industries from foreign products. Britain, on the other hand, restricted exports of certain technologies, in hopes of containing the diffusion process and maintaining control over advanced techniques [6]. Both the protection of infant industries and the control of technology diffusion have remained important topics for trade debates, for rich and poor countries alike. These problems demonstrate that free trade can have undesirable economic, political, and security costs.

For Third World consumers today, while "commercial benefits" from international trade exist, "dreadful misfortunes" also persist, due in part to problems in procuring good information, making appropriate choices, and obtaining fair redress when harmed.

INFORMATION

Problems of information flow represent a key flaw in the current circumstances of international trade, reflecting the general problem of the asymmetry of information between producers and consumers. Too frequently, Third World consumers have inadequate, inappropriate, or incorrect information. The flow of products from rich to poor countries generally precedes the flow of information, especially information on safety or health problems.

Sheer distance, both geographical and organizational, between producer and consumer in international trade can obstruct the flow of information. Once a product has been shipped from a rich to a poor country, individual consumers and even government agencies may lack the means to contact the company's home office for additional data. Private companies may lack an economic incentive to provide full information about a product, in part due to potential harm to sales. (For some products, however, full information may increase sales, if the information persuades consumers that a product is a comparatively better buy than existing products.) Moreover, providing additional information creates costs for the seller [35]. Similarly, the costs of search for information by Third World consumers are likely to be higher than those costs for consumers in rich countries (certainly relative to income), especially for products that originate in the rich countries.

The complexity of the distribution system for certain products in poor countries also tends to decrease the flow of information to the individual consumer or end user. Pesticides, for example, are commonly repackaged and sold in small quantities, with warnings on the original packages discarded [38]. Pharmaceutical products similarly are sold in small quantities with little information provided about indications for product use or potential hazards and side effects [10]. Package inserts for drugs, which could contain such information, may not be required or provided. Cigarettes may also be sold individually, so that any health warnings on packages are not passed along to the end consumer. For products sold in bulk in international trade, information about use and hazards tends not to be transmitted to the end user.

Language barriers between trading partners also reduce the flow of information to Third World consumers, especially if information on the product is provided in the language of the exporter rather than the importer. Multiple languages in a single country also create similar problems. In Kenya, for example, warnings about the use of pesticides are printed in only two (English and Swahili) of the 15 national languages [41]. Moreover, in many poor countries, high levels of illiteracy pose obstacles to information transfer and thus contribute to the misuse of pesticides and other toxic chemicals.

The lack of an effective international code of hazards also creates problems for consumers. Confusion about the meaning of a hazard symbol on fungicide-coated grain in Iraq produced a major disaster in the early 1970's. Farmers used mercury-coated grain intended for agricultural seed to make homemade bread, resulting in 6,000 reported cases of poisoning. The grain was tinted with brownish-red dye as a warning. Unfortunately, the dye was largely removed by water, leaving the mercury behind. The now untinted grain and the warnings on sacks written in a foreign language left farmers uninformed of the dangerous nature of the seeds. Similar poisonings reportedly occurred in Iraq in 1956 and 1960 [1].

In the early 1980s, one U.S. multinational corporation sought to develop an international code of warnings for toxic chemicals, called the "One World Communication System," to help illiterate or poorly educated farmers in the Third World. Unhappily, when faced with a lack of strong interest from relevant parties -- other U.S. firms, the trade association for agricultural chemicals, and the State Department -- the company gave up the project [39].

Multinational firms sometimes provide different information on the same product in different countries. A study of prescription drug labeling and promotion showed different indications for use and warnings about side effects for the same product in various countries. Compared to the United States, "with few exceptions, the indications included in the reference books [in Latin America] are far more extensive, but the listings of hazards are curtailed, glossed over, or totally omitted" [32]. The firms involved explained that countries impose different requirements about information packets on pharmaceuticals, resulting in varying information packets for the same product. Many countries, for example, do not legally require full disclosure to physicians of potential hazards or side effects [32]. As a result, both doctors and consumers in poor countries tend to receive less information about potentially hazardous consequences of products than consumers in rich countries.

International trade, by introducing large multinational corporations to small national markets, provides small economies with access to products that domestic enterprises cannot supply. But such trade also creates situations where companies have little incentive to invest in specific information for local consumers, especially when competition is limited. Foreign companies may have less interest in providing consumer information than domestic companies, reflecting a lower level of commitment to that particular market and perhaps different views on corporate social responsibilities. A foreign company, for example, may provide the same information as in a rich country, without taking into account the special cultural characteristics (including language) or different usage patterns for the same product. As a World Bank report noted about warnings on pesticides in Kenya, "Even if the user can read and understand the warnings, it is not easy to 'avoid contaminating rivers,' nor even to 'wash with soap and water after use.' Most users have never seen a physician, and certainly are not able to consult one 'immediately' as advised by the label" [41].

Another problem is that most corporate information provided to consumers comes in the form of advertising, noted for its bias in content. One review of several studies linked multinational corporations, and by implication international trade, with increasing levels of advertising in poor countries [19]. Increased advertising would provide consumers with more information than previously available, but not necessarily with full, appropriate, or honest information. A lack of government regulation of advertising contributes to problems of the quality of information conveyed in commercial messages.

The case of infant formula illustrates that the marketing message can reach poor consumers before the safety message reaches them. Companies have successfully portrayed this product as carrying prestige, modernity and health. The makers have not conveyed -- and may never -- the instructions for proper use to poor consumers as quickly or effectively. The controversy over infant formula resulted in an international code of marketing adopted by the World Health Organization in May 1981. The code sought to change the information content and format of corporate advertising in order to protect poor consumers in the Third World from getting the wrong message [42]. The infant formula controversy reflects the evolving socio-political environment and corporate strategy around the marketing of consumer products in poor countries [29].

In sum, the disjunction between the flow of information and the flow of products to Third World consumers contributes to the hazardous use of products in poor countries and to the diffusion of hazardous products. One must remember, however, that only a portion of products in international trade pose problems of health and safety. Moreover, the flow of information can catch up with the diffusion of products -- through the activities of consumer groups, international agencies, and national governments as described in the paper's final section.

CHOICE

A major constraint on consumer choice in poor countries is the lack of adequate information necessary for an individual to make an informed decision. As described in the section above, international trade can introduce new products into a country, without providing individual consumers with adequate information about the immediate or long-term consequences of choosing that particular product. If consumers possessed and understood more information on health and safety problems associated with certain products (for example, pharmaceuticals or pesticides), they might choose other less toxic products or might use the products more cautiously. Constraints on information flow to Third World consumers, therefore, have a critical impact on choice.

Third World consumers lack information on other aspects of international trade in addition to health and safety. Consumers may be unaware of how their choice of imported goods can affect domestic employment or production structure. For example, growing acceptance of imported plastic products could displace traditional domestic products, and thereby change local employment and production patterns in irreversible ways. Individual consumers, however, do not directly choose such irreversible changes. To the extent that imported products substitute for local products, international trade can reduce the scope of choice for consumers, in unintended and unexpected directions.

Consumer choice is also shaped by the information provided by foreign corporations, mainly through advertising. As Newfarmer concluded about the activities of multinational corporations in poor countries, "advertising does appear to bias consumer choice toward the advertised products and thereby shift consumption patterns to mirror those in the North" [19]. Increased advertising for foreign products in poor countries raises the potential for expanding the use of products that would be considered inappropriate for considerations of equity, culture, or safety and health [14].

Individual consumer choice can also be limited by government policy, for various reasons. Government policy may be used to achieve social objectives deemed more important than consumer choice. For example, a poor country might restrict its imports of pharmaceutical products for the public sector to a list of essential drugs purchased as generic items. That policy could increase the quantity and distribution of those essential drugs through the government health service, thereby increasing choice for some groups of consumers, such as poor rural residents who did not previously have access to government supplies of pharmaceuticals. But it would also necessarily limit choice for other groups, by reducing the number of available products and by removing brand-name drugs from government (or even market) supplies [25, 43]. The policy would alter the range of choice for different income and geographical groups, reflecting a government effort to increase social equity.

Such policies can raise bitter social and political controversies. Sri Lanka's pharmaceutical policy in the mid-1970s restricted public and private purchases to generic drugs and encountered stiff opposition from physicians as well as corporations. The physicians objected to government intervention that limited their professional choice of patient treatment and would, they asserted, negatively affect the quality of care through the use of lower-quality generic products [17]. With the change of government in 1977, Sri Lanka reverted to its previous approach of limited intervention and open borders for the pharmaceutical market.

The government's allocation of foreign reserves can also shape the scope of consumer choice for different income groups. For countries that have extremely limited foreign exchange reserves, an increasingly common problem for poor countries, government policy on imports is especially important in determining who gets what. Public policy could determine, for example, whether priority is given to the purchase of luxury automobiles for the urban elite or spare parts for public bus transportation. A country might allocate a limited sum of foreign exchange for pharmaceutical imports by the private sector, but if no further restrictions are applied, imports are likely to be high-profit-margin branded products for the urban market. When the pie cannot easily be expanded, more powerful groups in society will seek to expand their choice at the cost of weaker groups, unless government policy intervenes.

Government policy on imports can also have unintended consequences for consumer choice. A policy of open markets can expose consumers to potentially harmful products, especially if the country lacks appropriate regulatory policy or the capacity to implement policy. Government acceptance of food aid (as one element of international trade) can have the unintended consequence of undermining domestic agricultural production, by depressing the prices of local crops and discouraging local farmers [31]. Food aid can meet critical short-term needs, but the process can replace locally available and nutritious food over the long term, thereby restricting consumer choice and making poor consumers subject to the domestic and international political uncertainties of food aid [4]. Similar patterns exist for foreign assistance of pharmaceutical products, which can depress prices and disrupt local production.

Foreign assistance that requires purchases in the donor country also can reduce choice for recipient countries and consumers. This practice of tied aid illustrates the lack of voluntary contracting in government-mediated international trade and reduces efficiency and freedom from the recipient's perspective. Foreign assistance can result in a choice of technologies that poor countries are unable to maintain and operate due to limited technical and financial resources -- "poor-fit" or inappropriate technologies. Such technologies in the medical area include neonatal intensive care units in Egypt and high output x-ray equipment in various African countries. In these cases and others, the equipment has suffered severe operational problems, resulting from an inability to service and maintain the complex machinery and lack of effective plans to pay high recurrent costs [21]. Similar problems of technology choice exist in many poor countries [2]. Foreign governments thus can offer "assistance" which may seem to expand choices but may not represent the recipient government's real preferences and may not actually contribute to expanding the choices of most consumers in the country.

Governments and corporations thus exercise substantial influence in structuring individual consumer choice in poor countries [2]. But the criteria for decisions by governments and corporations are often ambiguous. The decisions may benefit organizational goals of various sorts and personal pockets of public and private officials, through corruption, more than the broader interests of consumers [37, 13]. Restrictions on consumer choice for the vast majority of the population in the Third World emerge from these social processes of international trade, as well as from the more fundamental problems of poverty.

REDRESS

When a Third World consumer is harmed by a product gained through international trade, the process of obtaining redress tends to be more complex than for a domestically produced good. An initial obstacle to redress is the lack of adequate information to link the harm with the product. For new kinds of products introduced from abroad, consumers may be unaware of potential injury and may have difficulty linking health effects with product use. For example, farm workers may develop skin ailments and other symptoms but not identify the cause as pesticide poisoning [28]. Similar problems can occur for pharmaceuticals, contraceptives, and industrial chemicals, as well as consumer products. The distance between producer and consumer can delay or obstruct information about potentially defective products from reaching all users, as in the case of the Dalkon Shield intrauterine contraceptive device made by the A.H. Robins Company and distributed worldwide. The difficulty of relating cause and effect is exacerbated by international trade that introduces unfamiliar products or that provides products without adequate information on hazards.

Even if a Third World consumer can link damage with some product, enormous hurdles must be overcome to achieve redress. Several features of international trade complicate that process. Most poor countries lack an adequate administrative capability to assist consumers harmed by dangerous or defective products. Governments have a difficult time protecting consumers from harmful products since regulatory policies tend not to be well developed or enforced. They also provide minimal services to persons who have suffered harm. Such services may include testing of suspicious products, legal assistance, and official contact with the company.

Many poor countries also lack a strong tradition of tort law, which might provide an avenue for redress in the legal system. India, for example, has a well developed legal system, but poorly developed tort law. The system is designed to discourage people from filing a damage suit for negligence by imposing high ad valorem court fees. The codification of common law in India in the late 19th century omitted tort law, and it has since remained outside the main stream of Indian law. The legal system is fraught by long delays, low recoveries, and the absence of contingency fees, all inhibiting access and legal innovation [9]. Poor people without access to money or legal resources are effectively excluded from the legal system. "Modern technology with its great injury producing capacities has arrived, but not a consciousness that these harms are going to be controlled by the legal system. Disasters large and small in India typically have no legal consequences" [9].

International trade complicates the legal process of redress by involving at least two legal jurisdictions and perhaps international law. These additional layers of complexity can place redress at even further distance from the individual consumer. Multiple actors and liabilities can stalemate legal proceedings and deny redress to persons harmed.

Finally, Third World consumers stand at a disadvantage in achieving redress by the weakness of consumer protection organizations and public interest groups. Not only do consumers lack individual resources to challenge governments and corporations, they also lack well developed organizational resources of assistance. In some poor countries, however, consumer organizations are emerging. One example is the Consumers Association of Penang in Malaysia which is actively fielding consumer complaints and helping persons harmed by defective products and deceptive companies [24]. The general weakness of consumer organizations in poor countries contributes to the difficulties of achieving redress from products that originate in international trade.

THE MARKET MODEL

The problems confronted by Third World consumers reflect broader issues that underlie the simple market model of international trade. This essay does not seek to evaluate all the shortcomings of that model, a task others have attempted in detail and from various perspectives [12, 7, 11]. But three key assumptions of the market model -- about information, voluntary contracting, and government intervention -- deserve brief review. These assumptions operate in the minds of some important policymakers, and a critical discussion can illustrate the gaps between image and reality of the market model of international trade. In a related review of the market images and realities in health care, Culyer concluded that "health care markets are always and everywhere so imperfect that the marketeers' image of the market for health is a completely irrelevant description of an unattainable Utopia" [5]. Similar conclusions may hold for international trade, especially from the perspective of Third World consumers.

The limitations of the market model help explain the problems of information flow, choice, and redress for Third World consumers.

Information

The market model assumes that participants have complete access to full information regarding current choices and future consequences. The model provides that both sides in a market transaction have equal access to and certainty of information.

The free flow of information is rarely achieved in international trade between rich and poor countries [12]. Capabilities for information gathering and analysis depend in part on organizational capabilities. Information management on a global scale can be achieved more effectively by the governments and large corporations of rich countries than by those of poor countries. Economies of scale also affect information management, so that it costs organizations in poor countries more to procure and analyze information than it would for organizations in rich countries.

Another restraint on information flow is the extent of control over certain kinds of information. Information contained in patents, for example, represents a legal form of monopoly. Patent restrictions impede the flow and increase the cost of information, but on the other hand can provide an incentive for innovation. Some technologies are not for sale on the market at all or are transferred only within a corporate organization, e.g., to a subsidiary in another country. Large areas of information of potential importance to poor countries, therefore, are not available or can be obtained only at premium prices.

Poor countries also lack adequate capabilities to assess the reliability of information received. Information assessment is affected by the factors noted above: relatively poor information management capacity, inadequate testing facilities, expensive costs of information, and proprietary obstacles to information flow. Problems of determining reliability are exacerbated when the sources of information have a vested interest in a particular interpretation.

Problems of information flow, therefore, represent a critical omission in the simple market model of trade between rich and poor countries. As Hans Singer reported: "Information, like technology, feeds upon itself. If you do not have enough information to begin with to know where to look for the information that you need, or to know what new information could be assembled, your initial inferiority is bound to be sharpened and perpetuated. . . This unequal bargaining situation will affect <u>all</u> relations between the investing and borrowing countries, whether labelled aid, trade, investment, transfer of technology, technical assistance, or any other" [33]. This inequality, however, probably poses more serious problems in some areas (new or proprietary technology) than in others (commodities).

Voluntary Contracting: According to the market model, exchanges occur through voluntary contracting among participants. In theory, this system results in an efficient allocation of resources (Pareto optimality) in which resources are used in their most valued uses and any redistribution would cause net harm to at least one participant.

Voluntary contracting has not always been a prominent feature of trade between rich and poor countries. The bargaining process has frequently been influenced by the unequal distribution of power. G.K. Helleiner noted the role of threats and bullying in ostensible market relationships, for example, "....in ex-colonial countries where there has been forced labor, where gunboats and the military have been employed for the preservation of 'order', and where even the law has been constructed for the explicit purpose of maintaining the market power of particular foreign enterprises" [12].

The use of coercion in such exchanges need not be so blatant or violent. Foreign aid programs have frequently required that purchases be made from firms in the donor country. This practice can result in increased prices, for the initial purchase and for continuing maintenance and parts, estimated by some to average 20 percent [3]. Such restrictions on foreign aid limit the receiving country's ability to shop for the best purchase through the market. Assistance projects by private voluntary agencies can also restrict the choice of products by recipients, with counterproductive results. In one project in India, the foreign donor's choice of the nutritional supplement as an imported product contributed to undermining the project's continuity and long-term success, by making it nearly impossible to procure the supplement once the project ended [22]. As another study concluded, "While most programs advocate the use of culturally appropriate foods in supplemental feeding programs, in reality many projects continue to use imported foods" [15].

Another constraint on voluntary contracting results from the growing role of transnational corporations in international trade. These complex multinational organizations allocate resources across national boundaries but within corporate boundaries. The largest companies in effect replace open market transactions with internal organizational procedures, as prices, products, and processes are determined more by corporate decisions than by market dynamics, especially in situations of limited competition [19].

<u>Government Intervention</u>: The conventional image of the market model assumes no government intervention, thereby allowing open competition to produce both efficient resource allocation and freedom. Government intervention is seen as creating barriers to entry, distorting the market, and enriching the protected parties.

Of course, governments do intervene in markets, in various ways and for all sorts of reasons. Governments intervene in markets to alter income distributions, for example, to lower the price of food for the poor as a means to achieve an equitable distribution of nutrient intake. Market proponents generally oppose this approach as rigging the market, creating inefficiencies, and reducing competition. They would prefer direct measures to redistribute income and thereby preserve the benefits of a competitive market.

Government intervention occurs for reasons of self-interest as well. Coercion and corruption can lead government officials to protect and favor certain private interests over others, thereby distorting in practice the principle of voluntary contracting. Government officials can also be persuaded to intervene in the market through the pressure politics of democratic societies, as illustrated by U.S. government policy to protect the incomes of domestic sugar producers from falling world prices.

From a global perspective, one problem with the market model is the lack of a world government that could act directly to alter the distribution of incomes and wealth between nations. Third World countries, in calls for a new international economic order, are seeking to use the United Nations to achieve fundamental changes in global institutions and to close the gaps between rich and poor nations. Although they have encountered many obstacles, including vetoes of the rich countries as well as dissension among their own ranks, some believe that the Third World demands will utimately prevail [11]; others have serious doubts.

Another constraint from a global view is the multiplicity of governments and their varying regulatory standards and implementation capacities. In general, poor countries tend to have less well developed regulatory systems and more difficulty implementing government standards, due in part to limited public resources. Many poor countries also lack adequate legal mechanisms for private citizens to recover damages when harmed by the actions of companies. Rich countries, on the other hand, tend to be better at controlling the undesirable activities of private companies in the market (for example, pollution and defective products) and at providing mechanisms of redress, although many problems remain.

International trade between rich and poor countries thus occurs in a complex reality of multiple government interventions -- far from the image of the market model. This complexity can have special consequences for Third World consumers, for example, when companies from rich countries take products that cannot be sold at home and sell them in poor countries.

CONCLUSION

A major conclusion of this analysis is the need to disseminate more information to Third World consumers to improve product choice and use, thereby reducing the likelihood of harm, and also to improve redress. In recent years, the problems of information flow to Third World governments and consumers have attracted increasing attention from national and international policy makers. In the late 1970's, the Carter Administration developed a uniform policy of notification for the export of hazardous substances, based on a principle of informed consent for the international trade of potentially hazardous substances [30]. That policy was promulgated in the last days of the Carter Presidency and rescinded in the first days of the Reagan Administration, reflecting a broader shift in philosophy and initiative back to the "magic of the marketplace."

In 1979, the U.N. General Assembly passed a resolution recognizing the need for global cooperation to prevent damage to health from the international trade of banned and restricted products such as hazardous chemicals and unsafe pharmaceutical products. The debate focused on the problems of poor countries that lack adequate information to assess imports. Various United Nations agencies have become involved in the flow of information to poor countries regarding hazardous products -- the International Labor Organization, the U.N. Environment Program, and the World Health Organization. The U.N. Environment Program, for example, is developing information on both scientific and regulatory aspects of chemicals, in its International Register of Potentially Toxic Chemicals.

The Organization for Economic Cooperation and Development (OECD) has also become concerned about the international "harmonization" of national approaches for regulating chemicals among industrial countries emphasizing the need to promote the international transfer of information on chemicals, especially between the OECD and poor countries [20]. The Committee on Consumer Policy of the OECD has also discussed the issue of hazardous exports. In 1974, the OECD established a voluntary notification system for member countries for a limited range of consumer products. The United States still remains the only country with legislation requiring export notification for hazardous consumer goods. According to one OECD Committee member, its member nations confront "enormous difficulties" on issues of principle and practice regarding the policy of rich countries toward the export of hazardous products to poor countries [27].

Some multinational corporations have also tried to improve the flow of information to poor countries. Some companies, for example, have developed educational programs on pesticide use and held meetings in poor countries. The U.S. National Agricultural Chemicals Association has cooperated with international organizations in efforts to reduce pesticide misuse and has sought to improve registration and safety programs in importing countries. The effectiveness of these efforts, however, is constrained by various factors over which the multinational companies have limited influence, including the practice of repackaging, the realities of government enforcement, and the existence of small local manufacturers [40]. A similar pattern has been reported for pharmaceutical products: informational reforms with respect to advertising and package inserts have been accompanied by continued abuses in prescribing practices [10].

Information flow to Third World consumers through international trade represents an important area of research. What do different social classes in different countries know about potentially hazardous pesticides or pharmaceutical products that are imported? What are the main sources of such information? How could national policies be adjusted to improve the flow of information? The costs of improving the provision of information to poor consumers in the Third World also need to be explored from an empirical perspective (what are the costs?) and a normative perspective (who should pay the costs?).

A second conclusion of this essay relates to the importance of consumer groups in poor countries and international consumer organizations. The 1970s witnessed the growth of an increasingly international consumer movement. Established consumer groups in the United States, Britain, Germany, and Japan turned to the environmental and health problems of poor countries. And developing countries began to establish and expand their own consumer and public interest organizations. The selection of a Malaysian president, Anwar Fazal, for the International Organization of Consumers' Unions -- the first Third World president -- reflected those two trends.

Several international organizations emerged in the 1980s to focus on specific products. Health Action International was formed in 1981 "to further the safe, rational and economic use of pharmaceuticals, to promote the full implementation of the World Health Organization's Action Programme on essential drugs, and to look for non-drug solutions to the problems created by impure water and poor sanitation and nutrition." A coalition of consumer groups has recently organized a regional program, Action for Rational Drugs in Asia, to promote similar goals in Asia. Pesticide Action Network, established in 1982, is another international coalition that addresses problems of pesticides. Consumer Interpol links consumer groups around the world to provide hazard alerts and scientific information on banned and restricted products. These initiatives by private voluntary organizations seek to improve information flow and to influence the decisions of governments and corporations that affect consumer choice and redress.

The role of Third World consumer groups and international consumer organizations deserves the attention of researchers. How have domestic and international groups affected the processes for putting consumer issues of international trade on the political agenda in Third World countries? What are the major strengths and limitations of these organizations? Social and political analyses are necessary to identify the strategies likely to be most effective in different national contexts. Contrasting approaches to international agencies and private corporations, ranging between collaboration and confrontation, need to be examined for their impact on setting the agenda of international trade issues for Third World consumers.

On problems of redress, consumers are being assisted in some countries by the growth of a public interest law movement. In India, for example, public interest litigation has been used to provide representation to groups of people who have not previously had access to the legal system [8, 9]. This approach could be used to provide consumers with more legal and political leverage in obtaining redress, for cases involving domestic products as well as international trade. Other poor countries, however, are still far from recognizing that the distribution of economic and political resources affects the ability of different groups to protect their interests through the courts, in both national and international arenas.

The International Law Commission of the United Nations is also studying issues of redress, under the title "International Liability for Injurious Consequences Arising out of Acts Not Prohibited by International Law." This effort particularly addresses harmful transnational environmental problems. One review of the Commission's work concluded that the group had progressed in defining the boundaries of the issues but left the fundamental issues of international liability unresolved, reflecting the complexity of the problems and the political sensitivity of possible responses [18]. Significantly, the Commission is considering problems of state liability for both public and private activities that cause harm in another country.

The area of redress leads to another important set of research topics, with both empirical and normative dimensions. How do different poor countries conceptualize and implement the processes of redress for consumers injured by imported (or domestically made) products? How do national policies for redress reflect broader social values in specific Third World countries? What opportunities exist for improving the processes of redress? This set of issues raises much broader questions about the universality of certain consumer values initially articulated by Western organizations. For example, do the seven consumer rights adopted by the International Organization of Consumers Unions apply to Third World countries? If so, with what consequences? And if not, do alternative consumer concepts or values emerge from specific Third World contexts with implications for consumer organizations in rich countries?

This analysis of the problems of international trade for Third World consumers also has implications for the development strategies of poor countries. It suggests that neither a market completely open to free trade nor a totally closed border of autarky is the answer [36]. Something like the concept of selective delinkage needs to be adopted [6]. The governments of poor countries need to identify the conditions under which a connection to global markets benefits the country. This pathway, between modernization and dependency models, poses problems of how to select products and how to implement policies, but it raises the potential of making international trade more efficient and more equitable [6]. Research topics in this area might include analyses of different types of trade (foreign assistance, advanced technology, private versus state-owned enterprises) and their consequences for consumers in poor countries.

Finally, this analysis suggests special responsibilities of rich countries and private corporations involved in international trade. As a minimum ethical standard, one could argue for a principle of informed consent in international trade [30]. But even that principle is fraught with difficulties: Whose consent? How much information? What constitutes consent and recognition of risk? To what extent do decisions of governments represent consent of consumers? Despite these problems, however, this discussion suggests that multinational corporations involved in poor countries have a social responsibility to provide information, especially when the government lacks a strong administrative capacity. Empirical studies on how different governments approach the principle of informed consent in international trade, and how different corporations design a policy of information flow in Third World countries, could be quite instructive for future debate on these topics.

One could argue that improvements in the processes of information flow, consumer choice, and redress in poor countries are in the long-run interests of both governments and companies of the rich countries. Indeed, making trade more sensitive to the welfare needs of consumers in poor countries would undoubtedly help reinforce international trade. That view, however, is often obscured by the short-term costs of making those improvements -- costs that can affect the political and economic standing of key public and private groups. Merely placing the issue of market imperfections of international trade for Third World consumers on the international agenda does not guarantee adoption of policy. Each country must consider the tradeoffs its consumers are willing to withstand -- a question that remains fundamentally a national process and a political issue, and about which we need to learn more.

REFERENCES

1. BAKIR, F. ET AL. (1973), "Methylmercury Poisoning in Iraq," Science, 181: 230-241.

2. BANTA, H. DAVID (1986), "Medical Technology and Developing Countries: The Case of Brazil," International Journal of Health Services, 16: 363-373.

3. BHAGWATI, J. (1970), Amount and Sharing of Aid, Monograph No. 2, Washington, D.C.: Overseas Development Council.

4. BISWAS, MARGARET (1985), "Food Aid, Nutrition, and Development," in Nutrition and Development, edited by Margaret Biswas and Per Pinstrup-Andersen, 97-119, New York: Oxford University Press.

5. CULYER, A.J. (1982), "The NHS and the Market, Images and Realities," in The Public/Private Mix for Health: The Relevance and Effects of Change, edited by G. McLachlan and A. Maynard, 23-56, London: The Nuffield Provincial Hospitals Trust.

6. DIAZ-ALEJANDRO, CARLOS F. (1978), "Delinking North and South: Unshackled or Unchanged?," in Rich and Poor Nations in the World Economy, Albert Fishlow et al., 87-162, New York: McGraw-Hill.

7. EMMANUEL, ARGHIRI (1973), Unequal Exchange: A Study of the Imperialism of Trade, New York: Monthly Review Press.

8. GALANTER, MARC (1983), "Making Law Work for the Oppressed," The Other Side, 3(2): 7-15.

9. _________ (1985), "Legal Torpor: Why So Little has Happened in India After the Bhopal Tragedy," Texas International Law Journal, 20: 273-294.

10. GREENHALGH, TRISHA (1986), "Drug Marketing in the Third World: Beneath the Cosmetic Reforms," The Lancet, ii: 1318-1320.

11. UL HAQ, MAHBUB (1976), The Third World and the International Economic Order Development Paper 22, Washington, D.C.: Overseas Development Council.

12. HELLEINER, G.K. (1979), "World Market Imperfections and the Developing Countries," in Policy Alternatives for a New International Economic Order, edited by William R. Cline, 357-389, New York: Praeger.

13. JAGANNATHAN, N. VIJAY (1986), "Corruption, Delivery Systems, and Property Rights," World Development , 14: 127-132.

14. JAMES, JEFFREY and STEPHEN LISTER (1980), "Galbraith Revisited: Advertising in Non-Affluent Societies," World Development, 8: 87-96.

15. KENNEDY, EILEEN and ODIN KNUDSEN, "A Review of Supplementary Feeding Programmes and Recommendations on Their Design," in Nutrition and Development, edited by Margaret Biswas and Per Pinstrup-Andersen, 77-96, New York: Oxford University Press.

16. KENNEDY, JOHN F. (1962), "Message to the Congress on Foreign Trade Policy," Jan. 25, 1962, Public Papers of the Presidents, 68-77. Reproduced in Meier, Gerald M. (1973), Problems of Trade Policy, 27-35, New York: Oxford University Press.

17. LALL, SANJAYA, and SENAKA BIBILE (1978), "The Political Economy of Controlling Transnationals: The Pharmaceutical Industry in Sri Lanka, 1972-1976," International Journal of Health Services, 8: 299-328.

18. MAGRAW, DANIEL BARSTOW (1986), "Transboundary Harm: The International Law Commission's Study of 'International Liability,'" American Journal of International Law, 80: 305-330.

19. NEWFARMER, RICHARD (1984), "Multinationals and Marketplace Magic in the 1980s," in The Political Economy of Development and Underdevelopment, 3rd Edition, edited by Charles K. Wilber, 182-207, New York: Random House.

20. NICHOLS, JOANNE K. and PETER J. CRAWFORD (1983), Managing Chemicals in the 1980s, Paris: Organization for Economic Co-operation and Development.

21. PERRY, SEYMOUR and FLORA CHU (1987), "Selecting Medical Technologies in Developing Countries," In Health, Nutrition and Economic Crises: Approaches to Policy in the Third World, edited by David E. Bell and Michael R. Reich, Boston: Auburn House.

22. PYLE, DAVID (1980), "From Pilot Project to Operational Project in India: The Problems of Transition," in Politics and Policy Implementation in the Third World, edited by M.S. Grindle, 123-144, Princeton: Princeton University Press.

23. REAGAN, RONALD (1986), "Opening Statement, Transcript of Reagan's News Conference After Tokyo Parley," The New York Times, (May 8): A10.

24. REICH, MICHAEL R. (1980), "Activism Malaysian Style," Environmental Action, (March): 14-17.

25. _________ (1987), "Essential Drugs: Economics and Politics in International Health," Health Policy, 7: 1-19.

26. RICARDO, DAVID (1978), Principles of Political Economy and Taxation, New York: Everyman's Library, (first edition, 1817).

27. RINGSTEDT, NILS (1983), "Hazardous Products - The Concerns and Views of OECD Countries," in Health, Safety & the Consumer, Proceedings of the IOCU Seminar, Ranzan, Japan, 6-9 April 1983, edited by Foo Gaik Sim, 89-92, Penang, Malaysia: International Organization of Consumers Unions.

28. SAHABAT ALAM MALAYSIA (1981), Pesticide Problems in a Developing Country: A Case Study of Malaysia, Penang: Sahabat Alam Malaysia.

29. SETHI, S. PRAKASH, HAMID ETEMAD, and K.A.N. LUTHER (1986), "New Sociopolitical Forces: The Globalization of Conflict," Journal of Business Strategy, 6(Spring): 24-31.

30. SHAIKH, RASHID, and MICHAEL R. REICH (1981), "Haphazard Policy on Hazardous Exports," The Lancet, ii: 740-742.

31. SHEPARD, JACK (1985), "When Foreign Aid Fails," The Atlantic Monthly, (April): 41-46.

32. SILVERMAN, MILTON (1976), The Drugging of the Americas, Berkeley: University of California Press.

33. SINGER, HANS (1975), "The Distribution of the Gains from Trade and Investment -- Revisited," Journal of Development Studies, 11(4): 376-382.

34. SMITH, ADAM (1976), An Inquiry into the Nature and Causes of the Wealth of Nations, Oxford: Clarendon Press, (first edition, 1776).

35. STIGLER, GEORGE J. (1961), "The Economics of Information," Journal of Political Economy, 69: 213-225.

36. TIMMER, C. PETER (1986), Getting Prices Right: The Scope and Limits of Agricultural Price Policy, Ithaca: Cornell University Press.

37. WADE, ROBERT (1985). "The Market for Public Office: Why the Indian State is Not Better at Development," World Development, 13: 467-497.

38. WEIR, DAVID and MARK SCHAPIRO (1981), Circle of Poison: Pesticides and People in a Hungry World, San Fransisco: Institute for Food and Development Policy.

39. WHITESIDE, DAVID (1983), Note on the Export of Pesticides from the United States to Developing Countries, Boston: Harvard Business School Case Services, No. 384-097.

40. _________ (1984), Velsicol Chemical Corporation (A) and (B), Boston: Harvard Business School Case Services, No. 9-385-021.

41. WORLD BANK (1984), World Bank Tobacco Financing: The Environmental/Health Case: Background for Policy Formulation, Washington, D.C.: World Bank, Office of Environmental and Scientific Affairs, Projects Policy Department, W0020/0087W/C2404.

42. WORLD HEALTH ORGANIZATION (1981), International Code of Marketing Breast-Milk Substitutes, Geneva: World Health Organization.

43. _________ (1983), The Use of Essential Drugs, WHO Technical Report Series No. 685, Geneva: World Health Organization.

Chapter 18

ABOUT THE AUTHOR

Jean-Pierre Allain is Special Assistant with IOCU, working out of IOCU's Asian-Pacific Office in Penang.He did undergraduate studies at the University of Sao Paulo and graduate and postgraduate studies at the University of Geneva. Allain has been associated with IOCU since 1980. He has played an active role in a number of global public interest campaigns dealing with the marketing of infant formula, pesticides, and medicines. His current responsibilities in IOCU pertain to training, fundraising, and documentation.

INTERNATIONAL TRADE: BOON OR BANE FOR THIRD WORLD CONSUMERS?

Jean-Pierre Allain

INTRODUCTION

The issues of international trade have long been of concern to consumers and their representatives. The International Organization of Consumers Unions (IOCU) and the European Bureau of Consumers Unions (BEUC) have recently produced a position paper on trade policy [1]. International trade does indeed create trade-offs for consumers, as Michael Reich has shown in his excellent paper. The questions are: "For which consumers?" and "Is the overall balance for consumers in developing countries positive or negative?"

This brief discussion paper will argue that the conventional view of the benefits of international trade, based on the principle of free trade, is not supported by reality. I will show the need for a wider analysis of the issue that extends beyond the effect of international trade on the individual consumer. A critique of some of the points of Reich's paper should lead to a broader view of the macro-economic consequences of international trade and its impact on consumers, particularly in the Third World.

SOME REACTIONS TO REICH

Reich convincingly argues that consumers in developing countries do not derive full benefits from international trade, due to faults in three main areas of the free market model which tend to affect them more than they do consumers in industrialized countries. These areas are (1) information, (2) choice and (3) redress.

Information

The problem here is not only that consumers in the Third World lack sufficient information. In fact, in some instances they may suffer from too much information. But the central questions are: How relevant is the information provided to the needs of Third World consumers? Is this information accessible to the great majority of consumers? Unfortunately, a large proportion of Third World inhabitants are illiterate. The most common and preferred means of communication is oral, leaving printed information on the use, misuse, dangers, and warnings inaccessible to most consumers. Furthermore, information about many imported products that cause harm to consumers, such as pharmaceuticals, pesticides, canned or powdered foods, toys, chemicals, is not part of the oral tradition. The old do not transmit "wisdom" about these products to the younger generation.

Quite apart from this information problem is the fact that many traded goods are not suitable for the needs and the conditions of consumers in Third World countries. Thus, even if sufficient information about them were available to consumers, the latter lack the means or conditions in terms of money, knowledge, equipment, etc. to use such goods appropriately. For this reason, many "inappropriate" products confer harm, waste and violence, instead of benefits. These "inappropriate" products ought not to be imported into developing countries for this and other reasons discussed below.

It is dangerous to view the main problem as stemming from a lack of information, because that view leads to the conclusion that, once information becomes available, the problem will be gone, regardless of whether the information is used and acted upon appropriately. This view also ignores the fact that most of the information about goods and services is provided by the producer via advertising and is thus inherently biased [8]. As Galbraith points out, the function of advertising is to "bring into being wants that previously did not exist" [3]. Information by itself is not enough to protect consumers or to insure the best choice [6, 10]. In my view, products that are harmful or wasteful should not be freely traded in the first place.

Choice

There is no doubt that the spread of international trade has widened the choice for consumers all over the world. Almost everywhere on earth now imported goods compete with domestic ones or complement the available choice. However, the free market philosophy does not deal with disposable income as the critical factor in making a large choice of goods possible [5]. The adverse influence of advertising and cultural alienation lead to poor consumer choices. In developing countries the waste from poor choices is more serious because it affects a large fraction of the smaller incomes in developing countries [4].

Reich also stresses the fact that choice is influenced by government decisions, notably those regarding the use of scarce foreign currency, as well as quotas, tariffs and other trade restrictions. Some of them may be imposed for social reasons, such as surcharges on imports of luxury items with an eye to reducing their importation and hence leaving more foreign currency available for imports of essentials. Another common practice is to tax alcoholic beverages and tobacco products heavily, both to discourage their consumption and to raise revenue. But such government action rarely is sufficient to alter the distribution of wealth in a country and therefore the basic composition of demand. A point raised by Reich and to which we shall revert later is the consequences of consumers' choice for employment and for the production structure.

Redress

The problem of redress is well described in Reich's paper. But it is worth pointing out also that in many developing countries there is no tradition of litigation. In many societies, problems, including conflicts between buyers and sellers, have traditionally been solved by long discussion and the use of "wise" arbitrators, but without any written laws. Contracts and written guarantees were -- and to a large extent are still -- unknown and "foreign." People trust each other more.

Another major obstacle to redress is the fault concept. In many countries a consumer, seeking redress through the courts after being harmed by a good or service, must not only document the harm inflicted, but prove that it was the fault of the producer or seller. This is virtually impossible under the laws of most Third World countries, especially since the information that might lead to a producer's conviction is in his hands, not the consumer's. Only recently some countries have started to change their laws to make consumer claims easier and less costly to settle. Brazil is one example. Earlier this year the Brazilian congress passed a bill that would simplify consumer court cases enormously and make proceedings free of charge to consumers. Further, it would allow consumer organizations and government agencies to obtain court injunctions against any goods or services harmful to consumers, even prior to a consumer complaint.

Influences on Consumers' Decisions

There is a tendency, when discussing trade and other relations between industrialized and developing countries, to treat countries as whole entities and not to emphasize individual consumers or citizens enough. This obscures the fact that import and export decisions for most goods and services and in most countries are made by corporations and individuals, not by governments. Admittedly, international trade operates within the framework of agreements, restrictions and distortions made by governments. However, apart from intergovernment trade in major commodities such as oil, the actual decisions to import or export a particular good or service are made by companies, based on the demand created by advertising and marketing activities. Thus individual consumer purchase decisions, often influenced by advertising more than needs [11], are of paramount importance in shaping international trade. This is why advertising and all commercial promotional activities are so crucial to the development process and have come increasingly under the scrutiny of both national and international authorities [7]. There are numerous examples of how promotional activities can mould consumer choices, particularly those of children and youth towards goods which do not suit their needs or their conditions [2]. An obvious and very good example of the detrimental consequences of this is the replacement of breast milk -- the ideal food for babies-- by manufactured powdered milk [5].

Reich points to the involvement of United Nations agencies in setting guidelines for international trade and advertising. It needs to be pointed out, however, that United Nations recommendations are addressed to governments and not individual citizens. UN actions are not binding laws. In fact, national governments tend not to act on UN recommendations and tend only to pass on information to consumers when sufficient public pressure exists. This pressure can come only from organized consumers. But in this regard, most developing countries have a long way to go. Their consumer organizations are usually small and weak, lacking the financial and technical strength of their counterparts in affluent countries. The solidarity manifested by the international consumer movement is essential to forestall harm to consumers in economically weaker countries. A noteworthy example is the Bangladesh Drug Policy which survived considerable international pressure because of support from consumer groups outside Bangladesh [9]. Unfortunately, most domestic and international governmental action to prevent or limit harm to consumers comes after the harm has been done. The development of new products and industrial processes by business tends to come before government action.

MACRO-ECONOMIC IMPLICATIONS OF INTERNATIONAL TRADE FOR CONSUMERS

It is a recognized fact that the terms of trade of developing countries have declined consistently over the past 40 years; that is, developing countries have been losing more from international trade than they have been gaining. Since these conclusions are based on average statistics, we concede that some countries or some business sectors may have gained more than they have lost. However, the stark result of this trend in international trade has been a slow but constant erosion of purchasing power of consumers in many developing countries and a concomitant increase in wealth of industrialized countries.

Again, statistics, usually supplied on a country-by-country basis, do not reveal the effects of international trade on individual consumers. However, observation of actual living conditions of consumers in Third World countries over the past 40 years confirms this impoverishment for the majority.

The international trade system is a reflection of the power structures of the world. It also expresses a continuation of the colonial relationships that dominated most of the Third World until the 50's and 60's. During the colonial period many Third World countries were forced to be the suppliers of raw materials for the industries of the colonial powers. They were forced to change their patterns of production so as to supply those materials the colonial powers wanted. In many cases, they were prevented from industrializing and pursuing their own economic development. Despite independence, the situation has changed little. The efforts of developing countries to export semi-processed and industrial products to the markets of industrialized countries have usually been hampered by trade restrictions imposed by the developed countries to protect their own markets and maintain their technological lead over the rest of the world. These tendencies allow the developed countries to continue their domination of world trade.

The problem with the trade system is, therefore, much more than a question of what goods and services reach Third World consumers and the impact they may have. It is the distortion of the whole production pattern in the Third World that prevents its consumers from achieving a higher standard of living and, with it, the education, the information, the legal system and the institutions that would allow them to make the best choices. By pursuing the present so-called "path of development," Third World countries are forever condemned to obtaining less from international trade than industrialized countries. They can never, therefore, offer their consumers the same advantages enjoyed by consumers in advanced industrialized countries!

By exporting raw materials or agricultural commodities mainly and importing industrial and highly processed consumer goods, developing countries are not getting much value added for what they produce and have to pay a much higher value added for what they import. This perpetuates the difference in incomes between industrialized and developing countries -- the infamous "gap" that, despite all development efforts, has not grown smaller. The fact that this is so is sufficient proof that the development model pursued today is a failure. The system is bad also because it allows a small minority of consumers in poorer countries to become richer and richer, while the vast majority gets poorer and consequently hardly benefits from the positive side of international trade.

This is not to say that international trade does not offer some gains to Third World consumers. There is no doubt that certain products, for instance some medicines or some industrial processes, have improved living conditions for Third World inhabitants. But "consumers" consist not only of those who buy because they possess the necessary purchasing power. <u>All</u> people are consumers. <u>All</u> suffer the consequences of industrialization, of pollution, of city overcrowding, or deteriorating health conditions, albeit to different degrees.

Granted, international trade has a few success stories to show --countries such as Singapore, Taiwan, South Korea, Hong Kong, where the majority of consumers have benefited. But the stories are few and these countries too are now facing increasing difficulties as their export outlets are closing. On the other hand, few people know that countries such as Paraguay, Brazil and Chile were, at one time in their history, nearly self-sufficient because of the high degree of industrialization they had achieved. But then they were very protectionist and hardly participated in international trade. Once they did, they lost more than they gained and slipped back into under-development.

CONCLUSION

International trade can benefit some consumers in the Third World. However, the potential benefits are restricted to those consumers with sufficient purchasing power, i.e., a minority, whereas the undesirable side effects of international trade affect most consumers. Some of these undesirable effects can be lessened by more, better and more relevant information to consumers, particularly independent unbiased information relayed by socially and culturally acceptable methods; by policies that lead to a better, not necessarily wider, choice of goods and services to satisfy the needs of consumers; and by fast, efficient, cheap and easily accessible means of legal redress.

International trade, in its present form, cannot confer a net benefit on the majority of consumers in the Third World, because it relies on and is the consequence of a system of unequal distribution of wealth and power, a system in which trading partners are not on an equal footing. This system is heavily biased by agreements and decisions that distort free trade and which have little to do with the needs of consumers or the wishes of trading partners. It is a system that forces the weaker partners to accept trade which, in the long run, causes them to lose more than they gain. International trade is part and parcel of a global imbalanced structure of powers which perpetuates the dependence of some countries on others and prevents consumers and governments from making free choices. It encompasses the issues of both external and domestic debts of developing and industrialized countries, the issues of so-called aid to developing countries, the issues of military expenditures and militarization, and the global management of the environment, among others. Trade protectionism and its impact on consumers, both in developing and industrialized countries, is but a manifestation of the reactions to this imbalanced structure. Yet it has attracted a lot of attention of late as protectionist measures have multiplied in many countries. The consumer movement too has joined in the debate. Thus, IOCU and BEUC (European Bureau of Consumers Unions) presented the views of consumers at an OECD Symposium on International Trade and the Consumer Interest. It is a subject that deserves a separate development.

Free trade does not exist and cannot exist in a world with such enormous differences in wealth, level of development, natural endowments, cultures and social values. Free trade does not even exist between highly industrialized and relatively similar countries. And it is even more improbable when a large part of international trade is conducted by huge transnational corporations and within them. But then, from a consumer viewpoint, absolutely free trade may not be desirable.

Changes and improvements in the system are possible and would benefit consumers everywhere, but their discussion is beyond the scope of this paper. Reich has already pointed to some of these, such as the need for a world government that could "act directly to alter the distribution of incomes and wealth between nations" and a greater role for and participation of national and international consumer organizations.

REFERENCES

1. ACTION GUIDE - CONSUMERS AND TRADE POLICY (1986). Ref. 65/86, IOCU, The Hague and BEUC, Brussels, April.

2. ADVERTISING AGE (1978). 6 February :2.

3. GALBRAITH, J.K. (1962). The Affluent Society, Harmondsworth: Penguin Books.

4. GREINER, T. (1975), "The Promotion of Bottle Feeding by Multinational Corporations: How Advertising and the Health Professions Have Contributed," Cornell International Nutrition Monograph Series, No. 2, Cornell University, Ithaca, NY.

5. JAMES, J. (1983). Consumer Choice in the Third World, New York: Saint Martin's Press.

6. KERTON, R., et al. (eds) (1983). Appropriate Products, IOCU/IDRC, Penang.

7. MURDOCK, G. and JANUS N. (1985). Mass Communication and the Advertising Industry, UNESCO, Paris.

8. STRIDSBERG, A. (1974). "Can Advertising Benefit Developing Countries?" Business and Society Review, (II) Autumn.

9. TIRANTI, D.J. (1986). Essential Drugs: The Bangladesh Example - Four Years on 1982-1986, Oxford: New Internationalist/IOCU/War on Want.

10. VAN GINNEKEN, W. and BARON C. (eds.) (1984). Appropriate Products, Employment and Technology: Case Studies on Consumer Choice and Basic Needs in Developing Countries, ILO, London: Macmillan.

11. WILLAT, J. (1970). "How Nestle Adapts Products to its Markets," Business Abroad, June.

ABOUT THE AUTHOR

Jean Kinsey is Professor in the Department of Agricultural and Applied Economics at the University of Minnesota. Kinsey received her Ph.D. in Agrcultural Economics from the University of California, Davis in 1976. Kinsey has been both a high school teacher and university professor, moving to the University of Minnesota upon completion of her Ph.D. Kinsey was President of ACCI in 1983 and is a member of the ACCI Research Committee. She has had foreign assignments in Rwanda and Barbados. Her research centers on food economics and consumer credit.

INTERNATIONAL TRADE AND TRADE-OFFS FOR THIRD WORLD CONSUMERS: A MATTER OF ENTITLEMENTS

Jean Kinsey

The economic position of consumers in developing countries is difficult to conceptualize. For many developing nations the time in the transition from a subsistence economy to a monetized market has been reduced from centuries to decades. Imported Western goods are highly sought after in the Third World because they are often believed to be superior. That they may malfunction, be hazardous or overpriced are not likely to be primary concerns to consumers who daily face absolute scarcity and deprivation.

By superimposing three of the consumer rights established in the Western World -- information, choice and redress -- on Third World markets, Reich has provided some important insights into the position of Third World consumers. Recognizing that these rights will be implemented with great difficulty in the Third World, he implies that those who export to Third World countries bear a special responsibility for the health and safety of their consumers. It is easy to agree with this proposition on ethical grounds. I suggest that establishing the mechanism and enforcing the responsibilities of exporters should be an integral part of the agenda for research in the interests of international consumers.

In this discussion paper, I will comment briefly on Reich's paper and suggest some additional trade-offs. Then I will propose a conceptual framework in which the incentives and costs associated with consumers' safety can be examined from a behavioral and an economic perspective. Finally, I will assess the role of national and international organizations that can in principle, act on behalf of consumers.

TRADE-OFFS AND TRADE

Although Reich's title includes "trade-offs," the benefits and costs of international trade to Third World consumers are not discussed. The potential contribution of imports to agricultural development, industrial employment, per capita income and health and sanitation are ignored. Many governments of developing countries would argue that these benefits outweigh the costs of accidents incurred through the use and misuse of individual products by individual consumers. For example, the early importation of DDT into Thailand dramatically decreased the incidence of malaria, opened up vast new areas of land to rice and corn production, increased local food consumption, improved nutrition, and facilitated agricultural exports. The U.S. Agency for International Development (U.S.A.I.D.) no longer allows its aid money to be spent on chemicals containing DDT. It does, however, allow the purchase and use of phostoxin, a biodegradable pesticide that is very dangerous to humans in the short run. Its safe use requires the wearing of special clothing which is generally not available. The decision to trade off the long-term, environmental hazards of DDT for the deadly, short-term hazards of phostoxin has clearly been made for Third World consumers, in this case by an international development agency. The example illustrates the real and difficult trade-offs facing Third World countries and their advisors. These trade-offs involve economic development (growth in national income and production) vs. environmental protection vs. the cost of accidents to individual consumers and society.

Trade-offs associated with Third World countries' promotion of exports are not mentioned by Reich. But they are real. For example, the resources used to produce exportable goods must compete with the production of food and other goods for local consumers. Exports, however, increase foreign exchange and enable Third World countries to buy and sell in the international market. It is no accident that the development of exportable commodities is a major goal of most Western development projects and of the countries in which they are sited.

POLICY CHOICES

Enforcement of the three consumer rights identified by Reich-- information, choice and redress -- require different types of policy solutions. Using the traditional two-pronged fork of consumer policy, improved information and choice clearly belong to the prong labeled "information" (or "education"). Redress requires the second prong -- "protection".

The provision and acquisition of better product information is a "market enhancing activity". It facilitates trade. Extremely good information enables consumers to protect themselves. However, given the dearth of product information in Third World markets, information search costs are very high. This implies that the price and quality of goods will vary a great deal [4]. Consumers in these markets will ultimately accept risky products without adequate information because the marginal cost of information will outweigh any perceived product benefit. Since consumers in most Third World countries are so far away from achieving any semblance of self-protection via information and education, protection -- as Thorelli argues [5] -- must be the policy priority if the costs and incidence of product related accidents are to be diminished.

Redress is also aided by information, but requires protection. Protection implies some form of government intervention and regulation. It implies altering the rules of the game. It implies--using Kerton's terminology [3], changing the institutional "framework" in which market transactions take place. More abstractly, it involves reassigning entitlements or "property rights." It means, at least for very risky products, that the market rules must be converted deliberately from "caveat emptor" to "caveat vendor".

TRADE-OFFS AND ENTITLEMENTS

A useful taxonomy for thinking about consumer rights -- the "entitlement" to prevail -- has been provided by Calabresi and Melamed [2]. Their approach blends the economic theories of social cost with legal property rights. These theories have been applied by natural resource economists as they speak about social costs or "externalities" [1]. Negative externalities in consumer markets include accidents which occur because of product hazards, malfunctions or misuse.

The theory of social costs may further be linked to trade theory by considering the relative profitability of trading in a particular country. Profitability is partially a function of institutional arrangements that specify which parties bear the social costs of consumers' accidents and which parties are responsible for the transaction costs of trade. Transaction costs are generally defined to include costs of search and negotiation while social costs are attributed to post-purchase phenomena such as the costs of misinformation, accidents, and waste. None of these costs are likely to be reflected in the selling price of products, but they are ultimately born by members of society.

Calabresi and Melamed's taxonomy, adapted for consumer product markets, is outlined in Table 1 [2]. It assumes a world where transaction costs are high and where some extra-market authority (a government?) is necessary to allocate resources consistent with the values of society. First, entitlement is assigned. Then, one of three types of rules is invoked to protect or change entitlements. These rules have major implications both for consumers' protection and for sellers' profitability.

The prevalent case in Third World consumer markets is case II on Table I where Seller B is entitled to prevail and that entitlement is protected by a property rule. That is, Seller B (or perhaps Developed Country B) can interfere with Consumer (or Country) A's lifestyle -- sell anything that Consumer A will buy -- until A takes action to stop B. Since the burden for initiating action to stop B or to change the entitlement rests with A, A's resource constraints, such as income and education, largely determine the probability that any action will be taken.

TABLE 1

Entitlement Belongs to:	Entitlement Protected By: Property Rule	Liability Rule	Inalienability
A. Consumer (Caveat Vendor)	I. A must consent to B's interference with his/her lifestyle (property). A must agree to accept risky products after full disclosure of characteristics and dangers.	III. A must be compensated for the actions of B, e.g., for harm done by the use of a defective product. A third party determines the fair compensation.	V. B may not interfere with A under any circumstances Stopping the sale of products that threaten life and limb would not be compensated.
B. Seller (Caveat Emptor)	II. B can act to interfere with A's lifestyle (property) and can be stopped only if A bribes B to stop.	IV. B can be stopped from selling harmful products but only if A compensates B for losses incurred due to stopping.	

If there existed a national or international organization capable of making and enforcing a change in property rule II, it could, for example, pass a law that no seller's goods could enter a Third World country until the seller disclosed to the official import authorities the potential hazards of using that product in that country. The import authorities (acting on behalf of consumers) must then give, or withhold, permission to sell in that country. This is a case of informed consent, a minimum ethical standard in international trade suggested by Reich. The burden of taking action, under property rule I, is on the seller, whose income and education constraints are far less severe than those of consumers. Shifting the responsibility for the transaction costs to the seller changes the entitlement, and "caveat vendor" replaces "caveat emptor." In either case, a market solution is implied.

Entitlements may also be protected by liability rules. They require a third party to determine the level of enforcement and compensation. Product liability rules under tort law in the United States are an example of liability rule III. Consumers are entitled to be compensated for harm caused by a defective product, the amount of which is determined either by an insurance company or the courts. A similar set of institutional arrangements would need to exist in the Third World for liability rules to be workable.

A modicum of safety and health may be viewed as an inalienable right of consumers who cannot be informed or otherwise be protected. Inalienability implies that some trades may not be allowed because "dreadful accidents" are intolerable and the transaction costs of preventing these accidents are so great that they would not be undertaken if only property or liability rules apply. Again, institutional arrangements such as an international, governing body would have to protect this right.

INTERNATIONAL AGENCIES AND CONSUMERS' RIGHTS

Reich lists some of the international organizations that have tried to increase the flow of information and a few that have tried to assist with a system of redress. While recognizing the political and developmental problems surrounding the evolution of governing bodies that have the will and the resources to change the form of consumer entitlements, a few candidates come to mind. As mentioned earlier, international development agencies such as U.S.A.I.D., the U.N. Food and Agricultural Organization (FAO), and the World Bank, have considerable influence in the countries where they work. They could, if so inspired, make aid contingent upon local enforcement of consumer rights. Several developing and socialist countries have foreign trade offices that monitor and control certain imports. They, too, if similarly inspired, could monitor the safety and efficacy of consumer products.

If, through the efforts of organized consumer groups, the mass media, other consciousness-raising agencies, world opinion leaders came to espouse basic consumer rights, some fundamental changes in the institutional framework in which Third World trade takes place could occur. Changing the rules of the game implies, however, a redistribution of costs and profits. Research could appropriately address questions about the direction and magnitude of that redistribution.

By the same token, changes in entitlements could increase sellers' costs, decrease profits, and potentially stop the importation of some products into the Third World. Research questions might be: (1) How much would the internalizing of transaction costs decrease sellers' profits? (2) What is the probability of an accident? What would it cost for the seller to reimburse a Third World consumer for harm or malfunction? (3) How much will it cost the government to enforce entitlements? Some puzzling methodological questions will also arise. For instance: (1) How does one calculate the value of life and limb in the middle of the Kalahari versus the heart of Santiago? (2) How do Westerners handle the problem of preferences for risky products in the face of absolute scarcity?

Reich's paper suggests several research questions, but it does not set a research agenda or lead us to a clear set of policy solutions. Perhaps this is for the better for optimal choices are not at all obvious. Some philosophical questions, as well as cross-cultural issues surround research into the trade-offs faced by Third World consumers. Careful benefit/cost analyses of different entitlement scenarios could provide useful information for international trade policy decisions but, ultimately, consumer rights, as defined by the Western world, will have to be enforced at the local level.

REFERENCES

1. BROMLEY, DANIEL W. (1978), "Property Rules, Liability Rules and Environmental Economics," Journal of Economic Issues, 12:43-60.

2. CALABRESI, GUIDO and A. DOUGLAS MELAMED (1972), "Property Rules, Liability Rules and Inalienability: One View of the Cathedral," Harvard Law Review, 85:1089-1128.

3. KERTON, ROBERT R. (1981), "A World View of the Consumer Movement Seen as Collective Consumer Search Capital," Proceedings of 27th Annual Conference of the American Council on Consumer Interests, 90-95.

4. STIGLER, GEORGE J. (1961), "The Economics of Information," The Journal of Political Economy, 69:213-255.

5. THORELLI, HANS B. (1981/3), "Consumer Policy for the Third World," Journal of Consumer Policy, 5:197-211.

Chapter 19

ABOUT THE AUTHOR

John E. Kushman is Professor and Chair in the Department of Textiles, Design, and Consumer Economics, University of Delaware. At the time of the Wingspread Conference he was Professor of Agricultural Economics and Agricultural Economist at the Experiment Station and Giannini Foundation at the University of California, Davis. An economist, Kushman received his Ph.D. in Economics from the University of North Carolina in 1974. Widely published, his articles deal with topics in consumer economics, health economics, aging, and the micro-economic functioning of markets.

INCREASING COMPETITION THROUGH DEREGULATION: DO CONSUMERS WIN OR LOSE?

John E. Kushman

SUMMARY

This paper addresses the impact on consumers of the broad array of deregulatory changes taking place in the U.S. economy. Neither the public interest nor the special interest theories of regulation are satisfactory as an explanation of regulation followed by deregulation. A synthesis of these theories is proposed as an explanatory theory of regulatory policy with emphasis put on understanding deregulation rather than on formal hypothesis testing. Types of regulation are defined, some better suited to defining "increasing competition through deregulation" and more likely to yield consumer gains from deregulation than others. The different types of regulation defined in this paper have different implications for cross subsidization of one part of the regulated product by another and the theoretical basis for analyzing the types of regulation is more or less settled, depending on the regulation. Deregulation of domestic airlines is taken as a case study. Overall, deregulation is thought to have benefited consumers. The extent to which consumers have benefited is related to how well their trips fit into the emerging hub-and-spoke system of air transport. A general perspective on research on deregulation in the consumer interest is offered in conclusion.

INTRODUCTION

Writing this paper was exciting and perplexing. It was exciting because deregulation is a source of major, some would have thought impossible, changes in the U.S. economy. Deregulation is also a rare instance in which academics have had a direct and evident effect on public policy.

The assignment was perplexing because it is not clear how to say anything conclusive about a phenomenon that is so recent, so complicated, and so broad. Deregulation is a fact or a matter of speculation in many sectors of the economy. Evaluating deregulation entails all the unresolved methodological issues represented in other sessions of this conference. Finally, deregulation is perplexing in itself.

Deregulation has come at a time which is awkward for scholars. Deregulation began in earnest just when conventional wisdom was holding that regulation was invulnerable to attacks of reason from academia or elsewhere and just when competing theories explaining regulatory entrenchment were being refined! All theories of regulatory entrenchment were thrown into question even before they could be winnowed to a few favorites.

My first task is to make the assignment less perplexing by defining the question in a narrow and exploratory context. I will define the notions of increasing competition, deregulation, and gain or loss to consumers narrowly. The process of narrowing the question will create an implicit research agenda.

In the first section of this paper I look among the current theories of regulation for a conceptual framework within which to evaluate the effects of deregulation on consumers. I conclude that even though we economists want to talk and act like positivistic scientists our methods are unsuitable for this objective. We make the greatest contribution to policy analysis by providing explanatory theories and qualitative analyses of efficiency. I propose an explanatory theory of regulation as a context for assessing deregulation and its effects on consumers.

The third section of the paper narrows the question of effects on consumers by delineating types of regulation and sectors of the economy in which they are found. Some types of regulation and some sectors are better candidates for deregulation than others. By "better candidates" I mean that our present state of knowledge and common sense logic are more persuasive that there are benefits to be had for consumers from deregulation. For some types of regulation the notion of increasing competition through deregulation is not meaningful. The last substantive section of the paper summarizes the empirical evidence on effects on consumers of airline deregulation. Airlines were an early instance of deregulation with relatively more time having elapsed to observe and to document the ultimate impacts of deregulation. Airlines were also a good candidate for deregulatory benefits to consumers.

My concluding remarks are directed to a research agenda on consumers and deregulation. These comments are my assessment of what we should try to accomplish, what we can expect to accomplish, and how the two should be related.

THEORIES OF REGULATION

I take up theories of regulation in this section in order to establish a conceptual basis for the question of whether consumers gain or lose from deregulation. If there exists some well-accepted theory of how regulation comes about, how it works, and how it comes to be undone, we can use it to conceptualize what is meant by increasing competition through deregulation and by deregulation's probable effects on consumers. This section extends Keeler's recent work [27] in some small ways and draws on the review of regulation by Joskow and Noll [26]. If the reader notes a sparsity of references, it is because those previous works and other contributors to this conference have summarized the literature so thoroughly.

Theories of regulation are imbued, or should be imbued, with the spirit of workable competition. That is, the major lessons of pure theory (Pareto optimality, second-best, the fundamental theorems of welfare economics, contestability, sustainability, etc.) are incorporated, but with their lessons interpreted in pragmatic terms. These lessons of pure theory are augmented by empirical evidence, subjective judgments when empirical evidence is insufficient, and explicit equity considerations. Theories of regulation are meant to be policy-relevant and policy does not wait on theory or definitive empirical studies! However, theories of regulation and the policies they support must be continually reconsidered and deregulation affords an excellent opportunity for reevaluation.

"Regulation" is taken to mean functions performed by administrative agencies. The antitrust laws and the court system are excluded except as instruments to achieve the ends of administrative agencies. Public utilities regulation and environmental protection are two examples of regulation as the term is used.

In broad terms, Keeler distinguishes between "public-interest" theories of regulation and "revisionist" or "special-interest" theories of regulation. Public-interest theories developed along with formal statements of general equilibrium and welfare economics. Keeler notes public goods and externalities as the theoretical basis of public-interest theories of regulation. Historically, this list is probably accurate, but I add market failures due to natural monopoly, insufficiency or asymmetry of information and externalities associated with income distribution or consumption interdependencies. The information-related motivations are pertinent to regulations that purport to protect consumers from unwise choices while externalities associated with income distribution are pertinent to the widely-recognized redistributive goals of some regulations.

The public-interest theories of regulation are positive (or descriptive) theories with normative (or prescriptive) ancestry. They grew out of the demonstration that ideal government intervention could restore the economy to the frontier of efficient resource allocations. Regulation could be at least part of the ideal government intervention. Once the economy was functioning on the frontier of Pareto-efficient resource allocations, a choice among those allocations could be made in accordance with some social welfare function. The operational version of this social welfare function gives positive weights to consumer and producer surpluses. In the first applied studies, distributional questions were ignored and total surplus was maximized. This approach, with its implicit equal weights for all surpluses, is obviously inadequate, and some welfare weights are required. Public-interest theory held that regulation takes whatever form maximizes social welfare.

Criticism of public interest as a positive theory of regulation has been that actual regulation is not Pareto-efficient (first or second best), or that the effect of regulation is to transfer surplus in ways that are inconsistent with widely held beliefs about the social welfare weights, or both. It has been argued that the magnitude of inefficiency and the consistently perverse direction of surplus transfers is irreconcilable with the public-interest theory. An alternative theory is in order.

The revisionists developed positive theories that predicted regulatory inefficiency and inequitable surplus transfers. The transfers were explained by positing that the regulatory process served the interests of bureaucrats, politicians, or the regulated producers, depending on the particular revisionist theory. Regulatory inefficiency resulted from institutional rules that insured that the public's control would be nullified. Thus, regulatory instruments were chosen not because they could efficiently achieve the avowed purpose of regulation but because they insulated the regulatory process from scrutiny and discipline by the public. Inefficiency was necessary to protect government failure. For instance, transfers by differential pricing were preferred to straight tax-and-transfer schemes because differential pricing was harder to detect and discipline.

Peltzman has developed a relatively formal model that serves well to represent the revisionist class [39]. In the Peltzman model there are no market imperfections or market failures that would rationalize government intervention in the public interest, but government fails in that it does not maximize social welfare. The regulatory agency charges different groups for a regulated product so as to maximize a political support function. Some groups are charged a high price to generate a profit which is then transferred to another group through a low price. The losers and gainers are chosen according to their influence on the political fortunes of the regulator (legislator, bureaucrat, or commissioner). Price differentials have the effect of reducing surpluses for the losing groups and increasing surpluses for the winning groups. Thus, Peltzman shows that differential pricing schemes and surplus transfers can arise solely from the imperfections and failures of government.

The revisionist theories represent an analytical advance. They brought the behavior of regulators under the paradigm of rational, self-interested behavior. They also recognized the asymmetry between failing market and infallible government that characterized the public-interest theories. These steps to bring theories of market failure and theories of government failure under the same paradigm were essential to further development of the theory of regulation. In time, the revisionist theories seemed to rout the public-interest theories in competition for the "truth" about regulation. Robert Lampman's account of the development of the consumer "Bill or Rights" at this conference [29] reflect some of the influence of the revisionists. Proponents of the revisionist theories can rightfully claim a role in the advent of deregulation.

Unfortunately for those who like stories with neat finishes, the victory of the revisionist theories was incomplete. In the important areas of environmental quality and product safety, regulations have increased in number and scope, and theoretical work has mostly supported government intervention. In the environmental quality and product safety areas history repeated itself. The chief sources of market failure in these areas were informational deficiencies. Theoretical developments began to elucidate the nature of market failure and the most straightforward remedies. Not surprisingly, the most straightforward remedies incorporated the assumption of an infallible, beneficent government to carry them out. Standards, liability rules, and other schemes could restore optimality <u>if correctly implemented</u>. Again, a normative rationale for regulation emerged as the foundation of a positive theory -- the positive theory of consumer protection. In this theory, government acts perfectly to remedy market failures due to information deficiencies.

General equilibrium and Pareto efficiency results were difficult to achieve in cases of informational deficiencies, so the normative standard in consumer protection theory was more likely to be partial-equilibrium analysis of how well actual consumer choices correspond to the choices of a fully-informed, rational consumer. To date, the theoretical literature is still dominated by normative models of government intervention in the environmental and consumer protection areas. In this volume, several papers review the development of consumer protection theory, especially as it relates to quality, and others deal with the state of knowledge about consumers and incomplete information [10, 11, 15, 16, 25, 36, 49]. The references in these papers reflect the state of theory and empirical work better than any list I could construct. This is not to imply that the authors agree with my summary of the state of affairs. If history fully repeats itself, these theories will see their own revisionists!

In more traditional areas of regulation -- public utilities, transportation, and communications -- the revisionist victory may be transient. Just as the revisionist theories gained ascendancy in these traditional areas, along came deregulation in trucking, railroads, airlines, telecommunications, natural gas extraction, petroleum, banking, and the securities markets. One school of thought holds that deregulation refutes the revisionists. This school emphasizes the testing of formal, rigorous statements of positive economic theories. In fact, both the public-interest and revisionist theories performed poorly in predicting regulation and subsequent deregulation. Critics view these theories as static, ahistorical, lacking social context, characterizing only polar cases, in short as tired apologies for inadequate theories. According to this school of thought, economists say nothing of interest about regulation or deregulation, since they lack a viable theory. This critique of economic theories of regulation can be seen as an extension of the problems of economic theory in general [24, Chapters 15 through 18]. Economic theories either predict regulatory entrenchment and fail in the face of deregulation, or they predict regulation in the public interest and fail in the face of regulations that violate this standard.

If one adopts a narrow positivistic perspective of finding a single "truth" by eliminating competing theories, then the rejection of both the public-interest and revisionist theories of regulation is correct. But this perspective would lead to the rejection of nearly all competing economic theories. Over the years many have noted that economists like to "talk" positivistic methodology, but that they implicitly reject it in application. The development of economic theory has placed more emphasis than most would admit on "verification" of theories by both formal and informal means [31] and on maximally explanatory theories [40, 41 and sources cited therein]. Only in a cumulative and informal fashion are theories actually discarded. In my view we are not yet in a position to discard either the public-interest or special-interest theories of regulation. Formal economic theories are only a starting place for a discussion that must move on to include dynamics, historical and social context, and nonpolar cases. Useful policy analysis proceeds in this less formal manner.

A synthesis of the public-interest and revisionist theories along lines suggested by Keeler seems consistent with theory and policy analysis in practice. This synthesis yields an explanatory theory of regulation. That is, it reveals a hidden mechanism at work behind regulatory change and leads to a number of useful analogies. This explanation or subjective understanding provides the basis for policy analysis and choice. Moreover, the synthesis is consistent with a broad array of formal and informal empirical evidence. A theory that offers understanding and is verified by a broad spectrum of evidence is subjectively appealing and logically consistent basis for policy analysis.

Just as the theories of public goods, externalities, and natural monopoly provide a formal basis for the public-interest theory of regulation, the Peltzman model provides a formal representation of the revisionist model. These theories, however, have symmetrical limitations. The public-interest theory postulates market failure and government perfection. The Peltzman theory postulates market perfection and government failure. That reality lies at neither pole hardly requires formal tests. Any useful theory must include failure in both markets and government and lie between the poles!

The common structure of the public-interest and revisionist theories makes it impossible to distinguish between them empirically. The public-interest model is closed by a social welfare function that attaches weights to the surpluses of members of society. The Peltzman model involves a political support function that attaches weights to the surpluses of voters or special interest groups according to their political power over the regulator and the extent to which regulations affect their surpluses. A political support function cannot logically exclude any party affected, even indirectly, by the regulations. In a general-equilibrium context with taxation and where all parties are potential consumers or producers of all products, all parties will be affected by all regulations. Hence, a political support function and a social welfare function have the same form and attach positive weights to the surpluses of all parties. The public-interest and special-interest theories will only be distinguishable, even in principle, if it is known that they imply different weights for specific surpluses.

There have been attempts to estimate the "policy preference weights" that are implied by regulations [13, 14, 30, 44, 45, 47, 51, 52], but it cannot be determined how these weights arise, so they cannot be used to test the public-interest theory against the special-interest theory. The authors typically regard the weights as the outcome of a bargaining process in which decisionmakers trade off special interests against the public interest. No independent source of social welfare (public interest) weights has been accepted. Research motivated by the special-interest theories has tended to identify those parties whose surpluses receive high weights in the political support function as those parties who benefitted from regulation. This sort of identification proceeds ex post and tautologically.

Since regulations can be rationalized by a public-interest argument or a special-interest argument given the right social welfare or political support weights and since the weights have only been identified ex post, it is impossible to discriminate empirically between the theories. Compounding this problem is the difficulty of measuring externalities, public goods, natural monopolies, and other market failures on one hand and special-interest benefits on the other hand.

One side of this analysis is the impossibility of discriminating between the public-interest and special-interest theories of regulation with our present tools. This difficulty arises from their common structure, but it is important only from the narrow positivistic perspective. The other side of the analysis is that, since the theories share a common structure, either theory or a synthesis of the two is equally useful as a context for policy analysis. Therefore, I take as the context of the question at hand a regulator who maximizes a political support function in which the surpluses of all parties get positive weights and in which some surpluses are increased by regulations that ameliorate market failures. A rational regulator has an interest in reducing inefficiencies and increasing all surpluses.

The synthesis of public-interest and special-interest theories of regulation suggests the following potential sources of deregulation:

1. Technological changes that (a) make deregulation more beneficial to consumers or producers, thereby giving them a greater stake in regulatory reform or (b) reduce the loss of surplus to consumers or producers from deregulation, thereby giving them a lesser stake in the regulatory status quo.

2. Changes in the political and institutional rules that (a) increase the political power of those who would gain from deregulation or (b) decrease the political power of those who would lose in deregulation. I confine these changes in political and institutional rules to those that may clearly be considered exogenous to the formulation of regulatory policy (like the enunciation of the one-man, one-vote rule for legislative districts by the Supreme Court).

3. Changes in preferences and incomes of consumers that (a) make deregulation more beneficial to consumers or producers, thereby giving them a greater stake in regulatory reform or (b) reduce the loss of surplus to consumers or producers from deregulation, thereby giving them a lesser stake in the regulatory status quo.

These forces for deregulation can occur simultaneously.

Analytically, the question whether consumers gain or lose from deregulation is whether the surplus they realize is greater under the new, deregulated regime than under a counterfactual old regime. If we have a plausible explanation of the source of deregulation in terms of 1-3 above, we have at least a presumption of whether consumers win or lose. Of course, not all consumers must benefit equally from deregulation.

TYPES OF REGULATION

In this section I review, very briefly, general types of regulation and the status of theoretical and empirical findings for each. I rely heavily on the excellent review by Joskow and Noll [26]. The taxonomy of regulation enables us to clarify the notion of increasing competition through deregulation and to identify sectors where deregulation is likely to substantially affect consumers.

Regulation of Entry, Exit, and Price in Industries with Competitive Structures

This category includes industries where, even under regulation, there are a large number of relatively small sellers of a reasonably homogeneous product. Examples of this type of regulation are agricultural price supports, limits on prices in banking and brokerage services, licenses and other restrictions in the learned professions, and, in some markets, airline, truck, bus, and taxi transportation.

The relevant theory for these markets seems to be competition or monopolistic competition versus oligopoly or monopoly, and the literature supports some rather strong generalizations about the effects of regulation. First, if efficiency criteria are invoked without contemplating distributional issues, the regulations produce inefficiencies. When entry is not barred or when barriers to entry are ineffective, potential rents to producers in the industry are dissipated through nonprice competition. That is, new entrants or expanding firms are prohibited from competing on price, so they compete on quality. This nonprice or quality competition (premiums for savings accounts, better meals on airplanes, etc.) is less efficient than price competition in the same way in kind transfers are less efficient than cash transfers in traditional public finance analysis. When entry is effectively barred, consumers share in ongoing losses due to noncompetitive restrictions of output. As Posner has pointed out [43] and others have elaborated [9, 32, 33], however, there also is a deadweight loss to society from activities that are not directly productive but that are necessary to secure and maintain the regulations that bar entry.

When price is restricted but there is free entry, or when entry is restricted but there is a competitive market for places in the industry, profits are reduced to normal returns by nonprice competition or expenditures on acquiring the right to enter. Consumers are worse off with regulation in either case, but their losses are mitigated by the benefits of in kind transfers when entry is free. (The reader shouldn't miss the satire of this whole line of inquiry by Dixit and Grossman [12].

The foregoing is the revisionist side of the story for industries with a competitive structure. The public-interest side is that regulation may be a way, even a relatively efficient way, to effect income redistribution through cross-subsidization of markets. Some regulations may have consumer protection benefits that counterbalance their costs. Cross-subsidization of small-town, rural and poor consumers has been a consistent theme in the explicit objectives of regulating transportation. Consumer protection objectives have been theorized for licensing restrictions, in health care for instance. The cross-subsidization argument is not convincing for regulations that fall in this class, however, unless some class of producers is the intended beneficiary of the subsidy. For instance, agricultural price supports seem much more plausible as subsidies to small, rural producers than as subsidies to any class of consumers.

The pure efficiency losses to consumers suggested by the revisionist perspective are supported by a large body of empirical evidence. As I pointed out in the previous section, the public-interest perspective cannot be rejected by the evidence, because it is not an empirically distinguishable hypothesis. Overall, the evidence seems to suggest that at best trivial cross-subsidy effects have occurred for consumers from this class of regulations. The absence of cross-subsidy effects is largely related to the absence of exit prohibitions (common carrier obligations and obligations to serve thin markets) in these competitively-structured markets. Indeed, exit prohibitions would not be workable with many small producers to monitor. Evaluation of the consumer-protection effects of the regulations is deficient at this time, for reasons that I will discuss further under "Qualitative Regulation" below.

To summarize, analysis of regulations that restrict entry, exit, and prices in markets with competitive structures rests on relatively well-established theoretical underpinnings, with the exception of consumer-protection considerations. The regulations have produced losses for many or most consumers from a pure efficiency perspective. In part, because there have been few exit restrictions, and none would be practical in competitively-structured markets, there have been no important redistributive effects of this class of regulations. The issue of potential consumer protection effects will be dealt with below.

This class of regulations is a good candidate for consumer benefits from deregulation if the caveats of redistributive and consumer protection effects are observed. "Increasing competition through deregulation" can be construed in these sectors as changing regulations to permit freer entry, exit, and pricing.

Regulation of Entry, Exit, and Price in Industries with Monopoly Structures

This category of regulation poses many more theoretical difficulties than the previous category. Historically, this category includes the public utilities and, arguably, some transportation types in some markets. The analytical difficulties arise from unsettled theoretical questions, some of which blur the boundary between this category and the previous category. First, the adequacy of the traditional concept of natural monopoly has been brought into question by the contestability and sustainability concepts. Whether these are new ideas or only refinements of old ideas is not important here. It is important that they raise the question whether regulation is necessary to control pricing in industries where, even in the absence of entry restrictions, there would be one or a few firms. If a market is perfectly contestable, ignoring potential intertemporal inefficiencies, regulation is unnecessary and wasteful. The unregulated market will yield a first-best Pareto optimal outcome [2, 3]. Sustainability is a generalization to a multiproduct context of the limit-pricing concept and also deals with whether regulation is necessary. If a natural monopoly exists and is characterized by a form of economies of scale and of complementarities in production, a Ramsey (second-best optimal) vector of prices and quantities will provide both financial viability for the monopolist and prevent entry. Furthermore, there is a weak presumption that the monopolist will operate at such a combination of prices and quantities, because to operate elsewhere runs a risk of not being sustainable [3, 38]. If there is no set of prices at which a single firm is economically viable and which will prevent entry (a sustainable monopoly), but there is a natural monopoly, then regulation of entry may be necessary.

Together, the unresolved theoretical and empirical issues of contestability and sustainability bring into question the desirability and necessity of regulated monopolies. Contestable markets should be lumped into the first category of regulations, making it competitively-structured and contestable industries. The theoretical details of contestability are not sufficiently well established and understood nor its empirical relevance sufficiently well documented to redefine the categories now.

Even if it could be established that regulated monopoly were necessary and desirable, there are important unresolved theoretical and empirical questions about the results of alternative regulatory schemes. Public utilities clearly are supposed to engage in cross-subsidization [42], so the equity issues mentioned with regard to the previous category of regulation also complicate evaluations of regulated monopolies.

More on the level of pure efficiency results, controversy continues around the theoretical and empirical relevance of resource distortions going generally under the heading of the Averch-Johnson effect, the tendency of utilities regulation to promote overinvestment in capital assets. Capital is part of the rate base, and the permitted earnings are tied to the rate base. The theoretical case for an A-J distortion depends heavily on a number of assumptions that are unrealistic. Changing the assumptions can change the implications for efficiency. Empirical estimates of the size of A-J distortions also vary. Beyond questions of allocative distortions like the A-J effect, Babilot, Frantz, and Green recently have pointed out that X-inefficiency (not operating on the cost or production frontier given the resources used) in regulated monopolies may add to the costs of regulation [1]. That is, firms that are sheltered from competition may tend to be internally inefficient as well as inefficient in allocation of inputs. Indeed, Babilot, Frantz, and Green cite findings that losses due to X-inefficiency may be about the same magnitude as losses due to allocative distortions.

Certainly all of the theory of regulated monopoly is not in turmoil. The desirability of peak-load or variable pricing for pure efficiency is generally regarded as settled. Peak load pricing has become more common and continues to spread. In this case, theory, empirics, and practice have moved a long way toward common ground.

"Increasing competition through deregulation" can still be defined for this category of regulation as freer entry, exit, and pricing, as it was for the previous type of regulation, but the consequences of deregulation for consumers are more ambiguous in the current category. More cross-subsidization has gone on through public utilities than in the competitively-structured sectors, so the distributional consequences of deregulation would be greater and more uncertain. Restrictions on exit (common carrier obligations and requirements to serve small markets) have been almost universal in this category of regulations. These exit restrictions are important in achieving redistribution.

Deregulation of single-seller markets that are sustainable and contestable would be desirable from a pure efficiency perspective, since at least the deadweight loss of regulatory activity and any X-inefficiency due to regulatory sheltering would be saved. In addition, resource distortions like the A-J effect might be avoided. If the market was not contestable, however, a sustainable monopoly could exploit consumers.

Revisionists tend to see contestability where public-interest proponents see unregulated natural monopoly and exploitation of consumers. The empirical evidence is still too fragmentary and too new to settle the question. Redistribution effects are likely to cloud the issue even if the pure efficiency results can be established.

The case for deregulation of regulated monopolies is theoretically and empirically weaker than the case for deregulating competitively-structured industries. The case for deregulation is weaker because regulation may be necessary to cross-subsidize and because there is only a weak presumption (a weak invisible hand theorem) that sustainable natural monopoly will achieve Pareto efficiency if unregulated. An exception to this general complexity and uncertainty about the consequences of deregulation is that markets in the present category rarely involve information problems that might justify regulation. Therefore, consumer-protection public interest theory is less relevant to regulated monopolies than to regulated industries with competitive structures. This contrasts sharply with the next category of regulation to be considered.

Qualitative Regulation

Environmental regulations, product quality regulations, and most health care regulations are examples of this last category of regulations. This category is distinctive in that entry and exit of firms and prices are rarely regulated. Instead, regulations focus on entry and exit of products and the characteristics of products or production processes. Many of these regulations are recently promulgated, and the agencies enforcing them tend to have broad scopes (e.g., EPA and the Consumer Product Safety Commission). The public-interest justification for these regulations typically involves externalities or information-related market failure or both. For instance, production processes in the toxic chemicals industries may have externalities that are misperceived by the public and by workers in the industry. An externalities problem is complicated by an information problem.

The prominent role of information failure in the public-interest justification for many recent regulations is understandable in the context of history of theory. The economic theory of markets with imperfect information is of relatively recent vintage, and the policy-relevant theoretical work is still characterized by the failing market/perfect government paradigm. This paradigm is likely to exert a powerful effect on regulation for some time to come, because the current empirical techniques of economics are insufficient to test it. When some or all parties are acting on the basis of imperfect information, market transactions will not reveal preferences and costs accurately, even when externalities and public goods are absent. Without some substantial advances in methods for measuring preferences when markets are characterized by imperfect information, qualitative regulations of almost any sort can be justified by strategic choice of assumptions about information failure.

Defining "increasing competition through deregulation" in the context of qualitative regulations is difficult. Many of these regulations do not impinge directly or importantly on the entry and exit of firms or on prices. Where qualitative regulations do affect these "competitive" aspects of markets, there are important questions of balancing anticompetitive effects against market failure and consumer protection that current theory and empirical work are inadequate to resolve. Thus, defining the question I have been assigned in the context of this last category of regulations is difficult. Answering that question is especially hard. The state of theory and empirical work relevant to information problems, which are at the core of my difficulty, is represented in this volume by many papers cited above. Those other authors have commented at greater length and with greater insight on this subject, rendering further comments by me unnecessary.

DEREGULATION OF AIRLINES

This section examines empirical evidence and special problems in evaluating the impact of deregulation of airlines on consumers. Domestic passenger airlines are an obvious illustrative case, since airline deregulation occurred early enough for us to guess at its ultimate effects by now. Airlines also have been touted as contestable markets. Although contestable markets were not treated as a separate category in the taxonomy of the previous section, they should behave like markets in category 1 --markets with competitive structures. Airlines should be a good candidate for consumer benefits from deregulation. However, under regulation many routes were served by one or a few carriers, thus better fitting in category 2 -- markets with monopoly structures. Like many category 2 industries, airlines were regulated initially to achieve cross-subsidization of smaller markets. Airlines illustrate well that taxonomies are likely to be imperfect. Most industries spanning the categories rather than fitting neatly within a single category.

The airlines first came under regulation with the Civil Aeronautics Board Act of 1938. Originally, the Civil Aeronautics Board (CAB) had economic and safety responsibilities, but by 1958 most safety responsibilities had been transferred to the Federal Aviation Administration. Generally, regulation was sought to support an air transportation system larger than the private market would support. In particular, there was an intention to subsidize short-haul and small-market flights from profits on long-haul and dense-market flights. Airmail service contracts were one means of subsidizing the system, but cross-subsidization was also to be used. The extent to which cross-subsidization represented the special interests of communities in the short-haul, small markets or the public interest in externalities and public goods aspects of the communication and transportation systems is unknowable, but both probably were involved. There also is evidence that the airlines' own special interest may have played a role in the types of regulations promulgated. As part of a "deal" including regulation there may have been some attempt to guarantee the airlines a greater than normal profit [5; 27, pp. 111-113]. More fairly, aspects of the regulations that tended to raise returns to the airlines were a response to the Depression-era fear of "destructive competition." Destructive competition may seem nonsensical to most economists today, but it made good sense to politicians familiar at first hand with Depression dynamics in an era when formal economics was in disrepute [46].

The major economic regulatory instruments of the CAB were rate regulation, route and service certification, and prohibitions on unfair methods of competition. Rate regulation means setting minimum prices for each type of service and route. Route certification denotes the allocation of the rights to serve a particular route while service certification refers to the right to operate as a regularly scheduled, unscheduled charter, or other type of carrier. Prohibitions on unfair methods of competition included controls on amenities offered in a bundle with basic transportation (meals, baggage storage, cocktails, and so forth). Rate regulation could suppress price competition, route and service allocations could control entry, and prohibitions on unfair competition could reduce nonprice competition.

In 1978 Congress formally began economic deregulation of the airlines with passage of the Airline Deregulation Act. Under the Act, route and service certification were discontinued on December 31, 1981, and rate regulation was discontinued on January 1, 1983. In January of 1985 the CAB was dismantled and its remaining functions were transferred to the Department of Transportation. Informal deregulation had begun as early as 1977 when the CAB began relaxing its control on routes and fares. Deregulation was generally faster than the official timetable.

Although CAB regulation is gone, air travel is not unregulated. The air traffic control system and airports are still regulated public enterprises. In addition to problems carried over from the air traffic controllers' strike, the system suffers from budgetary sleight of hand. Funds from ticket taxes, earmarked for improvements in airports and air controls under the Airport Development and Airways Program, have accumulated unspent as the Administration seeks to minimize aggregate government expenditures and, hence, the apparent Federal deficit. Thus, a key input to airline operations remains regulated in such a way as to be a bottleneck in the system. Beyond this dilemma, airports pose significant externalities, making it inconceivable that they will be deregulated. Takeoff and landing "slots" are allocated and constrained by Federal, state, and local authorities. A "buy/sell/trade" program started by the Department of Transportation in April, 1986 by which one airline could transfer its slots to another, was voted down by the U.S. Senate within two weeks. Peak-load pricing is almost entirely ignored in the allocation of slots. Safety-related regulations remain in effect.

The specific implication of remaining regulations in air travel is that "increasing competition" has a very restricted meaning in this case. The more general lesson is that the relevant question is not regulation versus deregulation but one form of regulation versus another. In the spirit of second-best, deregulating fares and routes may have little impact, or even a perverse impact, if slots and system capacity are regulated.

Any assessment of the current status of the airlines also must take into account adjustments in capital stocks and route patterns. There are economies of scale and economies of utilization in providing service on a given route. That is, average costs are lower when using larger planes at higher load factors [6, 7, 8, 18, 35, 50; and sources cited therein]. Deregulating routes has enabled carriers to move toward less costly route configurations, generally hub-and-spoke configurations for larger carriers, in which they can use larger planes at higher load factors. The extent to which this is desirable, however, is limited by passenger demand for convenient departure times and nonstop flights. Carriers are still adjusting their fleets of planes from the regulated route configuration, and further movement toward the hub-and-spoke system impends. The carriers also are still building new terminal facilities to accommodate their hubs. These continuing capital adjustments indicate that any changes observed since deregulation are likely to continue in the near future as the remaining adjustments are worked out.

It will help to organize the discussion of deregulation's impacts on consumers to ask why deregulation happened. The best answer seems to be that regulation was serving special interests badly, that technological and demographic changes made regulation of airlines less important to the special interests, and that these changes gave the people who were disadvantaged by regulation a greater stake in getting rid of it.

Regulation served the interests of the airlines badly. The CAB pursued its anticompetitive policy weakly and inconsistently, thus, not assuring high profits. The airlines had long periods of low profitability and in generally did not achieve high profit rates [5, 27, 37, and sources therein]. The CAB alternated its policy between pro-competitive and anti-competitive swings. During good times the CAB was generous in allocating new routes and creating competition. During bad times it did not make commensurate cuts in routes. Airlines found themselves competing on nonprice aspects of service (chiefly frequent and convenient flight schedules and inflight service) that drove up their costs on long hauls and potential high-density routes. At the same time, the CAB did not permit the airlines to cut back on service elsewhere. Since potential profits from the long-haul flights were eaten up by service competition, the CAB could not strictly enforce requirements to serve small communities and short-haul flights. Cross-subsidization was restrained but not eliminated. Neither the airlines nor the small-market, short-haul communities had a large stake in regulation. Meanwhile, growing population and higher incomes were increasing the demand for air travel and the stake of the public in deregulation. Changes in the highway system and auto/bus transportation also decreased the public interest in subsidies to smaller and short-haul markets. With population growth, some markets that would have required subsidization could support unsubsidized service. Thus, deregulation can be seen as a reaction to changing effects on the surpluses in the policy preference function.

We would expect deregulation to benefit consumers generally through lower prices and a switch from service (in kind) to price (cash) competition. We also would expect some redistributive effects in favor of long-haul, dense-market travelers and at the expense of short-haul, small-market travelers.

The first empirical question with regard to airline deregulation is whether there has been an increase in competition. In keeping with the taxonomy of the previous section, the key variable is whether there has been an increase in the number of carriers serving given routes or a decline in the concentration of service among carriers on a given route. This condition is not necessary for an improvement in performance if the markets are contestable. Unfortunately, the evidence to date is not sufficient to justify an assumption of contestability [18, 35, pp. 22-23].

Graham, Kaplan, and Sibley [18, pp. 119-121] and Moore [35, pp. 5-8] have presented convincing evidence that the structure of airline markets has become more competitive since deregulation. For example, Moore takes 1976 as the year preceding deregulation and compares that year to 1983. The number of certified passenger carriers more than doubled over this period. Most major city pairs also were served by more carriers, and even some smaller cities gained carriers. Graham, Kaplan, and Sibley use 1978 and 1981 as their comparison periods, and they find that the Herfindahl index of market concentration fell in most categories and did not increase in any market classification. To an important degree, this decline in concentration is due to an increase in the number of carriers on a route rather than to a reallocation of service among existing carriers. Moore [35, pp. 6-7] also finds a decrease in the Herfindahl index for his market classifications and study period. The structure of the airline industry has become more competitive under deregulation.

The second obvious question is what has happened to fares. Before proceeding to the evidence on that question, however, I want to point out that the data on money prices can be misleading if they are not considered in conjunction with other aspects of the product -- time prices, uncertainties about bookings and connections, information and search costs, and amenities. As others have pointed out in these sessions, the net impact on consumers of simultaneous changes in several of these product aspects is not easy to analyze. If all impacts are not in the same direction, some subjective comparison is necessary.

The best evidence, incomplete as it is, suggests that real overall fares are substantially lower than they would have been without deregulation. Between 1976 and 1983, Moore [35, pp. 8-11] found that real fares per mile fell 8.5 percent while costs increased by about 15 percent during the same period. There has been a dramatic expansion of the proportion of travelers on discount fares (on the order of one-fourth of passengers to three-fourths of passengers), and the number of markets served with discount fares and other fare alternatives has increased. This decrease in fares, however, has not been shared by all consumers. There appears to be substantial downward pressure on fares when flights fit into the hub-and-spoke pattern being adopted by the airlines. On flights that go between two smaller cities (two ends of spokes), however, there is some evidence of fare increases. This pattern is in keeping with eliminating cross-subsidization.

Probably the third question should be what has happened to time and convenience factors. Frequent departures were a major form of service competition under regulation, and it would not be surprising for deregulation to see fewer departures at higher load factors and lower money prices. Some small markets might lose service altogether. The number of departures must be considered along with closely related time and convenience factors - number of stops and number of changes between airlines required for a trip. Again, the effects of a shift to hub-and-spoke are evident, and the constraints posed by slots, especially at the eight or so completely slot-constrained major airports, affect the current situation.

There has been a substantial increase in total departures during deregulation with the figures varying widely with the type of market. Without separating the effects of deregulation from the effects of general economic and demographic growth, it is not possible to say exactly what part of the increase is attributable to deregulation, but it is reasonable to credit deregulation with some increase in departures. Some small cities have lost departures or lost service altogether. Small city departures to hubs, however, have increased. In fact, the proportion of flights requiring connections may have increased slightly with the hub-and-spoke system [35, pp. 7-8; 17, pp. 29-30]. This would indicate a decrease in convenience that would be greater the larger the proportion of such stops that involved a change of airline. Fortunately for passengers, there has been a noticeable increase in the proportion of connections that are made online. The balance appears to be in favor of the deregulated system. Again, however, routes that do not fit into the hub-and-spoke system are disadvantaged in departures and travel time.

The last question on which any evidence will be examined is what has happened to amenities -- the stuff of nonprice competition. The indicators are indirect for items like meal quality, entertainment, and space; but they suggest that the average level of amenities has decreased. The average for the industry is certainly lowered by many of the new entrants that charge extra for checked baggage, meals, and so forth, when only amenities included as standard with the fare are counted. Higher load factors and more seats in cabin-class compartments suggest more crowding, despite some adjustments to first-class cabins and different types of seats. Certainly the higher load factors and more seats put additional pressure on fixed common areas like restrooms, aisles, and gate areas. Airline spending on passenger service per mile fell by about 14 percent between 1976 and 1982 [35, p. 13]. It is apparent from the data and to anyone with gustatory senses that the airlines have economized on food.

There are important caveats with regard to this rather negative assessment of service amenities. Additional amenities are frequently available for a charge (meals on some lines, movie headsets on others), so that consumers have more choice among unbundled services. United Airlines recently started reserving the right to preselect seats to passengers not travelling on excursion fares. If planes are more crowded, aisle seats are more of an amenity and one for which United will be charging in its new system. Additional amenities also are available for first-class passengers. First-class fares have been restrained by competitive forces with deregulation, and a high proportion of first-class passengers are now flying with discount tickets. The net effect may well be to make approximately the same amenities available as before deregulation but a lower prices with some "unbundling" of services. In terms of excludable amenities it may be that passengers have more choice and better prices than before deregulation. With respect to nonexcludable or common resources like restrooms and loading congestion, however, I conclude that consumers are worse off.

There are two aspects of air travel that I will only indicate as having received little discernible attention from researchers to date. I suspect the lack of attention reflects the difficulty of developing applicable theory and sufficient data. The first of these "loose ends" is the reliability of connections, departures, and arrivals. Major delays can be occasioned by missed connections or delayed departures, with nontrivial consequences for time costs of travel. The second loose end is search and transactions costs. I am not aware of any research on changes in information available to consumers before and after deregulation, on consumer search (including the use of travel agents), and on costs of changing reservations. Ruppenthal and Toh have presented a preliminary analysis of the overbooking problem and the reservations system [48]. Since the diversity of travel opportunities may be increasing, the question of how and how well consumers can deal with information and transactions is important. As deregulation unfolds and the data accumulate, I hope to see new research incorporating these considerations.

Any assessment of the impact of airline deregulation on consumers is complicated by the simultaneous impacts of bottlenecks in the airways system and continuing adjustments of capital stocks. Changes in demographic and economic factors also must be separated out. To account for all of these effects formally is impossible, but the net effect of deregulation on consumers seems to be positive. That the net effect is positive will become more apparent as consumers learn how to use the various discount systems, airlines, and individually-priced amenities to better advantage and the airlines learn how to market their new services more effectively. There have been redistributive effects of deregulation, however. Small markets, short hauls, and, especially, travellers whose trips do not fit well into the emerging hub-and-spoke system have lost. Alternative modes for these trips are readily available, so the losses appear small relative to the gains. Elimination of system-level bottlenecks would substantially increase the gains from deregulation.

CONCLUSIONS

My assigned topic was "Increasing Competition Through Deregulation: Do Consumers Win or Lose?" I am tempted to take advantage of the syntax and answer, "Yes." If I must address the question, "Do they win or do they lose?" it would be safe to say, "It depends, and generally some lose and some gain." It depends on the type of regulation and how the regulation is being changed in general, and it depends on the specifics of each case. Having said all I can in conclusion about the assigned topic, I turn to a research question, "How can we analyze whether consumers win or lose from deregulation?"

Given the myriad possibilities for regulation and deregulation, specific answers to even my new question are impossible. But the following general guidelines for research on deregulation and consumers may facilitate the search for answers.

1. The problem is not one of regulation versus deregulation. Regulatory reform would be a more apt term than deregulation. The case of the airlines illustrates that interactions with other regulations and resource constraints are likely to be important. The researcher should remember that the most interesting problems are second-best problems and be parsimonious in his/her modelling.

2. The problem's many facets require an eclectic approach to evaluation. An all-encompassing formal model is unlikely to be successful when several product aspects are changed directly or indirectly by deregulation. Take part of the problem, and look over all of the useful analytical approaches. Especially, look beyond the literature on regulation. For instance, when deregulation replaces service competition with price competition, there is an analogy to a change from in-kind to cash transfers. The public finance literature deserves a thorough search in this regard. When the regulated market offers a menu of in kind adjuncts to the regulated product, e.g., premiums from different banks for savings accounts, the value of in kind competition may be greater to consumers than it would appear in thinking about only one aspect of the product. This is analogous to the value of a menu of in kind transfers. Deregulation often involves different

bundling or tying of services, so the entire literature from industrial organization on tying and bundling is relevant. This, in turn, suggests that the appropriate quantitative techniques may include models of discrete and discrete/continuous choice. The literature on information and search/transactions costs is relevant to nearly all deregulation affecting retail markets. The literature on formal general equilibrium models also is widening the situations which are known to be at least approximately Pareto-optimal to include monopolistic competition in large (many-times-replicated) economies [19, 21]. It appears that it may be easy to overestimate consumer benefits from deregulation.

3. Incorporate important, predictable market responses to deregulation. The market is ingenious in evading regulation and in softening changes from deregulation. For instance, if travelers between adjacent spokes are disadvantaged by a hub-and-spoke airline system, there may be adjustments in other modes of transportation to compensate. At least a sensitivity analysis is needed to determine the impact of potential offsetting reactions to deregulation in the market.

4. Use state-of-the-art measures of welfare gains and losses rather than the consumers surplus triangle approximations whenever the data will support more than Laspeyres or Paasche variations [20, 22, 28, 34, 53].

5. Include and distinguish among different types of losses from regulation or regulatory reform, including deadweight loss from output restriction, X-inefficiency, deadweight losses from rent-seeking activities, and allocative inefficiency.

6. Make redistribution effects explicit and incorporate them formally, if possible [54].

These general guidelines are obviously incomplete, but they are the best commandments I can concoct on such a broad and complex undertaking. The dogma would not be complete, however, without some "shalt not's." My "shalt not's" are meant to help economists stay the course as deregulation unfolds. Economists have had an important role in getting deregulation underway. We should see it through. So,

1. Do not be seduced by the emphasis on formal testing of obvious hypotheses that permeates degree and tenure seeking in academia. We know some coefficients are not zero, even when the null hypothesis cannot be rejected. We know that neither markets nor governments are perfectly anything. Concentrate on explanation and estimation rather than on seeking a single truth in the data. Your time and energy will have more impact on policy and, ultimately, on economic thought.

2. Do not engage in poor scholarship that will pass review only because of its ideological correctness. Two articles in a recent Journal of Law and Economics present analyses generally supportive of deregulation. These papers are ideologically well-suited to the journal in which they appeared, but each contains a fundamental flaw that invalidates its analysis.

3. Do not forget Hirschmann's warning about disappointment and changing allegiances of the public citizen [23]. Do not see the issues in terms of extreme alternatives. Set intermediate goals, recognize and appreciate partial fulfillment of objectives. Foresee the costs of public involvement realistically.

And a final suggestion: follow my advice better than I have!!

REFERENCES

1. BABILOT, GEORGE, ROGER FRANTZ, and LOUIS GREEN (1985), "Consumer Welfare and Inefficiency Among Regulated Industries," Journal of Consumer Affairs, 19(Fall): 207-221.

2. BAUMOL, WILLIAM J. (1982), "Contestable Markets: An Uprising in the Theory of Industry Structure," American Economic Review, 72(March): 1-15.

3. ________, ELIZABETH E. BAILEY, and ROBERT D. WILLIG (1977), "Weak Invisible Hand Theorems on the Sustainability of Multiproduct Natural Monopoly," American Economic Review, 67(June): 350-365.

4. ________, JOHN C. PANZAR, and ROBERT D. WILLIG (1982), Contestable Markets and the Theory of Industry Structure, San Diego: Harcourt Brace Jovanovich.

5. BROWN, ANTHONY (1985), "The Regulatory Policy Cycle and the Airline Deregulation Movement," Social Science Quarterly, 66(September): 552-563.

6. CAVES, DOUGLAS W.; LAURITS R. CHRISTENSEN, and MICHAEL W. TRETHEWAY (1982), "Airline Productivity Under Deregulation," Regulation, (November-December): 25-28.

7. _________, (1983), "Productivity Performance of U.S. Trunk and Local Service Airlines in the Era of Deregulation," Economic Inquiry, 21(July): 312-324.

8. _________, (1981), "U.S. Trunk Carriers, 1972-1977: A Multilateral Comparison of Total Factor Productivity," pp. 47-76, in Thomas G. Cowling and Rodney E. Stevenson (eds.), Productivity Measurement in Regulated Industries, New York: Academic Press.

9. CHERKES, MARTIN; JOSEPH FRIEDMAN, and AVIA SPIVAK (1986), "The Disinterest in Deregulation: Comment," American Economic Review, 76(June): 559-563.

10. CRANDALL, ROBERT W. (1988), "The Use of Cost-Benefit Analysis in Product Safety Regulation," Ch. 4 in this volume.

11. CURRY, DAVID J. (1988), "The Concept of Quality: New Insights, Unanswered Questions," Ch. 6 in this volume.

12. DIXIT, AVINASHI and GENE GROSSMAN (1984), "Directly Unproductive Prophet-Seeking Activities," American Economic Review, 74(December): 1087-1088.

13. FRIEDLAENDER, A.F. (1973), "Macro Policy Goals in the Postwar Period: A Study in Revealed Preference," Quarterly Journal of Economics, 87(February): 25-43.

14. FROMM, G. and P. TAUBMAN (1968), Policy Simulations with an Econometric Model, Washington, D.C.: Brookings Institution.

15. GEISTFELD, LOREN V. (1988), "The Price-Quality Relationship: The Evidence We Have, The Evidence We Need," Ch. 7 in this volume.

16. GERNER, JENNIFER L. (1988), "Product Safety: A Review," Ch. 3 in this volume.

17. GRAHAM, D.R. and D.P. KAPLAN (1982), "Airline Deregulation Is Working," Regulation, (May-June): 26-32.

18. _________, and D.S. SIBLEY (1983), "Efficiency and Competition in the Airline Industry," Bell Journal of Economics, 14(Spring): 118-138.

19. GUESNERIE, ROGER and OLIVER HART (1985), "Welfare Losses Due to Imperfect Competition," International Economic Review, 26(October): 525-545.

20. HANEMANN, W. MICHAEL (1984), "Welfare Evaluations in Contingent Valuation Experiments with Discrete Responses," American Journal of Agricultural Economics, 66(August): 332-341.

21. HART, OLIVER D. (1979), "Monopolistic Competition in a Large Economy with Differentiated Commodities," Review of Economic Studies, 46(January): 1-30.

22. HAUSMAN, JERRY A. (1981), "Exact Consumer's Surplus and Deadweight Loss," American Economic Review, 71(September): 662-676.

23. HIRSCHMANN, ALBERT O. (1982), Shifting Involvements, Princeton: Princeton University Press.

24. HUNT, E.K. (1979), History of Economic Thought: A Critical Perspective, Belmont, California: Wadsworth Publishing Co.

25. IPPOLITO, PAULINE M. (1988), "The Economics of Information in Consumer Markets: What Do We Know? What Do We Need To Know?" Ch. 11 in this volume.

26. JOSKOW, PAUL L. and ROGER C. NOLL (1981), "Regulation in Theory and Practice: An Overview," 1-65, in Gary Fromm (ed.), Studies in Public Regulation, Cambridge, Massachusetts: The MIT Press.

27. KEELER, THEODORE E. (1984), "Theories of Regulation and the Deregulation Movement," Public Choice, 44: 103-145.

28. KUSHMAN, JOHN E. (1987), "Comment on Welfare Evaluations in Contingent Valuation Experiments With Discrete Choices," American Journal of Agricultural Economics, 69(February): 182-184.

29. LAMPMAN, ROBERT J. (1988), "JFK's Four Consumer Rights: A Retrospective View," Ch. 2 in this volume.

30. MAASS, ARTHUR (1966), "Benefit-Cost Analysis: Its Relevance to Public Investment Decisions," Quarterly Journal of Economics, 79(May): 208-226.

31. MACHLUP, FRITZ (1955), "The Problem of Verification in Economics," Southern Economic Journal, 22(July): 1-21.

32. MCCORMACK, ROBERT E., WILLIAM F. SHUGHART II, and ROBERT D. TOLLISON (1984), "The Disinterest in Deregulation," American Economic Review, 74(December): 1075-1079.

33. _________ (1985), "The Disinterest in Deregulation: Reply," American Economic Review, 75(June): 564-565.

34. MCKENZIE, G.W. and I.F. PEARCE (1982), "Welfare Measurement--A Synthesis," American Economic Review, 72(September): 669-682.

35. MOORE, THOMAS GALE (1986), "U.S. Airline Deregulation: Its Effects on Passengers, Capital, and Labor," Journal of Law and Economics, 29(April): 1-28.

36. MORGAN, JAMES N. (1988), "Consumer Choice Is More Than Search," Ch. 13 in this volume.

37. MOTT, BASIL (1952), "The Effect of Political Interest Groups on CAB Policies," Journal of Air Law and Commerce, 19(Autumn): 379-410.

38. PANZAR, JOHN C. and ROBERT D. WILLIG (1977), "Free Entry and the Sustainability of Natural Monopoly," Bell Journal of Economics, 8(Spring): 1-22.

39. PELTZMAN, SAM (1976), "Toward a More General Theory of Regulation," Journal of Law and Economics, 19(August): 211-240.

40. PFOUTS, RALPH W. (1967), "Artistic Goals, Scientific Method, and Economics," Southern Economic Journal, 33(April): 456-467.

41. _________ (1973), "Some Proposals for a New Methodology for Economics," Atlantic Economic Journal, 1(November): 13-22.

42. POSNER, RICHARD A. (1971), "Taxation By Regulation," Bell Journal of Economics and Management Science, 2(Spring): 22-50.

43. _________ (1975), "The Social Costs of Monopoly and Regulation," Journal of Political Economy, 83(August): 807-828.

44. RAUSSER, GORDON C. and J.W. FREEBAIRN (1974), "Estimation of Policy Preference Functions: An Application to U.S. Beef Import Quotas," Review of Economics and Statistics, 56(November): 437-449.

45. REUBER, G.L. (1964), "The Objectives of Canadian Monetary Policy, 1949-1961: Empirical 'Trade-off' and the Reaction Function of Authorities," Journal of Political Economy, 72(April): 109-132.

46. ROBINSON, JOAN (1972), "The Second Crisis of Economic Theory," American Economic Review, 62(May): 1-9.

47. ROTHENBERG, J. (1961), The Measurement of Social Welfare, Englewood Cliffs, New Jersey: Prentice-Hall.

48. RUPPENTHAL, KARL M. and REX TOH (1983), "Airline Deregulation and the No Show/Overbooking Problem," Logistics and Transportation Review, 19: 111-122.

49. RUSSO, J. EDWARD (1988), "Information Processing From the Consumer's Perspective," Ch. 9 in this volume.

50. TAPLIN, JOHN H.E. (1983), "Regulation, Deregulation, and the Sustainability of Transport Monopolies," Logistics and Transportation Review, 19: 31-44.

51. THEIL, HENRI (1968), Optimal Decision Rules For Government and Industry, Amsterdam: North-Holland.

52. VAN EIJK, C.J. and J. SANDEE (1959), "Quantitative Determination of an Optimum Economic Policy," Econometrica, 27(January): 1-13.

53. VARTIA, YRJO O. (1983), "Efficient Methods of Measuring Welfare Change and Compensated Income in Terms of Ordinary Demand Functions," Econometrica, 51(January): 79-98.

54. WILLIG, ROBERT D. and ELIZABETH E. BAILEY (1981), "Income-Distribution Concerns in Regulatory Policymaking," pp. 79-107, in Gary Fromm (ed.), Studies in Public Regulation, Cambridge, Massachusetts: The MIT Press.

Chapter 20

Panel: The Issues in Regulation and Deregulation

ABOUT THE AUTHOR

Kenneth W. Clarkson is Professor of Economics and Director of the Law and Economics Center at the University of Miami. Clarkson received his Ph.D. in Economics from the University of California, Los Angeles in 1971. He was on the Economics faculty at the University of Virginia prior to moving to the University of Miami in 1975. For the year, 1982-83, Clarkson held an executive position in the Office of Management and Budget in Washington. His many publications include The Federal Trade Commission Since 1970: Economic Regulation and Bureaucratic Behavior (co-author), Industrial Organization: Theory, Evidence and Public Policy (co-author), and West's Business Law: Text and Cases (co-author).

THE CASE FOR MINIMIZING REGULATION

Kenneth W. Clarkson

OVERREGULATION: THE BASIS FOR CHANGE

In order to understand the potential benefits of deregulation, a review of previous regulatory efforts governing price, product information, product quality, terms of sale and other elements impacting on consumer outcomes is necessary.

Price

Consumers search for goods and services that offer them the best price/quality relationship. Federal and state authorities establish regulations to prohibit combinations or monopolies that may artificially increase price above the competitive level. Most scholars and commentators now are convinced that an analysis of the effects of alleged monopoly behavior is preferred to arbitrary rules that are designed to promote competition. A "rule of reason" is preferred to the "per se" approach in the regulation of entry, exit, merger and price.

Advertising

The main economic justification of advertising is that it reduces the costs and increases the effectiveness of consumer search. History teaches us that regulatory authorities have frequently set the wrong objectives for improving consumer information. Specifically, the regulators attempt to increase the reliability of <u>all</u> advertising, including that which consumers use as a complement or guide to their own product-search activities and that which they use as a substitute for their own search.

Until recently, the FTC prohibited any advertising that had a "capacity and tendency" to deceive under its authority to declare "unfair or deceptive acts or practices" unlawful. Under this standard, the FTC considered advertisements deceptive that would fool only a small number of gullible people yet, conveyed meaningful information to others, requiring no proof of actual harm to consumers. In other advertising enforcement. The Commission required sellers to prepare expensive "reasonable-basis" reports even for claims that are known to be true without prior substantiation. This represents a clear waste of resources. The FTC was able to adopt these rules because their application required relatively little effort on the part of FTC. The Commmission would win if before the ad was run, it could show that the advertiser lacked evidence supporting each interpretation of its advertising claims. The Commission justified this requirement by arguing that its adaption would yield great administrative savings as compared with operations under the earlier deceptive-advertising doctrine. In my judgment these administrative savings, however, were frequently less than the cost of the many needless reports that had to be prepared by advertisers -- a cost that was passed on to consumers. Under these conditions, some firms chose to avoid these costs by <u>not</u> running some useful advertisements.

Information Disclosure

This type of regulation might seem relatively innocuous and even beneficial when the information market is shown to have failed. Unfortunately, regulatory authorities have frequently made major mistakes in implementing disclosure requirements. They have, for example, been very lax in demonstrating the benefits of requiring disclosure as compared with the costs of gathering the required information. Indeed, they often believe that if some information is good, more must always be better.

Because information is of value to the consumer, the market will normally produce information. Sellers have incentives to inform consumers of the desirable qualities their products possess and of the undesirable properties they lack. Thus, when the cost of disclosure is small relative to the price of the product, the fact that particular information is not being disclosed strongly implies either that it will affect few purchasing decisions or that some barrier--such as monopoly, collusion, or regulation--prevents the market from functioning effectively. In some cases, regulations require the disclosure of information that is of little benefit to consumers. In other cases regulations prohibit certain information from reaching the public. For example, in the Vocational Schools Rule, the FTC told the industry that materials referring to job or earning opportunities must also disclose specific, costly-to-gather information on placement and salary data of graduates. Less information about job opportunities may be produced under such regulations.

Product Quality

In attempts to govern product quality, regulatory authorities frequently ignore the fact that consumers should expect to find some imperfect products. Preventing defects is not cost-free. Perhaps more important, products of different degrees of reliability compete with one another in the same market because consumers have different preferences for avoiding defects. Those who prefer risk, for whatever reason, will be most likely to purchase cheaper, less-reliable products. Those whose time, for whatever reason, is worth little may prefer relatively unreliable products since they incur only a small cost in obtaining repairs or fixing the goods themselves. In addition, those who plan to use the product for a very short time would also prefer a cheaper, less reliable product. By the same token, those whose time is more valuable may prefer more reliable products.

In attempting to coerce better quality, regulation interferes with the expression of consumer preferences that will occur so long as consumers have decent information about quality. If such search information is not available, the answer to the problem is to encourage disclosure of product characteristics. But by coercing better quality, consumers who prefer cheaper, less-reliable products are denied the opportunity of obtaining them.

Contracts

Some regulatory programs rest on the theory that disparity in bargaining power between consumers and producers justifies extensive intervention. This theory fails to explain why many contracts are take-it-or-leave-it and how these contracts harm consumers. If negotiations about consumers' rights in purchase transactions are rare, the costs of negotiation to either party are probably greater than the benefits available from negotiation. Most take-it-or-leave-it practices arise because transaction costs are too high relative to the benefit potential of tailoring the contract to the individual preferences of the bargaining parties. Prices would rise if bargaining were required in situations where it has not been engendered by market forces.

Certainly, problems may arise in the contract-information process. However, such legal doctrines as fraud and duress are the appropriate tools for dealing with them, not the sweeping bargaining-power approach. Although the administrative process might remedy some negotiating problems less expensively than private litigation would, these cases are certainly the exception to the rule.

Professional Licensing

Licensing requirements vary from occupation to occupation, usually stipulating some combination of (1) education, (2) apprenticeship, (3) written or practical examinations, (4) good moral character, and (5) citizenship or residency. Under a licensing system, the occupational board controls jurisdiction not only over entry, but also over such matters as accreditation and permissible forms of competition. Although licensing is intended to control and improve the quality of professional services, it frequently is used by various professions to restrict entry and to support monopolistic pricing schemes for their members. By controlling entry into professions, government-backed licensing restricts the quantity of services as much if not more than it assures the quality of services. Thus, it directly affects both the level of competition and the prices of services.

REGULATORY REFORM: ADMINISTRATIVE VERSUS PRIVATE LAW

In a country whose legal system is based on common law, regulation effectively implies the substitution of administrative law for private law. When we focus on the public interest theory of regulation, one lesson we learn is that administrative control of the public interest must be highly constrained. In the absence of such constraints, regulatory agents are free to pursue their own private interests. These may or may not coincide with those of the general public. In the choice between regulation or more administrative law versus deregulation or more emphasis on private law, several principles are likely to improve outcomes.

The burden of proof should be placed on the administrative agency to demonstrate that private law solutions are inefficient. Thus, in the promulgation of statutory rules, administrative regulations or hearings, the null hypothesis should be that private law is relatively more efficient.

In comparisons of outcomes between administrative and private law, consistency of assumptions should be maintained. Thus, infallible markets may be compared with infallible government in theoretical models or fallible markets with fallible governments in empirical estimations, but not fallible markets with infallible governments or visa versa.

Public interest regulation should first look to strengthening private law. In cases where the products or services have a high degree of the public good characteristic, public authorities should examine options that increase the ability of producers to exclude non-payers from consuming. When problems of reducing negative externalities exist, officials should consider broadening judicial standing to include directly affected parties. Such attention does not necessarily imply that all solutions will result in strengthening the private law, but the approach should begin there.

ABOUT THE AUTHOR

Thomas A. Durkin is Chief Economist and Director of Research of the American Financial Services Association in Washington. Durkin received his Ph.D. in Economics from Columbia University in 1973. Before taking his current position, Durkin was a member of the Finance faculty at Pennsylvania State University and then Senior Economist and Assistant to the Director of the Division of Research and Statistics at the Federal Reserve Board from 1979 to 1981. His research covers a wide array of topics in consumer credit. Durkin is a member of the Editorial Board of the Journal of Retail Banking and the Governing Board of the Credit Research Center of Purdue University.

FINANCIAL SERVICES REGULATION (NOT DEREGULATION) RULES

Thomas A. Durkin

We certainly hear and read a lot these days about the ferment in financial markets caused by deregulation. Some see deregulation as the solution to problems while others see deregulation as the cause. Deregulation is either harmful or beneficial to consumers and institutions, or maybe both, depending on what form the deregulation takes.

To me deregulation is a misnomer for the changes that are taking place in financial markets. The term, deregulation suggests that government officials, by conscious efforts, are reducing their control on actions of those regulated. Nothing, it seems, could be further from the truth. In my view, three other intertwined forces are directing change: technology and technological innovation, economic conditions including high and fluctuating interest rates, and regulation itself which functions economically like a tax on the financial sector. Like any tax, the regulation "tax" generates pressures to reduce tax rates by shifting resources toward untaxed enterprises.

Certainly, each of these three forces directing financial change -- technological innovation, economic conditions, and regulation itself -- is worthy of fuller discussion. In my limited space I will have to content myself with developing a little more fully my first point: simply that deregulation is a misnomer for what is happening in financial markets, at least if we are talking about Federal legal changes. Then I will speak briefly about important areas where tighter federal controls are pending to the disadvantage of consumers, in my view. This is in the area of entry into consumer banking.

THE DIMENSIONS OF REGULATION AND DEREGULATION

First, let us look at the pace of federal deregulation. As a result of a variety of historical forces and circumstances, American financial institutions labor under all sorts of controls. These include:

1) Entry restrictions like chartering, branching, and affiliation limits on banks and savings and loan associations;

2) Balance sheet requirements such as capitalization requirements for banks and savings and loans;

3) Activity limits such as restrictions on banks' ownership of equities;

4) Pricing rules such as the interest restriction on demand deposits;

5) Consumer protection rules including Truth in Lending, Equal Credit Opportunity, and the Electronic Fund Transfer Act;

6) Monetary policy requirements such as reserves on deposits.

Within this framework a veritable "squad" of agencies issues regulations, interpretations, guidelines, and enforcement actions. Some of the agencies are well known such as the Federal Reserve Board, the Federal Home Loan Bank Board, the Federal Deposit Insurance Corporation, and the Securities and Exchange Commission. Others are less well known but may be important in particular areas. As an example of the complexity that can result from so many agencies, eight separate federal agencies have enforcement authority under the Truth-in-Lending Act. Further the Act itself is a very complex law governing a very simple idea.

With all the recent talk about deregulation it is actually startling to see how little deregulation there has been at the Federal level. In matter of fact, the trend in the past half decade has been in the direction of tighter regulation, not deregulation, for four of the six regulatory areas I mentioned. In only two areas has the direction on balance been toward regulatory ease. Even in these areas the trend has reversed recently.

Let us consider each regulatory area again:

1) In the area of entry these has been no easing of federal restrictions on chartering or branching of depository institutions, except when failing institutions are involved. There has been some easing of state laws allowing interstate combinations. But, at the Federal level, there is a strong likelihood of tighter controls in a significant area: entry by nonbanks into providing banking-type services.

2) Capital requirements for depository institutions have tightened, not eased, in recent years, and regulatory proposals are pending to tighter them further.

3) Consumer protection laws are still fully in place. There has been no major reductions and currently there are no proposals to reduce any requirements of Truth in Lending, Equal Credit Opportunity, or other provisions of the Consumer Credit Protection Act. Quite the contrary. There are proposals in Congress to increase controls in a variety of areas: consumer leasing, funds availability on deposited checks, disclosures on deposits and credit cards, and community reinvestment.

4) Congress tightened monetary policy regulations in 1980 by extending reserve requirements to all depository institutions offering transactions accounts or nonpersonal time deposits. Currently, no one is proposing any easing of monetary policy regulations.

In only two areas -- pricing rules and activity limits -- has there been any reduction at all in federal controls:

5) Pricing rules on deposits other than demand deposits were phased out over six years, ending in March, 1987. Also, in 1980 Federal law superceded state controls on residential mortgage interest rates. But, Congress permitted the 1980 deregulation of state controls on business credit pricing to expire in 1983. Price deregulation did not affect consumer credit, although some states deregulated consumer credit rates. Currently, the only proposal pending at the Federal level is to increase controls, in particular over credit-card interest rates.

6) There has also been some easing of activity limits of depository institutions. Legal changes in 1980 and 1982

permitted new kinds of deposit accounts such as interest-paying transaction accounts or NOW accounts. Also, savings and loan associations and mutual savings banks received limited consumer and commercial lending powers outside the housing area. Currently, there are proposals pending in the Senate to give banks expanded powers in the areas of underwriting and selling commercial paper, municipal revenue bonds, collateralized mortgage obligations and mutual funds. My best guess is that these proposals will not pass, however, at least not this year.

In sum, financial deregulation at the Federal level has been very limited so far, despite popular perceptions. My view is that consumers would be well served by some further Federal deregulation, in particular by freer entry into the market for consumer financial services. This leads to my second area of discussion -- entry into consumer banking.

THE CASE FOR DEREGULATION

The advantage for consumers of freer entry is, of course, enhanced competition. The benefits of competition are well understood. But they bear repeating because they seem to be overlooked so often.

First, competition assures that products or services, including financial services, are available to those who demand them at minimum production cost for the quantity of service. This is the concept of efficiency. Simply stated, competition causes resources to be allocated to their best productive uses with minimum loss of resources along the way.

Second, competition also reduces potential conflicts of interest and concentrations of power that, along with higher prices, are the hallmarks of uncompetitive markets. To insure these benefits of competition, free entry into markets is an important prerequisite. As soon as substantial barriers to free entry are put in place, the competitiveness of markets begins to deteriorate and the benefits to consumers to decline. As competitiveness ebbs, the quality of service declines, prices rise, or both.

EASIER ENTRY INTO "BANKING" SERVES CONSUMERS BEST

In this context, it seems to me that consumers benefit from enhanced choice and competition in the market for financial services. Ultimately, this involves the question of entry into banking: specifically who may offer what kind of banking-type deposit services, where, and with what affiliates.

It is well known that current law, as well as the current opinion of the Federal Reserve Board, suggests that banks are "special." Since banks are special, entry into banking is closed to those in other businesses. And, banks themselves are generally prevented from affiliating with businesses not "closely related to banking." In effect, firms must choose whether they want to be "banks" or nonbanks. Having made the choice, they are prevented from entering the other area.

Two questions come to mind immediately: (1) Why should nonbanks want to enter banking in the first place? and (2) If nonbanks wish to invade banks' turf, does the public interest call for their exclusion?

The reason why banks and nonbanks want to invade each other's "turf" is the believed or feared existence of "economies of scope." Economies of scope are opportunities to reduce costs by producing services in combination rather than on a stand-alone basis. For nonbank financial firms, the hope and the fear of scope economies arises from technological change which is fusing asset and liability products. Let me explain.

At one time consumer credit "products" were distinct from consumer asset products like deposits and payments. This is no longer the case. Today newer credit products such as revolving credit, credit cards, and second mortgage or secured lending together with new asset products like ATM's (automatic teller machines), debit cards, and electronic transfers are bringing credit and payments together. In the future, scope economies may make joint provision of credit with asset and payment services even more important, possibly absolutely essential.

As a result, financial institutions that are frozen out of the payments system will be weakened. Not surprisingly, they seek access to the payments systems. But since the payments system has traditionally been the province of banks, it will be difficult to capture these scope economies if there is forced legal separation of banks from nonbanks. Hence, the institutional desire for entry into banking. Ultimately this is the reason why members of my Association, the American Financial Services Association, have vigorously pursued development of "nonbank banks" or consumer banks. These will be banks for consumer credit and payment purposes.

The remaining question is whether nonbank institutions should be prohibited from combining consumer banking and nonbanking if they want to do so. This issue has been widely enough discussed and debated. Those trying to preserve protected markets offer many arguments as to why permitting entry by nonbanks is a bad idea. Suffice it to say that these arguments are not very convincing, in my view, especially where they concern consumer banking. And, of course, they must be weigh again the clear public benefits of free entry and competition by innovative entrepreneurs. Unfortunately, opposing arguments live on because they have broad political appeal for groups whose turf they protect.

In conclusion, Federal financial deregulation has not proceeded very far. Important questions must be addressed before access to consumer banking is tightened.

ABOUT THE AUTHOR

Jeremy Mitchell is a Consumer Policy Advisor in London and was formerly Director of the U.K. National Consumer Council. For further biographical information, see Headnote in Chapter 14.

PRIVATIZATION, COMPETITION AND AIRLINE DEREGULATION: A VIEW FROM ABROAD

Jeremy Mitchell

As all of Kushman's 44 references and examples appear to come from United States sources, my comments will bear on regulatory issues as they present themselves to some of the residual 95 percent of the world's consumers who do not live in the USA.

Privatization Is Not Deregulation

The current political and public debate, in many of the Organization for Economic Cooperation and Development (OECD) countries, confuses the issues of privatization, competition and deregulation. Privatization involves the transfer of ownership of a monopoly (or partial monopoly) from public to private hands. The act of privatization may be unrelated to competition [3, 8]. In the United Kingdom (UK), for example, the privatization of British Telecom (BT) has increased competition by converting a monopoly in one industry -- trunk voice telephony and transmission -- into a partial duopoly, with some competition for business uers but none, as yet, for residential consumers. Similarly, the privatization of British Gas has increased competition in relation to supplying gas to large industrial users while leaving gas-consuming households unaffected. The point is that privatization was not an essential step in increasing competition. In both instances, a similar degree of competition, or indeed a greater one, could have been achieved without privatization. Conversely, if competition had really been a serious objective of the United Kingdom Government, BT and British Gas could have been broken up either functionally or geographically upon privatization. Instead, individual consumers of essential services from these industries are now faced with massive privately owned monopolies or partial monopolies. Thus, privatization involved the construction of new regulatory systems, not deregulation.

In the UK, these new regulatory systems are industry-specific. The enforcement of the government license issued to a now privately owned BT is the responsibility of the Director General of Telecommunications, who operates under statute with considerable independence from government. For a privatized British Gas, similar functions lie with the Director General of Gas Supply. These new regulatory systems are intended to be "light," or not intensive.

For BT, the regulation of prices for a transitional period will be accomplished by restricting annual price increases to no more than the percentage increase in the Retail Price Index minus 3 percent. A similar formula applies to British Gas. The UK Government prefers this to the rate-of-return control used in the US, expecting this formulation to encourage productivity.

Consumer anxieties in this situation focus on the possible inadequacies of the regulatory systems. It appears that one of the UK government's prime objectives in its privatization programme is to maximize the receipts from the sale of public assets to the private sector. This has meant that BT has been sold as a single entity, and the same has happened to British Gas. Combined with the prospect of a light regulatory regime, this means that the UK Government has simultaneously capitalized and captured future monopoly profits as the proceeds of the sale to the private sector. For consumers, both BT and British Gas will be privately owned monopolies with no alternative suppliers. While regulators will control overall prices for a transitional period, there is the possibility that prices to the individual consumer will be "loaded" to allow lower prices for large commercial customers. Also, monopoly profits might be increased by lowering the quality of service to individual consumers. We should note that the industry-specific regulatory authorities have uncertain responsibilities in relation to quality of service [4, 5].

CONSUMER ORGANIZATIONS SUPPORT AIRLINE DEREGULATION

From the above discussion one might be tempted to conclude that consumer protagonists usually press for "heavy" economic regulation. Air services provide an example of pressure in the opposite direction. In Canada, for example, the Consumers' Association of Canada (CAC) proposed that air transport be deregulated by 1 July 1987, allowing airlines to set fares in response to market forces. This followed a sample survey commissioned by CAC which showed that 11% who were commercial airline travellers in Canada began a flight from a U.S. airport during the proceeding two years. Their reason was to avoid the high rates charged by Canadian airlines [1].

In Australia, in 1985, the Canberra Consumers Organization proposed that all regulatory controls on airlines except those relating to safety should be removed immediately, on the grounds that consumers would benefit from more competition with airlines paying greater attention to passenger needs [2]. Another Australian organization -- the Consumers' Association --has called for complete deregulation, except for health, safety and security aspects, and a new competitive fare system. The United Kingdom National, Scottish and Welsh Consumer Councils have pressed for economic deregulation of air transport within the United Kingdom, coupled with explicit public subsidies for vulnerable routes whose maintenance is socially desirable [7].

The United Kingdom National Consumer Council (NCC) has carried out a major study of the international aspects of air transport regulation in western Europe as they affect the consumer [6]. The study reveals an extremely complex system of regulation, involving seven different components:

1. Bilateral, inter-governmental agreements often accompanied by confidential memoranda of understanding;

2. International, multilateral treaties between groups of countries;

3. Secret agreements between individual airlines -- One of these became public when it was reported that the state-owned Irish airline, Aer Lingus, had made a secret payment of $750,000 to KLM not to establish a route from Amsterdam to Dublin;

4. Collective agreements between scheduled airlines through their international association (IATA);

5. Regulatory activities by national authorities;

6. Regulations and agreements governing the operation of airports;

7. The Rules of the Treaty of Rome, including the competition rules, within the European Economic Community (EEC).

The NCC's conclusion, following a study of consumers' air transport needs in relation to access, safety, choice, information, redress, representation and value for money, was that airlines in Western Europe subvert, rather than serve, the interests of consumers.

> "Agreements between governments and between airlines restrict the journeys that travellers can

> make and the services they are offered, and artificially keep up the prices they are charged. These restrictions are operated in the interests of individual governments and some existing airlines. They largely ignore the interests of the travelling public - both those who do travel and those who wish to but are prevented by the present system" [6].

The Report goes on to argue that much of the rationale for the present system of regulation stems, not from significant economic differences between air transport and the rest of the economy, but from its historically political and diplomatic nature.

> "It is, of course, the consumer and taxpayer who pay the price of political and diplomatic intervention in what should be the simple commercial arrangements needed to fly from one place to another. It is also the consumer who pays when airlines come together in a cartel to agree on minimum fares and to restrict the services that will be provided."

The NCC recognizes the severe problems involved in dismantling international air transport regulation. Some European governments are unwilling to relinquish, unilaterally at any rate, the power they wield through route licensing, capacity control and price setting. Governments are loath to relinquish the prestige of sponsoring a national "flag carrier". Indeed, many of the major European airlines are wholly or partly state owned. Five-- Austrian Airlines, Air France, Olympic (Greece), TAP (Portugal) and Iberia (Spain) -- are totally (or virtually totally) state-owned. In four others -- Sabena (Belgium), Finnair, Lufthansa (W. Germany) and KLM (Netherlands) -- the national government has majority ownership.

The NCC concludes that the ideal solution -- replacing the many bilateral agreements that exist between European countries with a multilateral agreement which would allow European air transport to develop in response to consumer need -- is unlikely to be achieved in the short run through lack of political will. It, therefore, urges the United Kingdom government to take the initiative in taking air transport out of the political arena. It could achieve this by removing the anti-competitive aspects of its inter-governmental air service agreements and joining other willing European governments to form a block of countries that have liberal air service agreements.

The NCC report [6] on international air transport regulation demonstrates clearly the ambivalent role that governments play in regulatory activities, especially when regulation involves the interests of governments themselves or when perceived national interests are involved. Consumer protagonists need to discriminate between the health and safety aspects of regulation and the economic aspects, as the NCC report does.

From the consumer viewpoint the level of optimal economic regulation depends largely on whether or not there is a natural monopoly and, if not, whether effective competition is attainable in practice. Consumers are at risk for both extremes. Their economic interests will be damaged both by excessive economic regulation of industries where effective competition could better take care of their interests and by unregulated, or too lightly regulated, monopolies and cartels.

REFERENCES

1. CANADIAN CONSUMER (1984), Ottawa, July 1984.

2. CANBERRA CONSUMER (1985), Canberrra, December 2985.

3. GARNHAM, NICHOLAS (1985), "Telecommunications Policy in the United Kingdom," Media, Culture and Society, 7: 7-29.

4. MITCHELL, JEREMY (1983), "Consumer Performance Indicators in the Nationalized Industries," Journal of Consumer Policy, 6: 177-93.

5. _________ (1986), "Quality of Telephone Service and the Domestic Consumer," Proceedings of the European Communications Policy Research Conference, London.

6. NATIONAL CONSUMER COUNCIL (1986), Air Transport and the Consumer - A Need For Change? London.

7. NATIONAL, SCOTTISH and WELSH CONSUMER COUNCILS (1983), Freedom of the Air, London.

8. VICKERS, JOHN and GEORGE YARROW (1985/86), "The Privatisation of British Gas," Oil and Gas Law and Taxation Review, 4 (No. 8).

ABOUT THE AUTHOR

Helen Ewing Nelson is President of the Consumer Research Foundation in San Francisco. For further biographical information, see Headnote in Chapter 5.

THE ISSUES IN REGULATION AND DEREGULATION

Helen Ewing Nelson

Since each of the words, "regulation" and "deregulation" has many varying connotations, accurate communication becomes difficult.

THE VARIOUS "FACES" OF REGULATION

Regulation is a wonderous thing. One hears that it:

-- enforces competition;
-- invigorates competition;
-- limits entry;
-- prevents exit;
-- permits an industry to limit supply.

With governmental enforcement it:

-- grants monopolies;
-- requires disclosure, and
-- punishes fraud and deception.

Whatever form it takes, it is something that some level of government does "in the public interest".

Regulation is often urged upon government, typically by industry (another research project possibility), but sometimes by consumers, in these cases meeting more resistance. On rare occasions regulation is proposed to the peoples' government with the combined support of industry and consumers. (A research project studying these latter cases could be very illuminating.)

Deregulation is equally imprecise. Deregulation is alternatively a mood, an ideology, a mind set, a delusion, as well as a concrete act by government, lessening its control over an industry or parts of an industry.

This lessening may occur administratively, legislatively, or, as in the telephone case, through the courts.

To some, deregulation means a return to laissez-faire, where "anything goes." It could mean a "level playing field," not level between producer and consumer but between two or more competitors, both previously regulated but regulated differently, as in the case of trucks versus railroads or banks versus thrift institutions. Or, to some it makes it possible newly arisen price and service differences that expand consumer choice, but with fewer or lesser suppliers than before.

Further, deregulation may occur in a single limited area of an industry's activities. This was the case with banks when Regulation Q was lifted, freeing banks to set their own interest rates on savings. Other aspects of bank behavior continued to be regulated. Banks need charters to be in business, are subject to examination by the central banks, must meet reserve requirements set for them by the Federal Reserve and sister authorities, and are subject to the Truth-in-Lending Act. Moreover, recently several banks have been fined by the government for "laundering" money and, in Los Angeles, several banks have been charged by the Department of Justice with collusive price fixing of interest rates paid on savings.

A PARADOX: DEREGULATION IN BANKING YIELDS REGULATION

An interesting and unexpected outcome of partial deregulation in the financial services industry resulted from extensive deregulation of the savings and loan segment (S and L) of that industry.

In the first half of this century, S and L's were given charters by both state and Federal governments to accept savings and make home loans. In the recent move toward deregulation, the "fence" that restricted savings and loan associations to home lending was removed and the S and L's were turned loose to make loans for other purposes, commercial as well as consumer, and to offer checking accounts. Deposits in these "thrift institutions" have for decades been insured by the Federal Savings and Loan Insurance Corporation of the Federal Home Loan Bank Board, a sound program as long as the lending of the thrift institutions was limited.

Unfortunately, the new freedom conferred by deregulation sent many thrift institutions off on heady adventures. More than a few land developers and speculators saw the advantage of buying an S and L with all that cash rolling in regularly. The combination of economic forces and the desperate efforts of the Federal Savings and Loan Insurance Corporation to avoid failures has transformed the thrift industry and impinged irrevocably on the whole financial services industry. To avoid failure and further drains on its deposit insurance fund, the Federal Home Loan Bank Board is selling S and L's every week to the highest bidder, often receiving bids that are not "high." In short, the exigencies of deregulation in this industry have induced an unplanned form of regulation in the industries with consequences that have still to be finally resolved. To save its insurance fund, the Home Loan Bank Board does not shrink from selling a failing S and L to a non-failing one in another state, or to a bank in another state.

Thus, deregulation's "emergencies" are creating de facto interstate banking. For example, New York's Citicorp Bank now has a San Francisco headquarters building, having bought a large and failing S and L in California. The giant retailing firm, Sears Roebuck, is also providing bank services in California and other states sometimes through purchases of failing S and L's. Ironically, these developments are faits accompli while debates continue in Congress and state legislatures as to whether interstate banking should be permitted.

Thus, these unplanned and unexpected consequences of "deregulation" are generating a new form of regulation, the government-ordered merger. At the same time they are introducing a new form of deregulation, interstate banking. This is happening without explict action by our elected policymakers in Congress!

Has so called deregulation in the financial services industry benefited consumers?

Certainly savers have benefitted from the higher interest rates that came when ceilings were removed -- as long as their bank or thrift institution was not forced to close its doors.

Consumers may ultimately benefit from the increased competition arising in the more broadly defined "financial services" industry. But they may find this industry offering fewer or lesser services to consumers than before.

It is a disturbing fact that the number of consumers having bank accounts has decreased. There is evidence that banks, in their search for increased earnings, are sluffing off lower-income households' accounts -- the accounts these families used to pay for basic utilities and rent [1]. At the same time the financial institutions are engaged in an expensive competition to serve more accounts from high income households and to increase their credit card and personal loan business. Certainly those members of society who cannot find or afford accessible banking services have not benefitted from deregulation.

THE IMPROVEMENT OF REGULATION

My comments have focused on the financial services industry--and banking particularly--because this is the deregulation area with which I am most familiar. But in closing, let me allude to a larger vista. The last six or seven years of deregulation mania in the United States gives us a body of experience from which we can learn.

A global look-around reminds us quickly that governments and their nation's economy are going to be interactive in making economic decisions. For example, whether we sell subsidized U.S. wheat to Russia is a policy decision.

Sober reflection will tell us that there will always be government regulation because regulation is the essence of government. Regulation is even necessary to ensure that most honored shibboleth, competition! After all, the Federal Trade Commission has been in business for 75 years!

The real issue is not regulation vs. deregulation, but rather <u>what sort</u> and <u>what degree</u> of regulation will best achieve the results we desire.

Too often, given our generally negative attitude toward regulation, we institute regulation in shocked response to business failures or blatant abuses. In the crisis, discussion centers around whether to regulate or not with too little thought being given to the most effective form of regulation.

In my view much of our present day disaffection with government regulation should be directed toward the <u>form</u> and <u>functioning</u> of regulation and not to berating regulation itself.

How many courses today do our universities offer on regulatory theory? Let me propose a new profession--Regulations Architect. Training for this profession would, in my view, be multi-disciplinary with economics as its core. Our delicately balanced economy and our faltering faith in government are evidences of the need for such professional concentration. We have graduate programs in "Public Policy" and "Public Administration" at several leading universities. I hope some of them may soon be producing Regulations Architects.

Regulation we will always have, good or bad. Let us make good and bad regulation the subject of serious study. We have some regulatory structures that have stood up well over time, e.g., the Securities and Exchange Commission. We have some that are jerry-built. We have some that might best be razed and replaced. Architects of regulatory structures are needed. May the universities of the world make this a field of special study and training!

REFERENCES

1. FEDERAL REGISTER (1987), "Interagency Policy Statement on Basic Financial Series," Federal Financial Institutions Examination Council, 52, (44), March, p. 7024.

ABOUT THE AUTHOR

Frederick C. Thayer, Jr. is Professor in the Graduate School of Public and International Affairs at the University of Pittsburgh, a position he has held since 1969. Thayer received his Ph.D. in International Relations from the University of Denver in 1963. He has had visiting appointments at a number of universities including Syracuse University, the University of Southern California and the University of Calgary. He is the author of An End to Hierarchy and Competition: Administration in the Post-Affluent World (1981) and Rebuilding America: The Case for Economic Regulation (1984). Thayer serves on the Editorial Boards of Administration and Society and Politics, Administration, Change (Bangladesh).

THE OTHER SIDE: A BRIEF SERMON ON THE HISTORY AND NECESSITY OF ECONOMIC REGULATION

Frederick C. Thayer, Jr.

The allegedly "pro-consumer" approach of this volume attacks economic regulation; as such, the approach is a literal implementation of "consumer sovereignty." This theory, usually attributed to Keynesian Nobel winner Paul Samuelson, holds that unregulated competition compels producers to increase efficiency and reduce prices in order to attract individual consumers. The greater the number of producers per consumer, the greater the power of each consumer and, it follows, all consumers. The general concept is equally attractive to monetarist Nobel winner Milton Friedman, who wants each consumer to be "free to choose" among many producers, and to consumer advocate Ralph Nader, the loudest supporter of all-out antitrust enforcement. Among those who label themselves "consumer economists" or "consumer scientists," the approach has the status of a fundamentalist religion.

Tragically, the approach divides many individual citizens (the approximately 123 million constituting the official U.S. labor force) in two. In supporting the interests of the "consumers," economists ignore or oppose the interests of the "workers." The problem is that most "consumers" must first be "workers" in order to earn the wherewithal to buy. The attempt to help consumers, therefore, harms workers, thereby canceling most of the benefits allegedly achieved. Only those of independent wealth are helped. This is not surprising: after all, free market economics was invented in the age of slavery.

Economic theory, it follows, has the socially destructive effect of forcing groups of citizens into constant and bitter conflict with each other. Each individual consumer must first seek a stable income high enough to provide a satisfactory living standard for perhaps an entire family. That consumer also has an interest in reducing the incomes of all those who produce whatever she/he buys, and will support policies to reduce general price levels and increase his/her purchasing power. All consumers who work in other industries, of course, have an equal interest in reducing the income of that first consumer. The basic flaws of economic theory can be summarized and even broadened.

1. A theory that attacks workers was bound to incite the invention of a counter-theory, Marxism, in this case. The reactionary response is nothing more than a promise to turn the tables by supporting workers' interests over those of their employers and consumers. The strength of Marxism is its promise to unite the interests of workers and consumers.

2. The principle of competition, fundamental to economics, prescribes that at the time of each purchase, supply must greatly exceed demand if consumer interests are to be served, and the greater the excess of supply over demand, the better for the consumer. Because huge excesses of supply could not promise "efficiency," it was necessary to invent a corollary principle (Say's Law). It states that because supply automatically creates demand, total supply never can exceed total demand except in very brief periods of disequilibrium (length unspecified). Because the principle of competition (supply must exceed demand) and Say's Law (supply cannot exceed demand) are incompatible, one of them is incorrect; Say's Law is absurd. Despite their claims, Keynesians did not abolish Say's Law, but only revised it in trivial fashion. The Keynesians argued that in periods of too little demand, governments might have to "stimulate" demand to provide buyers for the supply, i.e., if Say's Law doesn't work automatically, make it come true. This preserved the basic economic myth that it is never necessary to restrict supply.

3. Given their acceptance of Say's Law, economists generally agree that chronically "excessive," "destructive" or "cutthroat" competition is impossible, as are "overcapacity," "overproduction" (in farming) and "industrial glut." From their perspective, unregulated competition always is a solution, never a problem, because all problems are caused by restraints on

> competition. It follows that if any industry was subjected to economic regulation at some time in the past, the action was a serious policy mistake that only "deregulation" can correct.

The issue "regulation vs. deregulation" is best understood with respect to entire national economies, even the global economy, and to all industries, one-by-one. The economists have managed to frame the debate by asking such questions as "Why should any one industry be an exception to the general norm that economic regulation is unnecessary and undesirable?" They have been successful in their use of this ploy, but they are at war with history, historians and the presidents who have tried to deal with the consequences of economic collapses.

COMPETITION CREATES DEPRESSIONS

Despite their presumably different economic philosophies, Herbert Hoover and Franklin Roosevelt used strikingly similar language to describe the roots of the economic crisis of the 1930s. "Destructive competition," noted Hoover in 1931, had brought "demoralization" to such industries as coal, oil and lumber. Coal production in that year, for example, required the services of only half the available miners. Two months after taking office in 1933, Roosevelt asserted that "We have found our factories able to turn out more goods than we could possibly consume," while condemning the "cutthroat" and "unfair" competition that was punishing workers with "long hours and starvation wages." Hoover sought immediate revision of the antitrust laws so that firms could restrict competition by consolidating [2, December 9, 1931] and Roosevelt promised to "encourage each industry to prevent overproduction" and to decrease the country's disastrous farm surpluses [2, May 8, 1933]. One result, the short-lived National Industrial Recovery Act, permitted firms in individual industries to jointly plan output, wages and prices -- in short, to engage in industrial self-regulation with minimal government oversight. The words and actions of these presidents are worth recalling, because the world now faces problems very similar to those that they blamed on industrial overcapacity and agricultural overproduction. Even the U.S. stock market has now "crashed" as it did in 1929. All of this is ignored by economists because it does not fit their theory, just as they have ignored the excessive railroad competition and follow-on collapse of the steel industry that triggered the great slump of the 1890's [1]. Unaware or intolerant of history, small wonder that economists led the way in the "deregulation fever" of the 1970s.

WHAT'S WRONG WITH DEREGULATION

Since I have written a book in defense of economic regulation [3], I outline only briefly here the consequences of deregulating such industries as finance, telecommunications, airlines, trucking and buses. It is usually forgotten that in most instances, beginning with the 1887 establishment of the Interstate Commerce Commission to oversee the U.S. railroad industry, economic regulation has been installed only after a major free market failure. The laws providing for regulation usually have given existing companies "grandfather" rights to continue operations, thereby introducing a long-term contradiction. Excessive competition causes the problem, but "grandfathering" ensures that the problem will not be solved. Indeed, regulatory agencies have been required to promote head-to-head competition even if, as in the case of the airlines, the government must subsidize the competitors. The history of such industries suggests that deregulation advocates are wholly wrong when they argue that all regulatory schemes preserve monopoly, and that the inefficiencies of regulation were traceable to monopoly rather than competition.

One airline president recently observed that "nobody expected deregulation to be this 'anti-people' in operation." He was not lobbying for re-regulation but only referring to the depression-type punishment that has been visited upon airline employees since deregulation. Typically anti-worker union-busting has been widespread, wages having been substantially slashed (up to 50%). Entire cadres of employees have been fired in favor of low-wage replacements. Some airlines have such poor labor relations that the federal government has instituted a special watch on the effects of bitterness and resentment upon performance. Airlines have disappeared at a moment's notice, leaving passengers and crews stranded en route. The principle of "equal pay for equal work" has vanished in favor of "two-tier" labor contracts that pay newer workers much less than older ones. Flight attendants of at least one major airline live eight per one-bedroom apartment in New York to be close enough to the airport to meet flying schedules; they cannot afford anything larger. Those who write about the "quality of work life" usually conclude that job security and predictable living standards are prerequisites to good performance. Unfortunately, deregulation destroys the "quality of work life." And, of course, when firms must keep on cutting costs, safety and ethics also are victims.

At this fundamental level, the supporters of deregulation become inadvertently callous and cruel. Professors long ago fought successfully for job security -- "tenure" -- because they believed that university administrators under pressure to cut costs would make inappropriate decisions, dismissing faculty unfairly. While some professors occasionally criticize tenure, they do so only because they believe their own performance is so outstanding that the absence of tenure would not threaten them, forgetting that everyone is threatened in such situations. Professors who condemn "protectionism" in other industries should ask about the consequences to themselves of a fifty percent salary reduction. They argue instead that their consumers (students) are better served by a tenure system that keeps professorial salaries (and university tuitions) higher than a free market would provide. True to their theology, they argue that other workers be punished. If they are going to preach the gospel of anarchy, and free market theory is unadorned anarchy, they must also argue for academic anarchy. Because they do not, they should be ignored instead of being asked to advise U.S. presidents. Put more directly, those who label themselves "consumer advocates" are among the worst enemies of consumers.

REFERENCES

1. FAULKNER, HAROLD U. (1959) Politics, Reform and Expansion: 1890-1900, New York: Harper and Row, p. 145.

2. NEW YORK TIMES, December 9, 1931; May 8, 1933.

3. THAYER, FREDERICK (1984), Rebuilding America: The Case for Economic Regulation, Lexington, Mass.: Praeger.

THE RIGHT

TO

BE HEARD

Chapter 21

Panel: Cross-National Perspectives: The Major Developments Internationally

ABOUT THE AUTHORS

Robert O. Herrmann is Professor of Agricultural Economics at The Pennsylvania State University. Herrmann received his Ph.D. in Agricultural Economics from Michigan State University in 1964. From the beginning his career has been in Consumer Economics, starting at the University of California, Davis in 1962 and continuing with his move to Penn. State in 1974. Herrmann has been one of the leading scholars of Consumerism and of the history of the consumer movement. He has been active and influential in ACCI, having served at various times as Board Member, President (1968-69), the Editor of the Journal of Consumer Affairs (1977-80). Herrmann also served on the Board of Consumers Union (1974-77) and is a Distinguished Fellow of ACCI.

Edward J. Walsh is Associate Professor of Sociology at The Pennsylvania State University. He received his Ph.D. from the University of Michigan in 1974. After graduating, he worked for a year as a field hand in Salinas County, California in order to study the farm labor movement firsthand, under a Ford Foundation grant. Walsh has written extensively on the citizen groups which sprang up in the area around Three Mile Island after the nuclear reactor accident there. His work has been financed by three National Science Foundation grants. Two of his articles on TMI are co-authored with Dr. Rex Warland. Walsh's findings are incorporated in a forthcoming book on the TMI activists.

Rex H. Warland is Professor or Rural Sociology at The Pennsylvania State University. Warland received his Ph.D. from Iowa State University in 1966. Warland has been involved in survey studies of the consumer movement since 1971. He pioneered in the development of consumer satisfaction/dissatisfaction research. The 1975 article by Warland, Herrmann and Willits was one of the first research articles on consumer complaining. He was Associate Editor of the Journal of Consumer Affairs from 1977-80. He currently is a member of the governing council of the Rural Sociological Society.

THE ORGANIZATIONS OF THE CONSUMER MOVEMENT: A COMPARATIVE PERSPECTIVE

Robert O. Herrmann
Edward J. Walsh
Rex H. Warland

A number of studies over the past 20 years have looked at the distribution of consumer concerns and support for consumer action among the public [37, 26]. The translation of these preferences for social change into action depends on the organization and mobilization of those who share these preferences. This job has been undertaken by a group of organizations which identify with the general goals of the consumer movement and seek to implement these goals [30, p. 1218].

The consumer movement, similar to most other social movements, includes a number of distinct organizations representing certain broadly held preferences but diverse subpreferences. Distinguishing consumer movement organizations from the movement of which they are a part forces us to recognize that the consumer movement, like other social movements, is represented by more than one organization each of which possesses distinctive characteristics. These characteristics include the goals toward which the organization is working and its resources -- money, facilities and public supporters or adherents.

This paper examines some of the organizations of the consumer movement and considers how the distinctive characteristics of each help explain its present situation and future prospects. Five different types of organizations are singled out for particular attention: local boycott groups, state and local consumer organizations, the Nader network, Consumers Union, and the American Council on Consumer Interests. These organizations differ with respect to views, financial support and tactics.

Previous studies have focused mainly on the public's attitudes on consumerism issues. These studies followed a traditional approach to the analysis of social movements, emphasizing the social and economic strains that gave rise to each movement. A recent and alternative approach emphasizes that structural conditions in a movement determine which strains find expression in an organization [29, p. 1]. This "resource mobilization" approach emphasizes the role of resources more than member consciousness as an important determinant in the development of a movement. This approach pays particular attention to the role of (1) social movement entrepreneurs, i.e., individuals who are able to recruit supporters by making them aware of the benefits of group action, (2) contributions of time and money from individual supporters and institutions, and (3) the role of the mass media as a source of support.

This paper surveys the five organizational groups, examining for each: (1) conditions underlying its historical development, (2) tactics used, (3) the resources available to it and how they were obtained, (4) its organizational and financial linkage to other organizations and, finally, (5) its prospects for success.

All of the organizations draw their financial support chiefly from members and individual supporters rather than outside organizations. This differentiates them from coalitions and confederations of organizations. The Consumer Federation of America (CFA) is the most notable example of an "organization of organizations" within the consumer movement. Because CFA's organizational structure is distinctly different, it will not be examined here. But it deserves more attention than it has received.

BOYCOTT GROUPS

Boycotts have been an important instrument in the protest repertoire of consumers for the last 20 years. Boycotts are often a response to some sudden strain rather than a long-felt concern. The motives reported by participants in the 1966 supermarket boycotts support this conclusion [12, p. 8]. When local groups leaders were asked their chief motives for participation, easing the strain on their own food budgets and helping the poor and others in the community were reported with almost equal frequency. The leaders did not see participation as closely linked to a desire to "assert themselves" or to "work with friends."

Resources

The boycott groups typically have had few resources except the time and efforts of the groups' leaders and the volunteer participants. The leaders in the 1966 boycotts were middle and upper middle class, relatively young married homemakers with at least some college education [12, pp. 5-8]. They were "joiners" and belonged to a number of social, civic and educational organizations. Few had previously participated in protest actions. The leaders believed that other key participants were also relatively young married women, with somewhat less education than themselves [12, pp. 9-10].

Tactics

A boycott may utilize a variety of tactics or combinations of tactics in addition to the boycott itself: picketing, letter-writing, pursuit of media coverage, meetings, and discussions. In the consumer boycotts from 1970 to 1980, producers and processors were found to be frequent targets, but consumer problems were the cause of only a fraction of the boycotts [13]. Boycotts for consumer causes included those aimed at price increases for sugar, meat, coffee and milk.

Boycotts work well when the target is close at hand and appeal to loosely organized groups with limited finances. Boycotts are cheap, relatively easy to organize since they often only last one day [13, p. 106] and provide an attention-getting topic that ensures news coverage.

The boycotters made heavy use of the news media [12, pp. 12-13] with media coverage varying directly with a group's level of action [33]. The media carried the boycotters' story to the public. At the same time, the media conferred legitimacy on the boycotters.

The leaders of the 1966 supermarket boycott considered boycotting and picketing to be their most effective means, along with radio and TV appearances [12, pp. 12-13]. Militant measures were thought to have been highly productive while moderate measures, such as letter-writing, meetings and discussion were thought less productive. A careful student of boycotts -- Monroe Friedman-- concluded that the two ends of the boycott militancy continuum -- a mere "announcement" that a boycott was being considered at the one end, and full-scale demonstrating/picketing at the other -- were substantially more successful than the intermediate steps -- "calling for" or "organizing" a boycott [13, p. 109].

Business leaders consider the boycott of companies or specific products to be more effective than other forms of consumer protest [25, p. 66]. The longer-run effects of boycotts may be open to question. The local leaders of the 1966 supermarket boycotts concluded a year later that their effect had been only short-term [12, pp. 14-15].

Linkages

Where the problem was a widespread one, local groups have sometimes had loose links to those in other areas. Most of the 1966 leaders said they coordinated their actions with other groups. The boycotts spread from city to city as the actions of one group became a model for others [12, p. 19]. The media carried the news of boycotts from one city to another. Successes led to emulation in other places.

Future

Most consumer boycott groups were short-lived. Only 15 of 64 groups from the 1966 supermarket boycotts were still active one year later. Only a minority of the leaders of the 1966 groups that had gone out of existence thought the group would reassemble in the future [12, pp. 15-16].

Friedman feels that the increased number of boycotts over time may cause this tactic to lose its effectiveness [13, pp. 115-116]. Survey evidence from 1982 shows broad public acceptance of the boycott instrument [26, p. 59]. Today there exist significant barriers to organizing and maintaining consumer boycott actions. In the past boycotts depended heavily on the volunteer efforts of younger, educated women. Increasingly this group is in the labor force and is less available for volunteer activities.

Participation in boycotts seems to be motivated both by personal gains and a desire to help others. These two purposes motivate two distinct constituencies: "beneficiary" constituents and "conscience" constituents [30, pp. 1221-1222]. The two groups are doubtlessly committed to a boycott action in differing degrees. Maintaining commitment over time appears to be a serious problem.

The boycott groups typically have dealt with single issues or a limited range of issues and their tactics frequently have been militant. In contrast, most other consumer organizations including local and state-level consumer organizations generally have had a broader range of concerns and have utilized less militant tactics.

LOCAL AND STATE ORGANIZATIONS

The hey-day of activity at the state and local level undoubtedly was the 1960s and 1970s. Of the organizations founded at that time, many have disappeared or gone inactive. In a 1983 survey which sought to identify state and local consumer advocacy organizations, 391 were studied [8]. Over 86 percent of the organizations were founded in the 1960s and 1970s, indicating a higher degree of longevity than might have been expected.

A 1972 survey of 21 state and local organizations across the country, ranging from the Oregon Consumer League to the Harlem Consumer Education Council, provides many insights [36]. The author of the survey, Philip Sorenson concluded that the impetus for these organizations typically was local [36, p. 11]. Their members had been brought together by a local incident or piece of legislation or on the initiative of a local leader. Because of their origins, they are diverse in concerns and organizational structure. They are also independent with each recruiting its own members, defining its own priorities and carrying out its own programs.

According to Sorenson, the organizations he studied did not have any complex ideology or philosophy. He concluded that such an intellectual base probably is not necessary for success. What is needed is simply "some general ideas and notions about the rights, powers and prerogatives of the citizen" [36, p. 9].

Resources

The organizations studied had few financial resources and were supported chiefly by members' dues, which were low [36, p. 15]. Each organization's accomplishments seemed to depend almost entirely on the quality of its leadership and not on its financial resources [36, p. 22]. In most local organizations the leadership was thin, consisting usually of one or a few persons. Even the best-financed organizations had only a part-time paid staff.

Membership activity also depended on the quality of leadership and its skill in using volunteer help. In most of the organizations only a handful of members were really active [36, p. 22]. The most active members usually were housewives, academics and lawyers. Active members often came out of fields or organizations which are consumer-oriented, such as labor unions or co-operatives. Getting an organization started is relatively easy, but acquiring significant numbers of members is difficult [36, p. 12].

One of the major problems for the state and local organizations was the lack of opportunity for volunteers to acquire the skills and expertise they needed [36, p. 29]. Many organizations included lawyers but they often lacked information on specific issues and needed help in getting it.

During the halycon days of the 1970s, the Federal government was a source of funds for many groups. Comprehensive Employment and Training Act (CETA) funds were used to pay employees and up to 85 percent of the budget of some groups came from government. Much of the balance was received from foundations [16, p. 222]. These sources have dried up in recent years.

Tactics

Sorenson noted three main areas of activity: lobbying, complaint-handling, and communicating consumer information and solutions to consumer problems [36, pp. 14-15]. Most organizations concentrated on just one of these activities. Lobbying typically took place at the state level while complaint-handling occurred locally.

Organizations of organizations were best at lobbying, Sorenson judged [36, pp. 13-14]. They typically had paid staff who could keep on top of legislation, which was hard for individual volunteers to do. Organizations of individuals, on the other hand, were more successful at tasks where volunteer help could be utilized, for example, educational and expose work, complaint-handling and price surveys. Another important function of state and local groups has been to legitimize action by sympathetic officials and legislators. "Just keep them [the state consumer organization in question] raising the issues and I can proceed to get something done on most of them," a state legislator in Oregon observed [36, p. 17].

The organizations differed in militancy: "In general, the more localized the group or the poorer the constituency, the more militant the organization" [36, p. 16]. One of the more militant groups was the Consumers Education and Protection Association (CEPA) in Philadelphia. CEPA was founded as a grass-roots consumer action group in 1966 with a largely lower-income, Black membership, [36, p. 3]. Its emphasis has been on group action to help solve individual consumer problems [22, p. 36]. CEPA has insisted that individual consumers get involved in helping solve their own problems rather than relying on others or outside agencies. Visits by delegations to offending merchants and educational picketing are the principal tools used. Boycotting is not used. Newsletters reporting individual cases are used to educate members to typical consumer problems [22, p. 38].

In a survey of CEPA membership in 1972, Ittig found that 57 percent of those responding had participated in a picket line and 43 percent had gone with a delegation [22, p. 94-96]. Although these activities were required of members, Ittig concluded that the rule was apparently not strictly enforced. Membership turnover in CEPA was high. Apparently many were active only while their case was handled [22, pp. 91-93] and thus appear to be "beneficiary constituents." Some middle and upper income members who never came to meetings should apparently be regarded as conscience constituents. While many whose problems are solved drift away, others stay for an extended period and form a devoted core. Some

6.5 percent of the respondents in Ittig's survey had been members for six or more years, while 40 percent had been members for less than a year [22, p. 52-53, 91-92].

Overall, the state and local groups generally have had good access to the press and know how to use it [36, p. 17]. Their press releases have been picked up by the media and they have had good relations with consumer journalists. Sorenson concluded that consumer needs may be best served by a larger number of groups, even with smaller membership than by fewer, large groups [36, p. 28]. The existence of many small groups creates an opportunity for a wide level of activism, he argued.

Linkages

It is difficult to document the linkages of the state and local groups. They undoubtedly vary in their strength and change over time. In a 1983 CFA survey of state and local consumer advocacy organizations [8] a number of linkages were found:

65 organizations belonged to the Consumer Federation of America

34 were affiliated with the Gray Panthers

39 were Public Interest Research Groups with student-financing and undoubtedly some links to the Nader network.

Some were part of other networks including ACORN, Citizen Action and the Citizen Labor Energy Coalition.

Future

The state and local groups form a diverse category with varying concerns. Although their fortunes have fluctuated, many have been surprisingly long-lived. They undoubtedly vary greatly in level of current activity, but even the moribund groups are of interest because of their potential for action if new local level issues arise.

The leadership of the state and local groups seems to represent a "conscience" constituency. The component of State-level groups that focus on lobbying are also likely to be conscience constituencies. Local groups, especially complaint-handling groups, probably includes a high proportion of beneficiary constituents and suffer from a high rate of membership turnover.

THE NADER NETWORK

The group of organizations associated with Ralph Nader has grown and changed in the two decades since he came to national attention. The changing composition and tactics of the "Nader network" reflect the change in Nader's own agenda. Nader's book, Unsafe at Any Speed [31] and his early efforts were aimed at convincing the public of the need for reforms in product safety and in the government regulatory process. Nader's "Raiders" had the same goals. The Raiders worked out of the Center for Study of Responsive Law, founded in 1969 which had tax-exempt status because of its educational emphasis [15].

In the early 1970's Nader moved to establish a non-tax-exempt organization to promote action on the problems which had been exposed. These efforts ultimately were located in Public Citizen, Inc., whose chief goals have been to provide a stable funding base for the network's activities. Public Citizen carries on an ambitious fund-raising campaign to support six different program groups including the Tax Reform Research Group, Congress Watch, and the Health Research Group.

By the mid-seventies the Nader operations had jelled into three fairly distinct parts including the, by then, much-diminished tax-exempt, research-oriented Center for Study of Responsive Law; Public Citizen with its emphasis on political action, and a small group around Nader which functions as a personal staff and is paid from personal funds [15]. With some changes, activities are still organized along these same general lines.

Resources

In their early stages, Nader's activities were financed by the large settlement resulting from his lawsuit against General Motors and by his speaking fees. The creation of the Center for Study of Responsive Law in 1969 provided a channel for foundation grants. The low-paid help of recent college and law school graduates also has been an important resource for the network. The turnover of student workers is high but their work is supervised by a stable staff of trusted lieutenants [15, p. 8].

Public Citizen has sought small contributions from the public with large-scale direct mailings. Currently, it has about 70,000 annual contributors [7, p. 2] and states that it has had over 200,000 supporters since its founding in 1971 [21, p. 198]. These figures suggest a good deal of turnover during the 13-year period covered. Public Citizen's funding comes chiefly from these contributors (the minimum suggested contribution in $20), and from payments for publications, litigation fees and foundation grants.

Nader himself has been a major contributor. Information filed with the Internal Revenue Service indicates that between 1964 and 1982 he contributed $300,000 to $500,000 to the tax-exempt groups he influences. Nader also says he contributed half a million dollars to the Congress Project, which is not tax-exempt [42, p. 8].

A 1972 nationwide survey sketched potential Nader contributors [19]. Respondents were classified into four categories depending on their attitude toward Nader and his efforts. Supporters, who had a favorable opinion and who had or were willing to contribute money, constituted 18 percent of the respondents. They tended to be younger, female and political liberals. Supporters were more concerned with business and marketing practices than were other groups.

The Supporters were politically active. They had signed protest petitions, contacted legislators, and contributed time and money to political causes and social action groups more frequently than had the other groups [19, pp. 13-14]. Support for Nader, it was concluded, "is part of a broader pattern of social and political activism" [19, p. 15].

Tactics

Up until about 1970, Nader and Nader's Raiders focused their efforts on the study of regulatory failures and unsafe products and environmental dangers, preparing exposes on their findings. While this research and expose work was still going on, parallel efforts were begun to influence the legislative and regulatory process to produce solutions. These activities began with a close scrutiny of the way Congress operates, including the records of individual members of Congress. At about the same time, efforts were initiated to found Public Interest Research Groups (PIRGs), funded from college student's fees. Research was shifted into a supporting role, and emphasis was placed on legal action, including lobbying, litigation on broad issues of law which could establish important precedents and intervention in regulatory agency actions [21, p. 199].

One of the secrets of Nader and his network's survival has been their continuing ability to identify new issues, to develop dramatic information about them and to time the release of these stories to the press for maximum impact [41, p. 568, 561].

Linkages

Early in his activist career, Ralph Nader was dubbed the "Lone Ranger of the Consumer Movement," and had no visible links to other consumer organizations. He did, in fact, receive some informational and financial aid from Consumers Union and was a member of its board of directors from 1967 to 1975. The Nader network generally has not, however, collaborated with other organizations of the consumer movement.

There are significant linkages between the organizations in which Nader still is regularly active and others which he helped organize but which now operate independently. The Center for Auto Safety was founded by Nader but became an independent organization in 1973 [15]. PIRG's have been founded with the help of Nader's Citizen Action Group, but each is independent with its own financing and directors. The organizations founded by the Nader network although independent are, however, still linked to it by their common interests and goals and by the interchange of personnel.

Future

Nader's support appears to come from a widespread liberally-oriented conscience constituency concerned about business practices and about social and economic changes. His opposition has come from conservatives and as Colston Warne has suggested, from "intellectuals ... alienated by the broad sweep of Nader's criticism and the over-eagerness of his followers for social change" [41, p. 568]. These comments suggest the need to consider the public's solution preferences as well as its concern with particular issues.

Some portions of the public favor policy solutions which tend to limit choices [24]. The proposals of the Nader network for banning of products and restricting the scope of corporate activity can be characterized as choice-limiting. Other groups concerned with improving consumer protection have favored solutions which seek to optimize individual choice--typical proposals include increased consumer information and warning labels. Support for choice-allowing solutions was found to be significantly higher among younger, more educated and higher income adults [24]. Support for Nader did not differ between those who favored choice-allowing proposals and those who favored choice-limiting proposals. It may well be, however, that some intellectuals, who are more familiar with the details of Nader's proposals than is the general public, may resist his choice-limiting solutions.

Although some journalists suggested a few years ago that Nader was in eclipse, he and his organizations still are clearly visible. Public Citizen, the organization on which information is most readily available had 70,000 supporters in 1985 and an operating budget of $1.9 million [7]. Membership turnover is, however, considerable and necessitates continuing recruitment efforts.

CONSUMERS UNION

Disagreement about the appropriate role for Consumers Union (CU) has arisen within the organization on several occasions during its life. In its early years there was considerable disagreement among the CU board and staff as to whether the organization should be a technical testing organization or a broad consumer organization. As the organization developed, the board and staff became increasingly aware of the problems of mixing technical testing and advocacy and tilted toward a scientific emphasis. This left some dissatisfaction. Colston Warne, in particular, wanted a broader role for CU and, in 1950, threatened to resign. The threat produced a compromise. Ultimately, the broader view found embodiment in the establishment of a CU Office in Washington devoted to lobbying and litigation [14, p. 483].

Consumers Union has continued to emphasize technically-based product-testing, primarily through the reports published in Consumer Reports (CR), in the belief that scientific evidence, dispassionately presented would help produce needed consumer protection reforms [34, p. 38]. It has been careful about making policy prescriptions and has distanced itself from advocacy groups [34, p. 125].

Resources

As part of its aggressive recruitment efforts CU has, over the years, financed market research studies of CR subscribers and aided academic research on them. The studies generally have agreed on the characteristics of subscribers. A 1970 survey found them to have much-above-average incomes and education, and managerial or professional occupations; they were also likely to be married and predominately in the 25-54 age range, [38, pp. 61-64]. Subscribers have been characterized as information-seekers who actively gather information from a wide-variety of sources, relying heavily on CR, especially for durable goods purchases [38, p. 79].

The evidence suggests that CR is valued chiefly for its test reports although it also includes articles on health, safety and other consumer issues. In a 1969-70 survey, the two most frequently given reasons for non-renewal were that the respondent was not in the market for the products tested and that they were in the market but were disappointed by the lack of relevant information [4, p. 176]. When the desired information is available, the 1969-70 survey results suggest it has a major influencce on the model chosen [5, p. 145].

The fluctuation of subscriber rolls with consumers' buying plans also supports the conclusion that CR is valued principally for its product reports by a significant portion of its subscribers. As a result of the recession of the mid to late 1970's, subscriptions fell from 2.2 million in 1972 to 2.0 in 1976. They have increased sharply in the relatively prosperous 1980's to 3.8 million in 1986.

There is other evidence that subscribers' principal interest is in the test reports. In the 1969-70 survey, only 14 percent of active and expired CR subscribers said CU's involvement in consumer affairs was their principal interest [4, pp. 176-77]. However, 40 percent of renewed subscribers and 20 percent of the expired did indicate the CR editorial and general interest articles were weighted as a positive factor in their subscription decision.

CR subscribers appear to favor choice-allowing rather than choice-limiting approaches to aiding consumers. In a comparison of Indianapolis subscribers to average consumers in the same city, subscribers tended to favor improvements in consumer information more frequently than did the average consumers. Average consumers more often favored consumer protection (presumably by government) and consumer education than did CR subscribers [38, pp. 88-90].

Overall, it appears that CR subscribers are more motivated by the benefits of participation to themselves rather than the benefits to consumers at large. We must, it appears, regard them as beneficiary constituents, rather than as conscience constituents, who will remain loyal subscribers so long as CU continues to provide test reports on products they are interested in buying.

Tactics

CU is a comprehensive organization with a sizable budget and a variety of programs. Its major thrust is, of course, providing information and advice on products, services, and financial matters. CU has come to regard itself as a consumer information-producer and disseminator rather than more narrowly as a product-testing organization. Its media involvement supports this self-assessment as does the position of CR among the 20 most widely circulated magazines in the country [11, p. 79]. In addition to CR, CU also publishes Penny Power (a consumer education magazine for secondary school children), Consumers Union News Digest (abstracts of articles on topics affecting consumers) and the recently added Consumer Reports Travel Letter. CU also distributes over two dozen books and is producing radio programs and cable TV specials.

Consumers Union maintains three advocacy offices (Washington, D.C.; San Francisco; and Austin, Texas) which work in the areas of litigation, legislation and regulation. Although CU refused for years to lobby for legislation and testified only on invitation, it recently changed its stance and now lobbies intensively. When CU takes cases to court it tries to maximize its leverage by focusing on issues with widespread impact [40, p. 194]. An example is its efforts to end prohibitions on advertising by lawyers [11, p. 79].

Another part of the CU program is to give aid to individual and group efforts to assist consumers. A significant part of this program has been to give financial aid and advice to consumer organizations both in the U.S. and abroad. Groups assisted by CU typically have been aided through an initial period, then nudged into independence.

Linkages

CU's linkages to other portions of the consumer movement have developed out of its grants program, begun in 1952, which has aided consumer organizations both in the U.S. and abroad and encouraged consumer education [40, pp. 185-86]. The program expanded after 1956 because of Internal Revenue Service threats that CU would lose its tax-exempt status unless it demonstrated its emphasis on public service.

Early on, CU's grants program provided $700 to aid in the founding of the Council on Consumer Information (now the American Council on Consumer Interests or ACCI) in 1953. ACCI continued to receive grant support until 1973. Grants also assisted the pioneer European product-testing organizations in Britain, the Netherlands and Belgium. Another early project was the founding of the International Organization of Consumers Unions (IOCU) which received an annual grant or membership fee of about $35 thousand during its earlier years [40, pp. 186, 195]. In addition to its aid to ACCI, CU worked on forming other links to education and on the strengthening of consumer education. Classroom use of CR was promoted, consumer education materials were developed and, more recently, the magazine for young consumers was established. A variety of consumer research also has been supported, including David Caplovitz's study of consumer credit practices in East Harlem [10], the weights and measures research effort headed by Leland

Gordon, and pioneer conferences on consumer behavior research in the 1950s [40, pp. 186-87].

Another thrust of the grants program was subsidizing the formation and development of state and local consumer organizations from California to Harlem, and collaborating with existing ones. In addition, CU played a leadership role in the creation of the Consumer Federation of America, the federation of organizations with consumer concerns.

When Colston Warne summarized the results of the grants program for the 1952-79 period, he indicated that a total of $1.496 million had been distributed. A listing of CU's financial contributions grossly understates its impact. Colston Warne, as well as many of the paid staff and board members carried perspectives developed at CU to other groups and provided time, energy and leadership to ensure their success.

Ralph Nader had significant links with CU from the earliest stages of his activist career. CU supplied materials from its labs for the preparation of <u>Unsafe at Any Speed</u> and later helped subsidize the Center for Auto Safety and collaborated with it on a number of projects [40, pp. 561-62]. Nader was elected to the CU board in 1967 and was, Colson Warne comments, "quite influential in establishing board policy when he was present" [41, pp. 561-562]. There were, however, continuing frictions between Nader and CU. Nader's lieutenants disturbed the CU staff with conclusions which they felt were, in some cases, overdrawn.

Although CU's Washington advocacy office was created as a result of Nader's influence, there was resistance to his proposals to further increase CU's legal advocacy efforts, and to deemphasize its consumer education activities. In 1974-75, CU experienced increasing financial strains confounded by major leadership changes. Nader, apparently convinced that CU was not a significant source of support for advocacy, resigned just as CU's difficulties were becoming clear.

In recent years grants to outside organizations have received reduced emphasis. Grants were reduced during CU's financial difficulties in the later 1970's. As CU's finances revived, additional funds were channeled into CU's advocacy offices and into efforts to influence public policy formation.

Future

While CU did not ultimately provide the kind and amount of aid to the consumer movement which Nader hoped for, it has provided an authoritative voice on consumer issues, one whose pronouncements are based on scientific objectivity. It seems highly likely that CU will continue to be a significant organization in the consumer movement because of its financial power, its human resources, it reputation and its legitimacy. Its subscribers' support seems to be based, in large part, on the benefits CU provides, not on conscience. While this support may fluctuate somewhat with consumers' buying plans, CU is not subject to the wide swings more typically found for organizations dependent on conscience constituencies.

PROFESSIONAL ORGANIZATIONS

Professional organizations consisting of academics, as well as corporate and government officials concerned with the consumer interest, differ significantly from the activist groups in their priorities and tactics but share their general concern with the consumer interest. There are several organizations of consumer professionals: (1) the American Council on Consumer Interests--made up chiefly of academics, (2) the Society of Consumer Affairs Professionals--made up of corporate consumer affairs executives, and the (3) National Association of Consumer Agency Administrators. ACCI is the oldest and will be the one singled out for particular scrutiny.

At its founding in 1953, a major goal of ACCI was to provide the public with analyses of consumer issues and consumer education materials in readable pamphlet form. The ACCI pamphlet series, modeled on the Public Affairs pamphlet series, included such titles as <u>Consumers Look at Farm Price Policies</u>. Despite the publication of a number of high-quality pamphlets, the plan ran into difficulties. The academic authors had trouble writing at the popular level and distribution proved complicated and limited.

Over the years, ACCI became increasingly centered on the professional concerns of its educator members. In the late 1960s, a few members pressed for a more activist stance, urging support for consumer legislation. Others argued that ACCI should serve as a professional organization for those in consumer education and consumer affairs. The die was cast when the decision was made in 1966 to publish a professional journal, <u>The Journal of Consumer Affairs</u>.

ACCI's principal emphasis is on the professional development of its members [27]. Its publications and annual conference serve as channels of communications to promote this development. ACCI has emphasized: (1) dissemination of information on current consumer research and education topics, (2) dissemination of policy proposals and analyses to encourage participation in the policy process. In its early years the organization gave major emphasis to consumer education. More recently, consumer research has come to be at least a co-equal concern.

ACCI has avoided political stands on consumer issues except for the funding of consumer education programs. While some individual members have been involved as activists, the membership has been reluctant to involve the organization as a whole. Topics of concern to consumer activists such as corporate power and monopoly, product safety and the performance of the regulatory agencies have not been major topics within ACCI. This neglect parallels the neglect of these topics in secondary education [18]. It should be noted that the topics considered by ACCI are decided by individual authors, editors, conference chairpersons and reviewers.

Resources

Over its life, ACCI has had only limited financial resources and has relied on a few part-time paid personnel to perform headquarters functions [27, p. 123]. The activities of the organization now are supported almost entirely by membership dues and subscriptions. Over the period 1953 to 1973, ACCI received annual grants from CU. Toward the end of this period, it received a major developmental grant to facilitate recruitment and became financially independent. The organization has accepted a few corporate and foundation grants for specific projects rather than to supplement regular operating funds.

ACCI's services and activities are made possible largely through the voluntary contributions of time and professional expertise of its members [27, p. 122]. Membership has drifted downward and in 1986 stood at about 1800, down from 2200 in 1979 [3]. These numbers include libraries, government agencies and businesses as well as individual members. A clearer picture of the non-institutional membership can be gained from a 1985 survey of a sample of individual members [2]. Of those responding, 44 percent were university faculty and another 16 percent were Extension specialists at the state and local level. Ten percent were students. Over half had Ph.D.s. A significant share of the membership is highly stable; 53 percent have belonged for 6 years or more [2].

Tactics

The ACCI organization puts major emphasis on disseminating information to its membership and facilitating communication among them. Publication costs take about half of revenues [27, p. 118; 1]. The annual conference is fully supported by registration fees [1]. The nine-times yearly newsletter includes an extensive bibliography of articles on consumer education topics and consumer issues as well as listings of new educational materials and is seen as a major benefit by members. The importance of the Journal of Consumer Affairs is recognized, but it probably is regarded as less essential by many members [2]. Although the annual conference has been important for ensuring face-to-face contacts and preserving the continuity of the organization, a majority of the members (51 percent) have not attended [2].

Linkages

The most important and tangible links of ACCI with other consumer organizations have been through its membership. Members of the ACCI board have served on the boards of a number of other consumer organizations, including the Consumer Federation of America, Consumers Union, the Conference of Consumer Organizations, the International Organization of Consumers Unions, the Association for Consumer Research and federal and state advisory committees and commissions [27, p. 123]. ACCI board members and general members were notably involved in the activities of the Office of Consumers' Education during its existence. ACCI is an organizational member of both the Consumer Federation of America and the International Organization of Consumers Unions and sends delegates to their conferences.

Future

The ACCI organization clearly is committed to the consumer interest, but has confined its activities to the consumer education and research fields. Its membership values the professional development services the organization provides and can be regarded as beneficiary constituents. Library, business and government subscribers also are, in a real sense, beneficiary constituents. Membership numbers have drifted downward in recent years but include a significant proportion of long-term members. This stability and the organization's financial health suggest that it will be a long-term presence within the consumer movement.

CONCLUSIONS

The picture of the consumer movement which seems to emerge from our analysis is of a decentralized movement with no binding ideology. The consumer movement is a diverse set of organizations with diverse concerns. These organizations appear to agree only on the general principle that more attention needs to be given to the interests of consumers. The use of the term consumer movement may, in fact, have misled us. We have reified the consumer movement, erroneously treating a diverse calculation of organizations and concerns as if it were a single, cohesive entity.

The Nature of the Consumer Movement

The Nader network organizations closely resemble the model of the professional social movement organization delineated by students of social movements [23, p. 535]. The Nader-linked organizations have arisen out of the efforts of an "entrepreneur" who recruited potential supporters by making them aware of the benefits of group action. Since consumer issues typically are not a central concern for most, it is possible to recruit large numbers only with extraordinary efforts and skills. Like other professional social movement organizations, the Nader network has paid professional staffs, a centralized, bureaucratic organizational structure and is highly skilled at recruiting support. Consumers Union shows many of the same characteristics and can also be regarded as a professional social movement organization. It differs in that it has used resources obtained from beneficiary constituents to finance advocacy programs of interest chiefly to a more limited conscience constituency among its membership.

Decentralized social movement organizations resemble the traditional idea of a social movement [23, p. 533]. They are guided by local leadership and are staffed by volunteers. Their resources come from their members who are drawn by the expectation of personal benefits. ACCI shows many of these characteristics as do the boycott groups and local consumer organizations. The state-level organizations stand somewhere in between the centralized and decentralized models.

Conscience constituencies might be expected to be less stable sources of support than beneficiary constituencies which are receiving continuing services. This appears to be the case. There appears to have been considerable turnover in Public Citizen, which clearly relies on a conscience constituency. By contrast, there has been greater stability in the support for CU and ACCI, both of which depend upon beneficiary constituencies and deliver a continuing stream of benefits that holds members. Support for the boycott groups and local and state organizations is drawn from both conscience and beneficiary constituencies. Support for the supermarket boycott groups has been short-lived, perhaps because they have been unable to deliver the results to their beneficiary constituency. There is little clear evidence on the stability of support for local or state organizations. The data on the Consumer Education and Protection Association of Philadelphia suggest a high rate of turnover among beneficiary constituents whose immediate needs have been satisfied. A survey including only five selected state and local organizations [35, pp. 68-69] found that they had grown substantially in membership, budget and staff between 1978 and 1982. It was suggested that this growth was due to their ability to deliver services to a beneficiary constituency.

Support of social movements has frequently displayed a cyclical pattern [20]. After achieving institutional recognition, movements typically fragment and decline. This pattern more nearly describes the developmental path of the consumer advocacy organizations, those with a conscience constituency. Those with a beneficiary constituency with continuing needs seem somewhat exempt from this set of forces.

The consumer movement consists of organizations that deal with multiple issues that change over time. The sole exception is the boycott groups. Their limited agenda may be the result of the boycott groups' brief lives. Conversely, their brief agendas may sentence them to short lives. While most consumer organizations focus on multiple issues, boycott groups typically concentrate in only one or a few major areas: health-safety, economic regulation-antitrust, participation in government decision making, price/quality relationships, redress, information and education. McCarthy and Zald have suggested a new corollary of Parkinson's Law: the issues considered will expand as resources and personnel permit [29, p. 23]. Not only do the concerns of the various parts of the consumer movement differ, their preferred solutions also differ, perhaps even more sharply. The Nader network, in particular, has emphasized choice-limiting solutions. Some of the other groups and CU, in particular, have put more emphasis on choice-allowing solutions.

The tactics particular organizations employ are closely linked to their resources. The boycotters, with virtually no resources except volunteer time and press coverage have been able to mount highly visible, but short-lived campaigns. The Nader network when its resources were more limited initially focused on expose work. Later, as more resources became available, it moved into advocacy, which requires a pool of expertise and continuing efforts. CU's history shows a similar pattern. Initially it limited itself to disseminating product test and other information and to publicizing product-related problems and hazards and providing expert testimony on invitation. More recently, more ample resources have made advocacy efforts possible.

Factors Associated with Success and Failure

A variety of measures can be used to judge the success of a social movement organization. One measure is simply its ability to survive. A surprising number of organizations from the 1960s and 1970s have met this basic test [8], although some may be moribund. Other tests of success include the delivery of benefits to members, success in changing power relations with target institutions, and success in making fundamental changes in the structure of society.

The decentralized consumer movement organizations seem to have had less dramatic success than the more centralized ones. The boycott organizations have been short-lived and have had little ultimate effect on prices. Economic realities may have made their goal an impossible one. Similar tactics applied to other consumer issues have had more success, as in the case of CEPA. Decentralized organizations are an effective way to organize grass-roots participation, but the evidence from the boycott local groups suggests that it is difficult to hold active memberships for very long. Decentralized organizations are well suited to quick-strike efforts where a long lasting organization is not appropriate or necessary. Attempts to formalize the organization of local, loosely-knit groups may, in fact, weaken them rather than strengthen them. The effort required to develop a formal structure may divert the group's limited energies from planned actions.

ACCI has survived and established itself, although with a reduced membership. While it has many of the characteristics of a decentralized organization, it is more structured and follows the professional organization model familiar to its membership. One reason for its survival is the continuing flow of valuable benefits it is able to provide: access to current professional thinking and literature and, in addition, professional visibility and recognition.

Some students of social movements have suggested that a centralized organizational structure is more efficient and reduces internal conflicts. They conclude that such organizations are more durable and produce longer-lasting results. The most centralized consumer organizations, CU and the Nader network, clearly have been successful in organizing the low-level concerns of large groups of consumer and giving assistance and advice.

Centralized social movement organizations are a relatively recent phenomenon. In the past, the decentralized-type of organization was considered more typical. The public interest and environmental organizations which sprang up in the 1960s and 1970s, helped to inspire the development of this newer model. One of the major advantages of the centralized organizational form is that it facilitates obtaining resources, which may be either tangible (money, facilities and means of communication) or intangible (knowledge, leadership and workers' effort). Centralized organizations have had notable success in tapping outside sources of help including foundations, the media and conscience constituencies. Not only has the Nader network been successful in coopting the news media, it also has developed its own media outlets. CU, of course, has been a publisher since its inception.

Media coverage has served the important function of providing legitimacy to consumer movement organizations. By giving them exposure it implies that they have a viewpoint worthy of attention. Using their media exposure, consumer spokespersons have called up powerful images of the abused public and the underdog and have demanded fair play and justice.

The Future of the Consumer Movement

Recent scholarly work on social movements emphasizes the key role of the political environment in their success [23, pp. 543-549]. The political environment in the U.S. after the 1964 election landslide clearly was conducive. Liberals in Congress were looking for issues and a group of activists were in place in Washington to help them. Furthermore, the media were receptive [32, pp. 13-20]. The White House welcomed consumer measures because of its desire to build a domestic program at minimal cost so as to avoid diverting funds from the Vietnam War [17, p. 59].

The political environment since 1980 has reduced the visibility of and funds for federal government efforts closely linked to the consumer movement. The Office of Consumers' Education has disappeared, CETA funds for local consumer groups are gone and the U.S. Office of Consumer Affairs has become less visible. Despite these governmental pullbacks, there are areas where progress seems possible. There is agreement across the political spectrum on the importance of consumer education [25, pp. 75-76], but apparently less agreement on how it will be paid for. There also is wide agreement on the importance of preserving and encouraging competition. The economic deregulation begun under Jimmy Carter has continued without interference. The Reagan administration does, however, seem to continue to underestimate the extent of public support for health-safety regulation.

Another factor which encourages the creation and growth of social movement organizations is the visible success of other organizations [23, p. 548]. This phenomenon clearly is present in the consumer movement. Nader's success undoubtedly led to the founding of the 10 other Washington-based consumer groups concerned with national issues which appeared in the 1968-1972 period [6, p. 34]. Many state and local organizations also were founded during or after this same period [8].

Social movement organizations must compete for the allegiance of what undoubtedly is a limited constituency (although there is no clear empirical evidence). Some of this group is potentially recruitable only on a single issue. Others may, perhaps, be recruited on several issues at once, or sequentially. Some members of the total activist pool have previous, or other, involvements, e.g., the anti-nuclear, antiwar, civil rights and women's movements [9, pp. 135-136]. A group with a wide range of experience in dealing with community issues and problems and in complaining about consumer problems does, however, exist [39]. This group's past experience and its above average levels of income and education make them potential recruits who could be expected to be highly effective.

The consumer movement organizations, like other public interest organizations, seem to have had their best success in recruiting membership from middle class professionals, housewives and students with discretionary time and/or income, from liberally-oriented foundations and from the mass media [23, p. 534]. Some of these resources may be becoming scarcer.

After looking at the consumer movement objectively, we can ask a normative question: has the movement been organized in the most effective way? The answer undoubtedly is no. A single centralized organization with local chapters probably would have been more effective. However, given the level of public interest, the diverse concerns and the disagreement over preferred solutions, what emerged probably is the best that could have been hoped for. The diverse set of organizations and organizational forms has provided ways for a wide variety of people to be involved at different levels. The resulting conglomeration of groups is an ideological and organizational muddle. Constant changes of issues, tactics, organizations and leadership make it hard to describe or pin down. These changes are confusing to the movement's sympathizers. They, undoubtedly, are even more confusing to the movement's adversaries who have to take aim at a constantly changing target.

REFERENCES

1. AMERICAN COUNCIL ON CONSUMER INTERESTS (1985), Audit Report of Barbara Scobee, C.P.A. Columbia, Missouri: American Council on Consumer Interests.

2. _________ (1986), Report of Future Directions Survey - 1985, unpublished tabulations, Columbia, Missouri: American Council on Consumer Interests.

3. _________ (1986), "Membership Statistics: American Council on Consumer Interests, April 1986," unpublished mimeo, Columbia, Missouri: American Council on Consumer Interests.

4. BENSON AND BENSON, INC. (1970), Survey of Present and Former Subscribers to Consumer Reports, Princeton, NJ: Benson and Benson, Inc. as cited in Thorelli, Becker & Engledow 1976: 176-77.

5. _________ (1970), Survey of Present and Former Subscribers to Consumer Reports, Princeton, N.J.: Benson and Benson, Inc. as cited in Maynes 1976: 145.

6. BERRY, JEFFREY M. (1977), Lobbying for the People: The Political Behavior of Public Interest Groups, Princeton, NJ: Princeton University Press.

7. BOLLIER, DAVID, editor (1986), "Public Citizen 1985: The Year in Review," Public Citizen, 6(No. 4; April);unpaged insert.

8. BROBECK, STEPHEN and GLENN NISHIMURA (1983), "Statistical Report on the Grassroots Consumer Movement, 1983," unpublished report, Washington, D.C.: Consumer Federation of America.

9. CABLE, SHERRY MONTGOMERY (1985), Differential Paths to Activism: A Study of Social Movement Organizations in Three Mile Island Communities, unpublished Ph.D. dissertation, University Park, PA: The Pennsylvania State University.

10. CAPLOVITZ, DAVID (1963), The Poor Pay More: Consumer Practices of Low-Income Families, New York, NY: Free Press.

11. CONSUMERS UNION (1986), "50 Years Ago: What Happened when Consumerism and Unionism, Two Great Social Movements of the 1930s, Collided?" Consumer Reports, 51(No. 2, February):76-79.

12. FRIEDMAN, MONROE P. (1971), "The 1966 Consumer Protest as Seen by Its Leaders," Journal of Consumer Affairs, 5(No. 1; Summer):1-23.

13. _________ (1985), "Consumer Boycotts in the United States, 1970-1980: Contemporary Events in Historical Perspectives," Journal of Consumer Affairs, 19(No. 1; Summer):96-117.

14. GORDON, LELAND (1980), "The Development of a Consumer Economist," in Erma Angevine (editor), They Made a Difference: The History of Consumer Action Related by Leaders in the Consumer Movement, Washington, D.C.: National Consumers Committee for Research and Education, 476-92.

15. GROSS, SUSAN (1975), "The Nader Network," Business and Society Review, No. 13 (Spring):5-15.

16. HARRIS, MARLYS (1982), "What Have Consumer Groups Done for You Lately?" Money, Vol. 11 (No. 10, October):218-228.

17. HERRMANN, ROBERT O. (1970), "Consumerism: Its Goals, Organizations and Future," Journal of Marketing, 34(No. 4; October), pp. 55-60.

18. _________ (1982), "The Historical Development of the Content of Consumer Education: An Examination of Selected High School Texts, 1938-1978," Journal of Consumer Affairs, 16(No. 2; Winter):195-223.

19. _________ and REX H. WARLAND (1976), "Nader's Support: Its Sources and Concerns," Journal of Consumer Affairs, 10(No. 1; Summer):1-18.

20. _________ (1980), "Does Consumerism Have a Future?" Proceedings of the 26th Annual Conference, American Council on Consumer Interests, Columbia, Missouri: American Council on Consumer Interests, 12-17.

21. INTERNATIONAL ORGANIZATION OF CONSUMERS UNIONS (1986), Consumer Directory - 1987, The Hague: International Organization of Consumers Unions.

22. ITTIG, KATHLEEN BROWNE (1973), Consumer Collective Action: A Study of Consumers Education and Protective Association International, Inc., Unpublished M.S. Thesis. Cornell University.

23. JENKINS, J. CRAIG (1983), "Resource Mobilization Theory and the Study of Social Movements," Annual Review of Sociology, 9:527-53.

24. KROLL, ROBERT J. and RONALD W. STAMPFL (1985), "Orientations Toward Consumerism: A Politically Based Theory and an Empirical Test," Proceedings of the 31st Annual Conference, American Council on Consumer Interests, Columbia, Missouri: American Council on Consumer Interests, 86-92.

25. LOUIS HARRIS AND ASSOCIATES, INC. and MARKETING SCIENCE INSTITUTE, (c 1977), Consumerism at the Crossroads: A National Opinion Survey of Public Activist, Business and Regulatory Attitudes Toward the Consumer Movement, Stevens Point, WI: Sentry Insurance Company.

26. _________ (1983), Consumerism in the Eighties, Los Angeles: Atlantic Richfield Co.

27. MAKELA, CAROLE J., KAREN STEIN and JOSEPH N. UHL (1979), "The American Council on Consumer Interests: Its Activities and Future Development," Journal of Consumer Affairs, 13(No. 1; Summer):117-27.

28. MAYNES, E. SCOTT (1976), Decision-Making for Consumers, New York: Macmillan.

29. MCCARTHY, JOHN D. and MAYER N. ZALD (1973), The Trend of Social Movements in America: Professionalization and Resource Mobilization, Morristown, NJ: General Learning Press.

30. _________ (1977), "Resource Mobilization and Social Movements: A Partial Theory," American Journal of Sociology, 82(No. 6; May):1212-1240.

31. NADER, RALPH (1965), Unsafe at Any Speed: The Designed-In Dangers of the American Automobile, New York, NY: Grossman.

32. PERTSCHUK, MICHAEL (1982), Revolt Against Regulation: The Rise and Pause of the Consumer Movement, Berkeley and Los Angeles, CA: University of California Press.

33. RICHARDSON, LEE (1969), "Mass Communications and the Consumer Movement," in Lee Richardson (editor), Dimensions of Communication, New York: Appleton-Century-Crofts, 459-61.

34. SILBER, NORMAN ISAAC (1983), Test and Protest: The Influence of Consumers Union, New York: Holmes and Meier.

35. SMITH, DARLENE BRANNIGAN and PAUL N. BLOOM (1986), "Consumerism Dead or Alice? Some Empirical Evidence," in Paul N. Bloom and Ruth Belk Smith (editors), The Future of Consumerism, Lexington, Massachusetts: Lexington Books, 61-73.

36. SORENSEN, PHILIP C. (1972), Report to Consumers Union Regarding State and Local Consumer Organizations, unpublished report to Consumers Union, Board Mount Vernon, N.Y.: Consumers Union,

37. STANLEY, THOMAS J. and LARRY M. ROBINSON (1980), "Opinions on Consumer Issues: A Review of Recent Studies of Executives and Consumers," Journal of Consumer Affairs, 14(No. 1; Summer):207-20.

38. THORELLI, HANS B., HELMUT BECKER and JACK L. ENGLEDOW (1975), The Information Seekers: An International Study of Consumer Information and Advertising Image, Cambridge, MA: Ballinger Press.

39. WARLAND, REX H., ROBERT O. HERRMANN and DAN E. MOORE, "Consumer Activism, Community Activism, and the Consumer Movement," in Paul N. Bloom and Ruth Belk Smith (editors), The Future of Consumerism, Lexington, Massachusetts: Lexington Books, 85-95.

40. WARNE, COLSTON E. (1980), "Consumers Union's Contribution to the Consumer Movement," in Erma Angevine (editor), They Made a Difference: The History of Consumer Action Related by Leaders in the Consumer Movement, Washington, D.C.: National Consumers Committee for Research and Education, 150-200.

41. ________ (1980), "The Nader Network for Consumer Impact," in Erma Angevine (editor), They Made a Difference: The History of Consumer Action Related by Leaders in the Consumer Movement, Washington, D.C.: National Consumers Committee for Research and Education, 554-68.

42. WILLIAMS, JUAN (1982), "Return from the Nadir," Washington Post Magazine, (May 23, 1982):6-15.

ABOUT THE AUTHOR

Mitsuaki Imai is President of Kinjo Gakuin University and also Professor of Consumer Economics. Educated in Economics at Nagoya University, Imai has been at Kinjo Gakuin University since 1968. Imai has played a prominent role in the development of consumer education and the consumer movement in Japan. He is President of the Japan Academy of Consumer Education. He also serves as a Director of the Japan Consumers Association and the Consumer Information Center in the Economic Planning Agency in Tokyo. Imai is the author of The Thought of Consumerism (1972) and Principles of Consumer Education (1984).

WHY CONSUMER EDUCATION IN JAPAN?

Mitsuaki Imai

My purpose is to discuss the types of consumer problems that the Japanese face today and to stress why consumer education is so needed now.

The economic and social environments facing Japanese consumers today may be summarized as follows:

(1) An economy of slow growth;

(2) The practice of product differentiation, based on ephemeral product features;

(3) A loan society;

(4) A service economy;

(5) An aging society;

(6) A newmedia society;

(7) An internationalized society.

THE IMPLICATIONS FOR CONSUMER EDUCATION

Consumer education is needed more than ever as a means to solve these problems encountered by Japanese consumers. In a slow growth economy, for example, the competition to win a share of the economic pie is very stiff. Door-to-door selling grows rampantly with consumer problems increasing proportionately. Many consumers, especially senior citizens, are falling victim to unfair contracts and dubious business practices.

Product differentiation poses another consumer problem in a slow growth economy. When sellers purport to add "something" to the product that does not contribute to its quality of the product, it does increase prices! And it contributes to a negative correlation between the quality and the price of the product. This in turn produces a need for product test information.

Increasingly Japan is becoming a "service economy" as labor is transferred from the household to the service sector. This new service emphasis in the Japanese economy creates additional problems for consumers. There is a need for consumer education and for consumer protection with respect to the provision of services.

Ours is an aging society, in which many senior citizens are falling victims to fraudulent estate planning businesses. Of course, the government is seeking to regulate pyramid sales, door-to-door sales and so on. Realistically it is difficult for laws and regulations to catch up with these new and harmful sales practices. Again, this situation contributes to a need for consumer education.

Not too long ago life expectancy in Japan was only fifty years. In just a short period of time life expectancy has increased to eighty years!! The adaptation of Japanese consumers to an eighty-year life calls for a new component in consumer education. What is an appropriate lifestyle for a 80-year life expectancy, as compared with 50 years?

Home ownership; especially of a one-family home, is an important goal for Japanese consumers. However, due to the high cost of housing, particularly of land, many consumers take on large debts to finance home purchases. These large debts present the need for consumers to arrange their finances so that expenditures, including debt payments, bear a reasonable relationship to income over the entire life cycle. In February 1987, I organized -- with the help of the Japan Institute of Life Insurance -- a support system for personal financial planning that advises consumers on how to make those decisions and reach their goals. Our approach utilizes the method of "system dynamics" and simulation.

As far as the internationalization of the market is concerned, deregulation has introduced Japanese consumers to many fraudulent brand-name products. While the strong yen has brought down the price of many imported items, others have remained high due to the inefficient distribution system. Japanese consumers must develop the ability to distinguish which items have come down in price and represent good value for money from those which have not.

Because of government regulations, all banks in Japan currently offer the same interest rate. If financial institutions are deregulated, internationalization of banking and other industries should make wider choices available to Japanese consumers. With greater choice the need for consumer education would be greater than ever.

Rather than consumer education taking a passive, defensive rule as the discussion above suggests, I see the need for consumer education to take a more positive stance. Through consumer education, I would like to see an environment in which corporations adopt self-regulation as an avenue to free and fair competition.

IMPORTANT ISSUES FOR CONSUMER EDUCATION IN JAPAN

Consumer education in Japan faces several issues that must be resolved. Some are philosophical in nature, and others concern the methods employed in dealing with consumers.

The first issue concerns the development of consumer education in Japan. In America the direction of development has been from educators to consumer groups, to government and then to industry. The direction of development in Japan has been almost the exact opposite. During the period of high economic growth in the 1960's, it started first in industry, then went into government through the enactment of the Basic Law on Consumer Protection in 1968, then to the consumer and, most recently and finally, it has become a part of education.

The second point has to do with the concept of consumer education. In the last twenty years there has been much discussion about basic concepts, philosophy and ideals under such headings as "What is Consumer Education?" This discussion was summarized in the 15 "Questions and Answers" regarding the essence of consumer education that were compiled by the President's Committee on Consumer Interest (PCCI) that was convened in 1968 and 1969. Method is important in consumer education. But methods must reflect ideals. Further, there has to be interplay between ideals and reality. The extent to which consumer education and consumer information are the same or different was dealt with by the PCCI. Consumer information is a knowledge of facts, while consumer <u>education</u> is the development of the ability to make decisions. This distinction is basic for our thinking about "What is Consumer Education?"

The third important point is related to methods. This problem is one that naturally evolves out of the relation between method and concept. Education in Japan tends to be knowledge oriented, focusing too much on the accumulation of facts. This results in a reliance on "one-way" lectures with little discussion. In America the concept of "life experience education" has been used to develop the decision making ability of students. This approach has taken the form of simulation games and role-playing.

Japan has long had a strong central government in which the Japanese people have believed and on which they have relied heavily. This means the have had very limited experience with citizens' social action movements such as your Boston Tea Party. Consistent with this tradition, education has been dedicated to developing consumers who work faithfully in furtherance of industry and production. Japan is behind other countries in creating the kind of consumer who works for himself and in developing "consumer consciousness".

Let me discuss another consumer problem that arises from traditional Japanese ways. In Japan, it is not customary to sign a contract. We Japanese consider contracts unnecessary because human relations should be based on honor and on mutual understanding. This idea comes from the homogeneity of the Japanese culture. This might appear strange to Americans. In the United States, people enter a contract to avoid unnecessary trouble. In Japan, because people's relationships tend to be emotional rather than rational, consumers are unfamiliar with contracts and this produces problems. Often they have trouble "later on" with contracts, as in the case of door-to-door sales which are increasing in Japan. This is another reason why consumer education is a vital task.

Consumer education should make people aware of their role and responsibility in building up a democratic economy and society where consumers exercise intelligent economic "votes" in their daily living.

Consumer education should be a driving force in helping consumers to become less dependent and more important in our economy. To me, consumer education should not only provide one with the ability to be economically independent. It should help individual consumers to become well-rounded, independent persons, reflecting the importance of individual human lives.

REFERENCES

1. IMAI, MITSUAKI (1984), "Consumer Education in Japan -- From the Viewpoints of Thoughts and Methods," Journal of the Japan Academy of Consumer Education, No. 4.

ABOUT THE AUTHOR

Peter Sand is Chief Scientific Officer of Consumers' Association, London and Research Director of the Research Institute for Consumer Affairs. He did his undergraduate work at the University of Cape Town and received a Master's in Social Research from the University of Surrey. His entire career has been with CA, starting as a project officer in 1963. Sand was instrumental in setting up CA's key research departments--the Survey Unit and the Laboratory. He has been a long-serving member of the IOCU Testing Committee and recently helped author the IOCU publication, The Principles of Comparative Testing.

CONSUMER ORGANIZATIONS AND REPRESENTATION IN THE DEVELOPED WORLD

Peter Sand

COMPARATIVE TESTING AND PRODUCT STANDARDS

My own perspective stems from my work over more than 20 years for Consumers' Association[1], perhaps more widely known by the name of its magazine "Which?"; from my involvement with European consumer organizations as Secretary of the European Testing Group (ETG)[2] and with IOCU[3] and BEUC.[4]

---

[1]Consumers' Association: the British consumer organization, publishes Which?, Holiday Which?, and Gardening from Which? as well as books. Total membership about 785.000. Address: 14 Buckingham Street, London WC2N 6DS, UK.

[2]European Testing Group: A group of 16 consumer organizations in Europe from 14 countries which meets three times a year to agree on a program of joint tests. Address: ETG Secretary: Peter Sand, 14 Buckingham Street, London WC2N 6DS, UK.

[3]IOCU: International Organization of Consumers' Unions, founded in 1960, with a membership of more than 160 consumer organizations from fifty countries worldwide. IOCU coordinates the skills and experiences of consumer groups around the world through information networks, seminars, workshops, etc. Address: Emmastraat 9, 2595 EG The Hague, Netherlands.

[4]BEUC: Bureau European des Unions de Consommateurs. European consortium of consumer organizations in the European community. BEUC pursues its aims through studies, contact with the European Commission officials, representation on the Consumer

Two of the main challenges which face consumer organizations today are:

- to provide good, comprehensive, independent information about consumer products and services

- to campaign effectively for better standards, for better trading practices and for better consumer protection over a wide field covering almost every aspect of daily life.

Comparative Testing

Product information based on independent comparative tests is the foundation stone for the work of most consumer organizations in Europe. For consumer organizations dependent on the income from the sale of their publications, the provision of topical, comprehensive and useful information about consumer products is a *sine qua non*.

Surprisingly, the nature of some of the problems of providing good information have not changed significantly since the days when consumer organizations were first set up.

First, there is the need for good test methods. Consumer organizations have developed great skill and scientific sophistication in designing and carrying out tests, to the extent that they can hold their own in discussions with manufacturers about technical aspects of product performance.

But some of the fundamental problems remain. The first, predictably, is *cost*. Routine test costs (that is the laboratory testing alone, *not* sample and associated research and editorial costs) on washing machines can be more than 2000 ($3,300) a sample in the UK and even more in some other countries; on a camera 1000 ($1,650) a sample. This means inevitably that even the richest organizations can rarely afford to test more than one sample of each variety, or brand-model, of a product. Elaborate and largely effective procedures have been devised for detecting and avoiding misleading results based on atypical samples. Nonetheless, there remains the small possibility that atypical samples may mislead the testing organization and its readers.

Consultative Committee of the European Commission and by lobbying the European Parliament and Economic and Social Committee of the EEC. Address: Rue Royale 29, Bte 3, B-1000 Bruxelles, Belgium.

A further limitation is that the very high costs of skilled laboratory staff time put great pressure on research staff to cut down the number and extensiveness of the tests themselves.

There is also a considerable pressure to standardize tests. This comes as a result of an internally generated need for reports to be consistent over time. It also arises from external pressures from manufacturers and official institutions which would like to control the work of consumer organizations.

Pressure from government organizations is obviously greater on consumer organizations such as Stiftung Warentest which receive subsidies from government. Wholly private organizations such as CA have so far resisted being straitjacketed into reporting only the results of standardized tests. There are great advantages to be gained from the use of good "standard" test methods. Unfortunately, standards institutions have largely failed to produce satisfactory, relevant and comprehensive test methods. Hence consumer organizations have had to devise their own tests. The failure of the standards organizations to produce test methods which meet the needs of consumer bodies is probably due to the shortsightedness of government and industry which have left standards-making to the voluntary effort of manufacturers. The vacuum cleaner provides an example of failure. Even three quarters of a century after its invention, laboratories, scientific institutes and standards bodies have still failed to devise test methods that give performance information with the desired degree of repeatability and relevance. This for a product whose technology has virtually stood still!

A general improvement in the safety and performance of established consumer goods is clearly to be welcomed, as is a decrease in the relative price of many consumer goods in relation to the cost of living. Indeed consumer organizations have contributed to that. Paradoxically, this also presents difficulties for product-testing organizations in terms of consumer testing and information. The fact that most washing machines (for example) wash well and are electrically safe means that exhaustive (and expensive) tests on performance and safety yield diminishing returns to both product-testing organizations and their readers. But does that imply that performance and safety can be taken on trust? Unfortunately not, since there may always be some makes of washing machines that wash ineffectively and do not meet safety standards in all respects. This forces a compromise on consumer organizations. They will probably do less performance testing e.g., tests of washing effectiveness and safety, and more examination of features, convenience and reliability.

Now the relatively low cost of many appliances gives the consumer a chance to "test" things by experience without incurring great losses or harm. In my judgement, consumer organizations should no longer devote resources and space in their magazines on tests of "cheaper" products such as electric toasters or kettles. (These now cost less than the price of a meal for one person in a medium-priced restaurant!)

A further modern phenomenon in the consumer market of the developed world is the problem of brand and model proliferation. As the champions of consumer choice, consumers and their organizations can hardly complain if choice for some products has become almost overwhelming. Some of the increase in choice is specious, composed of a large number of makes and models which, though basically similar, may have only small differences in performance and features. In the case of cars, it may be possible for the consumer to decide for himself which of the many available variants of a car will best suit his budget and aspirations. With domestic appliances an intelligent assessment and choice between all the small differences may not be possible. For consumer product testing organizations the existence of basically similar products produced by one manufacturer and sold in a number of varying forms under different labels presents an almost insurmountable problem. The organization faces a nasty dilemma: it can either take it on trust that the differences are too small to matter, or it can engage in much expensive and repetitive testing to find the answer.

How have consumer organizations responded to these inherent difficulties in comparative testing? One answer to the problem of the high cost of testing is for consumer organizations in different countries to engage in joint testing as they are doing in the European Testing Group (ETG). In ETG approximately 25 projects are conducted jointly by 4 or more organizations each year, and 45 by two or three organizations. For a few projects joint testing has encompassed more than one region. In 1980, consumer organizations from 14 countries collaborated on tests of 35 mm cameras. Obviously the joint testing is beneficial only if there is a reasonable degree of overlap in the brand-models offered in different national markets. This is more likely for photographic and some electronic goods than other types of products where there are still marked national differences. Joint testing strengthens consumer clout. When manufacturers that know results of tests will be published in several countries, they are more likely to sit up and take notice. Joint testing also means that consumer organizations will meet and agree on common test methods. This may put them ahead of the field in producing better tests. Joint testing can help smaller organizations by drastically reducing the cost of testing.

A partial answer to the problem of the need to standardize tests is for consumer organizations to produce their own test methods and use these as 'standards.' This has been done for some products by the ETG. These methods can be produced more quickly than by standardization bodies and can be reviewed periodically. This is only a partial answer because consumer organizations themselves lack the resources to develop good test methods for the wide range of products tested. Unfortunately no one else seems ready to devote the resources to this problem on the scale that is needed.

In my judgement there has been a good response by consumer organizations to such developments as changes in the quality and efficiency of products, the relative cheapness, and the increasing number of similar makes and models. Consumer organizations have found ways of improving the character of information provided (often after careful research among readers) so that it is more useful to consumers. The current emphasis on "What to look for," now a recognized genre of report in European product testing magazines, may be more helpful than a catalogue of test results although the two complement one another. Some consumer organizations have taken the bold and controversial step of listing the features and specifications of models they have not been able to test, thus making it possible for the reader to choose from practically all the models available, not just those that could be tested at the time. (Sometimes the tested models represent only a small part of the market.)

Product Standards

Product standards consist of the specification of minimum requirements of important dimensions of products, e.g., performance, safety, ergonomics, fitness for purpose. Consumer organizations have always been concerned about product standards. Indeed, for many consumer organizations the improvement of product standards is a formal aim, included in the organization's constitution. What commends product standards is that they affect all brands, not just those that are tested. The difficulty with standards is that they require consensus and are legislated by committees populated by highly diverse interests. Hence, standards take a long time to be produced even in a single country. For international standards, it is worse. For some products, standards have been under discussion for 15 years without reaching a satisfactory conclusion! Obviously such long delays may sometimes suit manufacturers since they can postpone almost indefinitely the adaptation of their products to meet such standards.

Although many consumer organizations actively campaign for better standards and participate on standards committees, it is doubtful whether existing standards procedures in most countries really reflect consumer interests.

There are a number of reasons for this. First, product standards at the international level are chiefly seen by governments as means of removing technical barriers to trade. This is particularly true in Europe where the EEC Commission is trying to sweep away national differences in product standards to achieve a common market. This usually means that the lowest standard in member countries prevails. Thus specific consumer protection measures painfully achieved in particular countries over many years may be sacrificed.

The situation is changing slowly. Perhaps by the next century better ways will have been found to make the consumer voice heard in the standards-making process.

At the international level - IEC[5] and ISO[6] - the making of standards is very much controlled by the multinational and big manufacturers. Consumer organizations lack the resources to participate effectively though there is nominal representation on some committees, either from national consumer organizations or IOCU.

Nonetheless, consumer organizations are quite active in standardization. Consumers' Association, for instance, sends representatives to about 50 different committees in the UK. Many other consumer organizations are similarly involved in their national standards committees. Internationally, IOCU has sent observers to a number of committees dealing with consumer products. In Europe BEUC, with some help from the EEC Commission, has started to coordinate the work of consumer observers on CEN[7] and CENELEC[8]

---

[5]IEC: The International Electrotechnical Commission. The main international standardization body for electrical and electronic goods.

[6]ISO: The International Organization for Standardization. The main international standardization body for other goods.

[7]CEN: The European Committee for Standardization comprises national standards bodies of 17 EEC and EFTA countries.

committees. A number of European countries have consumer policy or advisory committees within their standards institutes. These promote the consumer viewpoint in committees, liaising with other consumer organizations and advising the boards of the standards institutes. In some countries, e.g., the USA, ad hoc consumer panels have been set up. Progress in standards committees is slow. In the future consumer representatives may do better to devote their effort to international standards rather than to national ones. To do this effectively consumer policy and advisory committees which can operate at an international level will need to be set up and funded. At present it is not clear where the funds for such work will come from.

The main purpose of international standardization has been to remove technical barriers to trade. In Europe this means that it is increasingly difficult to impose effective mandatory standards. This is an added disincentive to consumer organizations to spend time on standards. Should the consumer organizations manage to improve the standards, it may still be possible for manufacturers to ignore them! Fortunately, the more established manufacturers take consumer safety seriously and comply voluntarily with the safety standards that exist. My view on the prospects for international standards is encapsulated in the old joke about a camel "being a horse designed by a committee." If in the 1980's a committee was set up, to develop an international standard for "horses" it is unlikely that they would get further than defining the first hump by the end of the century. Future generations of consumers may have to make do with one-humped camels instead of the two-humped models!

---

[8]CENELEC: The European Committee for Electrotechnical Standardization. The electrotechnical counterpart of CEN, comprises the national committee of EEC and EFTA countries.

ABOUT THE AUTHOR

Jean-Pierre Allain is Special Assistant in the Penang Office of the International Organization of Consumers Unions. For further biographical information, see Headnote in Chapter 18.

CONSUMER ORGANIZATION AND REPRESENTATION IN DEVELOPING COUNTRIES

Jean-Pierre Allain

The consumer movement in developing countries had its origins in the 1960s, notably in Asia, with concerns similar to those of consumers in industrialized countries.

Consumer organizers in developing countries soon realized, however, that in conditions of poverty and underdevelopment, price and quality of goods and services are concerns for only few consumers. Therefore, they became much more involved in addressing the more pressing problems of the day, such basic needs as health, safety, and the environment.

It is usually the more recently established consumer organizations that are working on these issues. The older organizations, notably women's and housewives' associations, have usually emphasized consumer education and protection programs. Increasingly, some of these, too, are becoming involved in health, safety and the environment.

TYPOLOGY OF CONSUMER GROUPS

A rough typology of consumer groups in developing countries would include the following:

(1) Housewive's or Women's Associations, usually more conservative with a membership gathered from the upper and middle classes;

(2) Traditional Consumer Organizations, dealing with testing of quality and with price comparisons;

(3) Government-Sponsored Consumer Protection Agencies, and

(4) Consumer "Activist" Groups, usually engaged in issue-oriented activities and campaigns.

These are not water-tight categories. Some organizations belong to more than one category.

The most exciting development in the consumer movement of the Third World in the past ten or so years is the realization by many organizers and consumers that the struggle for a better deal for consumers is an integral part of other movements: (1) the development movement; (2) the struggle for liberation from economic oppression and of efforts to achieve self-reliance. Third World consumers are in a different position from their counterparts in industrialized countries who, in their early stages of development, did not face the same avalanche of new products and technologies.

There are a number of government-sponsored consumer agencies in developing countries. Usually modeled on similar bodies in industrialized countries, they also frequently engage in consumer "activist" campaigning. They recognize that there is a huge task of educating consumers plunged abruptly into a modern world, in addition to protecting consumers through legislative and other means.

AN OVERVIEW BY REGIONS

A brief overview of the consumer movement in developing continents would give the following picture:

In Asia the consumer movement developed rapidly between 1965 and 1980 with new groups being formed in Malaysia, Taiwan, Indonesia, India, Sri Lanka, Thailand, the Philippines, Bangladesh, Singapore and Korea. In some countries already existing women's associations embarked on consumer education and protection programs while governments set up their own consumer agencies. Now many of these groups are going through a phase of consolidation and the rate of formation of new groups has slowed. In Malaysia alone there are 11 consumer associations, including the largest and most successful Third World consumer organization--the Consumers Association of Penang (CAP). Some of the consumer movement's ideas, ideals and actions are being spread by such "consumer" organizations as health and environment groups. Some of these later evolved into full-fledged consumer associations.

In Latin America, with many countries under dictatorial regimes in the 60s and 70s, there occurred widespread suppression of freedom of expression and association, with the result that the consumer movement developed later there. However, some women's associations, such as the Liga de Amas de Casa de Argentina, had been engaged in consumer education for a long time. Another exception is Mexico, where an independent consumer association was established in the early 70s and became so influential that it persuaded the government to establish its own consumer institute and a large consumer complaint agency.

Since the early 80s, the swing back to democratic regimes has given great impetus to the growth of the environmental and popular movements, particularly in poor urban areas. At the same time, the deep economic recession through which most of the continent has been going for more than a decade has made all groups poorer, including the middle class which has the ability to organize and to provide leadership in organizations. Together these two trends have produced a flowering of the consumer movement. New consumer groups have appeared in Argentina, Brazil, Uruguay, Peru, Colombia, Venezuela, Chile, Ecuador, Costa Rica, Guatemala and the Dominican Republic. In the English-speaking Caribbean (part of Latin America) some small consumer organizations have existed for a long time. Unfortunately their development has been hampered by financial difficulties and by the smallness of their countries.

Africa's consumer movement is still in an early stage. Nigeria and Kenya have had rather weak and ineffective consumer associations for several years. In Africa, as in Asia, groups working on health and environment issues are taking a holistic view of their goals and see themselves more and more as consumer protection organizations. New consumer groups have sprung up in Zimbabwe, Mauritius, Zambia, Kenya and Sierra Leone. The French and Portuguese-speaking countries are still far behind. Recently though, an African French-language magazine on consumer issues has appeared and is beginning to create some awareness among consumers.

IOCU AND THESE DEVELOPMENTS

The strong worldwide leadership of the International Organization of Consumers Unions (IOCU) has contributed to the integration of consumer organizations representing both industrialized and developing countries. Many consumer associations from the industrialized countries have given financial and technical support to the new organizations in developing countries, thus helping to fulfill one of IOCU's main objectives.

An innovation for the consumer movement since the late 1970s, has been its joining forces with other citizens groups organized through worldwide networks, thus amplifying the influence of all. This has been particularly true in developing countries and at the international level, the strategy being largely due to the vision and leadership of former IOCU President Anwar Fazal.

The role in consumer organizations in protecting consumers and in promoting a more harmonious, balanced economic development is now widely recognized by governments and by other organizations in both developing and industrialized countries. The consumer movement is also exerting a considerable influence within international bodies such as the United Nations. A recent illustration is the adoption of the UN Guidelines for Consumer Protection [1]. These guidelines are helpful to the consumer movement in promoting consumer legislation and protection in developing countries and also in tackling international consumer problems.

It is impossible to separate the problems of consumers in developing countries from those of industrialized countries. Many problems have their origins in products, services or habits that "travel" via international trade from industrialized countries to the rest of the world. Their solution requires cooperation by consumer organizations in all countries and by all governments. Research into the problems of consumers and consumerism in developing countries will hasten the solutions of these problems.

REFERENCES

1. GUIDELINES FOR CONSUMER PROTECTION (1986), United Nations, New York: DIESA.

ABOUT THE AUTHOR

Marie A. Orsini is Program Manager at the Center for Applied Studies in International Negotiations (CASIN) in Geneva. As Program Manager, she supervises research, organizes seminars, and produces studies and reports, all dealing with the impact of non-governmental organizations like those in the consumer movement on the international "system." Orsini received Bachelor's and Master's degrees in Political Science from the University of Grenoble and has done graduate work at the Graduate Institute of International Studies in Geneva. Before joining CASIN in 1985, Orsini was an assistant officer with the UN Center for Human Rights.

CONSUMER POLICY AND THE EUROPEAN ECONOMIC COMMUNITY (EEC)

Marie Antoinette Orsini

THE CONSUMER INTEREST AND EEC

When the Treaty of Rome established the European Economic Community (EEC) in 1957, it was thought that the best way governments could ensure the well-being of the people and their future was by expanding the economy, boosting trade and avoiding impediments to trade. The primary goal of the EEC was, and remains, the elimination of barriers to trade and investment among its member states. By design, EEC was to increase the free flow of goods and factors of production among member states and to develop common policies in certain areas. A consumer policy as such did not at that time constitute a primary objective for the establishment of an EEC.

The Community was given the authority to pass laws binding member states and preempting contrary national legislations. In principle, EEC can even require member countries to harmonize their national laws. "In the European system, harmonization means bringing national laws into agreement with common European approaches" [3]. While the Community has the legal authority to develop a community wide system of consumer law and policy, this power has been used sparingly. One can still say that the protection provided for consumers in the twelve member states essentially derives from national laws, the only possible exception being the future consumer policy of the most recent entrants--Greece, Spain and Portugal.

The first move by the Commission to recognize consumer interests came in 1962 when the Contact Committee for Consumer Questions, which lasted 10 years, was set up to represent consumers within the Common Market. This Committee was replaced in 1968 by a new "Consumer Affairs" unit within the Competition Directorate. With the entrance into EEC of the UK, Ireland and Denmark in 1972, the heads of state met in Paris and stated that "effective action in the social sphere has the same importance as the achievement of economic and monetary union" and that consumers and producers should have a greater role to play in the Community's decision-making on economic and social policy.

The Treaty of Rome makes no explicit mention of a consumer protection policy. Nonetheless, certain provisions of the Treaty furnished a legal basis for creating the Directorate General XI (DGXI), a special service to deal with environmental consumer protection and nuclear safety. One basis was the Preamble of the Treaty which states that one of the Community's basic objectives is "the constant improvement of the living and working conditions of their peoples." Article 39, dealing with the Common Agricultural Policy, lists among its objectives the assured availability of supplies and stabilization of markets and specifies that the aim of the policy is to "ensure that supplies reach consumers at reasonable prices." Article 86 cites as an example of abuse the practices of "limiting production, markets or technical development to the prejudice of consumers."

DGXI was created in 1973 and, along with it, the Consumer Consultative Committee (CCC). CCC consists of four organizations representing consumer interests: the Bureau Européen d'Union des Consommateurs (BEUC), The Committee of Family Organizations in the Community (COFACE), the European Community of Consumer Cooperatives (EUROCOOP) and the European Trade Union Confederation (ETUC).

In 1975 the first "Programme of the European Economic Community for a consumer protection and information policy" was adopted. Representing the most advanced thinking on consumer policy, it recognized five Consumer Rights to: Health Protection and Safety; Protection of Economic Interests; Redress; Information and Education, and Representation (the Right to be Heard).

A second program was adopted in May 1981 at the initiative of the Council of Ministers. It stressed the importance of "a better dialogue" and proposed "increasing consultation" between representatives of consumers, producers and distributors. This program put less emphasis on direct government intervention and encouraged more use of voluntary industry codes of conduct. This second program, adopted before the first had achieved, reflected a concern over the deepening of the world recession of the early

1980's. The program expressed concern over the falling purchasing power of the consumer and the need to help consumers make the maximum use of their incomes. Therefore the Commission planned to monitor the prices and quality of goods and services more assiduously than ever before and to ensure that the interests of consumers were taken into account in other community policies, e.g., community agricultural policy, competition and industrial policies.

ECC INSTITUTIONS DEALING WITH CONSUMERS

The EEC institutions dealing with consumer affairs are the Commission, the European Parliament, the Council of Ministers and the European Court of Justice. Major policies are routed through "directives." These directives are legislative acts which, according to Article 189 of the Treaty of Rome, require member states to make changes in their national laws within a specified time. The directive expresses a common objective but leaves to the member states the choice of form and methods to the member nations. The adoption of a directive involves three steps. First, the Commission drafts its proposal after consulting CCC. The draft directive goes next to the European Parliament for an opinion and finally to the Council of Ministers for adoption or rejection.

The consumer section of the Commission within DG-XI is a rather small unit composed of only 12 professional staff members. It is responsible not only for implementing the consumer program but also for ensuring that consumers' interests are taken into account in other policies. Though it can initiate actions, it has only done so sporadically. When regular meetings of the Ministers of Consumer Affairs were organized in 1983, the Commission started putting forward more consumer proposals.

The initially high momentum of the Parliament within the Committee on the Environment, Public Health and Consumer Protection faded quickly, largely due to the absence of proposals from the Commission.

The Council carries the real blame for the deplorable lack of achievement in the European consumer policy these past 10 years. This failure is due to its infrequent meetings, its very slow decision-making process, and overcautious government representatives. (Paradoxically, most of the problem is caused by the most "advanced" countries in the area of consumer protection -- UK, Germany and Denmark.)

The European Court of Justice plays a prominent role, monitoring the application and interpretation of Community Law.

The Court has often revealed the protectionist motivations behind certain supposedly consumer protection laws. Thus, on many occasions, it has been highly sensitive to consumer protection and health concerns.

THE EEC RECORD ON CONSUMER POLICY

The 10th anniversary of the consumer program in 1985 occasioned various comments on the Commission's activities. Most in the European Community agreed that the Commission's achievements fell short of expectations. Some critics characterized them as a "failure." Expressions of disappointment appeared even in the Commission's own report to the Council, which bore the title "A New Impetus for Consumer Protection Policy." A major excuse for the limited achievements was the deep economic recession of the decade, reflected in the decrease in the rate of economic growth from 4.6% in 1970 to -0.3% in 1981. This argument implicitly accepts the "promotion and protection of consumer interests as an activity to be pursued only when times are good... a fair weather phenomenon."

In addition, some are reluctant to support a community consumer policy due to their belief that legislation for consumer affairs is the domain of individual governments. Another obstacle has been that legislation concerning health and safety is perceived as an obstacle to the free movement of goods. Moreover, too many of the directives proposed and adopted -- See Appendix I-- prescribe rules for a restricted range of goods and ingredients. The negotiating process for these directives is highly technical and subject to strong producer lobbying. Therefore, progress is slow. In my view emphasis should be shifted to directives of a general nature to avoid recapitulation of similar negotiations pertaining to each individual product or category.

Articles 100 and 235 of the Treaty require unanimous votes for a law to be adopted. This has slowed progress on consumer issues. As an example, the Directive on Product Liability which was adopted in July, 1985 was first proposed in 1976! Moreover, a minor Directive on Doorstep Selling, adopted also in the second half of 1985, had been proposed in 1977. Adoption was slowed by the stolid and incomprehensible resistance of Germany, one of the few countries not to have legislation in this area. More frequent meetings of the Council for Consumer Affairs would accelerate and improve the decision making process within the community. Currently, the scheduling of these meetings depends too much on the goodwill of the President at the time.

The existence of pending draft directives at EEC has even served as a reason or pretext for delaying reforms in national laws. Similarly, the EEC goal of total harmonization has been used to postpone the adoption of reforms in member countries. Harmonization would force member countries with advanced legislation in certain fields to regress. In my judgement the Commission should adopt "minimal" directives that set out common standards, but leave individual countries the freedom to adopt stronger measures if they so wish.

There are two basic approaches to legal consumer protection. The traditional liberal approach views the functioning of the market as a "game" and the state as the referee whose role is to enforce the rules. Individuals enforce their rights in the courts. An alternative approach recognizes the need for direct forms of government intervention such as direct regulation of product quality and safety, continuing regulation of market activity by specialized agencies, the creation of more effective mechanisms for redress and expanded consumer participation in government decision making. Most of the twelve nations of the European Community agree on the need to go beyond the liberal approach. But they differ greatly as to which policy areas should be given priority. Some would give more emphasis to control of quality and safety in consumer goods, others to consumer credit. EEC member states vary substantially with respect to economic wealth and also have different legal traditions. Different constitutional structures make it difficult to reach unanimous agreements. So, too, do their different approaches to consumer protection. Some countries use administrative and criminal law while others rely on civil law. Some, like Denmark and the United Kingdom rely more on industry self regulation and voluntary 'codes of conduct' for business while others rely more heavily on the court system.

Consumer policy at the European level is linked to the implementation of a single EEC domestic market where the Four Freedoms of Movement of (1) people, (2) goods and (3) services and (4) capital, combined with competition, are intended to serve the needs of European citizens. The deadline for agreeing and implementing the main legislative proposals on consumer safety and rights is 1992, by which time it is planned to achieve a single EEC market.[1] In 1985, aware of the need for a "new impetus for

---

[1]The necessary steps to achieve the unification of the Common Market have been described in the "White Book" published by the Commission in 1985 during the presidency of Mr. Delors [COM (85)

consumer policy," the Commission set out policy guidelines with a detailed program to be completed by 1988. The political argument in favor of a consumer policy is that it concerns the daily life of 270 million people. The principal lines of action for the promotion and protection of consumer's interests can be stated as follows: (1) Products traded in the community should conform to acceptable health and safety standards; (2) Consumers must be able to benefit from the common market; (3) Consumers' interests should be taken into account in other community policies. The program proposed by the Commission in its communication to the Council, "A New Impetus to Consumer Protection Policy,"--See Appendix 2--needs translation into specific actions.

It is in the area of health and safety standards that EEC's effectiveness has been best established. Even here, specific legislation limited to particular goods has been insufficient to bring about a comprehensive EEC policy for product safety. The Commission faces the constant dilemma of conflicting objectives between a safe market and a free market. The new approach to technical harmonization of standards allows products for which safety requirements can be specified in common to be grouped together in Council directives. CEN/CENELEC, the European standards organizations, have been requested by the Commission to prepare common EEC standards that will become mandatory. Pending the completion of common European standards, existing national standards which satisfy the mandatory requirements will be circulated in the Community. The Community now operates a system under which a member state must first notify the Commission of proposed new standards or regulations. The Commission in turn notifies all other member states (Council Directive of March 1983). The Commission may order a stay of adoption of new measures if it believes they will create new barriers to trade and will cause further divergence between member states in technical specification for goods including consumer goods."

<u>The Matter of Dangerous Products</u>

A major achievement in the area of health was the creation in 1984 of the Early Warning System on Dangerous Products which so far has been relatively ineffective. In 1985 the Commission initiated a Data Bank on Domestic Accidents. The same year, the Directive on Product Liability was finally adopted after having been delayed by the UK, Italy and Germany. Member governments have three years to implement this Directive. The effectiveness of these tools

---

310 Final].

would be improved if the CCC legislation on product recalls passes. With regards to child safety, the toy Directive is still being held up by the European Parliament. It seems likely that the Commission will propose safety standards for children's equipment and measures to improve child safety at home. In June 1986 a conference was held in The Hague to develop a "multiannual program for consumer safety and for home and leisure accident prevention in the European Community, 1987 - 1991." Thus the debate to produce a general directive on consumer product safety appears to be underway. Several directives deal with the labelling, packaging and composition of foodstuffs. Traditionally a technical barrier to trade in foodstuffs resulting from mandatory national provisions could be eliminated by adopting a Community legislation of the same nature. The key directive in this area is the one on Labelling, Presentation and Advertising on Foodstuffs. Due to some 40 derogations and options, it allows member states to choose very divergent interpretations in its implementation. An EEC nutritional labelling scheme should be introduced in order to avoid further fragmentation of the market and confusion on the part of consumers. In late 1985 the Commission sent to the council a formal communication outlining its thoughts on how best to achieve the completion of the EEC internal market on foodstuff by 1992.

Several measures have been taken relating to the protection of the economic interests of the consumer. A directive relating to misleading advertising was adopted in 1984. It was designed to deal also with "unfair" advertising. Unfortunately during the negotiations member states could not agree on the definition of "unfair." Now preparatory work is being done to find a satisfactory definition. The Commission is also committed to a directive dealing with comparative advertising. This year a directive covering broadcasting advertising and copyright should be proposed. So far nothing has been achieved in setting European standards for consumer credit that would improve the transparency of credit terms, and in particular, the real cost of credit. Nor has anything been done with standard contract forms to protect the consumer against unfair contracts. While supporting access to courts for redress of consumer grievances, the Community has taken little concrete action in this area. As to consumer education in schools, the Commission has done a lot of research, but has not tried to establish "standard" European programs for consumer education in schools. As the result of a pilot school project, a series of conclusions were reached by the Commission in a draft resolution on education in primary and secondary schools which was forwarded to the Council. Finally, to complete this sketch of consumer policy in EEC, we should mention the special effort made in regard to price posting for common consumer goods. In 1979 the Council adopted a directive concerning the compulsory posting of the prices of food. Another directive, now being discussed, would apply similar requirements to non-food products.

SUMMARY

The European Community institutions have encountered many obstacles in trying to integrate consumer policy. These obstacles are chargeable to the dual concerns of (1) opening of borders to trade, and (2) protecting the consumer. An added difficulty is the lack of machinery to implement law at the European level. One should also note difficulties arising from the very small consumer representation in EEC. BEUC is the only organization that effectively (and beyond its capacities!)--represents the consumer movement at the European Community. One wonders how consumer representation can be increased in EEC while at the same time EEC representatives in EEC seek to respect, stimulate and base themselves on the ever important national consumer movements. One wonders, too, how to improve collaboration and cooperation with other organizations like COFACE and EUROCOOP which pretend to represent the consumers' interest.

APPENDIX I

PRINCIPAL INSTRUMENTS CONCERNING CONSUMER PROTECTION ADOPTED BY THE COUNCIL SINCE 1975

- Directive 75/318/EEC of 20 May 1975 on the approximation of the Laws of Member States relating to analytical, pharmaco-toxicological and clinical standards and protocols in respect of the testing of propriety medicinal products (OJ N° L 147, 9.6.1975)

- Directive 76/211/EEC of 20 January 1976 relating to the making-up by weight or by volume of certain prepackaged products (OJ N° L 46, 21.1.1976)

- Directive 76/621/EEC of 20 July 1976 relating to the fixing of the maximum level of erucic acid oils and fats intended as such for human consumption and in foodstuffs containing added oils or fats (OJ N° L 202, 28.7.1976)

- Directive 76/769/EEC of 27 July 1976 relating to restrictions on the marketing and use of certain dangerous substances and preparations (OJ N° L 262, 27.9.1976)

- Directive 76/768/EEC of 27 July 1976 relating to cosmetic products (OJ N° L 262,27.9.1976)

- Directive 76/893/EEC of 23 November 1976 relating to materials and articles intended to come into contact with foodstuffs (OJ N° L 340, 9.12.1976)

- Directive 76/895/EEC of 23 November 1976 relating to the fixing of maximum levels for pesticide residues in and on fruit and vegetables (OJ N° L 340, 9.12.1976)

- Directive 77/94/EEC of 21 December 1976 relating to foodstuffs for particular nutritional uses (OJ N° L 26, 31.1.1977)

- Directive 77/728/EEC of 7 November 1977 relating to the classification, packaging and labelling of paints, varnishes, printing inks, adhesives and similar products (OJ N° L 303, 28.11.1977)

- Directive 78/25/EEC of 12 December 1977 on the approximation of the laws of the Member States relating to the coloring matters which may be added to medicinal products (OJ N° L 11, 14.1,1978)

- Directive 78/142/EEC of 30 January 1978 relating to materials and articles which contain vinyl chloride monomer and are intended to come into contact with foodstuffs (OJ N° L 44, 15.2.1978)

- Directive 78/631/EEC of 26 June 1978 relating to the classification, packaging and labelling of dangerous preparations (Pesticides) (OJ N° L 206, 29.7.1978)

- Directive 78/663/EEC of 25 July 1978 laying down specific criteria of purity for emulsifiers, stabilizers, thickeners and jelling agents for use in foodstuffs (OJ N° L 223, 14.8.1978)

- Directive 78/664/EEC of 25 July 1978 laying down specific criteria of purity for antioxidants which may be used in foodstuffs intended for human consumption (OJ N° L 223, 14.8.1978)

- Directive 79/112/EEC of 18 December 1978 relating to the labelling, presentation and advertising of foodstuffs for sale to the ultimate consumer (OJ N° L 33, 8.2.1979)

- Directive 79/530/EEC and 79/531/EEC of 14 May 1979 on the indication by labelling of the energy consumption of household appliances (OJ N° L 145, 13.6.1979)

- Directive 79/581/EEC of 19 June 1979 on consumer protection in the indication of the prices of foodstuffs (OJ N° L 158, 26.6.1979)

- Directive 79/693/EEC of 24 July 1979 relating to fruit jams, jellies and marmalades and chestnut puree (OJ N° L 205, 13.8.1979)

- Directive 80/232/EEC of 15 January 1980 relating to the ranges of nominal quantities and nominal capacities permitted for certain prepackaged products (OJ N° L 51, 25.2.1980)

- Council Decision 84/133/EEC introducing a Community system for the rapid exchange of information on dangers arising from the use of consumer products (OJ L 70, 13.3.1984)

- Council Directive 84/450/EEC relating to the approximation of the laws, regulations and administrative provisions of the Mmber States concerning misleading advertising (OJ L 250, 19.91984)

APPENDIX II

TIMETABLE FOR THE EXECUTION OF ACTIONS: PROPOSED EXTRACT OF "A NEW IMPETUS FOR CONSUMER PROTECTION POLICY" [4]

	Proposal/ action	Adoption by the Council
Product Safety		
1. Report on general obligation to market safe products	1986	
2. Directive on counterfeit products	1987	1989
3. See Part Two of the Timetable annexed to the White Paper on Completing the Internal Market		

Information Campaigns

4. Campaign for child safety	1986/87	
5. Campaign for product safety	1987/88	

Protection of Economic Interests

6. Directive on unfair contract terms	1987	1989
7. Directive on calculating the rate of charge for consumer credit	1986	1988
8. Directive on unfair and comparative advertising	1987	1989
9. Proposal on new information technology affecting consumers	1988	1990
10. Proposal on electronic funds transfer	1987	1989
11. Proposals on guarantees and after-sales service	1986	1988
12. Directive on package tours	1985	1987
13. Report on public services	1985	

Information

14. Trans-border price surveys	ongoing from 1985	
15. Publication of guide on consumer rights to buy goods in other countries	1986	
16. Directive on price indications for services	1986	1988

Education

17.	Resolution on consumer education	1985	1986
18.	Publication of teaching manual on consumer education (in collaboration with national authorities)	1986	
19.	Report on pilot experiences in teacher training for consumer education	1988	

REFERENCES

1. BOURGOIGNIE, THIERRY (1982), "European Community Consumer Law: Actual Achievements and Potential for the Future," European Consumer Law: Prospect for Integration of Consumer Law and Policy Within the European Community. Bourgoignie T. (Ed.), Louvain la Neuve, Belgium: Centre de Droit de la Consommation.

2. BUREAU EUROPEEN D'UNION DES CONSOMMATEURS (BEUC) (1985), "A Sop to BEUC of a Genuine Commitment by the Commission," BEUC News, Special Dossier, No. 46, Brussels, July.

3. COMMISSION OF THE EUROPEAN COMMUNITIES (1985), "European Unification and Development," Bulletin of the European Community, 3, p. 27.

4. _________ (1986), "A New Impetus for Consumer Protection Policy," Bulletin of the European Communities, suppl. June.

5. _________ (1985), "Achievement of the Internal Market," COM (85) 310 Final, Brussels, Juin 14.

6. _________ (1985), "European Unification," European Documentation, Periodical, March.

7. KRAMER, L. (1986), EEC Consumer Law, Story Scientia, Collection Droit et Consommation, Brussels, pp. 432.

Chapter 22

ABOUT THE AUTHOR

Hans B. Thorelli is Professor of Business Administration at Indiana University. Thorelli received Law and Ph.D. degrees from the University of Stockholm. The major part of his career has been spent at Indiana University. Thorelli has been a leading scholar on the topics of consumer policy, consumer information systems, and consumer organizations for two decades. He is perhaps the only scholar to have undertaken research on consumer behavior in both developed and less developed countries, his domain including the U.S.A., West Germany, Sweden, as well as Thailand and the People's Republic of China. His books include Consumer Information Systems and Consumer Policy (Ballinger, 1975), The Information Seekers [1975], and Consumer Emancipation and Economic Development: The Case of Thailand [30].

CONSUMER PROBLEMS: DEVELOPED AND LESS DEVELOPED COUNTRIES

Hans B. Thorelli

SUMMARY

Although some consumer problems are self-inflicted, most originate in the marketplace environment. The ecological approach to the analysis of marketing systems is presented, comparing salient features of the consumer market setting in less developed (LDC) and more developed (MDC) countries. Next, consumer problems characteristically arising in these two market environments are discussed. Appropriate roles of three major types of consumer policy--protection, education and information--in the resolution of LDC and MDC problems are suggested, as is a tentative agenda for research.

SOME PARADOXES

A handful of paradoxes presage this analysis of consumer problems in less developed (LDC) and more developed (MDC) countries:[1]

---

[1]LDC and MDC are, of course, catch-all generic terms, each of which stands for a great variety of countries. There is no general agreement on exactly what countries belong in each category. Generally, we may say that the LDC or "Third World" includes over 100 countries with approximately three-fourths of the global population. While categorization may be debated, the Newly Industrialized

First, in the LDC the consumer is the forgotten man, in part in the supposed interest of long-term development. By contrast, in the U.S. and Europe (typical MDC), economies are so highly geared to satisfying current consumer demands that the rate of development has slowed remarkably. The consumer is "forgotten" in the LDC in that citizens do not generally think of themselves as "consumers" (they tend not to be consumer-conscious) and in that policy-makers--be they public or private--pay little heed to consumer problems or consumer rights.

Second, with regard to the elementary right to consume what one's income can buy, we may note that in the LDC consumers have little discretion, though products are substantially unregulated, while in the MDC consumers have much discretion, though products are substantially regulated.

Third, the consumer interest in the LDC is rather homogeneous but unarticulated, while in the MDC it is fragmented but articulated.

Fourth, consumer information about the market in the LDC is ephemeral to start with, but getting more available; in the MDC it is available (though often impenetrable), but becoming more ephemeral. This new ephemerality of consumer information in the MDC is due to the increasing turnover of products, models, and brands and the rapid growth of services, where the lack of consistency and standardization is frequently noted [2].

Fifth, most consumers have a modicum of discretionary income in all countries, no matter how poor. "Discretionary" income refers to income used for things other than "necessities of life" (or, at least, what MDC economists would think of as "necessities"!). Indeed, this statement also seems to be true with regard to saving, although this is somewhat less relevant here. Thus, it would be misleading to say about even the poorest consumers that they can, or will, not buy anything beyond the dire necessities of life. The ubiquity of lottery tickets among the very poorest in many LDC is but one illustration of this paradox.

Taking initial note of this set of paradoxes will be useful in the subsequent comparative discussion of consumer problems in both MDC and LDC.

Countries (NIC), as well as the socialist nations (including the USSR and the PCR), are more like the LDC than the MDC from a consumer point of view. There are industrialized enclaves in most LDC and less developed areas in virtually every MDC.

FOCUS: THE PROBLEMATICS OF BUYER-SELLER INTERACTION

The focus here is the complex of problems surrounding buyer-seller interaction in commercial transactions, whether they are open or regulated by public or private fiat. As will be developed later, the buyer-seller problems will be viewed broadly and will include trends in some important determinants of marketplace frameworks, e.g., the increasing scarcity of time, the individualization of life-styles (hence, demand) in the MDC, and the impact of hyperinflation and import substitution policies in the LDC.

It is customary to discuss consumer problems in the context of consumer rights. To a certain extent this tradition will be followed here. We abstain, however, from enlarging upon the right to consume what one's income can buy. We also do not deal with the numerous constraints imposed on this right in both MDC and LDC [32, Ch.2]. This topic deserves separate treatment. Largely an object of government regulation, the right to consume is not ordinarily at stake in buyer-seller interaction. It is also a surprisingly poorly researched subject.

There is no hard and fast way of defining, much less prioritizing, consumer problems. Most problems of consumers originate in the inability, or unwillingness, of producers to satisfy fully consumer needs and interests. Some consumer problems are self-inflicted. Consumer needs and interests are extremely varied, differing among cultures and, within cultures, from one individual and group to the next. Since the process of inclusion and exclusion of issues is necessarily arbitrary, it seems appropriate to indicate major areas that will not be treated here (or only referred to tangentially):

Environmental protection	Inflation
Quality of life	Taxes
Market "failure"	Health care
Industry self-regulation	Product liability
"Underground" economy	Drug trafficking
Motivation and incentive systems	Terrorism
Income distribution	Satellite advertising

To serve the dual purpose of concentrating attention on the focal topic of consumer problems in buyer-seller interaction and to facilitate cross-cultural comparison (in the present context between LDC and MDC), we need a model of marketplace ecology.

COMPARATIVE ECOLOGY OF MARKETS

Consumer problems originate in the local marketplace. Figure 1 views any national market ("macro-culture") as an open interaction system. This ecosystem is based on the structure-strategy-performance (SSP) approach [32, Part III]. The term structure refers to the seller and buyer subcultures as well as the products (services) and market infrastructure (distribution channels, media, transportation, etc.). Strategy refers to buyer-seller interactions, the nature of which is conditioned by the respective subcultures (values, size, asset mix, number and dispersion, and so on) and by the surrounding market environment. In turn, market system performance is largely determined by the strategic interaction process.

For present purposes, the key ingredients in market system performance are the consumer problems generated by the system. System performance also includes consumer and producer satisfaction level, as well as each party's relative power, productivity, innovation rate, environmental impact, effects on the value, aspiration, and motivation structure of buyers and sellers, and other factors.

To permit cross-cultural comparison, it is necessary to include in our model such framework variables as the local economic, social, political and technological environment, as well as the value, aspiration and motivation structure of the local culture. Over time, these layers of macroculture interact with the market system. It is important to realize that market systems exist in all societies, be they liberal or socialist, democratic or authoritarian [26]. Administrative regulation by government and/or business can eliminate <u>open</u> markets, but not the exchange system in any society based on the division of labor.

It is clearly not feasible to catalog, much less analyze, all the variables represented by the gross categories of our model. Our selection of variables for analysis is based on the twin criteria of relevance to (1) the problems of buyer-seller interaction and (2) ease of identification. Specifically, we compare LDC and MDC market systems on the following major dimensions:

* Consumer characteristics and values
* Products
* Consumer search strategies
* Seller strategies
* Market institutions
* Market system performance

FIGURE 1

THE ECOLOGY OF MARKETS:
A FRAMEWORK FOR CROSS-CULTURAL COMPARISON

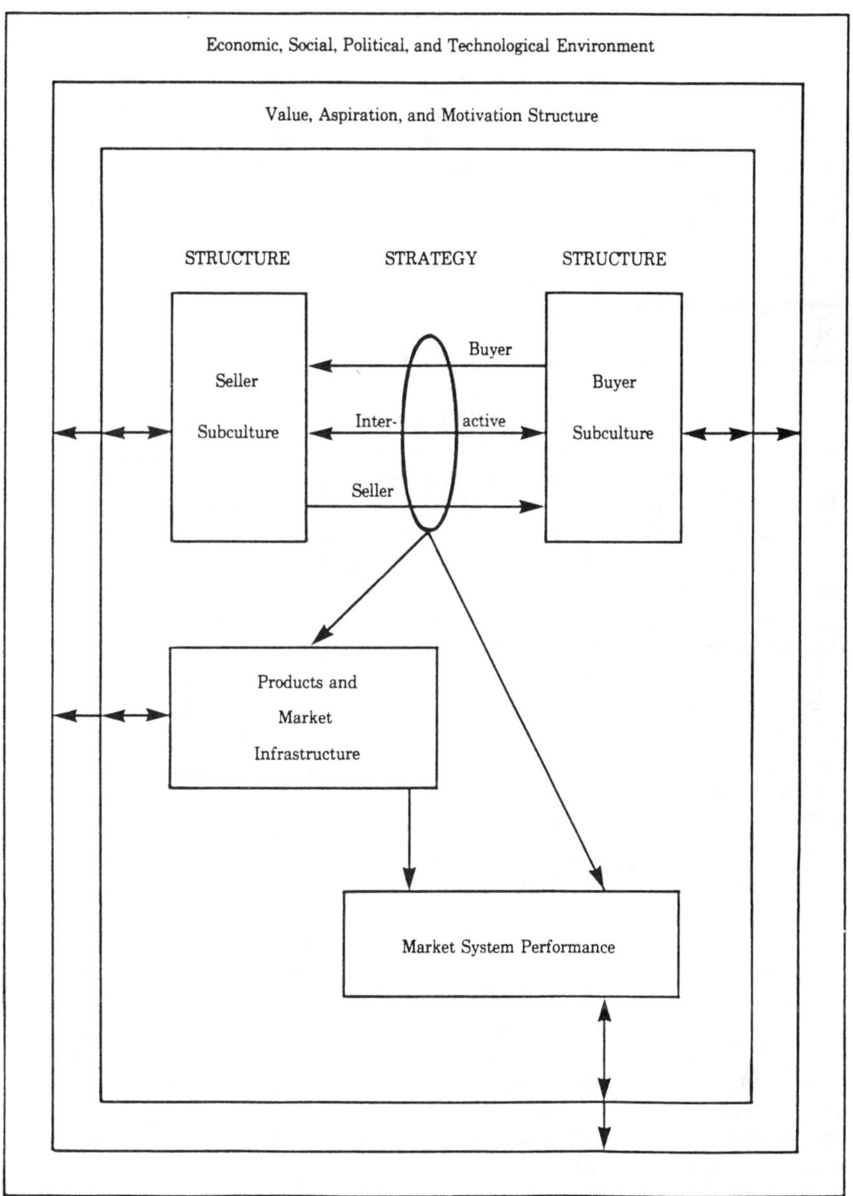

From this comparison we shall derive inventories of consumer problems believed to be characteristic of the LDC and the MDC, respectively.

CHARACTERISTICS OF LDC AND MDC MARKET SYSTEMS

LDC Background

The first major field study of the LDC marketplace from a consumer perspective was carried out in Thailand a decade ago [30]. Limited replications of that research have been made in Kenya and Turkey. Full-scale replications have just been concluded in Brazil [8] and South Korea [33], and preliminary results are on hand. Seller-oriented studies are more numerous (citations in [24]) and much anecdotal evidence exists. It is still true that remarkably little research has been done on LDC markets. Thus, it is logical to set the stage for comparison with an introductory view based mainly on our Thai study. Of course, the statements made will have varying degrees of validity from one LDC to the next.

The outstanding feature of the consumer buying process in the LDC is that it is fraught with high risk. This is due to market structure problems as well as to characteristics of sellers and buyers themselves. Three major structural factors, existing side by side, frequently reinforcing each other: (1) the lack of quality control in local manufacturing, (2) the equally striking lack of transportation and storage facilities suitable to the preservation of fresh foods, and (3) the predatory practices of sellers. In Thailand, as in many other LDCs, chicanery is not unethical--it is a game!

The single most important characteristic of the typical LDC consumer is, of course, that of poverty. This means that she--and I use "she" deliberately--can ill afford to make mistakes. Unlike many ghetto consumers in the MDC, the poor consumer in the LDC does not seem to resign herself to a state of stupor in facing the marketplace. Realizing her high-risk situation, she counters with a surprisingly intensive search effort.

From Bangkok down to the village level an important part of all Thai transactions are carried out in public market places which are generally privately owned and operated. In these market places, as in Middle Eastern bazaars, information is poor, scarce, and intensely valued. The search for information, laborious and uncertain as it may be, is therefore the central experience of life in the public market. Sellers and buyers often are as much interested in making search difficult for others as they are in making it effective for themselves.

The market system is one where relatively few things are prepackaged, and where packaged goods are often adulterated. There are few official product standards, and everything tends to be approximate. The veracity of weights and measures may well be questionable. In such an environment, almost any product is a search good. In the MDC comparative shopping is inter-product and inter-brand while in the LDC it is more often a cross-examination of several exemplars of the same product, brand or model. Distribution methods typical of the MDC (one-price-for-all, standardized packaging, homogeneous product offerings, etc.) are daily making greater inroads in the Thai system. They are epitomized by some of the department stores, hotels, and specialty stores opened in Bangkok in recent decades. Yet their penetration in the outlying municipalities and rural areas is modest.

Bargaining represents the classic--though not always prevailing--way of transacting business in the LDC. Often ascribed to other social and cultural factors, bargaining should be viewed as a natural outgrowth of the uncertain and heterogeneous market environment. It tends to be a time-consuming form of search. To many buyers as well as sellers it is also an enjoyable game aimed at teasing out information relevant to the final deal.

Simply because of the vicissitudes of the local environment, the average consumer in the LDC is an information seeker when it comes to routine, everyday goods. To a surprising extent, she also carries the search habit with her when buying major durables. On the other hand, such "nonfunctional" characteristics as style, beauty, fashion, and social approval seem to count even more than in the MDC, a relationship that appears especially strong with regard to consumers at the lower end of the social scale. As part of the consumer ecology we must also consider the social function of shopping. In the village the store(s) is often a natural meeting place and a clearinghouse for news and gossip. In the city, the stores by definition constitute the "downtown" area, and the bazaar or public market tends to be the center of excitement. This is especially so in those LDC where the penetration of TV is still modest.

This brief survey of the LDC marketplace from a consumer viewpoint has stressed information search as the prime means that LDC consumers use in fending for themselves. In a sense they all tend to be "information seekers." Unfortunately, the information they obtain tends to be ephemeral and unreliable: past experience has little learning value. In Kerton's [10] terms, LDC consumers must spend a large amount of time to build even a modest stock of consumer search capital. Not surprisingly, they differ markedly from the sophisticated "information seekers" we have identified in the MDC [28]. They also differ from MDC average consumers, who have better data more easily available and whose time premium generally precludes extensive search for any but major or hobby-oriented items.

Comparing the Consumer and the Marketplace in LDC and MDC

A highly condensed comparative overview of consumers and their marketplace in LDC and MDC is given by Figure 2. Our need to simplify will occasionally cause undue polarization. For instance, LDC buyers spend at least as much time as MDC buyers on the functional aspects of shopping. In addition they spend much more on the social aspects. Here Figure 2 will largely have to speak for itself [30].

Most of the items under the heading consumer have already been discussed. A preliminary analysis of the Korean data suggests an awareness of consumer rights in that developing country in 1985 was a bit more prevalent than in Thailand 10 years earlier. It is too early to say whether this is due to a difference between the countries themselves, their degree of economic development, or simply an effect of time.

When we say that products bought in the LDC tend to be necessities, the statement is culturally conditioned. In truth most products bought in the LDC are dire necessities that are needed for physical survival--staple foods, clothes and utensils. Accordingly, the assortment of goods in most stores tends to be both narrow and shallow.

The stress on personal sources of information search in the LDC, and impersonal ones in the MDC, is only a matter of relative emphasis. Personal sources are everywhere the sources most frequently reported as important in major purchase decisions. Relatively speaking, seller strategies in the LDC are more often differentiated on the basis of personal contacts and friendships than on a functional basis, such as differences in cost.

With the exception of certain aspects of fresh food marketing, the market system in the LDC is characterized by a kind of don't-rock-the-boat "cryptocapitalism" reminiscent of the medieval guild system in Europe. An important and unfortunate characteristic of this system (a feature also common in socialist countries, albeit for other reasons) is the existence of a chronic sellers' market in many consumer goods. As indicated under market institutions market system performance in Figure 2, such a system is not

FIGURE 2

THE CONSUMER AND THE MARKETPLACE IN LDCS AND MDCS[A]

	LDC	MDC
Consumer		
Standard of living	poor	well-to-do
Values	fatalistic easily satisfied	self-actualization hard to satisfy
Nature of shopping	social	functional
Frequency of shopping	many trips	few trips
Shopping criteria	price, economy quality, style product on hand to inspect location of dealer	durability, performance reputation of brand reputation of dealer
Awareness of market functioning	fair	fair
Awareness of consumer rights	poor	relatively good
Mobility	fair	high
Products		
Type	necessities	discretionary
Variety	limited	proliferation
Buying decision	specific (exemplar)	generic (brand)
Limitations, fraud	frequent	occasional
Quality	variable	standardized
Safety	poor	good
Information Search		
Product focus	all goods	"shopping" and "speciality"
Sources	personal	impersonal
Independent info	little or none	obtainable
Nature of info	relatively ephemeral	relatively permanent
Perceived risk	high	low
Time premium	low	high
Effectiveness of search	low	relatively high
Seller Strategies		
Differentiation	personal	functional
Deception	ubiquitous	frequent
Sales volume, market share	don't rock the boat	increase
Market Institutions		
System	cryptocapitalism employment buffer	open market
System reputation	poor	acceptable (or better)
Level of trust	relatively low	relatively high
Infrastructure (transportation, adv. & mkt. res. agencies, etc.)	poor	rich
Credit at all levels	poor, expensive inexpensive	available, relatively
Consumer protection	nonexistent	well-developed
Market Sytem Performance (also includes Consumer Problems)		
Productivity	low	medium
Complaint handling	poor	medium
Information flow	poor	medium
Competition	weak	strong
Dispersion of benefits	narrow	wide
Contribution to ec. dev.	none	driving force

conducive to economic development. Indeed, it is our view that reform of the marketing system--of which consumer emancipation will be an integral part--is a prerequisite to balanced development in Third World countries [30, Ch. XIII].

Finally, we note a few trends in the MDC that should help us to understand consumer problems there. Rising standards of living in the most affluent countries seem to be accompanied by greater individualization of styles of life and, consequently, in demand patterns and buying criteria. A natural result of such differentiation is the further fragmentation of consumer interests and of consumers' perceptions of what their problems are. The polarization between man's roles as producer and consumer is growing, due to increasing specialization and division of labor. The emigration of women from the home to the labor market has accelerated this trend. This polarization permits the individual at the same time to be a dissatisfied consumer and yet to produce goods of poor quality! He does this not only without any pangs of conscience but also without even seeing the connection between the two roles.

The increasing premium on time [11, 20] is stimulating reallocation of internalized and externalized consumer activities and decisions. We internalize more activities which we enjoy or which are simply becoming too cumbersome or expensive to be performed by others. We increasingly externalize activities, and even decisions, in such areas as financial services, tax accounting, exercise, meal preparation, and even the care of our appearance. The enormous growth in services markets reflects these developments. These trends, coupled with the increasing complexity of many products, are accompanied by another: the growing importance of what may be called the "software" aspects--provision of information, pre- and post-sales services, warranties, credit arrangements, "personalization" of standard products by owner magazines, hotlines for complaints or service advice, and so on--relative to the more traditional and functional "hardware" aspects. The software area has a rich potential for both generating and alleviating consumer problems.

CONSUMER PROBLEMS IN LDC AND MDC: AN IMPRESSIONISTIC VIEW

The overviews of the ecology of markets and the characteristics of LDC and MDC market systems provide the environmental setting where most consumer problems originate. A goodly number of such problems were, in fact, suggested merely by the inventory of market characteristics. An apology is in order for the occasional repetition that is unavoidable in this section. A more important caveat is that our examination of consumer problems in the LDC is based on large-scale field research in only one country, albeit enriched with much anecdotal evidence from others. In the MDC much survey research as well as consumer advocacy has been concerned with individual consumer problems (misleading advertising, complaint handling, unsafe products, unsatisfactory buyer or user experiences, etc.). We are unaware, however, of any systematic, research-based inventory of problems.

The picture presented is impressionistic, being both subjective and incomplete.

Self-Inflicted Problems

Before examining environmentally induced consumer problems, we note that some consumer problems are self-inflicted. If I go to the fanciest restaurant in town instead of McDonald's (which is more in tune with my budget), I have only myself to blame for any second thoughts. The right to choose freely implies some obligation to choose wisely. By smoking in bed, I incur the risk that the house itself may go up in smoke. The right to be safe implies some obligation on the part of consumers to observe "safety first." It is easy to enlarge the list of consumer problems by including those that are self-made, in whole or in part.

LDC Consumer Problems

As a group, the LDC constitute the part of the world where consumer problems are most urgent and least attended to. Consumer consciousness and aspiration levels are both low, relative to the MDC. A prime reason for this sad state of affairs is that consumers are all but forgotten in the calculus of development planners and also in the misguided discipline of "development economics"! Low consumer aspiration levels with regard to both the number and quality of products and services, and the relative ease with which these nondiscriminating demands are satisfied in an otherwise high-risk and unsafe market environment, are especially characteristic of LDC rural areas. If you add to this situation limited assortments and the prevalence of seller's markets, you wind up with consumers who are poorly motivated in their role as producers. This is especially true because farm output beyond subsistence is typically disposed of at governmentally fixed "low" prices calculated (1) to win the political allegiance of the metropolitan population and/or (2) to generate a surplus for the state (or public officials) in export trade.

Another macrolevel consumer problem area is the lack of power of consumers relative to producers in seller's markets, as reflected in unawareness or nonrecognition of basic consumer rights. Lacking the equal partnership in the marketplace and the kind of consumer emancipation this requires, a market system cannot be expected to pay much attention to consumer interests.

A large collection of LDC consumer problems may be subsumed under the heading of risk, be it actual or perceived. The single most important of these problems is product safety. Information gathered by the International Organisation of Consumer Unions (IOCU) and affiliated bodies [1] and by our own research, shows that product safety in the LDC is typically deplorable. Some examples include frequently adulterated food, unsafe appliances (e.g., kerosene stoves), "ethical" drugs freely sold on a nonprescription basis and, of course, in the public sector, unsafe water. The powdered milk formula episode also stresses the fact that preparations perfectly safe in one market environment may indeed be unsafe in another. A key feature in this case was the "hard sell" by leading multinational companies of powdered milk in disregard of the fact that local water in the LDC is frequently an unsuitable ingredient in baby milk formulas.

Somewhat related to product safety is the prevalence of fraudulent and imitation goods. Consumers all over the world buy products of a given brand on the basis of trust. In the LDC more often than in the MDC the product is a fraudulent and/or often poor-quality imitation of the original. This problem affects all kinds of products from Kleenex to medications to kerosene stoves and Russian-made Fiats. The lack of quality standards for mass-produced goods and, even more importantly, consistency in quality, is an unnecessary aspect and a major element of risk in LDC markets. Unhappily (but naturally), this phenomenon results in distrust of the quality of locally produced goods. Weights and measures and labels indicating contents may be untrustworthy due to chicanery or laxness on the part of sellers and inspectors.

False or misleading information or high noise-information ratio is characteristic of much advertising and packaging in the LDC. Generally, too, the flow of spontaneous, functionally-oriented consumer information is poor. This includes price information, often obtainable only through a time-consuming bargaining process. Inevitably, this state of affairs leads to discriminatory trade practices. In many LDC with weak concepts of trademarks and warranties, imitation brands and nonenforceable warranties are ubiquitous. In the People's Republic of China the trademark Panda, at least until recently, was used for a dozen different consumer products originating from as many different enterprises, creating confusion among consumers as to the origin of the goods.

Corruption, by distorting the linkage between honest effort and productive output, is a roadblock in the way of economic development. However, it may be even more of a consumer problem, generating distrust in the quality of locally made goods. Corruption is a serious block to consumer emancipation in the LDC. As long as bribes let sellers market imitation or fraudulent products, sellers can forget about quality control and the health and safety of their products. They can pollute the environment, use false weights and measures, and neglect warranties and consumer complaints. While rich countries such as the United States are able to absorb corruption as just another questionable business practice, the LDC can ill afford this luxury [22].

High marketing costs, relative to the value added by the local trade structure, is often an LDC consumer problem. The trade structure tends to be complex, with several layers of criss-crossing primary and secondary wholesalers, as well as retailers. Additional cost and complexity is added by the fact that marketing in general and retailing in particular often serve as an employment buffer for relatives and friends who otherwise would lack jobs. It does not help that individual traders frequently just eke out a meager existence for themselves: there are simply too many of them.

The rather nonproductive trade structure is only one aspect of what we call cryptocapitalism [30]. By this we mean a private enterprise system based on closed rather than open markets, a self-limiting, static system characterized by aversion to both risk and competition. To quote from Thorelli and Sentell [30, p. 20]:

> Risk aversion is manifested in requirements that capital invested be returned in three years or less. Local firms are generally family dominated, and the normal urge to grow is checked by the desire to maintain control. Political favor is courted to obtain protection against competing imports, tariff exemptions for the importation of machinery and components, sales to the government, foreign currency allocations, and so on--frequently by the use of bribery or special contacts. Generally, manufacturers in LDCs tend to produce what is best for them and then attempt to force it into the market at relatively high prices rather than practicing the marketing concept. This involves

> finding out what the market wants and needs and then providing reasonably priced goods to meet those needs. If good profits are being made, they will often be placed in overseas investments rather than plowed back locally.
> Thus, it is no wonder that "capitalism" in general and its field agents, the merchants, in particular, are in disrepute in most LDCs.

The lack of awareness of consumers about consumer rights (to the extent that they exist at least in theory) means that no one else needs to pay much attention to them. Consumer complaints are few, as they do seem to lead nowhere. Most LDC have witnessed little or no organized consumer action. An exception is the Penang consumer group which stimulated the creation of a regional office of the IOCU in Malaysia.

Hyperinflation is the source of serious consumer problems in several LDC. Inflation run amuck turns forecasting into a fairly random exercise, thereby significantly adding to consumer risk. Such inflation also distorts demand, inducing consumers to buy items in advance of need for fear they may no longer able to afford them when the need becomes critical. This kind of dysfunctional consequence was frequently observed in the Brazilian survey [8].

Finally, we note that many well-meaning people (as well as a number of not so well-meaning ones) in and out of the LDC regard multinational corporations (MNC) as such as an LDC consumer "problem." It is certainly true that some pointed examples of clearly undesirable behavior by MNC do exist, e.g., the old United Fruit Company and the baby milk formula case. But it is equally clear that literally hundreds of millions of LDC lives have been saved due to the medicines and vaccines provided by the MNC, that most technology transferred (and it is a huge volume) to date emanates from the MNC, and that these companies have been providing hundreds of thousands of job opportunities in the Third World. Certainly, Soviet programs of technology transfer have been a fiasco in comparison. Our view is simple: you do not throw out the baby with the bathwater, i.e., the actual and potential contributions of the MNC to the LDC are far greater than the abuse which may come from them. What is needed is mutually fruitful accommodation, not one-sided and unjustified condemnation.

MDC Consumer Problems

It is easier to compile an inventory of consumer problems in the MDC than in the LDC due to the larger amount of academic research and public policy debate. Space confines our selection of such problems to ten categories:

* Product safety
* Consumer information
* Consumer education
* Quality
* Nonmetropolitan markets
* One size fits all vs. individualization
* The decline of trust
* Consumer participation in marketplace decisions
* Changing quality of competition
* Prospects of consumer movements

Product safety. A multitude of unsafe products still exists around the MDC. No matter how many safety gadgets we force the manufacturers and users of chainsaws to accept, the fact remains that a footlong, razor-sharp chain, moving at hundreds of rpms will always be a dangerous instrument. A medicine may be life-saving to one person and life-threatening to another. Cocaine, heroin and other habit-forming and mind-boggling drugs (a major export from the LDC to the MDC!) are forbidden fruit in most MDC, but easily, if expensively, obtainable. Terrorists may yet turn to poisoning city water and other vital consumer products. But miraculously we have so far escaped this particular threat. Speaking generally, it may be claimed that, thanks to Ralph Nader and his followers around the Western world, most MDC have, by now laid a minimum foundation of protection in the product safety area. The groundwork is done; the superstructure will need amendments from time to time. Meanwhile, cost-benefit analysis will be applied to proposed measures, and the debate will continue, concerning the appropriate limits to regulation of the freedom to consume, e.g., of smoking.

Consumer information (CI). The increased volume and varieties of advertising in the last decade or two has undoubtedly raised the noise level of Western civilization appreciably. Though advertising is likely the single most important source of CI, one may doubt whether advertising in general has become more informative. With regard to sources of independent CI, the comparative testing organizations in countries such as the U.S., Germany, Holland, Belgium, Norway and Britain are enjoying continuing success. However, since we made our study of consumer information organizations in 16 North Atlantic nations some 15 years ago [31], informative labeling programs have stagnated and quality certification schemes have shown only modest progress. France, with its Minitel system, has seized the leadership in the development of videotext-based consumer information programs, though it is quite limited in its coverage of products and services and has a way to go to reach even two million homes [13]. Certainly, no country can boast of a comprehensive CI system. This seems a major consumer problem in an era when products and brands are proliferating and the average complexity of products is steadily increasing.

Consumer education. Only a bare handful of the 50 United States and, at most, an equal number of Scandinavian and other European nations have made consumer education obligatory at the secondary school level. Elsewhere, combinations with economics or home economics do exist. In such marriages, consumer education generally winds up the junior partner.

Quality. Millions of consumers feel that the quality of many American products has been declining, from Detroit cars to ladies hosiery. While this phenomenon may be due ultimately to complex changes in cultural values and styles of life, it seems definitely to be reinforced by producer-oriented "value analysis," (cost-shaving) that produces plastic forks that break at the touch of food and aluminum wrap that appears to leave the factory "equipped" with holes. Many of us are staking high hopes on the wave of quality concern now manifesting itself in American industry. We hope that other MDC will be able to avoid deterioration of product quality altogether.

In the meantime, all MDC are facing a common quality challenge in the burgeoning area of services. Maintaining consistency in service quality is particularly difficult in view of the critical roles played by employee training and morale, and customer-establishment interaction in the production of many services.

Nonmetropolitan markets. Few penetrating studies have been made of the functioning of local consumer markets in towns and rural neighborhoods beyond the pale of metropolitan areas. It is well known, however, that assortment tends to be narrower and competition weaker in nonmetro markets [13]. Many consumers view catalog and mail-order suppliers as insufficient substitutes. A town like Bloomington, Indiana, with 60,000 consumers has half a dozen hardware stores, all of which seem to obtain their supplies from the same wholesale co-op. The problem recurs in the liquor trade and many others. Generally, there is an unwillingness to order an item not in the standard assortment. Indeed, ironic in the age of "informatics," are the frequent cases of dealer stock-out with consumers often having to wait months before their shipment comes in.

It is not known to what extent these problems prevail in other medium and small American towns or, indeed, in other MDC. These issues are certainly crying for research. In the meantime, we note an interesting model in Sweden where the government lends some support to grocery and general stores in its "outback" areas in the far North. The purpose of this policy is more to maintain a minimum standard of consumer convenience than to subsidize retailers.

One size fits all vs. individualization. We have already discussed the trend towards individualization of demand associated with higher standards of living. In the last decade or two the American market has also evidenced the one-size-fits-all countertrend. This is especially true of hosiery, where it obviously means that the one size made available will not fit most consumers. In other products we have gone from providing several numbered sizes to small, medium and large. This may mean cost savings to producers, which do not seem reflected in consumer prices. If this is true, we are simply faced with a reduction in the standard of living.

The decline of trust, so very noticeable in urban U.S. markets, seems to affect most MDC. It is reflected in many ways, from requirements to prepay hotel room reservations to utilities employing "meter maids" to read water, gas and electricity meters rather than accepting customer readings. Credit card abuse and shoplifting, employee stealing and fraud, and the lackadaisical handling of repair and other services all serve to generate mistrust. Again, it is obvious that the decline of trust in the marketplace is not all due to sellers. A minority of unethical or dishonest consumers are also involved in making life just a bit more miserable for the rest of us.

Participation. A growing number of consumers feel that the remedies of "exit" (withholding or shifting patronage) and complaint handling--both negative and "ex-post" responses to grievance--are no longer sufficient means of actuating consumer power. Some would prefer more positive, "proactive" instruments of participation. They point out that marketing research is generally responsive to the short-term concerns of producers rather than to the long-term concerns of consumers. They believe that industrial customers have a lot more influence on product design and generally receive better information than final consumers. They feel that there should be greater consumer participation in the entire marketing process, from initial new-product conception to monitoring of complaints handling [23]. The issue of participation may well provide the next focus of MDC consumer movements.

The quality of competition may be deteriorating in a number of markets. For instance, in some mature markets imperfect information permits, and perhaps stimulates, the proliferation of too many, nearly identical products. This contributes to noise and confusion. In this case the cost savings of competition may be absorbed by promotional hoopla rather than in lower prices, better quality or other products. The solution to this consumer problem is more likely to be found in comprehensive consumer information systems than in drastic or detailed public regulation.

Mergers of firms in the same market are often a natural element of competition and create a consumer problem only when they increase monopoly power. More problematical are the kind of multimarket marriages that have given rise to the "merger mania" in countries like the U.S. and Sweden. Mergers of this type are associated with such phenomena as green mail (Son of Blackmail, i.e., the practice of paying off undesirable suitors in amounts and favors discriminating against regular shareholders), poison pills (e.g., the deliberate incurring of vast debts), and golden parachutes for managers whose jobs might be at risk. In these cases, financial "games" played by insiders become the key concern, rather than finding new ways of satisfying consumers. The same criticism may be applied to a number of leveraged buyouts of companies by incumbent management.

The prospects of consumer movements in the MDC have often been belittled by friends and critics alike. There has been a lull in the rate of progress in a number of countries in recent years, although such consumer testing groups as Consumers Union (U.S.) Consumers Association (U.K.) and Stiftung Warentest (W. Germany) have experienced steady growth. It may be that we are merely observing a downward swing in what may be a commonplace cyclical phenomenon. Public awareness of consumer problems is still high in the U.S. [7], and rapidly increasing in such a "nouveau-MDC" as Spain. Meantime, there are certainly things that could be done to accelerate long-term growth of consumer organizations, notably in cooperation with other interested parties.

LDC and MDC: Common Consumer Problems

Several of the problems classified as indigenous to either the LDC or the MDC above are, of course, common to both, though with significant differences in relative importance. Two problem areas of great significance to both are misleading advertising and protectionism.

Misleading advertising figures at or near the top of the list of consumer concerns in both LDC and MDC in one survey after another. It is likely that LDC lead MDC in the prevalence of outrageous varieties of misleading advertising and that LDC lead with respect to misleading claims in national advertising. Although no adequate statistics seem to exist, misleading advertising at the local level is still about as commonplace in such an MDC like the U.S. as it is in the LDC. Scherhorn [19] has indicated that consumer dissatisfaction on occasion may be projected into other areas than those in which the dissatisfaction originated. Thus, it might be that to some extent misleading advertising serves as the whipping-boy for other consumer concerns. That such advertising still exists in all cultures (including the East Bloc and PRC) is still beyond doubt.

Protectionism may well serve a purpose in fostering infant industries and in providing temporary relief for mature industries under pressure from international competition, such as the steel, textile and auto industries of many MDC. Even in these case consumers are likely to foot a large part of the bill. As soon as the "infant" industry has graduated from the kindergarten stage, or the mature industry has had a few years in which to adjust, protectionism becomes an instrument for special interest groups to "milk" consumers at large, as demonstrated in a number of studies [3; 21]. The cost to consumers takes the form of higher prices and lagging quality. This breeds distrust in local products, an area of considerable concern in the LDC.

The negligible concern about protectionism exhibited by the consumer movement worldwide underlines the diffuse nature of consumer interests.

CONSUMER POLICY AND POLICYMAKERS IN LDC AND MDC

Consumer policy may be defined as measures taken by parties other than individual consumers to promote consumer rights or other consumer interests or, generally, to resolve consumer problems. Consumer policy measures may be classified as protection, education and information [32, Ch. 2]. Consumer policymakers include consumer organizations, other citizen groups, business, government, educational institutions and the mass media. Protection, education and information may reinforce each other or be in a trade-off relationship; the same thing is true of policymakers.

Thorelli and Engledow [29] have argued that in the LDC the ordering of priorities among consumer policies should be protection, education and information, while in the MDC the order among these policy types should be the reverse. Our inventories of LDC and MDC consumer problems lend support to this proposition. Such key consumer concerns as product safety, integrity and consistency in quality have been given little attention in the LDC. On the other hand, organized consumer information programs demand a type of consumer sophistication not generally widespread in these countries. The proper attention to, understanding and use of most consumer information programs presupposes a minimum level of consumer education not yet found in the LDC. Two other important missions of consumer education: to raise consumer consciousness and to help consumers avoid self-inflicted problems in the marketplace.

Consumer emancipation must be an integral part of a program for balanced socioeconomic development. As the experience of the People's Republic of China indicates, a dramatic reform of the market system--and consequently of the motivation structure in a culture--can produce an amazing improvement in economic development and self-awareness among consumers even in the most distant rural areas.

In most MDC a minimum platform of product safety and other protective measures already exists. Standards of general education tend to be appreciably higher than in the LDC, and this is also the case regarding consumer consciousness and awareness of consumer rights. Even average LDC consumers are ready for simplified consumer information systems, and the MDC Information Seeker sophisticates can deal with comprehensive ones. In the MDC, consumer education is second in priority to consumer information.

The technology is already on hand for videotext-type and other advanced consumer information systems. The obstacles in the way are primarily economic and administrative. We submit a fundamental bottleneck is the lack of enthusiasm among consumer organizations. After 20-50 years, most of these groups are still too wary of losing their purity--or too skeptical of the business community--to wish to cooperate with other interests on a pluralist basis. In our view, this is also why the growth of many of these groups has slowed. Yet by now it seems obvious that the only hope for a comprehensive consumer information system lies in pluralist sponsorship, including consumer and standardization groups, business, independent economic, technical and marketing expertise, along with government representatives. This is the way to obtain necessary cooperation from all interested parties, as well as the credibility that is indispensable in the marketplace.

It is not the purpose of this paper to advance policy recommendations for all the LDC and MDC consumer problems inventoried [24]. In many areas further research is needed to provide the factual input needed in the policymaking process (see below). We will, however, mention a few areas where international cooperation is urgently needed. Fledgling LDC consumer groups need both technical assistance and economic support. In practice, this has meant support from IOCU and related organizations (such as Health Action International and Consumer Interpol), which in turn need greater resources for this kind of work. Technical assistance might also be provided by USAID and the Peace Corps and corresponding agencies in other MDC to a much greater extent than in the past. UN general policy declarations may morally strengthen forces in favor of consumer emancipation in the LDC and elsewhere. The UN should be cautioned against suggesting that any consumer policy measure adopted in one country be automatically transferable to others [25].

Global product and test methods standardization efforts must be stimulated at the cost of regional ones that often establish instant trade barriers. New ways must be found to secure consumer participation in standards work.

Clearly trade liberalization and the regulation of LDC- and MDC- originated dangerous drugs are also subjects in urgent need of international collaboration.

RESEARCH AGENDA

The analysis of this paper suggests the following as priority areas for future research:

* LDC market systems and consumer problems
* Marketing and motivation
* The open market experiments in the People's Republic of China
* The economics of pluralist-based consumer information systems
* Extent and significance of Speciality Seekers (as contrasted to general Information Seekers) in the MDC
* Consumer affairs and complaint handling systems
* Consumer participation in product planning and introduction

* Cross-cultural studies of the right to consume

* Cost/benefit analysis of protectionism from a consumer perspective

* Characteristics of nonmetro markets in the MDC

* Effects of particular consumer policies

* How people spend their time

* Cyclicality of advertising attitudes and advertising practices in economic development

* The ecology of self-regulation (e.g., regarding misleading advertising)

* Determinants of successful cross-cultural tranferability of consumer policies

Virtually all of these areas have seen some research. Yet they are all under-researched relative to the needs of intelligent policymaking. Researchers in this field will have the satisfaction of knowing they are working with problems of direct relevance to public and private consumer policy.

REFERENCES

1. BEARDSHAW, VIRGINIA (1983). Prescriptions for Change: Health Action International's Guide to Rational Health Projects, The Hague: International Organization of Consumer Unions.

2. BERRY, LEONARD L. (1980), "Service Marketing Is Different," Business (May-June), 24-29.

3. CRANDALL, ROBERT W. (1984), "Import Quotas and the Automobile Industry: The Costs of Protectionism," Brookings Review, 2 (Summer), 8-16.

4. DOWIE, M. (1983), "Unsafe At Any Price," IOCU Consumer Interpol Press Kit, Penang: International Organization of Consumer Unions.

5. FEDERAL RESERVE BANK OF NEW YORK, "The Consumer Cost of U.S. Trade Restraints," Quarterly Review (Summer), 1-12.

6. HARLAND, DAVID (1985), "Legal Aspects of the Export of Hazardous Products," Journal of Consumer Policy, 8 (September), 209-238.

7. HARRIS, LOUIS and ASSOCIATES (1983), Consumerism in the Eighties, Los Angeles, Atlantic Richfield Company.

8. JOHNSON, DENISE M. (1986), "The Impact of Risk Perceptions on Information Search in a Hyperinflationary Environment: The Case of Brazil," Unpublished doctoral thesis, Indiana University.

9. JUSTER, F. THOMAS and FRANK P. STAFFORD (1985), eds., Time, Goods, and Well-Being, Ann Arbor: Institute for Social Research.

10. KERTON, ROBERT R. (1981),"Consumer Search Capital: Delineating A Concept and Applying It to Consumers in Developing Countries," Journal of Consumer Policy, 4, 293-305.

11. LINDER, STAFFAN B. (1970), The Harried Leisure Class, New York: Columbia University Press.

12. MAYER, ROBERT N. (1986), Videotex in France: The Other Revolution, Salt Lake City: Working Paper #86.5, Division of Social Science Research, Center for Public Affairs and Administration.

13. MAYNES, E. SCOTT (1976), Decision-Making for Consumers, New York: Macmillan.

14. MELROSE, D. (1982), Bitter Pills: Medicines and the Third World Poor, Oxford: Oxfam.

15. MITCHELL, JEREMY (1983), The Information Society: A Strategy for Consumers, The Hague: International Organization of Consumer Unions.

16. RINGSTEDT, NILS (1986), "OECD, Safety, and the Consumer, Journal of Consumer Policy, 9, 57-64.

17. "SAFETY OF CONSUMERS IN EUROPE" (1985), BEUC News (September) 1985.

18. SCHERHORN, GERHARD, et al. (1975), Verbraucherinteresse und Verbraucherpolitik, Goettingen: Verlag Otto Schwartz.

19. _________ (1985), "Die Unzufriedenheit der Verbraucher," Stuttgart: Universitaet Hohenheim.

20. SCITOVSKY, TIBOR (1976), The Joyless Economy, New York: Oxford University Press.

21. TARR, DAVID G. and MORRIS E. MORKRE (1984), Aggregate Costs to the United States of Tariffs and Quotas on Imports, Federal Trade Commission, Washington, D.C.

22. THORELLI, HANS B. (1978), "Management Audit and Social Indicators: The MDC Through the Glasses of the LDC," Journal of Contemporary Business (Winter), 1-20.

23. _________ (1980), "Codetermination for Consumers?" Business Horizons (August), 3-6.

24. _________ (1981), "Consumer Policy for the Third World," Journal of Consumer Policy, 3 (Summer), 197-211.

25. _________ (1981), "Swedish Consumer Policy, Its Transferability and Related Research Implications," Advances in Consumer Research, 8, 467-73.

26. _________ (1983), "Concepts of Marketing: A Review, Preview and Paradigm," The Marketing Concept: Perspectives and Viewpoints, p. 15, Varadarajan, ed., American Marketing Association Workshop, Texas A & M University (February), 2-37.

27. _________ (1984), "Informatics: Impact on Marketing," The Collection and Analysis of Economic and Consumer Behavior Data: In Memory of Robert Ferber, Seymour Sudman and M. A. Spaeth, eds., Urbana, Illinois: Bureau of Economic and Business Research, University of Illinois, 171-184.

28. _________, H. BECKER and J. ENGLEDOW (1975), The Information Seekers, Cambridge, Mass.: Ballinger.

29. _________ and JACK L. ENGLEDOW (1980), "Information Seekers and Information Systems: A Policy Perspective," Journal of Marketing, 44 (Spring), 9-27.

30. _________ and GERALD D. SENTELL (1982), Consumer Emancipation and Economic Development: The Case of Thailand, Greenwhich, CT: Jai Press, Inc.

31. _________ and SARAH V. THORELLI (1973), Consumer Information Handbook: Europe and North America, New York: Praeger.

32. _________ and SARAH V. THORELLI (1977), Consumer Information Systems and Consumer Policy, Cambridge, Mass.: Ballinger.

33. YE, JONGSUK (1986), "The Experience, Attitude and Behavior of Consumers as Actors in the Marketplace of South Korea," unpublished doctoral thesis, Indiana University.

Chapter 23

ABOUT THE AUTHOR

Folke Olander is Professor of Economic Psychology at the Aarhus School of Business Administration and Economics in Denmark. A psychologist by training with a Ph.D. in Psychology from the University of Stockholm in 1963, Olander held positions at the Economic Research Institute of the Stockholm School of Economics (1959-72) and the International Institute of Management in Berlin (1973-74) before moving to Aarhus. A longtime leader in the consumer policy field, it was Olander who, in collaboration with Gerhard Scherhorn, organized the two Berlin Conferences on Consumer Action Research in 1974-75. Olander is Editor of the Journal of Consumer Policy and has also been a member of the Danish Social Science Research Council, serving as its Chairman in 1983-84. In research his main interests are consumer policy and consumer influence, new information technologies and the consumers, consumer decision-making.

SALIENT ISSUES IN CURRENT EUROPEAN CONSUMER POLICY RESEARCH[1]

Folke Olander

SUMMARY

European research in the consumer interest from 1980 onwards is presented in this review of recent contributions to the literature. Some of the fields in which European research appears to be strong are: consumer problems related to the market behaviour of producers; new technologies, media, and information systems; research into ways of organizing consumer interests. Several weak (even blind!) spots are identified.

Concepts and ideas from sociology and political science play a larger role in European research as contrasted with U.S. research where economics and psychology dominate. The paper ends with a call for more theoretical work, on both sides of the ocean, aimed particularly toward the development of "grand theories" of consumer policy.

---

[1]The author wants to thank Thierry Bourgoignie, Klaus G. Grunert, Jeremy Mitchell, Karl-Erik Warneryd, and Solveig Wikstrom for valuable comments and suggestions.

In March 1986, some 25 scholars and practitioners from consumer organizations and public agencies met at the Heiligkreuztal nunnery in southern Germany to present research results and discuss consumer policy. They came from twelve European countries and were supplemented by three North-American scholars.

* * * *

The papers presented dealt mostly with international issues (trade restrictions, export of hazardous products), with information technology and new forms of advertising, and with the efficiency (or lack of efficiency) of various forms of public consumer policy and of alternatives to legislation ("soft law," negotiations between producer and consumer organizations). Several of these papers will appear in the Journal of Consumer Policy and other international journals.

What led me to start this paper with a reference to that symposium was a small exercise undertaken at the end of the meeting. Participants were asked to list the most relevant consumer issues for the years ahead.

It was refreshingly unscientific. The format of answers was unspecified; no checks of interjudge reliability were made with regard to the categorization of responses; participants had little time to ponder upon their views before they listed them. Of course the responses were influenced by the context, including the papers that had been presented and the discussions that had taken place during the symposium. Some participants insisted that there was no one-to-one relationship between the relevance or importance of an issue and the priority that it should be given in a research agenda (not all important consumer problems being regarded as researchable). The respondent sample was a convenience sample with certain disciplines and countries more heavily represented than others and with only one representative from industry.

Thus, this little survey is not representative of consumer scholars and policymakers in Europe. It is interesting because it tells what some European researchers/practitioners regard as important consumer policy issues. Therefore, I have included this list of issues as an Appendix. Further, this paper is organized around the main categories developed from that conference.

There are two reasons for choosing this starting point for the presentation of European research. First, there are some divergencies worth noting between the topics given the highest priority on the Heiligkreuztal list and the research recently carried out in Europe. Some "blind spots" are discovered in this way.

Secondly, any review of research should be based on <u>some</u> taxonomy. To cover the research of a whole continent and, in principle, all the disciplines and fields covered by the Wingspread conference is a formidable assignment. It seemed to me that the classifications and priorities of 25 experts would provide a better basis for the undertaking than the idiosyncracies of a particular reviewer.

The paper is organized, then, according to the following outline:

- a <u>short discussion of the priorities</u> set by the participants in the Heiligkreuztal symposium;

- a <u>description of research</u> which fits into this list of priorities;

- a very summary <u>catalogue of other research</u> that is not easily categorized under the headings of the Heiligkreuztal list;

- <u>some reflections on similarities and dissimilarities</u> between European and U.S. consumer policy research.

CAVEATS AND LIMITATIONS

Before embarking on the first leg of this Tour d'Europe, I have however to insert certain caveats and to point to several limitations of my review.

First, it is presumptuous to pretend that a single person from a single country and a single discipline can know even the bulk of what is going on in multifarious Europe. In most fields, the European scientific scene is more diverse and less transparent than the U.S. scene -- by force of different research traditions in different countries, language barriers, and the lack of shared publication channels. When it comes to consumer policy, which is so "young" as a policy field and as a field of research, this tendency towards fragmentation and insulation is particularly pronounced. Public policies are usually <u>national</u>, rather parochial, more adapted to the conditions of the specific country where they have been instituted than designed to meet general principles. The national characteristics of policy also affects <u>research</u> aimed at providing a rationale for such policies or at monitoring their effects.

There have been attempts to achieve cooperation and integration in policies across Europe. Obvious examples occur within the European Community (EC); within that, by BEUC, the association of consumer organizations of EC countries; within the Council of Europe; within OECD; and within the Nordic Council of Ministers. Some of these efforts have led to a harmonization of policies across borders; others have turned out to be paper tiger.

Sorry to say, however, cooperation by researchers across borders is even less developed. It is somewhat surprising to find that, among European social scientists working in the consumer policy area, collaboration seems most frequent among law scholars, in spite of the difficulties of making legal research applicable to countries with basically different legal principles and traditions. The work of the European Law Group [37], the annual European Workshop on Consumer Law at Louvain-la-Neuve which even exposes legal scholars to the views of economists and other social scientists, and the brand new European Consumer Law Journal are cases in point. For the other social and behavioral sciences, communication and cooperation among European consumer policy researchers is incidental and irregular. The only exception is the Journal of Consumer Policy which seeks to link researchers on consumer policy from different countries and different disciplines.

For all these reasons, then, the present review of research is limited and biased. Many of the publications mentioned in the paper stem from the Nordic countries and from the Federal Republic of Germany. A more correct title of the paper would be "Salient Issues in Current North European Consumer Policy Research." In choosing areas and examples, I must confess that papers from the Journal of Consumer Policy have often been my first choice. Furthermore, in my search of examples I have mainly confined myself to the 1980s. For a rather extensive review of European research up to 1980, see [114].

This review does not deal with legal research in spite of its abundance in Europe and in spite of the fact that legal and social science papers are published side-by-side in the Journal of Consumer Policy, with at least an occasional attempt to integrate the two strands of research. Obviously, a law scholar would be needed to carry out this task. Hence, some of the legal issues considered at the Wingspread conference, such as product liability and product safety, are omitted from my review. Omitted also is research on access to justice for consumers, a rather well developed area in Europe [17]. I would like to point out, however, that not least the evaluation of "soft law," i.e., quasi-legal institutions and procedures for negotiations between consumers and producers, requires the collaboration of legal and social science researchers. A special issue of the Journal of Consumer Policy (Vol. 7, No. 2, 1984) describes in detail various attempts at initiating "soft law" consumer-producer dialogues in several European countries. So far, however, most research on soft law has been carried out by law scholars in isolation.

THE HEILIGKREUZTAL PROBLEM AREAS

Preliminaries discharged, here is the Heiligkreuztal list of important consumer policy issues for the years ahead (see Appendix for the fully detailed list):

1. Consumer problems related to market structure and market behavior;

2. Consumer problems related to regulated markets/systems;

3. Problems related to new technologies, new media, and new information systems;

4. Problems of disadvantaged consumers;

5. International/global dimensions of consumer issues;

6. Consumer issues in the service sector (private and public);

7. Consumers and economic affairs;

8. The organization of consumer interests.

A first, general observation is to note the importance given to <u>producer</u> action, both in individual firms and - not least - as collective action. Most of the subtopics mentioned under Categories 1 and 2 deal with the behavior of producers in the marketplace. So do most of the topics under new information technology (Category 3) as well as some under international/global issues and service sector problems (Categories 5 and 6). The organization of consumer interests (Category 8) is recognized as an important issue. It seems that few consumer problems are perceived as "self-inflicted" (cf. Thorelli's Wingspread paper) or curable by actions directed at <u>individual</u> consumers and households. The improvement of consumer education, consumer information and consumer decision-making were not identified as salient issues. One might say that consumer problems are externalized. In particular, it is coordination and cooperation on the producer side (lack of competition, concentration, the growing importance of multinational companies) that are believed to cause consumer problems. Related to this, consumer problems are seen as becoming increasingly internationalized. Trade and marketing cross the borders, and so also do the mass media, not the least being advertising, and companies themselves become international.

Consumer Problems Related to Market Structure and Market Behavior

Market Behavior

The consumer policy literature in Europe puts more emphasis on the behavior of producers in markets than on the structure of markets.

One line of research concerns the quality of supplier-provided information. A very comprehensive content analysis of advertising in Danish print media by Sepstrup [141] shows that advertisements contain little information with respect to product attributes and sales conditions and thus is of little assistance in helping consumers assess products and make decisions. A similar content analysis by Sepstrup showed TV advertising to be less informative than print advertising on the dimensions studied [142]. Nowak and Andren [109] assessed the relative importance of informative and persuasive elements in Swedish magazine advertising from 1950 to 1975. Towards the end of this period advertisements contained fewer persuasion "tricks." This does not imply that these advertisements became more informative. Instead, information about price and durability became less common while, for a global index of informativeness, no change occurred during the period.

A multifaceted research programme at the University of Hohenheim, developed a methodology for measuring the consumer information deficit in terms of failure of information sources to eliminate perceived purchase risks. The methodology is described in [27] and [50]. Applying this approach to sales brochures, advertisements, and sales talks for automobiles the Hohenheim group found the coverage of perceived risks to be unsatisfactory [27, 50]. They also found that nearly 50 percent of relevant supplier information in automobile brochures is wasted because the consumers do not understand it [44].

An offshoot of the same research program is a new procedure for identifying misleading advertising: the misleading components approach. Its central idea is to detect certain types of misleading messages that are found repeatedly in many advertisements. This approach avoids the problems associated with case-oriented methodologies [54]. For a thorough theoretical review of misleading advertising, see Durandin [35].

Another line of research at the University of Mannheim has dealt with the effects of comparative product testing by Stiftung Warentest on industry and trade [42, 121, 122]. The effects studied are Padberg's "non-use benefits"; i.e., effects on the actions of suppliers that benefit all consumers, not only consumers who actually use test results in their purchase decisions [117]. Clear effects on market behavior were reported, especially with respect to product, communication, and distribution strategies among manufacturers and with respect to product-line, communication, and distribution strategies in trade enterprises. As to effects on market structure and market performance, these researchers see some potentially negative effects in that large companies appear to derive more benefits from product testing than their smaller competitors. Further, innovation efforts can be led in the wrong direction and perhaps even throttled by product tests that are not always based on consumer criteria and that often are outdated. The authors outline various measures that would reduce such negative impacts.

Yet another line of research occupies itself with innovation and product development activities within industry. Early work by Lindhoff and Olander [85] and Czerwonka, Schoppe and Weckbach [26] developed the thesis that consumers have a very limited influence on new product development and suggested new avenues for communication between the two parties in order to see to it that consumer needs and ideas are considered to a greater extent in product development. (See also [39].) Empirical research is now under way in Germany to explore the possibility of an improved dialogue between individual consumers and individual firms during the product development process [57]. In Sweden, another route has been taken. Here, engineers have taken it upon themselves to develop prototypes of "user-oriented" products in a large number of areas (packaging, surface materials easy to keep clean, shoes and clothes for work and for elderly and handicapped consumers, equipment for personal hygiene which is also easy to use for elderly and handicapped consumers, and so on) [79]. Not surprisingly, the major problem encountered is convincing commercial producers of the marketability of these new or improved products.

Research regarding the communication between producers and consumers is being carried out also by company "consumer affairs" departments. For a survey of the situation in various European countries, and in West Germany in particular, see [58, 59].

Producer behavior in terms of the degree of adherence to voluntary, "soft law" rules and codes of conduct has also been examined in a number of contexts. For a sample of reports in English, see [11, 92, 120, 172].

Market Structures

Despite the fact that both researchers and practitioners at Heiligkreuztal identified changes in market structures as an issue of major concern to consumers, surprisingly few European studies, theoretical or empirical, have taken a hard look at market structures and performance from a consumer perspective. Because competition policy is normally oriented to the enhancement of the public interest rather than the consumer interest, it follows that much research on competition, market structures and market performance by economists and legal scholars is only partly relevant [71, p. 110; 15]. For a thorough treatment of whether and to what extent competition policy takes consumer interests and expectations into account, see several contributions in the Proceedings of the Third European Workshop on Consumer Law [45].

Some interesting papers by European researchers have recently dealt with the effects of imperfect consumer information on the structure and functioning of markets [19, 53, 60, 123, 124]. Illuminating as such papers are, it is difficult for this reviewer to conceive of all consumer problems as emanating from "information failure." There is need for more inclusive analysis of the possibilities and limitations of competition as a solution to consumer problems. For his part, Scherhorn [140, Sec. 2.2] is sure that competition and competition policy are necessary, but not sufficient. The instruments used in competition policy are often ineffective. Further they aim to influence the behavior of suppliers only, not that of consumers. When, as is the rule, consumers have few sanctions other than "exit" at their disposal, both individually and collectively, and when suppliers dominate the communication channels in the marketplace, seller competition is not sufficient to improve the consumer position and to solve consumer problems. According to Scherhorn, it is not sufficient to prevent cooperation among suppliers, one must also support cooperation among consumers.

There are also other rationales for consumer protection besides efficiency, viz., the equity rationale [124]. Here, the basic stance is that the correction of market failures is not enough. There are also social policy goals in consumer protection [14]. Solutions based on this rationale do not always coincide, of course, with solutions based on an efficiency rationale.

We can see, then, that although the Heiligkreuztal participants may have correctly diagnosed defects in market structures as a major and perhaps increasing cause of consumer problems, no easy remedy is around the corner.

Somewhat simpler solutions may exist in the area of international trade restrictions [110]. Consumer organizations in Europe have become very active in support of open trading, and an OECD symposium held in Paris in November 1984 provided an occasion for the organizations to assert vigorously the consumer interest in international trade policy [95]. Consumers' Association in the U.K. undertook research on the costs to consumers of protectionist measures [24]. A parallel effort has been started under the sponsorship of the Consumer Committee of the Nordic Council of Ministers [153].

A Nordic consumer policy, that may influence market structure modestly, is government support to small grocery and general stores in sparsely populated areas [36]. This program has also generated some cost-benefit research [72].

An aspect of market performance, dealt with in Geistfeld's Wingspread paper, concerns the possible consumer losses caused by low correlations between price and quality in consumer markets. For European contributions to this problem area, see [4, 5, 34], and the recent study by Hjorth-Andersen [62]. Some consumer policies designed to improve price and market transparency such as monitoring and publication of prices, and public price controls are investigated in papers presented at the Fourth European Workshop on Consumer Law [46].

Consumer Problems Related to Regulated Markets/Systems

When it came to consumer problems arising from government regulations and systems, the Heiligkreuztal participants thought at once of the systems providing food, drug and health care, and housing. Although much analysis has been undertaken in Europe of the way in which these systems function, very little of the research has been done under the rubric of consumer policy. This seems strange. One can hope that in the future, more attempts will be made to integrate such studies into the body of consumer policy theory. This becomes ever more appropriate as consumer organizations at both national and international levels become seriously interested in such areas, particularly drugs and health care. A brief introduction to the European drug market and its associated problems is provided by Reich [125], while Wikstrom [173] and Bolin, Meyerson, and Stahl [12] have analyzed problems relating to the Swedish food supply system.

In quite a different realm, the rather unique participation by consumers in decision-making in the U.K. nationalized industries has been described and evaluated by several consumer policy researchers

[70, 83, 157, 177]. Mitchell [94] reviews the use made of consumer performance indicators and targets within these industries. He suggests changes, including the adoption of a publicly declared set of targets and the development of recognized procedures for monitoring success or failure in meeting these targets.

Problems Related To New Technologies, New Media, and New Information Systems

At Heiligkreuztal, the discussion centered very much on the mass media and the new information technology, as can be seen from the set of issues listed under this heading in the Appendix. The discussion was instigated by three papers, two of which were presented by European researchers.

In one of these, Sepstrup [144] describes how the relatively peaceful life of TV advertisers has been disturbed by the advent of new information technology and documents empirically the "electronic dilemma of advertising" that has resulted: falling exposure due to consumer avoidance by means of zapping, videorecording, etc. He describes the measures taken by the media and the advertising industry to counteract this electronic dilemma, many of which have rather disastrous consequences from a consumer (as well as a cultural) point of view, e.g., strong story plots that do <u>not</u> focus on the products advertised, reducing the length of the commercial, split-screen-commercials, program-like advertising, and sponsoring.

In commenting on Sepstrup's paper, Grunert [52] assesses these findings from the perspective of economics of information. Here, it is assumed that information search by consumers is governed by costs and benefits and that the degree of use of information is a measure of its informativeness. If this is true, the pervasiveness of zapping clearly documents the low information value of advertising. Furthermore, economists usually assume that the supply of a certain type of information is by itself evidence of its usefulness. How is it then that large resources go into the supply of a certain type of information -- TV advertising -- that many consumers obviously regard as superfluous? At least one of the arguments of information/market economics must be wrong, maintains Grunert: either (1) consumer search is not a function of the usefulness of the information, or (2) the market does not yield the optimal amount of information through advertising.

One might argue that consumer organizations should see to it that citizens are well informed so they can choose wisely among the television <u>programs</u> that they watch. Further, these organizations should try to influence the quality of programming. This is surely as important as equipping consumers to choose their TV sets wisely. Yet, consumer organizations have been reluctant to wrestle with assessments and policies regarding this intangible consumer product. In another paper, Sepstrup [143] analyzes the reasons for this state of affairs. He also discusses the difficulties that consumer organizations have encountered when they have attempted to have a say in national and international media policies, e.g., with respect to the amount and types of television advertising that are acceptable. One of the difficulties has to do with the fact that consumer representatives from various European countries differ greatly in their evaluations of the problems caused by television advertising. This makes it extremely difficult to arrive at a common consumer stance with respect to advertising on TV.

In another Heiligkreuztal paper, Grønmo [48] argues that the development of new information technology (point of sales systems, bar code labelling, electronic funds transfer systems, home computers, videotex, etc.) will lead to the integration of functions, the concentration of power, and the homogenization of interests among the commercial and institutional actors within the distribution system. Conversely, it will lead to fragmentation of consumer behavior and heterogenization of consumer interests. Thus, Grønmo holds, as information technology marches on, the most powerful commercial and institutional actors are likely to strengthen their positions while simultaneously the consumers' position is weakened. To counteract such a development, consumers will have to utilize the new technologies actively, developing their own communication networks, fostering their common interests.

One new information technology, videotex, has often been hailed as a medium excellently suited for consumer information (unlimited capacity, easy to use by laymen without computer know-how, available day and night, use of home television screen as monitor, interactive features). Grunert [50, 51] carried out the most extensive field experiment to date in order to test the suitability of videotex for public consumer information -- for consumers choosing among different makes of cars. Although the participants viewed the intelligibility and usefulness of the system very positively, the quality of the purchase decisions as measured by Grunert did not improve compared to a control group lacking access to the videotex database.

Videotex development in France is very atypical since in France the medium reaches a much larger household audience than in all other countries, where diffusion has been much slower than expected. Thus, for those interested in videotex's potential for consumer information, it is important to follow the French development. Mayer [90] provides a detailed account of Teletel, the French videotex system in English. Good French-language sources for videotex are [30, 31, 97, 156] and, for new electronic media in general [20, 55], and [155].

Sepstrup and Olander [145] describe the experiences of various European consumer organizations in using videotex to provide product test and other consumer information. Both the very slow diffusion of this new technology and the difficulties of financing the generation and updating of information about goods and services in a large number of areas are factors that lead Sepstrup and Olander to be highly skeptical about videotex as a major future channel for disseminating consumer information from neutral senders. (See also [115]). Teletext -- a medium now spreading rapidly in a number of European countries -- and cabletext may stand a better chance. No matter which new electronic text medium prevails (if any!) it is clear that neutral consumer information will constitute a very minor part of the total supply of information in that medium. The vast majority of consumer information delivered by these new technologies will consist of advertising and sales promotions. Thus, consumer policymakers and researchers should concentrate on devising rules regarding commercial consumer information in these media.

The Heiligkreuztal group agrees with Mitchell and Murley views set forth in a monograph prepared for IOCU [96]. They believe that maximizing the advantages and minimizing the disadvantages of developments in information technology, will constitute a major challenge for consumer policymakers and researchers in the years to come.

Problems of Disadvantaged Consumers

The Heiligkreuztal document, identified numerous groups of disadvantaged consumers who need attention due to their vulnerable position in the marketplace: children, the poor, the unemployed, the elderly, immigrants, and ghetto consumers. In various European countries, the protection of such groups is one of the most important goals of government consumer policy. For this reason it is astonishing to find that academic research in Europe has paid little if any attention to the consumer problems with which these groups are confronted. Since 1980, Journal of Consumer Policy has published only one paper in which the investigator decidedly set out to study such a group. In this study, Wimmer (175) provides evidence that "the poor pay more" in the Federal Republic of Germany. Wimmer found that buying efficiency was lowest for consumers who are both old and come from the lowest social-economic stratum. For Germany the hypothesis ought to be rephrased: "The old and socially disadvantaged pay more."

As to children, the effects of television advertising upon children has been the subject of several European investigations. For some German studies see, [10, 152]. Several European contributions on this subject may be found in [165].

The dearth of consumer policy research dealing with disadvantaged groups does not mean that we lack European studies of the consumption habits and attitudes of various market segments such as the young and the elderly. The studies exist but, unfortunately, there is little contact between scholars in the consumer policy field and the economists, sociologists and psychologists carrying out such work. Nor have studies carried out by consumer agencies and organizations been used as inputs for academic research. I think here of British studies of physically disabled consumers, ethnic minorities, and low income consumer/social security claimants [98, 100, 101, 102, 174]; Belgian and French research on poor consumers (in Belgium, studies by the Centre d'Etudes et de Diffusion Economiques et Sociales in Brussels and by Fondation Roi Baudoin [40], in France [93, 113, 118]); as well as several Nordic investigations of the consumption and time use patterns of the young, summarized in a recent publication from the Consumer Committee of the Nordic Council of Ministers [160].

Bourgoignie and others [13, 28, 170] have advanced the general thesis that many policy measures intended to inform and protect consumers, in effect hurt low-income families by increasing the inequality among consumers.

Thus, the problems of disadvantaged consumers have been underexplored in Europe. It is noteworthy that neither was there a session at the Wingspread Conference dealing with the problems of disadvantaged consumers except possibly consumers from less developed countries. Is this a universal blind spot in the coverage of research that purports to be "in the consumer interest"?

International/Global Dimensions of Consumer Issues

Disconcertingly, one has to admit that European researchers have made very few contributions to the understanding of consumer problems in the third world or the development of consumer policy guidelines for such countries. European contributions appear largely to be limited to documentation of drug and pesticide problems caused by European exports [89, 21, 22], and to the analysis of legal possibilities for preventing such exports [16]. There are in the European literature no general treatises of third world consumer problems comparable to those of Thorelli [158, 159] and Kerton [80]. Nor does there seem to be any independent monitoring or evaluation of the intensified efforts of the International Organization of Consumers Unions (and several affiliated alliances) to organize and improve the lot of consumers in third world countries.

As to global issues discussed in earlier sections of this paper-- protectionism and internationalization of the mass media -- more European research has been done or is under way as indicated.

Consumer Issues In The Service Sector (Private and Public)

This again is a little-researched topic in spite of the fact that dissatisfaction and complaints with regard to services often rank high in consumer dissatisfaction surveys. Rosenberger's paper [130] on methodological problems in measuring the quality of services, the previously mentioned papers on consumer representation in the nationalized British industries, and a paper and discussion on optimal retail structures seen from a consumer perspective [32, 33, 47] are the only European articles to have appeared recently in Journal of Consumer Policy disregarding some exclusively legal papers. An empirical study of the users of the U.S. Consumers' Checkbooks appeared in a German working paper [61]. (The Washington and Bay Area Consumers' Checkbooks publish evaluations of a wide vareity of service providers ranging from dentists to florists.)

With respect to consumer problems with public services, it is regrettable that the rich theoretical framework by Young [176] has not become influential in triggering off and guiding consumer policy research. At a more practical level, attention should be drawn to a large-scale program set up by the Norwegian Ministry for Consumer Affairs. This program is intended to improve government services in several areas where citizens deal with public agencies and civil servants (social security agencies, hospitals, tax authorities, etc.). Some of the research that spurred these efforts is described by Jensen [67].

Consumers and Economic Affairs

Participants at the Heiligkreuztal symposium were concerned with the impact of economic trends and government economic policy on consumers at both macro and micro levels.

At the macro level, the question is to what extent consumer interests (as compared to those of industry and labor) are looked after when government economic and financial policies, industrial and regional policies, agricultural and housing policies, etc., are formed. In his Heiligkreuztal paper, Koopman [81], drawing on his experience in the Dutch administration, stressed the need for consumer interests to be represented in the decision-making process in the sectoral policies worked out in several branches of government. This represents the opening of a new topic for consumer policy research. An interesting beginning has been made in Germany by Schatz and his coworkers [131, 132] who set out to investigate the determinants of consumer influence in political decision-making. Schatz et al. undertook case studies of standard form contracts, drug safety, housing policy (tenants' protection), and technical standardization. Not surprisingly, government's decision-making was found to be bureaucratic. It also reflected an increasing dominance of legal and economic views over social considerations. Schatz et al found that consumer organizations played a very subordinate part in the process. Somewhat more formally, Pestoff [119] has described the representation of consumer interests in various political decision-making bodies in Sweden.

More interest -- and more research and practical work -- has dealt with the description and amelioration of the plight of the individual consumer or household caught up in microeconomic problems, e.g., consumers getting in over their heads with consumer credit. Since this is a relatively well-researched area I will limit myself to listing a set of recent studies and policy documents [23, 29, 38, 63, 78, 103, 163]. The other side of the coin, saving behavior and attitudes, has been studied extensively at the Stockholm School of Economics [75, 76, 86, 87, 116, 164, 167]. These studies also include analyses of household economic planning in general.

The tax burden was also mentioned in the Heiligkreuztal document. Although not seeing themselves as consumer policy researchers, a group of psychologists and economists, primarily from the U.K., the Netherlands, Sweden (and also the U.S.), have done considerable research under the heading of fiscal psychology. Their recent research has produced a series of empirical findings concerning attitudes towards taxes, tax evasion, the comprehensibility of the tax system to taxpayers, and the influence of taxation on the supply of labor. These are clearly relevant for any consumer policy-makers and researchers who want to enter this thorny arena. The book by Lewis [84] gives a good introduction to the field. A series of recent research papers on fiscal psychology appeared in two special issues of Journal of Economic Psychology (Vol. 2, 1982, No. 3; Vol. 3, 1983, No. 2); see also [25, 49].

The impact of inflation upon consumer well-being was another topic in the Heiligkreuztal document. Here again, the work of economic psychologists is worth looking into. Perceived rates of past and future inflation and their impact on intended behavior have been studied in [1, 2, 3, 8, 73, 74, 146, 154, 168, 169]. Several of these papers appear in a special issue of Journal of Economic Psychology (Vol. 7, No. 3, 1986).

By integrating these strands of research, it might be possible to test the hypothesis that increasingly big differences in consumption standards are coming into existence among families with equal nominal income, due to inequalities in the ability and opportunity to manage family economic affairs with respect to budgeting skills, price awareness, tax evasion opportunities, and black market participation. If this hypothesis is confirmed, it will also be necessary to study the consequences in terms of personal frustration and societal tension.

The Organization of Consumer Interests

This is definitely a field in which European consumer policy researchers have shown much interest in recent years.

In West Germany, Biervert, Monse and Rock [6, 7] completed an intensive study of consumer organizations from 1953 to 1980, based on analysis of existing documents and on qualitative surveys. The authors criticize what they call the depoliticization and increasing market orientation of consumer policy in Germany. They dislike the tendency by consumer organizations to see consumer policy as applicable only to micro relations in markets. There is no radical dissent in consumer organizations. Thus there comes about a convergence between government consumer policy and the activities of consumer organizations. According to these authors, consumer organizations have not recognized that economic development is jeopardizing the natural environment and desirable living conditions. The prevailing view reinforces an unfruitful polarization of grassroots-oriented forms of protest on one hand and traditional representation of the consumer interest on the other.

Nelles and coworkers [104, 105] have studied the appearance of various self-help groups (tenant groups, environmentalist groups, self-help health groups, etc.) to see if they reflect the beginning of a new and different consumer movement. Various types of new collective action are identified. According to Nelles, the relevance of these developments for consumer theory and consumer policy lies not only in the contribution that these new groups and movements make to the representation of consumer interests, but even more, they reveal how more and more activities outside our working time are being mediated and determined by consumption, demand, and the use of systematically produced goods and services. Consumer theorists and consumer policy-makers should ask themselves, says Nelles, whether this development represents a positive contribution to human well-being and happiness (the conventional view) or whether they should question and criticize it along the lines indicated by the protesters in the new movements.

Offe [111] has emphasized the well-known difficulties of forming effective consumer organizations and building consumer countervailing power that arises because "consumers" are not a particular segment of society that can easily be mobilized against other groups. He therefore proposes an integration of consumer interests with worker interests and advocates a shift of focus to a "production-centred" consumer policy that would take up such issues as the humanization of the workplace, environmental effects of industrial production processes, and product line decisions. He does not underestimate the conflicts that will appear in these spheres between employee and consumer viewpoints. But he does see more hope for consumers in a reintegration than in a continued differentiation of consumer and worker interests.

Studies critical of current consumer organizations and their goals have also been carried out in Scandinavia. In Denmark, Jensen [64, 66] concludes that few of the existing consumer organizations and institutions seek to solve what he calls the "structural" problems of consumers. This he ascribes to the fact that most consumer organizations adhere to one of two basic paradigms -- (1) consumer-controlled production or (2) interdependence between production and consumption. Only those few organizations and groups that embrace the paradigm of producer-controlled consumption as their ideological basis are critical of "normal" functioning of markets, and thus do not concentrate exclusively on (1) activities directed to consumers-- information, advice, education, or (2) remedying the damages done by individual, "naughty" sellers.

As to Norway, Stø [151] describes the crossroads at which a quasi-governmental organization such as the Norwegian Consumer Council stands. The work of the Council is based on financial support by government, but is governed by a body with representation from a number of independent, voluntary organizations. (A similar organizational pattern exists in several European countries.) According to Stø, a choice will soon have to be made between developing the Council into an arm of government (a public agency) or turning it into a totally independent organization. He outlines the pros and cons of both options.

Koopman [81], in his Heiligkreuztal paper, takes a forthright stand in this issue, arguing that the government ought to leave most consumer issues (but not all) to be solved by negotiations between producer and independent consumer organizations. At the same time government should provide consumer organizations with the financial resources to carry out these functions.

Blomqvist [9] makes a strong plea for the potentialities for consumer cooperatives to become the main organization representing the consumer interest. He finds it astonishing that consumer researchers, when searching for mechanisms whereby the consumers can represent themselves, almost always neglect consumer cooperatives. "Why reinvent the wheel?" is his rhetorical question. In discussing Blomqvist's paper, Nilsson [107], who has dissected the mechanisms of the consumer cooperative firm in two recent books [106, 108], is more skeptical about the role of consumer cooperatives in furthering consumer interests in general. Nilsson does not dismiss this possibility entirely, agreeing that cooperatives tend to be more consumer oriented than their competitors. Broadly speaking, there is a noticeable increase in research interest in consumer cooperatives, and especially in newly emerging forms, in all the Nordic countries.

OMNIUM GATHERUM

This, then has been the research that fitted the Heiligkreuztal categories. Let me finish with a terse catalogue of some European research which fits none of these categories. Because the emphasis in Heiligkreutztal list is on the production side, it is not surprising that most of the residual topics are related to the consumer side. The residual deals mainly with the situation of individual consumers and households and with the effects of consumer information, counseling, and education programmes.

Consumer Satisfaction and Dissatisfaction

The study of consumer satisfaction and dissatisfaction (and complaining behavior) has spread also to Europe. In some countries, such studies have been carried out by major institutions, e.g., National Consumer Council [99] and Office of Fair Trading [112], both from Great Britain. In the scientific literature, a number of findings have been reported. In a Danish study, Kristensen [82] found that consumers with less education were less likely to be dissatisfied -- but not less likely to complain when dissatisfied. Corroborating results from Norway were published by Stø [150]. Bruhn [18] uncovered a learning effect in complaining behavior:

positive experiences with earlier complaints have a clear impact upon later expectations and behavior. In the Netherlands, Richins and Verhage [129] found that situational factors seem to have a greater impact upon complaining propensity than attitudinal factors. A summary of the results from several of the European (and U.S.) studies on consumer satisfaction and consumer complaining behavior with an attempt at a theoretical explanation and integration has recently been provided by Scherhorn [139].

Consumer Attitudes

Whereas consumer satisfaction research mainly deals with satisfaction/dissatisfaction with particular products and services, there have also been a number of surveys of more general consumer attitudes towards the performance of business and various ways of regulating and organizing consumer affairs. Wikstrom [171] found that Swedish consumers are less worried about various consumer problems than their U.S. counterparts. Hansen and Olander [56] showed that Danish attitudes towards consumer policy issues had not changed much from 1976 to 1984 with the exception of a movement towards a more passive attitude when it comes to self-organization as a means of ameliorating the situation. Stø [150, 43] has identified a red, a blue, and a green consumer attitude segment in the Norwegian population. The red segment stresses social inequalities and wants to protect the weak consumer; the blue segment believes in the fairness of the market mechanism but approves of consumer information; the green segment gives protection of the environment and the preservation of natural resources the highest priority.

Consumer Information

In the Heiligkreuztal document, the responsibility for unsatisfactory product and service information has been assigned to the supplier of products and services. Similar ideas appeared in a Swedish Government Commission report in 1974 [128, 166], recommending the introduction of mandatory consumer information in advertising and marketing. This led to the introduction of a general clause about information responsibilities in marketing legislation. Wikstrom's report on the effect of this legislation is not encouraging [172].

This does not mean that the effects of information provided by neutral institutions and consumer organizations have been neglected in European research. In West Germany, much more than elsewhere, such research has been extensive.

A group of researchers at Mannheim University, led by Hans Raffee and Gunter Silberer, studied intensively attitudes towards, the exposure to, and the use and effects of product test information. The number of dependent variables in their most recent and most extensive, quasi-experimental investigation is so large as to defy summary here. Exposure to product test information seems higher than previously believed and occurs also among lower socioeconomic groups. The effects on purchase decisions seem, however, to be limited. The various investigations have led to a series of proposals for improved procedures on the part of product testing organizations. These include the recommendation that they publish two overall quality ratings for each product in order to sensitize users to the interdependence of attribute weights and overall ratings. The main publication from the project is Silberer and Raffee [149] (in German); papers in English are [147,148].

In a rare, full-fledged field experiment, Kaas and Tolle [77] found that providing consumers with subscriptions to Test (the German Consumer Reports) over a long period (14 months) turns readers into "information seekers" who make greater use of all kinds of information sources.

In the Hohenheim research program [27, 50], participants in a laboratory experiment made product choice decisions of a higher quality when a sheet with standardized information on risks perceived by consumers was included.

Consumer Counseling

Individual and group consumer counseling has also been the subject of a number of studies. A symposium report recently published in Germany [88] covers the entire spectrum of counseling activities. In an interesting "action research" project, Reifner and his coworkers experimented with the collectivization of both counseling and complaint action. This involved a procedure in which consumers were actively encouraged to bring their problems to advisory centres [127, 78, 126]. The Hohenheim group [27] found that group advice can be successful in changing the degree of risks perceived in a purchase situation, and in improving the knowledge about indicators that can be used to reduce certain risks of purchase. In a recent paper, the Swedish Consumer Ombudsman has described the shifting of the emphasis of Swedish public consumer policy towards devoting considerably more of the available resources to local advisory and complaint handling centres [41].

In a provocative paper, Scherhorn [138] questioned the use of consumer counsellors and advice centres to provide objective product information and purchase recommendations. According to Scherhorn, these obligations should be placed upon the producers. By contrast it should be the task of consumer agencies and organizations to stimulate, promote, and check information and recommendation standards set up by others. Personal advisory services should be restricted to decision counseling in a broader sense, teaching consumers how to attain greater autonomy and self-critical reflection.

Consumer Education

Consumer education in schools is a child of many sorrows. This is true because of (1) the very limited amount of consumer education that takes place in European schools and (2) the sparseness of research efforts aimed at improving and/or monitoring the effects of such education. Meyer [91] took stock of European consumer education in schools and advanced a number of conceptual educational guidelines. Jensen [65] reported on the results of an EEC pilot project designed to spur the development of new ways of teaching children consumer skills.

Consumers and the Environment

For years observers have predicted a merger of environmental and consumer policy. Except for the field of energy conservation (for a good survey see two special issues of Journal of Economic Psychology (Vol. 3, No. 3/4, 1983; Vol. 4, No. 1/2, 1983), few signs of such a merger have appeared despite certain forays by consumer organizations into environmental territory in the form of package recycling and other prevention of pollution, the control of hazardous products such as pesticides, etc.). A survey of the surprisingly sparse, consumer-policy related research on environmental issues is provided by Joerges [68, 69] and Uusitalo [161, 162].

U.S. AND EUROPEAN RESEARCH: COMPARING NOTES

Certain categories in the Heiligkreuztal list are obviously under-represented in current European consumer policy research. The most obvious of these are: (a) problems related to regulated markets and systems; (b) problems of disadvantaged consumers; (c) international/global problems; (d) consumer issues in the service sector.

It is interesting to see what differences in emphasis there might be between U.S. research -- as represented at the Wingspread Conference, and European research -- as reflected in the Heiligkreuztal Conference.

My impression is that economics of information and the notion of imperfect information and its effects on the functioning of markets are more topical issues "over here" (in the U.S.). So, too, consumer information processing. Europeans, on the other hand, are more preoccupied with the assessment of various ways of organizing the consumer interest and with the impact of mass media contents upon the socialization of consumers and on consumer policies to deal with this impact.

Taking a more sweeping view, one can dare to generalize that concepts and ideas from sociology and political science play a larger role in European research while concepts and ideas from economics and psychology are more dominant in U.S. research.

What is more striking to this reviewer is a shared shortcoming. In my opinion, too little consumer policy research in both European and North America is founded on a "grand theory" or is aimed at constructing such a theory. By a grand theory, I mean a general framework that encompasses the structure and behavior of producers, consumers, and their interaction in the marketplace; which deals with the goal conflicts between producers and consumers, and among consumers themselves; which interrelates the various criteria for consumer welfare (without the guidance of which no consumer policy can be evaluated); and which elucidates the role that is to be played by each and every major consumer policy instrument within the framework.

It is noteworthy, and in my judgement unfortunate, that even during as major an event as the Wingspread Conference, there was not a single session devoted to "the theory of consumer policy" during which various proposals for the underpinnings of such a "grand theory" could be pitted against each other.

The most ambitious European attempt to date to present such a theory, is attributable to Gerhard Scherhorn. First presented in 1973, it was amended and reformulated first in a major work [140] and then in a series of papers over the years [133, 134, 135, 136, 137]. It is a sign of the immaturity of our field that neither this nor any other comprehensive theory is the focal point of scientific debate and functions as the point of departure for empirical work. (That a good theoretical framework can function as a stimulus and a valuable guideline for empirical research is amply demonstrated by the unusual productivity of the Hohenheim group in several areas such as consumer information systems, consumer education, consumer counseling, and consumer socialization.)

I see no sign that consumer policy researchers on either side of the ocean are turning to theoretical work to a larger extent than has been the case during the last decade. I believe it would be beneficial for the long run development of the field -- and for practitioners of consumer policy, too -- if this were to come about.

At any rate, more should be done to broaden the interface between the scholarly activities on the two sides of the ocean. I can only repeat the final words of a previous review article: in the underdeveloped area of consumer policy research, insulation is a luxury that neither side can afford!

APPENDIX

SUMMARY OF VITAL CONSUMER POLICY ISSUES: HEILIGKREUZTAL SYMPOSIUM

What are the most relevant consumer policy issues in the years to come? This question was put to the participants of the symposium on "New Challenges for European Consumer Policy," held at the University of Hohenheim/Heiligkreuztal on March 17-20, 1986.

The participants of this symposium were research workers in the field of consumer policy or related disciplines, and policy makers from business, government, and consumer organizations, representing twelve European countries together with three overseas participants. The papers and discussions focused on the future development of the consumer role; the impact that changing technological, economic, and social conditions would have upon the consumer's situation; the organization of consumers; and consumer representation in government and business.

After two days of discussion, the participants were asked to list the three issues they saw as most relevant for consumers in the years ahead.

This is the summary of the statements from 25 participants. The issues varied in character and in the form they were presented. Some statements included several issues, others were one-dimensional. Some participants made a distinction between consumer problems and areas for research. The protocols used for summary purposes permitted a single statement to be the input for more than one problem area. On the other hand, all issues generated from one participant may in some cases have been placed in the same area. Naturally, some statements were difficult to interpret; some were ill matched with the problem categories. This means that "counting heads" when ranking the importance of the different areas is not possible. What is reported is how many times statements belonging to the different problem areas have been made.

The participants' statements have been classified under eight different problem areas, which are presented in order of their amount of support.

1. Consumer problems related to market structure and market behavior -- 15 statements on the following issues:

   Structural dimensions:

   - More business concentration;
   - More concentrated markets;
   - Growing influence of multinational corporations;
   - Increasing dominance from horizontal and vertical systems;
   - Effects of concentrated and regulated markets.

   Behavioral aspects:

   - Lack of competition;
   - Unfair competition;
   - Trade barriers and growing protectionism;
   - Problems related to unsatisfactory supplier/consumer communication or interaction;
   - Poorly working distribution systems;
   - Unsatisfactory supplier responsibility for product and service information.

2. Consumer problems related to regulated markets/systems -- 12 statements on the following issues

   - Agricultural and food system;
   - Health care, the drug market, drug prices, and drug consumption (especially overconsumption);
   - Housing and rents.

   The consensus was that these markets have become ineffective due to lack of competition or inappropriate regulation.

3. Problems related to new technologies, new media, and new information systems -- 9 statements on the following issues:

   - How to secure varied, high quality TV;
   - How to secure the consumer interest in the new media with a free flow of information, entertainment, and advertising;

- What will the impact of new information technology be on the consumer interest?
- How will computerization of daily life affect consumers?
- What kind of future for consumers will the new information technology offer? What will the role of advertising be?
- What about the cultural effects of the new electronic media?
- What will the new technologies offer when it comes to efficient consumer information systems?
- Will it be possible to maintain present standards of information in the new media?

4. Problems of disadvantaged consumers -- 9 statements on the following issues:

   Groups of consumers which are considered to need special attention:

   - Children;
   - The new poor;
   - The traditional poor (there is a tendency to forget these);
   - The unemployed;
   - The elderly;
   - Immigrants;
   - Ghetto consumers.

   Some of these seem to be growing in numbers, e.g., the new poor, the unemployed and the elderly.

5. International/global dimensions of consumer issues -- 9 statements on the following issues:

   These statements indicate that consumer problems have to be solved on an international basis.

   - International coordination of consumer law and policy;
   - Internationalization of communication networks and distribution systems -- implications for consumer information, consumer protection, and consumer organizations;
   - International trade policy;
   - Ways to solve the growing number of consumer problems which have an international anchorage (hazardous products, TV advertising).

6. Consumer issues in the service sector (private and public) -- 8 statements on the following issues:

   The emphasis is on public services which were seen as a growing problem area. How to protect the consumers when it comes to public utilities, how to get consumer representation, how to control public utilities in the consumer interest?

   Service areas especially mentioned were professional services, public transportation, communication, and health care;

   Within the private sector, marketing failure at the grass roots level is also seen as a vital consumer problem.

7. Consumers and economic affairs -- 5 statements on the following issues:

   The character of problems stated under this heading were as follows:

   - Tax burden and consumers: implications for economic well-being;
   - Inflation and its impact on consumer welfare: purchasing power and protection of savings;
   - The consumer's role and place in the economy;
   - Integration of consumer policy into general economic policy.

8. The organization of the consumer interest -- 5 statements on the following issues:

   The issues in this category were mostly in the shape of questions:

   - How to arrange for a more efficient consumer power;
   - How to create a clearer and more powerful consumer voice;
   - How to arrange for a more effective consumer countervailing power;
   - How to strengthen the consumer role;
   - Consumer chambers as a working solution.

Some overall comments are in order. First, the statements about what are the most vital consumer problem areas in the future reflect current economic and technological changes in society as a whole.

Second, maturing industries with overcapacity, new technologies for information and communication move consumer problems to the international arena. The problems no longer stay local or national. They are also more and more interrelated. Solving one problem may lead to other problems in another area or another country.

Third, problem areas not mentioned in these statements are also indicative of a change of perspective. Product safety and misleading advertising are no longer seen as vital problems: they are taken care of, more or less, by mature industries and by regulatory agencies. Even consumer education received little attention. Only one participant mentioned this field.

The new consumer problem areas are broader and more complex than the earlier ones. They call for an interdisciplinary approach, thus posing a new challenge to the scientific community.

REFERENCES

1. BATCHELOR, R.A. (1986), "The Psychophysics of Inflation," Journal of Economic Psychology, 7 (No. 3; September): 269-290.

2. BATES, JOHN B. and ANDRE GABOR (1986), "Price Perception in Creeping Inflation: Report on an Enquiry," Journal of Economic Psychology, 7 (No. 3; September): 291-314.

3. BEHREND, HILDE (1984), Problems of Labor and Inflation, London: Croom Helm.

4. BEIER, UDO (1978), "Entscheidungsbedingte Kaufkraftverluste: Formen, Umfang und verbraucherpolitischer Relevanz (Monetary Losses Caused by Uninformed Purchase Decisions: About Their Implications for Consumer Policy and Various Ways of Calculating Them)," Journal of Consumer Policy, 2 (No. 2; Spring): 159-171.

5. ________ (1979), "Zum Einfluss beschrankter Markttransparenz auf die Kaufentscheidungen der Privathaushalte (On the Influence of Limited Market Transparency on Purchase Decisions by Private Households)," Hauswirtschaft und Wissenschaft, 27 (No. 3, June): 108-117.

6. BIERVERT, BERND, KURT MONSE, and REINHARD ROCK (1984), "Alternatives for Consumer Policy: A Study of Consumer Organizations in the FRG," Journal of Consumer Policy, 7 (No. 4; December): 343-358.

7. ________ (1984), Organisierte Verbraucherpolitik (Organized Consumer Policy) Frankfurt: Campus.

8. BLOMQVIST, H.C. (1983), "On the Formation of Inflationary Expectations: Some Empirical Evidence from Finland, 1979-1980," Journal of Economic Psychology, 4 (No. 4; December): 319-334.

9. BLOMQVIST, K. (1984), "Cooperatives and Consumer Research," Journal of Consumer Policy, 7 (No. 3; September): 323-341.

10. BOCKELMANN, F., J. HUBER and A. MIDDELMANN (1979), Werbefernsehkinder (The Children of Television Commercials), Berlin: Spies.

11. BODDEWYN, J.J. (1985), "Advertising Self-Regulation: Private Government and Agent of Public Policy," Journal of Public Policy and Marketing, 4: 129-141.

12. BOLIN, OLAF, PER-MARTIN MEYERSON, and INGEMAR STAHL (1986), The Political Economy of the Food Sector, Stockholm: Studieforbundet Naringsliv och samhalle.

13. BOURGOIGNIE, THIERRY (1984), "Le consommateur oublie ou la protection du consommateur economique faible (The Forgotten Consumer or the Protection of the Economically Weak Consumer)," in Jeune Barreau de Bruxelles (ed.), Droit des pauvres, Pauvre droit, Louvain-la-Neuve: Cabay, 149-162.

14. _________ (1984), "The Need to Reformulate Consumer Protection Policy." Journal of Consumer Policy, 7 (No. 2; June): 307-321.

15. _________ (1985), "Theoretical Framework and Introductory Remarks," in Monique Goyens (ed.), E.C. Competition Policy and the Consumer Interest, Proceedings of the Third European Workshop on Consumer Law, Louvain-la-Neuve/Bruxelles: Cabay/Bruylant, 1-18.

16. _________ (1986), "Exports of Dangerous Medicinal Products from the Territory of the European Community to Third World Countries," paper presented at the symposium, "New Challenges for European Consumer Policy," held at Heiligkreuztal, March 17-20, 1986.

17. _________, GUY DELVAX, FRANCOISE DOMONT-NAERT, and CHRISTIAN PANIER (1981), L'aide juridique au consommateur (Legal Aid for the Consumer), Bruxelles: Bruylant.

18. BRUHN, MANFRED (1982), Konsumentenunzufriedenheit und Beschwerden (Consumer Dissatisfaction and Complaints), Frankfurt: Lang.

19. CAVE, MARTIN (1985), "Market Models and Consumer Protection," Journal of Consumer Policy, 8 (No. 4; December): 335-351.

20. CENTRE DE RECHERCHES INFORMATIQUE ET DROIT (1984), La telematique: Aspects techniques, juridiques et socio-Politiques (Telematics: Technical, Juridical, and Socio-Political Aspects), Bruxelles: Story-Scientia.

21. CHETLEY, ANDREW (1985), Cleared for Export, The Hague: Coalition Against Dangerous Exports.

22. _________ (1986), "Not Good Enough For Us But Fit For Them -- An Examination of the Chemical and Pharmaceutical Export Trades," Journal of Consumer Policy, 9 (No. 2; June): 155-180.

23. CONSUMERS AND DEBT (1983), London: National Consumer Council and Cardiff: Welsh Consumer Council.

24. CONSUMERS' ASSOCIATION (1979), The Price of Protection, London: Consumers' Association.

25. CULLIS, JOHN and ALAN LEWIS (1985), "Some Hypotheses and Evidence on Tax Knowledge and Preferences," Journal of Economic Psychology, 6 (No. 3; September): 271-287.

26. CZERWONKA, CHRISTINE, GUNTER SCHOPPE and STEFAN WECKBACH (1976), Der aktive Konsument: Kommunikation und Kooperation (The Active Consumer: Communication and Cooperation), Gottingen: Otto Schwartz.

27. DEDLER, KONRAD, INGRID GOTTSCHALK, KLAUS G. GRUNERT, MARGOT HEIDERICH, ANNEMARIE L. HOFFMANN and GERHARD SCHERHORN (1984), Das Informationsdefizit der Verbraucher (The Consumer Information Deficit), Frankfurt: Campus.

28. DELVAX, GUY and THIERRY BOURGOIGNIE (1981), "La fonction de consommation et le droit de la consommation: L'enjeu reel (The Function of Consumption and Consumer Law: The Real Issue)," Revue interdisciplinaire d'etudes juridique, (No. 7): 1-72.

29. DESSART, W.C.A.M., and A.A.A. KUYLEN, (1986), "The Nature, Extent, Causes, and Consequences of Problematic Debt Situations," Journal of Consumer Policy, 9 (No. 3; September): 311-334.

30. DE VALENCE, FRANCOIS (1985), "Les marches du videotex (Developments in Videotex)," Paris: Association Francaise de Telematique, Mimeo.

31. "DEVELOPPEMENT DU SERVICE TELEMATIQUE," (1986), Paris: L'Institut National de la Consommation, Mimeo.

32. DICHTL, ERWIN and MARIUS LEIBOLD (1983), "Adequate Provisioning - The Need For Revision of Domestic Trade Policy Orientations," Journal of Consumer Policy, 6 (No. 4): 419-435.

33. _________ (1984), "Trade Policy Orientations and Provisioning: A Rejoinder," Journal of Consumer Policy, 7 (No. 3; September): 403-407.

34. DILLER, HERMANN (1977), "Der Preis als Qualitatsindikator (Price as Indicator of Quality)," Die Betriebswirtschaft, 37 (No. 2): 219-234.

35. DURANDIN, G. (1982), Les mensonges en propagande et en publicite (Untruths in Propaganda and Advertising), Paris: Presses Universitaires de France.

36. EKHAUGEN, KNUT, SIGMUND GRØNMO and DAVID KIRBY (1980), "State Support to Small Stores: A Nordic Form of Consumer Policy," Journal of Consumer Policy, 4 (No. 3; Summer): 195-211.

37. EUROPEAN CONSUMER LAW GROUP (1984), Reports and Opinions (September 1977 - March 1984). Brussels: Cabay-Bruylant.

38. _________ (1986), "Report on Consumer in Debt," Mimeo.

39. FLEISCHMANN, GERD (1981), "Sources for Product Ideas: A Proactive View on the Consumer," in Kent B. Monroe (ed.), Advances in Consumer Research, Vol. 7, 386-390, Ann Arbor, MI: Association for Consumer Research.

40. FONDATION ROI BAUDOIN (1984), La protection juridique contre le surendettement (Legal Protection Against Getting Into Extreme Debt), Bruxelles: Fondation Roi Baudoin.

41. FREIVALDS, LAILA (1986), "Nya former for lokalt konsumentarbete i Sverige (New Forms of Local Consumer Work in Sweden)," in Ulla Aitta et al. (eds.), Vagar till konsumentinflytande, Copenhagen: The Nordic Council of Ministers, NEK-Rapport 1986:8, 239-261.

42. FRITZ, WOLFGANG (1984), Warentest und Konsumguter-Marketing (Product Testing and the Marketing of Consumer Goods), Wiesbaden: Gabler.

43. GLEFJELL, SIDSEL and EIVIND STØ (1986), "Holdniger til virkemidler og institusjoner i norsk forbrukerpolitikk (Attitudes to Instruments and Institutions in Norwegian Consumer Policy)," paper presented at Seminar on Consumer Research, Asker, June 11-12, 1986.

44. GOTTSCHALK, INGRID and IRIS SCHNEIDER (1983), "The Intelligibility of Supplier Information," Journal of Consumer Policy, 6 (No. 2): 161-176.

45. GOYENS, MONIQUE (ed.) (1985), E.C. Competition Policy and the Consumer Interest, Proceedings of the Third European Workshop on Consumer Law, Louvain-la-Neuve/Bruxelles: Cabay/Bruylant.

46. _________ (1986), Price Information and Public Price Controls, Consumers and Market Performance, Proceedings of the Fourth European Workshop on Consumer Law, Brussels: Story-Scientia.

47. GRØNMO, SIGMUND (1984), "Adequate Research on Provisioning?" Journal of Consumer Policy, 7 (No. 1; March): 85-90.

48. _________ (1987), "The Strategic Position of Consumers in the Information Society," Journal of Consumer Policy, 10 (No. 1; March): 43-67.

49. V. GRUMBKOW, JASPER, and KARL-ERIK WARNERYD (1986), "Does the Tax System Ruin the Motivation to Seek Advancement?" Journal of Economic Psychology, 7 (No. 2; June): 221-243.

50. GRUNERT, KLAUS G. (1984), "The Consumer Information Deficit: Assessment and Policy Implications," Journal of Consumer Policy, 7 (No. 3; September): 359-388.

51. _________ (1984), Verbraucherinformation in Bildschirmtext: Moglichkeiten und Grenzen (Consumer Information on Videotex: Possibilities and Limits), Grobenzell: Verlag Reinhard Fischer.

52. _________ (1986), "Comment on the Paper by Sepstrup," presented at the symposium "New Challenges for European Consumer Policy," held at Heiligkreuztal, March 17-20, 1986.

53. _________ (1986), "Price Transparency, Competition, and the Consumer Interest: Economic Reasoning and Behavioural Evidence," in Monique Goyens (ed.), Price Information and Public Price Controls, Consumers and Market Performance, Proceedings of the Fourth European Workshop on Consumer Law, Brussels: Story-Scientia, 23-48.

54. _________ and KONRAD DEDLER (1985), "Misleading Advertising: In Search of a Measurement Methodology," Journal of Public Policy and Marketing, 4: 153-165.

55. GUYOT, BRIGITTE and COLETTE LOUSTALET (1983), La telematique, literature "grise," elements de bibliographie (Telematics, the "Grey" Literature, Elements of a Bibliography), Paris: La Documentation Francaise.

56. HANSEN, FLEMMING and FOLKE OLANDER (1986), "Attitudes to Consumer Policy Issues in Denmark - 1976 to 1984," Journal of Consumer Policy, 9 (No. 4; December): 407-429.

57. HANSEN, URSULA (1986), "Dialogue Between Business and Consumers in the Process of Product Development," paper presented at the Symposium "New Challenges for European Consumer Policy," held at Heiligkreuztal, March 17-20, 1986.

58. _________ and INGO SCHOENHEIT (eds.) (1985), Verbraucherabteilungen in privaten und offentlichen Unternehmen (Consumer Affairs Departments in Private and Public Enterprises), Frankfurt: Campus.

59. _________ (1986), "Consumer Affairs Departments -- A Report on Their Development in the United States and Their Transferability to the Federal Republic of Germany," Journal of Consumer Policy, 9 (No. 4; December): 445-468.

60. HART, DIETER (1986), "On the Conditions of an Integrative Consumer Information Policy -- Comments on Grunert's Contribution," in Monique Govens (ed.), Price Information and Public Price Controls, Consumers and Market Performance, Proceedings of the Fourth European Workshop on Consumer Law, Brussels: Story-Scientia, 49-60.

61. HARTJENS, PETER G. (1983), "Das Washington Consumers' Checkbook: Modell eines lokalen Dienstleistungsbewertungssystems (The Washington Consumers' Checkbook: Model for a Local System of Service Evaluation)," Stuttgart: University of Hohenheim, Department of Consumer Economics, Working Paper.

62. HJORTH-ANDERSEN, CHR. (1984), "The Concept of Quality and the Efficiency of Markets for Consumer Products," Journal of Consumer Research, 11 (No. 2; September): 708-718.

63. HORMANN, GUNTER and KNUT HOLZSCHECK (1983), "Consumer Credit in the Federal Republic of Germany: Selected Findings From an Empirical Study," Journal of Consumer Policy, 6 (No. 4): 457-468.

64. JENSEN, HANS RASK (1983), Forbrugerpolitik og organiseret forbrugerarbejde (Consumer Policy and Organized Consumer Action), Copenhagen: Akademisk Forlag.

65. _________ (1985), "The ECC Pilot-Project on Consumer Education in Schools," Journal of Consumer Studies and Home Economics, 9 (No. 1; March): 1-10.

66. _________ (1986), "The Relevance of Alternative Paradigms as Guidelines for Consumer Policy and Organized Consumer Action," Journal of Consumer Policy, 9 (No. 4; December): 389-405.

67. JENSEN, THOR ØVIND (1986), "Forbrukerinteresser og offentige tjenester (Consumer Interests and Public Services," in Ulla Aitta et al. (eds.), Vagar till konsumentinflytande, Copenhagen: The Nordic Council of Ministers, NEK-Rapport 1986:8, 69-99.

68. JOERGES, BERNWARD (1981), "Okologische Aspekte des Konsumverhaltens-Konsequenzen fur die Verbraucherinformationspolitik (Ecological Aspects of Consumer Behaviour - Consequences for Consumer Information Policy)," Journal of Consumer Policy, 5 (No. 4; Fall): 310-325.

69. _________ (ed.) (1982), Verbraucherverhalten und Umweltbelastung (Consumer Behaviour and Burdens on the Environment), Frankfurt: Campus.

70. JONES, T.T. (1981), "Consumer Representatives on the Boards of Nationalized Industries," Journal of Consumer Studies and Home Economics, 5 (No. 2; June): 85-99.

71. _________ and J.F. PICKERING (1979), "The Consumer's Interest in Competition Policy. 1. Welfare Competition. 2. Policy Implications," Journal of Consumer Studies and Home Economics, 3 (No. 2; June): 85-126.

72. JONSSON, ERNST (1983), "Does it Pay to Keep Shops Open in Sparsely Populated Areas? A Cost-Benefit Analysis of a Hypothetical Shop Closure," Journal of Consumer Policy, 6 (No. 4): 437-456.

73. JONUNG, LARS (1981), "Perceived and Expected Rates of Inflation in Sweden," American Economic Review, 71 (No. 5; December): 961-968.

74. _________ (1986), "Uncertainty About Inflationary Perceptions and Expectations," Journal of Economic Psychology, 7 (No. 3; September): 315-325.

75. JULANDER, CLAES-ROBERT (1975), Sparande och effekter av okad kunskap om inkomstens anvandning (Saving and the Effects of Increased Knowledge About the Use of Income), Stockholm: The Economic Research Institute at the Stockholm School of Economics.

76. JUNDIN, SILJA (1985), "Adolescent Orientation Toward Saving and Economic Planning," Stockholm: The Economic Research Institute at the Stockholm School of Economics. Research Paper 6302.

77. KAAS, KLAUS PETER and KLAUS TOLLE (1981), "Der Einfluss von Warentestinformationen auf das Informationsverhalten von Konsumenten (The Impact of Product Test Information Upon Consumers' Information Processing)," Journal of Consumer Policy, 5 (No. 4; Fall): 293-309.

78. KAHLER, ANNETTE (1984), "Consumers and Debts in the Federal Republic of Germany," Journal of Consumer Policy, 7 (No. 4; December): 487-495.

79. KARRHOLM, MARIANNE (1986), "Konsumentinflytande genom brukarkravsutformning (Consumer Influence by Outlining Product User Demands)," in Ulla Aitta et al. (eds.), Vagar till konsumentinflytande, Copenhagen: The Nordic Council of Ministers, NEK-Report 1986:8, 151-176.

80. KERTON, ROBERT R. (1980), "Consumer Search Capital. Delineating a Concept and Applying it to Consumers in Developing Countries," Journal of Consumer Policy, 4 (No. 4; Fall): 293-305.

81. KOOPMAN, Joop (1986), "New Developments in Government Consumer Policy: A Challenge for Consumer Organizations," Journal of Consumer Policy, 9 (No. 3; September): 269-286.

82. KRISTENSEN, PREBEN SANDER (1980), "What Consumers Want and What They Get From Complaints Directed at the Place of Purchase," Journal of Consumer Policy, 4 (No. 1; Winter): 1-7.

83. LENZEN, RICHARD (1981), "Verbraucherbeirate in Grossbritanniens verstaatlichten industrien (Consumer Councils in the Nationalized Industries of the United Kingdom)," Journal of Consumer Policy, 5 (No. 3; Summer): 244-256.

84. LEWIS, ALAN (1982), The Psychology of Taxation. Oxford: Basil Blackwell.

85. LINDHOFF, HAKAN and FOLKE OLANDER (1971), "Konsumenternas inflytande pa foretagens produktutveckling (Consumer Influence on Product Development)," in Lars-Gunnar Mattsson (ed.), Manniskor och foretag i kommunikationssamhallet, Stockholm: Prisma, 147-193. Also available in English as No. 1/73-68 in the Preprint Series of the International Institute of Management, Science Center Berlin.

86. LINDQVIST, AALF (1981), Hushallens sparande (The Saving of Households), Stockholm: The Economic Research Institute at the Stockholm School of Economics.

87. ________ (1981), "A Note on Determinants of Household Saving Behaviour," Journal of Economic Psychology, 1 (No. 1; March): 39-57.

88. LUBKE, VOLKMAR and INGO SCHOENHEIT (eds.) (1985), Die Qualitat von Beratungen fur Verbraucher (The Quality of Consumer Counseling), Frankfurt: Campus.

89. MEDAWAR, CHARLES (1979), Insult or Injury? An Enquiry Into the Marketing and Advertising of British Food and Drug Products in the Third World, London: Social Audit.

90. MAYER, ROBERT N. (1986), "Videotex in France: The Other French Revolution," Salt Lake City, UT: University of Utah, Family and Consumer Studies, Working Paper 86-5.

91. MEYER, HEINRICH (1983), Europaische Verbrauchererziehung - Bestandsaufnahme und curriculare Konzeption (European Consumer Education - State of the Art and Curricular Concepts), Frankfurt: Lang.

92. MICKLITZ, HANS-W. (1984), "Three Instances of Negotiation Procedures in the Federal Republic of Germany," Journal of Consumer Policy, 7 (No. 2; June): 211-229.

93. MILANO, SERGE (1982), La pauvrete en France, Paris: Editions du Sycomore.

94. MITCHELL, JEREMY (1983), "Consumer Performance Indicators and Targets for Nationalized Industries in the United Kingdom," Journal of Consumer Policy, 6 (No. 2): 177-193.

95. ________ (1986), "Consumer Organizations' Fight Against International Trade Restrictions: Comment on the Paper by Dardis," Journal of Consumer Policy, 9 (No. 3; September): 261-267.

96. ________ and LOVEDAY MURLEY (eds.) (1984), The Information Society. A Strategy for Consumers, London: National Consumer Council.

97. NAHON, GEORGES (1985), "The Growth of Videotex in France Beyond the Forecasts," in Proceedings of Videotex International, Pinner, UK: Online Publications, 1-10.

98. NATIONAL CONSUMER COUNCIL (1976), Means Tested Benefits, London: National Consumer Council.

99. ________ (1981), An Introduction to the Findings of the Consumer Concerns Survey, London: National Consumer Council.

100. ________ (1981), Getting Around: The Barriers to Access for Disabled People, London: National Consumer Council.

101. ________(1982), Minorities in the Marketplace: A Study of South Asian and West Indian Shoppers in Bradford, London: National Consumer Council.

102. ________ (1984), Of Benefit to All: A Consumer Review to Social Security, London: National Consumer Council.

103. ________ (1985), Behind With the Mortgage. London: National Consumer Council.

104. NELLES, WILFRIED (1983), "Consumer Self-Organization and New Social Movements," Journal of Consumer Policy, 6 (No. 3): 251-272.

105. ________ and WOLFGAND BEYWL (1984), Selbstorganisation: Alternativen fur Verbraucher (Self-Organization: Alternatives for Consumers), Frankfurt: Campus.

106. NILSSON, JERKER (1983), Det konsumentkooperativa foretaget (The Consumer Cooperative), Stockholm: Raben and Sjogren.

107. ________ (1985), "Consumer Cooperatives as Consumer Welfare Organizations," Journal of Consumer Policy, 8 (No. 3; September): 287-301.

108. ________ (1986), Den kooperativa verksamhetsformen (The Cooperative Form of Business), Lund: Studentlitteratur.

109. NOWAK, KJELL and GUNNAR ANDREN (1983), Reklam och samhallsforandring. Variation och konstans i svenska popularpressannonser 1950 - 1975 (Advertising and Societal Change. Variation and Constancy in Swedish Magazine Advertising 1950 - 1975), Lund: Studentlitteratur.

110. OECD (1985), Costs and Benefits of Protection, Paris: OECD, Economic Policy Committee.

111. OFFE, CLAUS (1981), "Ausdifferenzierung oder Integration - Bemerkungen uber strategische Verbraucherpolitik (Differentiation or Integration - Remarks on Consumer Policy Strategies)," Journal of Consumer Policy, 5 (Nos. 1+2; Winter + Spring): 119-133. The article appears in English in John Keane (ed.), Claus Offe: Contradictions of the Welfare State, London: Hutchinson, 1984.

112. OFFICE OF FAIR TRADING (1986), Consumer Dissatisfaction, London: Office of Fair Trading.

113. OHEIX, G. (1982), Contre la precarite et la pauvrete (Against Uncertainty and Poverty). Paris: La Documentation Francaise.

114. OLANDER, FOLKE (1980), "Recent Developments in European Consumer Policy Research," in Jerry C. Olson (ed.), Advances in Consumer Research, Vol. 7, Ann Arbor, MI: Association for Consumer Research, 56-65.

115. ________ (in press), "Consumer Information in the Electronic Data Media," in Shlomo Maital (ed.), Applied Behavioural Economics, Brighton: Wheatsheat and New York: New York University Press.

116. _________ and CARL-MAGNUS SEIPEL (1970), Psychological Approaches to the Study of Saving, Urbana, IL: University of Illinois, Bureau of Economic and Business Research.

117. PADBERG, DANIEL I. (1977), "Non-Use Benefits of Mandatory Consumer Information Programs," Journal of Consumer Policy, 1 (No. 1; Winter): 5-14.

118. PAUVRETE--PRECARITE (Poverty -- Precariousness) (1985), Paris: Ministere de l'Economie, Secretariat d'Etat Charge du Budget et de la Consommation. With a very complete bibliography.

119. PESTOFF, VICTOR (1984), Konsumentinflytande och konsumentorganisering (Consumer Influence and Consumer Organization), Stockholm: Ministry of Finance, Report Ds Fi 1984:15.

120. PICKERING, J.F. and D.C. COUSINS (1983), "Corporate Reactions to Voluntary Codes of Practice: Results of a Survey," Journal of Consumer Policy, 6 (No. 3): 37-54.

121. RAFFEE, HANS and WOLFGANG FRITZ (1984), "The Effects of Comparative Product Testing on Industry and Trade: Findings of a Research Project," Journal of Consumer Policy, 7 (No. 4; December): 423-439.

122. RAFFEE, HANS and GUNTER SILBERER (eds.) (1984), Warentest und Unternehmen (Product Testing and Industry), Frankfurt: Campus.

123. RAMSAY, IAN (1984), Rationales for Intervention in the Consumer Marketplace. London: Office of Fair Trading.

124. _________ (1985), "Framework for Regulation of the Consumer Marketplace," Journal of Consumer Policy, 8 (No. 4; December): 353-372.

125. REICH, NORBERT (1986), "Paradoxes of Social Regulation - Or: Difficulties of Articulating the Consumer Interest in a Complex Surrounding (The Example of the European Drug Market), paper presented at the symposium "New Challenges for European Consumer Policy," held at Heiligkreuztal, March 17-20, 1986.

126. REIFNER, UDO (1985), "From Market Protection to Consumer Protection. Collective Legal Advice for Consumers," Hamburg: Hochschule fur Wirtschaft and Politik, Working paper.

127. _________ and SABINE ADLER (1981), "Moglichkeiten fur eine praventive und breitenwirksame Verbraucherberatung durch die Verbraucherzentralen (Consumer Advisory Centres: How to Make Their Activities More Preventive and Far-Reaching)," Journal of Consumer Policy, 5 (No. 4; Fall): 346-356.

128. REKLAMUTREDNINGEN (1974), Information i reklamen (Information in Advertising), Stockholm: SOU (Swedish Government Commission Reports), 1974:23.

129. RICHINS, MARSHA L. and BRONISLAW VERHAGE (1985), "Seeking Redress for Consumer Dissatisfaction: The Role of Attitudes and Situational Factors," Journal of Consumer Policy, 8 (No. 1; March): 29-44.

130. ROSENBERGER, GUNTHER (1981), "Die neutrale Verbraucherinformation uber die Qualitat von Dienstleistungen - Einige methodische Probleme (Independent Consumer Information About Quality of Services - Some Methodological Questions)," Journal of Consumer Policy, 5 (No. 4; Fall): 326-336.

131. SCHATZ, HERIBERT (1983), "Consumer Interests in the Process of Political Decision-Making," Journal of Consumer Policy, 6 (No. 4): 381-395.

132. _________ (1984), Verbraucherinteressen im politischen Entscheidungsprozess (Consumer Interests in Political Decision Processes), Frankfurt: Campus.

133. SCHERHORN, GERHARD (1977), "Uber die Bedeutung des Verbraucherverhaltens fur die Funktionsfahigkeit des Marktes (On the Importance of Consumer Behaviour for the Functioning of Markets)," Journal of Consumer Policy, 1 (No. 1; Winter): 20-31.

134. _________ (1980), "Implications of the Theory of Consumer Behaviour for Consumer Policy Research," in Jerry C. Olson (ed.), Advances in Consumer Research, Vol. 7, Ann Arbor, MI: Association for Consumer Research, 52-55.

135. _________ (1981), "Methoden und Chancen einer Beeinflussung der Konsumentzen zur rationalen Ueberprufung von Praferenzen (Methods and Opportunities of Getting Consumers to Reconsider Their Preferences)," in Reinhard Tietz (ed.), Wert- und Praferenzprobleme in den Wirtschafts- und Socialwissenschaften, Berlin: Duncker & Humblot, 171-194.

136. _________ (1983), "Die Funktionsfahigkeit von Konsumgutermarkten (The Functioning of Markets for Consumer Goods)," in Martin Irle (ed.), Marktpsychologie als Sozialwissenschaft, Gottingen: Hogrefe, 45-150.

137. _________ (1983), "Wie unubersichtlich durfen Konsumgutermarkte werden? (How Intransparent May Consumer Goods Markets Get?)," Mitteilungsdienst der Verbraucherzentrale Nordrhein-Westfalen, No. 1, 37-45.

138. _________ (1985), "The Goal of Consumer Advice: Transparency or Autonomy?" Journal of Consumer Policy, 8 (No. 2; June): 133-151.

139. _________ (1985), "Die Unzufriedenheit der Verbraucher (The Dissatisfaction of Consumers)," Stuttgart: University of Hohenheim, Department of Consumer Economics, Working paper.

140. _________, ELKE AUGUSTIN, HEINRICH GUSTAV BRUNE, GERD EICHLER, ANNEMARIE HOFFMANN, HARALD SCHUMACHER, CLAUS HENNING WERNER, and KLAUS WIEKEN (1975), Verbraucherinteresse und Verbraucherpolitik (Consumer Interest and Consumer Policy). Gottingen: Otto Schwartz.

141. SEPSTRUP, PREBEN (1981), "Information Content in Advertising," Journal of Consumer Policy, 5 (No. 4; Fall): 337-345.

142. _________ (1985), "Information Content in TV Advertising," Journal of Consumer Policy, 8 (No. 3; September): 239-265.

143. _________(1986), "Forbrugerindflydelse pa mediebilledet (Consumer Influence on Mass Media Politics), in Ulla Aitta et al. (eds.), Vagar till konsumentinflytande, Copenhagen: Nordic Council of Ministers, NEK-Rapport 1986:8, 37-50.

144. _________ (1986), "The Electronic Dilemma of TV Advertising," paper presented at the Symposium "New Challenges for European Consumer Policy," held at Heiligkreuztal, March 17-20, 1986. Part of the paper has subsequently been published in European Journal of Communication, 1986, 1 (No. 4; December): 383-406. The whole paper is available as Working Paper No. 2, Aarhus: Aarhus School of Business Administration and Economics, Department of Marketing.

145. _________ and FOLKE OLANDER (1986), Forbrugerinformation i de elektroniske medier: Forbrugeroplysning, reklame, salg (Consumer Information in the Electronic Media: Neutral Consumer Information, Advertising, Selling). Copenhagen: The Nordic Council of Ministers, NEK-Rapport 1986:6. A shorter version in the English language has been published in Journal of Consumer Policy, 10 (No. 3; September 1987): 283-305.

146. SEVON, GUJE (1984), "Cognitive Maps of Past and Future Economic Events," Acta Psychologica, 56 (No. 1-3): 71-79.

147. SILBERER, GUNTER (1982), "Marketing of Non-Commercial Test Institutions," Journal of Business Research, 10 (No. 1; March): 59-73.

149. ________ and HANS RAFFEE (eds.) (1984), Warentest und Konsument (Product Testing and the Consumer), Frankfurt: Campus.

150. STØ, EIVIND (1983), Forbrukermisnøye og klageatferd blant norske forbrukere (Consumer Dissatisfaction and Complaining Behaviour Among Norwegian Consumers), Oslo: Fondet for Markeds- og Distribusjonsforskning.

151. ________ (1986), "Forbrukerradet: Interesseorganisasjon eller forvaltningsorgan? (The Norwegian Consumer Council: Partisan Organization or Public Agency?)," in Ulla Aitta et al. (eds.), Vagar till konsumentinflytande, Copenhagen: The Nordic Council of Ministers, NEK-Rapport 1986:8, 213-238.

152. STEPENING, EDUARD (1981), Kind und Werbefernsehen (The Child and Television Advertising), Bonn: Abt Associates.

153. SUNDKVIST, EVA (1986), Handelshinder och hushallens ekonomi, (Trade Restrictions and the Economy of Households), Oslo: The Nordic Council of Ministers.

154. SVENSON, OLA and GORAN NILSSON (1986), "Mental Economics: Subjective Representations of Factors Related to Expected Inflation," Journal of Economic Psychology, 7 (No. 3; September): 327-349.

155. TELEMATIQUES ET COMMUNICATIONS: UN NOUVEAU DROIT? (Telematics and Communication: A New Legal Area?) (1985), Paris: Economica.

156. TEXIER, ALAIN G. (1984), "Teletel After Two Years of Commercial Service," in Proceedings of Videotex International, Pinner, UK: Online Publications, 33-43.

157. THOMAS, MICHAEL J. (1980), "Consumer Representation in British Nationalized Industries: Does It Work Effectively?" Journal of Consumer Policy, 4 (No. 4; Fall): 323-334.

158. THORELLI, HANS B. (1981), "Consumer Policy for the Third World," Journal of Consumer Policy, 5 (No. 3; Summer): 197-211.

159. ________ and SENTELL, GERALD D. (1982), Consumer Emancipation and Economic Development: The Case of Thailand, Greenwich, CT: JAI Press.

160. UNGES FORBRUG (Consumption of the Young) (1987), Copenhagen: Nordic Council of Ministers, NEK-Rapport 1987:3.

161. UUSITALO, LIISA (ed.) (1983), Consumer Behaviour and Environmental Quality, Aldershot: Gower.

162. ________ (in press), Environmental Impacts of Consumption Patterns, Aldershot: Gower.

163. VAAGBØ, OLA (1983), Spare- og laneatferd i nordiske hushold (Saving and Borrowing Behaviour in Nordic Households), Oslo: The Nordic Council of Ministers, NEK-Rapport 1984:6.

164. WAHLUND, RICHARD and KARL-ERIK WARNERYD (in press), "Aggregate Saving and the Saving Behaviour of Saver Groups in Sweden Accompanying a Tax Rate," in Shlomo Maital (ed.), Applied Behavioural Economics, Brighton: Wheatsheat and New York: New York University Press.

165. WARD, SCOTT, TOM ROBERTSON and RAY BROWN (eds.) (1986), Commercial Television and European Children, Aldershot: Gower.

166. WARNERYD, KARL-ERIK (1975), "The Problem of Putting More Information into Advertising," in Folke Olander and Gerhard Scherhorn (eds.), Proceedings of the Second Workshop on Consumer Action Research, Berlin: Science Center (I/1975-3).

167. ________ (1983), "The Saving Behaviour of Households," paper presented at the conference "Saving in a Time of Economic Stagnation," Scheveningen, June 9-11, 1983.

168. _________ and RICHARD WAHLUND (1985), "Inflationary Expectations," in Herman Brandstatter and Erich Kirchler (eds.), Economic Psychology, Linz: Trauner, 327-335.

169. WEBLEY, PAUL and RUSSELL SPEARS (1986), "Economic Preferences and Inflationary Expectations," Journal of Economic Psychology, 7 (No. 3; September): 359-369.

170. WIEVIOKA, MICHEL (1977), L'Etat, le patronat et les consommateurs (State, Business, and Consumers), Paris: PUF.

171. WIKSTROM, SOLVEIG (1983), "Another Look at Consumer Dissatisfaction as a Measure of Market Performance," Journal of Consumer Policy, 6 (No. 1): 19-35.

172. _________ (1984), "Bringing Consumer Information Systems Down to Earth," Journal of Consumer Policy, 7 (No. 1; March): 13-26.

173. _________ (1985), "The Swedish Food Supply System at a Crossroads - An Analysis of a Mature, Extensively Regulated Branch's Dilemma," Stockholm: Faradet, Working paper.

174. WILLIAMS, FRANCES (ed.) (1977), Why The Poor Pay More, London: National Consumer Council.

175. WIMMER, FRANK (1981), "Mengelnde Einkaufseffizienz einkommensschwacher Verbraucher - eine empirische Ueberprufung und inhaltliche Erweiterung der These "Die Armen zahlen mehr" fur die BRD (Lower Buying Efficiency Among Low Income Consumers - An Empirical Test and a Theoretical Extension of the Thesis "The Poor Pay More" with Respect to the Federal Republic of Germany)," Journal of Consumer Policy, 5 (Nos. 1+2; Winter + Spring): 64-87.

176. YOUNG, DENNIS R. (1977), "Consumer Problems in the Public Sector: A Framework for Research," Journal of Consumer Policy, 1 (No. 3; Summer): 205-226.

177. _________ (1982), "The Role of Consumer Councils in the Evaluation and Delivery of Public Services," Stony Brook, NY: State University of New York at Stony Brook, Institute for Urban Science Research, Working paper 82-108.

Chapter 24

ABOUT THE AUTHOR

Robert R. Kerton is Professor of Economics at the University of Waterloo, Canada. Trained in Economics with a Ph.D. from Duke University in 1969, Kerton has spent most of his career at the University of Waterloo. An active consumer scholar, Kerton has also been a prominent participant in the Consumers Association of Canada and in IOCU. In 1982 he spent a sabbatical at IOCU in Penang, Malaysia. Kerton's work on consumer search capital has been influential.

TIME FOR A "WINGSPREAD": THE CONTRIBUTIONS OF PROFESSORS OLANDER AND THORELLI

Robert R. Kerton

The two papers by Thorelli and Olander are valuable attempts to ask that the consumer research community "spread its wings" and fly.

The wide-ranging survey of European research on consumer policy prepared by Folke Olander is important because it makes this work available in a single review. In so doing, Olander alerts us to the greater role played by concepts from political science and sociology in European research in contrast to the more extensive use of economics and psychology in North American work. Two examples suffice: First, his review shows a distinctive approach to information and misinformation as exemplified in the work of Sepstrup, Grunert, Dedler and others. Second, he highlights the research into the way that product testing reports by consumer organizations affect the suppliers of goods (for example, Fritz, Raffee and Silberer). The review whets the appetite for more work on Swedish efforts by consumers, not producers, to design new and appropriate products. It is useful to learn of the extensive public model of consumer policy successfully employed in Norway even though we still lack an organized list of the full range of alternative consumer policies being tried in different countries. But Olander's compilation reveals the value of examining recent research.

THE ADVANTAGES OF THORELLI'S CONSUMER ECOLOGY MODEL

Thorelli's paper is an admirably succinct presentation of the consumer ecology model, utilized by Thorelli and associates in several well known books. The ecological perspective provides a rich field of vision on certain consumer issues. Its novel findings testify to the exhortation in the Olander paper for a "grander" theory on the grounds that "...a good theoretical framework can function as a stimulus and as a valuable guideline for empirical research...".

In the very difficult survey work done in Thailand, the ecological approach allowed Thorelli and Sentell to see, and to try to take account of, cultural variables. As one example, consider the effect on complaint behavior of the importance to Buddhists of being choei (imperturbable) and of maintaining the upper hand with dignity by demonstrating mai pen rai, roughly translated as "it doesn't matter" [3]. The consumer ecology approach could be equally successful in explaining the way that Indonesia has been able use the levers of religion and pride in persuading urban consumers to grow food in their front yards. This model is one avenue for making good the lack of contact between economists, sociologists, and psychologists and others, a shortcoming clearly explained by Olander. Another benefit of Thorelli's consumer ecology approach is its focus on consumer emancipation as a sine qua non of economic development. Think of the untold number of publications on economic development that pay attention exclusively to capital, natural resources, labor, and entrepreneurship. This "input fascination" is perverse wherever it occurs since it ignores the real goal of economic activity: consumer well-being.

"WOLVES" IN CONSUMER ECOLOGY

The consumer ecology approach as explained thus far has certain limitations. As it stands, it assumes that the economic environment is passive and benevolent. In my judgment, these assumptions urgently need to be extended in two major respects as they pertain to the LDC: (1) The economic environment may not be populated by benign creatures; instead, many of its inhabitants may be "wolves," i.e., certain sellers; (2) These "wolves" may exert undue influence on the "framework" in which we live, i.e., the institutions and the rules of play. Let me elaborate on these points.

Alfred Marshall, the great British economist and student of markets, used the ecological approach almost 100 years ago. He pointed out, ever so tellingly, that wolves thrive, not because they improve the environment, but rather because they learned to hunt effectively, in packs. In Marshall's view, it is a misunderstanding to believe that "....those organisms tend to survive which are best fitted to benefit the environment....those organisms tend to survive which are best fitted to utilize the environment for their own purposes" [2, p. 140]. The "wolves" in LDC are sellers (though not all of them!).

In 1982 I visited nine Asian LDC on behalf of IOCU. In each country I asked consumer leaders: "What is the most important thing you have been able to achieve?" The leaders were virtually unanimous in specifying changes that obliged their governments, producers, and sellers to take account of the consumer interest. These accomplishments of the consumer leaders were hardly easy, nor always successful, because of well organized and effective opposition. Evolution has its own rules. When the ecological model is used, it is important to recognize that some agents are very effective at helping to mold the environment itself, its institutions and its rules of play. It seems that the more ruthless participants -- the wolves -- exert disproportionate influence, creating institutions and rules that are often inimicable to the interests of consumers. In nature, ecology does not give its creatures quite so much power to decide on the fundamental laws of evolution.

Far better would be market laws that serve the general interest and/or which allow those firms to thrive which best serve the consumer. It is surprising how powerless consumer-serving firms seem to be. We lack the research that explains their lack of influence. For example, we lack a means of examining "investments" by domestic and foreign sellers who lobby against fair legislation dealing with international trade. As a single but important example, consider the efforts made to stop the publication of the United Nations Consolidated List of Products Whose Consumption and/or Sale Have Been Banned, Withdrawn, Severely Restricted or Not Approved by Governments [4]. This list is an important means of allowing consumer-serving firms to succeed rather than those which sell useless or harmful products. The list is efficient, on economic grounds, because it eliminates the need for low income consumers and for poor countries to re-discover known hazards and ineffective products. Olander is surely right in arguing that we should devote much more research to identifying and analyzing the influence of various economic "agents."

According to Thorelli, the ecological approach yields priorities that go from information (first) to education to protection (last), in "developed" countries, and exactly the reverse in developing countries. That places "protection" first for the LDC.

This is easier said than done. My own experience convinces me of the need to give high priority to research dealing with the economic framework (institutions and rules) intended to encourage fair exchanges in markets. This is especially important in developing countries. Without a framework, the consumer in an LDC is all too likely to become sustenance for the race of wolves. The enlargement of the consumer ecology model to include the framework "pressure" needed to create the basic rules for fair exchanges, enables us to see the naivete of attempts to transfer laws directly from industrialized countries to LDC's with different cultural and economic realities. First, we must appraise the environment of the LDC. Even taking this into account, there is no reason to believe that it will be easy to create the appropriate public and private support capital.

The Olander paper provides a synoptic review of existing research and concludes with a compelling case for a "grand theory." Thorelli supplies one such theory and shows how much it can achieve in developed and developing countries. This stocktaking is highly rewarding: It shows, to use the words of the prominent American social philosopher, Yogi Berra, "You can see a lot, just by looking." The stocktaking is most useful because it may help avoid wasting scarce research resources "rediscovering the wheel." Olander's conclusion that consumer research is at an early stage ("immature" in his phrasing) is humbling but also encouraging. First, it means that important discoveries -- including grander theories-- are yet to be made. Second, it gets us beyond ignorant certainty. Each paper is an eloquent demonstration that researchers can profit by leaving the security of the cultural cocoon. It is, to play on the title of the Conference Center, time for a Wingspread.

REFERENCES

1. ACKERLOF, G.A. (1970). "The Market for Lemons: Quality Uncertainty and the Market Mechanism," Quarterly Journal of Economics, 84, pp. 488-500.

2. MARSHALL, ALFRED (1899). Elements of Economics (Third Edition). Macmillan, London.

3. THORELLI, HANS B. and GERALD D. SENTELL (1982). Consumer Emancipation and Economic Development: The Case of Thailand. JAI Press Inc., Greenwich, Conn.

4. UNITED NATIONS (1984). Consolidated List of Products Whose Consumption and/or Sale Have Been Banned, Withdrawn, Severely Restricted or Not Approved by Governments. United Nations Secretariat, DIESA/WP1, July.

ABOUT THE AUTHOR

Gerhard Scherhorn is Professor of Consumer Economics at the University of Hohenheim. After receiving his Ph.D. in Economics from the University of Cologne in 1965, he joined the faculty of the Graduate School of Economics and Public Policy in Hamburg before moving to Hohenheim. Scherhorn has long been engaged in consumer and economic policy. Scherhorn and Olander together organized the two Berlin Conferences on Consumer Action Research in 1974 and 1975 that were the precursors of Wingspread. Scherhorn served on the German Council of Economic Advisers from 1974 to 1979 and as Board Member of Stiftung Warentest (the German Consumers Union) from 1974 to 1985. He is a Co-Editor of the Journal of Consumer Policy.

SELF-FULFILLMENT, CONSUMER POLICY AND CONSUMER RESEARCH

Gerhard Scherhorn

In considering Thorelli's comparative study of consumer problems in less versus more developed countries, I am struck by the notion that it is mainly the kind of consumer problems that changes with the process of economic development. Consumer problems as a whole show no decline in importance; many have become more complex.

So with regard to the importance of consumer problems there seems to be no significant progress from LDC to MDC. On the contrary, as aggregate income rises, consumption will increasingly have negative side effects: on consumers' upbringing, health, appearance, social relations, environment, satisfaction in life, etc. Furthermore, as aggregate income rises, the expenditures that consumers must make just in order to maintain their level of living will increase [5].

Even the recognition of "Consumer Rights"--which we have every reason to celebrate--does not resolve consumer problems. It just compensates for earlier aggravations. Historically, the emergence of consumer rights is to be seen as the reaction to two closely connected developments: (1) increasing acceptance by consumers of the need, even the duty to buy consumer goods,[1] and the realization of the individual consumer's impotence at the micro

---

[1]This is the consequence of the mass of advertising and other "messages" assaulting consumers everyday.

level, i.e., the inability of consumers to obtain good value for money [8].

A PARADOX: THE MORE CONSUMERS GET, THE MORE DISSATISFIED THEY BECOME

I therefore propose to add another paradox to those of Thorelli's paper. Consumers seek economic progress and more consumption even though the result is often greater feelings of consumer dissatisfaction. What accounts for this paradox? On the one hand, consumers want and support economic development and growth in consumption because they always have problems they expect to be solved by rising income and greater consumption. On the other hand, one of the side effects of greater consumption will be consumer problems that detract from their expected higher quality of living. Many consumers, it appears, measure the quality of their living by the quantity of goods and services they consume. These consumers fail to recognize that the consumer problems they deplore may be causally connected with the growing quantity of consumption they desire -- in their thinking "consumption" and "consumer problems" are placed in different compartments. So, paradoxically, they continue to support economic progress even while feeling frustrated by it!

The reason for this dissociated perception, or compartmentalization, can be traced to the father of modern Economics, Adam Smith. He took it for granted that men (and women, too) are fundamentally governed by the drive to improve their position. Further, he argued that men invariably measure their status by the degree to which they achieve (1) the necessities of life, and (2) approval by others. He concluded that wealth, since it confers influence as well as goods, serves as <u>the</u> unique and universal means of improving one's position [6]. By these assumptions Smith established a tradition of dealing with economic behavior as if it were in fact confined to a certain set of motives, namely, to (1) "existence needs" and (2) "relatedness needs" [1]. These beliefs by themselves would indeed prevent people from realizing that increasing wealth may contribute more to consumer "problems" than to their solution.

THE ULTIMATE GOAL OF ECONOMIC ACTIVITY: SELF-FULFILLMENT

It is only in the recent decades that we have begun to learn that it is inappropriate to view man in this restricted, materialistic way. Men are also guided by "growth needs," e.g., by desires to develop their skills, enlarge their awareness, actualize or "fulfill their potential" [7]. In the view of Kurt Goldstein, who first used the concept of self-fulfillment or, as he called it, "self-actualization," human behavior is explained best by the assumption that "the only drive or basic tendency of the organism is to actualize itself according to its potentialities in the highest possible degree" where the possible degree is defined by the given situation [4, p. 140].

According to Goldstein, the tendency to release tension--which economists customarily identify with the fulfillment of specific material needs via consumption -- is not characteristic of human behavior in general. Instead, it seems to be a characteristic expression of a defective, deprived, or otherwise endangered organism [4, p. 141]. "Defects" and "deprivation" among humans include disease, poverty, being threatened by insecurity, or being stressed by fear of sanctions.

It is generally held that economic progress and growth release people from material deprivation and insecurity. They also enlarge the individual's freedom of action by weakening societal sanctions that have proved to be unnessarily strict and narrowing. In this sense economic progress increases the potential for self-fulfilling behavior. Self-fulfillment in turn depends upon:

1. An awareness of all relevant needs and feelings (none repressed);

2. A preference to undertake activities for their intrinsic values, not just to obtain a reward.

So, under favourable conditions consumption may serve as a means of self-fulfillment. In the course of economic progress consumers come to learn that consumer goods do not generate utility themselves. Instead, it is the consumer's own activities that produce utility [2]. The more satisfying an activity, the more likely it is intrinsically motivated [3]. Increasingly people are striving for more satisfying activities, at work and at home. In other words, the probability may rise that consumers will behave in a "growth-motivated" way.

On the other hand one cannot overlook contrary tendencies as indicated, for instance, by the growing frequency of neurosis, obesity, addiction, suicide. These, too, are outcomes of economic growth. Even they can be viewed as manifestations of a desire (though misdirected) for self-fulfillment. They can also be seen as symptoms of compulsion or, as John Watkins has pointed it, of "inner heteronomy" [10]. Consumer behavior of this kind is currently excluded from consumer theory as deviant and pathological. In my view it should be integrated into the study of "ordinary" consumer behavior.

The main point I wish to make is that the concept of self-fulfillment enables us to view consumption and consumer problems as integral parts of consumer behavior. It is not consumer goods people want, but instead self-fulfilling experiences. Those experiences are far more subject to interference by the side-effects of consumption than are consumer goods. Therefore, as self-fulfillment becomes more accepted, the tendency to support economic growth, regardless of its negative consequences, will lessen.

SOME CONSEQUENCES CONCERNING POLICY AND RESEARCH

Does an acceptance of self-fulfillment imply that people will be more inclined to support consumer policy? Probably yes. Self-fulfilling behavior does imply that consumers are aware of their role relations to producers, sellers, as well as to local and state governments. It implies also that people are aware of their situation, as shaped by (1) the natural environment, (2) other public goods, (3) their life-styles and standard of living, and (4) other habits and values. Last, but not least, it implies that they are aware of their self, that is, the preferences and reactions of their own body, heart and mind. Growth of awareness may lead consumers to give more weight than before to problems related to their situation and self, in contrast to problems related to their role. Traditionally consumer policy has focused on consumers' roles as the weaker partners in an exchange relation. Self-fulfillment would lead consumers to take a broader view of consumer policy.

As we learn from Olander's paper, research and analysis on consumer policy continue to be centered around the role the consumer plays in the marketplace. Attempts to enlarge the scope of consumer policy to include the consumer situation have so far been unsuccessful, even in the case of environmental problems. "The Environment" has come to be the domain of different organizations and authorities. Consumer organizations, consumer policymakers, and consumer researchers have been reluctant to invade into what seems to be territory staked out by others. These leaders are in danger of losing the opportunity of integrating the treatment of consumer-producer relations with the treatment of provision of public goods.

In my judgement consumer policy research should be extended to take account of how consumers become more highly aware of their self, viz. their own bodily and mental reactions [9]. If we view self-fulfillment as a concept which can advance understanding of consumer behavior, we can no longer exclude from research the extent to which consumers are aware of what they themselves, after thorough consideration, would call their "true" needs or interests. We would exclude neither the question of how consumers suppress part of their emotions nor the question of how consumers, by increasing awareness of their own feelings, gradually obtain a better understanding of their own intrinsic motivation and, in many cases, even reduce their own mental or physical defects.

The center of consumer theory would then shift from buying behavior to consumers' experiences, activities, and life. In consumer policy the role-centered approach would be replaced by a somewhat broader view of the consumer interest, a view affected not only by the traditional consumer "problems" but also by consumer's ability to behave in a self-aware, intrinsically motivated way.

REFERENCES

1. ALDERFER, CLAYTON, R. (1972) Existence, Relatedness, and Growth. New York: Free Press.

2. BECKER, GARY S. (1976) The Economic Approach to Human Behavior. Chicago, Ill.: University of Chicago Press.

3. DECI, EDWARD L. (1975) Intrinsic Motivation. New York: Plenum Press.

4. GOLDSTEIN, KURT (1940) Human Nature in the Light of Psychopathology. Cambridge, Mass.: Harvard University Press.

5. HIRSCH, FRED (1976) Social Limits to Growth. Cambridge, Mass.: Harvard University Press.

6. HIRSCHMAN, ALBERT O. (1977) The Passions and the Interests. Political Arguments for Capitalism Before its Triumph. Princeton, N.J.: Princeton University Press.

7. MASLOW, ABRAHAM H. (1968) Towards a Psychology of Being. New York: Litton Educational Publishing.

8. MAYNES, E. SCOTT (1972) "The Power of the Consumer," in B. Strumpel et al. (Eds.). Human Behavior in Economic Affairs. Essays in Honor of George Katona. Amsterdam: Elsevier.

9. SCHERHORN, GERHARD (1985) "The Goal of Consumer Advice: Transparency or Autonomy?" Journal of Consumer Policy, 8, 133-151.

10. WATKINS, JOHN, W.N. (1956) "Three Views Concerning Human Knowledge," in H.D. Lewis (Ed.), Contemporary British Philosophy, Third Series. London: Allen & Unwin. Reprinted 1963 in: K.R. Popper (Ed.), Conjectures and Refutations, chapter 3. London: Routledge & Kegan Paul.

Chapter 25

ABOUT THE AUTHOR

Claes Fornell is Professor of Business Administration at the University of Michigan. A Swede who earned his Doctor of Economics degree from the University of Lund in 1976, Fornell has spent most of his professional career in the U.S. with successive appointments at Duke University, Northwestern University, and the University of Michigan (1980--). Fornell's research interests embrace, in addition to consumer affairs, marketing strategy, and multivariate analysis. He is a member of the Editorial Boards of the Journals of Marketing Research, Consumer Research, and Marketing Science. In 1987 he was Visiting Professor at INSEAD, France and the Stockholm School of Economics. Fornell has served as consultant to many firms in the U.S.A. and in Europe.

CORPORATE CONSUMER AFFAIRS DEPARTMENTS: RETROSPECT AND PROSPECT

Claes Fornell

INTRODUCTION

The establishment of special organizational units within business corporations to handle consumer affairs was in large measure a result of strong consumerism pressures in the late sixties and early seventies. A substantial number of companies organized corporate consumer affairs departments (CAD) between 1970-1975 primarily as a response to considerable consumer discontent and frustration in the marketplace. There was dissatisfaction with product quality, high prices, warranties, services, and, perhaps most evident, with the difficulty encountered by consumers in trying to voice their problems to companies. The rise of self-service retailing, the declining quality of sales employees, the interposition of computers between the customer and the organization, and the inherent difficulties of dealing with bureaucracies all contributed to consumer dissatisfaction [1].

The CAD was designed to address these problems. Beyond the steps taken by individual firms, those in consumer affairs responded by forming their own professional association. The Society for Consumer Affairs Professionals in Business (SOCAP) was founded in 1973 to "foster the integrity of business in its dealings with consumers; and advancing the consumer affairs profession." This organization has grown to include more than 1,500 members (750 companies) today.

Most of the new CADs in companies such as Whirlpool, Giant Foods, Corning Glass Works, Ford, Eastman Kodak, RCA, Pan Am, J.C. Penney, Zenith, Toyota, and others were involved in at least one, and usually more, of the following activities:

- Handling, resolution, and analysis of consumer complaints and inquiries;

- Serving as an internal consumer ombudsman and consultant on consumer matters relevant to the company;

- Developing and disseminating to consumers information on the use of products sold by the company;

- Providing liaison with consumer-interest groups outside the company.

A few years later, the idea of the CAD function in business had spread to Europe, where several firms set up their own departments with responsibilities similar to their U.S. counterparts [8].

In view of increasing consumer activism and government pressures, the background and rationale behind the emergence of CAD are clear enough. What may not be as clear is the relationship between the CAD and the consumer interest. Is the establishment of Corporate Consumer Affairs Departments in the consumer interest? If so, how? What might the scope and limitations be? And, how have the CADs in fact performed? These are some of the questions to be discussed in this paper.

In order to analyze what, if anything, CAD can contribute to the consumer, we have to specify what is meant by the "consumer interest." From this starting point it may be possible to determine what a CAD can and cannot accomplish. As a part of a profit-seeking enterprise, it is immediately clear that a CAD cannot pursue consumer interests that are perceived by corporate management to be inconsistent with the firm's (profit) objectives. Therefore, the part of consumer interest that can be met by a CAD is confined to what is in the interest of the firm. The potential contribution of the CAD to the consumer interest must also serve the company (like marketing, production, selling, etc.). If no intersection of interests exists between consumer and company, the CAD will not exist. This is the main difference between CADs and independent consumer organizations. If a meaningful intersection of consumer and company interest does exist -- my position -- the questions become:

How can this intersection be described or understood? Can it be enlarged?

Thus, to analyze the relationship between CADs and the consumer interest, one must also look at the interest of the firm. In fact, if one assumes that the profit motive is the ultimate driving force in firms, the issue becomes one of establishing a causal link between the enhancement of the consumer interest via the CAD and profitability. Let us begin with the consumer interest.

THE CONSUMER INTEREST

The "consumer interest" is a concept that does not lend itself to a simple definition. The related terms--consumer welfare and consumer satisfaction--albeit somewhat easier to define, are not sufficiently broad. Welfare (in economics) has to do with efficient allocation of resources in the economy. As such, it can only be part of the "consumer interest." Satisfaction, while also an ingredient of the "consumer interest," is in large part determined by the consumer's subjective expectations.

At the very least, then, the "consumer interest" is determined by both individual and collectively shared values and beliefs. As a result, people are likely to differ on what they consider to be in the best interest of consumers in much the same way they differ with respect to political opinion and general philosophy. Nevertheless, there are some widely shared values about some basic principles. For example, few would disagree that it is desirable to provide consumers with the "rights" to safety, to be informed, to choose and to be heard, as spelled out by President Kennedy in his address to the Congress on March 15, 1962. But we must ask: How much of each of the above is desirable? What should each cost? Who should pay for each? The answers to these questions will always remain debatable in attempting to define "what is in the consumer interest". Consequently, it may be necessary to adopt an <u>ad hoc</u> position for each specific issue under study. In determining the potential impact of CAD on consumer interests, it is obvious that CAD can potentially affect safety, information, etc. In doing this, it also seems that most of the direct costs will be assumed by the firm. Staffing, information development, complaint handling, etc. are all activities that demand resources from the firm. For the consumer the costs of interacting with the CAD will involve some of his/her resources -- money, time and energy. Obviously, both parties would like a high ratio of output to input.

For the firm, the output is economic performance (e.g., profit); for the consumer, it is utility. If consumers were perfectly homogeneous with respect to utility, it would be straightforward to proceed with an analysis of "the consumer interest." Unfortunately, utility is a subjective property that varies from individual to individual. Nevertheless, even without specifying utility per se, we can say that in order for the outcome to be positive, the consumer must depart from the interaction with a utility gain. That is, the consumer must have acquired something in terms of money, information or products, and/or services from the firm that exceeds his/her costs. If the consumer gains nothing at the individual level, the consumer interest can only be enhanced if the interaction affects the future behavior of the firm (in terms of lowering prices, improving quality, changing advertising content, etc.). Nevertheless, it seems unlikely that a CAD will be long-lived unless it provides individual consumers with some form of extra utility. By the same token, the return to the firm must exceed its investment.

Thus, there are two countervailing forces at work, as in most negotiations or business affairs. The investment (input) of the firm affects the gain (output) to the consumer. If the firm's investment is high and its return low, the CAD will eventually be abolished. If the firm's investment is meager, the return to consumers will be too small, also leading to the abolishment of the CAD.

This is illustrated in Figure 1. If the relationship between firm performance and consumer utility is negative (as illustrated by the line with CA1 and CA2 as endpoints), the successful CAD must find a point of trade-off between the interests of the firm and those of the consumer. The problem is that whatever resources the firm invests in the CAD translates into a consumer gain, but without any return to the firm. It is doubtful that the CAD can survive under this scenario.

Consider now the case where the relationship between firm performance and consumer utility is positive (as indicated by the dotted lines). Again, there is a tradeoff between the parties (as determined by the slope of the line), but as long as the line is positive the trade-off is between gains--not losses. The successful CAD will strive outwards (as indicated by the arrow going from CA3 to CA4).

These two perspectives reflect fundamental differences among writers in the consumer affairs area. In the first case, the CAD is viewed as a cost without payoff and the situation is very much like a zero-sum game where A's gain is B's loss. Under such conditions, the firm will tend to (eventually) locate its CAD in Figure 1 in such a way that the consumer utility is very small. This view is represented by a "Conflict Model" as argued by Wimmer [32], Bergstrom [3], and recently by Stark [25].

FIGURE 1

CONSUMER AND COMPANY RETURNS FROM CAD

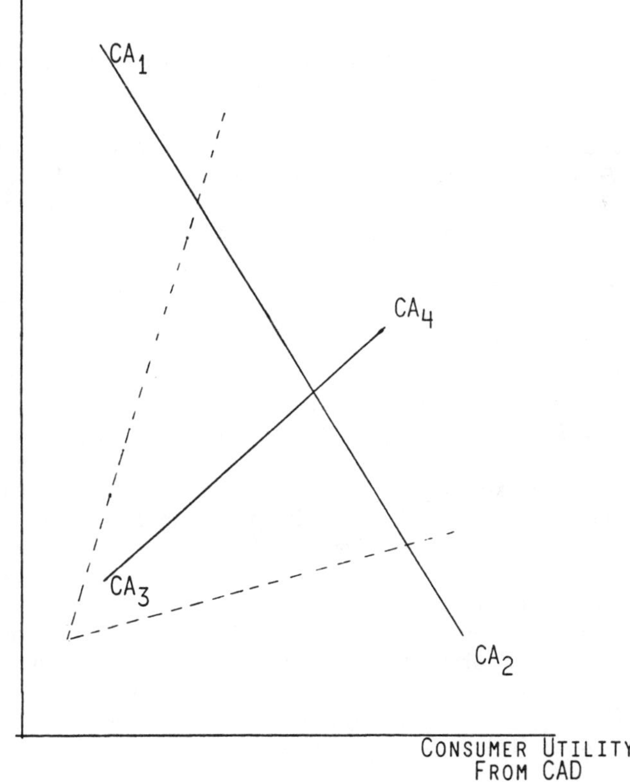

The contention here is that the interests of the firm and the consumer are so disparate that the profit maximization objective of the firm is achieved at the expense of the consumer. The absence of a conflict model, does not, however, imply a "Harmony-of-Interest Model." This would only be the case if the slope of the line is 45 degrees, which seems unlikely in the general case. With any other positive slope, there is trade-off, although contrary to the conflict situation, the trade-off is with positive returns. The amount of gain is not equal, but there is a gain. Since this is the only scenario under which the CAD can exist in the long run, this is the kind of situation we will analyze further.

Because the CAD is a part of a profit-seeking organization, it cannot be expected to free itself from the economic conditions of the firm. The only way, then, for the concept of CAD to survive and be successful is for it simultaneously to provide economic benefit to the firm as well as to the individual consumer. The more direct and tangible the economic gain is, the more persuasive the case. A major purpose of this paper is to demonstrate how such a gain can come about, that is, how the CAD can be profitable for both the consumer and the firm.

THE COMPANY INTEREST

The CAD, like other functions within profit-seeking organizations, must be able to justify its existence in terms of its contribution to the organization's well-being. A general finding in the organizational behavior literature is that a function's or department's degree of influence on the behavior of a business firm of which it is a part is proportional to its contribution to the performance of the firm [6, 15, 31]. It seems reasonable to assume that the greater the influence a CAD has, the greater the consumer voice within the firm. Therefore, we focus on ways in which the CAD acquires power and influence within the business organization. We note also that, while CAD power and influence is not synonymous with consumer influence, it is a necessary prerequisite. If the CAD has no influence on the corporation, the consumer can have no influence either via the CAD.

THE BASES FOR CONSUMER AFFAIRS INFLUENCE

There are two basic ways in which the CAD can contribute to the profitability of the firm, without losing sight of the consumer interest, via its position in the organization. First the CAD as a recipient of communications from consumers, can have an <u>indirect effect</u> by discerning and transmitting important messages from consumers to management. Second, the CAD, acting as a "problem-solver" for consumers, can have a direct effect by strengthening customer loyalty and reducing customer turnover. Let us examine the indirect effect first.

The Effect of Communications

A fundamental requirement for consumer welfare, as understood in economics, depends on the ability and willingness of buyers and sellers to communicate effectively. There must be a communication system that allows for two-way communications between the parties involved. As long as we restrict the analysis to direct buyer-seller negotiations, there is no problem. Each party has an opportunity to talk as well as to listen. However, whenever the manufacturer is removed from direct interactions with the ultimate consumer and/or when there is a large number of consumers (mass markets), the communications systems become more complicated and, as it turns out, less effective. In part, the problem is technological, but there are other facets involved as well. Consider the application of communications theory [e.g., 24, 19, 23, 30], which has been extensively applied in helping the firm develop and disseminate one-way communications (e.g., advertising), but is not used to help the company receive and interpret communications. Traditionally, market communications have been viewed as a means of influencing consumer behavior. However, there is nothing inherent in economics or in the theory of the firm to suggest that altering the behavior of consumers is always more desirable than altering the behavior of the firm. There are probably many cases in which it would be more profitable for the firm to change its behavior instead of attempting to change that of its potential customers. The implication is that market communications models must not automatically cast the firm as the sender and the consumer as the receiver of communications, but must instead recognize an alternation of communicative roles in a process that is continual and interactive. We cannot focus on characteristics of a consumer audience without taking into account the consumers' opportunities to perform sender activities and the firm's abilities to receive and process the messages [7].

It is in this context that we will now examine CAD: As a channel for two-way communications. We will focus on the consumer-to-firm communications provided via CAD relative to two other ways in which consumers have input into the decisions and behaviors of firms: (1) consumer purchase choices and (2) market research. Let us begin with the former.

Consumer Purchase Choices as Communications to the Firm

In competitive markets, consumer desires are communicated to the firm in the form of purchase choices. According to classical economics, when a firm fails to meet consumer expectations, it is punished by consumer withdrawal or a shift in consumer patronage. The process is illustrated in Figure 2.

FIGURE 2

CONSUMER PURCHASE CHOICES AS COMMUNICATIONS

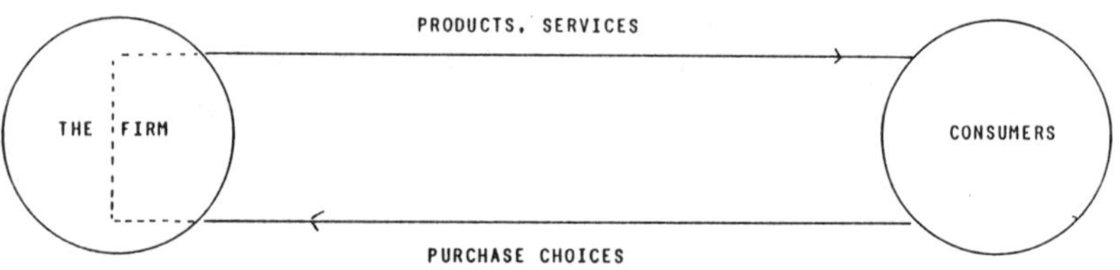

Even though this is the only form of consumer-to-firm communication that classical economic theory relies upon, it has many limitations in terms of the information it provides. It does not make a distinction between consumer needs and desires on one hand and preferences on the other. A choice presumes alternatives. If all alternatives are poor, a choice of one of them does not reflect much about needs and wants. It reveals preference.

The most severe limitation of purchase choices as communications is the fact that they are limited by the offerings of the industry. If the consumer does not like any of the offerings, he may refrain from buying or he may choose the alternative which is the least distant from his needs. Such decisions, however, do not necessarily provide much consumer influence on company behavior. In terms of information, this type of communication relies on the efficacy of competition. Consumer patronage switching or refusal to purchase causes shifts in revenue among competing firms and sets into motion market forces such that firms that fail to meet consumer expectations will either improve or face eventual elimination from the market [16].

Clearly, the informative value of consumer purchase choices increases in competitive markets. Nevertheless, the information is typically communicated to the firm in the form of aggregated sales statistics where the individual pieces of data are often binary (purchase/no purchase). As such they rarely produce a complete picture of consumer needs, wants, or desires, let alone sufficient insight into the behavior of consumers and its causes. While the firm may notice a revenue decline, the information says nothing about the cause of the decline.

Market Research as Communications to the Firm: Ex Ante Design

In view of competitive imperfections and the limitations of consumer purchase choices as communications in general, many business firms look to various forms of market research to aid their decision making. It is important to make a distinction between market research for competitive advantage *per se* and market research as a vehicle for consumer influence into the organization, because the effectiveness of market research in terms of consumer influence depends, to a large extent, on the type of research that is done. For example, advertising copy testing, test marketing, and field and lab experiments essentially measure consumer reaction to a stimulus set up by the firm, that is, the communication is of a feedback nature. It is initiated and, to a large extent, controlled by the firm. The purpose as well as the method of the specific market research project define the extent of the feedback. Questions posed in a survey present the stimuli; the nature of the response format (e.g., open-ended, multiple choice, scales, etc.) determines the scope of the feedback.

Consumer influence in market research is thus restricted by research purpose and methodology in the sense that it cannot go beyond the operational definitions of the phenomena investigated. And it is the firm that determines what those phenomena are. The limitation of market research is due to the fact that it needs some form of problem statement as a point of departure. The burden of defining the problem falls on the firm. The consumer role is basically reduced to reaction; the firm assumes the role of initiator of the communication process. Certainly, some market research methods allow for more consumer "participation" than others, but even the most exploratory designs involve a selection by marketers for the firm of topic, subjects, and timing, thus assigning a relatively passive role to the consumer.

As is shown in Figure 3, communications from consumers to the firm now include both purchase choices and market research. Both, however, incorporate strong elements of feedback communications. Feedback can be thought of as a measure of communication effectiveness, typically in terms of behavioral or attitudinal changes. Since the firm is the dominating participant and the consumer is more passive, it is the behavior and attitude of the consumer--not the firm--which are monitored.

The drawbacks for the firm of being the initiator and the dominating participant lie in the demands of having primary responsibility for creating the communication in the first place, determining who it should communicate with, and what the subject matter ought to be. Because of these requirements, it is not surprising that market research is usually a better tool for studying "known" problems rather than discovering "new" problems. Because the role of the consumer is mostly passive and reactive, there is always a risk that market research omits important consumer concerns.

Consumer-to-Firm Communications via Consumer Affairs: Ex Post Interpretation

Although both purchase choices and market research fill important roles as communications from the consumer to the firm, they impose restrictions on consumer sovereignty: purchase choices are confined to industry offerings and market research is coupled to specifications and requirements determined by the firm. For effective two-way communications between consumers and firms, a mechanism is needed that would allow the consumer to play a greater role in initiating the process and establishing a dialogue with the firm without these restrictions. As illustrated in Figure 4, this is what CAD can be designed for.

The CAD is responsible for managing unsolicited consumer communications. They can be complaints, inquiries, or suggestions. Compliments have been reported as well. These are essentially consumer-initiated communications. As opposed to purchase choices, they are not restricted by industry offerings. Contrary to market research, they represent consumer action--not reaction.

As shown in Figure 4, CAD receives communications from consumers which are analyzed and interpreted within the department. The information is subsequently transmitted to management (there are some important barriers in this transmission, a problem to which we will return) and a response will be made to the consumer. The firm's response is now the feedback communication that the consumer can use to evaluate the effectiveness of his action. There are two modes of feedback: one is directed at the individual

FIGURE 3

MARKET RESEARCH AS COMMUNICATION

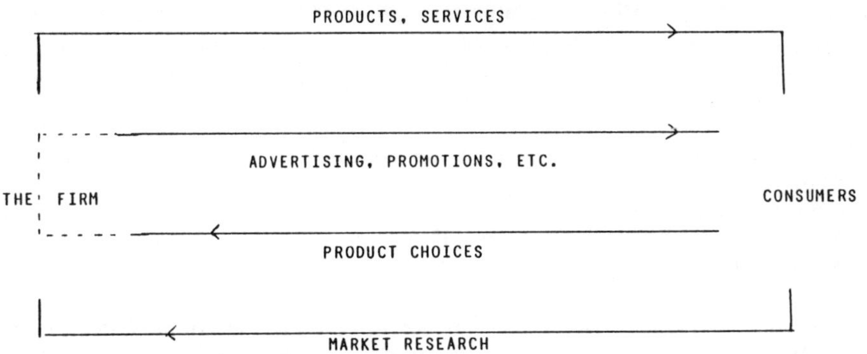

FIGURE 4

COMMUNICATIONS VIA CONSUMER AFFAIRS

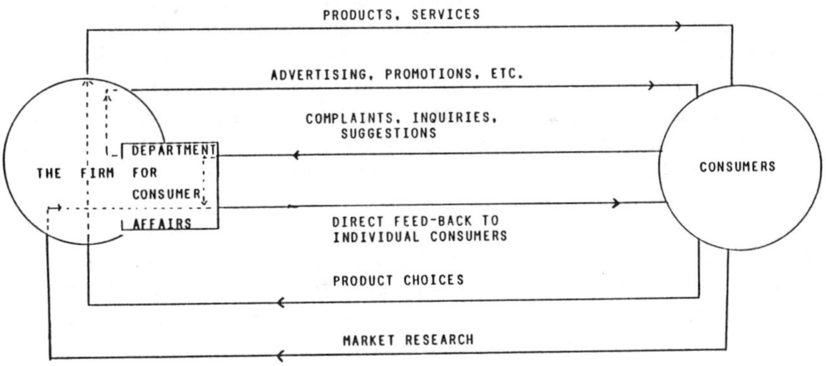

consumer who initiated the process; the other is a response to some aggregate of consumers (e.g., segment, market). The first type obviously deals with each individual consumer. If we are dealing with a consumer inquiry, the appropriate information is provided; if we are dealing with a complaint, appropriate remedy is given. The second type goes beyond the case-by-case analysis and may result in changes in company behavior that are reflected in price, quality, advertising, etc.

Consider now the information properties of consumer-initiated communications. We can classify these properties in terms of the implications of reversing the roles of action and reaction between the firm and the consumer on (1) problem awareness, and (2) errors in communication.

If one views communication as a two-way continual process, it is probably not possible to identify the initiator in an absolute sense. For the purpose of our analysis, it will, however, be sufficient to let the initiator be the party who exercises predominant control over the content of the communication, the choice of channel, the timing and responsibility for the communication that takes place. In market research, the firm controls most of these. In consumer purchase choices, the consumer can be said to control a part of the message (purchase/no purchase); the firms control another part (the purchase alternatives). The other decisions are also jointly determined by the firm and the consumer; the degree of control would, however, vary from case to case. It is in this sense that a consumer's complaint, inquiry, or suggestion is a method of communication which is unsolicited by the firm and initiated by the consumer. The channel is basically determined by the consumer (CAD, independent consumer action groups, government agencies, industry associations, etc.). Further, these communications are not restricted by the (research) designs of the firm, nor by the product offerings by the industry. Their content is caused by consumer perception of seller behavior in general and is beyond company control. Let us now examine in more detail what the implications are in terms of (1) shifting the responsibility of "problem awareness" from the firm to the consumer and (2) errors in communication.

(1) Shifting The Requirement of Problem Awareness

> -In consumer-initiated communications, the "awareness of a problem" is a "responsibility" of the consumer. (This is the case for most communications of the type discussed in this paper with the exception of compliments, which obviously do not emanate from

problems.) In order to put this into perspective, consider market research in the form of a survey--a company-initiated communication. A carefully formulated problem is a necessary starting point for any research. The problem, as defined, drives the design of the research (e.g., sample design, questions or variables to include, operationalizations of variables, data analysis techniques, and so on). Consumer-initiated communications, on the other hand, do not require the firm to be problem conscious in the same sense. Information about consumer concerns enters the CAD as the problems are perceived by the consumers themselves, free from potential preconceptions and prejudgments of the firm. It is the difference between ex ante design and ex post interrelation of correlation signals. The process, from the firm's point of view, is one of "data-to-conceptualization," which is the reverse of most market research communications. It does not mean that consumer-initiated communications are superior to other forms of consumer-to-company communications, but it does mean that the CAD is in a position to become quickly exposed to specific consumer interests, concerns, and problems that may otherwise be overlooked by market research.

(2) Effect on Communication Errors

-Errors in the survey method are usually categorized as (1) sampling error, (2) nonresponse error, and (3) response error. The sampling error cannot be controlled without the use of probability sampling. In consumer-initiated communications, there is "self-selection sampling," raising the possibility that the information provided is unrepresentative of the population. Non-response error, as usually conceptualized in survey research, does not exist in consumer-initiated communications. In consumer-initiated communications, it is the responsibility of the firm to respond--not the consumer. By the same token, response error does not exist either (on the part of the consumer). There are, however, errors that are similar in kind. One is ambiguity in communication, the other is inaccuracy. Ambiguity has to do with errors in the transmission of data. In terms of communication theory, these are errors in encoding and decoding of signals.

Figures 5A and B illustrate the sources of the encoding and decoding errors. In the survey communication, there are at least three sources of each error. The process of evolving from the discovery of a problem to defining it more precisely involves encoding. Developing a research instrument, say a questionnaire, to measure the relevant variables is another form of encoding. Finally, the respondent must encode the stimuli with which he or she is presented (e.g., questions in a questionnaire). The decoding process includes recording the responses, submitting them to analysis, and, finally, interpreting the results. As is shown in the figure, encoding tasks are eliminated in consumer-initiated communications. Thus, the errors associated with encoding are also eliminated. This does not imply, however, that consumer-initiated communications contain fewer errors than, say, survey communications. In fact, the problems with decoding are probably increased. It seems reasonable to assume that an unstructured message is more likely to be ambiguous than a highly structured message (such as a response to a multiple-choice question). By and large, consumer-initiated communications are not as structured as survey communications because they are not coordinated across consumers. Instead, each individual consumer has principal control over message content and format. As a result, the interpretative skill of the firm as "receiver" is put to a more difficult test. On the other hand, there are some advantages in decoding consumer-initiated communications as well. Some of those arise from the reduced problem of inaccuracy. Inaccuracy may result from either the inability or the unwillingness of the consumer to provide the desired information. The common survey biases from yea saying, memory loss, lack of interest, or perceived invasion of privacy do not appear to be serious problems in consumer-initiated communications. By definition, if the consumer initiates a communication, he or she is willing to share information.

The problem with ability is a different matter. This problem is probably exacerbated in consumer-initiated communications. Compared to market research, these communications require more effort from the consumer. Not only must he or she be able to formulate opinions effectively, but he or she must also possess the motivation and knowledge to voice them through an appropriate channel (such as CAD).

FIGURE 5A

CONSUMER SURVEY COMMUNICATIONS

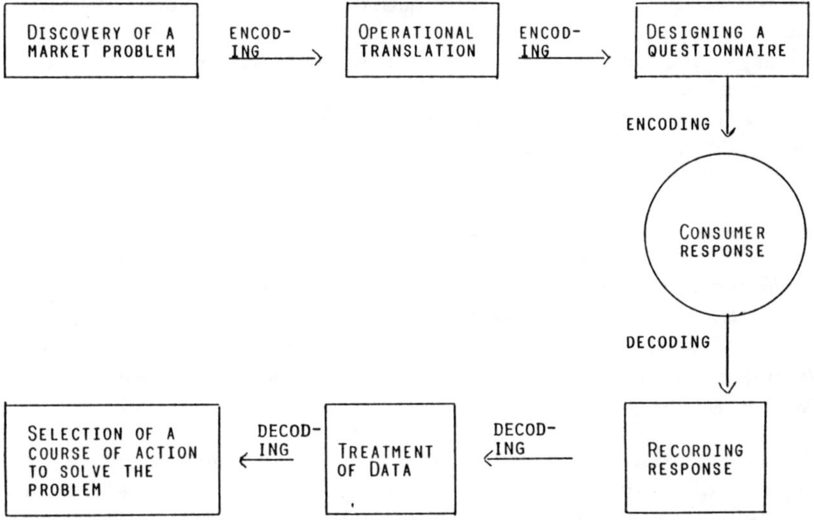

FIGURE 5B

CONSUMER-INITIATED COMMUNICATIONS

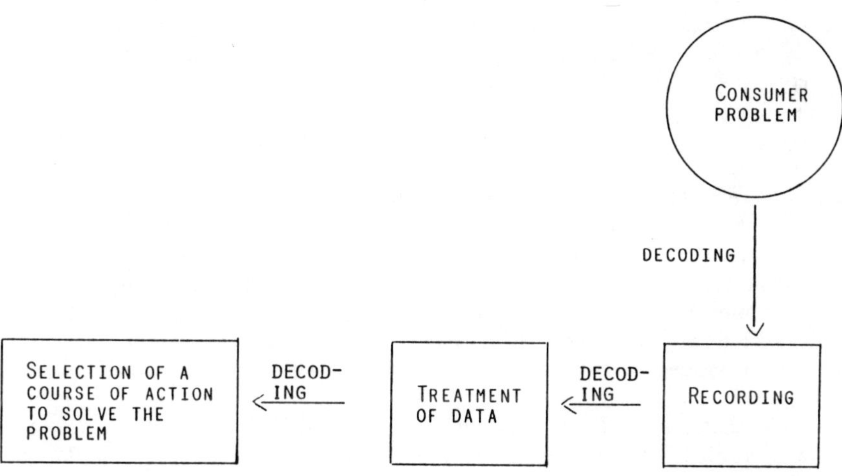

Recapitulation

Some consumer-to-firm communication is necessary for the functioning of any firm. We have now discussed three types of such communications and the information about consumer concerns that they each provide. Consumer purchase choices produce essentially binary data; as communications these signals contain little in terms of explanations for purchase behavior. Consumer decisions to purchase or not to purchase show the direction and magnitude of sales development. Causes and explanations have to be sought elsewhere.

With respect to market research as communications to the firm, it was concluded that consumer opinion via this type of communication is essentially a feedback device that is dependent upon the firm. Consumers do not decide what to research, which issues to address and or the scope and limit of inquiry. There is no guarantee that the issues examined correspond to what consumers view as essential.

With respect to unsolicited consumer communications, it was found that these communications have strengths where market research information is weak - and vice versa. If a certain deficiency or error in communication is likely in communications to CAD, it would be less severe or less likely in market research. On the other hand, if it is common in market research, it would be less frequent in communications to CAD. Where one type of communication is weak, the other is strong. Thus, one would expect that consumer influence depends, to a considerable extent, on the degree to which the firm uses market research and CAD as complementary information sources.

The Effect on Revenue

We have discussed the potential impact of CAD in terms of the information it can provide to the firm. This information, it was shown, has certain properties that are lacking in other types of consumer-to-firm communications. If the firm recognizes its value, the consumer voice is heard in management decisions. Let us now show how CAD can also have a more direct effect on company performance.

Instead of analyzing all types of consumer-initiated communications, let us narrow the focus to consumer complaints and their relationship to company revenue. The linkage between the firm's complaint processing and company performance is vital; it is the strength of that relationship that ultimately determines the status of CAD and consumer influence via CAD. In order to make clear this relationship, it is necessary to understand the firm's reaction to consumer complaints. Let us look at three categories of reactions:

Primitive Reaction to Complaints by Sellers

Manifestation: "Silent treatment," legal gimmicks, intimidation, "stonewalling," etc.

Typical objective or attitude: "Don't waste time on complainers."

Complaint Handling

Manifestation: rapid, fair, and accurate handling of complaints.

Typical objective or attitude: Minimize the number of complaints.

Complaint Management

Manifestation: Rapid, liberal, and generous compensation.

Typical objective or attitude: Maximize the number of complaints (relative to dissatisfaction).

Although the first category is one that every consumer has probably encountered at least once, it is of limited interest for this discussion. In the long term, it is obvious that such an attitude cannot be in the interest of the competitive business firm although in a monopoly, this may, of course, not be so. Nevertheless, let us proceed by looking at firms operating in competitive markets. As described in the second category, "complaint handling" is perhaps the most common. Here, efficiency usually refers to the procedures involved and the steps taken to ensure rapid turnover of complaints, accurate and fair responses to consumers, and low complaint processing costs. On the surface, this approach makes intuitive sense but it has a dysfunctional aspect to it. The problem is that it does not consider the opportunity cost of not receiving a complaint from a dissatisfied customer. Instead, reductions in the ratio of complaints to sales are seen as desirable and complaint reduction is a typical objective. Sometimes a management bonus is tied to the number of complaints in such a way that executive paychecks increase with fewer complaints.

Complaint management is the more enlightened approach. It differs from complaint handling in that it incorporates objectives that are reflected in customer retention as well as complaint volume. Contrary to the narrow focus of complaint handling, it is now realized that a complaint is but one expression of dissatisfaction. Another expression of dissatisfaction is "exit," to use Hirschman's [16] term. Exit implies that the dissatisfied consumer deserts the company in favor of a competitive firm or stops purchasing from the industry altogether. It is clear that the firm would want to prevent exit because it results in a direct revenue loss. It is also clear, albeit less obvious, that the firm should encourage complaints. Complaints do not involve revenue losses; instead they give the firm a chance to recover a potentially lost customer. There are, of course, costs associated with processing complaints (staffing, analysis, consumer compensation, etc.) but whenever the revenue loss is greater than the cost, if a sufficient number of the complainants decide to remain customers, complaints should be encouraged. This leads us to the following proposition: there are general circumstances under which company profitability and increased consumer communications in the form of complaints may well go hand-in-hand.

The positive relationship between complaint management and company performance (as measured by market share and profit) has been analytically demonstrated by Fornell and Wernerfelt [12]. For example, it has been shown that if all firms in an industry fall into the first two categories of complaint reaction and one firm begins to pursue complaint management, the "complaint managing" firm will gain substantial market share.

Empirical evidence also demonstrates that a <u>satisfied</u>, complaining consumer becomes more loyal and will generate positive word-of-mouth about the firm to other consumers [14]. As discussed earlier, the complaining consumer expects a response from the firm that will make the effort of complaining worthwhile. A part of that response concerns compensation. Let us now illustrate, by way of a simple example, how both the firm and the consumer can gain from the activities of the CAD. Specifically, we will show how the firm can enjoy increased market share and, at the same time, be quite generous in its consumer compensation.

Consider the market for mid-sized automobiles. Annual industry sales is approximately two million units. On the average, let us assume that 20% of the buyers are less than satisfied with their purchase. (This percentage corresponds roughly to what has been found in nationwide surveys on dissatisfaction with cars.) If industry growth is negligible, each firm looks at a pool of .2 x 2 million = 400,000 customers who are prone to exit. Again, if there is no growth in the industry, this pool constitutes the sole source of increased sales for the individual firm. Firm A manufactures a car in the mid-size market that has a market share of 16% (which implies sales of 320,000 units). If its share of dissatisfied customers is equal to the industry average, the firm will have 64,000 (.20 x 320,000) dissatisfied customers. These are the customers that are likely targets for the competitors' marketing efforts. The issue now is: how many of these customers can firm A retain and what is the cost of retention? In order to analyze this problem in detail, we need more information about the severity of the dissatisfaction, the nature of competition, consumer expectations, and so on. However, we can still gain important insight by keeping the problem simple. Let us assume that retention is strongly affected by the compensation that the CAD provides to the complaining customer. From the consumer's point of view, it would be desirable to have the firm provide generous compensation without taking the time to investigate the validity of the complaint. As it turns out, this would probably be desirable for the firm as well. For the sake of illustration, let us say that 47% (again, this number corresponds with data from empirical studies) of the dissatisfied car buyers complained. For firm A, this would mean 30,080 complaints. Firm A calculates the average compensation amount to be $50. It investigates every complaint and finds that a large number, let's say 40%, are not what the firm considers "valid". On the average, the investigation costs amount to $25. Accordingly, the cost for firm A is:

Compensation .60 x 30,080 x $50	=	$902,400
Investigation Cost 30,080 x $25	=	$752,000
TOTAL		$1.65 mill.

Now, consider what happens if firm A decides not to investigate at all. The costs would be:

Compensation 30,080 x $50	=	$1.5 mill.

Clearly, in this example it would be more profitable for the firm to compensate every complaining customer without investigation. How general is this case? There are strong arguments to suggest that it is quite general and that the example understates rather than exaggerates the effect. The reason: it seems unlikely that as many as 40% of all complaining consumers are willing to take the effort to complain without a valid reason. If, for example, 9 out of 10 complainants had valid claims and the average cost of investigation was still $25, it would not be cost-effective for the firm to investigate unless the compensation exceeded $250. If the cost of investigation was $100, it would not be profitable to investigate unless the compensation exceeded $1,000. As can be seen from the formula below [4], it is only when a majority of complainants (more than 60%) have invalid claims that it pays to investigate:

$$C = I + (P \times C)$$

where,

C is consumer compensation measured in dollars
I is investigation costs measured in dollars
P is the fraction of valid complaints.

Given that, for most companies, the likely percentage of invalid complaints is below 20% [4], it is probably safe to say that the firm "wins" by issuing credits or refunds without questioning the customer's integrity. This argument is further bolstered by the effect on customer retention. If the firm can make the complaint process less unpleasent by requiring less extensive documentation or less questioning the truthfulness of the customer, a good deal of consumer exit can be prevented. In our example, firm A stands to gain a maximum potential of 64,000 customers directly and additional customers via the effects of word-of-mouth. Similar conclusions are obtained where the customer retention rate was modeled as a function of compensation [12].

ACTUAL PERFORMANCE: CONSUMER AFFAIRS DEPARTMENTS IN OPERATION

A CAD, to be successful, must serve two masters successfully. It will not be allowed to pursue consumer interests that are inconsistent with the objectives of the firm; it will be rejected by consumers if it does not increase their utility. We concluded earlier that this role is viable at least in principle: (1) CAD can render the consumer a voice in management decision making while at the same time the firm gains valuable information that is otherwise inaccessible to it, and (2) CAD can reduce consumer frustration by facilating consumer redress while at the same time the firm gains from reduced customer turnover.

Let us conclude our analysis by looking at how CADs actually perform. Do they function as described here? The empirical evidence on the performance of CADs is not large, but there has been a continuous stream of research over the years. One of the earlier accounts (1969) is provided by Cohen [5] who had her students examine the impact of consumer-initiated communications in a range of different industries. She concluded that "it was evident that most of the companies viewed a consumer communication channel as performing a public relations function of minimizing or relieving consumer complaints, rather than as a means of implementing the consumer orientation concept which is concerned with securing information helpful in providing consumer satisfactions" [4, p. 184].

A few years later -- in the early 1970's -- the Conference Board published an essentially descriptive study by McGuire [21], but from his discussion it appears that CAD did not have a major impact on management decisions. Most of the evaluative research that followed [18, 7, 1, 17] found the typical CAD to be rather isolated within the company, not being integrated into the decision-making structure and with little say in marketing or production matters. Five years later, a major study for the U.S. Office of Consumer Affairs entitled "Complaint Handling in America" conducted by Technical Assistance Research Programs (TARP) in 1979, presented a more positive picture. Leading companies in several major industries looked upon consumer complaints not as a nuisance but as a marketing asset. Overall, however, TARP's conclusion was less encouraging. In most firms complaint handling was given a low priority, complaints were rarely solicited, and the reporting of complaint data to management was either nonexistent or very poor. Since then, TARP has conducted a large number of consulting projects for individual firms and has probably had some influence in making CADs more effective and improving their status within the firm. This, at least, is the conclusion by TARP in a 1986 follow-up report to the original study.

This is not to suggest that the remaining problems are small or that most CADs are performing up to potential. In fact, there is little evidence to make such a claim. Ross and Gardner [22], for example, did a study that involved the collection from CAD's of statistics on consumer-initiated communications. In many cases, the CAD did not even compile fundamental statistics and the data sought by the researchers were often not available. Further, Ross and Gardner concluded that many consumer affairs directors have a misconceived view of the inferences one can draw from complaint data. As many as 73% of the respondents attributed changes in complaint frequency to a change in consumer dissatisfaction, just to take one example. In fact an increase in complaint frequency could mean more dissatisfied consumers or it could mean fewer simply because exit has become less attractive for some reason.

While there may have been some progress in specifying the relationship between CAD and company performance [9, 12, 27, 28], there are at least four major problems that deserve attention. As Goodman and Malech point out [14], a firm's distribution channel is often ill equipped to transmit consumer complaints from the retailer to the manufacturer. The complaint data may never reach the manufacturer. Another problem is the "vicious circle of consumer complaints." A 1984 study of CADs [13] found that company responsiveness to complaints depends on the extent of the sampling consumer criticism. Perversely, the more complaints (relative to more positive consumer communications, such as inquiries and compliments), the less the firm's willingness to respond positively. This tendency results in a vicious circle where high levels of consumer complaints tend to isolate the CAD within the company and, because of its isolation, the CAD cannot affect company behavior in order to reduce future consumer problems. Thus the level of complaints remains high, further isolating the CAD, and perpetuating the cycle. The reason for this vicious circle: the reluctance of people in corporations to transmit "bad news" to management [13].

A third frequently encountered problem is a conflict of labor/production versus consumer interests. An example is the restaurant that closes for lunch, thus easing things for owners and employees, but not serving consumers. In some cases the "product" is defined in terms of production, forgetting consumption. Lovelock [20] gives an example of a bus company. Passengers, standing at marked bus stops waiting in line to board, complained that the bus would come by half-empty, the driver would smile, wave, and continue without stopping!! The company "explained" to the would-be-passengers that it was not possible to keep to its schedules if drivers had to stop and pick up people at every bus stop!! Though extreme, this example makes the point.

Finally, much needs to be done in terms of improving the analysis of aggregate consumer-initiated communications as well as integrating it with other types of data. For management to draw the correct inferences and in order to best utilize the information, it must be processed in such a way that its strengths are realized and weaknesses compensated for. There have been tremendous advances in both hardware and software that make it possible to do this. Unfortunately, it seems that it is only the hardware component that has made its way into business corporations. Most of the recently developed multivariate analysis techniques are still waiting to be applied. This is especially true for the more powerful and sophisticated techniques of the "second generation of multivariate analysis" [10, 11].

Although there are individual CAD exceptions, and some evidence that things are improving in general, the empirical evidence still suggests that CADs have a long way to go before they realize their full potential and begin to resemble the type of department that has been outlined in theory.

REFERENCES

1. AAKER, D.A. and G.S. DAY (eds.) (1974), Consumerism: Search for the Consumer Interest (2nd ed), New York, The Free Press.

2. ANDREASEN, A.R. and A. BEST (1977), "Consumer Complain - Does Business Respond?" Harvard Business Review, 55, No. 4, pp. 93-101.

3. BERGSTROM, S. (1979), "Some Reflections on Fornell's Paper on Corporate Consumer Affairs Departments, JCP, 2, 1978, 4," Journal of Consumer Policy, 3, pp. 166-167.

4. BLANDING W. (1984), "Complaint Handling: Can you Afford to Give Away the Store? Perhaps you can." Customer Service Newsletter, 12, No. 7, pp. 1-6.

5. COHEN, D. (1969) (ed.), Communication Systems Between Management and the Consumer in Selected Industries. Hempstead, New York: Hofstra University Yearbook of Business.

6. CROZIER, M. (1964), The Bureaucratic Phenomenon. Chicago: University of Chicago Press.

7. FORNELL, C. (1976), Consumer Input for Marketing Decision - A Study of Corporate Departments for Consumer Affairs. New York: Praeger.

8. _________ (1978), "The Corporate Consumer Affairs Function - A Communication Perspective," Journal of Consumer Policy, vol. 2, No. 4, December, pp. 289-302.

9. _________ (1981), "Increasing the Organizational Influence of Corporate Consumer Affairs Departments," Journal of Consumer Affairs, Winter, pp. 191-213.

10. _________ (1986), "A Second Generation of Multivariate Analysis: Classification of Methods and Implications for Marketing Research," in M.J. Houston (ed.) Review of Marketing, forthcoming.

11. _________ (1982) (ed.), A Second Generation of Multivariate Analysis, Vols. 1 & 2, New York: Praeger.

12. FORNELL, C. and B. WERNERFELT (1987), "Defensive Marketing Strategy by Maximizing Consumer Complaints," Journal of Marketing Research, November, 10-27.

13. FORNELL, C. and R.A. WESTBROOK (1984), "The Vicious Circle of Consumer Complaints," Journal of Marketing, Summer, pp. 68-78.

14. GOODMAN, J.A. and A.R. MALECH (1985), "Using Complaints for Quality Assurance Decisions," TARP working paper.

15. HICKSON, D.J., C.R. HININGS, C.A. LEE, R.E. SCHNECK and J.M. PENNINGS (1971), "A Strategic Contingencies Theory of Intraorganizational Power," Administrative Science Quarterly, No. 2, Vol. 16, pp. 216-229.

16. HIRSCHMAN, A.O. (1970), Exit, Voice, and Loyalty: Responses to Decline in Firms, Organizations and States. Cambridge, Mass.: Harvard University Press.

17. HISE, R.T., P.L. GILLETT, and J.P. KELLY (1978), "The Corporate Consumer Affairs Effort," MSU Business Topics, Summer, pp. 17-26.

18. KENDALL, C.L. and F.A. RUSS (1975), "A Warranty and Complaint Policies: An Opportunity for Marketing Management," Journal of Marketing, 39, April, pp. 36-43.

19. LASSWELL, H.D. (1948), "The Structure and Function of Communications in Society" in L. Bryson (ed.), The Communication of Ideas, New York: Harper & Row, pp. 37-51.

20. LOVELOCK, C.H. (1985), Presentation on Services Marketing Given Before the American Marketing Association's Boston Chapter, November.

21. MCGUIRE, P.E. (1973), The Consumer Affairs Department: Organization and Functions. New York: The Conference Board.

22. ROSS, I. and K. GARDNER (1985), "The Use of Consumer-Initiated Communication as Marketing Research Data: The View of Consumer Affairs Professionals," Working Paper, School of Management, University of Minnesota.

23. SCHRAMM, W.L. (1954), The Process and Effects of Mass Communications, Urbana, Illinois: University of Illinois Press.

24. SHANNON, C.E. and W. WEAVER (1949), The Mathematical Theory of Communication, Urbana: University of Illinois Press.

25. STARK, A. (1986), "Consumer Reporting Should Evaluate Organizations From the Consumers' Point of View. Objections to the Paper by Kasper and Scheuder," Journal of Consumer Policy, 6, pp. 91-94.

26. TARP (1979), Consumer Complaint Handling in America: Final Report. Washington, D.C.: U.S. Office of Consumer Affairs.

27. ________ (1983), The Bottom Line Benefits of Consumer Education: A Preliminary Exploratory Study Conducted for the Industry and Consumer Affairs Department of Coca Cola USA.

28. ________ (1983), "The Bottom-Line Implications of Unmet Customer Expectations and How to Measure Them." Working paper, June.

29. ________ (1986), Update: Consumer Complaint Handling in America, Washington, D.C.: U.S. Office of Consumer Affairs.

30. THAYER, L. (1968), Communications and Communications Systems. Homewood, Illinois: Irving.

31. THOMPSON, J.D. (1967), Organizations in Action, New York: McGraw-Hill.

32. WIMMER, F. (1979), "Corporate Consumer Affairs Departments: Are They Really in the Interest of the Consumer? A Comment on Fornell in JCP, 2, 1978 4." Journal of Consumer Policy, 3, pp. 91-95.

Chapter 26

ABOUT THE AUTHOR

Meredith M. Fernstrom is Senior Vice President-Public Responsibility at American Express Company. The holder of a Master's in Consumer Economics and Marketing from the University of North Carolina at Greensboro, Fernstrom has had a highly diversified career, starting as a home economics teacher, followed by stints with an advertising agency in Washington, as Director of Consumer Education in the District of Columbia, Special Assistant to the Secretary and Director of Consumer Affairs in the U.S. Department of Commerce (1976-80). She joined American Express as Vice President-Consumer Affairs in 1976 and became Senior Vice President in 1982. Fernstrom served as President of the Society of Consumer Affairs Professionals in 1985-86. She is a member of the Editorial Policy Board of the Journal of Retail Banking.

CONSUMER AFFAIRS: A VIEW FROM BUSINESS

Meredith M. Fernstrom

According to Claes Fornell, the corporate consumer affairs department in order to be successful, must serve two masters simultaneously. It will not be allowed to pursue consumer interests that are inconsistent with the objectives of the firm; it will be deserted by consumers if it does not increase their utility.

This "balancing act" between the consumer and the company interest has been the central feature of my last thirteen years as a consumer affairs professional. First, for seven years in City and Federal government, and then, for six years in a major corporation, I have walked that fine line between trying to serve the consumer's interest and that of my employing organization.

This brings us to two important questions: Can people like me -- the consumer affairs professional in business -- really serve the consumer interest inside the corporation? Can anyone realistically serve two masters?

SOME BACKGROUND

My answer is that many of the corporate consumer affairs professionals I know -- and myself among them, I hope -- can and are performing this balancing act very effectively.

Fornell concluded, on the basis of several studies, that corporate consumer affairs departments "have a long way to go before they realize their full potential." With that conclusion I agree. But it is appropriate to single out several factors which have hampered the achievement of that potential until now and, in many cases, will continue to do so in the future.

First, corporate consumer affairs as a profession is relatively new--dating back to the early 1970's for most companies, and much more recently for others. Many of these consumer affairs units were established, as Fornell correctly notes, as defensive moves against the consumer activism of the late 60's and early 70's. Unfortunately, this origin put in place among many corporate executives an erroneous mindset. In their eyes consumer advocates and government representatives were "the enemy." By extension, many even began to see the consumer, our customers, as the bad guy causing all our problems.

Thus, also by extension, the first consumer affairs offices were viewed in the narrowest terms: their sole functions were to appease complaining customers and to avoid the "shrinkage" of corporate profits that consumer advocates might achieve through restrictive anti-business legislation, boycotts, media exposes, etc. Very few consumer affairs offices were created from a more positive perspective -- aiding the Company's marketing strategies, for example.

This attitude prevailed in many companies throughout the '70s, reinforced by the continuing stream of "pro-consumer" legislation and regulation that occurred during that decade.

Gradually, some consumer affairs departments expanded their functions to become more proactive, e.g., by producing and distributing consumer information and by establishing relationships with consumer leaders. Developments such as these were not general, but were often dependent upon the abilities and attitudes of particular consumer affairs individuals, and more importantly, on the attitudes of his or her management.

The second major factor hampering the development of consumer affairs offices has been the variety of functions and responsibilities assigned to consumer affairs. Most departments perform the basic function of responding to customer inquiries and complaints. Most also provide management with reports on the nature and cause of complaints and with recommendations for reducing "problems."

Beyond these basic functions, however, there is extreme diversity among our offices. We might do one or more of the following:

-- produce and distribute consumer information;
-- review advertising copy;
-- develop liaison with consumer organizations and other public interest groups;
-- participate in legislative activities;
-- give media interviews or speeches;
-- advise management on product design, policy development, or marketing strategies.

But again, the specific range of our responsibilities is most often determined not by how well we perform, but by how creative and persuasive we can be, and how enlightened our management is. Obviously, these factors vary widely from person to person and from company to company.

It is my strong view that consumer affairs professionals <u>can</u> serve the consumer interest inside the corporation <u>IF</u>:

-- the corporation wants it to happen;
-- the corporation provides sufficient resources;
-- the person in consumer affairs is "right" for the job;
-- our constituents, both consumer and corporate, give us a fair shot at making it work.

Let me expand these "ifs" and give a few examples from my experience at American Express Company as to how we're addressing them.

MAKING CORPORATE CONSUMER AFFAIRS WORK

Corporate Commitment

First and most important, the corporation must want consumer affairs to work. Senior management, and especially the chief executive officer, must be philosophically committed to seeking customer and consumer opinion and to factoring those views into the company's policy decisions as well as the design and marketing of its products. The consumer affairs office must be viewed as an integral part of the company's overall marketing philosophy and strategy, not as a defensive, adversarial or public affairs "add-on."

At American Express, we are blessed with a senior management that is consumer-oriented. Our Chairman, Jim Robinson, frequently attributes the success of American Express to the fact that we are "customer-driven": that is, we believe it is in our best <u>business</u> interest to serve the <u>consumer</u> interest, and serve it better than our competition does! Thus, the Consumer Affairs Office is expected--even encouraged -- to represent the consumer perspective in our policy decision-making even when the views we express differ from other views within the Company. As Mr. Robinson puts it, the purpose of consumer affairs is to provide a system of "checks and balances," consumer affairs offsetting the position of others whose views "may be dominated by the ring of the cash register."

At the same time, we must be alert to capitalize on those situations where there is a mutuality of interests between consumers and our Company--the "win-win" situations. As an example, our on-going campaign to inform women about their credit rights is such a win-win situation. We perform a useful and appreciated public service while at the same time achieving the important marketing goal of adding more women to the ranks of American Express card members.

<u>Giving Consumer Affairs Sufficient Resources</u>

Now to my second "if." If appropriate resources are made available to them, corporate consumer affairs professionals <u>can</u> serve the consumer interest.

In these competitive times, corporations are taking whatever measures they can to hold the line on costs. This means trimming any "fat" that exists and requiring greater productivity from everyone. More than ever, consumer affairs offices--like other parts of the corporation--must justify their worth to the company if they are to maintain or expand their share of company resources.

What makes this requirement especially difficult is the challenge of quantifying the impact of consumer affairs activities on profits. In many companies progress has been made in assessing the costs and benefits of effective customer complaint handling. But other aspects of our programs, such as providing consumer information or enhancing the company's image, are much more qualitative in nature, resistant to easy quantification of benefits.

Regardless, management must be willing to back its commitment to consumer affairs by providing adequate resources. While the primary resources I have in mind are the number and status of positions in the consumer affairs office and its total operating funds, there are other important resources that must be made available as well. These include the access by the consumer affairs professional to senior management and to the company's information network, both formal and informal. If the company provides this access and it is used judiciously, it can be one of the most powerful tools for effectively representing the consumer interest.

Access is largely determined by the placement of the consumer affairs office within the organizational structure and by the seniority accorded the person in charge of consumer affairs. My position is illustrative. I am one of the few corporate consumerists at the senior vice president level. I report to an executive vice president who in turn reports directly to the Chairman. My responsibilities are both corporation-wide and world-wide. In addition, the corporate culture at American Express allows me to have frequent contact with our Chairman, our President, and other senior officials.

Another invaluable resource of the corporate consumer affairs professional is the authority granted to him or her by the company. While most of us in consumer affairs do not actually make final policy decisions within our companies, many of us do recommend new or revised policies. Many of us are frequently responsible for implementing and evaluating them. The extent of authority accorded to consumer affairs needs to be clearly spelled out and made known throughout the company.

As one example, my office is responsible for assuring compliance with American Express' voluntary "Privacy Code." This code establishes standards for the collection, use and retention of personal information about our customers and employees. In addition, I serve on the Advertising Review Board of our Travel Related Services Company. This Board must approve all marketing communications, print and electronic, before their final production. This provides an important avenue by which I can directly influence what we say to our customers, and how we say it.

This example illustrates a difficulty of evaluating corporate consumer affairs programs: actions taken may be invisible to the outside observer. You may not always see direct, tangible results of our actions. When we prevent mistakes or misinformation from occurring, you are unlikely to have heard about it. Nonetheless, visible or not, we have performed one of our most effective and cost-efficient functions, both for company and customers.

Professional Qualifications of Consumer Affairs Professionals

Now to my third "if." Corporate consumerists can serve the consumer interest if the individual holding that position is "right" for the job.

Because the consumer affairs profession is still relatively new, it is often defined and understood on a case-by-case basis within each company. Misconceptions about its true purpose frequently occur both within and outside the corporation, necessitating a continual education process.

The Society of Consumer Affairs Professionals in Business, SOCAP, now in its fourteenth year, is gaining both in number of members and in visibility. Equally important, it is providing extensive professional development programs that help clarify the role of the consumer affairs manager and enhance our effectiveness.

To me, the most important criteria for a consumer affairs professional is having a strong philosophical commitment to representing the consumer perspective in the corporation. In this regard, it is useful for consumer affairs professionals to have some experience outside of business--in government, consumer advocacy, the media, etc. On the other hand, to be effective in our jobs, we must have credibility inside the company. We must represent the consumer's voice in corporate decision-making, being branded neither as "Pollyanna" or adversary.

Constituent Support

This brings me to the final "if" on my list. Corporate consumerists can serve the consumer interest if our constituents give us a fair chance to make it happen.

Who are our constituents? Certainly, consumer leaders, government representatives and academicians are among our most important constituencies. We look to these groups to provide the "cutting edge" perspective on issues that may not yet be widely known by the general public, and to give us extra insights from more studied analyses of the issues.

Our customers are also a major constituency. On some issues, the views of consumer affairs professionals and theirs may not be in agreement. Our job is to weigh and represent fairly all such opinions. At the same time, we must understand and acknowledge the many other "special interests" the company must serve: its shareholders, employees, community organizations, business partners and so on. But it is our special responsibility to see to it that the consumer perspective is represented clearly and effectively.

We may not accomplish everything that our constituents -- or we -- would like to accomplish. But our presence inside the corporation is vital if we are to help bring about the goal of an enlightened private sector responding fully to its public responsibilities.

I applaud the growing list of consumer organizations, government agencies and universities that are entering into cooperative relationships with corporate consumer affairs offices. In my view, such collaboration can work to the mutual benefit of company and consumer without compromising either organization.

Summary

Can corporate consumer affairs professionals really serve the consumer interest? Yes, if:

...the corporation is committed to it;

...the company provides sufficient resources;

...the person(s) in consumer affairs is "right" for the job;

...constituent groups are supportive.

ABOUT THE AUTHOR

Irene M. Vawter is Assistant Director for Consumer and Business Education in the Bureau of Protection at the Federal Trade Commission. Vawter received her Master's in Journalism from Marquette University and has done post-graduate work at the University of Iowa. For the past 15 years she has worked in government communications, developing national campaigns in consumer, business, energy, and worker education at the General Services Administration, the Department of Energy, The Office of Personnel Management, and the Department of Labor. She began working at the Federal Trade Commission in 1980.

CONSUMER AFFAIRS: A VIEW FROM GOVERNMENT

Irene M. Vawter

As I read Claes Fornell's thoughtful analysis of Corporate Consumer Affairs Departments: Retrospect and Prospect, my mind kept jumping to the many obvious parallels between corporate consumer affairs departments (CADs) and those located in Federal agencies. Federal consumer affairs offices also started up in the 1970's as part of the growing consumer movement and were integrated into the bureaucracy in 1979 by Executive Order. In fact, when I entered government from a university position in 1971, it was to establish a new consumer affairs office in a Federal agency. Although we in Federal consumer affairs offices do many of the same tasks and have many of the same problems as corporate CADs, our work and problems have a slightly different twist.

My intention today is to address the relevant Federal twists, to analyze some of the apparent conflicts raised by Fornell, and to suggest some strategies for moving Federal consumer affairs offices toward the full potential of Fornell's theories.

My judgments reflect my six years of experience with the Federal Trade Commission (FTC), managing its Office of Consumer and Business Education within the Bureau of Consumer Protection. The Bureau of Consumer Protection enforces a variety of consumer protection laws enacted by Congress, as well as trade regulation rules issued by the Commission. Its activities include investigations of individual companies and industries, administrative and federal court litigation, rulemaking proceedings, and consumer and business education. The work of my office is rooted in the Bureau's efforts and reflects its priorities. Operating from the Bureau Director's office, I coordinate with the Bureau's five divisions -- Advertising Practices, Credit Practices, Enforcement, Marketing Practices, and

Service Industry Practices -- and work to supplement and enhance their enforcement activity through consumer and business education. Through such efforts, the Bureau aims to promote self-help on the part of consumers and compliance on the part of industry.

MAKING THE INTERSECTION

The early questions in Dr. Fornell's paper afford an excellent starting point for an analysis of consumer affairs within Federal agencies. To focus their work, managers of consumer affairs in Federal agencies must ask and answer:

> "At what point does an intersection exist between the consumer interest (as defined by Dr. Fornell) and my Federal agency's interest?"
>
> "Where is the point of mutuality between my Federal agency's good and the consumer's good?"
>
> "How can I make this intersection visible for the good of each?"

The easy answers come by simply citing the law that established the agency. For example, one of my easy answers would cite Section 5 of the FTC Act which gives the FTC power to prohibit "unfair or deceptive acts or practices in or affecting commerce." The hard answers come by looking at two further questions.

> "What does my Federal agency do, or have knowledge about, that would provide for the consumer interest?"
>
> "What effective, tangible consumer programs/ products can I put into place, given my budget, staff, and other limitations, that also would further the work of my Federal agency?"

Providing Important Information

By asking and answering such questions, Federal consumer affairs managers can begin to formulate a plan to provide consumers with important agency information. This, Dr. Fornell said, was one basis for measuring corporate CAD influence. Therefore, each year, consumer affairs managers must re-ask and answer the question:

> "Given my Federal agency's work priorities, what consumer information programs can I put into place to provide important consumer information?"

For clarity, let me say how a fiscal year plan might be developed.

Step 1. Collect data about any new consumer-related efforts occurring in divisions for which you have responsibility. Find out what work will be completed during the year that would justify new consumer information. For me, this would mean:

-- talking with budget officers about money and staffing levels;
-- talking with key program attorneys about any special enforcement emphasis or any anticipated changes in rules or statutes;
-- reviewing the agency's regulatory agenda;
-- reviewing relevant agency studies or market research;
-- checking Headquarters and Regional Office computerized complaint statistics about companies and products;
-- reviewing current FTC publications to determine any need for revisions or deletions;
-- contacting appropriate outside organizations -- government agencies and the private sector -- to find opportunities for joint ventures.

Step 2. Draft a plan, based on the collected data, listing new potential consumer information topics for each division. I send the draft to division management and schedule a meeting for the plan's discussion. Division managers can react to the plan and add or delete topics. In this way, I get their reaction and enlist support for their attorneys' staff time.

As an added strategy, I list and report about incomplete on-going projects, but also list completed ones to demonstrate success.

Step 3. Prepare a final plan, which goes to division management requesting final comment. I also tell division directors when I intend to send the plan forward for official approval.

Step. 4. Prepare monthly status reports and send them to appropriate officials to keep them informed. I make status reports brief by simply listing topics under categories, such as: completed; in production; in final review; in development; under consideration.

The "under consideration" category is a continual source of new work, unless a topic is displaced by a new one of higher priority.

Step 5. Prepare a year-end accomplishment report and distribute it appropriately. I also suggest sending out brief periodic information memos about consumer affairs successes to appropriate officials agency-wide, with new publications attached.

Using such a yearly-plan strategy is only one example of how a Federal consumer affairs office might structure itself within the agency to provide important consumer information and extend the agency mission. Obviously, given the diversity of Federal consumer affairs offices, any plan would need adaptations, and no plan will project the whole responsibility of the office. The point is, each year Federal agency consumer affairs managers need to analyze and plan creatively. They need to discipline themselves to contribute visibly to the consumer interest and to the agency's mission. Otherwise, the office may become a "o" in any cost-benefit equation.

Satisfying the Public

The second basis for corporate CAD influence, according to Dr. Fornell, is effective complaint handling to reduce customer turnover. In a Federal parallel, effective customer relations might translate into ensuring that the public is satisfied with the agency's work. Any dissatisfaction with an agency or its consumer affairs office may be expressed in complaint letters to agency officials or to Congress.

To maintain a satisfied public and to resolve disputes effectively, the Federal agency and its consumer affairs office must operate with a substantive rationale to explain and justify their policies and performance. At any point when the public disagrees with such policies and performance, it may voice their disagreements with their vote, just as customers voice complaints to companies by switching brands.

The public nature of our work tends to raise official sensitivities to public opinion. For that reason, if for no other, the consumer interest can prevail. Any serious complaints about the performance of an agency or a consumer affairs office escalates quickly to the highest level, especially if the complaint is published in the morning paper or comes as a Congressional inquiry.

I have had my share of public complaints to resolve in my six years at the FTC, but the funniest and most rewarding was the monster dispute.

Just before I arrived on the job, the consumer education office had done a poster concerning unordered merchandise which said, "If something shows up in the mail that you didn't order, you can keep it for free." To capture attention, the poster showed the unordered merchandise, in this case a toothy dragon which was featured by the Washington Evening Star on its front page. It became news because Time/Life felt that the dragon disparaged its negative option sales program and stood ready to sue.

My first day on the job I was told to "fix it." Thus our joint-venture program with industry was born.

In general, I agree with Dr. Fornell. Our Federal consumer affairs offices have not yet approached theoretic perfection. But I see a strength developing in these offices that goes beyond "hype," our developing strength is the result of experience and honest communication, especially that which exists among government, business, and academic communities.

I don't know what Dr. Fornell was doing in 1971. But, if he had written his paper then and I had read it, it would have saved me from making some honest mistakes early in my Federal consumer education career.

ABOUT THE AUTHOR

Dianne McKaig, an attorney, is a partner in Jones and McKaig, a consumer interest law firm in Washington, D.C. McKaig has law degrees from the University of Kentucky and Harvard University. McKaig spent ten years with the U.S. Department of Labor, ultimately becoming Chief of the Legislation and Standards Division of the Women's Bureau. She started her consumer career as the first Director of the Office of Consumer Services in the U.S. Department of Health, Education and Welfare. Subbsequently, she was Executive Director of the Michigan State Consumers Council. In 1972 McKaig became Vice President for Consumer and External Affairs of the Coca-Cola Company. She has served on the Boards of many Consumer Affairs Committees for business and public interest organizations. She is a former President of the Society for Consumer Affairs Professionals in Business.

CONSUMER AFFAIRS PROFESSIONALS AND THE CONSUMER INTEREST

Dianne McKaig

What I like about Claes Fornell's paper is his upbeat approach. He assumes that it is possible for a corporate consumer affairs department to function in the consumer interest, and proceeds to develop techniques for achieving this -- building blocks, if you will.

I too, am upbeat. But I would like to go back a step and consider the strength, or weakness, of the underpinning of this "construction." The assigned subject of this session was "Consumer Affairs Professionals and the Consumer Interest" which Fornell interpreted as consideration of "Corporate Consumer Affairs Departments." How did he get from the first to the second? Since one of the discussants has corporate experience, his may have been the interpretation intended. At any rate, this confusion in nomenclature sets the stage for what I have to say.

There are many experienced people in the field of consumer affairs who are employed in activities other than business. At the same time, there are many consumer affairs people in corporations who have little experience in consumer affairs. They are "professionals" only because the title is conferred by eligibility for membership in the Society of Consumer Affairs Professionals in Business - SOCAP. Ironically, SOCAP's sole requirement for membership is a job in a consumer affairs department (CAD) in a profit-making organization.

The co-opting of the term "professional" for CAD representatives in business was by no means invidious. On the contrary, it expressed a very positive aspiration.

But, in fact, SOCAP was not established by, nor is it an arm of, the business community. In the beginning, after a get-acquainted meeting sponsored by the Better Business Bureau, a group of some 200 people set about establishing a professional organization of individuals with safeguards for organizational independence. It was not a trade association with business memberships. Instead, the concept was to:

-- develop professionalism among members;

-- develop an expertise not otherwise available to the corporation;

-- position CADs to use their expertise to achieve a balance in decisions affecting consumers.

Much has been accomplished. SOCAP has grown from 200 to 1300 members, representing consumer-related programs in most of America's major corporations. Many of these programs work from positions of strength, developing balance between companies and consumers, two-way communications, and other activities consistent with Fornell's building blocks.

On the other hand, some of the supposed consumer programs are more fancy than fact, just complaint departments operating out of basements. Worse, some have been abolished, due either to a change in management, or a decision by management based on a judgment that CADs were not cost-effective. This is a disheartening loss of opportunity if true, and if attributable to a failure to develop the professionalism to which SOCAP and its members aspired.

A profession, according to Dean Norma Compton of the School of Consumer and Family Sciences at Purdue, has three primary characteristics:

1. A professional organization and code of ethics;

2. An orientation of altruism or service rather than self interest;

3. A body of knowledge applicable to the practical problems the profession faces.

Strictly speaking, SOCAP has none of these. The first, a code of ethics, is not at variance with Fornell's observation that a CAD's pursuit of consumer interests must be viewed as contributing to the corporation's profits. The "profit" goal should not be sneered at. Socially profits are "good." They are what keep the corporation, its stockholders, and the economy going. And the corporation -- at least an establishment corporation -- will have its own standards or ethics as to how those profits may be achieved.

Moreover, the corporations employ many people besides consumer affairs people who are concerned with ethics or standards -- the lawyers, the accountants, the quality control people. If their behavior does not conform to the standards of their professional associations, they are not making the contribution they were hired to provide.

The second characteristic, -- an altruistic or service orientation -- implies the obligation to represent the balance betweeen consumers and company about which Fornell was speaking. It also implies a willingness to engage in some judicious risk-taking as part of that representation. How can someone, lacking training or experience, recognize a balance, much less represent it? How can that person find the individual strength or organizational strength to represent a balance vigorously when they come without credentials?

One key to a successful CAD program is its positioning within the corporation. After lengthy discussion SOCAP's founders agreed on the need for CADs to be positioned outside of public relations. Their reason: so that CADs could focus on substance outside of the units that would find substance peer-threatening, close enough to the top management to get important messages communicated to top management. It was anticipated that developing professionalism would furnish the credentials to help achieve this positioning.

To be fair about it, some individuals, lacking experience in consumer affairs, but endowed with determination and insight, have established or continued very effective consumer affairs programs after some on-the-job training. Remember Betty Furness?[1]

---

[1]Betty Furness currently does three consumer spots a week on NBC's Today Show as well as being the central figure in Action 4 Consumer News, the daily consumer show of NBC's anchor station in New York, WNBC.

Our pioneers, of whom Betty Furness is representativve, were simply particularly capable individuals. By and large, our profession would benefit from training for those who chose to enter it. This brings me to the third characteristic of a profession - the body of knowledge which is educationally communicable.

It is disturbing that the body of knowledge necessary to effective functioning in the consumer affairs field has never been defined or, in some instances, even recognized. It will not be recognized as long as there is an "any-woman-with-a-shopping-cart-will-do" syndrome. It will not be recognized as long as consumer affairs in the corporation is viewed as a throw-away, reserved for a VIP's cousin or for a former secretary to the Chairman.

Nor will it be defined as long as we accept, as a "professional development" program of SOCAP or other associations that offer training, a session now and again on currently "in" subjects, without any concern for the basics, or "what every person in this discipline should know."

In other words, it is inappropriate to pursue the "electives" until the requirements are covered. Unfortunately, there is no consensus currently as to what the requirements are among those who are doing the hiring in consumer affairs.

My reason for raising this issue is that two-thirds of you attending this Conference are educators. Educators have a key role to play in developing professionalism based on a common body of knowledge.

John Burton, Associate Professor of Consumer Studies at the University of Utah, has done several studies of the correlation between consumer science studies in the universities and careers in the field, not just careers in business but careers across the full spectrum of consumer affairs. He observed that each university's courses were based on its own self-definition of consumer program. Evaluated by objective criteria, some programs were acceptable, some were provisionally acceptable, and a few served the requirements of the profession not at all.

In other words, while our universities are seeking to address this need, they are floundering to some extent in terms of course content. Anecdotal evidence of university people complaining that there are no openings for their graduates, and also of potential employers complaining that the graduates are not trained to meet their needs, underscore the point I am making.

It seems odd that there has never been a concerted effort by consumers affairs professionals and university educators to work through the basic questions together. It is my concern that the long term SOCAP aspirations for professionalism will never be fully achieved until we receive more help from educators, the only people qualified to develop course content. In my view, some students are not receiving the help they need while, at the same time, employers -- business people and some in government or the community or elsewhere -- find themselves doing more on-the-job training than is desirable. Finally, I am concerned that a structure be put in place to support the research and refinements that can be provided by people like Claes Fornell.

Chapter 27

Panel: Market Research and the Consumer Interest

ABOUT THE AUTHOR

David B. Eastwood is a Professor in the Department of Agricultural Economics and Rural Sociology at the University of Tennessee. An economist, Eastwood received his Ph.D. from Tufts University in 1972. Before going to Tennessee in 1977, Eastwood was on the Economics Faculty at the University of Lowell. Since 1984 Eastwood has been Editor of the Journal of Consumer Affairs and has been a member of the Editorial Board of the Journal of Behavioral Economics since 1977. He is the author of The Economics of Consumer Behavior (Allyn and Bacon, 1985) and many articles on demand analysis and consumer theory.

ADVERTISING: A CONSUMER ECONOMICS PERSPECTIVE

David B. Eastwood[1]

It is the thesis of this paper that we have a very limited economic theory of consumer demand and an even more limited appreciation of how marketing, and advertising, in particular, fits into consumer decision making.

CONSUMER SOVEREIGNTY AND ADVERTISING

Implicit in the vast majority of economic analyses of consumer behavior and of the functioning of markets is the assumption of consumer sovereignty. However, the explosion of consumer goods has made it impossible for consumers to be knowledgeable about all products. Furthermore, mass communications and advances in advertising technologies enable producers to take more active roles in determining preferences. This environment permits situations in which sellers have the potential for providing information which may not lead to optimal purchases or even for manipulating consumer preferences.

Producers are assumed to be profit maximizers. This is not equivalent to utility maximization, and we need to recognize the difference. The two do not have to be incompatible. Rather, it means that advertising research, as well as advertising, may be oriented to the seller's interest instead of the consumer interest.

---

[1]John Brooker and Jean Kinsey provided helpful comments on an earlier draft.

We need to develop and test models of consumer choice that incorporate advertising. In my view the best way to achieve advertising that contributes positively to consumer decision making is to develop appropriate theoretical models, confirmed by empirical evidence.

THE ECONOMICS OF CONSUMER CHOICE AND ADVERTISING

Economists have developed two basic models of consumer demand -- (1) the traditional model, and (2) the derived demand model. The two models have the following common features. Observed consumer behavior is considered to be a result of rational choice. Consumer decisions are interrelated, thereby necessitating a systems approach to modeling and estimation. Preferences change causing shifts in demand curves, as traditionally drawn, and the two ways of allowing for this are referred to as translating and scaling.[2] These adjustments are consistent with dynamic versions of both types of demand models.

The distinction between the models centers on the arguments of the utility function. Traditional demand models are defined as those in which utility is generated directly by marketplace goods.[3] Derived demand models are defined as those in which the purchases of marketplace goods comprise an intermediate stage in the utility maximization process.[4]

The difference between the types of models has significance for advertising, because distinct demand equations are associated with each approach. If traditional theory is followed, then the prices of marketplace goods, income, and demographic variables are the determinants of demand. If the derived demand approach is followed, then either the prices of characteristics or inputs of household production, income, demographic variables, and factors

---

[2]As noted by Green [9] and Johnson, Green, Hassan, and Safyurtlu [11], translating refers to incorporating socioeconomic variables into parameters of the utility function. Scaling refers to transforming consumers into adult equivalents.

[3]Johnson, Green, Hassan, and Safyurtlu [11] present an excellent survey of complete demand system models.

[4]These include characteristics models and household production models. See Eastwood [7, ch. 11] for an overview of these models, Terry [26] for an example of the former, and Bryant [1] for an example of the latter.

that affect the transformation of market goods into other products which generate utility are the determinants. Therefore, the model type limits the ways in which advertising can affect consumer purchase decisions.

When advertising is incorporated into consumer choice models, a dynamic framework is needed. A consumer must be exposed to an ad. Then, the ad must affect the decision making criteria. If the ad is effective from the consumer's perspective, then a higher level of utility is achieved because of the ad. Furthermore, an ad's impact may extend beyond the current period. These features of advertising complicate the already formidable modeling problems with respect to consumer behavior.

Advertising alters three basic features of consumer theory. One is perfect knowledge. Just the number of products alone makes it impossible for a consumer to be knowledgeable about each of the goods available.[5] Many of these products, particularly durable goods, are purchased so infrequently that the consumer cannot be familiar with them.[6] Furthermore, the technologies embodied in many products change rapidly, and it is difficult to keep abreast of all the changes. Consequently, the inclusion of advertising in consumer theory should reflect the range of impacts from familiar goods to little known products.

The second feature is the presence of price variation within the same shopping area. This was initially analyzed by Stigler [24] and has led to subsequent work such as that of Maynes and Assum [18], Moore and Lehman [19], and Olshavsky and Rosen [21]. It has also fostered a series of food price studies such as Lesser and Bryant [16]; Devine and Marion [6]; McCracken, Boynton, and Blake [17]; and Boynton, Blake, and Uhl [3]. Spatial considerations, also consistent with price variation, have been examined by Faminow and Benson [8] who assume retailers attempt to achieve geographic control of markets. Such analyses suggest that theoretical consumer models need to include the benefits as well as the costs of additional search.

A third feature is that price may not reflect all of the relevant information consumers need. Based upon the search, experience, and credence attributes of goods, advertising is directed toward

---

[5]For example, a grocery store in Miami, Florida carries over 400 fresh produce commodities.

[6]See Chern [4] for an example.

informing consumers about these properties. Imagine a continuum of the ways in which goods generate utility in the traditional model or of production technologies for transforming market goods into commodities in the derived demand approach. For example, with the derived demand approach at one extreme are goods that require little household effort before they generate utility, e.g., a charcoal broiled steak. At the other extreme, expert input may be required before the commodity is attained. This is the case with "good health." This continuum is consistent with the information content of goods. Search attributes have the most direct transformation into utility, experience attributes are more involved and have less straightforward transformations, and credence attributes have poorly understood transformations. Advertising, from this perspective, has an important role to play in decision making, but its usefulness depends on how well it provides information about household production.

Economists are beginning to incorporate advertising into consumer choice models. With respect to the classical demand approach, the effects must be introduced into the utility function or the budget constraint. Green [9] has proposed an innovative model. This is a modification of the recently developed almost ideal demand system of Deaton and Muellbauer [5]. Utility maximization is analyzed through the dual problem of minimizing the cost of attaining a given level of utility, the cost function. It has potential for estimating the impacts of advertising on income and price elasticities while at the same time accounting for the simultaneity of the decision making.

Derived demand models also have potential for incorporating the effects of advertising. This could occur in three ways through: (1) the utility function, (2) the budget constraint, and (3) the production function. It follows that a consumer good should not be viewed in terms of a one-to-one correspondence to search, experience, or credence attributes. That is, a particular good should not be considered as exclusively related to one of the three categories Eastwood [7]. Stigler and Becker [25], and the ensuing work of Nichols [20], pursue the idea that consumer tastes are invariant and advertising affects the household production of commodities. Kihlstrom [13] and Pope [22] view advertising as a means of changing the consumer's distribution of perceived characteristics associated with goods. Research in the area of the economics of information, such as by Kinsey, Senauer, and Roe [15] pertains to the hypothesis that information changes the parameters of the utility function. These lead to shifts in demand curves. Also, research by Russell and Thaler [23] considers the imperfect transformation of information into the optimal consumption bundle.

With respect to derived demand models, this mapping pertains to translation of preferences for characteristics into optimal purchases of marketplace goods. A next step in these models is to relate advertising's impacts to the continuum of production technologies.

EMPIRICAL WORK

Although existing models have limited views of advertising's impacts on consumer choice, there are indications that economists are beginning to tackle this difficult and complex choice situation. Most of the theoretical and empirical work on consumer demand has been done by agricultural economists. Certainly, this group has been the beneficiary of extensive Federal and state research support. In addition, the agricultural commodities consumers purchase are well defined with large bodies of cross-section and time-series data. Although these data may not always be ideal, they have traditionally been the best available data for testing consumer demand theory.

Even within the agricultural economics community, advertising research has generally taken the profit maximizing perspective. As Tilley has noted [27], the bulk of the empirical work lacked a theoretical foundation in consumer economics and has tended to use ad hoc single-equation estimation. Dynamic adjustment to advertising on the part of consumers has been incorporated via lagged measures of advertising. Kinnucan [14] summarizes the time-series analyses as having little theoretical guidance regarding the length or structure of lags.

Cross-section data have been used generally to determine the effectiveness of advertising campaigns. Specific socioeconomic groups or regions are targeted, and results are measured in terms of sales. Longitudinal data are becoming available, so future research can take on more of a dynamic focus. Studies by Ward and Davis [28] and Ward and McDonald [29] are examples of using pooled household data to estimate advertising impacts from a business perspective. Grigsby [10] provides an excellent summary of analyses based on successful agricultural promotional programs.

Current agricultural marketing research includes analyses of generic versus brand advertising. It has been possible to develop models that account for substitutes and complements. Generic advertising provides general information about a product and entices a consumer to try it, whereas brand advertising is directed toward choosing among alternatives and developing brand loyalty. Tilley [27] raises the interesting question of whether the increased generic promotion of products can be successful from a profit maximization perspective with products that have close substitutes (e.g., milk, eggs, and cheese). A variant of this focus is the interest in fresh produce. The issue here is whether locally grown fresh produce can be advertised and sold as a "brand."

Most food commodities have search and experience components. The household production of meals requires well defined capital goods and labor inputs. These considerations suggest that initial forays into advertising's impacts on consumer choice may be handled most easily with food. Certain aspects of food advertising are directed toward utility function parameters, while others are directed toward providing information about alternative meal production possibilities. Similarly, durable goods advertising seems to be aimed at household production technologies.

RESEARCH AGENDA

Problems that need to be addressed are complex and difficult to handle, but have the potential of identifying the role of advertising in consumer behavior. Certainly, more realistic theoretical models which incorporate the effects of advertising within the simultaneity of decision making have to be developed. The spatial distribution of consumers and stores needs further examination. Information problems regarding stores, products, and advertising should be addressed. More attention should be given to durable purchases.

Better data are also needed. Testing the household production derived demand approach requires much more information about resource allocation "beyond the threshold." Juster, Courant, and Dow [12] have proposed a theoretical framework for the requisite data. However, substantive research is needed to develop the methodology for tracking resource allocation within the home, defining the units of output, and use of capital goods.

Advertising introduces additional data considerations. Appropriate measures of advertising have to be identified. Those which are available have well-known limitations of differing advertising productivity by advertiser and media. Improved theoretical models may be of some assistance here in defining the appropriate measures from the consumer's decision making perspective. However, there is the additional problem of measuring the effect of advertising on consumer choice. Clearly, this calls for measures of advertising which permit hypothesis testing with respect to utility maximizing choice.

An enhanced understanding of the consumer economics of advertising has the potential of improving consumer well-being.

Products should be promoted on the basis of criteria that matter to consumers. Better standards for advertising could be established. The information content of ads should be more relevant for decision making. Consumer education programs could be developed around the appropriate view of the role of advertising. Progress toward these goals raises the possibility of a market system more in line with consumer sovereignty and an enhanced quality of life.

REFERENCES

1. BRYANT, W. KEITH, JENNIFER L. GERNER and URSULA HENZE (1983), "Estimating Household Production Functions: A Case Study," Proceedings of the 29th Annual Conference of the American Council on Consumer Interests, Karen P. Goebel (ed.): 179-83.

2. BUSINESS WEEK (1986), "And Now a Wittier Word from Our Sponsors," (March 24): 90-94.

3. BOYNTON, ROBERT D., BRIAN F. BLAKE and JOE E. UHL (1983), "Retail Price Reporting Effects in Local Food Markets," American Journal of Agricultural Economics 65(1): 20-29.

4. CHERN, WEN S. (1986), "Issues and Methodologies for Modeling Demand for Durable Goods," Proceedings of the 32nd Annual Conference of the American Council on Consumer Interests, Karen P. Schnittgrund (ed.): 118-23.

5. DEATON, AUGUS and JOHN MUELLBAUER (1980), "An Almost Ideal Demand System," American Economic Review, 70: 312-326.

6. DEVINE, D. GRANT and BRUCE W. MARION (1979), "The Influence of Consumer Price Information on Retail Pricing and Consumer Behavior," American Journal of Agricultural Economics 61(2): 228-237.

7. EASTWOOD, DAVID B. (1985), The Economics of Consumer Behavior, Newton, Mass.: Allyn and Bacon.

8. FAMINOW, MERLE D. and BRUCE L. BENSON (1985), "Spatial Economics: Information for Food Market Response to Retail Price Reporting," Journal of Consumer Affairs 19(1): 1-19.

9. GREEN, RICHARD (1985), "Dynamic Utility Functions for Measuring Advertising Response," Proceedings from Research on Effectiveness of Agricultural Commodity Promotion Seminar, Walter J. Armbruster and Lester H. Meyers (eds.), Arlington, Va., Farm Foundation and USDA (April): 80-88.

10. GRIGSBY, S. ELAINE (1985), "Empirical, Analytical, and Measurement Issues in Evaluating Effectiveness of Advertising and Commodity Programs: Cross-Section and Pooled Analysis," Proceedings from Research on Effectiveness of Agricultural Commodity Promotion Seminar, Walter J. Armbruster and Lester H. Meyers (eds.), Arlington, Va., Farm Foundation and USDA (April): 123-37.

11. JOHNSON, STANLEY R., RICHARD D. GREEN, ZUHAIR A. HASSAN and A.N. SAFYURTLU (1986), Food Demand Analysis: Implications for Future Consumption, Blacksburg, Va.: Virginia Tech Agricultural Experiment Station: 1-33.

12. JUSTER, F. THOMAS, PAUL N. COURANT and GREG K. DOW (1981), "A Theoretical Framework for the Measurement of Well-Being," Review of Income and Wealth, 27(1): 1-31.

13. KIHLSTROM, R. (1974), "A Bayesian Model of Demand for Information about Product Quality," International Economic Review, 15:O 99-118.

14. KINNUCAN, HENRY W. (1985), "Evaluating Advertising Effectiveness Using Time Series Data," Proceedings from Research on Effectiveness of Agricultural Commodity Promotion Seminar, Walter J. Armbruster and Lester H. Meyers (eds.), Arlington, Va., Farm Foundation and USDA (April): 105-22.

15. KINSEY, JEAN, BENJAMIN SENAUER and TERRY ROE (1986), "Imperfect Mileage Information and Changing Utility," The Journal of Consumer Affairs, 20(2): 155-172.

16. LESSER, W.H. and W.K. BRYANT (1982), "Predicting the Direct Benefits of a Food Price-Reporting or Preference-Changing Program," American Journal of Agricultural Economics 64(1): 129-133.

17. MCCRACKEN, VICKI A., ROBERT D. BOYNTON and BRIAN F. BLAKE (1982), "The Impact of Comparative Food Price Information on Consumers and Grocery Retailers," Journal of Consumer Affairs 16(2): 224-240.

18. MAYNES, E. SCOTT and TERJE ASSUM (1982), "Informationally Imperfect Consumer Markets: Empirical Findings and Policy Implications," Journal of Consumer Affairs, 16(1):62-87.

19. MOORE, WILLIAM and DONALD LEHMANN (1980), "Individual Differences in Search Behavior for a Nondurable," Journal of Consumer Research, 7(3): 296-307.

20. NICHOLS, LEN M. (1985), "Advertising and Economic Welfare," American Economic Review, 75: 213-218.

21. OLSHAVSKY, RICHARD W. and DENNIS L. ROSEN (1985), "Use of Product-Testing Organizations' Recommendations as a Strategy for Choice Simplification," Journal of Consumer Affairs, 19(1): 118-139.

22. POPE, RULON D. (1985), "The Impact of Information on Consumer Preferences," Proceedings from Research on Effectiveness of Agricultural Commodity Promotion Seminar, Walter J. Armbruster and Lester H. Meyers (eds.), Arlington, Va., Farm Foundation and USDA (April): 69-79.

23. RUSSELL, THOMAS and RICHARD THALER (1985), "The Relevance of Quasi-Rationality in Competitive Markets," The American Economic Review, 75(5): 1071-1082.

24. STIGLER, GEORGE (1961), "The Economics of Information," Journal of Political Economy, 69: 213-225.

25. STIGLER, GEORGE J. and GARY S. BECKER (1977), "De Gustibus Non Est Disputandum," American Economic Review, 67(2): 76-90.

26. TERRY, DANNY E. (1985), "An Evaluation of Characteristic Theory: Implicit Prices and the Demand for Nutritional Attributes," unpublished Ph.D. dissertation, University of Tennessee.

27. TILLEY, DANIEL S. (1986), "Consumption Dynamics and Evaluation of Advertising Impacts," Proceedings of the 32nd Annual Conference of the American Council on Consumer Interests, Karen P. Schnittgrund (ed.): 124-28.

28. WARD, RONALD W. and JAMES E. DAVIS (1978), "A Pooled Cross-Section Time-Series Model of Coupon Promotions," American Journal of Agricultural Economics, 60: 393-401.

29. WARD, RONALD W. and WILLIAM F. MCDONALD (1986), "Effectiveness of Generic Milk Advertising: A Ten Region Study," Agribusiness, 2: 37-90.

30. WARD, RONALD W. and STANLEY R. THOMPSON (1985), "Commodity Advertising," Agribusiness, 1(4): 269-276.

ABOUT THE AUTHOR

Robert Imowitz is Manager of Market Research for the Health and Beauty Aids Division of Chesebrough-Pond's. Imowitz received an undergraduate degree in Agricultural Economics from Cornell University in 1965 before taking Graduate Work in Marketing at City College of New York. He has held a succession of positions in Marketing and Marketing Research with Audits and Surveys, Colgate-Palmolive, Johnson & Johnson, and General Foods before joining Chesebrough-Pond's in 1979. Imowitz served on the Grace Commission on Cost Control in 1982.

MARKET RESEARCH IN THE CONSUMER INTEREST THE VIEWS OF A PRACTICING MARKET RESEARCHER

Robert Imowitz

Market research has four facets, all entailing research among the public: political polling, opinion research, consumer research, and advertising research. I will attempt to show how market research helps consumers, and to demonstrate that the public is well served by market research. Even though, many times, it is unaware that it is served at all!

Consumer research, in my lexicon, consists of research conducted with the public (or some part of the public) that is devoted exclusively to a product which the public can use (if it wishes). The word, "product," is used here in its broadest sense. We include not only consumer packaged and durable goods, but also services such as transportation, medical facilities, and education. We also include services offered by government or by a non-profit operation such as a medical service or a local entity such as a library, as well as the myriad products of private enterprise, usually offered on a for-profit basis.

CONSUMER RESEARCH: GOVERNMENT VERSUS BUSINESS

It is our thesis that market research not only assists the purveyors of all these goods and services, but also helps to insure that the public gets what it wants.

It is useful to define what I mean by "the public interest." By this term I mean all the end results of market research that benefit the public (or a part of it) in terms of offering an increase in well-being, either factually real or perceived. An improved bandage for a wound, for example, is a factually real benefit. Improved automobile styling may be more a matter of perception. As a part of "the consumer interest," I include all those things which the consumer perceives as a part of his/her interest.

The two most important practitioners of consumer research are the government and private business. Each takes a fundamentally different approach to research. Each approach is appropriate to each kind of organizatin, given their different purposes. It makes sense for us to understand each approach.

The government does research with the avowed purpose of supporting augmenting, or initiating public policy, in other words, for the public's benefit. It spends public money to do so, since it has a mandate -- or sees itself as having one -- to act "in the public good." Because of this philosophy, government sponsored surveys tend to have large samples and to adhere more closely to the strict rules of random sampling than does the private sector. There have been cynics who say that the government cares little about the substantial expense that this adherence to the mathematical rules mandates. There may be some truth to this. But if the government is to use survey findings in formulating public policy, those survey findings must be as accurate as possible.

The business world takes a different approach. Most of its research is undertaken as a financial investment in knowledge which it needs for the pursuit of its business goals. As with any financial investment, the critical question is: How much investment for what return? If, for example, a new product concept or idea is to be tested for viability, how much money must be spent so that the decision to proceed to the next phase -- prototype developments-- will be an informed one? For this purpose it is not necessary, and would be financially absurd, to conduct a survey of the dimensions usually used by government agencies.

Some looking at business research from the outside fail to understand that a cost-benefit when the small samples and the limited analysis is always in order in considering research. It is always necessary to know what business decision will be the outcome of it or what risk is incurred if a wrong decision is made. It is poor business practice to spend more money to reach a decision than that decision warrants.

This stricture does not, of course, absolve the business community from using proper sampling and questioning practices in conducting its research. A necessary balance must be struck between excessive expense in the pursuit of accuracy and the need for dependable data for decision making.

THE DIVERSITY OF MARKET RESEARCH IN THE CONSUMER INTEREST

Instances of market research being used in the consumer interest are found in almost every aspect of daily life. Research is conducted by almost every conceivable group: by private companies, trade associations, common interest groups (for example, "Consumers Against Smoking"), government agencies, community groups (research of a neighborhood), and many more.

I mention briefly a few market research surveys in the public interest from diverse sources, including two examples of work conducted by my own company, Chesebrough-Pond's.

The best known use of market research in the public interest, of course, is the Decennial Census. Conducted every ten years, it forms the basis of government planning in many different ways, on a national and a local level, as well as being the basis for many business decisions.

In 1977, the Food and Drug Administration (FDA), prompted by adverse findings from Canada, proposed a ban on saccharine. The controversy had been going on for years. Public outcry against this proposal was such that the Congress temporarily prohibited it, a prohibition that still holds. The public reaction to the FDA's proposal was measured and reported by market research surveys, conducted by private industry interested in the marketing of food and beverages containing saccharine. It was also measured and reported by surveys of the medical profession which felt the product was essential to the management of diabetes, obesity, heart disease, hypertension and dental caries. What is significant to us is the role of market research to make the public's wishes and concerns known to the Congress.

During the 1960's and 1970's, the U.S. Department of Agriculture conducted a series of market research studies of the U.S. population to ascertain the existence of nutritional problems and, particularly, groups at risk, nutritionally. This research turned up a number of interesting findings. There were indeed groups at risk -- particularly the elderly poor, young children of poor families, and perhaps more surprising, many women of childbearing age. Many of the latter were adversely affected by the widespread practice of dieting. In addition, the U.S.D.A. reported that many Americans were ingesting insufficient calories per day to maintain energy levels and less than RDA's of some vitamins and minerals.

This series of studies revealed an interesting paradox. While many Americans profess interest in and concern about nutrition, few know much about it and few take steps to find out about it. An important and long term outcome of this research was the mandatory ingredient labeling of food products, designed to help consumers determine what they were eating and to help them adjust their daily intake of various nutrients.

In the private sector, trade groups or professional associations conduct market surveys to help their members. The Supermarket Institute, for example, has conducted surveys over the years to examine customers' needs in terms of store layout, check cashing, in-store pharmacies, availability of general merchandise including clothes, hardware, auto supplies and the like. The purpose of these surveys is to help the industry to serve the customer better.

The automobile industry is one of the biggest investors in market research surveys. Its surveys cover many subjects related to its primary interest of selling automobiles. When applied to particular companies, that interest becomes one of serving the public by competing successfully with other automobile manufacturers and thus maximizing profit. However, they have also conducted surveys of the public's attitudes toward seat belts and safety bags, making the public's views known in testimony before congressional agencies concerned with public safety.

It is, of course, appropriate to ask whether the automobile companies conducted safety restraint research out of concern for the public good or out from a need to counteract demands on them made by government officials who believed themselves to be acting "in the consumer interest." The auto companies probably did it for both reasons. If the consumer really wants safety restraints, the automobile companies would be perfectly happy to provide them. Competitively, they would eventually have to offer them. If, on the other hand, the government declares that the public wants safety restraints while market research indicates otherwise, the issue changes. We then face the oldest question asked of a democratic government: Does it have the right to insist on something "for the public good" that the public does not want? To debate this would take an entire book. So we return to market research.

Community groups survey their communities to plumb reactions to local issues. A group in my town has recently been surveying the citizenry on the adequacy of garbage pickups.

The over-the-counter drug industry uses market research to position a new product so that consumers can understand what it will do for them. When time-release capsules were first introduced to the public as a non-prescription medication, market research showed that people did not understand the the concept of timed release despite their claims that they did. In fact, consumers were fearful that time-release capsules were unduly strong because their effects lasted for eight hours or more. The market research alerted Contac to this misapprehension. Contac then introduced these first time-release capsules in a way that allayed the users' fears.

This list could go on endlessly. Market research facilitated the introduction of stannous fluoride toothpaste; it helped position the contraceptive pill when it was introduced; it has been instrumental in the development of pregnancy tests; it went hand-in-hand with the introduction of caffeine-free products. Let me tell you about how we at Chesebrough-Ponds use market research.

TWO EXAMPLES FROM CHESEBROUGH-POND'S

Salt reduction in diet has become an important issue for many people over the past couple of years. Many concerned about heart and other stress related problems, have reduced their intake of this ingredient as part of their management of such health hazards. Consumer research indicated to us that there was a need to offer a salt-free version of our product, Adolph's Meat Tenderizer, while of course maintaining its function and quality. For ten consecutive months prior to our introduction of a line extension of this product, we uncovered a small but consistent demand from users of the regular Adolph's Meat Tenderizer for a salt-free version. By using this consumer research information, we simultaneously responded to consumer demand and extended the market for our total line of meat tenderizer. Thus, market research served consumer and company.

By contrast, our research disclose little interest in a reduced salt spaghetti sauce. As a result, our Packaged Foods Division did not go ahead with low-salt product spaghetti sauce. On the other hand, we were able to show that consumers were very interested in buying a spaghetti sauce that contained "chunky" pieces of different vegetables and other ingredients. This led to Ragu introducing its Chunky Gardenstyle Spaghetti Sauce in 1983. Subsequently, Chunky became the third most popular item in the Ragu line.

Other consumer studies indicated that consumers would "go for" spaghetti sauces in which the pasta was already present. A product with pasta and the sauce already prepared and mixed together and only needing to be heated would be an enormous convenience to those consumers having to make a meal in a hurry, particularly homemakers. Products of this type already existed, but they suffered a major defect: the texture of the pasta was unacceptably mushy. Our research and development people solved this problem, again making it possible for us to respond to a palpable consumer need and at the same time extend the market for our total line of spaghetti products, just as in the earlier example.

One other example is worth the telling. It involves nail polish. For years through an unending series of focus group disccussions, women had told us that the difficulty of application was a major problem with nail polish. We knew, too, that a nail polish must dry swiftly or it would never sell. The solution to these problems uncovered by market research, was the development of a polish "pen," by which the users applies the nail polish through a pen-like device. We struggled long and hard with the fast-dry requirement and finally perfected it. This enabled us to meet a consumer need and at the same time extend our Aziza line of cosmetics/nail polishes.

Some critics may feel that while market research has benefitted the consumer in all the instances I have given, its raison d'être is profit maximization. They are correct. Private industry listens to the consumer because it must. It is far too costly to introduce a product or service that the consumer does not want, has no use for, cannot adapt to its needs, or does not understand. To paraphrase, the road to hell is paved with such products. Firms have gone out of existence for lack of understanding this lesson. Market research is the best insurance, in fact the only real insurance, against such financial folly, against such a hazard to the continued existence of an enterprise.

Let me end with a negative example that is telling. A few years ago, one of my associates was involved with an intriguing product concept that did not pass the makret research test: sliced peanut butter. You peeled the paper off a slice of peanut butter just like a slice of American cheese, put the peanut better between two slices of bread, and ate it. Presto! Who could resist it? Well, consumers could. Market research indicated that this was a sure-fire loser: the sooner forgotten, the better. The company listened, and "sliced peanut butter" quietly sank into corporate oblivion. Maybe its day will come, but it has not arrived yet.

ABOUT THE AUTHOR

Sidney J. Levy is Professor of Behavioral Science in Management and Chairman of the Department of Marketing at Northwestern University; and the Charles H. Kelstadt Distinguished Professor of Marketing. A psychologist, Levy received his Ph.D. from the Committee on Human Development at the University of Chicago in 1956. His research examines social memberships, cultural influences, symbolic interaction, and complex motivation in personality. Widely published, his articles have appeared in most of the major Marketing journals. In 1981 the American Marketing Association awarded him the Maynard Award for the best theoretical article in the Journal of Marketing. Levy is the author of Marketplace Behavior--Its Meaning for Management (American Marketing Association, 1978).

MARKETING RESEARCH AS A DIALOGUE

Sidney J. Levy

As a teacher and marketing researcher, I encounter a wide variety of people in the marketplace--students, marketing practitioners, other executive and professional personnel, and consumers, in both business and non-business settings. The issues and problems that relate to the interest of the consumer as they interact with the interests of those who offer their goods and services are many. It is my theme that the marketplace is a dialogue, both harmonious and contentious. The conflicts between marketing research and the consumer interest arise from differences in goals, the discrepancy between ideals and practice, and the conflicts among basic values.

CROSS-PURPOSES IN THE DIALOGUE

Marketing research is carried out by great numbers of people whose aims and ethical concerns range considerably. In general, they are supposed to be guided by the purposes and codes of ethics provided by such groups as the American Marketing Association and the Marketing Research Association.

All these virtuous directives take for granted that marketers have the right to conduct marketing research in the first place. Further, it is a fundamental tenet that marketing research is essential to serving the consumer's interest. As Kotler states it, "...companies can serve their markets well only by researching their needs and wants, their locations, their buying practices, and so on [2, p. 64]."

The guidelines of the American Marketing Association call for the betterment of society, presenting goods, services, and concepts honestly and clearly, supporting free consumer choice, accountability. The Marketing Research Association specifies numerous though different goals: objectivity, accuracy, protecting anonymity and confidentiality, promoting trust among the public, avoiding misrepresentation, etc.

From such statements we might suppose that there would be no difficulties with the consumer interest, as everyone presumably has it in mind. But that would be naive. There is no single view of the consumer interest nor is there a single path to the betterment of society. It is more realistic to recognize that there are diverse interests. The market may be viewed as a place where people communicate by language and action to arrive at mutually satisfactory consummations. But it may also be viewed as an arena where they contentiously express their individual and group aims, even when these are not satisfying to others.

Marketing research is one part of this communication process, a dialogue that may be both harmonious and contentious. Such a dialogue cannot entirely produce accord because the objectives of the participants are not the same, and because there is no final resolution to the differences that arise about specific methods and how they relate to people's objectives and to their underlying values.

Much marketing research is harmonious with a general concept of the consumer interest, either gathering innocuous information or data that clearly serves consumer goals. Marketing researchers often share the same goals as consumers, clearly seeking information that will benefit consumers. Examples of market research that serves both consumers and market researchers would be efforts to learn what product improvements are desired, what new products are sought, what information consumers want, how well they interpret the language being addressed to them.

Then again, marketers may have other goals in mind of which consumers would not approve, such as learning how to increase consumption of a product widely regarded as "bad," or testing advertising appeals that would reduce store inventories even though stockpiling at home might not help the consumer, or learning about "unconstructive" consumer motives in order to exploit them.

IDEALS VERSUS PRACTICE

It is possible to feel virtuous about one's aims as a market researcher and to desire the best for consumers without adhering to the standards of the AMA and the MRA. For example, many researchers have no qualms about "borrowing" the names of survey respondents to generate lists of potential customers. Why should one suffer pangs of conscience, if one believes the product is a good one that will benefit the people on the list?

Researchers differ as to what kind of respondent briefing should be done. Should respondents be told who is sponsoring the research study? It seems only right to do that; speaking personally, I would like to know. But knowledge of sponsor's identity may interfere with people's spontaneity or objectivity. Worse, it might jeopardize their willingness to respond. On the other hand, do they not have to be interviewed in order "to be heard"? Presumably not, since the right to be heard certainly includes the right <u>not</u> to be heard. Against this is the requirement of some democracies that citizens must vote!

Should market researchers seek to elicit information only when respondents are clearly aware of the information they are providing? Sometimes the understanding sought in research might best be gained indirectly, under conditions where the respondent is providing information without being aware of it. This is often the purpose of unobtrusive measures, participant observation, and projective techniques. Here the respondents or consumers may not realize that their behavior is being watched; they will not know how their projective responses or behavior will be interpreted.

The idea of interpretation is itself a thorny one. Some people object to methods that could reveal information that respondents themselves would prefer to deny or to be concealed. A counter argument is that interpretation is applied to most human communication; even the information that the respondent gives knowingly is subject to interpretation. Is it much different to interpret information obtained without the respondent's direct knowledge and consent? Further, some argue that structured questions and rating scales, brief check-off questionnaires, or the chance to make a few remarks in a focus group interview do not represent genuine two-way dialogues. To be ethical, Ted Karger argues that researchers can best serve the public, their organizations, and their own professional development by understanding consumers fully. "Then, much more often, they would probe deeply into the hearts, minds, and behaviors of the people--would employ comprehensive personal dialogues to serve as penetrating diagnostic interviews--so that the vox populi becomes vividly clear." [1]. Karger's argument thus justifies the use of indirect means, lacking respondent consent, as a means of fully understanding the consumers and thus responding to them.

In some fields, standards for research with human subjects require that subjects be de-briefed or provided with information about the results of the study. Sometimes, some kind of de-briefing may occur in marketing research. Usually, however, respondents are dismissed with thanks. Often their participation is induced by a monetary incentive that heightens cooperation and reduces criticism. Paying people to be interviewed could be taken as a way of corrupting them, perhaps interfering with their desire to avoid the interview. Then again, such payment may be taken as a sign of the urgency of the desire to elicit the consumer's voice, of the importance of the research to its sponsor.

THE CONFLICT OF VALUES

Underlying these and other troubling matters in the conduct of marketing research are fundamental conflicts of values. Marketing research is a quest for information and understanding. It takes advantage of an implied freedom of inquiry. Whether this freedom should extend to commercial inquiry probably depends upon whether one believes that commercial speech is protected. For example, Laczniak and Michie approve of government's constraints on business practices, and express anxiety about the use of "marketing" methods to disseminate concepts they term "ethically charged" and "controversial" because "when someone 'markets' an idea, the first amendment limits the level of restraint that is possible" [3, p. 225].

<u>Advertising Age</u>, conversely, worries that William Rehnquist's nomination as Chief Justice may represent the end of an era for advertisers who welcomed the expanded First Amendment protection in Supreme Court decisions of the 1970s and '80s.

Should marketing research help consumers achieve greater freedom of choice? Should they be asked what they want? Marketing research is often used to study the needs and wants of marketing segments with an eye to providing them with new products. There are several sources of controversy here. Many critics believe that it is fine to <u>satisfy needs</u>, but that marketing research is often in the position of <u>creating wants</u>. It is not clear why the creation of wants is <u>per se</u> a bad thing, although it is easy to cite horendous or seemingly undefensible examples. Others argue that the task of defining "needs" versus "wants" is a semantic hornet's nest, something not worth the pain. Still others feel that once we progress beyond primitive man's cave, club, fire, and mate, all other products and services represent wants that were "created" -- by some force in our society.

Some assert that it is not in the consumer interest to widen the boundaries of choice, as this is economically inefficient and wasteful of resources. In their view marketing research should be used to learn what the boundaries of choice should be. Inquiring into consumer choice implies an encouragement of private spending, and interferes with the more publicly useful ways money might be spent, as J.K. Galbraith has so often reminded us. This implies that consumers may not know their own interests, at least not in the aggregate, and therefore should not be asked what they want. Instead they should be given what is good for them. Of course, then it might be useful to do marketing research with those who have (or take?) the responsibility of determining what is good for the consumer.

The many issues that put the desirability of marketing research into question could be taken as a basis for drastic inhibition of marketing research. In my view these problems should not prevent the conduct of inquiries by marketing managers. They should be free to carry out marketing research without revealing their identity and entire aims as long as their business is arguably legitimate and their purposes no more harmful than the society is willing to tolerate at that time.

As a teacher of students studying for a Master's Degree in Management, I seek to make them aware of these issues and to encourage them to work out their own position (with which I often disagree). As a research supplier, I reserve the right to work for clients whose goals I support and to avoid those whose values I reject. In undertaking market research, I consider myself free to ask consumers any questions that seem appropriate to the problem and that fit my values concerning courtesy, respect for the dignity of respondents, and for their right to respond as they wish. The interpretion of their responses to questionnaires or other instruments, is my responsibility. I seek to convey their "true" feelings or views as accurately as possible.

As a consumer and potential respondent, I support the right of organizations to conduct marketing research even though I find some of it annoying. I consider myself free to refuse to fill out questionnaires I receive in the mail, to do them hastily or partially, to avoid interviewers or to talk freely, to guard my responses as my personality dictates, perhaps even to tell whatever lies I can tolerate in myself when I answer questions, to put my answers in the best light I can, and in general to protect my interests as I see them. I expect the respondents in my researches to do the same.

REFERENCES

1. KARGER, TED, "'Your Opinion Counts'--Only If Researchers Really Listen," Marketing News, July 4, 1986, 2.

2. KOTLER, PHILIP, Marketing Management: Analysis, Planning, and Control, Prentice-Hall, 1984.

3. LACZNIAK, GENE R., and DONALD A. MICHIE, "The Social Disorder of the Broadened Concept of Marketing," Journal of Academy of Marketing Science, Summer, 1979, Vol. 7, No.3 214-232.

4. LEVY, SIDNEY J. and PHILIP KOTLER, "Toward a Broader Concept of Marketing's Role in Social Order," Journal of Academy of Marketing Science, Summer, 1979, Vol. 7, No. 3, 232-238.

ABOUT THE AUTHOR

Patrick E. Murphy is Associate Professor of Marketing at the University of Notre Dame. Murphy received his Ph.D. in Marketing from the University of Houston in 1975. His career has involved faculty positions in several universities--Bradley, Houston, Marquette where he was Chairman of the Department of Marketing, and now Notre Dame. In 1980-81 Murphy served as Consumer Behavior Specialist in the Bureau of Consumer Protection at the Federal Trade Commission. Widely published, Murphy serves as Editor of Journal of Public Policy and Marketing and on the Editorial Boards of the Journals of Marketing, Health Care Marketing and Macromarketing. He is the author of Marketing Ethics: Guidelines for Managers (with Gene Laczniak) and Marketing (with Ben Enis).

HOW CAN MARKETING RESEARCH CONTRIBUTE TO THE CONSUMER INTEREST?

Patrick E. Murphy

This question has been addressed many times over the last two decades. The consumerism movement of the 1960's and early 1970's was fueled, in part, by more precise measurement of what the consumer interest entailed. Both national and local surveys were conducted on the topic. The 1980's has seen the consumerism movement wane somewhat with certain authors suggesting that it is in the "maturity" [2] or "decline" [4] stages of the life cycle. Although not as newsworthy today, consumerism is in my judgment an enduring social force that is in an "extended" maturity stage. Consumers' perceptions of declining product quality, unsatisfactory repairs and services, and companies' failure to handle complaints are continuing sources of consumerism [6].

This paper seeks to explore two methods by which marketing research can contribute to the consumer interest. The first is by providing inputs into the public policy formulation process. Government agencies and consumer groups can use marketing research as a mechanism for influencing policy decisions. In recent years the lack of funding for consumer interest research has limited its impact. The second method involves the use of marketing research by corporations to measure the general consumer interest. This may occur in a variety of ways. For example, national surveys can be funded, environmental scanning can be employed to ascertain trends in the larger consumer environment, and companies can consider the societal marketing concept.

MARKET RESEARCH AS INPUTS TO PUBLIC POLICY

The consumer interest should be a major component of public policy decisions. Recognizing this, public policymakers have long realized the importance of obtaining objective information regarding consumer issues. A frequently used mechanism to achieve this goal is marketing research. Several consumer researchers [16, 5] have urged that marketing research be used as a basis for public policy. Too often, they believe, the adversarial and legalistic positions taken by government agencies did do a poor job of representing the consumer interest. Wilkie and Gardner argue that researchers should "lead rather than lag" public policy issues. Dyer and Shimp have proposed guidelines for increasing the impact of researchers in the policymaking process. They feel that cooperation between marketers and public policy officials would improve the regulatory environment. Futhermore, a book devoted to government marketing [11] includes six papers summarizing the role of marketing research in the policymaking process.

The Federal Trade Commission (FTC) is the federal agency that has used marketing and consumer research most extensively. The FTC has employed marketing researchers as advisors or staff members for about 15 years. [For a review, see 14]. Initially marketing researchers served as advisors on advertising cases and rules. In 1978 the Office of Impact Evaluation was instituted within the Bureau of Consumer Protection. This office serves a marketing research function within the FTC. Its objective is to assess the impact of proposed regulations, both retrospectively or prospectively [1]. The influence of this office has declined in recent years because of a lessening of rulemaking and the general deregulatory climate at the FTC. In addition, the analysis of economic impact has replaced marketing research as a favored activity of the agency.

Surveys of the public utilizing marketing research and especially survey research techniques have been proposed as useful inputs into public policy development [8, 10]. The Post Office, FDA, CPSC and Department of Energy are some of the government agencies that have utilized consumer research to guide decision making. Consumer interest projects and specific marketing research have been reduced in the face of budget cutbacks at other agencies, just as they have at the FTC.

This reduction in marketing research at the FTC and other agencies shows that regulatory interests shift with the prevailing political climate. It also reinforces the fact that marketing research is a fragile activity. The question becomes: How can one institutionalize marketing research in the public policy deliberation process? Unfortunately, there are no easy answers.

State and local levels of government as well as consumer organizations also have a need for researching the consumer interest. But they lack resources conduct these studies. Most of the individuals employed by these organizations do not have a background in marketing or consumer research. Therefore, it is difficult for them to develop a proper research design that will be useful for lobbying or policy development.

One illustrative joint project involving both a Federal and state/local organization took place in 1981 Montgomery County, Maryland in 1981.[1] The local Office of Consumer Affairs (OCA) received a $4,000 grant from the FTC to conduct a study of local residents regarding their experiences with service providers. The Office collects complaint information about firms in the area and makes it available to local residents. The Director of the OCA wanted to provide more extensive information regarding users' satisfaction with firms. It was with this objective in mind that she approached the FTC.

The author, a staff member at the time at FTC, became involved with the project, being assigned responsibility for the research and questionnaire design of the project. OCA handled mailing, editing and analysis of the results. Unfortunately, the FTC and Montgomery County officials decided jointly to publish only part of the information collected. Even for the limited experiment the reactions of media, general public and agencies involved in this project were favorable. Budget considerations kept this one-shot project from becoming an ongoing program. Once again, the issue of how to sustain marketing research inputs in policymaking has not been resolved. (For a detailed discussion of this study, see [12]).

CORPORATE MARKETING RESEARCH

Business firms engage in marketing research daily. However, their research tends to focus on the short term interest of

---

[1]Data similar to those collected in the Montgomery County Experiment are collected and published in Washington, D.C. by the Washington Consumer Checkbook and in the San Francisco area by the Bay Area Consumers' Checkbook. These quarterly publications have circulations of 35,000 and 17,000 respectively. For a discussion of Checkbook and Which? (publication of Consumers' Association in Great Britian) see [13].

customers or potential customers. Because of the profit motive and quarterly financial considerations, firms tend to look to marketing research for immediate feedback. Three mechanisms that can be used by companies concerned about the broader "consumer interest".

The first is to sponsor a national study to examine issues of a global nature. For example, Sentry Insurance supported a study in 1976 entitled Consumerism at the Crossroads and in 1982 ARCO funded a similar project conducted by Louis Harris, Consumerism in the Eighties: A National Survey of Consumer Attitudes. Another national study on consumers, focusing on perceptions of product quality, was funded by Whirlpool in 1983 [15]. The funding in 1988 of a replication and extension of the 1982 study would represent an admirable project for a large company seeking to serve the consumer and the public interest. Ideally, such a study would utilize the same techniques to achieve comparability and even reinterview identical respondents. Given the necessary scale of such studies, funding is likely to be limited to major corporations.

Other possibilities for research into the consumer interest might consist of joint projects sponsored by organizations such as the Marketing Science Institute, Direct Selling Foundation and others. These projects should deal with long-term issues relating to "consumer interest." They would help both companies and consumer organizations to obtain answers to questions that may be of interest to both groups. A specific example is Market Facts' (Chicago marketing research firm) sponsorship of a longitudinal "Index of Consumer Sentiment toward Marketing." This Index measures consumers' reaction to general and specific marketing practices [7].

Within the corporation, it may be advantageous to examine macro consumer interest issues that might guide the future directions of the firm. The technique of environmental scanning which monitors relevant trends in the external environments is used by many large organizations to examine forces which may influence the company in the future [17]. The consumer environment is one that should obviously be monitored closely. Emerging issues such as disadvantaged consumers, "good taste," and new media [3] should be monitored by national advertisers and agencies to more fully understand these trends. A better understanding of consumer interest issues should lead to product and marketing strategy changes. Ultimately, this activity would enhance the firm's long term profitability.

Companies are sensitive to "societal marketing [9] would want to explore the consumer interest more deeply. This concept places long-term social welfare above short-term consumer satisfaction.

Firms such as Volvo with its long-standing advocacy of auto safety in the design and promotion of its cars and Giant Foods' commitment to informative labeling illustrate this approach. Companies that believe that they should give consumers what they "need" as well as what they "want" might employ this operating philosophy. What seems to differentiate these organizations from others is that their "corporate culture" tends to reflect a basic commitment to a broader social values. Research is an important component of this approach, because the long term consumer interest may not be evident, even to the most socially-enlightened manager.

CONCLUSION

Marketing research can and has contributed to the consumer interest. In this era of declining government involvement, the use of sophisticated marketing research by government policymakers is on the decline. Thus, it essential that both government and consumer organizations think creatively about their options for measuring enduring consumer issues. For consumer organizations, joint work with industry, especially through foundations or independent research institutes, may be a more viable alternative in the future. Certain corporations also have demonstrated a concern for the consumer interest. More will have to be done in the future if a deeper level of understanding is to be gained.

REFERENCES

1. BERNHARDT, KENNETH L. (1981), "Consumer Research in the Federal Government," in Government Marketing, M. P. Mokwa and S. E. Permut, eds., New York: Praeger, 252-263.

2. BLOOM, PAUL and STEPHEN GREYSER (1981), "The Maturing of Consumerism," Harvard Business Review, (November-December), 130-139.

3. BODDEWYN, J. J. (1985), "Advertising Regulation: Fiddling with the FTC While the World Burns," Business Horizons, (May-June), 32-40

4. BOX, JO M. F. (1984), "Consumerism in an Era of Decline," European Journal of Marketing, 18 (4), 24-35.

5. DYER, ROBERT F. and TERENCE A. SHIMP (1977), "Enhancing the Role of Marketing Research in Public Policy Decision Making," Journal of Marketing, 41 (January), 63-67.

6. EVERS, MYRLIE (1983), "Consumerism in the Eighties," Public Relations Journal, (August), 24-26.

7. GASKI, JOHN F. and MICHAEL J. ETZEL (1986), "The Index of Consumer Sentiment toward Marketing," Journal of Marketing, 50 (July), 71-81.

8. KERR, JOHN R., JAMES M. STEARNS, ROGER R. MCGRATH and DEAN BLOCK (1981), "Program Planning and Evaluation: A Citizen-Oriented Approach," in Government Marketing, M. P. Mokwa and S. E. Permut, eds., New York: Praeger, 205-217.

9. KOTLER, PHILIP (1972), "What Consumerism Means for Marketers," Harvard Business Review, (May-June), 48-57.

10. MAY, PETER J. (1981), "Sample Surveys as Feedback Mechanisms for Guiding Municipal-Level Decision Making," in Government Marketing, M. P. Mokwa and S. E. Permut, eds., New York: Praeger, 218-232.

11. MOKWA, MICHAEL P. and STEVEN E. PERMUT (1981), Government Marketing: Theory and Practice, New York: Praeger.

12. MURPHY, PATRICK E. and STEVEN C. ROSS (1986), "Local Consumer Information Systems for Services: A Test," Journal of Consumer Affairs, (Winter), 249-266.

13. ________ (1987), "Evaluating Service Firms: An Approach with Policy Recommendations," Journal of Consumer Policy (December), 361-379.

14. PRESTON, IVAN (1980), "Researchers at the Federal Trade Commission--Peril and Promise," in Current Issues and Research in Advertising 1980, J. H. Leigh and C. R. Martin, Jr., eds., Ann Arbor: University of Michigan, 1-15.

15. WHIRLPOOL CORPORATION (1983), America's Search for Quality, Benton Harbor, MI: Whirlpool.

16. WILKIE, WILLIAM L. and DAVID M. GARDNER (1974), "The Role of Marketing Research in Public Policy Decision Making," Journal of Marketing, 38 (January), 38-47.

17. ZEITHAML, CARL P. and VALARIE A. ZEITHAML (1984), "Environmental Management: Revising the Marketing Perspective," Journal of Marketing, (Spring), 46-53.

ABOUT THE AUTHOR

Michael Warren is Director of Research for the Central Office of Information in London. At the time of the Wingspread Conference, he was Head of the Survey Unit at Consumers' Association. Warren started his career as a newspaper journalist, followed by a period in the theater before drifting (his word) into survey research in the early 1970's. He spent 10 years with a market research firm, Research Services, Ltd. before joining Consumers' Association in 1980. While with RSL, Warren carried out a very large scale "Survey of Consumer Concerns" for the National Consumer Council. He has presented papers before a number of survey research and consumer seminars in the U.K. and elsewhere.

SURVEY RESEARCH ON BEHALF OF THE CONSUMER: A VIEW FROM THE UNITED KINGDOM

Michael Warren

INTRODUCTION

This paper describes some of the survey work that my organization undertakes. Unlike the majority at this Conference my viewpoint is neither that of the academic, nor that of the manufacturer or service provider. It might be useful, to explain my viewpoint and provide perspective, to begin this paper with a brief description of the Association for Consumer Research and its Survey Unit.

Consumers' Association (CA) is a British research-based publishing and campaigning organization that operates on behalf of consumers. We publish a variety of magazines, books and tapes, our prime source both of income and expenditure being the product test magazine, Which?. This is a monthly magazine, sold only on subscription, with a current circulation of over 900,000, or some 4% of British households. The average monthly readership is estimated at some 3,000,000. Typically, a copy of Which? consists of 48 pages, many in colour, containing 12-14 major reports plus a number of shorter items. The areas covered include consumer durables, personal finance, motoring, home improvements, and health and leisure. Holidays and gardening, though occasionally covered in Which?, are primarily catered for in the two specialist magazines also published by CA, Holiday Which? and Gardening from Which?. In addition, CA publishes a number of books and is involved, successfully, in "campaigning" for legislative changes for the consumer's benefit. CA is funded, almost exclusively, from the sale of its product test and other research information, i.e., primarily by subscriptions.

In summary, CA tries to arm consumers with the information they need to help themselves. In addition, by exerting pressure on policy makers in government and business, CA seeks to alter "the rules of the game" when these are unfair to consumers.

The Survey Unit (TSU) is the department of CA responsible for producing survey-research-based data for inclusion in Which? in CA's other publications, and for our campaigning. We have a staff of 14, including in-house coding and computing. We undertake some 100 separate projects a year. We are survey research specialists who work for a magazine rather than journalists who do surveys, an important distinction in terms of magazine publication. Much of our work relies on samples from CA's subscribers, although we utilize samples from the general public whenever there is a campaigning element in our research. Our sample sizes vary from as few as, say, 30 (subscribers who vacationed in the Maldive Islands, for example) up to the 23,000 or more questionnaires that we process annually for our Car Reliability Survey. Our samples of subscribers are almost invariably randomly drawn from the current subscriber base. Aside from its work within CA, The Survey Unit is also an independent research institute, and undertakes survey-based projects for a variety of government and public sector clients. In this its practices differ from those of the Survey Research Unit at Consumers Union.

LABORATORY AND SURVEY RESEARCH

A major foundation-stone of CA continues to be the comparative testing of products and buying advice based on those tests, although the balance of work has changed to some extent over the years with the development of service and policy-related survey projects. Most of CA's product testing is carried out in our own Laboratories at Harpenden, 25 miles northwest of our London headquarters. These tests are designed to ascertain the quality of the product: does it do what it claims to do?; does it do what it ought to do? In particular CA examines such factors as:

- Safety: How safely will it perform?
- Ease of use: This takes account of storage, transportation, switches, controls, instructions, doors, displays, maintenance, cleaning, etc.
- Comfort: How comfortable are the handles, switches, etc. to use?

-- Performance/ efficiency: How well does it do the job?

-- Adjustability: How easy is it to adjust the product to fit the user (who may be tall or short, thin or fat) and how satisfactory are these adjustments?

As the papers in this book make clear, a great deal of work remains to be done on such questions as whether, how, and to what extent these and other factors are combined when the potential purchaser is coming to a decision to buy. We might want to know what proportion of Which?'s readers are "data-seekers," looking for as much information as possible to help them in deciding what to do, as opposed to "delegators" who prefer, in effect, to be told what to buy. Whatever the reality may be however, our research on readership and the success of Which? both suggest that laboratory tests remain an important element of our work. Our tests are designed and developed as necessary to ensure that CA's laboratory work conforms to accepted scientific standards as applied to realistic conditions. This emphasis on day-to-day life in the home, the garden, the shop, and in the car or on the train is also inherent in much of the research carried out by The Survey Unit.

The techniques of The Survey Unit are the practices of survey research, accepted throughout the developed and democratic world. Essentially, a sample of people (fewer than, but representative of, the total number who are of interest) is contacted and asked questions about their experiences, or views, or behaviour. If the correct number of people, selected in the right way, is asked the right questions, the data obtained can give an accurate guide to the total group's attitudes or knowledge. Much of TSU's work relies on samples drawn from CA's subscribers while the majority of our data is obtained using mail questionnaires. In the next section of this paper, we look at two areas in which CA has found survey research to be particularly useful.

PRODUCTS AND SERVICES: ALTERNATIVE APPROACHES

A paper of this length is necessarily highly selective. This section gives a summary -- no more -- of two applications where CA's survey research has been of particular help.

a. Product reliability and servicing. Here products are monitored over months and years rather than the hours or days of a laboratory study. Increasingly important, the performance of manufacturers and others in providing after-sales service is also monitored.

b. Service industries of various types, i.e., for examining those things which cannot be tested in a laboratory - the service given by holiday tour companies, television, Britain's health service, or the insurance industry, and to look at what people want as well as their responses to the services they receive.

Since the mid-1950's the emphasis of consumer research into household durables - washing machines, refrigerators, televisions, etc. - has moved from performance to reliability. For the first issue of Which? in 1957, CA tested kettles and reports of tests of durables have appeared in most issues since then. Now, by and large, products do what they claim to do. Greater sophistication in manufacturing techniques, strong and international competition, legislation, and - let us hope - the impact of the consumer movement in increasing purchasers' sophistication, have all discouraged the production and sale of rogue products. The occasional new product may leak, or may be electrically unsafe, but in general the emphasis in our work has shifted from questions like "Does it work?" to matters of safety and ease of use, and to questions like "How long does it work well?" and (a change in emphasis from the product to the service that goes with it) "If it develops a fault, what happens?".

CA obtains frequency-of-repair information from a panel of more than 15,000 subscribers, comprising the Which? "Monitoring Team." The panel members are recruited via a monthly omnibus survey mailed out by TSU to a random sample of 2000 subscribers. Panel members fill in diaries about any problems and faults with their appliances as they happen. Whenever any of their appliances are repaired, they fill in an additional questionnaire relating to the particular repair.

The Monitoring Team provides CA regularly with information (among other things) on the repairs and servicing of some 7,000 washing machines, 4,500 color television sets, and nearly 2,000 dishwashers. While the main aim of this project is to obtain data about brand and, if possible, model reliability, it is also allowing CA to build up data on the quality of repair services encountered.

Inevitably, there are occasions on which a single research method - a panel or ad hoc survey - is insufficient and a variety of complementary techniques have to be used. An example of this is research done several years ago to investigate the service given by

British Rail. Travellers by rail in the UK can be classified in a number of different ways, but CA concentrated on two types, the InterCity traveller and the commuter. It was relatively straightforward to contact a good sample of InterCity travellers, though it was costly since only 17 percent of the population travel InterCity in a year. We overcame this difficulty by using one of the multi-client surveys carried out regularly by Britain's market research agencies.

The problem of sampling commuters was more daunting. To any rush hour traveller the supply of commuters seems inexhaustible. But, in fact, as compared with the total population of London, commmuters are a smallish group. Interviewing on rush-hour trains would have been impractical, given the crush and congestion, even if British Rail had permitted it. Another alternative, using area probability sampling and personal interviews in households would have been time-consuming and costly. The compromise adopted was to select a random sample of stations at which we obtained names and telephone numbers of returning commuters. The actual interviews were undertaken within two or three days, by telephone.

To supplement this assessment of British Rail service, CA sent out inspectors to evaluate station cleanliness and food specialists to look at -and taste - the food and drink provided by BR. A final aspect of this complex project was to telephone a sample of British Rail enquiry offices to find how easy it was to get through and how comprehensive was the information that was then obtained.

The bulk of our projects are more conventional, single-technique research projects. Every year, for example, we carry out a car reliability survey, the main aim of which is to provide reliability information on a model-by-model basis for CA's annual Car Buying Guide, a separate 64-page supplement to Which? magazine. The 20-page questionnaire booklet is mailed to a random sample of about 45,000 Which? members. This number is usually supplemented by re-surveying owners from the previous year of brand-models with very small market shares. Our purpose was to obtain a sample size for each model that would provide at least a minimally acceptable level of precision.

Given such a large sample of members, it is tempting to send out an additional questionnaire on a different subject in the same package. In The Survey Unit we succumb to this temptation regularly. We have "piggy-backed" the car reliability study with questionnaires on house or car insurance for each of the last five years. It is a reflection on CA's dedicated members that response rates have been maintained at a comfortable 70% for this project, despite the increasing demands or "requests" we make on respondents.

CAVEATS AND CONCLUSIONS

Consumers' Association spends some $660,000 annually on survey research of one sort or another (£ = $1.65). To facilitate product testing of the "right" modes, CA spends a further $230,000 on "market intelligence," designed to find out who makes, imports, distributes, and sells the large number of products with which we are concerned. The organization's investment and belief in market research is therefore substantial, and is likely to increase. In my judgment TSU's work has proved its worth and its usefulness to CA. Whether most of it is equally useful to our readers is less clear. It is almost certainly true that in subscribing to _Which?_ our members are purchasing far more than just a buying guide. In addition to serving its prime purpose of generating data that is useful, our surveys crucially provide information that is interesting -- "a good read." As public opinion organizations, polling companies and newspapers well know, survey research provides splendid copy. CA is happy to capitalize on this, both for its own purposes of informing and entertaining readers and also to encourage media interest in its work.

Ironically, it is in the area of product reliability that particular problems remain with survey research. Small-scale experiments carried out by TSU have suggested that panel and ad hoc projects, ostensibly measuring the same variables, in fact generate some slightly but significantly different results. Our current view is that the panel method is probably the more accurate of the two techniques but that accuracy _per se_ is perhaps not our primary purpose. Most of our product reliability work concerns comparative assessment of different brands and models. For this it is the _relative_ position of brands or models, not the _absolute_ position that counts. We believe that our methods of measuring reliability are acceptably accurate for assessing _relative performance_ of brands. Thus, we are happy to provide the consumer with survey-based assessments of the most reliable brand or brands, model or models.

But do manufacturers feel that we are fairly and accurately measuring reliability? The cynic might say that those manufacturers who do well in our surveys think we do, while those who do less well have grave doubts about our work. It is certainly true, and hardly surprising, that we receive most complaints from manufacturers whose products emerge less favorably from our survey research. The main criticisms, however, center on the unrepresentativeness of our sample (which, as noted above, is of CA members only: this is a criticism that we strongly challenge but that need not be gone into here) rather than the postal technique or the questionnaires that we use. Significantly, many manufacturers who are initially critical of our work eventually purchase further, more detailed analysis of our surveys for their own internal use.

Our ideal, of course, would be to obtain reliability data for models as well as brands, and to publish it in Which? soon after the product is first offered on the market. Unfortunately, this is the source of our problem. It is clear that reliability simply does not exist until a given model has been on the market for, say, a couple of years. Unhappily, for some products, by the time reliaiblity data are available, the models may no longer be purchased. If we cannot provide up-to-date information on <u>models</u>, can we talk about historical <u>brand</u> reliability as a surrogate? Is it fair? On balance, we believe that it is. Our reliability results are, by definition, based on old data but our first responsibility is to the consumer. If we have any information of use to them, or any doubt about a particular model or brand, it is our responsibility to pass it on. How many of us, if we knew a particular brand had a bad reliability record, would discard this information as irrelevant and buy that manufacturers' latest model? We must remember that individual consumers have no other sources of information about reliability: our data are unique.

It is also worth noting that for some fields, product development is currently so rapid that even our timetables of laboratory tests and publication are being overtaken. This is particularly true of home electronics (home computers, compact disc players and similar items). Leading manufacturers of home computers revise their product range every 9-12 months, or about the same time that it takes the major consumer organizations to buy and test the products, and to then write, verify, edit and publish the testing-based report. So reliability is not our only problem. By the time even some basic test reports are published, the brand-models tested may no longer be found in retail outlets. It remains to be seen whether this problem pertains only to "young" products or whether it will become a general problem.

Our work, of course, continues. One of our major goals is to develop laboratory and in-house tests yielding useful reliability data that is available early in the product or model life cycle. Developmental work continues on our survey techniques. We would welcome the opportunity to describe our progress when ACCI next examines the research that is being undertaken, worldwide, "in the consumer interest."

THE RIGHT

TO

REDRESS

Chapter 28

ABOUT THE AUTHOR

Alan R. Andreasen is Professor and Chair, Department of Marketing, California State University, Long Beach. After receiving his Ph.D. in Marketing from Columbia University in 1964, Andreasen served on the faculties of SUNY-Buffalo, the University of Illinois and UCLA before moving to Long Beach in 1987. His university career was interspersed with foreign assignments with the Indian Institute of Management of Calcutta (1972) and the European Institute for Advanced Studies in Management in Brussels (1978-79). Andreasen is a member of the Editorial Boards of the Journal of Marketing, Consumer Affairs, and Health Care Marketing. He is the author of Talking Back to Business (with Arthur Best), The Disadvantaged Consumer and Strategic Marketing for Nonprofit Organizations (with Philip Kotler) as well as numerous journal articles.

CONSUMER COMPLAINTS AND REDRESS: WHAT WE KNOW AND WHAT WE DON'T KNOW

Alan R. Andreasen

SUMMARY

A review of the major research studies on consumer complaining behavior reveals a declining interest in the topic despite the existence of major unanswered questions of interest to business people, public policymakers and consumer interest specialists. The research base has deepened in its ability to explain complaining behavior, its sophistication in quantitative analysis and its coverage of developed and nondeveloped marketplaces. Provided we are precise in our definition of the occasion for complaining, we can now conclude that consumers experience problems in about 20 percent of their purchases, complain to the seller (rarely to third parties) 40 percent of the time and perceive that they have received satisfaction from this complaining behavior 60 percent of the time.

Research has identified the major characteristics of the kinds of problems likely to be voiced and the kinds of consumers likely to do the voicing. Biases in volunteered complaints data strongly suggest the need for direct surveying by those who need such feedback for strategic planning purposes. Future studies should also serve to increase our understanding of such issues as the role of blame and post-purchase emotions on complaining behavior, the under-complaining in the service sector, how consumers estimate the probability of success of their complaints and the role of other family members and/or friends in motivating and directing complaint behavior.

* * * *

Since 1975, over five hundred papers have been prepared with some immediate relevance to the issue of consumer satisfaction/ dissatisfaction and complaining behavior.[1] There have also been nine annual conferences held on the topic between 1976 and 1985. In the main, this literature has focused on three topics: (a) satisfaction with exchanges and its determinants; (b) responses to dissatisfaction and their determinants; and, more recently, (c) institutional responses to voiced dissatisfaction.

The present paper focuses on responses to dissatisfaction sometimes touching, tangentially, on the other two topics.[2] To make the subject manageable, the paper has been restricted in two other ways. First, the focus here is on consumer complaints, leaving to others [Rao, 24] the exploration of business-to-business complaints. Second, this paper emphasizes complaints to sellers and/or official third party complaint handlers such as the Federal Trade Commission or the Better Business Bureau, ignoring other responses such as negative word-of-mouth or brand or outlet switching.

The paper addresses five critical questions:

1. To what extent are consumers confronted by purchase problems for which they might seek redress or wish to be heard?

2. How frequent, in what cases, and with what methods-- both formal and informal -- do consumers seek to be heard or to exercise the redress option?

---

[1] Much of this material is summarized in two lists prepared by H. Keith Hunt who with Ralph Day has been instrumental in sustaining interest in this field. See [50, 51].

[2] Swan [94] and Woodruff, Cadotte and Jenkins [104] offer useful perspectives on the literature on consumer satisfaction. Fornell has several studies of corporate responses to dissatisfaction [e.g. 31]. Kasper [53], Resnick and Harmon [75] and Fornell and Westbrook [33,32] have also provided more recent studies on aspects of this topic. Review papers on the topic of complaining by Singh and Howell [90] and Robinson [83] were useful in preparation of the present paper.

3. How frequent are they successful (in their view)?

4. What factors determine whether a consumer will speak up or seek redress in a particular situation?

5. What are the implications of these findings for key interested parties:

   a. Businesspeople?
   b. Regulators and consumer activists?
   c. Consumer theorists and researchers?

The paper is based on two important premises. First, as supported by the evidence below, it is assumed that consumer complaining behavior is, in the main, based on valid grievances. There are undoubtedly cranks who like to "cause trouble" and cases where consumers do not understand the nature of their problem or the seller's responsibilities. Still, it is clear that these represent only a very small proportion of the overall experience.

Second, it is assumed that consumer complaint behavior is driven by one of four basic sets of factors. The cost-benefit model assumes that dissatisfied consumers more or less objectively evaluate the extent of present dissatisfaction, the costs and benefits of complaining and the probability of success and decide to act or not act on the basis of this analysis.

The personality model assumes that dissatisfied consumers, while paying attention to costs and benefits, are mainly driven to or restrained from action by the kind of people they are. The learning model assumes that, over time, consumers learn to become active or inactive complainers depending on the success of failure of their earlier attempts. Finally, the restraints model suggests that the rate and type of consumer complaining is affected not by what consumers wish to do but what they are able to do in the presence or absence of personal handicaps or actions by sellers to discourage complaining.

The paper is intended to be a working document for those interested in these issues. The initial sections, therefore, are necessarily devoted to systematically laying out essential background material drawn from the major studies in the area relevant to an understanding of consumers' experiences with problems, voicing and complaint-handling. Once this groundwork is laid, the paper then seeks to summarize what we know and do not know as well as the normative and prescriptive issues posed by the working of the redress process.

THE EVIDENCE

"Problems"

This paper focuses on what happens following a negative evaluation of a purchase. A first question, therefore: just how often do such negative evaluations arise? A review of the literature on dissatisfaction and complaint behavior, unfortunately, confronts one with a wide variation of definitions of negative evaluations.[3] Most studies begin with some explicit or implicit scale of dissatisfaction. Explicit scales ask respondents for ratings on a 4- or 5-point scale from, say, very satisfied to very dissatisfied [47,73,15]. Implicit scales ask about instances in which the respondent was "ever" highly dissatisfied [6,23,24], "had cause for complaint," [68] found "problems," or "ways it could have been better for your household" [15]. All presumably identify cases that would have been on the negative end of some explicit scale.

The measures differ also in specificity as to both time and category. Some ask about a more or less precise time period, others ask "in general." Some ask about a specific recent purchase of a single item or single service (e.g. a camera or bicycle purchase or an airline flight), others ask about broad categories (e.g. food, medical care, or clothing).

Finally, as Andreasen pointed out in an early discussion of taxonomies of consumer satisfaction/dissatisfaction measures [5], the measures differ in the extent to which they seek subjective or objective measures of dissatisfaction. Subjective measures require some insight into consumer cognitions. Objective measures are those that are susceptible to external verification, such as complaint letters. Subjective measures of dissatisfaction can seriously overstate the true level of "dissatisfaction." For example, Andreasen and Best [4] found significant numbers of subjectively "dissatisfied" respondents who were simply upset about the high cost of the purchase. That they were "dissatisfied" was not in dispute. However, the high prices generating their dissatisfaction were attributable to inflationary pressures rather than by actions by the seller, either wholesale or retail. For public policy purposes, it is

---

[3]Note that we are focusing here on dissatisfactions and complaining behavior with respect to acquisitions of goods or services. We do not consider dissatisfaction and complaining with respect to other aspects of the marketplace such as pricing, advertising, salesforce misrepresentation and the like.

important to remove such elements from consumer satisfaction/ dissatisfaction measures.

These measurement differences have important ramifications for our ability to estimate both the extent of dissatisfaction and the frequency with which consumers complain and how they complain. Obviously, ceteris paribus, one would expect to find more dissatisfaction with a group of items each of which could be a source of problems than with a single purchase. Similarly, more dissatisfaction will be registered if high prices or abrasive clerks are permitted to influence the judgment. Similarly, one would expect to see more active complaining if respondents are asked about cases in which they were "highly dissatisfied" or "recently had cause for complaint" than if they were asked about more vaguely defined episodes of "dissatisfactions."[4]

Clearly then, there are several ways in which we might phrase the question about how much dissatisfaction there is out there:

1. How often are specific purchases found to be unsatisfactory or to present "problems"?

2. How often does a particular category lead to dissatisfaction or problems?'

3. How often does a particular consumer encounter any dissatisfaction or problems of any kind?

This paper does not address these questions in detail. Fortunately, the first two questions do not appear to yield greatly differing results, although the differences are in the predicted directions. For example, Andreasen and Best addressed the first question [4]. They asked respondents whether in the last year or two they had purchased something in each of 34 product and service categories and then asked whether there was any problem with the purchase or whether there was "any way it could have been better for your household" (a probe). Based on this type of questioning, the study reports a relatively consistent problem rate (after eliminating price-related problems) of 20 percent for the three major summary categories; infrequently and frequently purchased products, and services.

By contrast, Leigh and Day [61], using a relatively broad category definition, report dissatisfaction on the part of about 15

---

[4]A good discussion of these issues is found in [104].

percent of their respondent households for frequently purchased products. Using the same definition, Day and Bodur [24] report somewhat higher averages in the 25 percent range for sets of professional and personal services and repairs and general services although similar 14 per cent rates for financial and insurance services.

Using even broader categories, the Office of Fair Trading in Great Britain found that 28 percent of their respondents reported "cause for dissatisfaction" with goods they had bought in the previous 12 months [68]. Twenty-four percent reported dissatisfaction with services.[5] Forty-eight percent had a problem with either a good or service, a figure very similar to that found by Zussman in Canada in 1979 [106] and Leigh and Day [61, p. 177]. These rates may be specific to the countries studied. Lower rates on a subjective dissatisfaction measure in West Germany were reported by Meffert and Bruhn [66]. Using categories drawn from the Andreasen/Best study, they found dissatisfaction levels of one to 13 percent across 23 product and service categories. On the other hand, Thorelli reports much higher levels of "disappointment" with durables in Thailand [96] and the People's Republic of China [97].

Data from the Andreasen and Best study are reported in Table 1. It is clear from the data presented in the first column that problems are not uniformly distributed across purchase categories. Low problem rates were found for cosmetics, blankets and sheets and medical/dental care. High problem rates were found for auto and appliance repairs, mail order purchases, automobile purchases and toys. Similar variation was reported for Great Britain [68]. There, highest problem rates were found for household appliances, building services, public utilities and transport and footwear.

From a review of this type of information [4], it would appear that about 40 to 50 percent of consumers, depending on the category and the country, will have experienced some form of dissatisfaction in the preceding year. Within a purchase category, the rate of dissatisfaction or "problems" appears to be between 15 and 25 percent on average.

---

[5]Respondents in this study were given a list of 10 categories for goods and 12 categories for services for guidance.

Table 1

Problem, Voicing, Complaint-Satisfaction and Residual Dissatisfaction Rates for Selected Product and Service Categories[e]

Purchase Category	Problem Rate[a]	Voicing Rate[b]	Complaint-Satisfaction Rate[c]	Residual Dissatis-faction Rate[d]
Mail Order Purchases	31	59	68	60
Books and Records	13	51	75	61
Washers, Driers	23	47	81	62
Cameras	17	50	71	64
Television Sets	21	58	61	65
Automobile Purchases	32	57	56	68
Automobile Repairs	35	60	50	70
Appliance Repairs	30	66	36	77
Floor Covering	19	35	47	83
Film Developing	19	35	45	84
Toys	31	22	69	84
Vacuum Cleaners	27	29	48	86
Blankets, Sheets	12	22	56	88
Medical/Dental Care	15	33	35	89
Cosmetics	9	14	69	90
Car Parking	23	24	30	93
All Purchases	20.2	42.3	58.9	75.1

[a]Percentage of purchases that resulted in a nonprice "problem" when consumers were asked "Was there a problem?" or "Was there any way the productor service could have been better?"

[b]Percentage of nonprice problems voiced to sellers or to official complaint- handling agencies.

[c]Percentage of voiced nonprice problems that were resolved to the consumer's satisfaction. Cases still pending were deleted from the base.

[d]Percentage of nonprice problems either not voiced plus those that were voiced and not satisfactorily handled.

Source: [4].

Inaction

Given that consumers experience product dissatisfaction relatively frequently, how often do they report not doing anything about it? This would include having no negative changes in intentions (although there may be negative changes in attitudes) and no attempts to seek redress or speak out to others.

Again analysis is plagued by the problem of the differing nature of the dissatisfaction base from which subsequent action is investigated. That is, the wording of questions asked may cause consumers only to report cases where they actually complained.

Further the definition of "inaction" varies from study to study. Some leave the definition to the consumer; thus, consumers who changed their intentions would say they did "nothing." Other studies consider only attempts to secure redress either directly or through third parties as "action."

The effects of these differences in definitions can be seen in comparisons of three major studies. In England, the Office of Fair Trading asked consumers whether they had "any reason to complain in the last 12 months" and, not surprisingly found inaction in only 24 percent of both product and service purchases [68]. Similarly, when Thorelli and Puri asked Norwegian consumers whether they complained in a case when they found a product defect (as opposed to a "problem" or "dissatisfaction"), they found that only 26.4 percent did not complain [98]. These approaches are similar to the findings of Warland, Herrmann and Willitts [101] who asked about cases where consumers "got good and angry" about a problem with a purchase.

In Bloomington, Indiana [23, 24] and Canada [6], researchers asked about instances where the consumer was "highly dissatisfied." As indicated in Table 2, these studies found about the same level of inaction in the two locales in the order of 40 percent (except for services in Bloomington where inaction was only 22 percent). A study in Istanbul, Turkey, replicating the Bloomington methodology for a specific set of services, found inaction levels almost double that in Indiana and Canada [16].

As noted above, Andreasen and Best asked about "problems" [4,15] and utilized a narrower concept of "voicing" which included only attempts at redress through sellers or third parties. Two of their findings are relevant to this discussion of methodology. First, they asked about "problems" both with and without a probe. Adding a probe significantly increases the rate of reported inaction:

Effects of Question Probe on Percent Nonvoicing

	Problems Reported		
	Before Probe	After Probe	Total
Infrequently Purchased Goods	37.5%	62.4%	50.5%
Frequently Purchased Goods	55.4	73.1	64.7
Services	45.4	61.4	52.3
TOTAL	48.0%	67.5%	57.7%

These data make it clear that the more "serious" the problem analyzed, the more likely consumers will be found to be taking an action. This conclusion is supported by the national TARP study [45,95]. In this study, consumers were asked whether they complained about the most serious of a set of problems they reported encountering in any product category. TARP found that only 31 per cent of their sample did not complain (although presumably many of the remainder changed intentions).

On the other hand, if one assumes a ratio of voicing to nonvoicing action (such as changing intentions) of 3 to 2, as the analyses below suggest is reasonable, then the Andreasen and Best data seem consistent with the Bloomington and Canadian findings. Thus, one may conclude that, if one considers all the problems consumers have with goods and services, they will take some action about a third of the time. If one restricts one's consideration to the relatively more serious problems, then consumers seem to act about 60 percent of the time. This rate is consistent with the findings of Robinson in 1981 [83].

The available evidence also makes it very clear that complaint rates, like problem rates, vary significantly across purchase categories. The second column of Table 1 reports voicing rates across categories to be lowest for less expensive goods such as toys, cosmetics, vacuum cleaners, and blankets and sheets and highest for two services, appliance and automobile repairs. In England, voicing was highest for repairs of various kinds and for furniture and floor coverings [68]. Although across studies, services seem to evoke some of the highest voicing rates, it is clear that one cannot generalize. Andreasen and Best [4] found, for example, very low voicing rates for services such as legal, medical and dental and car parking. Overall, the data make it clear that the use of average voicing rates across areas (or even across broader categories within studies) is unwise because the averages may conceal highly differing rates across particular kinds of services.

Active Responses Taken

As noted earlier, those who acted could choose exit or voicing. Unfortunately, as noted here, few studies exist to indicate the relative frequency of the two classes of responses or to the subcategories within each. Two exceptions are the Bloomington and Canadian studies. As noted in Table 3, in these studies voicing appears to outnumber exit by about three to two, at least in cases of "high dissatisfaction." This table, of course, indicates total responses. Table 2 earlier, however, indicated the proportion of respondents in the two studies making each type of response, duly allowing for multiple responses. The larger Canadian data base indicates that perhaps 50 percent or more of customers intend to change patronage when highly disappointed. This obviously is a serious problem for sellers. Negative word-of-mouth information can be highly damaging. About forty percent of those dissatisfied warned others about unsatisfactory durables and nondurables. This rate was 50 percent for services where, of course, quitting the service may not always be an option (e.g., refusing to patronize a hotel in a distant community to which one is unlikely ever to return).

Although it is not reported in Tables 2 and 3, other studies confirm that complaints to so-called third parties are very infrequent. In Andreasen and Best's national study, third parties were contacted for only 1 1/2 percent of all problems (or in 3 1/2 percent of all complaint actions) [15, p. 118]. In Day and Ash's Bloomington study, only about three percent of those with high dissatisfaction with durables contacted third parties. The figure was lower for nondurables with only one case out of 147 involving a third party [23]. Even in the TARP study [95], with its focus on single instances of "significant" problems, only nine percent of first contacts were with third parties (although unreported later contacts may have been). These represented only 6 percent of all "serious problems."

Table 2

Responses to High Dissatisfaction:
Did Nothing, Exited, Voiced, Bloomington and Canadian Studies

	Nondurables		Durables		Services	
Response	Blmgtn	Canada	Blmgtn	Canada	Blmgtn	Canada
Did Nothing	40%	46%	39%	42%	22%	41%
Exited:						
Quit the brand	37	50	27	40	--	--
Quit the product	14	25	13	16	17	22
Quit Store/supplier	17	18	17	20	33	47
Voiced:						
Warned others	34	39	27	38	38	50
Sought redress	27	39	41	34	44	30
Complain to store	17	29	27	41	20	17
Complain to manufacturer	7	7	11	12	--	--
No. of cases of dissatisfaction	(60)	(388)	(37)	(288)	(36)	(374)

Source: [25, p. 90].

Table 3

Responses to High Dissatisfaction:
Exit vs. Voice' Bloomington and Canadian Studiesa

	Nondurables		Durables		Services	
	Blmgtn	Canada	Blmgtn	Canada	Blmgtn	Canada
Exited:	44%	45%	35%	38%	33%	41%
Voiced:						
Warned Others	22	19	17	19	25	29
Sought redress	18	19	25	17	29	18
Complained	16	17	23	26	13	11
Total Voicing	56%	55%	65%	62%	67%	59%
Total	100%	100%	100%	100%	100%	100%
No. of Actions Taken[a]	(90)	(803)	(60)	(578)	(55)	(611)

[a]Multiple answers permitted.

Source: Recomputed from [25, p. 90].

Satisfaction with Complaint Handling

Of major concern to consumers and to policymakers is the question of how effective the private redress system is in resolving consumer problems. In the Andreasen and Best study, complainants' verbatim responses were categorized as satisfactory, unsatisfactory, "mixed" or pending with the following result [15].

Complainant's Satisfaction with Disposition of Problem	Infrequently Purchased Products	Frequently Purchased Products	Services
Satisfactory	57.5%	65.8%	43.9%
Unsatisfactory	24.3	23.1	28.7
Mixed	14.5	6.5	9.5
Pending	3.7	4.7	5.3
TOTAL	100.0%	100.0%	100.0%

The lower rate of satisfaction in the services category is mirrored by experience in the United Kingdom. The U.K. Office of Fair Trading reported satisfaction with complaint outcomes in 74 percent of the cases involving goods as contrasted with 34 percent of the cases involving services. Canadian experience was similar with Ash and Quelch reporting 34.2 percent satisfaction among Canadian complainers for three services (rentals, public transportation and utilities) [6]. In the TARP study [45, 95], respondents reported the following:

Largely Satisfied	42.6%
I received more than I asked for	1.1
I was completely satisfied	21.4
I was not completely satisfied, but the solution was acceptable	20.1
Largely Dissatisfied	53.9%
I was not completely satisfied, but I did get something	12.8
I was not at all satisfied	41.1
Other/Don't know	3.5
TOTAL	100.0%

The relatively low frequency of complete satisfaction may be ascribable to the lack of clear expectations on the part of complaining consumers. Gilly [37] classified consumers' expectations as (a) ideal, (b) deserved, (c) minimum tolerable, and (d) expected and was surprised to find 26 percent of her respondents "didn't know" what to expect at all. This result may depend on the level of the channel of distribution with which one is dealing. Kelley [54] found an 11 percent "don't know" rate for problems with retailers and 33 percent for problems with manufacturers. Gilly also found that expectations affected perceptions of the outcome, those with "ideal" or "deserved" expectations being significantly less likely to perceive the outcome as satisfactory.

Other research suggests factors other than the legitimacy of the complaint that may affect the likelihood of obtaining a favorable resolution. Boschung [17] found that manufacturers of supermarket products responded more favorably to consumers with higher education. This may be a function of expository skills since Pearson [72] found that the quality of a complaining letter positively affected response. However, these findings were not replicated in a later study by Resnik, Gnauk and Aldrich [76], although the nonreplication may have been the consequence of using students to write complaint letters. Presumably, students are characterized by low variance in letter quality and socioeconomic characteristics.

Finally, satisfaction with complaint disposition depends on the kind of problem that was voiced as shown in the following data from Best and Andreasen [15].

Type of Problem	Percent Satisfied with Disposition of Problem	Problem	Percent Satisfied
Freshness	81.5%	Workmanship	55.8%
Stitching	76.7	Slow/late/omitted	53.8
Partial breakage	64.0	Other	53.3
Total breakage	63.4	Wrong good/service	51.0
Shrinking/fading	62.1	Materials	41.8
Fit/size	61.0	Ease of use	41.5
Clerical error	60.3	Misrepresentation	38.8
Durability	57.1	Loss of property	38.3
		Design	36.2

Problems that are "manifest" or obvious such as "freshness" and/or are easily correctable -- replacement of broken items -- are more likely to be resolved to the satisfaction of the complainant.

Residual Dissatisfaction

A major concern of business, government and consumers should be with the amount of dissatisfaction that still remains <u>even after</u> the complaint process has run its course. Consumers can be satisfied with the exchanges they make if they are initially satisfied or if they are initially dissatisfied but seek redress and are satisfied with the outcome of this step. An important policy question then is: how often do consumers feel dissatisfaction and <u>either</u> do not seek redress <u>or</u> seek redress and are not satisfied with the outcome. This figure is surprisingly high. For example, the TARP study reports: "Nearly 70 percent of the most serious problems reported in the national sample were <u>not</u> satisfactorily remedied" [45, p. 498]. This estimate corresponds closely to the data of Andreasen and Best who reported residual dissatisfaction as follows [15, p. 100]:

	Type of Purchase		
Responses Collected:	Infrequently Purchased Products	Frequently Purchased Products	Services
	Percent Remaining Dissatisfied		
Before Probe	67.2[a]	70.9	78.7
After probe	74.5	80.4	76.7
All problems	70.9	70.9	77.7
No. of cases	(1,418)	(2,690)	(1,594)

a The table reads: "Of those reporting 'problems' with infrequently purchased products before probing, 67.2% remained dissatisfied with the disposition of their problem."

REASONS FOR INACTION

Why do 60 percent of consumers with problems take no action -- a major source of this residual dissatisfaction? The decision not to take action is, as noted above, a consumer choice and, like other consumer choices, is a function of individual attitudes (weighted perceptions of the costs and benefits of action), the influences of others, and situational factors. For someone not to take action, it will be because they: (a) have judged the benefits too small and/or the costs too great (see [60]), (b) been discouraged by others (possibly including the seller) from complaining, or (c) had some other intervening factor delay or prevent action (such as a family crisis occurring or the consumer leaving town).

Past research has paid very little attention to the influence of others, including sellers, in discouraging complaints.[6] Thus, the available evidence tends to reflect the other two sets of factors, cost/benefit and situational. The literature also suggests that personality and socioeconomic characteristics also affect complaining behavior. We shall consider first the costs and benefits and then return to consider exogenous factors including situational, personality and socioeconomic characteristics.

[6]For an exception, see Richins [79].

Benefits and Costs

The costs and benefits consumers seem to consider may be divided into economic and psychological. Factors that have been suggested as reasons for inaction within each of these domains include the following:

A. Economic Benefits and Costs

1. The value of the item or service involved may be too small to justify taking action. This may be because the purchase involved a very small expenditure of time and/or money or, in the case of certain more expensive purchases, was of a type where the consumer considered a "problem" as one of the risks one takes with such a purchase. Thus, it may be that consumers buying certain services, shopping at certain outlets (e.g., deep discount merchants) or for very low prices may say to themselves, "Well, it serves you right for making that transaction!" It has been suggested by Caplovitz [19] and Andreasen [1] that one of the reasons that the disadvantaged have lower rates of problem perception and action is that they see "problems" as one of the "necessary" concomitants of shopping where they do.

2. The problem is perceived as "trivial" and the consumer can live with it.

3. The objective costs of seeking redress are perceived to be too great. This could be a result of ignorance or of calculations based on knowledge. Among the objective costs of voicing are the following [78]:

    a. Special trips to lodge a complaint;

    b. Time and effort to raise the issue, fill out forms, etc.;

    c. Foregoing product use during redress.

4. The consumer may perceive the response as likely to be inadequate. This may be seen as having two components: the probability that the process will yield any of several outcomes (repair, repayment, apology, etc.) and the value of that outcome.

B. Psychological Benefits and Costs

Richins [78] has also identified a number of psychological costs of taking action:

1. Fear of being treated rudely or unpleasantly;

2. Fear of being blamed for the problem;

3. Dislike of having to "hassle" someone over the problem;

4. Fear of being labeled a "complainer" (by others including the seller);

5. Fear of being embarrassed when complaining;

6. Apprehension of feeling guilty about complaining after the fact.

On the other hand, it is likely that the complaint process will be undertaken in many cases because the consumer foresees such psychological benefits as:

7. Feeling one is a good "consumer citizen";

8. Feeling one has caused sellers discomfort or actual economic costs;

9. Feeling good about oneself "not holding it in";

10. Feeling one can brag to others about one's assertiveness;

11. Feeling one has learned a skill that can be used in future and/or passed on to others.

C. Research Evidence

The evidence explaining consumer inaction points most clearly to the monetary importance of the problem involved as a determinant of action or inaction. The evidence below from Best and Andreasen [15] demonstrates the importance of both purchase cost and problem cost and the interaction between the two on voicing rates[7] as follows:

	Percent Voiced
Both purchase and problem usually expensive	58.1%
Purchase usually expensive, problem usually inexpensive	48.9
Purchase usually inexpensive, problem usually expensive	41.5
Both purchase and problem usually inexpensive	31.7

The importance of cost is verified by Richins [82] and by Bearden and Oliver [9]. The latter found a very strong correlation between the cost of the product failure and the extent of complaining behavior. This finding is supported further by a number of studies in which inactive consumers say that complaining just was not worth it. Day, Grabicke, Schaetzle and Staubach [25], supply data from both Canadian and Bloomington studies, showing that for purchases of goods the major reasons for inaction were that the goods or the problems involved in comparison to the costs of taking any action made it such that complaining "was not worth it." As Table 4 indicates, this was more often the case for goods than for services. For services, inaction was more often attributable to the respondent's expectation that the seller's response was not likely to be worth the trouble.

[7] Assignment of purchases and problems to "expensive" and "inexpensive" categories was carried out by the researchers. Their assignments may be found in Best [14, p.124].

Table 4

Reasons for Taking No Action, Bloomington and Canadian Studies

	Nondurables		Durables		Services	
	Blmgtn	Canada	Blmgtn	Canada	Blmgtn	Canada
Not worth time and effort	52%	41%	43%	40%	28%	27%
Never got around to it	8	13	6 13	0	6	
Wouldn't make any difference	25	40	35 38	50	58	
Didn't know what to do	15	6	16 9	22	9	
	100%	100%	100%	100%	100%	100%
No. of cases	(60)	(388)	(37)	(288)	(36)	(374)

Source: [25, p. 98].

These conclusions tend to be supported by the Office of Fair Trading study [68]:

	Goods	Services
Can't be bothered/threw out	22%	14%
Didn't have time	5	3
Too far to go	4	-
Fixed myself or elsewhere	5	5
Not think it would do any good	18	31
Will act later	10	6
Other	39	17
Don't know	17	24
TOTAL	100%	100%

Richins attempted to identify the possible contribution of attitudinal factors to complaining behavior with a convenience sample of 171 middle and upper-middle class consumers who had experienced dissatisfaction with a clothing or appliance purchase in the last six months [78]. Richins presented them with a list of 10 costs and 11 benefits that "would be incurred should the respondent complain about the dissatisfaction in question." Richins concluded [78, p. 51]:

> Respondents, on the average, found it more likely than unlikely that they would have to make a special trip to the store to complain, take time and effort to fill out forms, forego use of the product while it was being repaired, and have to 'hassle' someone in making their complaints. On the other hand, respondents on the average considered it particularly unlikely that they might become embarrassed while making their complaint or would feel guilty about complaining. This finding may be due in part to the higher than average social class of the respondents.
>
> As far as the benefits likely to accrue as the result of a complaint action, the only benefit seen as particularly probable was that the consumer would feel s/he had asserted his or her rights as a consumer. This finding may also be reflective of the respondent's social class. It is of note that respondents, as a whole, did not feel it particularly likely that the complaint would be remedied, either by product repair or replacement or by refund of the purchase price.

Using a model similar to those of Fishbein and Ajzen [22] and Bagozzi [7], Richins asked her respondents to rate the various costs and benefits in terms of how desirable or undesirable they were and how likely they were to actually occur should a complaint be made. Richins then computed a values-times-expectancy index for each cost and benefit and then correlated each index with the respondent's reported <u>actual</u> complaining behavior with respect to clothing and appliance purchases. In general, these correlations made clear that the model has considerable explanatory power with point biserial correlations ranging as high as .39. Only eight costs and benefits out of the original 21 were statistically significant overall. There were also differences between the two purchase categories. Complaining behavior for appliances was predicted by one objective cost (time and effort to fill out forms) and two psychological benefits (seeing a chance to assert rights as a consumer and feeling guilty about <u>not</u> complaining).

These same three factors affected clothing complaints. However, in this case, two other economic costs were also significant (having to make a special trip to the store and forgoing use of the garment) and two psychological costs (fear of being treated rudely and of being considered a "complainer"). Multiple regression analysis within the two product classes indicated that the attitude variables could explain 22 percent of the variance in appliance complaint behavior and 25 percent of the variance in clothing complaint behavior.

Other research findings support the argument that consumers do not complain because they have calculated the relative costs and benefits of the action and decided that it would not be worth their time and effort. These include the following:

1. Andreasen and Best (as reported above) found that the nature of the problem affected voicing behavior [15]. They classified problems reported by their respondents into those that were manifest such as breakage of a product, late delivery, clerical errors or the wrong product or service provided and those that were judgmental or subject to possible dispute such as poor workmanship, misrepresented, not durable, or poorly designed. Their respondents voiced complaints for manifest problems 59 percent of the time and for judgmental complaints only 33 percent of the time.

2. In an experimental study with undergraduates, Didow and Barksdale, Jr. [26] found that, among three factors varied in a fully factorial conjoint design, price accounted for 80 percent of the variance in hypothetical complaining behavior[8], while the opportunity for complaining as indicated by the number of outlets carrying the item accounted for only 18 percent. The latter factor -- the availability of complaint opportunities -- is suggested by Day et al to be an important contributor to differences across countries in complaining behavior [25,p. 103].

3. Grønhaug [39] found that the higher the perceived financial, health and social risk in a product purchase, the more likely a consumer was to voice a complaint.

4. Oster [71] employed a model derived from an economic cost/benefit framework to predict the rate of complaining to New Haven's Better Business Bureau. Controlling for

---

[8]Students were given hypothetical scenarios varying in the price of the item involved, the number of retail outlets carrying the item and whether the item was purchased for the student, family or as a gift. They were then asked to rank the 27 combinations according to how likely they would be to complain given the particular scenario.

purchase frequency in the category, Oster found that the number of reported complaints increased with the price of the good, the probability of achieving a favorable outcome from complaining, the rate of price increase at the time (which it was hypothesized would cause consumers to overestimate the value of a good), infrequent purchasing (giving fewer occasions for exiting), industries with smaller firms and less local advertising (which would make consumers less informed as to what they could expect) and greater purchases by low income groups (arguing that these groups would somehow more often make "mistakes" in consuming the good). Oster found that these variables explained 49 percent of the variance in complaining for 72 product categories. The model was somewhat less successful for services, explaining only 32 percent of the variance.

Socio-economic Determinants

A number of studies and speculative models have suggested that socio-economic characteristics may provide additional explanatory power for complaint behavior, although in many cases the importance of these socioeconomic factors has been modest (e.g. [10]) or absent altogether [46]. For example, Warland, Herrmann and Willitts [101], Grønhaug [39], Liefeld, Edgecombe and Wolfe [64], Zaichkowsy and Liefeld [105], Bearden [10] and Kraft [57] found that higher socio-economic status--typically measured by income and education--was positively correlated with complaining behavior, particularly when that complaining behavior involved steps beyond the minimal such as writing complaint letters, contacting third parties [86] or contacting the chief executive officer of an organization (see also [84]).

Several explanations have been offered for the relationship between higher socio-economic status and complaining behavior. First, higher income may simply mean that the purchase in question was more expensive and, as noted above, the more expensive the purchase/problem, the higher the voicing rate. Alternatively, as Grønhaug and Zaltman [40, p. 84] suggest, higher income may simply mean that the household has more resources to complain.

Second, higher socio-economic status, particularly higher education, is presumably associated with greater knowledge of complaint alternatives. Inaction may simply be a matter of knowing nowhere to turn (as was the case for 15 to 22 percent of those in the Bloomington study and 6 to 9 percent of those in the Canadian study as shown in Table 4).

The problems of the undereducated in protecting their consumer rights have been well documented by a long history of consumerism studies. Perhaps the best known is Caplovitz's classic study, The Poor Pay More [19]. Caplovitz found ignorance of where to turn "if you were being cheated by a merchant or salesman" to be strongly correlated with education, a traditional neighborhood orientation to shopping and, most significantly, whether the respondent had actually experienced problems [19, pp. 175-177]. This theme of the lack of coping skills is amplified in more recent writings by Andreasen [1], Best [14] and Laura Nader [67].

Caplovitz also found that race was related to lower voicing levels for New York Puerto Ricans, a finding replicated by Villareal-Camacho for Mexican-Americans [99]. The latter study found that Mexican-Americans were also more likely to have negative attitudes toward complaining, to take more private actions, including changing their intentions, and to blame themselves more often when there is a problem.

The role of experience in producing complaint action is highlighted in Grønhaug and Zaltman's 1981 study [43]. In this study, the authors found that previous buying experience was more important than income, education and age in predicting who would be an activist consumer. Although, the demographic variables did predict complaning as shown in a number of other studies, Grønhaug and Zaltman suggest that this may be because they are related to marketplace experience. Grønhaug and Zaltman offer the same explanation as to why Wall, Dickey and Talarzyk [100], Granbois, Summers and Frazier [46] and Duhaime and Ash [27] found sex to be a significant predictor (i.e., women were more active shoppers in categories where sex was found to be significant). Sex was also found by Strahle and Day [93] to be an important moderator variable. Indeed, for this reason, Bearden [8] explicitly used sex as a covariate in his study of auto repair complaining behaviors.

Experience in the marketplace, however, may be best defined as a generalized characteristic, probably associated with knowledge. Fornell and Didow [34] found that the more often the consumer interacts with a particular seller, the less likely he or she is to voice complaints. This variable may be a surrogate for loyalty which, according to Hirschman [48], is likely to suppress voicing.

Age has been found to be negatively associated with complaining. This finding has been demonstrated by Grønhaug and Zaltman [43] and replicated by Bearden, Teel and Crockett [11] and Bearden [8]. Many of the studies have focused on the problems of the elderly [e.g. 13, 55]. In a recent summary of this literature,

Bernhardt [13] has pointed out that the elderly are not only likely to perceive fewer problems but are less likely to do something about them. These conclusions are consistent with Grønhaug and Zaltman's contention that complaining behavior may be carried out most often by <u>those with the resources to complain</u> whether these resources be health, income or knowledge [43]. However, Bernhardt suggests another, simpler hypothesis, namely that, like sex, age may simply be a covariate. Bernhardt found that the elderly purchased less than the general population and that, <u>when purchasing levels were controlled</u>, the elderly were just as often dissatisfied and complained just as often as others.

Finally, it should be noted that the majority of findings upon which the above conclusions are based contrast the characteristics of those who claimed on a survey to have taken action with the characteristics of those who were known through some other data base to have submitted some sort of formal complaint either to the seller or to a third party complaint handler like the Better Business Bureau. It appears that the further one carries a complaint, the more likely one is to be upscale economically, well educated and younger.

<u>Personality</u>

It has been suggested -- most often by businesspeople -- that a great many consumers complain because that is the kind of people they are. Indeed, many seem to feel that complaints are produced by a relatively small set of chronic "cranks." Both Day and Bodur [24] and Andreasen and Best [4] lay that myth to rest. The latter found the following distribution of complainers and complaints in their national study:

Number of Complaints	Percent of Complainers	Percent of Complaints
1	47.9	23.5
2	24.4	23.8
3	15.4	22.6
4 or more	12.4	30.0

In the words of Andreasen and Best: "[a]lthough there is a 'heavy half' of complainers who generate three-fourths of the objections, this does not appear to be an excessive concentration when compared with other aspects of consumer behavior" [4, p. 98].

On the other hand, some studies have found that personality traits - or generalized predispositions -- are associated with complaint activity. At the simplest level, several studies (e.g. Richins [78]) have found (somewhat redundantly) that complaint activity is associated with generally favorable attitudes toward complaining. Consistent with this, Bearden, Teel and Crockett [11] found that 48 percent of the variance in propensity to complain was explained by two variables, sex and attitude toward complaining. As Richins [78] points out, the direction of causation here is not clear. It may be that consumers complain because they are predisposed by some more pervasive underlying trait that is unaffected by complaint experiences. On the other hand, as self-perception theorists suggest, it may be that people become favorably disposed toward complaining because that is what they see themselves doing. A third possibility is that a favorable predisposition may simply be a learned trait resulting from a series of favorable outcomes from actual complaining. None of these hypothetical relationships has been explored in the literature to date.

Positive attitudes toward complaining are also apparently associated with a larger constellation of attitudes toward being socially concerned [18] and with supporting other consumerist issues [10]. This position is most strongly argued in a recent paper by Warland, Herrmann and Moore [103]. Basing a theoretical model on the work of David Horton Smith [91], they argue that "complaining behavior can more properly be regarded as a component of an overall pattern of political, social and economic behavior" [103, p. 65]. First, they note that consumers tend to use multiple channels when they do complain and so these researchers use the number of different methods of complaining as their dependent variable in a multiple regression model. Their community involvement index, measuring the extent to which respondents attempted to promote social change, did add considerable explanatory power over the traditional demographic variables of age, education and income, reducing the latter's impact substantially. The authors interpret this finding as suggesting that community involvement acts as a facilitator of complaining actions (e.g. for the elderly or less educated) by making consumers more aware of and comfortable using complaining methods and institutions. However, another possibility is that both promoting social change (the authors' actual measurement) and complaining may be related to underlying personality or lifestyle traits (and/or possibly to group pressure) that make some more active in many domains than others. This interpretation would also be consistent with Smith's model.

Research, however, is not uniform in this regard, especially as more sophisticated multivariate techniques are brought into play.

Recently, Bearden and Oliver [9] used LISREL, a sophisticated multivariate technique for modelling causal relationships, to investigate not just action/inaction but the extent of complaining.[9] In their study they found that a personal trait, the propensity to complain, was related to the extent of either public or private actions.[10]

Early studies in this area (e.g. Warland, Herrmann and Willitts [101], and Bearden and Mason [12]) suggested that a sense of alienation from society might be part of the constellation of attitudes that predict complaint actions. Those with more alienation tend to complain less. Bearden and Mason suggest that this may be because they perceive more constraints in registering their complaints. On the other hand, in a recent multivariate analysis using sex and general life satisfaction as covariates, Bearden found that alienation did not discriminate between complainers and noncomplainers [10].

On the other hand, studies do show that complaining is associated with trust in others and possibly with perceived self-confidence. Those with less trust complain more often [10]. However, the findings on self-confidence are mixed. Bearden [10] found those with less generalized self-confidence tended to complain more. In either case, the literature makes clear that attributions of blame affect complaining. As Krishnan and Valle [58] indicate, consumers less often voice if they feel that they are partially or wholly to blame for the problem.

A positive attitude toward complaining has also been found to be associated with assertiveness according to studies by Fornell and Westbrook [33] and Richins [80].

---

[9]This was operationalized by counting the number of complaint actions. A different approach was used by Bearden and Teel [8] who measured intensity of complaint actions by scaling the following responses to automobile service problems in order of increasing intensity: (1) warned family and friends, (2) returned vehicle for rework and/or complained to management, (3) contacted manufacturer, (4) contacted formal third party group, or (5) took some legal action.

[10]Perhaps discriminant analysis is the more appropriate technique for this issue in that propensity to complain should only be expected to predict complaining at all, not the extent of complaining.

Finally, in a study in Mannheim, West Germany, Grabicke, Schaetzle and Staubach [44] used a set of seven personality measures to predict complaining behavior for a durable electric product. They found that three (unnamed) variables accounted for 36 percent of the variance in complaining behavior when the remaining four variables were treated as suppressors.

Situational Factors

Richins [77, p. 505] points out that "perceptions of some aspects of specific complaint situations may overpower nonspecific attitudes in determining actual complaint behavior." We have already noted the importance of situational factors on complaining behavior. That is, voicing is significantly affected by the type of purchase and by the type of problem one has encountered. Further, Fornell and Didow [34] point out that the availability of alternatives to voicing will suppress the latter. By contrast, the alternatives for voicing were suggested as one explanation of different voicing rates across countries. Indeed, it may be that more frequent responses of knowing where to get help in Bloomington as compared to Canada noted in Table 4 may be due to an absence of third party complaint handlers in that Indiana community. Further, Levy and Surprenant [62] argue that consumers' lack of knowledge may also explain lower complaint levels for services. In their study, consumers had a much better sense of the hierarchy of complaint avenues for products than they did for services.

The type of retail outlet is likely to affect complaining behavior. Consistent with this, Andreasen and Best (Table 1), found that the likelihood of satisfactory response to a voiced complaint varies significantly across purchase categories. Similarly, Strahle and Day [93] found that voicing rates varied across type of outlet. Presumably they also vary significantly among different retailers of the same type. This squares with Bearden and Oliver's [9] and Richins' [81] common finding that the use of private voicing channels was inversely related to satisfaction with firm response. The literature abounds with examples of specific outlets notorious for their ill-treatment of consumers, particularly the disadvantaged [1, 67].

Finally, research by Bearden and Teel [8] showed clearly that the level of dissatisfaction, a situational variable, will affect how much a consumer complains. That is to say, the further the reality of consumption experience is from one's expectations, *ceteris paribus*, the more one is likely to do something about it.

SUMMARY

The Research and Conceptual Base

A historical overview of the evolution of research on consumer complaining behavior since 1975 reveals several noteworthy trends:

1. The quantity of research appears to have followed a classic product life cycle pattern. The most significant aspect of this observation is that the issue now appears to be in the decline phase. To take the series of Conferences on Consumer Satisfaction and Dissatisfaction as an indicator, the number of published papers has fallen from a high of 28 and 31 at the second and fourth conferences to 8 and 6 at the last two.

2. The domain of the research appears to have progressed from early papers on conceptual and measurement issues to papers on major, broad based, descriptive studies and, finally, to papers on more narrowly focused, convenience sample studies seeking explanation rather than description.

3. The quality of the research has progressed most notably in explanatory studies where early bivariate analyses have been supplemented by complex, multivariate approaches.

4. The locale of the research has expanded from early work in the United States to encompass studies now in at least nine other countries.[11]

The conceptual base on which the research stream rests can be divided into two broad domains, measurement and explanation. Although both have been addressed continually over the history of the topic, they are still in need of further refinement. The gaps in the two areas are different in character. In the measurement domain, we have paid too little attention to the base used when tracing complaining behavior. If studies across countries and across purchase categories are to be comparable and are to permit aggregation of our knowledge, more attention must be paid than in the past as to whether we are studying:

---

[11]The countries are: Canada, China, Denmark, Sweden, Norway, West Germany, Turkey, Thailand and the Netherlands. See particularly [70, 96, 97].

1. Subjective dissatisfaction or objective ("verifiable") problems;

2. Situations of any type (e.g., a recent case when an individual had any problem, felt cheated, and so on) or the most recent case in a specified purchase category.

If we are to avoid confounding our findings about how often consumers complain, who complains and in what manner, we must not permit consumers the freedom to choose the occasion of dissatisfaction we will explore.[12] Useful beginnings in regard to standardization have been made by Day [22], Ross [87] and Ross and Oliver [88]. However, attention to consistency and uniformity should be an unstated requirement of all future work in this domain.

In the area of explanation, a considerable number of models have been developed by Landon [60], Day [21], Andreasen [5] Grønhaug and Arndt [42] and others. However, we have been remiss in three respects. First, we have not fully utilized the range of consumer behavior theory that might be adduced to explain the phenomena in question. Second, we have not been careful enough to specify the role played by those variables we have already identified. Third, we have limited our scope of interest to less than the full range of problem situations and complaining processes to which we might address ourselves. These are issues we shall return to in the concluding section.

The Extent and Character of Complaining Behavior

Attempts to make generalizations across studies are fraught with danger because problem, voicing and complaint satisfaction rates vary significantly across purchase categories. It would appear, however, that perhaps fifteen to twenty-five percent of all purchases involve some sort of dissatisfaction and that about one-half of all consumers will report some incidence of dissatisfaction in, say, a year's time. Of these problems, perhaps one-half are sufficiently serious that consumers will recall them without prompting.

---

[12]The exception, of course, would be if there were sound theoretical grounds for doing otherwise, for example, if one wished to explore really serious incidences of dissatisfaction. However, in the past, researchers have been guilty of studying the latter while apparently believing they were studying general levels of dissatisfaction.

When dissatisfaction occurs, about 40 percent of the time consumers will complain to the seller or, more rarely, to official third party complaint handlers. In perhaps twenty percent of the cases they will instead respond in the form of negative word-of-mouth or actual or planned brand or store switching. When they do complain, it appears that they are satisfied with management's responses fifty to sixty percent of the time. The combined effect of 60 percent nonvoicing and 40 percent dissatisfaction with managements' responses suggests that in perhaps seventy-five percent of all cases where dissatisfaction with the exchange is initially perceived consumers are in some sense finally dissatisfied.

Analysis indicates that consumers are more likely to voice a dissatisfaction if the dissatisfaction has one or more of the following characteristics:

1. The purchase was expensive;

2. The purchase involved economic, social or health risks;

3. The correction of the problem was likely to be expensive;

4. The negative disparity between performance and expectations was large;

5. The problem involved loss of use of the product;

6. The problem was manifest rather than a matter of judgment;
7. Blame for the problem was attributed to the seller rather than the consumer;

8. Complaint channels were well understood;

9. The complaint handler was perceived to be likely to make a favorable response;

10. The problem involved a seller to whom the consumer might not be loyal.

Consumers are more likely to voice a problem if the consumer has one or more of the following characteristics:

1. Higher than average income;

2. Higher than average education;

3. Younger;

4. Not Spanish-American;

5. Views complaining favorably;

6. Does not fear "hassling" the salesperson;

7. Does not fear being labelled a "complainer";

8. Supports consumerism and other social actions;

9. Is assertive;

10. Is less trusting of others;

11. Is more experienced in the purchase category.

Problem and consumer characteristics interact. For example, those with higher social status will have more experience with the category, will purchase more expensive items and will be more knowledgeable about complaint channels.

IMPLICATIONS

The research reported in this paper and summarized in the preceding paragraphs, despite considerable diversity in conceptualization, methodology, reference periods and geographical sites, reflect considerable congruence. The research, therefore, has important implications for three groups, businesspeople, consumer protection specialists and consumer researchers. We shall address the concerns of each in turn.

Businesspeople

Consumer complaints present managers with a dilemma because of their dual potential impact on business. On the one hand, consumer complaints represent irritations in the smooth running of the corporate enterprise. They confront managers with unhappy or irate individuals -- or at least their correspondence. They tell management that the organization and/or its agents have failed in some greater or lesser fashion. And they represent costs that management will have to incur to investigate, process and either make good on or defend against the complaint. In this guise, consumer complaints are something management would like to minimize or, better still, eliminate altogether. They tell of weakness and managers do not wish to hear of this.

But this would be a mistake! Consumer complaints can represent valuable marketing research information. Objective managers ought to seek out consumer complaints for four reasons. First, complaints can provide crucial early warning information on failures or imperfections in product or service offerings. Second, complaint levels can provide important monitoring information to help management compare various departments or channels of distribution, reward or criticize individual performance and assess progress (or the lack of it) over time. Third, unresolved dissatisfaction -- estimated at 75 percent in this review -- can, if invisible, effectively destroy a product, service or organization's reputation. Fourth, if complaint data are also collected about competitors (as General Motors does), they can reveal important strengths and weaknesses on both sides that can serve as major input for corporate strategy.

As noted at the outset, this paper has deliberately not focused on management's responses to consumer complaining (however, see [41, 52, 63]). Although it is the author's experience that too many managers see complaints solely in their "irritant" guise and that a significant remainder of managers are at least schizophrenic about them, we shall assume that managers wish to utilize complaint data in a positive way. What, then, does this review indicate?

1. Volunteered complaints data are clearly unrepresentative of all dissatisfaction facing the organization at any point in time even when that dissatisfaction involves major manifest objective problems. As Andreasen and Manning [3], Day [20] and others have emphasized, complaints data represent a biased sample of an important reality. Managers are less likely to hear about problems in certain purchase categories or for certain kinds of outlets, e.g., where consumers feel complaining would do no good. Judgment problems may not be reported because consumers are not sure their evaluations are right or they fear a "hassle" if they try to express them to sellers. Yet, surely management would wish to know about such problems lest they drive these customers to a competitor.

2. Volunteered complaints are unrepresentative of who is dissatisfied. Clearly underrepresented are lower social status groups, the undereducated and racial minorities. To the extent that any of these groups constitute major market segments, the use of complaints data for strategic planning purposes would risk alienating key groups through ignorance or misperception of their concerns. Perhaps of more general significance to management is

> the finding that those less loyal to the organization and its offerings are less likely to voice. In most product categories (as in politics), it is these "swing" purchasers who can make the difference between success and failure.

It should be noted that volunteered complaints data, although biased, are not worthless. They can serve two important functions. First, they can alert management to serious problems, especially those involving manifest complaints. Management does not need a representative sample to discover problems with handles that break, instruction books that are incomprehensible, merchandise that is stale and so on. It takes only a few irate and vocal customers to put management on notice that something must be done.

Second, voiced complaints can serve a tracking function. They obviously constitute a biased measure of performance. But, if the nature of the bias is understood from periodic direct studies of <u>all</u> consumers and if it can be assumed that the nature of the bias stays constant over time, then statistically valid changes in levels of voiced complaints can signal important improvements and/or deterioration in performance within a product category. Although this evaluation role is supported by this review, the data also clearly should not be used to compare performance <u>across</u> categories. We know that voicing rates differ significantly across product categories. And while we have some notion of why voicing rates are high or low in general, the present review makes it clear that our level of knowledge is insufficient to enable us to understand and therefore factor out the different biases that affect different purchase situations to make data from different purchase categories comparable for evaluation purposes.

In the final analysis, direct field surveys will be needed to give management crucial diagnostic, evaluation and planning information. Such surveys are also important to tell management how the organization's complaint handling procedures are performing. We have seen that there exists a very high level of residual dissatisfaction in the marketplace. It is obviously in management's interest to know to what extent this dissatisfaction is potentially damaging to its future either through direct loss of future sales to disgruntled customers or indirect losses caused by the rippling waves of ill will spread by dissatisfied patrons. If residual dissatisfaction is potentially damaging, it is also important to understand the extent to which this is due to low voicing rates or low satisfaction with the organization's complaint handling operations.

As noted, many managers may be reluctant to try to <u>stimulate complaint voicing</u>. In my view this may well be a very desirable step to take (see also Olander's comments [69]). The resulting data can be useful in reducing residual dissatisfaction and thus avoiding negative word-of-mouth. Perhaps most important, considerable strategic benefits can accrue to the organization that is actively solicitous of the reactions of the customers, viewing their patronage -- and therefore opinions -- as critical to company success. Certainly, the data suggest that consumers seem to behave reasonably objectively in pursuing their complaints, weighing the costs and benefits of action. Further, it is clear that there are not a lot of "cranks" out there waiting for the opportunity to complain to management if given half a chance. If sellers make it easier for consumers to complain and encourage those more hesitant about their gripes to do so, they will not be inundated with a rash of unjustified complaints, as many managers seem to fear.

Consumers, Consumer Activists and Regulators

The key "bottom line" question for those concerned with the two consumer rights outlined at the beginning of this paper is: do we have _enough_ consumer complaining? As noted, this question can be addressed at the micro and macro levels. That is, we can ask: (a) Do consumers as individuals get "adequate" redress? and (b) Does the redress _system_ "adequately" police the marketplace? We discuss each of these issues in turn.

1. Individual Redress

Do individuals who would like redress -- and who by some "objective standards" deserve it -- actually secure fair compensation? At first glance the data would suggest that the answer is "no." After all, it appears that 75 percent of all occasions of dissatisfaction remain "final dissatisfactions." However, several pieces of data from this review suggest that this figure may seriously overstate the problem in some respects although understating it in others.

Consider first those who did complain and how they perceived the outcome. Forty percent were _not_ satisfied. It is, however, not possible to estimate what percentage of these consumers "deserved" not to be satisfied because their complaints were not justified. In the TARP study [45], over one-half of those who indicated satisfaction were in fact less than fully satisfied. Certainly, the fact that 35 to 40 percent of the problems with something as presumably uncontestable as breakage,[13] wrong fit or clerical errors were unsatisfactorily resolved [15] may suggest business is less than fully forthcoming. One possibility is that the seller may effectively block consumer access [see, e.g. 1, 14, 89].

Assuming arbitrarily that cases where redress is improperly incomplete balance cases where consumers have no objective grounds for being dissatisfied with the handling of their complaint, then we may conclude that at least 16 percent[14] of instances of dissatisfaction are not adequately handled by the redress system. What, then, of the cases where no redress is sought? Taking the data from Canada's national sample reported in Table 4 as representative, one may hypothesize that in 50 to 55 percent of cases of "high dissatisfaction" with goods, the cost/benefit analysis militated against voicing. This figure is 30 to 35 percent of service problems.

Thus, we may speculate that 45 to 50 percent of goods problems and 65 to 70 percent of service problems are not voiced because potential complainers do not know what to do or think that it wouldn't do any good. Of this group, the 5 to 10 percent who don't voice out of ignorance clearly represent cases of residual dissatisfaction about which we should be concerned. The remaining 38 to 58 percent who feel complaining would be futile present a problem since we do not know whether this represents the potential complainer's judgment that (a) the odds are against an objective evaluation in the complainer's favor or (b) sellers in general or this seller in particular will not respond responsibly and ethically or whether the response is really another way of saying that a cost/benefit calculation reveals that the complaint effort isn't worth it.

Making a heroic assumption that either misperception of the seller's likely favorable reaction or a feeling of intimidation about sellers in general or this seller represents 20 percent of the cases where dissatisfied consumers say they "didn't think it was worth it," then we can conclude that a further 20 percent of service problems and 16 percent of goods problems are not adequately redressed. Accepting all of these assumptions and adding cases where a voiced complaint was improperly deflected yields an estimate of perhaps 30

---

[13]It is recognized that there may still be questions of warranty coverage or contributory negligence on the part of the consumer and/or the consumer's household.

[14]40 percent dissatisfaction with the 40 per cent of problems that were voiced.

to 35 percent of all cases of dissatisfaction where the individual redress system breaks down.

Two points need to be made here. First, as noted throughout this study, we have taken dissatisfaction as a given. But as Olander articulately points out, consumers may underperceive dissatisfaction [69]. That is, it may be that consumers in general are not critical enough to see the "real" problems that are out there. For instance, this may explain why disadvantaged consumers seem to perceive fewer problems despite the view of many outsiders that they "ought" to see more. Society and even manufacturers might be better off, Olander implies, if we trained consumers to be fussier.

Second, the fact that a consumer with a legitimate complaint does not obtain direct redress from the manufacturer does not mean that he or she is totally unhappy with the outcome. The discussion above has assumed a process driven by logic and objective cost/benefit analysis. But as Richins and others point out, consumers act and do not act often for emotional reasons. Thus, many consumers -- if asked -- may state that they are not totally unhappy with the way things turned out because they (a) were satisfied just to speak up and be a responsible consumer-citizen; (b) were satisfied to have caused the seller a lot of bother in dealing with the complaint process; or (c) believed the seller would suffer from lost patronage from the potential complainant and/or others to whom the dissatisfaction was communicated.

Finally, the assembled evidence seems to suggest that, whatever the degree of residual legitimate dissatisfaction, it is not uniformly distributed. There are clearly inequities. The poor and uneducated are less often helped by the redress system and many argue this applies to the elderly and racial minorities as well. Further one can argue that certain problems (e.g., stale food, clerical errors or misfitting goods) are a greater burden on the disadvantaged and so, even if their problems with redress were equal to the nondisadvantaged, special attention to them is clearly merited.

2. System Policing

Albert O. Hirschman, in a major theoretical contribution to this area [48], has pointed out that markets are policed by consumers in two major ways, exit and voice. Traditional economists from Adam Smith onward have emphasized the exit option -- the "invisible hand" -- as the basic instrument that makes markets efficient. Exit behavior is supposed to police errant practices and drive evil or high cost producers out of business. But, as Hirschman points out, there are many situations in which such a regulatory mechanism will break down. In purchase categories with long repurchase cycles, consumers may have a long time to wait before they can effect their policing action. In some markets, few alternatives may exist for action or there may be no better alternatives. Finally, even in markets with many exit options and short repurchase cycles, the dissatisfaction of exiting consumers may be imperceptible to marketers because the influx of new customers or random switchers from competitors effectively masks a loud exit signal.

Voicing may also not work if consumers who "ought" to voice do not, either for personal reasons (e.g., fear or ignorance) or institutional reasons (e.g., sellers' inaccessibility or inhospitality). Voicing also is ineffective if sellers do not respond satisfactorily to legitimate complaints.

Andreasen and Manning [3] have proposed an approach to monitoring markets based on the types of data that can be gathered in consumer surveys like those reported here. They suggest that, once norms have been established, regulators or other interested parties may partition markets along three dimensions as to whether they score high or low in (a) problem perception; (b) voicing and (c) satisfactory complaint handling. Markets may then be categorized into one of eight cells ranging from the ideal where problem perception is low, and voicing and satisfactory complaint handling rates are high to the worst case where the problem rate is high and voicing and complaint handling satisfaction are low.

An allocation of selected cases reported in Table 1 above to these eight categories is offered in Table 5 below. It should be noted that the recommendations in the last column do not argue for regulatory intervention in all but the ideal case. For example, in Case I, although problem rates are high, it is recommended that regulators resist intervention because the industry seems to be effective in handling its own problems. Further, the recommended interventions vary depending on whether market imperfections seem to be more attributable to voicing or complaint-handling problems. It does seem clear, however, that there are potential needs for:

a. Continuing monitoring of complaint performance along these three dimensions over time to maintain a pulse on industry performance (a suggestion originally made by Professor E. Scott Maynes);

b. The creation of national third-party complaint handling institutions to supplement or replace local or state agencies for those industries where self-regulation appears not be be working.

Consumer Researchers

We have learned a number of lessons over the last ten years about how to do consumer complaint research and have refined our understanding of what it is we do not know. Briefly, what we know is the following:

1. Studies cannot be compared if they use different concepts of "consumer dissatisfaction" (e.g., defining it as problems, high dissatisfaction, any dissatisfaction, worst recent experience and so on) since this definition will determine both the frequency and nature of the complaining process that will be "discovered."

2. Studies cannot be compared across stages of the complaint process. Carrying a verbal complaint to a seller is one thing; carrying it beyond to letter writing, third party intervention or legal action narrows the type of people involved and, presumably, changes the processes that drive these higher level actions.

Table 5

A Taxonomy of Market Problem Response With Recommended Agency Intervention[a]

Case	Problem Rate	Voicing Rate	Satisfaction Rate	Purchase Example	Recommended Agency Action
I	High	High	High	Mail order, Washer/drier	Resist pressure to act: Market works
II	High	Low	High	Toys	Encourage voicing
III	High	Low	Low	Car parking	Reduce problems, encourage voicing, improve complaint handling
IV	High	High	Low	Appliance	Reduce problems; improve complaint handling
V	Low	High	High	Books, records	No action, ideal case
VI	Low	Low	High	Blankets Cosmetics	No action, problems minor, industry responsive
VII	Low	Low	Low	Medical/Dent.	If important, encourage voicing, improve complaint handling
VIII	Low	High	Low	None	Probably important, improve complaint handling

[a]Source: [3].

3. Controls for purchase frequency must be included or else one will falsely conclude that variables such as sex, age and income are determinant where they are really only surrogates for the opportunity to experience problems.

4. Studies across markedly different cultures are probably risky, given how little we understand cross-cultural differences.

5. A wide array of factors have been shown to predict complaining behavior. As noted in the introduction, these can be grouped under four models that may best characterize a given post-dissatisfaction process:

    a. The Cost/Benefit Model. This model assumes that each problem occasion is unique and that dissatisfied consumers more or less objectively evaluate the extent of present dissatisfaction, the costs and benefits of complaining and the probability of success and decide to act or not on the basis of this analysis.

    b. The Personality Model. This model assumes that, while consumers may objectively calculate what the costs and benefits might be, they are mainly driven to or restrained from action because of the kinds of people they are. They complain because they are assertive, they attribute blame to others, they have self-confidence about their own position, they support this kind of social/consumerist intervention in other domains and/or they have few fears that complaining will lead to "hassles" or will stigmatize them as "cranks."

    c. The Learning Model. This model has not been made explicit by researchers to date. It says that, like other consumer behaviors, complaining is a learned response to dissatisfaction. Whatever it is that drove the first complaint --cost/benefit calculations or personality -- subsequent attempts at complaining when dissatisfaction again occurs will be largely determined by how successful the first outcome was.

    d. The Restraints Model. This model suggests that the rate and type of complaining is driven not by what consumers wish to do but by what they are able to do. That is, consumers who are motivated to

> complain by cost/benefit calculations, personality or learning, do not do so because they either lack the personal health, income or information to carry out their complaint urge in <u>this</u> case or that they are effectively diverted or discouraged by the seller from doing so.

Despite the years of work in this area, we also have major gaps in our knowledge base. Major issues that ought to be addressed in future research include the following:

1. Studies to date have tended to focus on finding <u>single models</u> that best explain a given set of complaining behaviors. Yet the consumer behavior research literature makes it clear that almost always markets are segmentable. Since we have a considerable array of data supporting each of the models outlined above and experience at measuring most of the key variables, it is time to turn our attention to discovering under what circumstances <u>and for which consumer segments</u> each model applies.

2. We have also ignored the findings in the traditional consumer behavior literature that <u>others</u> have an important effect on what consumers do. These "significant others" (e.g., family members, co-workers, friends and so on) may be important sources of information, motivation or inhibition.

3. The learning model, as noted, has not been the focus of research despite its track record in the convenience goods area. Clearly, more attention needs to be paid to past successes and failures in complaining on future complaint actions.

4. Since the restraints model highlights the potential role of external inhibitors, more research would seem desirable on how consumers estimate the probability of complaint success.

5. The recent trend toward more sophisticated multivariate models should be continued given the complexity of the processes uncovered here.

6. Blame is a concept that should be important in complaint research, yet it has been rarely introduced in complex models. It may be useful to utilize the more recent

research on consumer information processing in this regard. For example, it may be hypothesized that consumers may blame themselves if, in some sense, they have undergone incomplete information processing prior to acquisition.

7. The models reported in this review were much less successful in accounting for complaining behavior with respect to services. It is hypothesized that this may be due to a lack of clarity as to appropriate complaint channels. It is apparently also due to consumer judgments that little may be accomplished by complaining. Clearly, the domain of services is one in which more work is needed. In addition to studying services more intently, it would make our findings more generic if we also focused some attention on nonmarket exchanges to which marketing concepts have been applied -- such as charitable giving or blood donations.

8. Models in this area and the research supporting them would be made more realistic if they accommodated the possibility suggested in this review that many of the phenomena being studied are multidimensional, not unidimensional. Thus, satisfaction may be better conceived as satisfaction on several dimensions, some of which may give rise to complaining, others of which may argue against it. (For early work in this direction, see [47, 73].) Similarly, as Day and his colleagues have shown, complaint actions are clearly part of a _set_ of responses to dissatisfaction. And finally, as suggested here, satisfaction with complaint handling may have several components, some of which the consumer likes, some of which he or she doesn't.

9. Exit behavior in most studies is treated as affectless in that the purpose of it is rarely explored. Thus, one does not know whether a given intention to switch products, brands or outlets is designed to be punitive or self-protective. Our abilities to predict such behavior should improve materially if this distinction were monitored in future. More generally, empirical tests of available models would be enhanced if we studied more often consumers' _motivations_ when they undertake complaining behavior. It seems reasonable to expect that the personality dimensions used with less than satisfying results in the past would prove more potent in future if the voicing

process were studied in terms of what the behaviors and outcomes mean to the actors in terms of their own goals.

10. Finally, in future studies, we must place more emphasis on normative issues at the micro level. Consumer complaint behavior is supposed to benefit individuals as well as society. Yet at the individual level, we tend to observe and explain what happens rather than focusing on what can make it better. Thus, we do not yet have a tradition of studies directed at answering the question: How can consumers be successful at complaining? A modest beginning in this direction could go far in meeting our challenge to help achieve the consumer rights the International Organization of Consumers Unions has said we are all entitled to.

REFERENCES

1. ANDREASEN, ALAN R. (1976), The Disadvantaged Consumer, Glencoe, IL: The Free Press.

2. _________ (1985), "Consumer Response to Dissatisfaction in Loose Monopolies: The Case of Medical Care," Journal of Consumer Research,12,2, pp. 135-141.

3. _________ and JEAN MANNING (1980), "Information Needs for Consumer Protection Planning," Journal of Consumer Policy, Vol. 4, No. 2, pp.115-126.

4. _________ and ARTHUR BEST (1977), "Consumers Complain--Does Business Respond?" Harvard Business Review, Vol. 55, pp. 93-101.

5. _________ (1977), "A Taxonomy of Consumer Satisfaction/Dissatisfaction Measures," Journal of Consumer Affairs, Vol. 11, pp. 11-23.

6. ASH, STEPHEN B. and JOHN A. QUELCH. (1980), "Consumer Satisfaction, Dissatisfaction and Complaining Behavior: A Comprehensive Study of Rentals, Public Transportation and Utilities," in Refining Concepts and Measures of Consumer Satisfaction and Complaining Behavior, eds. H. Keith Hunt and Ralph L. Day, Bloomington, Indiana: Bureau of Business Research, pp. 120-130.

7. BAGOZZI, RICHARD P. (1981), "Attitudes, Intentions and Behavior: A Test of Some Key Hypotheses," Journal of Personality and Social Psychology, pp. 607-627.

8. BEARDEN, WILLIAM O. and JESSE E. TEEL (1983), "Selected Determinants of Consumer Satisfaction and Complaint Reports," Journal of Marketing Research, Vol. 20, pp. 21-28.

9. _________ and RICHARD OLIVER (1985), "The Role of Public and Private Complaining in Satisfaction and Problem Resolution," Journal of Consumer Affairs, Vol. 19, pp. 222-240.

10. _________ (1983), "Profiling Consumers Who Register Complaints Against Service Repair Services," Journal of Consumer Affairs, Vol. 17, pp. 315-335.

11. _________, JESSE E. TEEL and MELISSA CROCKETT (1980), "A Path Model of Consumer Complaint Behavior," Marketing in the 80's, ed. Richard P. Bagozzi, Chicago: American Marketing Association

12. _________ and J. BARRY MASON (1983), "Empirical Evidence on the Market Alienation Scale," Journal of Marketing Management, pp. 6-20.

13. BERNHARDT, KENNETH L. (1981) "Consumer Problems and Complaint Actions of Older Americans: A National View," Journal of Retailing, Vol. 57, pp. 107-118.

14. BEST, ARTHUR (1981), When Consumers Complain, (New York: Columbia University Press).

15. _________ and ALAN R. ANDREASEN (1977), "Consumer Response to Unsatisfactory Purchases: A Survey of Perceiving Defects, Voicing Complaints, and Obtaining Redress," Law & Society Review, Vol. 11, No.4, pp. 701-742.

16. BODUR, MUZAFFER, ESER BORAK and KEMAL KURTULUS (1982), "A Comparative Study of Satisfaction/Dissatisfaction and Complaining Behavior with Consumer Services: Bloomington and Istanbul," in New Findings on Consumer Satisfaction and Complaining Behavior, Ralph L. Day and H. Keith Hunt, eds. Bloomington, IN.: Department of Marketing, Indiana University, pp. 73-79.

17. BOSCHUNG, MILLA (1976), "Manufacturers' Response to Consumer Complaints on Guaranteed Products," Journal of Consumer Affairs, 10, pp. 86-90.

18. BOURGEOIS, J. C. and JAMES G. BARNES (1979), "Viability and Profile of the Consumerist Segment," Journal of Consumer Research, Vol. 5, pp. 217-228.

19. CAPLOVITZ, DAVID (1963), The Poor Pay More, Glencoe, IL.: The Free Press.

20. DAY, RALPH L. (1980), "Research Perspectives on Consumer Complaining Behavior," in Theoretical Developments in Marketing, eds. C. W. Lamb and P. M. Dunne, Chicago: American Marketing Association, pp. 211-215.

21. _________ (1984), "Modeling Choices Among Alternative Responses to Dissatisfaction," in Advances in Consumer Research, Vol. XI, ed. Thomas Kinnear, Provo, Utah: Association for Consumer Research, pp. 496-499.

22. _________ (1983), "The Next Step: Commonly Accepted Constructs for Satisfaction Research," in International Fare in Consumer Satisfaction and Complaining Behavior, eds. Ralph L. Day and H. Keith Hunt, Bloomington, IN: Bureau of Business Research, Indiana University, pp.113-117.

23. _________ and STEPHEN B. ASH (1979), "Comparison of Patterns of Satisfaction/Dissatisfaction and Complaining Behavior for Durables, Nondurables, and Services," in New Dimensions of Consumer Satisfaction and Complaining Behavior, eds. Ralph L. Day and H. Keith Hunt, Division of Business Research, Indiana University, pp. 190-195.

24. _________ and M. BODUR (1978), "Consumer Response to Dissatisfaction with Services and Intangibles," in Advances in Consumer Research, Vol. V, ed. H. Keith Hunt, Chicago: Association for Consumer Research, pp. 263-272.

25. _________, KLAUS GRABICKE, THOMAS SCHAETZLE and FRITZ STAUBACH (1981), "The Hidden Agenda of Consumer Complaining," Journal of Retailing, Vol. 57, pp. 87-106.

26. DIDOW, NICHOLAS and HIRAM C. BARKSDALE, JR. (1982), "Conjoint Measurement Experiment of Consumer Complaining Behavior," Journal of Business Research, 10, pp. 419-429.

27. DUHAIME, CAROL and STEPHEN B. ASH (1980), "Satisfaction, and Complaining Behavior: A Comparison of Male and Female Consumers," in Refining Concepts and Measures of Consumer Satisfaction and Complaining Behavior, eds. H. Keith Hunt and Ralph L. Day, Bloomington, IN: Bureau of Business Research, pp. 102-111.

28. ENGEL, JAMES and ROGER BLACKWELL (1984), Consumer Behavior (4th ed.), New York: The Dryden Press.

29. FISHBEIN, MARTIN and ISAAC AJZEN (1975), Belief, Attitude, Intention and Behavior: An Introduction to Theory and Research, Reading, MA.: Addison-Wesley.

30. FOLKES, VALERIE (1984), "An Attributional Approach to Post-Purchase Conflict Between Buyers and Sellers," in Advances in Consumer Research, Vol. XI, ed. Thomas Kinnear, Provo, Utah: Association for Consumer Research, pp. 500-503.

31. FORNELL, CLAES (1978), "Corporate Consumer Affairs Departments: A Communications Perspective," Journal of Consumer Policy, vol.2, No.4, pp. 289-302.

32. _________ and ROBERT A. WESTBROOK (1981), "The Relationship Between Consumer Complaint Magnitude and Organizational Status of Complaint Processing in Large Organizations," in New Dimensions of Consumer Satisfaction and Complaining Behavior, eds. Ralph L. Day and H.Keith Hunt, Bloomington, IN: Bureau of Business Research, pp. 95-98.

33. _________ (1979), "An Exploratory Study of Assertiveness, Aggressiveness, and Consumer Complaining Behavior," in Advances in Consumer Research, Vol. VI, ed. William L. Wilkie, Chicago: Association for Consumer Research, pp. 105-110.

34. _________ and NICHOLAS M. DIDOW (1979), "Economic Constraints on Consumer Complaining Behavior," Advances in Consumer Research, Vol. VI, ed. William L. Wilkie, Ann Arbor: Association for Consumer Research, pp. 105-110.

35. FRANCKEN, DICK A. (1983) "Post-Purchase Consumer Evaluations, Complaint Actions, and Repurchase Behavior," Journal of Economic Psychology, Vol. 3, pp. 273-290.

36. GILLY, MARY C. (1981), "Complaining Consumers: Their Satisfaction with Organizational Response," in New Dimensions of Consumer Satisfaction and Complaining Behavior, eds. Ralph L. Day and H. Keith Hunt, Bloomington, IN: Bureau of Business Research, Indiana University, pp. 99-102.

37. _________ and BETSY GELB (1982), "Post-Purchase Consumer Processes and the Complaining Consumer," Journal of Consumer Research, Vol. 9, pp. 323-328.

38. _________ (1980), "Complaining Consumers and the Concept of Expectations," in Refining Concepts and Measures of Consumer Satisfaction and Complaining Behavior, eds. H. Keith Hunt and Ralph L. Day, Bloomington, IN: Bureau of Business Research, Indiana University, pp. 44-49.

39. GRØNHAUG, KJELL (1977), "Exploring Complaining Behavior: A Model and Some Empirical Results," in Advances in Consumer Research, vol. 4, ed. William Perrault, Atlanta: Association for Consumer Research, pp. 159-165.

40. _________ and GERALD D. ZALTMAN (1981), "Complainers and Noncomplainers Revisited: Another Look at the Data," in Advances in Consumer Research, Vol. VIII, ed. Kent B. Monroe, Ann Arbor: Association for Consumer Research, pp. 83-88.

41. _________ and JOHAN ARNDT (1980), "Consumer Dissatisfaction and Complaining Behavior as Feedback: A Comparative Analysis of Public and Private Delivery Systems," in Advances in Consumer Research, Vol. 7, ed. Jerry C. Olson, San Francisco: Association for Consumer Research, pp. 263-272

42. _________ and JOHAN ARNDT (1980), "Consumer Dissatisfaction and Complaining Behavior: A Model and Some Empirical Results," in Advances in Consumer Research, Vol. VI ed. Jerry C. Olson, San Francisco: Association for Consumer Research), pp. 324-328

43. _________ and GERALD D. ZALTMAN (1981), "Complainers and Non-Complainers Revisited," Journal of Economic Psychology, Vol. 1, pp. 121-134.

44. GRABICKE, KLAUS, THOMAS SCHAETZLE and FRITZ STAUBACH (1982), "The Influence of Personality Factors on Complaining Behavior," in Conceptual and Empirical Contributions to Consumer Satisfaction and Complaining Behavior, eds. H. Keith Hunt and Ralph L. Day, Bloomington, IN: Bureau of Business Research, Indiana University, pp. 26-31.

45. GRAINER, MARC A.. KATHLEEN A. MCEVOY and DONALD W. KING (1979), "Consumer Problems and Complaints: A National View," in Advances in Consumer Research, Vol. VI ed. William L. Wilkie, Ann Arbor: Association for Consumer Research, pp. 494-499.

46. GRANBOIS, DONALD, JOHN O. SUMMERS and GARY L. FRAZIER (1977), "Correlates of Consumer Expectation and Complaining Behavior," in , Consumer Satisfaction, Dissatisfaction and Complaining Behavior, ed. Ralph L. Day, Bloomington, IN: Department of Marketing, Indiana University, pp. 18-25.

47. HANDY, CHARLES R. (1976), "Monitoring Consumer Satisfaction with Food Products," in Conceptualization and Measurement of Consumer Satisfaction and Dissatisfaction, ed. H. Keith Hunt, Cambridge, MA.: Marketing Science Institute, pp. 215-239.

48. HIRSCHMAN, ALBERT O. (1970), Exit, Voice and Loyalty: Responses to Decline in Firms, Organizations, and States, Cambridge: Harvard University Press.

49. HOWARD, JOHN and JAGDISH N. SHETH (1969), The Theory of Buyer Behavior, New York: John Wiley.

50. HUNT, H. KEITH (1983), "A CS/D & CB Bibiography --1984 Update," in Consumer Satisfaction, Dissatisfaction and Complaining Behavior, eds. H. Keith Hunt and Ralph L. Day, Bloomington, Indiana: Department of Marketing, Indiana University, pp. 105-106.

51. ________ (1983), "A CS/D & CB Bibiography -- 1982," in International Fare in Consumer Satisfaction and Complaining Behavior, eds. Ralph L. Day and H. Keith Hunt, Bloomington, IN: Bureau of Business Research, Indiana University, pp. 132-155.

52. JACOBY, JACOB and JAMES J. JACCARD (1981), "The Sources, Meaning, and Validity of Consumer Complaint Analysis," Journal of Retailing, Vol. 57, pp. 4-24.

53. KASPER, HANS (1984), "Consumer Complaints as an Input into Corporate Decision Marketing Processes," in Consumer Satisfaction, Dissatisfaction and Complaining Behavior, eds. H. Keith Hunt and Ralph L. Day, Bloomington, Indiana: Department of Marketing, Indiana University, pp. 86-93.

54. KELLY, J. PATRICK (1979), "Consumer Expectations of Complaint Handling by Manufacturers and Retailers of Clothing Products," in New Dimensions of Consumer Satisfaction and Complaining Behavior, eds. Ralph L. Day and H. Keith Hunt, Bloomington, IN: Bureau of Business Research, Indiana University, pp. 103-111.

55. KOESKE, RANDI D. and DAJINDRA SRIVASTAVA (1977), "The Sources and Handling of Consumer Complaints Among the Elderly," in Consumer Satisfaction, Dissatisfaction and Complaining Behavior, ed. Ralph L.Day, Bloomington, IN: Bureau of Research, University of Indiana, pp. 139-143.

56. KOTLER, PHILIP and ALAN R. ANDREASEN (1987), Strategic Marketing for Nonprofit Organizations (3rd Ed.), (Englewood Cliffs, N.J.: Prentice-Hall, Inc.)

57. KRAFT, F.B. (1977), "Characteristics of Consumers as Complainers and Complaint and Repatronage Behavior," in Consumer Satisfaction, Dissatisfaction and Complaining Behavior, ed. Ralph L. Day, Bloomington, IN: Bureau of Business Research, University of Indiana, pp. 79-84.

58. KRISHNAN, S. and VALERIE A. VALLE, (1979), "Dissatisfaction, Attributions and Consumer Complaint Behavior," in Advances in Consumer Research, Vol. VI, ed. William I. Wilkie, Provo, Utah: Association for Consumer Research, pp. 445-449.

59. _________ and MICHAEL K. MILLS (1981), "Dissatisfaction with Retail Stores and Repatronage Behavior," in New Dimensions of Consumer Satisfaction and Complaining Behavior, eds. Ralph L. Day and H. Keith Hunt, Bloomington, IN: Bureau of Business Research, Indiana University, pp. 124-128.

60. LANDON, E. LAIRD (1977), "A Model of Consumer Complaint Behavior" in Consumer Satisfaction, Dissatisfaction and Complaining Behavior, ed. Ralph L. Day, Bloomington, IN: Bureau of Business Research, pp. 31-35.

61. LEIGH, THOMAS W. and RALPH L. DAY (1981), "Satisfaction, Dissatisfaction and Complaint Behavior with Nondurable Products," in New Dimensions of Consumer Satisfaction and Complaining Behavior, eds. Ralph L. Day and H. Keith Hunt, Bloomington, IN: Bureau of Business Research, Indiana University, pp. 170-183.

62. LEVY, DANNA and CAROL SUPRENANT (1982), "A Comparison of Responses to Dissatisfaction with Products and Services," in Conceptual and Empirical Contributions to Consumer Satisfaction and Complaining Behavior, eds. H. Keith Hunt and Ralph L. Day, Bloomington, IN: Bureau of Business Research, pp. 43-49.

63. LEWIS, ROBERT C. (1983), "Consumers Complain -- What Happens When Business Responds?" in International Fare in Consumer Satisfaction and Complaining Behavior, eds. Ralph L. Day and H. Keith Hunt, Bloomington, IN: Bureau of Business Research, Indiana University, pp. 988-94

64. LIEFELD, JOHN P., H. C. EDGECOMBE and LINDA WOLF (1975), "Demographic Characteristics of Canadian Consumer Complainers," Journal of Consumer Affairs, Vol. 9, pp. 73-80.

65. MASON, JOSEPH BARRY and SAMUEL H. HIMES, JR. (1973) "An Explanatory Behavioral Profile of Consumer Action With Selected Household Appliances," Journal of Consumer Affairs, Vol. 7, pp. 121-127.

66. MEFFERT, HERBERT and MANFRED BRUHN (1983), "Complaining Behavior and Satisfaction of Consumers - Results from an Empirical Study in Germany," in International Fare in Consumer Satisfaction and Complaining Behavior eds. Ralph L. Day and H. Keith Hunt, Bloomington, IN: Bureau of Business Research, Indiana University, pp. 35-48.

67. NADER, LAURA (1980), No Access to Law, New York: Academic Press.

68. OFFICE OF FAIR TRADING (1986), Consumer Dissatisfaction: A Report on Surveys Undertaken for the Office of Fair Trading, London: Office of Fair Trading.

69. OLANDER, FOLKE (1977), "Consumer Satisfaction -- A Skeptic's View," in Conceptualization and Measurement of Consumer Satisfaction and Dissatisfaction, ed. H. Keith Hunt, Cambridge, MA.: Marketing Science Institute, pp. 409-452.

70. _________ (1980), "Recent Developments in European Consumer Policy Research," in Advances in Consumer Research, Vol. VII, ed. Jerry C. Olson, Provo, Utah: Association for Consumer Research, pp. 56-65.

71. OSTER, SHARON (1980), "The Determinants of Consumer Complaints," The Review of Economics and Statistics, pp. 603-609.

72. PEARSON, MICHAEL M. (1976), "A Note on Business Responses to Consumer Letters of Praise and Complaint," Journal of Business Research, pp. 61-68.

73. PFAFF, MARTIN (1977), "The Index of Consumer Satisfaction: Measurement Problems and Opportunities," in Conceptualization and Measurement of Consumer Satisfaction and Dissatisfaction, ed. H. Keith Hunt, Cambridge, MA.: Marketing Science Institute, pp. 36-72.

74. RAO, SUSHILA (1982), "Dissatisfied Computer Users -- What Do They Do?" in Conceptual and Empirical Contributions to Consumer Satisfaction and Complaining Behavior, eds. H. Keith Hunt and Ralph L. Day, Bloomington, IN: Bureau of Business Research, Indiana University, pp. 37-42.

75. RESNICK, ALAN J. and ROBERT R. HARMON (1983), "Consumer Complaints and Managerial Response: A Holistic Approach," Journal of Marketing, Vol. 47, pp. 86-97.

76. _________, BRIAN GNAUK and RODNEY ALDRICH (1977), "Corporate Responsiveness to Consumer Complaints," in Consumer Satisfaction, Dissatisfaction, and Complaining Behavior, ed. Ralph L. Day, Bloomington, Indiana: Bureau of Business Research, pp. 148-152.

77. RICHINS, MARSHA L. (1981), "An Investigation of Consumer's Attitudes Towards Complaining,"in Advances in Consumer Research, Vol. IX, ed. Andrew Mitchell, St. Louis: Association for Consumer Research, pp. 502-506.

78. _________ (1980), "Consumer Perspectives of Costs and Benefits Associated with Complaining," in Refining Concepts and Measures of Consumer Satisfaction and Complaining Behavior, eds. H. Keith Hunt and Ralph L. Day, Bloomington, IN: Bureau of Business Research, pp. 50-53.

79. _________ (1983), "Word-of-Mouth as an Expression of Product Dissatisfaction," in International Fare in Consumer Satisfaction and Complaining Behavior, eds. Ralph L. Day and H. Keith Hunt, Bloomington, IN: Bureau of Business Research, Indiana University, pp. 100-104.

80. _________ (1983), "An Analysis of Consumer Interaction Styles in the Marketplace," Journal of Consumer Research, pp. 73-82.

81. _________ (1983), "Negative Word-of-Mouth by Dissatisfied Consumers: A Pilot Study," Journal of Marketing, Vol. 47, pp. 68-78.

82. _________ (1985), "The Role of Product Importance in Complaint Initiation," in Consumer Satisfaction, Dissatisfaction and Complaining Behavior, eds. H. Keith Hunt and Ralph L. Day, Bloomington, IN: Department of Marketing, Indiana University, pp. 50-53.

83. ROBINSON, LARRY M. (1981), "Consumer Complaint Behavior,: A Review with Implications for Further Research," in New Dimensions of Consumer Satisfaction and Complaining Behavior, eds. Ralph L. Day and H. Keith Hunt, Bloomington, IN: Bureau of Business Research, Indiana University, pp. 41-50.

84. _________, GEORGE G. TREBBI and ROY D. ADLER (1983), "Taking it to the Top: A Profile of Customers Who Complain to the CEO," in International Fare in Consumer Satisfaction and Complaining Behavior, eds. Ralph L. Day and H. Keith Hunt, Bloomington, IN: Bureau of Business Research, Indiana University, pp. 95-99.

85. _________ and ROBERT L. BERL (1979), "What About Compliments: A Follow-up Study on Consumer Complaints and Compliments," in Refining Concepts and Measures of Consumer Satisfaction and Complaining Behavior, eds. H. Keith Hunt and Ralph L. Day, Bloomington, IN: Bureau of Business Research, pp. 144-148.

86. _________, HUMBERTO VALENCIA and ROBERT L. BERL (1982), "Profiling Third Party Complaints and Complainers: A Comparison of Two Nationally Projectible Studies," in New Findings on Consumer Satisfactionand Complaining Behavior, eds. Ralph L. Day and H. Keith Hunt, Bloomington, IN: Department of Marketing, Indiana University, pp. 55-62.

87. ROSS, IVAN (1985), "Consumer Initiated Information Audit," in Consumer Satisfaction, Dissatisfaction and Complaining Behavior, eds. H. Keith Hunt and Ralph L. Day, Bloomington, IN: Department of Marketing, pp. 73-81.

88. _________ and RICHARD D. OLIVER (1984), "The Accuracy of Unsolicited Consumer Communmications as Indicators of 'True' Consumer Satisfaction/ Dissatisfaction," in Advances in Consumer Research, Vol. XI, ed. Thomas Kinnear, Ann Arbor: Association for Consumer Research, pp. 504-508.

89. SCHRAG, PHILIP G. (1972), Counsel for the Deceived, New York: Pantheon.

90. SINGH, JAGDIP and ROY D. HOWELL (1985), "Consumer Complaining Behavior: A Review and Prospectus," in Consumer Satisfaction, Dissatisfaction and Complaining Behavior, eds. H. Keith Hunt and Ralph L. Day, Bloomington, IN: Department of Marketing, Indiana University, pp. 41-49.

91. SMITH, DAVID HORTON (1980), Participation in Social and Political Activities, San Francisco: Jossey-Bass.

92. STEELE, ERIC H. (1975), "Fraud, Dispute, and the Consumer: Responding to Consumer Complaints," University of Pennsylvania Law Review,pp. 1107-1184.

93. STRAHLE, WILLIAM and RALPH L. DAY (1985), "Roles, Lifestyles, Store Types and Complaining Behaviors," in Consumer Satisfaction, Dissatisfaction and Complaining Behavior, eds. H. Keith Hunt and Ralph L. Day, Bloomington, IN: Department of Marketing, pp. 59-66.

94. SWAN, JOHN E. (1983), "Consumer Satisfaction Research and Theory: Current Status and Future Directions," in International Fare in Consumer Satisfaction and Complaining Behavior, eds. Ralph L. Day and H. Keith Hunt, Bloomington, IN: Bureau of Business Research, Indiana University, pp. 124-129.

95. TECHNICAL ASSISTANCE RESEARCH PROGRAM, INC. (TARP) (1979), Consumer Complaint Handling in America: Summary of Findings and Recommendations, Washington, D.C.: TARP.

96. THORELLI, HANS B. and GERALD D. SENTELL (1982), Consumer Emanicipation and Economic Development: The Case of Thailand, Greenwich, Conn.: JAI Press.

97. _________ (1983), "China: Consumer Voice and Exit," in International Fare in Consumer Satisfaction and Complaining Behavior, eds. Ralph L. Day and H. Keith Hunt, Bloomington, IN: Bureau of Business Research, Indiana University, pp.105-111.

98. _________ and YASH R. PURI (1977), "On Complaining in Norway and the Role of The Information Seekers," in Consumer Satisfaction, Dissatisfaction and Complaining Behavior, ed. Ralph L. Day, Bloomington, IN.: Department of Marketing, Indiana University, pp. 130-137.

99. VILLAREAL-CAMACHO, ANGELINA (1983), "Consumer Complaining Behavior: A Cross-Cultural Comparison," 1983 American Marketing Association Educators Conference Procedings, eds. Patrick E. Murphy, et al, pp. 68-73.

100. WALL, MARJORIE, LOIS E. DICKEY and W. WAYNE TALARZYK (1977), "Predicting and Profiling Consumer Satisfaction and Propensity to Complain," in Consumer Satisfaction, Dissatisfaction and Complaining Behavior, ed. Ralph L. Day, Bloomington, IN: Bureau of Business Research, University of Indiana, pp. 91-101.

101. WARLAND, REX H., ROBERT O. HERMANN and JANE WILLITTS (1975), "Dissatisfied Consumers: Who Gets Upset and Who Takes Action," Journal of Consumer Affairs, Vol. 6, pp. 148-163.

102. _________ (1977) "A Typology of Consumer Complainers," in Consumer Satisfaction, Dissatisfaction, and Complaining Behavior, ed. Ralph L. Day, Bloomington, IN: Bureau of Business Research, pp. 144-146.

103. _________, ROBERT O. HERMANN and DAN E. MOORE (1984), "Consumer Complaining and Community Involvement: An Exploration of Their Theoretical and Empirical Linkages," Journal of Consumer Affairs, Vol. 18, pp. 64-78.

104. WOODRUFF, ROBERT B., ERNEST R. CADOTTE and ROGER L. JENKINS (1983), "Charting a Path for CS/D Research," in International Fare in Consumer Satisfaction and Complaining Behavior, eds. Ralph L. Day and H. Keith Hunt, Bloomington, IN: Bureau of Business Research, Indiana University, pp. 118-123.

105. ZAICHKOWSKY, JUDITH and J. P. LIEFELD (1977), "Personality Profiles of Consumer Complaint Letter Writers'" in Consumer Satisfaction, Dissatisfaction, and Complaining Behavior, ed. Ralph L. Day, Bloomington, IN: Bureau of Business Research, pp. 124-129.

106. ZUSSMAN, D. (1983), "Consumer Complaint Behavior and Third Party Mediation," Canadian Public Policy, Vol. IX, No.2.

Chapter 29

ABOUT THE AUTHOR

W. Keith Bryant is Professor in the Department of Consumer Economics and Housing at Cornell University. After receiving his Ph.D. in Agricultural Economics at Michigan State University, Bryant was a member of the faculty in Agricultural Economics at the University of Minnesota from 1963 to 1974 before moving to Cornell. He had visiting appointments with the President's National Advisory Commission on Rural Poverty (1966-67), the University of Wisconsin (1970-71), and the University of Wageningen (1980-81). Widely published, Bryant has served on the Editorial Boards of the Journals of Consumer Affairs, Consumer Research, Consumer Studies and Home Economics and the American Journal of Agricultural Economics. He is President of the American Council on Consumer Interests.

CONSUMER COMPLAINTS AND REDRESS: SOME DIRECTIONS FOR FUTURE RESEARCH

W. Keith Bryant

Alan Andreasen has done us a great service in summarizing what we know about consumer complaints and redress. I much appreciate his careful winnowing of the glut of descriptive studies on consumer dissatisfaction and complaint behavior. I will spend my time and space dealing with explanatory models and the gaps in the literature. In doing so, I will emphasize four themes: (a) the need for multivariate analyses of dissatisfaction and complaint behavior; (b) the desirability of tests to reveal which explanatory models compete with or complement each other; (c) that manufacturer and seller behavior have as much to do with consumer dissatisfaction and complaining as consumer behavior; and, (d) that the law circumscribes and affects both consumer and seller behavior having to do with consumer dissatisfaction and consumers' responses to it.

MULTIVARIATE CAUSAL ANALYSES

Andreasen calls for more multivariate analysis of consumer dissatisfaction and complaint behavior. I agree completely. However, the program should not simply be to identify the net, or *ceteris paribus*, effects of each of a group of variables on complaint behavior. The multivariate research program should also deal with the determinants of consumer responses to dissatisfaction as a simultaneous system.

Consumers are satisfied or not with post-sale product performance. Responses to dissatisfaction include discarding the product, doing nothing, exiting, complaining to friends and neighbors, complaining to the firm, complaining to third party agents, and filing suit. Typically these responses have been analyzed separately. At most, the conditional nature of the responses have been dealt with by sample selection. This occurs when complaint behavior is analyzed conditional on dissatisfaction or when third party complaints have been analyzed conditional on first complaining to the firm. My own research in the area suffers from this myopia [2].

Andreasen has ably discussed the sample selection biases that result from the viewpoint of complaint managers. What remains unrecognized is the fact that the variety of responses to dissatisfaction are all part of the same system. It follows that better understanding of the phenomena will come only when the full system of endogenous and exogenous variables are modelled statistically and estimated simultaneously. In doing so, the sample selection biases commented on by Andreasen can be adjusted for statistically. Maddala's [5] new textbook on limited and qualitative dependent variables is the single most complete reference for such statistical models.

MODEL TESTING

Andreasen usefully groups the many explanations of consumer dissatisfaction and complaint behavior under four models: the cost/benefit model, the personality model, the learning model, and the restraints model. He then argues that we need to find out under what circumstances and for whom each of these models applies. Unfortunately, since most of the work has been univariate and only loosely tied to theory, it is not clear how many of the correlates of dissatisfaction and complaint behavior are causally related to the phenomena. Rather, in my view most of the factors evoked by these four models are simply competing explanations of the same variance.

Multivariate analysis will further confound the situation if it simply strings together the known factors in an almost unending equation to which step-wise regression is applied. What is needed is a complete model which encompasses Andreasen's four models along with other elements to be discussed below in an internally consistent manner. Constructing such a model is a necessary step in establishing what is complementary and what is competitive in the present array of explanations.

PRODUCER AND SELLER BEHAVIOR

Consumer dissatisfaction arises out of experience with post-sale product performance that is largely but not completely determined by firms. Whether and how consumers voice their dissatisfaction depends in part on the complaint systems established by firms. It is naive in the extreme, therefore, not to include manufacturer and retailer behavior in models that seek to explain consumer dissatisfaction and complaint behavior. Indeed, the very idea that complaining might be productive of nonfinancial redress rests on such an hypothesis. Research in the area must model and investigate empirically firm as well as consumer behavior if we are to be successful in understanding consumer dissatisfaction and complaints.

As a beginning some elements of firm behavior that need to be related to consumer dissatisfaction can be identified. First, the possibility of segmenting markets implies differing firm behavior with respect to each segment. Thus, we can expect segmentation along product performance lines as well as along other dimensions. Consumer dissatisfaction and complaint behavior, therefore, will also be segmented. Second, appliance firms and other manufacturers consciously manipulate product price, in-plant product testing, and warranty costs during product "burn-in" periods. Consumer dissatisfaction and complaint behavior will vary as firms manipulate these cost and return elements.

One might argue that such firm behavior is held constant by holding constant product type. But firm and retailer behavior create important differences within as well as between product categories. Furthermore, wherever product type has been dealt with in the literature to date, it has been justified on the basis of consumer, not supply-side behavior.

Some articles useful in modelling firm and consumer behavior simultaneously are Akerlof's market for "lemons" [1], Darby and Karni's piece on optimal fraud [4], and Courville and Hausman's work on warranties [3]. Akerlof concentrates on the effects of instances of poor quality on the prices of good quality items and on the existence and competitiveness of markets where poor quality exists. Darby and Karni develop a supply-side explanation as to why certain markets are ripe for consumer exploitation. Courville and Hausman concentrate on the relationship between warranties and product reliability. Each of the models developed in these articles is capable of being re-worked to reveal their implications with respect to dissatisfaction and complaint behavior.

So long as consumer dissatisfaction and complaining are regarded solely as consumer related, it is difficult to move policy beyond questions of equity. When the firm's role in consumer dissatisfaction and complaining is developed, questions of efficiency can be more effectively addressed.

LEGAL IMPLICATIONS

The law affects consumer dissatisfaction and complaints through both consumer and firm behavior. Poor product performance is covered under warranty law and, in extremes, under products liability. Whether consumers are dissatisfied and how they respond depend partly on their knowledge of the law. Since both warranty and products liability law differ widely from state to state, dissatisfaction and responses to it can also be expected to vary systematically from state to state.

The legal environment undoubtedly affects firm more than consumer behavior. Products liability law requires firms to maintain large legal departments or legal firms on a retainer basis, turning much legal advice into fixed costs. Consequently, firms' legal departments have become more involved not only with product liability cases but with cases of consumer dissatisfaction as well. The legalities, therefore, are emphasized, the redress process becomes more adversarial, and the costs of various possible legal procedures and outcomes are factored into firms' responses. From both explanatory and policy perspectives, therefore, much more work needs to be done on how the law impacts consumer dissatisfaction and redress.

REFERENCES

1. AKERLOF, G. (1970) "The Market for 'Lemons': Quality Uncertainty and the Market Mechanism," Quarterly Journal of Economics, 84:488-500, August.

2. BRYANT, W. K., and GERNER, J. L. (1978), "The Recent Television Purchaser Survey: A Descriptive Analysis," Chapter 3 in Consumer Durables: Warranties, Service Contracts and Alternatives, Vol. III, Appliance Warranties and Service Contracts: Consumer Experience, CPA-78-14/Vol. III, Cambridge: Center For Policy Alternatives, M.I.T.

3. COURVILLE, L., and HAUSMAN, W. H. (1979), "Warranty Scope and Reliability under Imperfect Information and Alternative Market Structures," Journal of Business, 52(3):361-378.

4. DARBY, M. and KARNI, E. (1973), "Free Competition and the Optimal Amount of Fraud," Journal of Law and Economics, pp. 67-88, April.

5. MADDALA, G. S. (1983), Limited-Dependent and Qualitative Variables in Econometrics, Cambridge: Cambridge University Press.

ABOUT THE AUTHOR

Robert O. Herrmann is Professor in the Department of Agricultural Economics and Rural Sociology at Pennsylvania State University.

For biographical details, see About The Author in Chapter 21.

CONSUMER COMPLAINTS AND REDRESS--WHAT WE KNOW AND WHAT WE DON'T KNOW

Robert O. Herrmann

The tasks imposed on the authors in this volume are truly Herculean. Unfortunately for Andreasen, he was assigned to the Augean stables. Let there be no doubt: putting the Consumer Satisfaction/Dissatisfaction field (CS/D) in order is a demanding task. Wisely, Andreasen narrowed the scope of his review and succeeded in finding some pattern in the plethora.

In focussing on publicly voiced complaints, he has, however, put aside a number of interesting questions about private complaining, such as whether friends and acquaintances warn away some consumers from potential problems. Casual observation suggests that in some segments of society consumer experiences are a more acceptable and frequent topic of conversation than in others. Could it be, therefore, that the lower level of dissatisfaction observed in down-scale groups arises partly because they are better "avoiders?" Andreasen has also deliberately sidestepped the whole issue of complaints about price, suggesting that they are not "real" complaints. Such complaints certainly are in a different class from such "manifest" problems as breakage or non-delivery. But even if they are judgmental, price-quality complaints do seem to be legitimate, both as cause for dissatisfaction and as a subject of research.

Despite Andreasen's monumental efforts to put CS/D in order, it is disappointing how little can be said with certainly after 500 papers and nine annual conferences! The field is clearly complex. And the decision to complain is undoubtedly as complex as the original decision to purchase, involving many steps. Complexity aside, another factor contributing to CS/D's failure to produce clear-cut results may be its extraordinarily rapid growth and decline. Before the field peaked out, research approaches and methodology never really were codified, despite some significant contributions. Now a more orderly research approach seems possible, for those who are still interested. Despite the massive volume of research completed there still exist a number of significant unanswered questions.

MARKET STRUCTURE AND CS/D

In this era of deregulation it seems useful to ask whether market structure has any relationship to consumer satisfaction. Is satisfaction higher in competitive markets, as economists would insist, or not? Albert Hirschman's seminal work [6] on exit and voicing has evoked little interest among economists and tends to go unread by the CS/D researchers who tend not to be economists.[1] As a result, this question of market structure has been addressed to only a limited extent.

Andreasen's formulation in Table 5 seems to suggest that the problem rate, the voicing rate, and the ultimate satisfaction rate is higher in more competitive markets (e.g., blankets and sheets, cosmetics) than in loose monopolies (medical/dental services). Although it would be interesting to see the effects of different levels of competition on satisfaction, Andreasen has moved beyond this question, to the more important policy issue: "What needs to be done to make particular markets work better?"

THE GOALS OF CS/D

While CS/D researchers may have thought they were addressing questions of social import and consumer welfare, much of the work really has been driven by the concerns of marketers and their clients, individual sellers. For this reason, the salient questions behind much of the research work have been, "Are complainers and their complaints representative of the broader population of the dissatisfied?" "How seriously should we take them?" This is a <u>marketing policy</u> issue. It is <u>not</u> the way the question would be formulated by those concerned primarily with the consumer interest.

CS/D does, however, provide some insights for consumer policymakers. With Andreasen's help, we get partial answers at least to some questions:

- How many unresolved problems are there out there? Or, as Andreasen has usefully framed the question, "How much residual dissatisfaction is there?")

---

[1]Best and Andreasen's use of exit and voicing in their 1975 study is a welcome exception [4].

- What kinds of products seem to "produce" most problems and the most residual dissatisfaction?

- Does something need to be done about residual dissatisfaction for particular product categories?

There are a number of other things which policymakers might like to know, including relative levels of dissatisfaction with different types of problems. Are problems arising from the "side effects of drugs" more serious than auto safety recalls? Where does auto rust rank? If through regulation we wish to minimize consumer dissatisfaction, then we need to know more about the relative importance of problems. Although public opinion polls have told us how many people are "concerned" about particular problems, they have left us guessing about the depth of their concern.

While CS/D has helped consumer policymakers somewhat, it has provided little for consumer educators. It does provide insights into the question of what groups should be encouraged to complain and what kinds of problems consumers need to be encouraged to complain about. But, as Andreasen notes in closing, CS/D offers little which can tell consumers how to become more effective in complaining. The few insights available, although useful, make only the barest beginning in helping consumers to be more effective. For example:

-- Send a typewritten letter rather than using a pencil and lined paper [5];

-- Use good grammar in framing the complaint letter [5, 7];

-- If several problems are involved, concentrate on the "manifest" ones rather than the judgmental ones in order to justify repairs, replacements or refunds [3, p. 133].

Unfortunately, the question of how consumers can complain more effectively seems to be attacked most easily with an experimental approach. Experimentation upon uninformed complaint-handling departments involves some very real ethical questions and seems little more justifiable than experimentation on uninformed consumers.

Although some early work focussed on satisfaction and its dimensions, the main body of CS/D research has focussed on dissatisfaction. This emphasis seems one-sided. We could, perhaps, learn a good deal from studying the antecedents of satisfaction. Consumer educators would find it very useful to know what attitudes, knowledge and behaviors lead to satisfaction, and how these differ from those leading to dissatisfaction. Some consumers end up satisfied, despite purchases in categories where others frequently are dissatisfied and despite the fact that with experience they have developed high standards of performance. Can something useful be learned from these consumers? How did they succeed in achieving satisfaction where so many others failed?

REFERENCES

1. ANDREASEN, ALAN R. (1977), "A Taxonomy of Consumer Satisfaction/ Dissatisfaction Measures," Journal of Consumer Affairs, Vol. 11 (No. 2, Winter): 11-23.

2. ________ (1985), "Consumer Responses to Dissatisfaction in Loose Monopolies," Journal of Consumer Research, Vol. 12 (No. 2, September): 135-141.

3. BEST, ARTHUR (1981), When Consumers Complain, New York: Columbia University Press.

4. ________ (1976) and ALAN R. ANDREASEN, Talking Back to Business, Washington: Center for the Study of Responsive Law.

5. BOSCHUNG, MILLA (1976), "Manufacturer's Response to Consumer Complaints on Guaranteed Products," Journal of Consumer Affairs, Vol. 10 (No. 1, Summer): 86-90.

6. HIRSCHMAN, ALBERT O. (1970), Exit, Voice, and Loyalty, Cambridge, MA: Harvard University Press.

7. PEARSON, MICHAEL M. (1976), "A Note on Letters of Praise and Complaint," Journal of Business Research, Vol. 4 (No. 1): 61-68.

Chapter 30

ABOUT THE AUTHOR

H. Keith Hunt is Professor of Business Management at Brigham Young University and Executive Secretary of the Association for Consumer Research. Hunt received his Ph.D. in Marketing from Northwestern University in 1972. Before going to Brigham Young University in 1975, Hunt held appointments at the University of Iowa, the Federal Trade Commission, and the University of Wyoming. Hunt was Co-Founder, with Ralph L. Day, of the Annual Conferences on Consumer Satisfaction and Dissatisfaction. Hunt was President of the Association for Consumer Research in 1979 and is a member of the Editorial Boards of the Journal of Consumer Research, the Journal of Consumer Affairs, and the Journal of Public Policy and Marketing.

CONSUMER SATISFACTION/DISSATISFACTION AND THE CONSUMER INTEREST

H. Keith Hunt

ABSTRACT

Consumer satisfaction and dissatisfaction (CS/D) continues to be a high-interest, low-progress topic of research in the consumer interest. In this paper progress is assessed for each area in which CS/D is applied. Numerous problems with CS/D research are discussed, including the emotional component, the "right" to be satisfied, when the disadvantaged aren't dissatisfied, highly skewed distribution, imperfect perceptions, and intention to repurchase as a CS/D measure.

INTRODUCTION

During the past ten years the formal study of consumer satisfaction, consumer dissatisfaction, and consumer complaining behavior has developed phenomenally both in volume and in sophistication. I can remember quite clearly when there was very little published information on consumer satisfaction/dissatisfaction and complaining behavior. I can remember hustling the grant proposal for the first consumer satisfaction conference. It was necessary to explain what consumer satisfaction/dissatisfaction was and what its potential uses would be, when more fully developed. Today it is a rare marketing, consumer economics, or consumer research conference which does not have at least one paper, often a session, on consumer satisfaction/dissatisfaction and/or complaining behavior.

If, in 1973 when the Federal Trade Commission first expressed interest in consumer satisfaction/dissatisfaction, someone could have polled consumer researchers to ask them what they thought of consumer satisfaction as a topic for research and what progress might be made by 1987, I believe even the most optimistic prediction would have fallen far short of actual accomplishments. Up to 1972 there had been only 7 papers on the topic. In the 1982 CS/D & CB Bibilography [11] there were 560 consumer satisfaction/dissatisfaction and/or complaining behavior papers. Now there are nearly 700 papers on the topic! In terms of numbers, our most optimistic expectations have been wildly exceeded. So, as we rehearse the numerous problems and concerns faced by CS/D research, I ask you not to lose sight of the tremendous progress made thus far.

The first consumer satisfaction/dissatisfaction conference was held in 1976, sponsored by the Marketing Science Institute and funded by the National Science Foundation. It was while working on this conference that I tired of writing "consumer satisfaction and dissatisfaction" and shortened it to "CS/D" which becomes CS/D & CB when also discussing complaining behavior. Some claim (tongue in check I hope!), that this has been the major breakthrough in the topic so far. The following year, 1977, Ralph L. Day hosted a similar conference at Indiana University. Since then Day and I have co-hosted annual, lately irregularly spaced, conferences on CS/D & CB leading to published conference proceedings. In the early years these conference proceedings volumes were the primary literature base for CS/D & CB. Papers on these topics eventually began to be accepted into the journals, thus calling greater attention to the topic. Today the journals are totally open to good papers on both CS/D and CB. It is safe to say that CS/D and CB have become mature research topics.

Over time various interest groups have waxed hot and cold toward CS/D. The first interest came from the public policy domain, with the Federal Trade Commission's Office of Policy Planning and Evaluation getting credit for the initial impetus to the topic. The FTC's goal was to achieve an alternative and superior source of dissatisfaction data to the complaint data generated by the Better Business Bureau. Soon after, the Office of Consumer Affairs and the Consumer Product Safety Commission became interested. While two major U.S. studies and one Canadian study grew out of this early interest, there is no evidence that any consumer-related public policy is directly traceable to these studies. Consumer groups never have expressed much interest in CS/D. Academics, primarily from consumer research and marketing, became highly active in CS/D but now their interest seems to be waning. Today business is the group expressing the strongest interest in CS/D and CB research and ideas as individual firms seek to enhance their marketing position by carefully monitoring CS/D and CB.

CS/D has now achieved considerable recognition in texts on consumer behavior. For example, William L. Wilkie's recent consumer behavior text devotes an entire section, complete with references and supplementary material, to CS/D and CB.

CONSUMER/PUBLIC INTEREST APPLICATIONS OF CS/D

Over the past decade CS/D has been proposed for several uses: (1) as a social indicator, (2) in policy planning, (3) in specific regulatory matters, (4) in consumer legislation, (5) in support of consumerism, (6) in theories of consumer behavior, and (7) in marketing management. It is a source of satisfaction to note that these were the primary applications proposed in the initial grant request to the National Science Foundation. They have continued to receive intermittent attention since then. We will now consider what progress has been made for each of these uses over the past decade.

CS/D as a Social Indicator

One of the earliest proposed uses of CS/D was as a social indicator, to be used with other such indicators to assess the functioning over time of our economic and social systems. While consumer satisfaction was generally accepted as a basic value of our society, we had no objective measure for monitoring the level of consumer satisfaction over time. In the words of Charles R. Handy: "While we can measure the growth of our economy, efficiency of resource use, and product flows, we have virtually no information indicating the extent consumers feel the products and services available to them actually conform to their preferences and needs" [10]. While the CS/D social indicator would provide some information about the current level of satisfaction, its greatest contribution was expected to be as a longitudinal measure for noting changes in the general level of CS/D for society and for segments of society over time.

Ironically, despite the large amount of research on CS/D in the past decade, none of it dealt with CS/D as a social indicator. This potential application, which was so salient a decade ago, now elicits no serious interest either in its development or in its use. What happened? Perhaps it is a simple chicken-egg problem: since no one wants to use CS/D as a social indicator, there has been no incentive to develop the necessary methodology; since no methodology has been developed, no one thinks of it as a possible social indicator.

The development of CS/D as a social indicator poses quite different problems than its development for other uses. For "other" uses CS/D can largely be developed and tested on a small scale by an individual or a small group of individuals with minimal financial investment. The social indicator use, to be anything more than an intellectual exercise, requires a national effort with a representative sample. Otherwise it could not be compared to or combined with other social indicators already in use. Testing and perfecting CS/D as a social indicator requires substantial resources and a long testing period, both of which have not been available to the CS/D academic researchers of the last decade. The longitudinal or time series nature of the social indicator application does not match the limited time horizon of most academic researchers.

Finally, we must recognize the political reality that those with political power have exhibited little interest in measuring consumer satisfaction or dissatisfaction. It appears that, since consumer satisfaction is expected as a "right" of all consumers, a series of studies which confirm consumer satisfaction offers little political value to politicians. Conversely, the discovery that consumers are dissatisfied might bring great harm to the party in power. So there is no political advantage to finding satisfaction and there is great potential harm to finding dissatisfaction. Any political party would be foolish to put CS/D in place as a regularly monitored social indicator.

Thus, what was originally expected to be a significant and important use of CS/D has turned out to be a blind alley. This verdict is likely to hold for the forseeable future because all the reasons for its nonuse will continue.

CS/D as an Alternative to Complaints in Policy Planning and Evaluation

For several years in the early 1970's, many government agencies were complaint driven -- that is, they were moved to action primarily by large numbers of complaints, registered by consumers themselves or by their representatives. While complaint-driven action may be superior to no action, some leaders in these agencies, along with many consumer activists, recognized that there are substantial flaws in this mode of operation. One problem is that the number of complaints on a particular problem can be greatly increased through intelligent use of the mass media [8, 9]. On the other hand, consumers can remain blissfully unaware of genuine problems, thus not complaining about serious problems in design, health, and safety factors. Thus, complaint-driven consumer protection is, by itself, an inadequate mode of operation.

Much of our research in CS/D is traceable to 1973 when the Federal Trade Commission (FTC) targeted various areas of consumer abuse for attention. The targeting was based on Better Business Bureau complaint data, consisting of the number of complaints for each product/service category, supplemented by interpretive comments by FTC staff members. Although the FTC staff realized that the Better Business Bureau complaint data were imperfect, they were still the best data available at that time on consumer problems. As the FTC budget process neared completion, the staff decided to request a "National Study of Consumer Satisfaction." Its purpose would be to find out if the Better Business Bureau complaint data were truly representative of consumer dissatisfaction. Ralph L. Day, joined by E. Laird Landon, pursued this research agenda first at the Federal Trade Commission and later at the Office of Consumer Affairs with some support from the Consumer Product Safety Commission. Three major studies of consumer satisfaction/dissatisfaction grew out of this awareness of a need for something more than Better Business Bureau complaint data. The Bloomington, Indiana study, the TARP study, and the Consumer & Corporate Affairs Canada study were each undertaken to test a CS/D survey as a means of measuring the degree of consumer satisfaction or dissatisfaction over a wide array of product categories and services. Each study demonstrated a methodology that was workable.

Unfortunately, as is so often the case, the "good news" was also the "bad news". The "catch" in this case was that these surveys uncovered areas of substantial consumer dissatisfaction. Complaint driven data typically reveal a limited number of problem areas demanding immediate attention. What would happen if CS/D surveys "discovered" many complaint categories characterized by CS/D levels ranging from serious dissatisfaction to mild dissatisfaction? Would every possible consumer interest group use those CS/D levels to justify agency programs on its behalf? What was needed next was the identification of acceptable and unacceptable ranges of dissatisfaction, with each portion of the range identifying the relative seriousness of the problem. This was necessary to forestall indiscriminate arguments to the effect that any degree of dissatisfaction merits government efforts to eradicate it.

On the other hand, during periods of retrenchment in the consumer protection activities of government, the problem for policymakers is not one of new directions, but of an orderly retreat during which it is definitely undesirable to uncover new problems. The last thing an administration wants under these conditions is formal evidence of consumer discontent that might have to be explained to a negative Congress or an annoyed Executive. For the consumer protection agency it is a no-win situation. One solution is to show no interest in CS/D and instead to limit consumer protection activities to those initiated by the most vocal complainers. Summing up, during good times CS/D is a positive tool for identifying problems that need attention; during times of retrenchment CS/D research is risky and will be avoided.

CS/D in Specific Regulatory Matters

CS/D has the potential to help the regulatory process in two ways: (1) by comparing levels of dissatisfaction across products and services and (2) by over time determining whether the regulatory efforts expended on particular problems have decreased consumer dissatisfaction. We have no evidence that regulators have used CS/D in either of these ways.

CS/D and Consumer Legislation

Legislators have to make far-reaching decisions affecting consumer satisfaction with no objective measure of the seriousness of the problem they are dealing with other than consumer complaints and lobby/PAC pressures. Were CS/D to develop it would provide legislators with a comparison figure which would enable them to assess which problems are worth serious consideration and which are mere flashes in the system.

Also, legislators are responsible for overseeing the different consumer-impacting services regarding their activity in the consumer and public sector. The CS/D measure, when fully developed, will enable the legislators to assess whether the agency has been dealing with trivial or substantial issues and, maybe in the longer run, whether its actions have led to increased satisfaction.

CS/D in Consumerism Activities

Consumerism becomes an active force when consumer dissatisfaction reaches a sufficiently high level that some citizens are willing to expend considerable effort and resources to attempt to bring the consumer satisfaction level back to what they consider to be an acceptable level. Sometimes these efforts come from single individuals or small groups. Other times the efforts come from large consumer organizations. Both can be effective. But both are handicapped by the lack of CS/D data. Such data could constitute critical ammunition in consumerists' attempts to influence policy and legislation. Arguments based on high measured levels of dissatisfaction would have more substance than activists' anecdotal evidence or assertions that consumers are unhappy with things as they are. CS/D data could help consumer activists and consumer groups to focus their efforts on those consumers incurring the highest levels of dissatisfaction.

Despite the arguments just made, consumerists continue to be complaint-oriented and complaint-driven. And understandably so. Complaints show graphically that there are people out there who are dissatisfied and who want something done about it. And the complaints are actual stories, not abstract CS/D measures. It is easier to get oneself and others fired up about stories and complaints of how consumers have been harmed by some product or service than to get excited on the basis of a general CS/D measure. With complaints the consumerist does not need to defend his/her involvement because others are also hearing similar complaints. With CS/D it is necessary to explain and defend the methodology and the underlying ideas. Further, CS/D research is quite costly, usually being based on a representative sample of the total population whereas data on complaints are inexpensive: they come to you. Because many consumer activists and their organizations tend to be underfunded, the less expensive complaints are perhaps the only dissatisfaction indicators they can afford to use. Finally, in terms of publicity, complaints make good stories in the media. It is important that consumer activists keep their causes in the public view.

It is worth elaborating why complaints make for better stories than CS/D. The more concrete the issue and action, the more consumers and the general public can clearly comprehend them and recognize their relative importance. Together these make complaints more media-ingestible. If a problem is too complex or fuzzy, the media won't put forth enough effort to understand and simplify and report it. So complaints, being more simple and more inherently interesting, are much more useful and usable for consumer activists than is CS/D information. By the same token, complaints are more personal and more emotion evoking. Is there anyone who is not moved by the story of the mother whose child was killed because her car accelerated instead of braking? Is there much sympathy for the auto manufacturer who solemnly declares they can find nothing wrong with the automatic shift mechanism? To ask these questions is to answer them.

For all these reasons it is unlikely that consumerists are going to become seriously interested in CS/D as a substitute for complaints. Of course they will use CS/D information which suits their purposes. But they are unlikely to be initiators of CS/D research because complaints are less expensive to obtain, are more media-ingestible, and mobilize emotions more effectly than CS/D data.

CS/D and Theories of Consumer Behavior

Theories of consumer behavior implicitly or explicitly state that consumers consume because it is expected to be satisfying and consumers repurchase brands which they perceive to be more satisfying than competing brands. As the understanding of consumer behavior expands, we are recognizing that consumer satisfaction is only one of many reasons for purchasing and consuming. As more and more is learned about consumer satisfaction and consumer dissatisfaction, we will in turn understand more about how this purchase/consumption evaluation affects future purchases of specific items as well as the consumer's overall satisfaction with marketplace performance. It will also give us insight into the adequacy/inadequacy of the consumer as an effective purchasing agent for his/her and other's needs.

CS/D and Marketing Management

Business has been proclaiming the "marketing concept" as its ideology for a couple of decades, the essential message being that the function of business is to satisfy consumers, at a profit. Profit, both in conceptualization and measurement, is well developed. Only now is consumer satisfaction getting attention. Only as CS/D is developed and implemented for each firm can the firm ascertain how well it is adhering to the marketing concept.

Attention to CS/D issues should conserve freedom of action for firms. As Charles R. Handy put it, "...consumer satisfaction information could be of additional use to the private sector by the encouragement of voluntary action and self-regulation of business practices. Legislation and regulations, once enacted, tend to impose universal behavior and values on all. Voluntary action enables business firms to retain greater flexibility in responding to the many minority interests and market segments they seek to serve" [10]. CS/D has the potential to provide an early warning measure to business that all is not well and that corrective action is needed allowing business the option of voluntary action forestalling legislation and regulation.

CONSUMER INTEREST PROBLEMS WITH CS/D

Had most of the problems associated with CS/D been solved, this paper could have been much shorter. Unhappily, the opposite is more nearly true. Over the past ten years the rate of arrival of new problems has exceeded the rate of resolution of old ones. This may often be the case with developing bodies of knowledge.

There are numerous measurement problems in CS/D. This paper will deal with them only to the extent that they affect the broader questions regarding the broader consumer interest. This is not to say that measurement problems are not in the consumer interest, only that I have chosen to address the more general problems associated with CS/D research and the consumer interest.

Probing the Emotional Component of CS/D

Most CS/D researchers believe that, under any conceptualization, CS/D must represent a combination of cognitive and emotional elements. However, only recently has anyone begun to probe the emotional component. Until now, all the CS/D research has been focused exclusively on the cognitive component, especially on rating scales, factor structures and the like. Having finally turned our attention to emotion we are brought up short by how little we know about it. We are not unique. Researchers in other areas of consumer behavior have been coming to this same realization. Westbrook has been involved in almost all of the useful work on the emotional component of CS/D. Yet even he readily admits to our barely having scratched the surface, and, even at that, we are not sure we are scratching in the right spot. But, whatever the emotional component finally turns out to be, we are sure that whatever else CS/D is, it is in part an emotional phenomenon. Omit the emotional element from CS/D and it becomes sterile and uninteresting, bearing little similarity to what we observe in ourselves as we experience CS/D. CS/D requires some degree of getting stirred up, getting emotional. This, of course, is a very real threat to the simple expected-minus-actual definition of CS/D. So we are not just looking into some different perspective when we insert emotion into CS/D. We are changing its whole conceptualization and measurement, shifting its direction from the emphasis of the last ten years towards something unknown. When the mainline CS/D researchers become nervous about the emotional component, they have good reason. The exploration of the emotional component may overturn much of the past research in the field. Emotion is certainly the critical research area in CS/D for the immediate future.

It is clear that our initial thinking about emotion has not led us to any great breakthroughs. Our failure so far is attributable to the superficial approach taken to emotion. Westbrook, the leading worker in this domain, is the first to acknowledge our primitive level of understanding. So far, no one has been moved to undertake the detailed study of emotion to the relationship of CS/D, to see how the emotional and the cognitive work in tandem to explain CS/D as experienced by the individual consumer. To those wanting to pursue this avenue, I commend a reading of all Westbrook's papers, as well as discussions with him. This is a domain that merits a high priority.

Do Consumers Have a "Right" to be Satisfied?

Do consumers have the right to be satisfied? That all depends on what "satisfied" means. If we define satisfied as "actual" equals expected satisfaction, -- and if we remember that aspirations/expectations rise to higher levels as we attain the current level, then the right to be satisfied is the right to have ever increasing "actual" equal the ever increasing "expected"! Thus, the consumer has a right to more and more and more. Or, if declining expectations dominate, we become more easily satisfied. The plight of some poor and some elderly illustrate this. Some of them come to view conditions that once would have been intolerable to them as actually satisfying.

The same relationship is true of expectations for all the consumer rights. Any current assessment is influenced by expectations. As we get more and more consumer information, we anticipate even more information and are somewhat dissatisfied with our current level because we have learned to expect increasing levels of information. As we achieve more consumer choice, we expect still more consumer choice. Yet, with all of these dimensions of consumer satisfaction, we need to recognize that their achievement incurs social and money costs. In a welfare sense, there needs to be some tradeoff analysis done between the cost of continually attaining consumer satisfaction, sometimes at higher and higher levels and costs, and the individual and social benefit of those higher levels of satisfaction. While one or another consumer right might be better achieved by a policy or development, we must take account of both costs and satisfactions in judging whether a policy or development really improves consumer welfare.

Further, we have the socio-philosophical question of whether it is ethically appropriate to continue the quest for elusive consumer satisfaction in our country when some consumers in other parts of the world are attaining a most meager existence at best. CS/D measures implicitly assume that the overall good is maximized as individuals seek their own satisfaction. And in theory I accept that premise. But the absolute inequity involved in measuring consumer satisfaction with food in the United States and consumer satisfaction with food in starving Africa should make us mindful that these measures are all completely insular: they possess no cross-cultural validity whatsoever. When post-meal leavings in one country would be a fine feast in another, it is not meaningful for consumer researchers to compile CS/D from the two areas with respect to food and then to compare the findings. In my mind this discussion raises serious consumer interest questions about the appropriateness and the morality of continually striving for higher and higher consumer satisfaction with food, health, childcare, etc. in one nation while other nations are literally starving, diseased, dying, etc..

The CS/D measure is very highly specific -- to a particular individual or to an extremely homogeneous set of individuals, to a particular socio-cultural-economic group, to a particular time. It is not some all-purpose measure of consumer well-being. This does not make CS/D worthless. It is just an explicit assertion that CS/D must be used very carefully. And, of course, it also shows that there is no satisfactory way to compare reported satisfaction levels between individuals or groups which have differing resources at their command.

Some have thought that once we obtain a CS/D coefficient we then have a base-free measure which can be compared to any other base-free measure, making it possible to compare a satisfaction score for apples with a satisfaction score for Chevrolets or Levi 501's. In my judgment there is no ground to justify comparisons of CS/D scores between diverse items. At least, we have no research findings to justify such a supposition.

When the Disadvantaged Are Not Dissatisfied

Aspiration theory tells us that if we consistently fail to meet our expected performance, we will lower our expectations. What of the disadvantaged consumers who, day after day, have their noses rubbed in the fact that they possess fewer of the many nice things other people possess and the things they do possess are less nice. Andreasen [1] and Olander [23] were the first to alert us to this phenomenon. The lowered expectations of the disadvantaged are deep in the "dissatisfied" range for most other consumers. Yet when we obtain our CS/D measures from disadvantaged consumers, they appear to be "satisfied." And, by our definition; they are satisfied. But, from the consumer and public interest viewpoint, we recognize that CS/D for the disadvantaged will be misleading. Handling this problem requires (1) recognizing the nature of the problem, and (2) devising a clever design to forestall it. You have to somehow bring all respondents to the same recognition of the true state of nature and the true state of possible heights of satisfaction before any kind of valid measure can be taken.

CS/D Distributions Are Highly Skewed

Distributions of satisfaction are usually highly skewed toward high satisfaction. This alerts us to the need to use a scale which differentiates more finely among the "highly satisfied". This might be accomplished by offering more categories, e.g., "very very good" and "absolutely delighted."

Another problem is that respondents say they are "highly satisfied" when perhaps they should not be. An as example, consider the research on consumer satisfaction regarding funerals that was presented in the public hearings on the proposed Funeral Rule at the Federal Trade Commission several years ago. As reported, consumer satisfaction was in the high 90's. Was it "really" as high as reported? Perhaps. But, perhaps the high satisfaction reported is due more to psychological factors. How does one admit to oneself that the funeral he/she planned for a loved one was "bad?" What base of experience do we have for comparing funerals? What would the satisfaction level have been if survey participants had first been educated as to the pricing structure, markups, and "required" services common in the funeral industry? Is CS/D even the appropriate measure in this situation, where comparison of actual with expected doesn't necessarily tell us the social value of the transaction? The introduction of a more discriminating measurement scale does not answer this type of question.

Imperfect Perceptions and CS/D

Too little attention has been paid to the two perceptions compared in any CS/D analysis -- (1) what is expected, and (2) what is actually obtained. The consumer's expectation may be quite precise and well grounded in reality, or it may be lacking on either of those dimensions. If it is imprecise, we have a hard time comparing it to actual because it is so vague. If it is an unreal expectation because of a lack of reality, a good product may be dissatisfying or a poor product may be satisfying. The other perception is that of the actual product or service. Its accuracy will depend on how precisely the consumer can judge and what experience and knowledge he/she brings to the judgment. Sometimes the consumer may consider a product "good" when in fact there are much better products available at the same price. When one stops to consider how many opportunities there are for a misperception of expected to couple with a misperception of actual in any CS/D comparison it becomes clear why this is such a major problem in CS/D research. This is a problem that has received zero attention in the CS/D literature.

In many aspects of consuming it is unlikely that most consumers will ever know enough to make any type of correct CS/D assessment. Consider the case of medical services where patients and families may well end up with strong emotional CS/D but that CS/D is all based on their poor understanding of health and medical knowledge. Most consumers have no basis for knowing whether an operation is needed, for knowing what the alternatives are, for knowing the probabilities and degrees of success associated with each alternative, and finally, for knowing after it is done whether the operation was a success or not, as it could have been much better or much worse and the consumer would have had no basis for knowing. Even in death we may express satisfaction because the alternative was a loved one being hooked to a machine to sustain life or the loved one would live in constant pain, yet that wasn't what we bargained for in the beginning when considering the operation, if we even had a choice. This leads directly into the question of CS/D with different stages of the consuming process or with levels in the channel of distribution for a product.

CS/D with Different Stages in the Consuming Process or Levels in the Channel of Distribution

Heart attack. Proposed Action: By-Pass surgery. Doesn't work: Hooked to life-sustaining machine. Satisfied or not? The question is, CS/D with what stage of the process. CS/D could be measured for each of the stages in the process, but we often fail to consider the stages and instead just take one overall CS/D measure. Once that overall measure is obtained there is no way to know what it refers to, whether to the whole process or to the end of the process or to some part in between, or, if to the whole process, how the different stages were weighted to obtain the final measure. Is there any way a measurement can be taken for any of the pre-final stages without the final outcome affecting the other evaluations? CS/D can be used at any stage, but the researcher has to be very careful to recognize the affect of outcomes at earlier stages and expected outcomes at later stages. Once these confounding effects are included, any CS/D measure may raise more questions than it answers.

Often, even though several different parties have had an impact on the overall satisfyingness of a product, we tend to attribute our total CS/D evaluation, positive or negative, to only one of those parties. For example, someone buys a new automobile, a fairly standard model. After 25,000 miles things start to go wrong with the car. What is the focus of your CS/D evaluation? the manufacturer? the retailer? the designer? even the whole production/economic system? The focus of your dissatisfaction leads to different reactions and actions on your part. If you can reach in any way the party you think is responsible for your problem, you will probably express dissatisfaction with that party. But what if there is no way you can reach the party you think is responsible. Then your CS/D focuses on some other party. For example, perhaps the problems are because of inferior design work. But you can't focus on the designers, so you focus instead on the manufacturer in general. Also, in terms of attribution, you tend to express dissatisfaction with the person or firm you think was responsible for the failure. So, if you were one of the unfortunate many who bought GM diesel engines in automobiles your primary dissatisfaction is toward the designer of the engine, as it is hard to believe that GM would deliberately design such a bad engine. But you can't reach the designer and it wouldn't give you any satisfaction if you did, so you instead express your dissatisfaction with GM or maybe with the particular GM dealer where you bought the car with the diesel engine. On the other hand, sometimes the problem causing the dissatisfaction is well known to the manufacturer who decides to do nothing about it, maybe even cover it up, so we have problems with Corvair stability and Pinto gas tanks which were fully known to the manufacturer but which the manufacturer chose deliberately to not correct. There the CS/D rests solely on the manufacturer.

Intention to Repurchase as a CS/D Measure

Despite the attention paid to sophisticated measures of CS/D, it is worth remembering that intention to repurchase is a simple and close substitute measure for CS/D. Intention to repurchase suffers from many of the same problems, e.g., insufficient awareness of information or alternatives. Its value lies in the fact that it is a composite measure of CS/D, reflecting the same influences, without having to identify those influences. It says, in essence, given the real world and your psychological world, what choice will you make next time? If a repeat purchase is intended, it implies that all things considered, the previous choice was satisfactory enough to merit repeating. Thus, intention to repurchase mirrors CS/D without measuring CS/D directly.

CONCLUDING COMMENTS

CS/D remains a ripe area for consumer research. However, it has become obvious that CS/D research has to be much more broadly based than was initially expected. CS/D measurement has developed much more rapidly than has CS/D conceptualization. As CS/D conceptualization catches up with CS/D measurement, it may be that much of what we believe we "know" in CS/D measurement will have to be reconsidered and perhaps redone. Czepiel and Rosenberg [2] commented at the first conference on the conceptual develop- ment that seemed to be needed. Their 1976 comments are as appropriate today as they were ten years ago:

> "What we seem to need is a good dose of qualitative research."
>
> 1. What does the presence or absence of satisfaction mean to consumers?
> 2. What are the social or psychological factors which affect the importance of satisfaction in the consumer's meaning system?
> 3. What are the subconscious or symbolic attributes to which satisfaction is related?
> 4. Where does satisfaction lie in the value structure of the individual consumer in this society?
> 5. In what ways does the consumer perceive and discern satisfaction? What are the experiential manifestations of satisfaction?
> 6. How do consumers relate to, refer to, and evaluate satisfaction generating experiences?
> 7. From the viewpoint of its effect on consumers, what alternative ways of looking at, of understanding, satisfaction are there? [2]

In 1976 we were much more advanced in measurement than in conceptualization. Now, ten years later, the exact questions can still be raised, plus many more, and it is painfully obvious that while we have learned a lot about CS/D, there are still major basic questions that remain unaddressed. Yes, this is still a ripe research area, awaiting further development.

REFERENCES

1. ANDREASEN, ALAN R. (1977), "A Taxonomy of Consumer Satisfaction/Dissatisfaction Measures," Conceptualization and Measurement of Consumer Satisfaction and Dissatisfaction, H. Keith Hunt, ed., Cambridge, Massachusetts: Marketing Science Institute.

2. CZEPIEL, JOHN A. and LARRY ROSENBERG (1977), "The Study of Consumer Satisfaction: Addressing the 'So What' Question," Conceptualization and Measurement of Consumer Satisfaction and Dissatisfaction, H. Keith Hunt, ed., Cambridge, Massachusetts: Marketing Science Institute.

3. DAY, RALPH L. (1977), Consumer Satisfaction, Dissatisfaction and Complaining Behavior, Bloomington, Indiana: Division of Business Research, Indiana University.

4. _________ (1977), "Extending the Concept of Consumer Satisfaction," Advances in Consumer Research, Vol. 5, Ann Arbor, Michigan: Association for Consumer Research.

5. _________ (1977), "Toward a Process Model of Consumer Satisfaction," Conceptualization and Measurement of Consumer Satisfaction and Dissatisfaction, H. Keith Hunt, ed., Cambridge, Massachusetts: Marketing Science Institute.

6. DAY, RALPH L. and H. KEITH HUNT, eds., (1979), New Dimensions of Consumer Satisfaction and Complaining Behavior, Bloomington, Indiana: Division of Business Research, Indiana University.

7. _________ eds., (1982), New Findings on Consumer Satisfaction and Complaining, Bloomington, Indiana: Division of Business Research, Indiana University.

8. DIENER, BETTY J. (1977), "Consumer Communications -- Should They Be Encouraged?" Consumer Satisfaction, Dissatisfaction and Complaining Behavior, Ralph L. Day, ed., Bloomington, Indiana: Division of Business Research, Indiana University.

9. _________ (1977), "The Fulfillment of Consumer Promotions as a Source of Consumer Dissatisfaction," Conceptualization and Measurement of Consumer Satisfaction and Dissatisfaction, H. Keith Hunt, ed., Cambridge, Massachusetts: Marketing Science Institute.

10. HANDY, CHARLES R. (1972), "Implications of the Index of Consumer Satisfaction for Pubic Policy Pertaining to Market Performance," Proceedings of the Third Annual Conference of the Association for Consumer Research, M. Venkatesan, ed.

11. HUNT, H. KEITH (1983), "A CS/D & CB Bibliography - 1982," International Fare in Consumer Satisfaction and Complaining Behavior, Ralph L. Day and H. Keith Hunt, eds., Bloomington, Indiana: Division of Business Research, Indiana University.

12. _________ (1977), Conceptualization and Measurement of Consumer Satisfaction and Dissatisfaction, Cambridge, Massachusetts: Marketing Science Institute.

13. _________ (1978), "Consumer Satisfaction and Dissatisfaction as Normative and Descriptive Expressions of Marketing Responsibility," Future Directions for Marketing, George Fisk, Johan Arndt, and Kjell Gronhaug, eds., Cambridge, Massachusetts: Marketing Science Institute.

14. _________ (1977), "Consumer Satisfaction and Dissatisfaction (CS/D) and the Public Interest: Conceptualization, Measurement Problems, and Applications," Marketing and the Public Interest, John Cady, ed., Cambridge, Massachusetts: Marketing Science Institute.

15. _________ (1982), "Consumer Satisfaction/Dissatisfaction: Of Continuing Interest? To Whom? Why?" Consumerism and Beyond: Research Perspectives on the Future Social Environment, Paul N. Bloom, ed., Cambridge, Massachusetts: Marketing Science Institute.

16. _________ (1977), "CS/D: Bits and Prices," Consumer Satisfaction, Dissatisfaction and Complaining Behavior, Ralph L. Day, ed., Bloomington, Indiana: Division of Business Research, Indiana University.

17. HUNT, H. KEITH and RALPH L. DAY, eds. (1982), Concept and Theory in Consumer Satisfaction and Complaining, Bloomington, Indiana: Division of Business Research, Indiana University.

18. _________, eds. (1982), Conceptual and Empirical Contributions to Consumer Satisfaction and Complaining Behavior, Bloomington, Indiana: Division of Business Research, Indiana University.

19. _________, eds. (1985), Consumer Satisfaction, Dissatisfaction, and Complaining Behavior, Bloomington, Indiana: Division of Business Research, Indiana University.

20. _________, eds. (1980), Refining Concepts and Measures of Consumer Satisfaction and Complaining Behavior, Bloomington, Indiana: Division of Business Research, Indiana University.

21. MILLER, JOHN A. (1972), Satisfaction and Modes of Response to Dissatisfaction for Supermarket Customer Segments, Unpublished doctoral dissertation, Indiana University.

22. _________ (1977), "Studying Satisfaction: Modifying Models, Eliciting Expectations, Posing Problems, and Making Meaningful Measurements," Conceptualization and Measurement of Consumer Satisfaction and Dissatisfaction, H. Keith Hunt, ed., Cambridge, Massachusetts: Marketing Science Institute.

23. OLANDER, FOLKE (1977), "Consumer Satisfaction -- a Skeptic's View," Conceptualization and Measurement of Consumer Satisfaction and Dissatisfaction, H. Keith Hunt, ed., Cambridge, Massachusetts: Marketing Science Institute.

24. WESTBROOK, ROBERT A. (1983), "Consumer Satisfaction and the Phenomenology of Emotions During Automobiles Ownership Experiences," International Fare in Consumer Satisfaction and Complaining Behavior, Bloomington, Indiana: Division of Business Research, Indiana University.

25. WILKIE, WILLIAM L. (1986), Consumer Behavior, New York: John Wiley & Sons.

Chapter 31

ABOUT THE AUTHOR

Jennifer L. Gerner is Associate Professor in the Department of Consumer Economics and Housing at Cornell University. For further biographical information see "About the Author" for Chapter 3.

RESEARCH ON CONSUMER SATISFACTION AND DISSATISFACTION

Jennifer L. Gerner

Hunt, in his review of research on consumer satisfaction and dissatisfaction, overviews potential uses of some measures of consumer satisfaction and dissatisfaction, and identifies some of the problems with research in this area. Rather than comment specifically on his paper, I would like to identify some additional problems with the research on consumer satisfaction and dissatisfaction in general. The problems that I see in research in this area arise because of the general failure to identify the role that consumer satisfaction and dissatisfaction plays in consumer behavior. Because of this, much of the research in this area is less useful than it might be.

CS/D AS PART OF A THEORETICAL "SYSTEM"

Consumer satisfaction and dissatisfaction do not exist in a vacuum. Hunt refers to "the expected minus actual disparity" as the motivating force behind consumer satisfaction and dissatisfaction. This is shorthand for a complicated process from which consumer satisfaction arises. Consumers, equipped with certain expectations about the product or service in question, realize that these expectations are met, exceeded, or frustrated. Consumer expectations themselves are formed as a result of the experiences and psychological makeup of the consumer, the information available about options and about the product itself, and the resources available to him/her. When expectations about product performance or product characteristics exceed the actual level of performance, consumer dissatisfaction is generated. Presumably, the greater the disparity between expected performance and actual performance, the stronger the dissatisfaction.[1]

---

[1]Whether this is the case is an empirical matter, and should be an issue addressed by the research in this area. This issue is underresearched, if researched at all.

If this describes something like the system that results in reported consumer satisfaction or dissatisfaction, then the reports of consumer satisfaction will change if any of the variables that determine expectations change or if the perceived characteristics of the product changes.

With this view of how satisfaction and dissatisfaction arises, it is easier to understand why the original use of consumer satisfaction and dissatisfaction, as a social indicator, never reached fruition. Without a clear idea of how consumer satisfaction is formed, and what sort of changes have led to changes in the degree of consumer satisfaction, the relationship between measures of consumer satisfaction and consumer welfare is unclear. It may be that consumer expectations have changed, or it may be that product characteristics have changed. Either of these changes can lead to changes in the measure of consumer satisfaction. Both are of interest, but each has different implications for consumer welfare.

This helps explain why disadvantaged consumers are often found to be satisfied. Although the research posits that disadvantaged consumers must have low expectations about product performance, it does not systematically concern itself with an examination of the expectations formation process itself, and the interaction between that process and satisfaction. Nor does it consider how expectations differ among consumers with different characteristics. Without a systematic theoretical and empirical examination of the process that leads to consumer satisfaction, measures of satisfaction are rather arbitrary and difficult to interpret.

If we had some better understanding of how consumer satisfaction and dissatisfaction are formed, some types of comparisons among consumers and across products might be possible. This is crucial if policymakers are to find measures of consumer satisfaction and dissatisfaction of much use. Policymakers can use these measures of satisfaction and dissatisfaction to pinpoint areas where regulation might be needed only if they can distinguish between those situations where real product quality problems exist and those situations where information about product characteristics and product performance are at fault. These two sources of dissatisfaction require quite different policy mechanisms.

CS/D AS A DETERMINANT OF SUBSEQUENT PURCHASE BEHAVIOR

Understanding how satisfaction is formed is only half of the story. What remains is the role of satisfaction and dissatisfaction in subsequent consumer behavior. There is a body of research relating consumer satisfaction and dissatisfaction to complaining behavior. It is difficult to imagine how any meaningful discussion of consumer satisfaction and dissatisfaction can ignore its importance in subsequent consumer behavior.

There are a variety of actions that consumers can take in the face of satisfaction or dissatisfaction. Consumers can complain in several ways. They may complain to friends and neighbors. They may use established complaint mechanisms. They may have access to the court system. They may choose not to repurchase the product. Here consumer satisfaction is just one of many elements that act together to determine what action consumers will take. Researchers dealing with consumer satisfaction and dissatisfaction and its relationship to some consumer action have tended to focus on only one sort of outcome, complaining.

To understand the role of consumer satisfaction fully we must consider the whole range of outcomes and their relationships to each other. Although some parts of this complicated behavior have been developed[2] in diverse fields, each piece omits important elements. For example, the economic literature on repeat purchases largely ignores the role of consumer satisfaction. But the consumer behavior literature fails to take into account the possible multiple outcomes. There are now statistical techniques that deal with the joint determination of several outcomes. These techniques, used together with a well conceived notion of how the outcomes are determined, could help us learn a great deal about the role of consumer satisfaction in determining subsequent consumer behavior.

In addition to taking multiple responses to dissatisfaction into account, research considering the importance of dissatisfaction has not adequately dealt with the role producers play in determining consumer satisfaction or dissatisfaction. Producers, after all, provide the products about which consumers are satisfied or dissatisfied, and they are largely responsible for the information provided to consumers about these products. Producers may choose to tolerate a certain level of dissatisfaction if eliminating it through either better information or higher quality products is more expensive. It is this with which the economic models of fraud are concerned.

---

[2]For example, see M. Darby and E. Karne, "Free Competition and the Optimal Amount of Fraud," Journal of Law and Economics, pp. 67-88, April 1973, and P. Nelson, "Information and Consumer Behavior," Journal of Political Economy, Vol. 78, March 1970.

What appears to be missing in the research in this area is a clear idea of how the entire system works. That is, how consumer satisfaction and dissatisfaction is affected by product performance, to what extent consumer purchase and complaining behavior is determined by dissatisfaction, and how product design and information provided by the producer responds to consumer dissatisfaction. Without a clear and systematic understanding of these mechanisms, the measurement of consumer satisfaction and dissatisfaction plays but a small role in helping us to understand consumer behavior.

ABOUT THE AUTHOR

Folke Olander is Professor of Economic Psychology at the Aarhus School of Business Administration and Economics in Denmark. For further biographical information, see Headnote for Chapter 23.

CONSUMER SATISFACTION/DISSATISFACTION AND THE CONSUMER INTEREST

Folke Olander

The astonishing amount of research that has been devoted to consumer satisfaction/dissatisfaction (CS/D) during the last decade forced Keith Hunt to adopt a bird's-eye view in his review. His necessity gives a felicitous result: it is much easier to discern the main trends of the research and, above all, to discover the many difficulties involved in using CS/D for consumer policy purposes. Hunt makes many astute observations and, in general, I am very much in agreement with his conclusions. If anything, I am probably even more skeptical than Hunt regarding the value of CS/D to "the consumer interest." Below I will outline the grounds for my skepticism.

SOME LIMITATIONS OF THE PAPER

What I miss much in Hunt's paper is a basic taxonomy of the phenomenon at stake. Early in his paper, Hunt refers to "consumer satisfaction/dissatisfaction and complaining behavior." But in the subsequent discussion, consumer complaints go largely untreated. A shame. The paper would have gained in generality and interest for policymakers had it included all forms of individual consumers' appraisal of their situation. In particular, I miss a reference to perceived consumer problems, regarding which there have been large-scale investigations, particularly in the U.K. and Sweden. As a dependent variable, consumer problems share many limitations with CS/D ratings and actual complaints. But this approach has the advantage of being based on representative samples (in contrast to complaints data) while at the same time allowing for more substantive explorations of consumer situations than do the rating scales usually used in "pure" CS/D research.

It is unfortunate that Hunt does not distinguish between satisfaction with macro-marketing and the micro-marketing systems, respectively. From a consumer viewpoint, one of the weaknesses of much CS/D research is that it focuses excessively on satisfaction/dissatisfaction with individual products, shops, manufacturers. Since consumer policymakers are often concerned with macroperformance -- market structure and performance, lack of competition, changes in the distribution system, advertising and information, safety and liability, environmental effects, etc., -- is it wise -- as does Day [1], for example -- to exclude consumer attitudes towards such matters from the research domain? Is there research evidence showing that dissatisfaction with purchase/use-- the facet that dominates CS/D research -- is what bothers most consumers most? For micro-marketing dissatisfaction, it is also the case that we have alternative measures: repurchase rates, buying intentions, complaints, and so on. For macro-marketing dissatisfaction, it is less obvious that there are alternative measures, at least as far as subjective indicators go.

I have already commended Hunt for his pertinent observations on the reasons for the non-use of CS/D measures by public agencies and consumer organizations. But he is guilty of a major inconsistency. On p. 741 he states "....these measured are completely insular: they possess no cross-cultural validity whatsoever." Later on the same page, he asserts that "....there is no ground to justify comparisons....between diverse items," outlining the reasons for his doubt. Nonetheless, temptation is too much and in the section on "CS/D and Consumer Legislation" (p. 736), he argues for the CS/D data to guide legislators in deciding which consumer products are worthy of policy considerations. Unfortunately this proposed use undoubtedly calls for the "cross product comparisons" he denounces later in the paper!

Keith Hunt is right in pointing to business as the primary interest group for CS/D research, as presently conceived. I would have wished for some concrete examples of such use. Unfortunately, the section on "CS/D and Marketing Management" is declamatory rather than illustrative. Perhaps an equally intensive examination of industry would have disclosed as many reasons for lack of applications in that sphere as in government/consumerism. Again, one of the reasons for non-use may be CS/D's focus on product performance, for which industry may have cheaper and -- from their viewpoints -- equally valid or more valid indicators, for example, "manifest" complaints, attitude data, purchase intentions, sales figures. CS/D's early warning function mentioned by Hunt on p. 738 may indeed be more important when it comes to other company practices, consumer reactions to which may not be so easily revealed by traditional instruments.

Few would question that satisfaction (or reinforcement) has an impact on the likelihood of repurchase. So it is only natural that researchers should try to increase their understanding of how expectations and norms are formed with regard to product and service performance, how these affect the actually experienced performance, and how this, in turn, affects the re-purchase intentions and later purchases. Hunt expresses concern that CS/D has become too cognitive, and that the emotional or affective part of the CS/D experience has been neglected. He may be right. But I see no reason to disparage attempts to model the relationships between the various constructs that presumably are needed. To my mind, we have seen much theoretical progress in the short period history of CS/D research. No doubt, the models I have in mind make sense also from a psychological point of view, especially as in the "actual minus expected" conception, the "expectation" component, hitherto mostly thought of as based exclusively on previous personal experiences, to an increasing extent is becoming supplemented by other comparison standards (norms, ideals, aspirations, equity, etc.).

As for the role of affect/emotion and the much discussed issue of whether emotions precede a cognitive judgment of satisfaction or result from the process of evaluation, it is not too much to predict that links will soon be established to the debate in psychology regarding the "mere exposure" phenomenon and the primacy of affect versus the primacy of cognition [9, 8, 3]. Such a rapprochement might be quite illuminating.

FUTURE USES OF CS/D RESEARCH IN THE "CONSUMER INTEREST"

I ended the previous section on a positive note. As far as product and brand choice is concerned, the understanding of individual consumer behavior will undoubtedly benefit from further research on factors determining, and being determined by, CS/D. Nevertheless, even though consumer agencies and organizations ought to benefit in the long run from an increased understanding of factors determining consumer choice, there seems to be little reason to expect that they will exhibit much interest in CS/D, especially formalized ratings. Nor is there any reason why they should.

Hunt has already stated many of the strategic or tactical reasons why such use is not to be expected. He has also touched upon some of the problems of interpretation of CS/D data for normative purposes. Two papers of mine a decade ago make the case against use of CS/D data for normative purposes [4, 5]. No significant counter-arguments seem to have turned up since then. Let me review this case against.

Very briefly, CS/D reports are plagued by a "Pollyanna" tendency to skew ratings in the direction of "high" satisfaction (an effect acknowledged by Hunt) and they also suffer from "expectancy" effects: in certain situations respondents feel it is better not to express one's true feelings. Both factors cast doubt on the validity of CS/D reports. But even if we believe CS/D ratings to be valid, there remain problems of interpretation. If satisfaction is dependent upon comparison with standards, and these standards clearly differ between various groups of consumers (due perhaps to differences in current living standards, in previous experiences, in the reference groups that are used), it becomes very difficult to conclude that one group of consumers expressing satisfaction is indeed better off than a second group reporting dissatisfaction (a factor also acknowledged by Hunt). In addition, the tendency to reduce dissatisfaction in order to avoid cognitive dissonance may be greater in some parts of the population, e.g., among those who find it especially difficult to express their discontent in other ways, such as by the launching of formal complaints.

Equally problematic, however, is the fact that many consumers are badly informed about alternatives to their present choices and/or life styles. Thus in reporting satisfaction people are on unequal footings: some consumers are aware of better alternatives and thus express discontent while others remain unaware and express satisfaction. It seems plausible that the very introduction of new information will often induce dissatisfaction. This constitutes a grave difficulty in interpreting CS/D data normatively.

Steps might be taken to offset these invalidating effects. One approach would be to try to offer information about alternatives, a possibility mentioned by Hunt. This requires different questionnaire techniques than those customarily employed in consumer surveys. Usually we allow the respondent no time for preparation and reflection and provide little or no information about alternatives and their characteristics. The alternative mentioned might require a more qualitative approach, adapted to the individual respondent. So the correction of this defect is not without cost.

While acknowledging that consumer protection agencies are unlikely to be very interested in using CS/D measures in times of "retrenchment" (since at least their political masters are not interested in hearing about consumer dissatisfaction), Keith Hunt maintains that in "good times," CS/D is a suitable tool for discovering problems that need attention. Again, for the reasons mentioned above, I am skeptical about this use, too. Dissatisfaction with certain product or service areas may seem large simply because groups of citizens prone to registering dissatisfaction frequent these areas (e.g., the highly educated). Or the citizenry as a whole may be quite satisfied (as measured) with some private or public sector performance simply because it does not realize that better alternatives exist -- in another country or culture, for example.

Nor is it obvious that a consumer protection agency ought to be happier with a situation in which all or most consumers are satisfied than with a situation in which many are dissatisfied. When voicing dissatisfaction, consumers prove that they are critical consumers, and dare to pass on their requests to the agency, and, hopefully, also to business. Satisfied consumers are really of little use to a consumer agency. (To be more precise, there is presumably an optimal level of dissatisfaction in the consumer population which lies somewhere in between total satisfaction and infinite, paralyzing dissatisfaction.) Elimination of the problems causing present dissatisfaction must be the target for agency action, while at the same time it should encourage vigilant consumers to discover new sources of dissatisfaction.

Another problem is that CS/D ratings focus very much on individual experiences, the consumer's personal well-being. Hunt recognizes this problem. Again, the micro orientation of most CS/D research makes it unlikely that respondents will be asked to judge the satisfaction/ dissatisfaction with their own consumption, taking into account the effects that their own consumption may have on other citizens, other nations, or the environment. Irrespective of whether or not consumers as a rule pay attention to such matters in evaluating their own satisfaction or happiness, one cannot neglect them if contemplating the use of CS/D data for normative, public policymaking purposes.

In the long perspective, perhaps both consumer researchers and consumer policymakers stand to gain more from an increased understanding of the role that different kinds of consumption play in the configuration of life satisfaction. This would mean abandoning the exclusive emphasis on the micro (and macro) marketing systems in favor of a more global approach. Although there have been some attempts to merge CS/D with social indicators and quality-of-life research, in the brief CS/D research "tradition," such attempts have been largely viewed as digressions.

If we are to believe Scitovsky [7] and Scherhorn [6], the permanence of human dissatisfaction can only be allayed if consumers/citizens turn from satisfying their "restitutional" or "deficit" needs to satisfying "stimulation" or "growth" needs. In the latter case, the increase in welfare, or "general satisfaction" depends upon the ability to increase self-fulfillment by personal development and by expanding one's knowledge and abilities, not upon an increase of the material living standard. While the objects needed to satisfy restitutional or deficit needs are subject to the law of diminishing marginal utility, this is not true for activities satisfying stimulation needs.

Hunt calls attention to the ethical issue involved in reconciling the constants striving for higher consumer satisfaction in the affluent parts of the world with concomitant starvation in other nations. One solution might be to try to redefine the whole issue along the lines indicated by Scitovsky and Scherhorn. At some point, the improvement in material living standards seems to lead to no further increase in satisfaction or "happiness." (This does not necessarily hold true for improvements in one's position relative to others, but apparently for standards improvement over time.) Not even the acquisition of "positional goods" [2] helps in the long run. At that point, improvements in "consumer satisfaction" will come not from additional material goods with their ever decreasing marginal utility or even with steadily improving quality, but rather from the provision of other, non-material kinds of need-fulfilling stimuli and activities.

Obviously, the search for such stimuli and activities -- and the documentation of the diminishing role that products and services play in the lives of citizens in the affluent nations -- would imply a major reorientation of the work of both consumer researchers and consumer organizations. It is not a reorientation that is likely to occur soon. And it may not be an option that readers of this book are very interested in pursuing.

Nonetheless, I could not resist my prerogative as a discussant to raise the question of what the ultimate goals of research -- or policymaking -- in "the consumer interest" should be. (For this is what it boils down to). It may be impossible to pinpoint the elusive role of consumer satisfaction studies in consumer policy research without first considering carefully the fundamental question of what goals or criteria to use in defining the "consumer interest." In effect, the CS/D field may be a good starting-point for such a discussion.

REFERENCES

1. DAY, RALPH L. (1982), "The Next Step: Commonly Accepted Constructs for Satisfaction Research," in Ralph L. Day and H. Keith Hunt (eds.), International Fare in Consumer Satisfaction and Complaining Behavior, pp. 113-117, Bloomington, IN: Indiana University, School of Business, Division of Research.

2. HIRSCH, FRED (1977), Social Limits to Growth, London: Routledge & Kegan Paul.

3. LAZARUS, RICHARD S. (1984), "On the Primacy of Cognition," American Psychologist, 39 (February): 124-129.

4. OLANDER, FOLKE (1977), "Consumer Satisfaction: A Skeptic's View," in H. Keith Hunt (ed.), Conceptualization and Measurement of Consumer Satisfaction and Dissatisfaction, 409-452, Cambridge, Massachusetts: Marketing Science Institute.

5. _________ (1977), "Can Consumer Dissatisfaction and Complaints Guide Public Consumer Policy?" Journal of Consumer Policy, 1 (Spring): 124-137.

6. SCHERHORN, GERHARD (1985), "Die Unzufriedenheit der Verbraucher (The Dissatisfaction of Consumers)," Stuttgart: Hohenheim University, unpublished working paper.

7. SCITOVSKY, TIBOR (1976), The Joyless Economy, Oxford: Oxford University Press.

8. ZAJONC, ROBERT B. (1984), "On the Primacy of Affect," American Psychologist, 39 (February): 117-123.

9. _________ and HAZEL MARCUS (1982), "Affective and Cognitive Factors in Preferences," Journal of Consumer Research, 9 (September): 117-123.

ABOUT THE AUTHOR

Robert A. Westbrook is Professor of Marketing at the University of Arizona. After receiving his Ph.D. in Marketing from the University of Michigan in 1975, Westbrook was a faculty member in Marketing at Duke University before moving to the University of Arizona in 1978. Westbrook's research interests include Emotional Phenomena and Processes in Consumption Behavior, Affective Advertising, Consumer Satisfaction and Complaining Behavior, and Consumer Information Search and Shopping Behavior. His articles have appeared in the Journals of Consumer Research, Marketing Research, Marketing, and Retailing.

CONSUMER SATISFACTION: AN AFFIRMATION OF POSSIBILITIES

Robert A. Westbrook

In recent years, consumer satisfaction has received increasing attention from marketing, family economics, health care administration, and consumer affairs. Behind this emergent interest is the apparently widely-held view that assessments of subjective consumer well-being constitute an important consideration in the formulation of both private- and public-sector consumer policy. In essence, appraisals of consumer satisfaction are viewed by some as a form of performance evaluation of the market system from the perspective of its consumer participants [30]. Much as a physician relies upon his patients' reports of symptoms as a basis for prescribing appropriate therapy, the consumer policy analyst may examine consumers' reports of satisfaction/dissatisfaction in order to identify the need for and nature of marketplace remedies "in the consumer interest."

In this light, Hunt raises a number of fascinating and timely questions about the extent and propriety of satisfaction research relative to the consumer interest. His skepticism is valued because intelligent policy-making in any area of human affairs requires an openmindedness about the limitations of one's basic premises. Hunt correctly points out the limited use to date of satisfaction research in furtherance of the consumer interest in the U.S.. What we as students of the consumer interest hold self-evident has yet to be accepted in the broader realm of American public policymaking and consumer advocacy. Interestingly, the political barriers to using satisfaction data for consumer policymaking seems not to have been the case in Western Europe [22].

Hunt also provides an appropriate discussion of various important conceptual problems which complicate the use of consumer satisfaction data for policymaking purposes. Despite the growing body of satisfaction research accumulated over the past decade, these problems have persisted. Clearly they are not trivial issues and applied researchers must face up to them as they undertake further study of satisfaction processes.

Hunt's insightful review could leave the unintended impression that the study of consumer satisfaction/dissatisfaction is so fraught with problems that its viability and perhaps even propriety for research in the consumer interest might be questioned. Indeed, some have already argued this postion [21, 7]. Lest this impression prevail, my Comment seeks to provide a complementary perspective in support of CS/D research.

This Comment deals with two vital issues in the application of consumer satisfaction research in the public sector:

1. What is the present state of knowledge of consumer satisfaction? Is it sufficient to justify its use in the determination of what lies in the consumer interest?

2. Should it matter to society whether its consumer citizens are satisfied or dissatisfied with their possessions, income and experiences in the marketplace?

The first of these questions will be addressed through an assessment of the points of major agreement as reflected in the literature of consumer satisfaction. The second, however, is a normative question whose answer ultimately depends on one's philosophical and value orientation.

CURRENT KNOWLEDGE OF CONSUMER SATISFACTION

To appraise current knowledge of consumer satisfaction, this review considers four topics: conceptualization, measurement, determinants and effects (or correlates).

Conceptualization of Satisfaction

There is emerging agreement that the concept of consumer satisfaction pertains to a distinctive subjective, evaluation of consumer experiences with particular marketplace objects, persons, institutions, or activities. This evaluative response is believed distinct from the cognitive process which precedes and determines it. In the cognitive process the nature of the experience as perceived by the consumer is compared to some standard or norm of evaluation. It is also agreed to be distinct from the outcomes of the experience itself, which may consist of pleasure, enjoyment, accomplishment, etc. The resultant response -- satisfaction -- is generally understood as having cognitive, affective, and conative properties, rendering it similar in nature to the more familiar notion of attitude. However, product and brand attitude are distinct from satisfaction in that they entail a broader focus, not necessarily requiring direct experience with the object or activity in question as does the notion of satisfaction.

As a post-consumption or post-experience evaluative response, satisfaction is generally agreed to be a pervasive aspect of consumer phenomenology. However, it need not be an inevitable consequence of all consumer experiences, some of which may remain unevaluated [6]. From a teleological perspective, satisfaction serves a "control" function in the regulation of consumer cognitive and behavioral learning, corresponding to the second "test" phase in Miller, Pribram & Galanter's [18] Test-Operate-Test-Exit model of adaptive behavior. As these views imply, satisfaction is necessarily a context-bound judgment, critically dependent on its antecedent cognitive and emotional inputs.

Satisfaction has been conceptualized as appropriate to a broad range of consumer experiences, ranging from the consumption of particular goods and services [37, 17], to shopping and purchasing at retail outlets [Westbrook 1982, 17], to overall participation in particular local product markets [42] and the overall market system [27]. While this flexibility in the usage of the satisfaction concept appears justifiable given its predominant conceptualization, it may at the same time create an undeserved impression that the concept lacks focus. In this regard, it is not dissimilar from other psychological notions that apply to a wide range of stimuli, such as beliefs, emotions and attitudes.

Measurement of Satisfaction

Despite early uncertainties about the feasibility of measuring such a subjective phenomenon, a number of excellent measures of satisfaction have been developed and found to possess suitable psychometric properties. Chief among these is the Delighted-Terrible (D-T) rating scale [1] which has been successfully validated in numerous consumer domains, being used for the assessments of the purchases of products and services as well as retail outlets [38, 39]. For examining consumer satisfaction at the level of the overall marketing system, Lundstrom and Lamont [15] have developed a reliable multi-item instrument which has met several validation tests and found some application to date. In fact, the use of the instruments mentioned above is by no means univeral, the empirical literature documenting the use of a variety of different satisfaction measures. There is certainly ample indication that accurate measurement of consumer satisfaction is feasible. Progress has even been made in developing aggregate indicators of consumer satisfaction across the market basket, using highly disaggregated product level data [26].

Doubts are often expressed about the "contamination" of satisfaction data by extraneous sources of variation such as social desirability bias, coincident mood states, general personality tendencies, and concurrent satisfaction judgments in other experiential domains. Examination of the literature provides no evidence that these presumed effects are anything more than that. Consider as an example Andrews and Withey's study of social indicators [1]. They found the validity coefficients of the D-T scale "high" by absolute standards (.8 and better). Further, Westbrook found satisfaction ratings with particular products/services to be uncorrelated with (1) the social desirability response set, (2) general personality, (3) optimism/pessimism, and (4) current mood, and only weakly related to marketing system CS/D assessments for unrelated products and services [37].

Determinants of Satisfaction

There is substantial agreement in the literature that the judgment of satisfaction is in large part the result of a cognitive process which involves the mental computation of some type of "disparity." The greatest exploration has centered about the disparity between consumer belief expectancies of the product or experience, and corresponding beliefs about the outcomes "actually" received in consumption, such as product performance, retailer service, etc. This disparity has been termed expectancy disconfirmation. Substantial support has been shown for this conceptualization of the satisfaction judgment process [23, 37, 3], along with the independent effects of initial expectancies, which appear to function as an anchor for the subsequent satisfaction response [24].

However, numerous other disparity models have been suggested, reflecting cognitive comparisons of outcomes received to needs [43], aspirations [4], social norms [19], and composite reference points [14]. Beliefs about the equity of the exchange have also been proposed as determinants of satisfaction [11, 33], as well as beliefs about the desirability of pre-choice alternatives which were also considered [32]. In only one instance has support been adduced for a non-disparity satisfaction determination process [5], and in this case a number of methodological issues clouded the credibility of the finding.

Although comprehensive testing to establish the simultaneous contributions of these alternative explanatory models has not yet appeared, the empirical support for these diverse antecedents suggests that there may not be a single, invariant psychological process at work determining satisfaction judgments. Instead, it would appear that consumers may apply a variety of different types of evaluative standards in reaching a particular satisfaction appraisal depending on product, use situation, and/or individual differences. In addition, some recent work indicates that satisfaction judgments may also reflect the integration of discrete emotional experiences during consumption in addition to cognitive comparisons of the sort previously noted [41].

While satisfaction is most likely determined by various cognitive and affective variables, the level of explanation achieved in empirical research suggests that many of the principal influences have indeed been identified and studied. Typically, satisfaction studies, using extant theoretical models, are able to account for over half the observed variation in satisfaction responses. Although much remains to be done for a complete understanding of satisfaction processes, the progress to date is noteworthy.

Effects of Satisfaction

Judgments of the degree of satisfaction experienced by consumers have been shown to influence a wide range of post-choice behavior. The theoretical basis of these findings adds a further measure of contruct validity to the notion of satisfaction itself. With respect to related aspects of cognitive structure, satisfaction has been found to mediate post-choice changes in consumer attitude and purchase intention toward products and services [23, 3]. Satisfaction has been variously related to consumer complaint behavior, showing that dissatisfaction is apparently a necessary but not a sufficient condition for complaining [2, 3, 28]. Dissatisfaction has also been shown to be related to negative word-of-mouth communications by consumers [28]. Satisfaction is also directly correlated with repurchase loyalty and inversely with brand switching, although intervening situational factors appear to moderate the magnitude of the relationships [13]. Finally the extent of satisfaction with a particular purchase choice is reliably linked to the extent of deliberation and search undertaken in future purchase decisions [12, 20].

Various studies of the consumer demographic correlates of satisfaction/dissatisfaction have been reported in the satisfaction literature. Typically these have not been strong statistical relationships and have varied in strength and direction, depending on product category. Age, for example, bears a weak negative relationship to consumer satisfaction with major household appliances [36], a positive relationship to housing satisfaction [25] and to satisfaction with health care providers [35], and a zero relationship to clothing satisfaction [31].

CONCLUSIONS

Although numerous research questions remain unanswered, the current state of knowledge with respect to consumer satisfaction/dissatisfaction is quite encouraging. On balance, there exists substantial agreement on the central meaning and scope of the construct of satisfaction as well as relatively suitable measures for its study. Further, there is substantial theoretical agreement and empirical support for the antecedent processes behind satisfaction judgments. Finally, satisfaction/dissatisfaction responses display predictable effects on other forms of consumer behavior.

Has sufficient knowledge been accumulated to warrant the use of satisfaction/dissatisfaction studies for public and private consumer policy formulation? My answer is "yes," supported by the affirmations above as well as a large number of satisfaction studies cited in Hunt's bibliographies [9, 10]. Hunt identifies several problem areas: imperfect perceptions, rising aspirations, the paradox of the "satisfied," disadvantaged consumers. In my judgment these reflect the inevitable limitations of all subjective indicators. They are <u>not</u> the consequence of our limited knowledge of consumer satisfaction. All social indicators, subjective and objective, suffer limitations. But, as Pfaff [26] points out, subjective social indicators were proposed to replace their more "objective" counterparts in policymaking. Their use was to enhance the information available to decisionmakers. Do consumer satisfaction/dissatisfaction measure accomplish this objective within acceptable levels of accuracy? The evidence of many studies supports a "yes" answer.

Does Consumer Satisfaction Really Matter?

Apart from doubts about the quality of satisfaction/ dissatisfaction assessments, some also question the appropriateness of employing satisfaction data in the determination of consumer policy [21, 7]. In essence, they argue that inevitable human frailties affect individuals' perceptions of market conditions and hence their assessment of satisfaction. Thus, even if the satisfaction could be measured exactly as it is experienced by consumers, it would have little practical relevance for the pursuit of the consumer interest.

First, it is argued that consumers lack information on the possible alternatives to their marketplace experiences. In the absence of such perspective, they practice the well known positivity bias -- the Pollyanna Principle [16] -- in reporting judgments of satisfaction. Alternatively, their satisfaction responses may be unduly inflated due to favorable anchoring of the judgment owing to the expectancy effect. This tendency more than offsets any negative disconfirmation, resulting from unfavorable "actual" experiences. Regardless of mechanisms, consumers are thus viewed as incapable of discerning product or market problems that truly warrant attention. Accordingly, the task of identifying policies in the consumer interest falls, by default, to experts who draw on more "objective" data than reports of satisfaction/dissatisfaction. Pfaff [26] has criticized this line of argument. In essence, the question is whether or not consumers themselves are likely to be the best judges of what is best for them, or, alternatively, whether others are in a position to know what is better for consumers. This is obviously a philosophical issue for which no ultimate answer exists. It has been variously answered by different societies at different points in their development. In Western civilization, however, there appears to be at least some agreement that the individual is entitled to (or carries responsibility for) a considerable say as to what lies in his/her interest. It would therefore seem inappropriate on philosophical grounds to discount the use of systematically-gathered satisfaction/dissatisfaction data for consumer policy determination. Although perhaps limited in perspective, there is reason to believe that the reported satisfaction of consumers is reasonably indicative of the consumer's own psychological reality. As such, it deserves some weight as public policymakers consider program priorities.

Interestingly, this issue seems to have been nicely resolved in the private sector by firms involved in new-product development. Here marketing managers combine evidence of consumer satisfaction/dissatisfaction with respect to particular product/service categories and/or market place experiences, with other marketing data, to estimate the demand for the new products they are exploring. Product concept testing, use testing, and regional test marketing all seek to assess satisfaction [44, 34, 29]. Obviously, policymakers need more than satisfaction/dissatisfaction data. But data on satisfaction plays a central role since it is believed that only highly satisfied consumers will purchase new products that are initially costly.

A second argument advanced for not using satisfaction/dissatisfaction data in consumer policy formulation is known as the phenomenon of rising aspirations or expectations. In essence, it is argued that social policy directed toward meeting consumer needs and wants will inevitably lead to dissatisfaction. The reason: aspirations are forever rising as prior levels are met. Since we can never be fully satisfied, it is fatuous to use satisfaction as a criterion. This is a specious argument. Progress requires intermediate goals to focus activity. Satisfaction/dissatisfaction data offer an important intermediate goal and thus provide focus for policymakers. Even if the use of satisfaction data result in improvements which later consumer participants take for granted and underappreciate, registering no higher levels of satisfaction than the original consumers voiced prior to the improvements, progress has occurred in some objective sense. Hence satisfaction may represent a useful intermediate criterion.

Third, some argue that satisfaction/dissatisfaction data may provide misleading signals. Instead of reflecting changes in the performance or quality of experiences rendered by products, institutions or marketing practices, changes in satisfaction may result from changes in consumer expectations or aspirations. This limitation does not preclude the usefulness of these data. Rather, it only indicates the need to understand <u>why</u> satisfaction/dissatisfaction reports are <u>what</u> they are. A simple resolution would be to also monitor the level of consumer expectations and/or aspirations and thus make possible the appropriate diagnosis of any changes in satisfaction/dissatisfaction level. Implicit in this discussion, of course, is the need for longitudinal or repeated cross sectional data collection.

In the final analysis, satisfaction/dissatisfaction represents a form of direct citizen input into consumer policy formulation, whether by public officials, private decision makers, or consumer advocates. While a single evaluative response may not convey the complexity of consumer problems, its simplicity makes it useful in mobilizing action "in the consumer interest." And, as the pursuit of the consumer interest attests, such mobilization is often the means to progress.

REFERENCES

1. ANDREWS, FRANK M. and STEPHEN B. WITHEY (1976), Social Indicators of Well Being: Americans' Perceptions of Life Quality. New York: Plenum Press.

2. ANDREASEN, ALAN R. and ARTHUR BEST (1977), "Consumers Complain - Does Business Respond?" Harvard Business Review, 55, 93-101.

3. BEARDEN, WILLIAM and JESSE E. TEEL (1983), "Selected Determinants of Consumer Satisfaction and Complaint Reports," Journal of Marketing Research, 20, 21-28.

4. BRINK, SATYA and KATHLEEN A. JOHNSTON (1979), "Housing Satisfaction - The Concept and Evidence from Home Purchase Behavior," Home Economics Research Journal, 7, 338-345.

5. CHURCHILL, GILBERT and CAROL SUPRENANT (1982), "An Investigation into the Determinants of Customer Satisfaction," Journal of Marketing Research, 19 (November) 491-504.

6. DAY, RALPH L. (1977), "Extending the Concept of Consumer Satisfaction," in William D. Perrault, Jr., eds., Advances in Consumer Research, 4, Ann Arbor, MI: Association for Consumer Research, 149-154.

7. ENGLEDOW, JACK L. (1977), "Was Consumer Satisfaction a Pig in a Poke?" Business Horizons, April, 87-94.

8. HUNT, H. KEITH (1976), "CS/D - Overview of Future Research," in H.K. Hunt, ed., Conceptionalization and Measurement of Consumer Satisfaction and Dissatisfaction, Cambridge, MA: Marketing Science Institute, 455-488.

9. ________ (1983), "A CS/D and CB Bibliography - 1982," in Ralph L. Day and H. Keith Hunt, eds., International Fare in Consumer Satisfaction and Complaining Behavior, Bloomington: Indiana University School of Business.

10. ________ (1985), "A CS/D and CB Bibliography - 1984 Update," in Ralph L. Day and H. Keith Hunt, eds., International Fare in Consumer Satisfaction and Complaining Behavior, Bloomington: Indiana University School of Business.

11. HUPPERTZ, JOHN W. (1979), "Measuring Components of Equity in the Marketplace: Perceptions of Inputs and Outcomes by Satisfied and Dissatisfied Consumers," in Ralph L. Day and H. Keith Hunt, eds., New Dimensions of Consumer Satisfaction and Complaining Behavior, Proceedings of the 3rd Annual CS/D and CB Conference, 140-143.

12. KATONA, GEORGE and ERA MUELLER (1954), "A Study of Purchase Decisions," in Lincoln H. Clark, ed., Consumer Behavior, New York: New York University Press, 30-87.

13. LABARBERA, PRISCILLA and DAVID MAZURSKY (1983), "A Longitudinal Assessment of Consumer Satisfaction/Dissatisfaction: The Dynamic Aspect of Cognitive Process," Journal of Marketing Research, 20 (November), 393-404.

14. LATOUR, STEPHEN A. and NANCY C. PEAT (1979), "Determinants of Consumer Satisfaction: A Field Experiment," in Ivan Ross, ed., Proceedings of the Division 23 Program, 87th Annual Convention of the American Psychological Association, September 1-5, 1979, New York City.

15. LUNDSTROM, WILLIAM J. and LAWRENCE R. LAMONT (1976), "The Development of a Scale to Measure Consumer Discontent," Journal of Marketing Research, 13 (November), 373-381.

16. MATLIN, MARGARET and DAVID S. STANG (1978), The Pollyanna Principle: Selectivity in Language, Memory and Thought, Cambridge, MA: Schenkman Publishing Co.

17. MILLER, JOHN A. (1976), "Store Satisfaction and Aspiration Theory (A Conceptual Basis for Studying Discontent)," Journal of Retailing, 52 (Fall), 65-83.

18. MILLER, GEORGE A., E. GALANTER and KARL H. PRIBRAM (1960), Plans and the Structure of Behavior, New York: Holt.

19. MORRIS, EARL W. and MARY WINTER (1975), "A Theory of Family Housing Adjustment," Journal of Marriage and the Family, February, 79-88.

20. NEWMAN, JOSEPH and RICHARD STAELIN (1971), "Multivariate Analysis of Differences in Buyer Decision Time," Journal of Marketing Research, 8, 192-198.

21. OLANDER, FOLKE (1977), "Recent Developments in European Consumer Policy Research," in H. Keith Hunt, ed., Conceptualization and Measurement of Consumer Satisfaction and Dissatisfaction, Proceedings of the 1st Annual CS/D and CB Conference, MSI, April 11-13, 1976, 409-452.

22. _________ (1980), "Recent Developments in European Consumer Policy Research," in Jerry C. Olson, ed., Advances in Consumer Research, Vol. VII, Proceedings of the 1979 Annual ACR Conference, 56-65.

23. OLIVER, RICHARD L. (1980), "A Cognitive Model of Antecedents and Consequences of Satisfaction Decisions," Journal of Marketing Research, 17 (November), 460-469.

24. _________ (1981), "Measurement and Evaluation of Satisfaction Process in Retail Settings," Journal of Retailing, 57 (Fall) 25-48.

25. PECK, CAROLYN and K. KAY STEWART (1985), "Satisfaction with Housing and Quality of Life, Home Economics Research Journal, 13 (June), 362-372.

26. PFAFF, MARTIN (1977), "The Index of Consumer Satisfaction: Measurement, Problems and Opportunities," in H. Keith Hunt, ed., Conceptualization and Measurement of Consumer Satisfaction and Dissatisfaction, Proceedings of the 1st Annual CS/D and CB Conference, MSI, April 11-13, 1976, 36-72.

27. RENOUX, YVES (1973), "Consumer Dissatisfaction and Public Policy," in Fred C. Alline, ed., Public Policy and Marketing, Chicago: American Marketing Association, 53-65.

28. RICHINS, MARSHA L. (1983), "Negative Word of Mouth by Dissatisfied Consumers: A Pilot Study," Journal of Marketing, 47, 68-78.

29. SCHWARTZ, DAVID A. (1984), "Concept Testing Can Be Improved," Marketing News, (January 6), 22.

30. SHEPARD, LAWRENCE (1978), "Toward a Framework for Consumer Policy Analysis," Journal of Consumer Affairs, 12 (Summer), 1-11.

31. SPROLES, GEORGE B. and LOGEN V. GEISTFELD (1978), "Issues in Analyzing Consumer Satisfaction/Dissatisfaction with Clothing and Textiles," in H. Keith Hunt, ed., Advances in Consumer Research, Vol. V, Ann Arbor, MI: Association for Consumer Research, 383-391.

32. SWAN, JOHN E. and FREDRICK TRAWICK (1982), "Satisfaction, Disconfirmation and Comparison of Alternatives," in H. Keith Hunt and Ralph L. Day, eds., Conceptual and Empirical Contributions to Consumer Satisfaction and Complaining Behavior, Proceedings of the 6th Annual CS/D and CB Conference, Indiana University, Bloomington, Indiana, October 1-2, 1981, 17-24.

33. _________ and RICHARD L. OLIVER (1985), "The Factor Structure of Equity and Disconfirmation Measures Within the Satisfaction Process," in H. Keith Hunt and Ralph L. Day, eds., Consumer Satisfaction, Dissatisfaction and Complaining Behavior, Proceedings.

34. TAUBER, EDWARD M. (1973), "Reduce New Product Failures: Measure Needs As Well as Purchase Interest," Journal of Marketing, 37 (July-August), 61-70.

35. WARE, JOHN E., JR., W. RUSSELL WRIGHT, MARY K. SNYDER and GODWIN C. CHU (1978), "Consumer Perceptions of Health Care Services: Implications for Academic Medicare, Consumer Perceptions of Health Services, 839-848.

36. WESTBROOK, ROBERT A. (1977), "Correlates of Post Purchase Satisfaction with Major Appliances," in R.L. Day, ed., Consumer Satisfaction, Dissatisfaction and Complaining Behavior, Bloomington, Indiana University, School of Business, 85-91.

37. ________ (1980), "Intrapersonal Affective Influences on Consumer Satisfaction with Products," Journal of Consumer Research, 7, 49-54.

38. ________ (1980), "A Rating Scale for Measuring Product/Service Satisfaction," Journal of Marketing, 44, 68-72.

39. ________ and RICHARD L. OLIVER (1981), "Developing Better Measures of Consumer Satisfaction: Some Preliminary Results," in Kent B. Monroe, ed., Advances in Consumer Research, Vol. 8, Ann Arbor, MI: Association for Consumer Research, 94-99.

40. ________ (1981), "Sources of Consumer Satisfaction with Retail Outlets," Journal of Retailing, 57 (Fall), 68-85.

41. ________ (1987), "Product/Consumption-Based Affective Responses and Postpurchase Processes," Journal of Marketing Research, 26 (August), 258-270.

42. ________ and JOSEPH W. NEWMAN (1978), "An Analysis of Shopper Dissatisfaction for Major Household Appliances," Journal of Marketing Research, 15 (August), 456-466.

43. ________ and MICHAEL D. REILLY (1983), "Value Percept Disparity: An Alternative of the Disconfirmation of Expectations Theory of Consumer Satisfaction," in R.P. Bagozzi and A.M. Tybout, eds., Advances in Consumer Research, Ann Arbor: Association for Consumer Research.

44. YUSPEH, SONIA (1975), "Diagnosis: The Handmaiden of Prediction," Journal of Marketing, 39 (January), 87-89.

Chapter 32

ABOUT THE AUTHOR

George L. Priest is Professor of Law and Director of the Program in Civil Liability at Yale Law School. After an undergraduate degree in Economics at Yale, Priest received his J.D. from the University of Chicago in 1973. He has held successive faculty positions at the University of Puget Sound (1973-75), Chicago (1975-77), SUNY-Buffalo (1977-80) and Yale (1980--). Notable among his numerous publications are "The Rise of Law and Economics," forthcoming in the Journal of Legal Education, "What Economists Can Tell Lawyers About Intellectual Property," forthcoming in the Journal of Research in Law and Economics. Priest is currently working on a book on product liability.

THE DISAPPEARANCE OF THE CONSUMER FROM MODERN PRODUCTS LIABILITY LAW

George L. Priest

I. INTRODUCTION

The Role Research on Consumer Markets Might Have Played

Every court today affirms that the goal of modern products liability law is to protect consumers, but no court today attempts seriously to identify the needs, interests or preferences of the consumers it hopes to protect. The now-extensive and far-reaching corpus of modern products liability law has been and continues to be defined without any attention at all to specific characteristics of consumers or of consumer product markets. The vast bibliography of research on consumer markets is totally unknown to the courts. Indeed, courts currently make no effort to understand the operation of the markets of the products in litigation before them. As a consequence, the substance of modern products liability law is largely uninformed. Moreover, neither courts nor students of the law have a clear way to determine the extent to which modern products liability law helps or hurts either consumers in the aggregate or any particular consumer subset.

The law has not always neglected consumers in this way. The doctrinal foundation of modern products liability law is the Restatement of Torts (Second) Section 402A [1]. Section 402A was recommended to the various state courts as an approach to the product injury question by the American Law Institute in 1965.[1] As framed by the drafters of the Restatement, the identification of the consumers of a particular product, of the preferences of those consumers, and of their concerns about product safety as they relate to specific product uses was to be the central focus of the new approach that they were recommending.

In order to appreciate the centrality of the definition of consumer interests to the Restatement recommendation, it is helpful to look at products liability law more broadly to see where the precise definition of consumer interests can possibly play a role. Under the Restatement approach, liability for a product-related injury attaches only when the product is found to be both unreasonably dangerous and defective. Among other justifications, the requirement that the injured consumer demonstrate that the product is unreasonably dangerous establishes a sharp limitation of manufacturer liability short of absolute liability. The requirement that the product also be defective is redundant in many cases, but serves to distinguish products (such as chain saws) that are inherently dangerous, but fully and adequately operational. Although these distinctions were somewhat vaguely understood in 1965, it is well established now that a product can be defective and unreasonably dangerous in three separate ways: (1) it can deviate from the standard production run of products (now called a manufacturing defect); (2) it can be misdesigned in a way that makes all items of the production run equally defective (a design defect); or (3) it can be inadequately labeled or explained in terms of harm-causing characteristics (a defect in product warning). Restatement Section 402A establishes strict liability for injuries resulting from each of these three types of defects.

Given the requirement of showing both defectiveness and dangerousness, the precise definition of the characteristics of consumers of the product and of consumer preferences for safety is chiefly important with respect to the second defect category, design defects. With respect to the first defect category, manufacturing defects, it is unnecessary to make careful efforts to identify the relevant set of consumers since the product could be regarded as defective solely by comparison to other items in the production run itself.

Similarly, although there are important questions of consumer definition in the advanced law of product warnings today, the

---

[1]For a discussion of the history leading to the adoption of Section 402A, see [22].

drafters of the Restatement, envisioning only limited contexts for warning law [22], did not emphasize the need for careful specification of the consumers potentially affected by a warning. The drafters saw the warning issue as relating chiefly to latent product dangers, of which the normal set of consumers would be ignorant. In their Comments to the Restatement, the drafters allude to the need for consumer identification only as exculpatory: the Comments state that manufacturers should not be required to warn the small set of consumers with common allergies. Instead, a warning is required where "the ingredient is one whose danger is not generally known, or if known is one which the consumer would reasonably not expect to find in the product" [1]. The drafters of the Restatement have in mind here situations characterized by widespread consumer ignorance. Here a more precise definition of the consumers affected would not advance appreciation of the problem.

It is with respect to the second category of dangerous product defects--design defects--that a careful definition of consumer markets and consumer preferences is most clearly required. The drafters defined as standards the requirement that the product be shown to be both "defective" and "unreasonably dangerous" in terms of the interests and preferences of the relevant set of product consumers. "Defective condition" is defined in Comment g as "a condition not contemplated by the ultimate consumer, which will be unreasonably dangerous to him." Similarly, "unreasonably dangerous" is defined in Comment i as "dangerous to an extent beyond that which would be contemplated by the ordinary consumer who purchases it, with the ordinary knowledge common to the community as to its characteristics."

One might have thought that the definitional focus of the Restatement's strict liability standard on consumers and on consumer expectations would have encouraged attention to the careful definition of consumer product markets in the years following the near-universal adoption of Section 402A by various state jurisdictions. Unfortunately, the vast expansion of products liability law since 1965 has been accomplished almost entirely by ignoring consumers, consumer markets, and consumer expectations. Today, most courts in the United States resolve design defect issues without serious reference at all to the characteristics of the consumers of the products under consideration.

This paper attempts to demonstrate how modern products liability law systematically ignores consumer preferences and the characteristics of consumer markets in the resolution of design defect litigation. It also attempts to show how more informed understanding of consumer interests in safety and of the operation of consumer markets can substantially improve legal rules that benefit consumers. Part II describes the development of liability standards in design defect cases. It describes how many courts have explicitly rejected reference to consumers. They do this by increasingly focusing on manufacturer decision-making, and adopting risk-utility (cost-benefit) tests for product defects. Part II also tells how other courts have allowed standards based on consumer expectations to be transformed into risk-utility tests, and how still other courts, while asserting the importance of defining consumer expectations, have allowed the standard to degenerate into meaninglessness. Part II reaches the conclusion that, today, the operational significance of consumer expectations in the resolution of modern products liability litigation is negligible.

Part III attempts to resuscitate the role of the consumer in modern law. Part III draws on research concerning the characteristics of consumer product markets. It attempts to show the importance of careful definition of the interests of relevant sets of consumers to the objective of controlling the level of product-related injuries. Part IV describes briefly the set of consumer research issues that must be addressed to help courts achieve this objective.

II. THE DECLINE AND DEATH OF THE CONSUMER EXPECTATION STANDARD FOR DESIGN DEFECTS

This Part charts shifts in emphasis to consumer preferences in design defect cases. It starts with the Restatement, where consumer expectations about design were the central focus, and moves on to current law, where the consumer expectation standard has been abandoned by most jurisdictions and reduced to meaninglessness by the remainder. This Part shows how courts have supplanted the consumer expectation standard with a standard that purports to weigh the risks of dangerous product characteristics against the utility of product design. Although a risk-utility or cost-benefit test could conceivably be sensitive to consumer interests, in practice the standard has shifted the attention of courts and juries to purely mechanical or technological issues. Today, the risk-utility standard is implemented by putting to the jury little more than the question of whether to believe the plaintiff's expert witness or the defendant's expert witness who disagree over the technological feasibility of some alternative product design. Data on the relevant set of consumers of the product, their uses of the product, and their interests in product safety, are totally absent from modern legal concern.

As indicated in the previous Part, the Restatement suggests that the issue of appropriate product design should be resolved chiefly by the definition of specific consumer expectations with respect to produce safety. In retrospect, it is not clear whether the Restatement's emphasis on consumer expectations derived from a vision of the importance of understanding the operation of consumer markets or, more plausibly, from the heritage of warranty law that preceded the adoption of the strict liability standard. Evidence strongly suggests that the drafters saw the strict liability standard as only slightly different from the part-contract, part-negligence regime in force through the 1950s. This interpretation was important chiefly because it eased recovery in manufacturing defect cases [22]. The vast changes in the law that followed were surely unanticipated and probably unintended.

But the drafters had consciously set product injury law upon a new course even if they were uncertain of the ultimate destination. The important point is that the centrality of consumer expectations in the interpretive Comments to the Restatement provided an opportunity for the development of understanding of consumer product markets as products liability law grew in the succeeding decades. The opportunity for introducing research on consumer markets into the legal discourse, however, was never realized. Courts rapidly abandoned interest in consumer preferences: some explicitly by viewing the consumer expectation standard as inadequate; others unintentionally either by failing to define the standard carefully or by laxly delegating issues raised by the standard to the jury.

The first problems with the consumer expectation standard for design defects arose in cases in which the dangerous characteristics of the product were fully obvious to the consumer or user. The Supreme Court of Oregon, for example, had very early adopted a consumer expectation standard for design defects [13], but lost faith in the standard when faced a few years later with a case in which a lumber worker was injured allegedly because of the absence of a safety guard that the worker knew had not been installed [21]. In this case, the safety characteristics of the machine did not violate the consumer's (user's) expectations; the worker knew exactly how dangerous the machine was. The Oregon Supreme Court, nevertheless, thought that the manufacturer should be held liable. Thus, the consumer expectation text had to be revised.

Courts in other states confronted similar situations. The Supreme Court of Minnesota, for example, faced a case in which an electrical worker was injured when the aerial ladder on which he was riding struck a power line [15]. Here again, there was no question that the worker knew that the ladder was made of metal, the power line was live and dangerous and that contact between the two should be avoided. Rather, the electrical worker claimed that the ladder should have been insulated, just as the lumber worker in Oregon claimed that the guard should have been installed.

Cases of this nature posed difficulty for the consumer expectation standard for design defects because the standard seemed to exonerate manufacturers of dangerous products where the danger was obvious to the consumer or user. To have interpreted defective design in this manner, however, would have rendered the strict liability standard indistinguishable from the negligence standard that it replaced. Prior to the adoption of the Restatement, one of the principal defenses to the claim of manufacturer negligence in design was that the alleged design defect had been open and obvious to the product user. Under a negligence regime, the demonstration of the injurer's negligence only leads to liability if the victim has not been contributorily negligent. The claim that the defect was open and obvious was a charge that the victim was contributorily negligent in not preventing or avoiding the injury. Even if manufacturer culpability were firmly established, recovery was denied, seemingly without regard to the ease with which the manufacturer could have averted the injury.[2] Legal rules of this nature had served as the impetus for the adoption of strict manufacturer liability. Thus, to interpret the consumer expectation standard for strict design liability in a manner equivalent to negligence would have defeated the objective of the reform.

It is, thus, not surprising that courts generally -- although not universally[3] -- rejected this interpretation of the Restatement's consumer expectation standard. Most courts abandoned the consumer expectation standard altogether by adopting what has become known as the risk-utility test for product defects [10]. The risk-utility standard for design defects is today by far the dominant interpretation of the Restatement.

A small minority of jurisdictions, however, have sought to retain some attention to the consumer and to consumer expectations in design defect litigation. The remainder of this Part will describe the law of these jurisdictions which reveals, I believe, that, despite the seeming concern for consumer expectations and the operation of consumer markets, the actual role of the consumer in design defect

---

[2]See, for example, <u>Tyson</u>, 1959 [32].

[3]See, for example, <u>Vincer</u>, 1975 [33].

litigation is non-existent. Some jurisdictions have adopted standards which they claim are consistent with a consumer expectations standard but which are indistinguishable for a risk-utility standard. Others affirm a consumer expectations standard but define it in non-consumer, risk-utility terms. Other jurisdictions define a consumer expectations standard so loosely as to make it vacuous. Finally, still other jurisdictions employ multi-varied standards in which consumer expectations actually play no essential role.

1. Standards said to resemble consumer expectations. An example of a jurisdiction which claims to acknowledge consumer expectations, while actually ignoring the characteristics of consumer product markets, is Oregon. In the case involving the lumber worker aware of the absence of the machine guard, the Oregon Supreme Court rejected the consumer expectation standard as inadequate [21]. In its place the court adopted a standard for evaluating claims of design defects that looks to the design decision of the manufacturer. According to the court, a product will be regarded as defective in design if a reasonable person would not have put the product into the stream of commerce knowing of its harmful characteristics. Strict liability establishes the presumption that the manufacturer knows all of the product's harmful characteristics.

The Oregon Supreme Court argued that this "manufacturer expectation" test was equivalent to a consumer expectations test.

> [A] seller acting reasonably would be selling the same product which a reasonable consumer believes he is purchasing. That is to say, a manufacturer who would be negligent in marketing a given product, considering its risks, would necessarily be marketing a product which fell below the reasonable expectations of consumers who purchase it. The foreseeable uses to which a product could be put would be the same in the minds of both the seller and the buyer unless one of the parties was not acting reasonably [21].

However congruent in theory are the ultimate objectives of the manufacturer and consumer, a manufacturer expectation standard is likely in practice to differ substantially from a consumer expectation standard. The evidentiary requirements for the two standards are vastly different. To fully appreciate the range of consumer expectations with respect to product safety, it is necessary to determine who the relevant set of consumers of the product are, how they plan to use the product, and what alternative methods they have beyond use of the product for achieving their ends. In contrast, the evidence relevant to determining the expectations of the manufacturer with respect to product safety will largely address alternative technological designs to achieve a similar marketing objective. Indeed, later in its opinion in the lumber worker case, the Oregon Supreme Court conceded that "It is necessary to remember that whether the doctrine of negligence, ultrahazardousness, or strict liability is being used to impose liability, the same process is going on in each instance, i.e., weighting the utility of the article against the risk of its use."

2. Consumer expectations interpreted as risk-utility. Even jurisdictions that have retained the consumer expectation standard as the principal method for adjudicating design defect litigation give little attention to the characteristics of consumer product markets. Several jurisdictions have great difficulty knowing how to define a consumer expectation standard. The Supreme Court of Washington, for example, has strongly embraced a consumer expectation standard for design defects as superior to a risk-utility standard. Nevertheless, in a 1982 decision interpreting the Supreme Court's consumer expectation standard, a Washington Court of Appeals held that there was sufficient support to uphold a jury verdict finding the design of an airplane carburetor defective under the consumer expectation standard, since the jury has been presented, in addition to evidence of the user's ability to avoid danger and his awareness of inherent dangers, evidence of

> the product's utility, safety aspects, available alternatives, feasibility of eliminating unsafe characteristics, [and] feasibility of spreading potential losses. . . . The expert testimony showed a feasible alternative one-piece design which allowed for testing after assembly of the carburetor to determine if the positive retraction device were present. No such testing was available with the [defective] two-piece design. . . . [35].[4]

Obviously, the product's general utility, the feasibility to the manufacturer of eliminating unsafe characteristics and the feasibility of risk spreading have nothing to do with consumer expectations

---

[4]Note that there was no discussion of whether the consumer could have done the testing.

and, indeed, are unrelated to the specific characteristics of consumers using the product.

The Washington Supreme Court, in a more recent decision has cemented this approach. In Lenhardt v. Ford Motor Co. [17], the court rejected the relevance of industry manufacturing or design standards in design defect litigation. According to the Court, the focus in design defect cases must be upon the expectations of the consumer not the actions of the seller or manufacturer. To introduce evidence of industry or manufacturer customers would make the issue one of the reasonableness of the defendant's design choice which is a negligence rather than a strict liability concept.

Nevertheless, in its definition of considerations relevant to determining the content of consumer expectations, the court includes factors that bear solely on the risk-utility calculus:

> In determining the reasonable expectations of the ordinary consumer, a number of factors must be considered. The relative cost of the product, the gravity of the potential harm from the claimed defect and the cost and feasibility of eliminating or minimizing the risk may be relevant in a particular case. In other instances the nature of the product or the nature of the claimed defect may make other factors relevant to the issue [17].

The tendency to interpret the consumer expectation standard in risk-utility terms is not confined to the State of Washington. The Supreme Court of Ohio's consumer expectation standard for design defects [16] was recently interpreted by the 6th Circuit to regard as sufficient evidence to uphold a jury verdict against a car manufacturer, encroachment of the roof into the passenger area of the car on a roll-over [28].[5] Similarly, a U.S. District Court in South Carolina, invoking the Restatement's consumer expectation test, held a boat engine manufacturer not liable for injuries on the basis of cost-benefit calculations of the effectiveness of such switches by (1) an expert witness retained by the defendant and (2) independently, by the Coast Guard [31]. According to the court, the absence of the kill-switch did not constitute defective design because the Coast Guard had calculated "that the prospective cost per life saved by the device [if the Coast Guard were to order its

---

[5]There was no independent testimony introduced with regard to consumer expectations of a roll-over.

installation] would be $1,600,000. This was determined not to be 'cost effective'."

These opinions demonstrate confusion over the differences between a consumer expectation and risk-utility standard for product design defects. Although the courts allude to the importance of the role of the consumer, the issues relevant to liability are technological in nature alone. There is no serious attention to the definition of the relevant set of consumers of the product, their uses, their abilities, and their alternatives.

3. <u>Pure consumer expectation standards -- and their vacuousness</u>. Some few courts have totally resisted the encroachment of risk-utility considerations in their interpretation of the consumer expectation standard for design defects. But these jurisdictions have failed to specify any independent content for the consumer expectation standard. Issues involving design defect litigation are merely passed to the jury, for its independent evaluation. The Connecticut Supreme Court, for example, has held that a manufacturer's compliance with a consumer expectation standard is a question of fact for the jury, and that little additional evidence is needed for the jury to determine that a product deviated from expectations common to the community from which it is drawn. In an early case, for example, the court affirmed a jury verdict finding the design and manufacture of a (then used) automobile unreasonably dangerous on the basis of evidence that the car was two-years old, had been driven 46,000 miles, was alleged by two previous owners to pull to the left and by a mechanical engineer to have broken spot welds in his inspection after the accident. According to the court, this evidence is sufficient because "the jury can draw its own reasonable conclusions as to the expectations of the ordinary consumer and the knowledge common in the community at large" [27]. In a subsequent case involving a gas furnace, the court took the same approach. The design issue was one for the jury given its appreciation of community standards [11]. No additional testimony was needed.

Other courts have interpreted the consumer expectation standard in the same way. An Arizona court, interpreting the consumer expectation prong of its design defect standard, held that it was unnecessary to introduce any testimony with respect to the relationship between a commercial emission control device and consumer safety expectations with respect to design, as explained by a professional emissions tester. It was sufficient in the mind of the court that the jury was shown pictures of the machine and informed how the accident happened [19].[6] The California Supreme Court, on consumer expectation grounds, held that a woman who claimed that a bus was defectively designed after she fell from her seat in the absence of a handrail, need only introduce as evidence photos of the bus and her account of the injury. According to the court, "[t]he need for a 'grab bar' or pole to steady oneself when a bus turns a sharp corner is a matter within the common experience of lay jurors. . . . Since public transportation is a matter of common experience, no expert testimony was required to enable the jury to reach a decision. . ." [6].

Questions of design suitability, of course, are ultimately factual. Our judicial tradition delegates questions of fact to juries. These cases, however, illustrate how courts invoke the consumer expectation standard in a manner that provides no guidance whatsoever to juries. Juries are not instrucrted as to how to evaluate the complicated considerations involved in design defect litigation. Here, therefore, the consumer expectation standard is meaningless. The jury is given nothing in the way of research on the operation of consumer product markets, either generally or for the specific product involved in the litigation. Nor is the jury instructed how to conceptualize the problem of the formation of consumer expectations, the determinants of consumer product selection, or the influences on consumer product use. Each of these, however, is a factor relevant to optimal design of the product from the standpoint of the consumer.

4. Multivariable tests that include consumer expectations. Courts have responded to the weaknesses of the consumer expectation standard by supplementing it, most commonly with a risk-utility or cost-benefit standard, but sometimes with other standards as well. The justification for such an approach in situations involving obvious dangers is readily understood. A product with obvious dangers may not violate the consumer's expectations, but it might be found defective and unreasonably dangerous on other grounds. Many states have taken this approach. The most prominent and influential case is Barker v. Lull Engineering Co., Inc. [2]. In this case the California Supreme Court adopted a two criteria standard for design defects: (1) whether the product failed to perform as safely as an ordinary consumer would expect; (2) whether the benefits of the challenged design outweigh the risk of danger inherent in such design. Barker has been widely

[6]For other cases of the same nature, see [3], [14].

followed, both explicitly[7] and conceptually. For example, Louisiana courts begin analysis of design defect problems with a consumer expectation standard. They then invoke an Oregon-like manufacturer expectation standard for cases in which the consumer expectation standard is viewed to be inadequate [18]. Other courts, however, have adopted multivariable standards of much less rigor [20].

It seems quite clear that one principal effect of the adoption of a multivariable standard for design defects is to increase the likelihood that a claim will reach a jury rather than being dismissed or no suit brought due to insufficient evidence to support the claim. For the same reasons, a verdict in favor of a plaintiff is more likely to be affirmed on appeal: multiple criteria increase the chances that there is <u>some</u> evidence that supports the verdict.

By the same logic, the consumer expectation component of a multivariable standard has become a residual ground of liability, approaching absolute liability. In a recent California case, for example, involving the structural design of a tractor cab, the jury was instructed on both consumer expectation and risk-utility grounds. The jury rendered a plaintiff verdict. By special verdict, however, the jury also reported its view that the utility of the design outweighed the risk of danger inherent in the design. The defendant challenged the verdict. It argued that the jury had found in favor of the defendant on the risk-utility prong of the standard and that the plaintiffs had presented no testimony concerning consumer expectations. The California Court of Appeals, nevertheless, affirmed the plaintiff's verdict. According to the court, although the jury's verdict seems inconsistent, the jury could have found that the expectations of consumers about the structural strength of a tractor cab (the cab had flown off the road after running over a cow) were violated even though the defendant had proved that the design of the cab was cost-effective [7]. Here, where there was no evidence whatsoever introduced relating to consumer expectations, it is clear that the consumer expectation standard serves to legitimate any plaintiff verdict.

5. <u>The product-conduct distinction as central to strict liability</u>. To my mind, the definitive evidence of the absence of the consumer from modern products liability law is found in what has become the dominant theme of the products liability field. As described earlier, the drafters of the Restatement had only a vague idea of the implications of the changes they had introduced. The

---

[7][16].

text of Section 402A and the Comments to the text are suggestive of directions and approaches that the law might take, but are surely not definitive prescriptions of the outcomes of specific cases. This unformed character of the textual foundation of modern products liability law, however, proved unsettling to the courts. In the early years following endorsement of the Restatement, courts struggled to define a unifying theme that would clearly distinguish the new strict liability approach from the now-obsolete negligence approach.

The desire to define a distinctive theory or conception for strict liability was particularly acute in the design defect field. The product design process involves subtle judgments on the part of the manufacturer. The evaluation of the manufacturer's choice among competing designs under the strict liability standard is hard to distinguish from the evaluation of the manufacturer's choice under a negligence standard. Similarly, the evaluation of the relative costs and benefits of alternative designs appears to involve similar concerns and evidence, whether the standard is strict liability or negligence.[8]

The concept that has evolved to firmly differentiate strict liability from negligence in the mind of the judiciary is the distinction between product and conduct. It has become ritual in products liability cases to affirm that, in contrast to the focus of negligence on the conduct of the parties to an accident (injurer and victim), the focus of strict liability is on the product itself, irrespective of the culpability of the behavior of either of the parties leading to the injury. The product-conduct distinction has now become a catch-phrase endlessly repeated: e.g., "In a strict liability case we are talking about the condition (dangerousness) of an article. . . , while in negligence we are talking about the reasonableness of the manufacturer's actions. . ." [21]. Or, "The liability of the manufacturer is measured solely by the characteristics of the product he has produced rather than his behavior. . ." [17].[9]

---

[8]Indeed, there are several scholars who argue -- with excessive emphasis on the design defect cases, in my view -- that strict liability is indistinguishable from negligence. See [25, pp. 454-64]; [26, pp. 971-73]. Also see [Epstein, p. 90] where it is argued that negligence can be more exacting than strict liability.

[9]See also quotation from the Washington Supreme Court, text at n. 4-5, <u>supra</u>.

The product-conduct formulation has proven to be a very effective means of distinguishing strict liability from negligence. The distinction, however, has the inevitable effect of channelling issues in products liability litigation into considerations solely of technical and engineering problems. Expert testimony in modern products liability litigation is dominated by designers and engineers who know little about consumer preferences or the operation of consumer product markets. Sole attention to questions of engineering and technical detail treats the consumer as an undifferentiated, passive medium which the product either serves adequately or injures on some random basis. The technological issues of modern litigation, thus, are remote from the question of how the joint behavior of the manufacturer and consumer in manufacture and use of the product can reduce the accident rate. As a consequence, the modern triumph of the product-conduct distinction signals the near-total abandonment of the consumer in products liability law.

My next Part will attempt to resurrect the consumer. It sketches the issues central to what I believe to be the only important concerns in the context of product law: how to reduce the injury rate and how to provide optimal insurance for personal or product losses.

III. THE RETURN OF THE CONSUMER TO MODERN PRODUCTS LIABILITY LAW

The previous Part demonstrated the movement of our courts in design defect cases away from the consumer expectation standard toward the technological-based risk-utility standard. In my view this shift reflected a decline in interest in the operation of consumer product markets and a disregard of specific concerns about consumer preferences. It is important, however, to be clear in identifying the failings of the risk-utility standard for design defects. How precisely does the risk-utility approach ignore consumer markets and consumer interests? Will not the judicial focus on available alternative designs place incentives on manufacturers to provide products most suitable for consumers? Why would consumers not want courts to implement a cost-benefit standard? The answers to these questions should suggest how research into the operation of consumer markets can contribute to a more sophisticated, consumer-oriented approach in the product defect field.

In evaluating the operation of the modern risk-utility standard for design defects, one should first distinguish between careful cost-benefit analysis in practice and the risk-utility standard as currently implemented. In current law, the risk-utility approach constitutes an amalgam of considerations that only vaguely resembles, even in formulation, the form of semi-rigorous cost-benefit calculation of modern public policymaking. The most widely adopted formulation of the risk-utility standard in products liability law is a list of seven relevant factors set forth in 1973 by one of the architects of the Restatement, Dean John Wade. Wade offered these seven factors to provide grounds for determining whether a product should be regarded as abnormally dangerous:

1) The usefulness and desirability of the product -- its utility to the user and to the public as a whole;

2) The safety aspects of the product -- the likelihood that it will cause injury, and the probable seriousness of the injury;

3) The availability of a substitute product which would meet the same need and not be as unsafe;

4) The manufacturer's ability to eliminate the unsafe character of the product without impairing its usefulness or making it too expensive to maintain its utility;

5) The user's ability to avoid danger by the exercise of care in the use of the product;

6) The user's anticipated awareness of the dangers inherent in the product and their avoidability, because of general public knowledge of the obvious condition of the product, or of the existence of suitable warnings or instructions;

7) The feasibility, on the part of the manufacturer, of spreading the loss by setting the price of the product or carrying liability insurance [34].

Wade's seven factors are redundant. None is seriously irrelevant, but the unrigorous formulation, in contrast to the simple consideration of whether the manufacturer or consumer could have prevented or insured for the loss at lower cost (described more fully below), has contributed to inconsistent decisions because of the necessarily greater range of discretion afforded to juries.

I strongly believe, however, that even if courts were to adopt more rigorous forms of cost-benefit analysis of product design, the inquiry would be too narrow and the outcomes skewed. The design decisions of the manufacturer constitute only one of many determinants of the rate of product injuries. In order to fully regulate the injury rate, a more comprehensive understanding of the product failure problem must be achieved. More precisely, the crucial contribution of the consumer must be added to the calculus.

Let me begin by proposing an uncontroversial definition of social objectives with respect to product quality: to optimize consumer preferences for product uses subject to the costs of product-related losses, the costs of preventing such losses, and the costs of insuring for losses.[10] This statement is given an economic cast, but the analysis is not constrained by the narrow normative approach of economics. My concern is with effects. Regardless of the values that courts or regulators seek to vindicate, a judgment or regulatory policy with regard to product quality can have only two long-term economic effects: (1) it can influence the accident rate (here I refer both to accidents causing personal injury and product failure), and (2) it can influence the provision of insurance for product-related accidents. These two effects, on the accident rate and on insurance for accidents, are the sole economic consequences on product quality of any legal or regulatory policy.

Most discussions of product defects in the economics literature regard the probability of a product-related accident (again whether involving personal injury or only product failure) as inherent in the product and influenced solely by decisions or investments of the manufacturer.[11] The manufacturer, of course, can influence the rate of product accidents by investments in design, quality control, appropriate marketing, and appropriate warning and by instruction on product use.

Independently of manufacturers, however, consumers also influence the rate of product injuries and the rate of product failures. Indeed, there is no meaningful way to consider any product accident or defect without reference to consumer investments in selection, maintenance, and use of the product [8]. Consumers influence the rate of product accidents by the initial choice of the product suitable for their expected use, by the nature and extent of maintenance of the product over its useful life, by the determination of the rate of use, and by the manner of product use in specific contexts.

---

[10]Derived from Calabresi, 1970. I ignore here administrative costs which, for the purposes of the discussion of alternative design defect standards, are unimportant.

[11]See, [29, 4, 12].

Virtually all discussions in the products liability literature and virtually all decisions in products liability litigation (except for the very small number of consumer misuse cases) ignore the role of the consumer in affecting the rate of product injuries. Yet there is growing evidence that the consumer's role is a very substantial one. For many products the consumer's role swamps the range of alternative technological investments available to the manufacturer [24; Viscusi, 1984]. Moreover, there is very substantial evidence that a focus on the average consumer of a product provides a very inaccurate view of the manufacturer-consumer relationship. Recently completed studies show wide variations in the characteristics and, presumptively, the preferences of the set of consumers of any product [9]. Where consumers are heterogeneous in preferences for product quality and reliability, the product safety question becomes very complex, whether for the manufacturer or for the court.

A 1983 study commissioned by the Federal Trade Commission, for example, showed significant differences between consumers of the same and of different products that are likely to generate different preferences for product quality and product insurance. The study investigated the personal characteristics of purchasers of a sample of 10 products, roughly representative of consumer products generally, from automobiles to televisions, washers, power tools and watches. The study showed substantial differences both within products and across products in personal characteristics of purchasers in terms of age, sex, education, and income. To give brief examples, of purchasers of color televisions, 8 percent are less than 25 years of age, but 21 percent between 35 and 44 years, and 14 percent older than 65. Forty-eight percent of air conditions are purchased by females, 31 percent by males, and 20 percent by couples. Of purchasers of clothes washers, 13 percent did not finish high school, although 33 percent attended college, and 8 percent took graduate study.

There are substantial differences in the personal characteristics of purchasers across different consumer products. Individuals 45 to 54 years of age comprise 14 percent of purchasers of vacuum cleaners, but 25 percent of purchasers of food processors. Female heads of households purchase 64 percent of all watches, but only 27 percent of automobiles. Persons with college educations purchase 24 percent of window air conditioners, but 38 percent of cameras.

These differences among the consuming population of a product are likely to translate into different preferences for product quality. Males and females, the young and old, the more or less extensively educated are likely to differ in the way they use products, in personal facility for product maintenance and repair, and in experience and expertise with products of different types. In each respect, these differences may lead to different preferences for product reliability. The 8 percent of purchasers of power tools over 65 years of age may very well prefer a different level of product safety than the 25 percent aged 25 to 34. The 13 percent of male heads of households purchasing clothes washers may have significantly different levels of expertise, and so demand different forms of quality reassurance, than the 55 percent of female washer purchasers.[12]

The most striking finding of the FTC study, however, is the extraordinary differences within products and across products in purchasers' income. Legal rules that require manufacturers to provide insurance for lost income as part of the product package will harm the relatively low income consumers within the product insurance pool, because they will be required to pay premiums greater than their expected losses. This point is irrefutable in theory, but its empirical importance depends upon the extent of income differences among purchasers of a given product. If, for example, all purchasers of a product were of the same income level, no subsidization of the high-income by the low-income would occur.

The FTC study, however, shows extraordinary differences in income levels for <u>every</u> product reported. These differences, first, are likely to signal differences in desired levels of product reliability. Although the determinants of consumer demand for reliability are not well known, they are likely to differ by income class, for we routinely observe different purchasing patterns across different income classes of brands of products of different levels of reliability. Second, income differences across purchasers are likely to generate different preferences for product insurance unrelated to coverage of lost income. In most property insurance situations, for example, persons with relatively high incomes purchase different levels of insurance than persons with relatively low incomes, obviously because the costs of self-insurance differ between these two classes of consumers. Thus the 18 percent of camera purchasers with incomes under $10,000 are likely to prefer a different level of product insurance than the 29 percent with incomes greater than $30,000.[13]

---

[12]For similar findings, see [24].

[13]For a more thorough discussion of the unfortunate insurance effects of modern products liability law, see [23].

Third, differences in income will greatly affect preferences for safety and for insurance for personal injury related to product use. Of purchasers of power tools, for example, 10 percent have incomes under $10,000, 27 percent between $10,000 and $20,000, 28 percent between $20,000 and $30,000, and 35 percent over $30,000. Similarly, 10 percent of automobile purchasers have incomes under $10,000, 21 percent between $10,000 and $20,000 28 percent between $20,000 and $30,000, and 41 percent over $30,000. Again, for products of this nature, for which safety is most relevant because of the relatively greater potential for personal injury, the regressive redistributional effects of liability rules or agency regulations requiring uniform product insurance are most serious.

The demonstration that consumers can influence the rate of product injuries and that consumers differ substantially in personal characteristics and in preferences for product reliability and safety suggests the importance of closer attention to the contours of consumer product markets in products liability litigation. In its current form, modern products liability law regards the consumer as a single, undifferentiated unit that has no role to play in the prevention of loss. The declining importance of the consumer expectation standard in design defect litigation and, more generally, the triumph of the product-conduct distinction are illustrative. This view of the consumer and the resulting emphasis on manufacturer technological investments alone cripple the ability of courts to regulate the product-accident rate effectively. The judicial power to control risky products would be substantially aided by closer attention to the characteristics of consumer product markets.

IV. HOW CONSUMER BEHAVIOR RESEARCH CAN CONTRIBUTE TO REFORM OF THE LAW

Consumer researchers can aid the judicial effort to influence product design to control the accident rate. In order to sensitively evaluate the appropriateness of a product design, these research questions must be addressed:

> Who are the relevant set of consumers for which the product has been designed? What are their characteristics and their preferences for safety and reliability? How successfully has the manufacturer segregated this set by design and marketing from the set whose uses of the product are likely to increase the accident rate? Can the court aid this segregation?
>
> How does the relevant set of consumers of a product expect to maintain and use it? How has the manufacturer aided this

expected use by warning or instruction? How can the court contribute to providing incentives for consumers to use products in ways that reduce the accident rate?

Modern products liability law ignores consumer product selection and product maintenance. It pays little attention to consumer product use. The law holds a manufacturer liable for product accidents related to any foreseeable use of the product. It is obvious that such liability provides an incentive for the manufacturer to homogenize the product making it less useful to sets of consumers with more specific product preferences. Many design issues in the product context involve what are essentially problems of controlling adverse selection. More selective products liability standards can aid rather than obstruct manufacturer efforts to control adverse selection. In a world of heterogeneous consumers, the greater the control of adverse selection, the more consumer welfare will be enhanced. Greater attention by courts to the characteristics and operation of consumer product markets will contribute to this objective.

REFERENCES

1. AMERICAN LAW INSTITUTE (1965), Restatement of Torts (Second) Section 402A.

2. BARKER V. LULL ENGINEERING CO., INC., 143 Cal. Rpts. 225, 573 P.2d 443 (1978).

3. BRADY V. MELODY HOMES MFG., 121 Ariz. 253, 589 P.2d 896 (Ariz. App. 1978).

4. BROWN, JOHN P. (1974), "Product Liability: The Case of An Asset with Random Life," American Economic Review, 64: 149.

5. CALABRESI, GUIDO (1970), The Costs of Accidents: A Legal and Economic Analysis, New Haven, Conn.: Yale University Press.

6. CAMPBELL V. GNL. MOTORS CORP., 32 Cal. 3d 112, 184 Cal. Rptr. 891, 899-900, 649 P.2d 224 (1982).

7. CURTIS V. ST. OF CALIF., 128 Cal. App. 3d 668, 180 Cal. Rptr. 843 (1982).

8. DONOHUE, JOHN J. III and PRIEST, GEORGE L. (forthcoming, 1987), "The Determinants of the Rate of Product Injuries."

9. FEDERAL TRADE COMMISSION (1983), Warranties, Rules, Consumer Followup Study, Draft Final Report.

10. FRUMER & FRIEDMAN (1986), Products Liability, 2, Section 3.03.

11. GIGLIO V. CONN. LIGHT & POWER CO., 180 Conn. 240, 429 A.2d 486 (1980).

12. HEAL, (1977), "Guarantees and Risk-Sharing," Review of Economic Studies 44: 549.

13. HEATON V. FORD MOTOR Co., 435 P.2d 806 (Oregon, 1967).

14. HOHLENKAMP V. RHEEM MFG. CO., 134 Ariz. 208, 655 P.2d 32 (Ariz. App. 1982).

15. HOLM V. SPONCO MFG., INC., 324 N.W.2d 207 (Minn. 1982).

16. LEICHTAMER V. AMER. MOTORS CORP., 67 Ohio St. 2d 456, 424 N.E. 2d 568 (1981).

17. LENHARDT V. FORD MOTOR CO., 102 Wash. 2d 208, 683 P.2d 1097 (1984).

18. LERAY V. ST. PAUL FIRE & MARINE INS. CO., 444 So. 2d 1252 (La. App. 1983).

19. MOORER V. CLAYTON MFG. CORP., 128 Ariz. 565, 627 P.2d 716 (Ariz. App. 1981).

20. O'BRIEN V. MUSKIN CORP., 94 N.J. 169, 463 A.2d 298 (1983).

21. PHILLIPS V. KIMWOOD MACHINE Co., 535 P.2d 1033 (Oregon, 1974).

22. PRIEST, GEORGE L. (1985), "The Invention of Enterprise Liability: A Critical History of the Intellectual Foundations of Modern Tort Law," Journal of Legal Studies 14 (January): 461.

23. _________ (1986), "The Current Insurance Crisis and Modern Tort Law," mimeo, Program in Civil Liability.

24. _________ (1981), "A Theory of the Consumer Product Warranty," Yale Law Journal 90: 1297.

25. SCHWARTZ, GARY T. (1979), "Foreward: Understanding Products Liability," California Law Review 67, 435.

26. _________ (1981), "The Vitality of Negligence and the Ethics of Strict Liability," Georgia L. Rev. 15, 963.

27. SLEPSKI V. WILLIAMS FORD, INC. 170 Conn. 18, 364 A.2d 175 (1975).

28. SOURS V. GNL. MOTORS CORP., 717 F.2d 1511 (6th Cir. 1983).

29. SPENCE, A.M., (1974), Marketing Signaling, 88-90.

30. SUTER V. SAN ANGELO FOUNDRY & MACHINE CO., 81 N.J. 150, 406 A.2d 140 (N.J. 1979).

31. TISDALE V. TELEFLEX, INC., 612 F.Supp. 30 (D.C.S.C. 1935).

32. TYSON V. LONG MFG. CO., 249 N.C. 557, 107 S.E.2d 170 (1959).

33. VINCER V. ESTHER WILLIAMS ALL AMERICAN SWIMMING POOL CO., 69 Wisc.2d 326, 230 N.W.2d 794 (1975).

34. WADE, JOHN W. (1973), "On the Nature of Strict Tort Liability for Products," Miss. L.J. 44: 825, 837-38.

35. WAGNER V. FLIGHTCRAFT, INC., 31 Wash.App. 558, 643 P.2d 906, 910-11 (1982).

Chapter 33

ABOUT THE AUTHOR

Nancy L. Buc is a Washington lawyer specializing in products liability and regulatory law. After receiving her law degree from the University of Virginia in 1969, Ms. Buc joined the Federal Trade Commission becoming Attorney-Adviser to the Chairman and Assistant Director of the Bureau of Consumer Protection. Shifting to the private sector in 1973, she became Associate and then Partner (1977 --) in Weil, Gotschal & Menges. In 1980-81 she was Chief Counsel for the Food and Drug Administration. Ms. Buc is on the Editorial Board of the Food, Drug and Cosmetic Law Journal and the Journal of Products Liability. She is a Fellow of Brown University.

PRODUCTS LIABILITY: THE VIEWS OF A PRACTICING ATTORNEY

Nancy L. Buc

My perspective is difference from that of Professor Priest. I spend much of my time talking to clients who seek counsel on two types of problems related to products liability. The first consists of clients who believe that the FDA or the Consumer Product Safety Commission will be breathing down their necks if they do or do not take a certain action. They call me because they feel vulnerable to attacks by FDA or CPSC. It sometimes comes as a surprise when I inform them that the more significant threat comes not from the Federal Government (perhaps less activist in recent years), but from products liability problems. In my view products liability law has turned out to be a far more serious problem in reaching business decisions than has been generally recognized.

The second set of product liabilities problems that I confront consists of "appropriate" labels, advertising, manuals, and consumer instructions. By "appropriate" I mean materials that will protect my client from adverse actions by the FTC or from products liability lawsuits.

So it is in these two contexts that I generally get involved with products liability. I should add that this is the most frustrating legal counseling I do because the law is such a mess. So confused!! From the standpoint of the average corporate client, it may often seem hopeless to do anything! Given the state of the law, defendants expect to lose. Even though these expectations are too pessimistic, their fears have grounds in reality. Their incentives in dealing with a product liability situation gives rise to a paradox:

no matter what a company does to make its product safe or to improve its advertising, it will lose. The "message" these product liability cases send is that improvement is not really worth the effort.

Let me explain. Firms feel that the court's responses to improved products or advertising will, in essence, be: (1) Good! You recognized a problem and responded by using technology to make your product safer or by writing more understandable instructions. (2) And then the killer: you didn't go far enough!! Hence you lose.

THE PROBLEM OF CLEAR INSTRUCTIONS

Consider as an example the clarity of instructions. This is an area I have long thought would make a difference, not only as a defense in a products liability case, but might (as I tell clients on my optimistic days) actually make the safe use of the product more likely. The goal is to explain how a product works carefully enough so that somebody can use it, obtaining its benefits without getting his head blown off. Unfortunately, good instructions are not foolproof! I am mindful of a famous case that we talk about in teaching young lawyers about FTC law. The FTC sued the Benrus Company for false advertising. So Benrus conducted some market research on the problem and came back and announced proudly that 80 percent of the people who had seen the ad understood it. The Commission's dismissal: Sure, 80 percent understood it. But, by your own data, 20 percent did not and were therefore "deceived." The verdict: you lose.

The negative potential of products liability far exceeds that of a "simple" FTC case. In an FTC case, the losing defendant signs a consent decree, promising to abstain from the prohibited action. No money changes hands; nobody gets hurt. Turning to the products liability situation, let's suppose, hypothetically, that you start with an instruction manual that 50 percent of the people can understand. By doing research and then more research, you get the percent understanding up to 70. That is impressive: you have improved understanding by 40%. Unfortunately, despite your best efforts, there remain 30 percent of the population who do <u>not</u> understand it. You can bet that <u>some</u> of this 30 percent will be injured, using the product. You can bet that some of those injured will sue. It is a very difficult situation!! And some of those will point to the instruction manual and your data showing some people did not understand it. Keep in mind that, had you never done the research, you would have no data to come back and bite you.

It is a situation that all of you have a real interest in resolving. If we could agree on an acceptable standard for a "safe" product or "clear" instructions, there would be a lot more money directed to this kind of research. But in my judgment this will not happen. And this is unfortunate because this is an area where research could contribute to real improvements in products and in ads.

FOR WHOM IS THE PRODUCT INTENDED?

Research might also solve one of the other problems that Priest talks about -- deciding who the product is for. Even after reading Priest's paper and hearing his explanation, I am still uncertain as to exactly what it is that Priest wants the courts to do. If the courts are supposed to be establishing the difference between abuse and reasonably foreseeable abuse and <u>not</u> the difference between foreseeable abuse and real outright misuse, that is one question. I think that a lot of information cited in cases is anecdotal and possibly apocryphal. It still leaves a question about who products are supposed to be for and how the instructions are supposed to be drafted. One of the issues I would raise is <u>when</u> the research on these points is supposed to be done -- <u>before</u> or <u>after</u> the accident. Is this kind of information supposed to be available to the manufacturer, or to the court at a later date? What do you do when you have figured it all out and you have defined the market for your product, when other people buy the product, despite your prediction?

I would like to hear more about <u>when</u> this research input is supposed to occur and whether it is limited to instruction manuals or whether there is a broader application. I would also like to hear more discussion of how we decide who the product was for and what functions the product is supposed to serve. How should these concepts work in practice? Or is it just something the courts should think harder about, realizing that they have not done good jobs in the past?

I don't want you to despair believing that my clients are spreading untruths in their ads. But I want you to understand their problem. This is a time when the legislative debate on products liability is raging and also a time when Federalism is relatively strong, as compared with 20 or 30 years ago. Federalism is one of the sources of confusion that confronts firms in dealing with products liability. It is very difficult to give a client an inexpensive answer about "what The Law is" when you must explore the statutes of 50 states, few of which are easily available. I suggest that these costs have enormously important political consequences. They represent another factor that must be taken account of.

You may be wondering what a practicing attorney on products liability can do in seeking to provide legal counsel for clients. He/she employs "common sense" and hopes that to be right! There is not much else one can do. Summing up, we certainly ought not to have laws and court decisions -- as in products liability today-- that act as disincentives to firms' efforts to improve products, simply because everybody feels hopeless about this area of the law.

ABOUT THE AUTHOR

David I. Greenberg is a Washington attorney with the law firm of Arnold & Porter. His practice involves product liability law and legislation at the state and national level among other topics. Greenberg received both M.B.A. and J.D. degrees from the University of Chicago in 1981. Prior to law school, he was a lobbyist for Ralph Nader. From 1981 to 1984 he was Legislative Director and General Counsel of the Consumer Federation of America. With Arnold & Porter, his clients have included Philip Morris, State Farm and the American Red Cross. He is a member of the Steering Committee for a Products Liability Project that seeks to negotiate products liability reform among business, labor, insurance and consumer groups.

THE REALITY OF MODERN PRODUCT LIABILITY LAW: COMPENSATING THE INJURED CONSUMER

David I. Greenberg

I comment on this issue based on nearly a decade of experience in the political and legal wars relating to product liability. I sport a number of battle scars. In the consumer movement I was known as the lawyer the corporate guys loved. Now as a member of a corporate law firm, I am known as the guy consumer groups love. So my position is unique: I couldn't get it "right" either time!

I agree with Professor Priest that the debate about the law is in a big mess. So, too, the law itself. And that is very troubling. In my judgment it is groups like this one -- expert consumer researchers -- that provide us with hope of resolving the products liability problem over the long run.

Watching the legal and political debates on product liability reminds me of a comment by one of the famous 19th century robber barons; he summed up his goal in life as follows: "All I ever wanted was a little unfair advantage!" That phrase sums up Washington, D.C. these days. In my view, both sides in the product liability debate -- consumers and business -- have been seeking a little unfair advantage. Priest characterizes the debate as between one set of consumers and another. I wish his interpretation were more widely understood in Washington, because this is certainly not the way the debate is played out politically.

Priest's analysis is interesting, insightful and essentially correct as far as it goes. But the real question is, "What do we do about it?" Further, if we can come up with a sensible solution, can we sell it? At present, we are failing on both those points.

THE CENTRAL FACT: COURTS WILL COMPENSATE THE INJURED

When you examine what courts and juries do in product liability cases, you must face up to the central fact that many simply will not let seriously injured people walk out of court without substantial compensation regardless of whether the defendent(s) did anything wrong. Until we address this reality, we are not going to get very far in resolving the problem.

Accordingly, there is a strong argument that we must create societal mechanisms to compensate injured people on a net loss basis. Whether the ultimate solution takes the form of disability systems, compensation systems, or a variant of tort law really does not matter. But to the extent that other compensatory arrangements are nonexistent or insufficient, the courts will fill the gap. Professor Priest is currently engaged in important research to ascertain how real and how large that gap is. If you talk privately with Federal judges and legal historians, they will tell you they perceive the gap to be huge. It is for this reason that they take the view that "I will not let this poor person walk out of my court uncompensated, if the person was injured by a product, regardless of fault." This is not a message that my clients like to hear, but I believe it is realistic.

The courts actually are usually a lot smarter than we believe. They know what they are doing. From a lawyer's viewpoint, the language they use often fails to make sense because there is no doctrinal or legal rationale for their actions. Whether one agrees or disagrees, wipe away all the inexplicable language and you see courts trying to serve injured people as humanitarian, rather than strictly legal, institutions.

One of the main reasons that Congress and state legislatures have been unsuccessful in addressing the real tort problem is that the consumer movement -- where I spent seven out of the last 15 years -- has totally failed to recognize some of the long-run costs of the current product liability system: (1) products that stay on the drawing board; (2) innovative research that, because of its risks, has not been carried out; (3) products that have been priced out of the market. I am critical of many of my former colleagues and of many of the positions I took in this debate. It is vitally important that consumer researchers try to answer some of the questions that arise in product injury discussions. This is important because the quality of discussion on product liability is low, often reading like some comic strip. Nor has the quality of discussion in Washington improved over the six or seven years of the debate. This criticism applies equally to the corporate and consumer sides of the debate.

If what the courts are doing now is taking money from one hand and putting it into another hand, we have to face the fact that there must be a cheaper way of performing this task! If such transfers are going to be the ultimate social purpose of our tort system, we should simply find another mechanism that is more economical.

ABOUT THE AUTHOR

Thierry-Michel Bourgoignie is Professor of Law and Director of the Consumer Law Research Center at the University of Louvain-la-Neuve, Belgium. After taking an undergraduate degree in Economics from Louvain, Bourgoignie earned Master's and Doctorate degrees in Law from Yale and Louvain respectively. The Consumer Law Research Center was established by Bourgoignie in 1978. Since 1981 the Center has sponsored yearly "European Workshops on Consumer Law" that have usually resulted in books. Besides numerous books and articles, Bourgoignie is the Editor (with D. Trubek) of Consumer Law, Common Markets and Federalism in Europe and the United States (New York: de Gruyter, 1986. Bourgoignie is a member of the Editorial Board of the Journal of Consumer Policy and the General Editor of the European Consumer Law Journal.

PRODUCT LIABILITY: OLD ARGUMENTS FOR A NEW DEBATE?

Thierry Bourgoignie

PRODUCT SAFETY AS A PROBLEM

Product liability is only one facet of the reforms by which EC consumer entrepreneurs in the European Community (EC) have been asked to compensate for losses resulting from defective and/or dangerous products and services circulating in its common market. Across EC, there are more than 30.000 deaths and about 40 million injuries each year caused by accidents in the home.[1] In addition to individual financial and moral losses, the social cost of dangerous or defective products is immense in terms of sickness and disability benefits, unemployment benefits, loss of taxable revenue, etc. With the present crisis of social security in Europe, it makes sense to avoid accidents in the first place. The EC open borders policy[2]

---

[1]BEUC News, n° 47, September 1985, The Safety of Consumers in Europe, p. 6-7.

[2]Completing the internal market, White Paper from the Commission to the European Council (Milan, 28-29 June 1985), COM (85) 310 final, 14 June 1985. This paper provides for the removal of physical barriers (border controls of goods and of individuals), technical barriers (free movement of goods, technical harmonization and standard policy, approximation of laws for sectorial products, free movement for labor and the professions, common market for services and capital movements, creation of suitable conditions for industrial cooperation) and fiscal barriers (harmonization of the rates and structures of indirect taxes such as VAT and excise duties). Its

makes it even more essential to provide national consumers with effective protection against dangerous products and services. New products imported from other EC countries may not meet the standards of quality, safety or performance imposed on products produced in the home market. The free-trade rules of the Rome Treaty make it possible for products whose sale is prohibited or restricted in one member State to be exported to another. This may result in "negative integration" effects or "regulatory gaps" for those consumers in the home market who otherwise benefit from higher national standards of protection in their home market.[3] Advertising, packaging and labelling rules may vary from one member State to another, thus reducing the transparency of the market for prospective buyers and users. The creation of the enlarged EC economic entity, based primarily on market mechanisms, entails a greater risk in terms of safety and information gaps to the disadvantage of the consumers. Social policy considerations require that a high level of protection be granted to consumers in any market system, especially when health and safety are at stake.[4]

The EC authorities have indeed recognized these legitimate concerns in the 1975 and 1981 Council Resolutions on a Community

---

Annex provides for a 34-page long timetable for completing the internal market by 1992, enumerating more than 350 initiatives to be taken by the Community authorities within the next 5 years to ensure that goal. This fundamental objective and priority action of the Community for the coming years is formally recognized in the text of the new Treaty of Rome as amended by the 1986 European Single Act, Articles 8A to 8C (in force since July 1, 1987).

[3]On the "regulatory gap" thesis, see Th. Bourgoignie, "Consumer Law and the European Community: Issues and Prospects," in Th. Bourgoignie, D. Trubek, Consumer Law, Common Markets and Federalism in Europe and the United States, W. de Gruyter, Berlin, 1986, 2-7; Th. Bourgoignie, the need to reformulate consumer protection policy, Journal of Consumer Policy, 1984, p. 310.

[4]Motivations which explain the rise of Community involvement in the consumer field have always combined economic and social considerations. See Th. Bourgoignie, "Consumer Law and the European Community," op. cit., 110-124; Th. Bourgoignie, "Vers un droit europèen de la consommation? Possibilites et limites," Revue Trismestrielle de droit europèen, 1982, p. 14-22.

program for a consumer protection and information policy:[5] "Goods and services offered to consumers must be such that, under normal or foreseeable conditions of use, they present no risk to the health or safety of consumers. There should be quick and simple precautions for withdrawing them from the market in the event of their presenting such risks... The consumer should be protected against damage to his economic interests caused by defective products or unsatisfactory services. To this end, the Commission will submit appropriate proposals to the Council, namely in order to harmonize the law on product liability so as to provide better protection for the consumer...".[6] However, despite pressure from consumer representatives, the European Parliament's Committee on the Environment, Public Health and Consumer Protection, and the Commission itself, there has been little progress in implementing these particular provisions of the Community consumer protection programs.

There is no such thing as a framework safety legislation at the EC level.[7] Private standardization bodies, which have responsibility

---

[5]Council Resolution of 14th April 1975, O.J. of 25th April 1975, C 92/1; Council Resolution of 19th May 1981, O.J. of 3rd June 1981, C 133/1.

[6]1975 Programme, para. 15; 1981 Programme, para. 12.

[7]Such framework legislation on consumer safety remains the exception at the level of the Member States either. Only France and the United Kingdom have adopted a comprehensive piece of legislation to deal with the treatment of defective and dangerous products put on the market: UK Consumer Safety Act of 1978 (on this, read M. Whincup, Consumer Legislation in the United Kingdom and the Republic of Ireland, Van Nostrand Reinhold Co., London, 1980, p. 96 et sv.; R. Cranston, Consumers and the Law, Weidenfeld and Nicolson, London, 2nd, 1984, p. 311-325); this Act was abrogated and replaced by a new legislation in May, 1987: the Consumer Protection Act 1987 (on this, reads, Weatherill, "Legislation on Consumer Safety in the United Kingdom," European Consumer Law Journal, 1987, 87-104; Loi du 21 juillet 1983 sur la sècurité des consommateurs, in France (Journal Officiel, 22 July 1983) (on this, read: G. Cas, D. Ferrier, Traité de droit de la consommation, PUF, Paris, 1986, p. 214-227; J.C. Fourgoux, "Le projet de lois sur la sècurité des consommateurs: un projet dangereux pour les citoyens?" Gazette du Palais, 1 and 2 April 1983, p. 2-4; D. Berges, "The New French Legislation on Product Safety," BEUC News, n° 30 December

and even a quasi-legislative role in formulating European norms applicable to industrial products,[8] do not always have safety requirements as a priority concern. Nor do they provide for adequate representation of consumer interests in their own decision-making process.[9] Except in the pharmaceutical area,[10] EC legislation provides no recall procedure for products that prove to be defective or dangerous.

In order to get the facts on accidents, an experimental Community-wide system of information on accidents involving

---

1983, p. 1-5; R. Loosli, France: "The Consumer Safety Legislation of 21 July 1983 and the Consumer Safety Commission," BEUC Legal News, n° 11, July 1985, p. 1-5.

[8]The European Commission has concluded an agreement in November 1984 with CEN (European Committee for Standardization) and CENELEC (European Committee for Electronical Standardization) about mutual cooperation (L. Kramer, EEC Consumer Law, E. Story-Scientia, Bruxelles, 1986, p. 260). It has also announced its intention to rely more heavily on the works of private standardization bodies as a valuable alternative for harmonization regulations and directives: CEE, Technical harmonization and standardization: a new approach, Communication of the Commission to the Council and the European Parliament, COM (85) 19 final, 31 January 1985. The Council agreed with this new approach in a resolution of 7 May 1985, O.J. of 4 June 1985, C 136.

[9]In the agreement of November 1984 between the European Commission and CEN/CENELEC, it is provided that CEN and CENELEC would make it possible for interest groups (in particular public authorities, industry, consumers and trade unions) to participate effectively in the elaboration of European standards. One consumer "observer" - without any power to vote - does participate in the meetings of the technical committees. L. Kramer, op. cit., p. 261-262.

[10]Directive of 75/319 concerning proprietary medicinal products, O.J. 1975, L. 147/13. BEUC, Withdrawal and recall of dangerous products in the European Community and the Member States, Bruxelles, 1984.

products used in the home was established.[11] It was only in 1986 that the Council formally decided to develop a Community data collection system on accidents caused by consumer products.[12] This system will remain temporary until 1990 and will work on a limited scale only, collecting data from 90 hospitals throughout the EC territory. The Community-wide system is far less comprehensive than those already operating in the U.K. (Home Accident Surveillance System) and the Netherlands (Pors). Gathering information on dangerous products makes sense if the information is shared and acted on by member States. In 1985 a rapid notification system for dangerous products came into effect.[13] Member States will alert the Commission and each other about the dangerous products. This "interpol" system remains strictly informational and voluntary: member States are not obligated to act on the information nor do EEC officials possess authority to impose Community-wide products bans or recalls.[14]

Thus, while everybody will agree that injuries from faulty goods should be prevented, much remains to be done by EEC authorities. Within the recent months, new policy statements have been made in the field of safety and make this an absolute priority concern in consumer law and policy. In its July 1985 communication to the Council concerning policy measures to be developed at the Community level as a follow-up to the previous programs of action

---

[11]O.J. of 13 August 1981, L 229/1. On this pilot experimentation scheme, L. L. Kramer, op. cit., p. 108-109; Y. Domzalski, Les interpols des associations de consommateurs, Report to the Conference "Product Safety in the European Community" (Bruxelles, 17-18 May 1984), doc. BEUC/113/84, p. 12 et sq.; M.C. Heloire, La politique de la Communauté économique européenne à l'égard des consommateurs, Thèse, Université de Paris I (Panthéon-Sorbonne), 1986, p. 722 et sq.

[12]O.J. of 26 April 1986, L 109/23.

[13]O.J. of 13 March 1984, L 70/16.

[14]L. Kramer, op. cit., p. 110, R. Milas, "La signification juridique de l'institution d'un système communautaire de'échange rapide des informations sur les dangers découlant de l'utilisation de produits de consommation," Revue du Marché Commun, 1984, p. 71 et sq.

towards consumers.[15] Recently, the European Commission called for the following measures:

(1) The definition of a general norm, requiring manufacturers to market "safe" products in the Community;

(2) A program of cooperative actions between national administrative authorities charged with the formulation and the enforcement of safety laws;

(3) The creation of Community facilities for surveillance and control of health and safety risks posed by the use of consumer goods;

(4) Information and education programmes and campaigns on safety issues and related matters.[16]

In a June 25, 1987 Resolution on consumer safety,[17] the Council decided to support all these initiatives and to reach concrete and comprehensive results by the end of 1982.

The need for reconciling market integration objectives with safety requirements is explicitly recognized by the Single Act, which does amend the text of the Treaty of Rome as of July 5, 1987:[18]

---

[15](footnote missing)

[16]Idem, p. 10.

[17]O.J. of 4 July 1987, C 176/3.

[18]The Heads of State and Government of the Member States of the European Community have agreed, for the first time since the Treaty of Rome was signed in 1957, to amend some of its provisions and add new items in the text of the Treaty. Namely, the protection of the environment is now integrated within the Treaty as an official Community policy; consumer protection continues not to be explicitly mentioned in the Treaty provisions as a particular Community policy. All amendments are contained in a document-- the so-called "European Single Act" -- which has been signed by the representatives of all Member States early in 1986 and is due to ratified by all national Parliaments. For a first comment on the Act and its impact on consumer policy, see L'Acte unique européen, Institut d'études européennes, Université Libre de Bruxelles, 1986. Read also: M.C. Heloire, "Community Policy Towards Consumers:

the accelerated decision making-process and majority voting system which is introduced under Article 100 A for harmonization measures which contribute to the completion of the Community internal market is indeed compensated by the admissibility of national provisions which prove to be fully justified by imperative requirements such as the protection of human health and public safety (Art. 100A, al. 4) as well as by the possibility of safeguard clauses providing for temporary measures in case of imminent danger (Art. 100A, al. 5).[19] European consumer groups and researchers also

---

The Conditions for New Impetus," European Consumer Law Journal, 487, 3-18.

[19]Article 100A of the Treaty, as amended, reads as follows: "By way of derogation from Article 100 and save where otherwise provided in this Treaty, the following provisions shall apply for the attainment of the objectives of Article 1 (which calls for the Community to adopt measures intended progressively to establish the internal market in the course of a period expiring on 31 December 1992): the Council shall, acting by a qualified majority on a proposal from the Commission after consulting the European Parliament and the Economic and Social Committee, adopt the measures from the approximation of such provisions laid down by law, regulation of administrative action in Member States as have as their object the establishment and operation of the internal market... The Commission proposals for the approximation of laws on health, safety, environmental protection and consumer protection will be based on a high level of protection....If, after adoption of a harmonization measure or a decision by the Council acting by a qualified majority, a Member State deems it necessary to implement national provisions on grounds of major needs as referred to in Article 36 (among these, the protection of human health and safety), it shall notify the Commission thereof. The Commission shall confirm the provisions involved after having verified that they are not a means of arbitrary discrimination or disguised restriction in trade between Member States....The harmonization measures referred to above shall, in appropriate cases, include a safeguard clause authorizing the Member States to take, for one or more of the non-economic reasons referred to in Article 36 of the Treaty, provisional measures subject to a Community control procedure."

plea for a clear commitment of the Community institutions to prepare and to adopt an EEC framework product safety directive.[20]

THE COUNCIL DIRECTIVE OF JULY 25, 1985

When injuries cannot be prevented, consumers harmed by defective products should get effective redress and adequate compensation. The Council Directive 85/374/EEC of 25 July 1985[21] pursues this goal. Member States must adapt their own legislation to its provisions by July 1988.

The new regime that this Directive introduces is described below.[22]

(1) The principle of no-fault is adopted on the part of the producer in case of safety defects (Art. 1). Importers are viewed as producers (Art. 3.2.) while traders are held responsible only in exceptional circumstances, namely when they market a product under their own brand name or where the producer or the importer of the product cannot be identified (Art. 3.3.);

(2) The new liability regime concerns products. "Products" include all movables except primary agricultural products and games (Art. 2). However, Member States can include these products into their national legislation under Article 15. No provision is made for nor envisaged for services.

(3) A product is defective when it does not provide the safety which an average user reasonably expects (Art. 6). The concept is subjective since it is based on consumer expectations. But it relies on the expectations of a

---

[20]BEUC, BEUC's plea for a consumer safety directive, BEUC News Legal Supplement, n° 14, June 1986, p. 7-9; H.W. Micklitz, "Perspectives on a European Directive on the Safety of Technical Consumer Goods," Common Market Law Review, 1986, 617-640.

[21]O.J. of 7 August 1985, L 210/29.

[22]For a more detailed legal analysis, one should read: N. Reich, Product safety and product liability. An analysis of the EEC Council directive of 25 July 1985 on the approximation of the laws, regulations and administrative provisions of the Member States concerning liability for defective products, Journal of Consumer Policy, 1986, p. 133-154; see also L. Kramer, op. cit., p. 276-294.

typical or average consumer, not a particular consumer whose expectations the manufacturer has no reason to know. "Expectations" take into account all circumstances including the appearance of the product, reasonable use of the product, warnings and instructions for use.

(4) Damage to property (with a lower threshold of 500 ECU or 500 U.S. dollars) as well as personal injury and death are covered but any redress for damage to the defective product itself is excluded (Art. 9).

(5) A limited list of defenses is allowed for manufacturers. They include "state of the art," the product's conformity to regulations imposed by member governments, development risks, and contributory negligence (Art. 7).

(6) Provisions limiting the producer's liability or exempting him from liability are banned (Art. 12).

(7) Liability is unlimited. However, member countries may, for dealth or personal injury damages resulting from the same defect, impose a liability ceiling not less than 70 million ECU (or 90 million U.S. dollars) (Art. 16, 1). At present there is no ceiling for liability throughout the Community under general tort liability systems. The sole exception is pharmaceutical products in Germany. Here both strict liability and a liability ceiling have been introduced.[23]

(8) Liability for development risks is excluded (Art. 7, e). But Member States may impose manufacturer's liability for

---

[23]Arzneimittelgesetz of 24 August 1976 (BGBL, 1976, I, p. 2445) On this, read N. Reich, H. Micklitz, Consumer legislation in the Federal Republic of Germany, Van Nostrand Reinhold Co., London, 1981, p. 187-194; E. Von Hippel, Verbraucherschutz, J.C.B. Mohr, Tübingen, 1986, p. 74-83. On main consumer products injury compensation plans existing outside of EC Member States, one should read: J. Fleming, "Drug Injury Compensation Plans," American Journal of Comparative Law, 1982, p. 297-323; M. Whincup, "Compensation for Accident Victims: the Exemplary Model of New Zealand," Journal of Consumer Policy, 1984, p. 497-504; J.J. Ottley, B. Ottley, "Product Liability Law in Japan: An Introduction to a Developing Area of Law," The Georgia Journal of International and Comparative Law, 1984, p. 29-59; M. Fallon, Les accidents de la consommation et le droit, Bruylant, Bruxelles, 1982, p. 187-194.

> such defects (Art. 15, 1, b). This exclusion of development risks will be reexamined in 1995 (Art. 15, 3). This provision is responsive to the frequently advanced argument that it is unfair to hold a producer liable when rapid changes of scientific and technical knowledge at the time the product was designed make it difficult or impossible to discover the existence of the defect.

In general, consumer representatives in Europe welcome this new Directive. But it is not beyond criticism especially when one compares the final "product" with the expectations of the mid-1970s. In particular, severe criticisms are made concerning the way the question of development risks was solved. The history of this Directive also illustrates weaknesses of the EC decision-making process in the field of consumer protection.

First, the process has been horrendously slow, especially when one notes that discussions on product liability in the EC started in 1973. In 1976 the Commission proposed a directive on product liability.[24] Another three years passed before the European Parliament expressed its views on the proposal.[25] The legal competence of the Community to act in this field was questioned and substantial criticism of the substance of the Directive was offered by three bodies: the European Parliament, the Economic and Social Committee[26] and the Consumers' Consultative Committee.[27] In 1979, the Commission amended its proposal[28] and then a long debate started at the level of the Council of Ministers. Various proposals and amendments were made in order to reach the consensus required for harmonization measures under Article 100 of the Rome Treaty. The main issues were (1) whether to include development risks, (2) whether to put a financial ceiling on liability and (3) whether the directive should be considered as a minimal

---

[24] O.J. of 14 October 1976, C 241/9.

[25] O.J. of 21 May 1979, C 127/61.

[26] O.J. of 7 May 1979, C 114/15.

[27] Consumers Consultative Committee, Comments to Second Draft Directive concerning the approximation of the laws of Member States relating to product liability, CCC/156/75/rev. 2.

[28] O.J. of 26 October 1979, C 271/3. In 1980, the Consumers Consultative Committee drafted a new opinion on the amended version: CCC/10/80/rev. 2.

one, thus allowing Member States to adopt stronger national product liability rules.[29] The need for a unanimous vote by the Council of Ministers goes a long way in explaining why this decision-making process is so time-consuming.

Other factors explain why EC consumer protection proposals face such great obstacles. Consumer protection is a field where economic and social interests are highly conflicting. Because the consumer interest is still underorganized and underrepresented at the Community level,[30] there is an obvious imbalance in bargaining power between the interested parties. In the debate on product liability there have been countless statements against the proposed directive from a wide range of national or Community-based industry and trade pressure groups while representatives of the consumer interest have contributed to only six documents. These include three opinions from the Consumers' Consultative Committee, one 1981 statement by BEUC, one 1980 statement by the U.K. Consumers in the European Community Group and one 1977 opinion of the European Consumer Law Group.

Second, it may be that, as one compromise has been succeeded by another result falls short of consumer needs and expectations. Indeed, it may even result in adverse effects for consumers of particular member countries. The pursuit of legal uniformity or integration across the community could leave consumers in some countries worse off. The approximation of national rules could result in legislation that embodies the "lowest common denominator" instead of being drafted according to the standards of the most advanced countries.

While for some countries -- Italy, Greece, Spain and Portugal-- the Directive represents a dramatic change from traditional

---

[29]Th. Bourgoignie, "Where We Stand on Product Liability," BEUC News, n° 32, February 1984, p. 7-10.

[30]Consumer interests remain poorly organized at the Community level; they are underrepresented within the European Commission administrative structure; severe gaps and limits do affect existing consultation procedures in the consumer field at the Community level; consumer participation to the enforcement process of Community consumer law and policy remains extremely low, especially because of a lack of access of consumer groups before the Court of Justice of the EC. Th. Bourgoignie, "Consumer Law and the European Community," op. cit., 189-199; id., "Vers un droit...?," op. cit., p. 62-72; L. Kramer, op. cit., p. 312-40, 355-364.

liability concepts based on negligence, for most it appears to be mainly a codification of existing case law. The EC Directive does not constitute a major step forward for France, Belgium, Luxemburg, Denmark and Germany.[31] For these countries, the exclusion of development risks seriously undermines the scope and the relevance of the reform. Further, in those countries where stricter product liability schemes have been seriously considered,[32] the Directive will most likely dampen the efforts of national policymakers to adopt the stricter patterns that do include development risks.

Adverse effects may also result from the fact that the EC initiative prevents member States from keeping or enacting stricter, though not necessarily uniform, laws. The Product Liability Directive does not allow member States to enact stricter product liability rules,[33] (although such a provision was included in the earlier Commission Proposal). For example, this prevents member nations from enacting laws that excuse consumers from the burden of demonstrating the existence of a defect or requiring that it be born by the manufacturer.[34]

---

[31]M. Whincup, "Product Liability in Common Market Countries," Law Review, 1982, p. 52 et seq.; id., Product Liability, Gower, 1985, p. 131 et seq.; B. Dahl, "An Introduction to Liability Debate," Journal of Consumer Policy, 1979, p. 14-28

[32]See especially: in the United Kingdom, Liability for de Reports of the Law Commission and the Scottish Law Commission, HMSO, Cmnd 6831; Royal Commission on Civil Liability and personal injury (Pearson report), 3 vol., 1978, HMSO, Comnd 7, France, final report of the Commission de Refonte du Droit de mation: J. Calais-Auloy, Propositions pour un nouveau droit de la consommation La Documentation francaise, Paris 1985, p. 66-67. On this Commission and its final report, Th. Bourgoignie, "Proposals for a New Consumer Law in France," BEUC News. Legal Supplement, n° 12, November-December 1985, p. 1-11.

[33]The technique of minimal directives is frequently used in the fields of environmental protection and social policy. For examples in the consumer field, see L. Kramer, op. cit., p. 47-48.

[34]This provision has been proposed in France in a draft text on product liability suggested by the Commission de Refonte du Droit de la Consommation: J. Calais-Auloy, Propositions pour un nouveau droit de consommation, op. cit., p. 86 and Article 166, p. 186.

It is worth noting the influence that U.S. experience and discussion of product liability has had on the European scene. There has been much deceptive lobbying in this matter. The product liability debate in Europe has been unjustifiably clouded by emotive reactions, most originating in the U.S.. The alleged product liability "crisis" in the U.S. was used, as early as the mid-70s, as a "Frankenstein monster" to convince European and national public authorities not to adopt a strict liability system. Recent partisan publications have described the "virtues" of recent U.S. developments, e.g., the Kasten bill, in order to influence Community legislators.[35] In my judgment, any parallel with the U.S. situation must be seriously qualified and treated very carefully.

(1) Although it is true that insurance premiums covering product liability sharply increased in the U.S. between 1974 and 1976, the actual link between this increase and the introduction of a no-fault system has been questioned by many observers, including the U.S. Interagency Task Force report. Estimates of complaints were grossly exaggerated. Further, no convincing study confirmed the fears expressed of the negative impact that the product liability system would have on international trade.[36] Indications in Europe are that the costs of product liability will be minimal. It is wrong to claim that the extension of no-fault liability and the coverage of development risks would bring about an unacceptable increase in insurance costs. Estimates quoted by the German Central Association of Liability, Accidents and Sickness Insurers (Hika-Verland, 1977) show that the directive would have little impact, even if development risks are included in insurance premiums. "European insurers gave evidence to the European Parliament of the expected additional costs. In every case but one, they were a fraction of 1% of turnover. The only product category where the cost of insurance might go as high as 1% was explosives... The German insurance industry estimated that the cost of introducing strict liability for pharmaceutical products, probably the most "difficult" area, amounts to 1/2 of 1% of turnover. It is difficult to

---

[35]A good example of this is W. Jebb, "The EEC's Proposed Directive on Products Liability: A Call for Reappraisal in Light of the Model Uniform Product Liability Act," Boston College International and Comparative Law Review, 1983, p. 315-353.

[36]B. Dahl, op. cit., p. 23-25; M. Fallon, op. cit., p. 179-186.

> estimate the marginal cost of the new regime precisely until there exists a specific piece of legislation. Nonetheless, all reports suggest that the extra costs are unlikely to have serious effects on the price of products. It is widely suggested that any increase in insurance premiums for general engineering products is likely to amount to 0.1 percent of turnover. Such costs are minuscule as compared with spending on advertising and promotion."[37]

Another potential cost might be the eventual threat to innovation. It seems to me, however, that the relatively remote risks of a claim are unlikely to act as a deterrent to development and production. The proposed Directive would, moreover, provide an incentive for better quality controls and improved safety standards with a view to avoiding claims. The use by manufacturers of development risk as a defense might actually harm their sales. It hardly increases consumer confidence in a new product if its maker says, "This product is in the process of development; therefore, I won't be responsible if it proves defective and injures you!"[38]

(2) The final version of the text of the Directive differs in important ways from the 2d Restatement of Torts, § 402 A. The Directive (1) makes the Community product liability scheme less rigorous than the U.S. one; (2) it does not cover intermediate links in the distribution chain; (3) some defenses such as contributory negligence, state-of-the-art and development risks are made explicit; (4) there is a 10-year time limitation; (5) some damages such as damages caused to the product itself, as well as exemplary and punitive damages are not covered (6) member States are allowed to provide for a financial limitation of the producer's total liability for damage resulting from death or personal injury.

---

[37]R. Thomas, The Consumer Interest in a Strong Products Liability System, National Consumer Council, London, 1981, p. 7. M. Fallon quotes figures as low as 0.8% to 2% (op. cit., p. 185). G. Sanders, in "The Development of Compensation Systems for Victims of Defective Products," Products Liability International, 1984, p. 88, reports that neither the German nor the Swedish strict liability system for pharmaceutical products has led to any significant increase in compensation claims (quoted by L. Kramer, op. cit., p. 292).

[38]R. Thomas, op. cit., p. 6.

(3) Finally, several aspects of the legal environment and social systems in the countries of the European Community differ sharply from those of the U.S. The list of differences includes: (1) the existence of comprehensive social security systems in the European countries; (2) the higher cost of expertise in the U.S., resulting from the free choice of experts by the parties; (3) the contingency fee system in the U.S. by which the victim pays attorney's fees, usually a fixed percentage of the award, only if the case is won; (4) the greater generosity of U.S. juries in making personal injury awards. Another major difference is the availability in the U.S. of a potentially more effective collective redress mechanisms for consumers: class actions. This instrument, unknown in Europe,[39] makes the protection of the new product liability rules less formal and illusory for consumers.

For all these reasons, a European product liability "crisis" appears unlikely. This, despite the fears repeatedly expressed by industry during the long product liability debate in Europe.

Several legal analysts have stressed the rather modest gains the directive brings to consumers:

> Norbert Reich: "On the whole, one might argue that the promulgation of the directive after ten years of discussion is a consumer victory over the resistance of Member States, of industry and trade because it imposes the principle of strict liability for defective products. On the other hand, the progress made by the directive with regard to compensation is minimal and will help the injured consumer only in a limited number of cases."[40]
>
> L. Kramer: "...the directive's liability rules appear as (the fixation of a traditional and

---

[39]Collective redress mechanisms for consumers under the form of group actions or class actions remain extremely undeveloped in the European countries: see the report of the European Consumer Law Group on this topic, in <u>European Consumer Law Group Reports and Opinions (1977-1984)</u>, Cabay/Bruylant, Bruxelles/Louvain-la-Neuve, 1984, p. 245-279 (in English) and p. 281-321 (in French).

[40]N. Reich, <u>op. cit.</u>, p. 150-151.

> individualistic system) which hardly promotes the development of liability law, in particular in the products."[41]

The Community Directive falls far short of introducing a collective, social and comprehensive risk allocation system among producers, distributors, consumers and citizens in general for accidents and damage caused by contemporary mass-consumption processes. It appears to me that a comprehensive product safety and liability reform, including a collective compensation scheme is the best and only answer to the problem of defective and dangerous products circulating on the market.[42] As M. Whincup puts it: "The certainty of a reasonable and immediate insurance provision (is) infinitely preferable to the speculation and gains and losses of years of litigation."[43]

The present Directive will bring a pause in the product liability debate at least until 1995, when its provisions will be reexamined. This period of time should be used for collecting the data necessary for a more persuasive assessment of the issue, based on facts rather than on emotions, taking into account worldwide experience, both preventive and corrective, in dealing with defective and dangerous products and services. This has been a goal which proved impossible to reach by 1985.

---

[41]L. Kramer, op. cit., p. 293-294, quoting B. Dahl, P-pilleskader og produktansvarsreform, in Forbrugeradet: Forbrug pa mange mader, Festkrift Munch-Pedersen, Copenhagen, 1983, p. 82.

[42]Suggesting such a comprehensive treatment, Th. Bourgoignie, La protection du consommateur en matière de produits et de services défectueux ou dangereux, in La protection du consommateur: Consumer protection, Centre international de'études et de recherches européennes (Luxembourg, courses, 1983), ed. UGA, Kortrijk/ Bruxelles/Namur, 1984, p. 129 et seq., spéc. p. 171-172.

[43]M. Whincup, op. cit., Consumer Market Law Review, 1982, p. 539-540.

THE RIGHT

TO

CONSUMER EDUCATION

Chapter 34

Panel: The Role of Various Organizations in Consumer Education

ABOUT THE AUTHOR

D. Hayden Green is Chairman of the Business Department at Oak Park and River Forest High School in Oak Park, Illinois. After receiving Bachelor's and Master's in Business Administration and Business Education, Green received his Ed. D. from Northern Illinois University in 1978. A high school teacher in Illinois since 1971, Green has been a leader in developing consumer education. He is the author of a high school text, Consumers in The Economy, and has made numerous presentations to professional and educational groups. Green spent 1982-83 with the Consumer Education Resource Network in Rosslyn, Virginia, developing curriculum modules for consumer education.

THE ROLE OF SECONDARY SCHOOLS

D. Hayden Green

Consumer Education in the public schools at the secondary level has a long history. This history is marked by a waning and waxing of interest in this subject at the secondary level. With each phase the subject has been reinvented, reexamined, renewed, and in this paper, reviewed. In no way does this paper pretend to be an exhaustive treatment of the subject. It is confined to those aspects of consumer education at the secondary level with which the author, a secondary school teacher himself, has come into contact.

WHAT EACH INSTITUTION HAS DONE

To understand the state of consumer education requires a brief examination of the historical development of this imperative need. The earliest attention to consumer concerns can be found at the turn of the century when the American Home Economics Association was founded [21]. Consumer education won rapid acceptance in the thirties and early forties because the dominant educational philosophy of the period encouraged the study of real concerns of everyday life. Numerous consumer courses sprang up throughout the curriculum. In addition to home economics, other subject fields, such as mathematics and business, made attempts to see what contribution they could make. During this period consumer education sought to prepare students for the dual role of producer and consumer. Early textbooks [18, 19] emphasized buymanship for the consumer and knowledge of merchandise for the producer or seller.

The decade of the fifties was an inactive period for consumer education because the economy was growing and because of the relatively strong economic position of individuals in society. During the fifties, Sputnik touched off an intense campaign for a new educational philosophy that promoted the purely intellectual disciplines and accorded particular attention to the ablest students. This new educational thrust resulted in new curriculums in science, mathematics and languages. Consumer education gave way to a more theoretically oriented "economic education."

By the mid-sixties, by contrast, the focus in education shifted to the needs of the less academic students and school dropouts. And by the mid-seventies, many students, parents and educators were seeking "relevance" in the school curriculum. This concern led to a search for curriculum content, consumer education, for example, that lies close to the realities of life. The educational and philosophical currents of the 60s and 70s, were reinforced by a burgeoning consumer movement. As it gathered new strength, it provided another impetus for the teaching of consumer education. In the seventies consumer education differed from former years. Since the greater majority of Americans were able to meet their basic needs, consumer education focused more on helping consumers to achieve satisfaction in the marketplace [22]. A major emphasis during this period was on inequalities in the marketplace created by producer power and the need for a proactive consumer voice to correct this imbalance.

Very little curriculum innovation occurs in the public schools without financial support. The 1960's and 70's were times for sharing in government revenues. Two small Federal programs supported consumer education. The first was the Consumer and Homemaking Education Program, administered under the Vocational Educational Act of 1968. The second, much smaller but given a much freer rein, was the Office of Consumers' Education (OCE) administered by the Department of Education [23].

OCE asked leaders in the field to prepare "needs assessment" papers. In his 1977 "state of the art" paper, Lee Richardson wrote, "While a generally understood concept, consumer education is not precisely defined enough to assure uniform understanding among the persons who could implement it" [20]. This lack of clarity and consensus regarding the definition and scope of consumer education had long plagued the field. In 1978, OCE identified the lack of definition as one of the major weaknesses of the field [23].

To correct this problem, OCE took a giant step toward meeting the basic needs of consumer educators on a national scale by contracting with the Michigan Consumer Education Center, the National Consumers League, and the New Careers Training Laboratory of the City University of New York to collaborate on the planning and implementation of a Consumer Education Development Program (CEDP). One task of CEDP was to conduct research to define the field and its major concepts. As a result, an acceptable definition evolved, along with an orderly classification of concepts:

> Consumer education is the process of gaining the knowledge and skills needed in managing consumer resources and taking actions to influence the factors which affect consumer decisions [2].

This contract also resulted in a 56-page booklet, The Classification of Concepts in Consumer Education [2]. The Classification now sets the parameters of consumer education and reduces confusion, both within and outside the field, as to what consumer education is, and how it differs from other areas of study.

BODY OF KNOWLEDGE

From the general definition, The Classification of Concepts in Consumer Education identifies the concepts which establish the content of consumer education. The concepts are arranged into a taxonomy of three primary categories (Decision Making, Resource Management and Citizen Participation), eight second-level concepts and numerous sub-concepts. This classification puts the concepts of consumer education into an organized and useful structure. It provides, for the first time, a master framework which serves as a base document for materials and curriculum development. In fact, the Classification has been used in textbook development, research studies, and curriculum development.

CONSUMER EDUCATION OBJECTIVES

As educators, we all know that every educational program must have clearly defined goals and objectives. Consumer education, too. A survey of the large body of consumer education literature reveals a philosophical purpose commonly expressed by most proponents of consumer education. My gleaning of the literature yielded five distinctive goals and objectives of consumer education [10]. A good consumer program must:

(1) Produce competent buyers and users of goods and services;

(2) Produce competent financial managers;

(3) Produce an understanding of the economy;

(4) Generate an acceptance of consumer responsibilities along with an assertion of consumer rights;

(5) Help young people examine their values in order to develop a philosophy enabling them to achieve satisfaction within the resources they possess.

WHAT EACH INSTITUTION CURRENTLY DOES

In describing what the secondary schools are currently doing in consumer education, one must remember that educational policymaking takes place locally. Policymaking occurs in fifty states and over 7000 school districts. Thus, it is an understatement to say that general conclusions are difficult to reach! But Wilhelms [27] cogently summarizes the dilemma for consumer education in the secondary schools.

> The introduction of a new content into the crowded curriculum, against the pressures of the established subject, is difficult enough even when the new subject has a clean-cut identity, can be "inserted" in one piece, and has a ready-made cadre of expert teachers to back it. When, as in the case of consumer education, a field lacks identity as a "subject," when it has almost no corps of full-time specialists and must depend on the good will and (at best) loosely coordinated efforts of specialists from other fields, the difficulties multiply [27].

To further illustrate the problems of identifying consumer education as it exists in the secondary curriculum, there are two other obstacles: (1) a lack of standardized course title terminology, and (2) the frequency with which, when consumer education concepts are integrated or infused into traditional subject, it is assumed that a student has also "received" consumer education.

The lack of standardized terminology causes confusion as to the objectives, identity, and contents of consumer education. Listed below are some commonly used course titles which may or may not contain the essential elements of consumer education:

- Consumer Education
- General Business
- Consumer Economics
- Personal Economics
- Consumer Economic Education
- Personal Finance
- Consumer and Home-making
- Money Management
- Economics or Applied Economics
- Free Enterprise

Frequently, consumer education concepts are integrated into traditional courses such as mathematics, English, home economics, business, social studies, and industrial arts, etc., rather than being offered as a separate course. Although this approach is better than no consumer education at all, it confounds the task of identifying consumer education in the curriculum. Even more significant is the problem posed when educators or researchers claim that this approach constitutes "consumer education." The problem becomes acute when researchers try to measure changes in attitude, consumer knowledge or behavior after instruction in consumer education. When there is little or no common terminology or little common exposure to the concepts that constitute the body of knowledge, measurement of the effects of consumer education seems destined to failure.

EDUCATIONAL REFORM: IMPLICATIONS FOR CONSUMER EDUCATION

The current national discussion on education in the United States was initiated by A Nation at Risk [17], the report of the National Commission on Excellence in Education, and has been sustained by numerous other school studies, such as the Carnegie Report, Paideia Report, National Science Board Report, Goodlad Report, and the National Academy of Science Report. Unquestionably the major impact on consumer education of the current educational reform movement lies in the area of curriculum.

Consumer education is not recognized in the mainstream of education and therefore, has not warranted discussion in the same way as mathematics, science, English, and computer education. There is no mention of consumer education in any of the national studies mentioned above. But consumer education is implicated in some reports by such statements as "Twenty-five percent of the credits earned by general track high school students are in physical and health education, work experience outside the school, remedial English and mathematics, personal service and development courses, such as training for adulthood and marriage" [17]. Another example from the same report says that "in 13 states, 50 percent or more of the units required for high school graduation may be electives chosen by the student. Given this freedom to choose the substance of half or more of their education, many students opt for less demanding personal service courses, such as bachelor living" [17].

If 1983 was the year of the educational reports, then 1984 and 1985 were the years of state legislative action in education. Since the publication of A Nation at Risk, some 44 states have made changes in high school graduation requirements, mandating an increase in math, science, English, and foreign language. The result of increasing graduation requirements has been to reduce or limit the number of elective courses, such as vocational subjects, arts, and personal development courses, like consumer education.

Although A Nation at Risk did not include "economics" in its recommendations, other reports do. For example, the Task Force on Education for Economic Growth, Action For Excellence, by the Education Commission of the States, includes economic competencies, along with reading, writing, speaking, listening, mathematical, scientific, basic employment and computer literacy competencies. In his concluding remarks at the National Forum on Excellence in Education, then Secretary of Education T. H. Bell stated that "to vote intelligently today, one must have a grasp of the fundamentals of economics, taxation, and the great ideas of free enterprise" [3]. Clearly the study of economics has gained greater acceptance among mainstream educators and the public than has consumer education. This is partially the result of organizational, financial and programmatic support provided by the Joint Council on Economic Education in recent years. In part, it may also be the result of a public perception that consumer education is "soft" while economics is perceived as rigorous, or "hard."

Consumer educators should have no quarrel with the linkage between consumer education and economic education. Consumer educators cannot afford to become embroiled in a battle over consumer education or economic education. Both are essential areas of study and the marriage is a natural one. In fact, the linkage helps change the public perception of consumer education as a soft, nonessential subject. An example of the shift toward economic education occurred in California with the passage of the Hughes-Hart Education Reform Act of 1983. This act requires that pupils must complete a one-semester course in economics. A close examination of the Model Curriculum Standards for Economics in California shows that the model economics course contains a substantial consumer education/personal finance component.

Although it is easy to agree philosophically with the linkage between consumer and economic education, it is a marriage that, unfortunately, seldom occurs at the implementation level. Instead, depending upon the academic preparation of the teacher and the curriculum plan, the instructional emphasis tends toward either consumer or economic education, not both, not integrated.

Another case illustrating the shift away from consumer education and toward economic education can be seen in the educational reform legislation in Illinois. Illinois House Bill 730 established a definition of schooling which includes outcome statements in comparative economic systems and the American economic system. As to consumer education, the legislature did not repeal the consumer education mandate. But it did pass a provision whereby students who pass a State-developed proficiency examination in consumer education are excused from the required consumer education course or equivalent.

Following is a summary of the State Mandates for Economic Instruction in 1985-86 prepared for the Joint Council on Economic Education by the Center for Economic Education, University of the Pacific [5]. The purpose of the project was to update a 1981 survey whose goal was to determine the existence of mandates for instruction in economics, free enterprise and/or consumer education at the elementary and secondary school levels within the fifty states. As of March 1, 1985, the status of state mandates for economics instruction in the various states was as follows:

(1) Twenty-seven states mandated <u>some form</u> of instruction in economics;

(2) Fifteen states required at least a semester course in economics for high school graduation;

(3) Four states required that high schools offer an elective economics course;

(4) Twenty-four states had an Economics/Free Enterprise mandate.

(5) Ten states mandated consumer education.

Since the 1981 survey, Hawaii, New Hampshire, New York, and Pennsylvania have added mandates for economics instruction while Kentucky and Wisconsin have withdrawn their mandates.

WHAT EACH INSTITUTION SHOULD DO

Recently there has been increasing awareness among consumer educators of the importance of measuring the "bottom line benefits of consumer education." This is reflected in such documents as the Report on the First National Consumer Education Roundtable sponsored by the U.S. Office of Consumer Affairs [12]. One of the key points emerging from this Roundtable was: "....Roundtable leaders agreed that we need a broad base of information that establishes costs and benefits of consumer education in order to show evidence for investment -- by all sectors -- in the production and delivery of consumer and economic education" [12]. The Dearborn Roundtable on Consumer Education, sponsored by Avon Products, Inc., further emphasized the need to establish a research based benefit from consumer education [1].

In a speech during National Consumers Week (1985) Michael MacDowell, President of the Joint Council on Economic Education, repeated this call for a demonstration of the benefits of consumer and economic education: "Effective and well educated consumers are the best friends that private enterprise has. We know this. We must prove it." [15]

Why can't educators prove the bottom-line benefits of secondary-level sponsored academic consumer education? Several doctoral studies have examined the question [11, 13, 16, 25]. Traditional assessments of consumer education have included pretest-posttest, quasi-experimental designs which measured the effect of consumer education in terms of knowledge gained, attitude change or by direct questioning on behavior in the marketplace. Most of the studies utilized student populations for which the effects were measured immediately following the completion of a consumer education course. Several studies utilized quasi-experimental designs and compared the change in consumer knowledge of students enrolled in consumer education to a control group not similarly enrolled. Langrehr reported significant differences in consumer economic competency among high school economics, consumer education, and control classes, with the consumer education class having the highest scores. Garman, McLaughlin, McLaughlin, and Eckert [9] compared university students enrolled in a consumer education course to a control group and found a significant difference in gain scores between the two. On the other hand, Bibb [4], Clair [8], Thomas [25] and Waddell [26] found no differences in consumer competency. Studies which measured cognitive change as a result of consumer education have often found demographic variables such as age, mental ability, prior knowledge, and sex of the student to be significant predictors of consumer competency [14]. Carsky,

Lytton, and McLaughlin [7] found major field of study and sex to be significant in assessing differential knowledge gains among university students enrolled in a consumer education course.

No easy answer is at hand as to what caused these conflicting research findings. But I would like to posit some suggestions for future research. It seems to me that the lack of adequate testing instruments in the field of consumer education poses a major obstacle for researchers and educational practitioners. Let me cite an example from Illinois. Reviewing commercial examinations, the Illinois State Board of Education found none acceptable for a variety of reasons. In the judgment of a committee and staff, most were unacceptable with respect to coverage, consumer education objectives, and degree of rigor.

As a result, the Evaluation Section of the Illinois State Board of Education found it necessary to start afresh to develop a consumer education proficiency examination. When this test is finished, it may measure some degree of proficiency as defined for and by the staff of the Illinois State Board of Education. The point is a simple one. Until the community of academics who call themselves "consumer educators" devise a reliable, valid instrument(s) that measures the commonly accepted concepts and objectives of consumer education, it will not be possible to measure the bottom line benefits of consumer education, whether cognitive, attitudinal, or behavioral.

The most imperative research need at this point is a test that will: (1) measure the scope and sequence of the field; (2) rigorously measure the topics that are essential components of consumer education, such as insurance, nutrition, housing, credit, investing, consumer law, economic understanding, decision making, etc.; (3) distinguish those who have studied formal consumer education from those whose knowledge is purely experiential; and (4) be based upon the Classification of Concepts in Consumer Education. A measurement instrument(s) based on the Classification of Concepts, is a means to ending the diversity of instruction and disparate interests that plague consumer education at the secondary school level.

Consumer educators should be able to reach agreement on what constitutes the core of knowledge representing competency in consumer education. They should also be able to identify competent consumer behavior. Our colleagues in English, mathematics, science, and other areas of study can do so at various levels, from elementary grades and advanced placement examinations to certification examinations in numerous occupations and for advanced degrees. Consumer educators should be able to do the same!

Prior to the development of a widely accepted definition and taxonomy of concepts in consumer education, it may have been necessary and understandable for researchers to establish their own objectives and questions, giving rise to various and conflicting research results. Now the time has come for academics to develop a scope and sequence of knowledge that can be tested and measured reliably. Such a test(s) would: (1) further define consumer education for curriculum implementation at the secondary level; (2) eliminate the ambiguity resulting from the lack of uniformity of course titles and instructional content; (3) help researchers as they attempt to determine the effects of instruction in consumer education; and (4) finally prove the bottom-line benefits of consumer education.

REFERENCES

1. AVON PRODUCTS, INC. (1985), Should There Be A National Agenda For Consumer Education? Avon Products, Inc., Consumer Information Center, New York, New York.

2. BANNISTER, ROSELLA and CHARLES MONSMA (1982), Classification of Concepts in Consumer Education, Cincinnati, OH.: South-Western Publishing Company. Monograph 137.

3. BELL, TERREL H. (1983), "Summary Remarks," National Forum on Excellence in Education," Indianapolis, Indiana. Unpublished speech.

4. BIBB, F.G. (1971), "A Comparative Study of Knowledge of Three Aspects of Consumer Information Possessed by Selected Indiana, Illinois, and Wisconsin University Freshmen." DeKalb, Il.: Northern Illinois University, College of Business. Unpublished Doctoral dissertation.

5. BRENNAN, DENNIS C. (1986), A Survey of State Mandates for Economics Instruction 1985-86. New York, New York: Joint Council on Economic Education.

6. CALIFORNIA DEPARTMENT OF EDUCATION (1985), Model Curriculum Standards For Economics. Curriculum Instruction and Assessment Division, Sacramento, CA.

7. CARSKY, M.L., R. LYTTON and G. MCLAUGHLIN (1984), "Change in Consumer Competency and Attitudes: Do Student Characteristics Make a Difference?" in K. Goebel (Ed.), Proceedings of the Thirteenth Annual Conference of The ACCI, Atlanta, GA: April.

8. CLAIR, R.C. (1973), "An Analysis of Economic Education and Consumer Education Knowledge of Kansas High School Seniors," Manhattan, KS.: Kansas State University. Unpublished Doctoral dissertation.

9. GARMAN, E.T., J.S. MCLAUGHLIN, G.W. MCLAUGHLIN and S.W. ECKERT (1983), "Measuring Change in Comprehension and Attitude in Consumer Education for Postsecondary Students," Proceedings of the Twelfth Annual Southeastern Regional Family Economics-Home Management Conference.

10. GREEN, D. HAYDEN (1985), "The Role of Consumer Education in the General Education of All Students," Kyoto Conference on Consumer Education, Japan Academy of Consumer Education, Kinjo Gakuin University. Unpublished speech.

11. HAWKINS, CALVIN H. (1979), "A Study of the Use of Consumer Education Concepts by High School Graduates," The Journal of Consumer Affairs, Summer.

12. KNAUER, VIRGINIA H. (1985), "Leaders Leading the Way," Taking Responsibility For Consumer Education, Washington, D.C.: U.S. Office of Consumer Affairs.

13. LANGREHR, FREDERICK W. (1979), "Consumer Education: Does It Change Students' Competencies and Attitudes?" The Journal of Consumer Affairs, Summer.

14. LANGREHR, F.W. and B.J. MASON (1977), "The Development and Implementation of Consumer Education," Journal of Consumer Affairs, Winter.

15. MACDOWELL, MICHAEL (1985), "Networks That Work for Consumer Education," Taking Responsibility For Consumer Education, Washington, D.C.: U.S. Office of Consumer Affairs.

16. MIESELWITZ, ROLT (1968), "A Study to Determine the Extent of Consumer Education Knowledge of Secondary School Students Related to Family Finance." National Business Education Quarterly.

17. A NATION AT RISK: THE IMPERATIVE FOR EDUCATION REFORM (1983), Washington, D.C.: The National Commission on Excellence in Education.

18. REID, M. (1942), Consumers and The Market, New York, New York: Appleton-Century-Crofts.

19. REICH, E. (1937), Consumer Goods-How to Know and Use Them, New York: Appleton-Century-Croft.

20. RICHARDSON, LEE (1977), Consumer Education -- A Position Paper on the State of the Art, Washington, D.C.: U.S. Office of Education, Office of Consumer's Education.

21. ROYER, GAYLE L. and NANCY E. NOLT (1980), Education of the Consumer: A Review of Historical Developments, Rosslyn, VA.: Consumer Education Resource Network.

22. SCHERF, G.W.H. (1974), "Consumer Education As a Means of Alleviating Dissatisfaction," Journal of Consumer Affairs, 8 (No. 1, Summer), 61-75.

23. SLAGEL, MICHELLE L. (1982), The Implementation of a Discretionary Project Program: A Case Study of the Office of Consumers' Education, Washington, D.C.: George Washington University, School of Government and Business Administration. Unpublished Doctoral dissertation.

24. TARP (Technical Assistance Research Programs, Inc.) (1983), The Bottom Line Benefits of Consumer Education, The Industry and Consumer Affairs Department of Coca Cola Company, Atlanta, GA.

25. THOMAS, LILLIE RUTH (1969), "A Comparative Study of the Effects of Course Organization on Achievement in Consumer Education Concepts," Tempe, AZ.: Arizona State University, College of Education. Unpublished Doctoral dissertation.

26. WADDELL, F.W. (1981), "The Effects of Experimental Consumers Education on Subsequent Performance in the Marketplace," Blackburn, VA.: Virginia Polytechnic Institute and State University. Unpublished Doctoral dissertation.

27. WILHELMS, FRED T. (1979), Consumer Education Project: A Final Report, Denver, CO.: Education Commission of The States.

ABOUT THE AUTHOR

Lillian H. Mohr is Assistant to the President for Contract Administration and Professor and Director, Center for Economic Education, at Florida State University, Tallahassee. Mohr has had a varied career in teaching, advertising, consumer education, and government. She received her Ph.D. from Syracuse University in Social Sciences/Economics in 1966. Her career involved service to Family and Consumer Economics at Syracuse and Florida State Universities. She has been a leading figure in Consumer Education for the Federal Government in two administrations, the Ford and Reagan (1981-83) Administrations. She is the author of Frances Perkins, "That Woman" in F.D.R.'s Cabinet, and many articles on consumer education.

THE ROLE OF THE FEDERAL GOVERNMENT

Lillian H. Mohr

THE RIGHT TO CONSUMER EDUCATION

In November, 1975 at the first Consumer Education "Catch-Up" Conference conducted by the U.S. Office of Consumer Affairs (OCA), Special Assistant to the President Virginia Knauer presented President Gerald Ford's statement on Consumer Education:

> In the last decade, the Buyer's Bill of Rights has become a way of life in our country. These rights include information, choice, safety and the right to have complaints satisfactorily resolved.
>
> The time has now come to recognize a fifth right -- one without which consumers cannot gain the full benefit of the other four. This is the right to consumer education.
>
> It is my earnest hope that consumer education will become an integral part of regular school instruction, community services and educational programs for people out of school. Only in this way can we ensure that consumers have the assistance necessary to plan and use their resources to their maximum potential and greatest personal satisfaction.

The problem with general statements of purpose like this is that they are subject to wide variations in interpretation. So, too, with the right to information, to choose and to have complaints satisfactorily resolved. The Consumer Product Safety Commission with its commitment to "safe" products can attest to different responses to "How safe is safe?" from its various Commissioners, manufacturers of products, and targeted consumers.

PRESIDENT FORD'S ASSERTION OF THE RIGHT TO CONSUMER EDUCATION

President Ford's statement does not place responsibility for consumer education on the Federal Government. Nor does it specify how consumer education will become an integral part of regular school instruction, community services and continuing education. Implicit in any Presidential statement, however, is the notion that the Federal Government will provide some leadership and that this leadership will find considerable acceptance at the grass roots level. Of course the best evidence of an administration's true commitment to Consumer Education would be a well-funded agency with consumer education as its primary mission.

Early in 1975 the Office of Consumers' Education was established in the then U.S. Office of Education (USOE) in the Department of Health, Education and Welfare (HEW). With a budget of $3.1 million for fiscal year 1976, staffed by a director, two or three assistants, and a small support staff, its major responsibility was to award grants and contracts to educators and community leaders who would experiment with or devise new ways to educate consumers. Three months after advertising the availability of and specifications for grants to consumer educators in the Federal Register, the Office of Consumers' Education received 858 project proposals!! Requests for funding came to $75 million. The selection process utilized judgments of outstanding consumer educators from academia and community groups. The criteria applied in allocating the $3 million were the projects most likely to (1) be productive and (2) make a difference in the field. Sixty-six out of the 858 submissions, or 7 1/2%, were funded in 1976-77. A number of specific projects deemed high priority by the Director were funded through Requests for Proposals (RFPs). These included a treatise on the state of the art, and somewhat later, the establishment of a Consumer Education Resource Network (CERN). (Currently, CERN is little more than a library service in the Department of Defense.) Over its 6-year existence, the Office of Consumers' Education funded hundreds of projects targeted for community, university, elementary and secondary school, bi-lingual, poverty and continuing education levels.

Prior to the establishment of the Office of Consumers' Education (which went out of existence in 1982), consumer educators received funding from other sources. The Title I Higher Education Act named consumer education as a priority for funding by the state granting agencies. However, some states chose to ignore this category, because of other needs they deemed more urgent. A Federal agency for education, be it an Office or a Cabinet Department, can urge educators to follow a course of action. But the only coercive pressure it can exert is the withholding of certain supplemental funds. Thus, agencies in the Federal Governement can exhort while the critical decisions are made in the 17,000-plus local school districts in our 50 states. In addition, State Departments of Education and Boards of Regents, can also exhort. But, to repeat, the final decisions are largely made by the local school board, the school superintendent, and the curriculum specialists, and within the schools themselves, by the principal, department chairpersons, and finally, the classroom teacher.

Other consumer education funds came from the National Science Foundation, the Consumer and Homemaking Education Program under the Vocational Education Act, and -- for specified research -- from such agencies as the U.S. Office of Consumer Affairs and the Food and Drug Administration.

In-House Programs

My position as a senior officer in OCA in 1975-76 and again in 1981-83 provides me with a basis for commenting on Federal agencies with a role in consumer education. In my view civil servants with a role in consumer affairs have shown tremendous dedication and commitment. As long as they have the support of their superiors, they have and will extend themselves, trying to maximize the productivity of the dollars allocated to various projects.

Budgets have typically been too small for the job to be done on a national level, making it necessary to establish linkages among various Federal agencies, and between the Federal agencies and the business community. In recent years particularly, the budget cuts, the constant threat of personnel cuts, and shifts in priorities have increased the pressures on government workers at all levels.

In earlier years the U.S. Office of Consumer Affairs developed "model" consumer education programs such as the All-Indian Pueblo and the District of Columbia Teacher Training programs, conducted "catch-up" conferences for newcomers to the field who had proposals funded, and special conferences to explore current issues such as the energy problem, health care cost containment, or counterfeit products.

Increasingly OCA has served as a catalyst, inspiring other people to take initiative at the grass roots level. What was "National Consumer Education Week" under Esther Peterson was broadened under Virginia Knauer with the result that each year a Presidential Proclamation declares the third week in April to be "National Consumers Week." All the Federal agencies represented on the Consumer Advisory Council seek to make this "awareness" event as spectacular as possible. Their primary role, however, is to get schools, universities, libraries, hospitals, community groups, labor organizations, corporations, and state and city agencies to participate by showcasing their consumer activities, developing forums, conferences and fairs, offering special courses, and in general, publicizing the importance of consumer education and the sources and materials available to the public. One will recognize this deference to the private sector as a hallmark of the Reagan Administration.

In 1986 OCA developed a Teachers' Lesson Plan to accompany the Consumer's Resource Handbook. It is not as significant as the curriculum guide developed by OCA under Virginia Knauer's leadership in the early Seventies. However, with the proliferation of curriculum guides, that need has already been met.

CONSUMER EDUCATION MATERIALS FROM OTHER FEDERAL AGENCIES

Josephine Turner's comments highlight the contributions to consumer education of the U.S. Department of Agriculture's Cooperative Extension Service. Extension agents all over the country have been educating consumers for decades. They warrant special kudos for working in the field when virtually no one else was around.

The Department of the Treasury provides educational materials for all age levels. Its major thrust has been Financial Management Service material on Direct Deposit. The U.S. Customs' brochures advise consumers to familiarize themselves with import information before traveling abroad. The U.S. Mint provides coin collectors with information as well as selling coins.

The Federal Deposit Insurance Corporation (FDIC) has a toll-free Consumer Telephone Hotline which enables the public to ask about their rights in relation to FDIC banks. This helps avert disputes stemming from confusion or misunderstanding of banking practices. The FDIC also provides booklets on "When a Bank Fails" and on protective credit legislation.

The district Federal Reserve Banks produce many excellent educational materials that are available for classroom distribution. For anyone teaching taxes, the Internal Revenue Service's Understanding Taxes tabloid for students and the matching teacher's manual stand out as exceptional materials.

The Consumer Product Safety Commission (CPSC) formerly had a large-scale educational program developed by outstanding educators for classroom use. Unfortunately, this staff has been virtually eliminated, and along with it, most of the educational material on how to buy safe products and use them correctly. The only free material listed in the Consumer Information Catalog, Spring 1986, is a 3-pager on kerosene heaters. The 11-page Home Electrical Safety Audit, 9-page Home Fire Safety, 29-page Safety for Older Consumers and 20-page children's comic book on fire hazards cost fifty cents each.

The Food and Drug Administration still produces quantities of free material on medical problems; most titles appear to be 3 and 4 pages long. The U.S. Department of Agriculture offers free publications on food safety, but more of their titles involve a 50 cents charge.

Consumers may have a "Right to Consumer Education." But, increasingly, they must purchase educational materials from the Federal Government rather than receiving them free. Starting five years ago, the Consumer Information Center (CIC) was required to impose user fees. This means no charge for one free booklet, but 2 or more free booklets incur a $1.00 charge. However, up to 25 different free booklets can be ordered for that $1.00. The list of sales booklets exceeds that of free materials; almost half cost 50 cents, and others run from $1.00 to $7.00. The consumer should be warned: some of the pamphlets sold are not good values. Thirty-six federal offices sponsor publications sent out by the Pueblo, Colorado facilities of CIC. The Consumer Information Catalog is available at no cost on a regular basis to educators, libraries and non-profit groups in quantities of 25 or more.

Other Aids

Teachers in the District of Columbia and environs have access to the personnel in Federal offices to ask questions, and to obtain speakers. If travel budgets permit, government speakers are available without charge for major conferences on consumer-related subjects.

A number of Federal offices provide their expertise if classroom materials need to be evaluated for accuracy before publication. Occasionally agency heads will write an introductory statement or an endorsement but this requires careful consideration.

SHOULD GOVERNMENT EDUCATE CONSUMERS?

Should the federal government compete with the private sector in purveying educational material and information? Obviously, it should not compete with educational publishers. But if they, or business and/or the media fail to provide current educational material about U.S. Savings Bonds, direct deposit of Social Security checks, hazardous substances, quackery and scams, most of us feel the government has an obligation to do so. Also if obtaining sound, objective information is too costly for middle- and low-income consumers, or if distribution is too limited, the government should fill the void.

In 1977 Virginia Knauer presented a proposal for a privately-funded National Foundation for Consumer Education that would function as a resource, research and referral center. A single such institution would serve educators well, forestalling excessive duplication of effort and doing the job efficiently. The coordinative function of a consumer education "headquarters" would contribute immeasurably to the development of the field. Since the private sector is unable or unwilling to undertake certain kinds of research, government support for such an undertaking is needed.

CONCLUSION

Finally, the trend away from protective legislation and the regulation of industries constitutes a powerful argument for reemphasizing that the consumers' best protection is knowledge of the marketplace and awareness of its pitfalls. Consumer education helps prevent problems. As a cost-effective way of reducing marketplace failures, it not only warrants but requires governmental support. Until consumers themselves insist on being educated as consumers or until they develop the cohesiveness that gives them the clout of "countervailing power," it makes economic sense for the Federal Government to further the objectives of consumer education through dissemination of information, coordination and support of research.

ABOUT THE AUTHOR

Grace E. Richardson is Vice President of Consumer Affairs at Colgate-Palmolive Company. Educated initially in Home Economics Education at Simmons College and then in Textile Chemistry with a Master's from Cornell University, most of Richardson's career has been in consumer affairs, starting with J.C. Penney, followed by positions as Director of Consumer Affairs at Consolidated Edison, Chesebrough-Pond's, and now Colgate-Palmolive. She has assumed leadership roles in the Society of Consumer Affairs Professionals (Board Member, 1984-88), consumer education (Board of the National Coalition for Consumer Education), and alumni affairs at Cornell (member of the Council, 1982-88 and Vice Chairman, Cornell University Administrative Board, 1986-88). While Director of Consumer Affairs at Chesebrough-Pond's, Richardson was instrumental in establishing financial support for the Wingspread Conference.

THE ROLE OF BUSINESS

Grace E. Richardson

My role as a Consumer Affairs Professional in business is to answer the question, "Why is business involved in consumer education anyway?"

HISTORICAL PERSPECTIVE

Historically, product promotion was the reason many companies sponsored consumer education programs. Though varied, some programs were quite elaborate, including company-run seminars or courses with instructors and textbooks. A conspicuous example was the sewing schools conducted by the Singer Company for purchasers of Singer machines.

Other programs focused on the preparation and distribution of bulletins, buying guides, and other collateral consumer information materials. Food companies provided recipes, furniture companies developed interior design guidelines and consumer product companies furnished "how to" information.

Over the years many companies have been involved in the production of consumer education materials for use in the classroom. Most of these materials provide up-to-date, realistic information that is difficult to obtain from other sources.

The activist consumer movement of the 60's and 70's with its emphasis on the consumer and consumer legislation spurred business to become even more involved in consumer education.

Periodically, however, business' role in consumer education has prompted controversy. Sheila Harty put the critical view succinctly in her 1979 book, Hucksters In The Classroom published by Ralph Nader's Center for the Study of Responsive Law. Harty wrote, "Corporations are inappropriate sponsors of educational materials precisely because they have something to sell" [8].

Admittedly, some business programs have been too promotional and self-serving. But for the most part, business is a supportive and appropriate partner in the consumer education process.

WHY IS BUSINESS INVOLVED IN CONSUMER EDUCATION?

The reasons for business' involvement in consumer education have changed during the last 20 years. Examples from my own career dramatize some of these changes.

My first Consumer Affairs position in 1966 was with the J.C. Penney Company. There our goals were (1) to help consumers explore issues and influence change in society, and (2) to provide educational programs and materials as a service in communities with J.C. Penney stores. It was the Company's belief that, "We owe something to the communities where we do business." This philosophy guided the entire J.C. Penney consumer education program.

Next, I held the position of Director of Consumers Affairs at Consolidated Edison, New York City's major utility company. Con Ed and other utilities viewed consumer education as a means of expressing good corporate citizenship. Utilities generally concentrate their education efforts on conservation and customer information programs.

At Chesebrough-Ponds the goal was to help position the company in the eyes of the public and purchasers of our products as a family- and consumer-oriented corporation. This was accomplished through consumer information materials and financial support for consumer education programs and organizations.

In my current position as Vice President of Consumer Affairs for Colgate-Palmolive, our role in consumer education is to provide consumer information on products.

Other companies sponsor consumer education programs as a means of presenting a company or alternative perspectives on policy issues or to explain and justify the practices of their company and/or industry [2].

As you can see, multiple reasons account for business involvement in consumer education. But the most fundamental reason is that consumer education is just plain "good business." Research supports this enlightened self-interest motivation. Various studies find that consumer education programs conducted by business provide increased consumer confidence, positive "word-of-mouth" publicity, increased sales, reduced consumer "problems" and need for service, enhanced perception of quality, reduced liability and better acceptance of new products [7].

Truly effective Consumer Education is obviously in the interest of consumers. It can be argued that it is critical to the success, if not the survival, of our American market economy, a position cogently argued by Professor Gwen Bymers [3].

WHAT ARE THE WAYS BUSINESS IS INVOLVED WITH CONSUMER EDUCATION TODAY?

There are many ways business is involved in consumer education; some will be obvious to you, others less so:

(1) As in the past, the most common form of business consumer education is consumer product information. While a 1982 General Electric study showed that today's consumers are more sophisticated and discriminating than in the past, they have less time to educate themselves about their options and to comparison shop. As a result, they seek quality information, especially during the pre-purchase period. Companies seek to fill this need by providing more accurate, useful, consistent, credible and reliable consumer information [6]. Surveys show that consumers respond enthusiastically to the new, more accessible information sources such as 800 numbers and do-it-yourself repair manuals.

(2) Another popular business involvement in consumer education is the development of classroom materials in the form of films, filmstrips, teachers guides, brochures, student activity sheets, etc. My own company, Colgate-Palmolive, has long been involved in providing dental education programs and classroom materials to improve dental health in kindergarten through fourth grade.

To guide business in developing materials that are appropriate in an educational environment, our professional association, The Society of Consumer Affairs Professionals in Business (SOCAP), developed "Guidelines for Business Sponsored Consumer Education Materials" [10]. The objectives of these guidelines are to help business develop educationally sound and worthwhile materials and to present content standards that SOCAP believes are appropriate to educational programs.

(3) Businesses are now working cooperatively with consumer, government and academic groups to co-sponsor the development and distribution of consumer education materials and programs in joint ventures. For example, a "Mail Order Rights" booklet was developed by American Express in cooperation with the U.S. Postal Service, the U.S. Office of Consumer Affairs and the General Services Administration's Consumer Information Center.

(4) Another way corporations get involved in consumer education is by sponsoring conferences that promote consumer education. Such a Conference was sponsored by Avon Products Inc. in 1984 for consumer education specialists from business, education, consumer organizations, community groups, and government. The purpose of the Conference was to explore and define the needs for a national consumer education agenda [1].

(5) In addition to sponsoring consumer education conferences, companies often provide support to consumer education through financial contributions or in the form of the time, effort and expertise of their employees. Such was the case with the National Consumer Education Round Table which was co-sponsored by the U.S. Office of Consumer Affairs, the Detroit Testing Laboratory and the University of Detroit in 1984. Key business consumer affairs professionals provided their expertise at the Round Table and the Zayre Corporation financed the publication of the Report [11].

Another appropriate example is the financial support provided for this ACCI Conference at Wingspread by the Consumer Affairs Departments of Chesebrough-Pond's, American Express, and the Shell Oil Company. The Conference also received financial support from the Johnson Foundation.

(6) Still another way business supports consumer education is by <u>sponsoring workshops and seminars for educators</u>. J.C. Penney was a long time leader in this effort, sponsoring workshops for secondary teachers across the country. Penney also sponsored annually the "Consumer Affairs Forum," a week-long, issue-focused seminar for consumer professionals in higher education and government.

(7) <u>Research</u> provides yet another avenue by which business supports consumer education. For instance, the Coca-Cola Company recently sponsored a study to document the corporate benefits of consumer education and to determine the effectiveness of educational materials in modifying consumer attitudes toward product utilization.

The results of the Coca-Cola study show that there can be definite cost-effective, bottom-line benefits to corporate sponsors of consumer education programs. These benefits include: (1) increased confidence in the sponsoring company; (2) more purchases of the sponsoring company's products; (3) fewer complaints [5].

(8) <u>Award Programs</u> constitute another avenue for business support of consumer education. Chesebrough-Ponds, for example, sponsors the American Home Economics Association's (AHEA) "Teacher of the Year Award". This supports consumer education indirectly since home economics teachers frequently assume leadership roles in consumer education programs. The Texize Corporation provides an AHEA award specifically targeted to consumer educators.

(9) Corporations are also <u>involved in national organizations that support consumer education</u> such as the National Coalition for Consumer Education. The Coalition's long range goal is to promote consumer education in schools, in the community and in the marketplace. Business' commitment to the development of the Coalition has been evident in the time and energy business people have devoted to the Board and in financial donations for national conferences and programs. This commitment remains strong today as business people are actively involved in keeping the Coalition alive.

(10) Finally, consumer affairs professionals in business have a responsibility to provide <u>internal consumer education</u>. This means educating their colleagues with differing

business philosophies and backgrounds to the advantages of working together with government, education and consumers. Ultimately, we believe that what is in the consumer interest is also in our company's long term interest [4].

QUESTIONS FOR FUTURE RESEARCH

Business will continue to work in partnership with education, government and consumer groups to develop innovative, high quality consumer education materials and programs. A major focus of this Conference has been to pose questions and issues that need to be addressed by future researchers. There are many unanswered questions relating to business' involvement in consumer education. Some of the biggest issues concern consumer education itself:

1. How can we rekindle interest in consumer education at the local and national level? What should be the role of business, government and consumer educators to help make consumer education "come alive?"

2. Can we identify or develop new methods that are more effective in educating consumers? Are we too attached to our "old ways?" Is there a "right teachable moment?"

3. With less government funding for consumer education, what can business do, collaborating with government, education and consumer groups, to aid the achievement of the Right to Consumer Education?

REFERENCES

1. AVON PRODUCTS INC. (1984), Should There Be a National Agenda for Consumer Education? Consumer Information Center, 9 West 57th Street, New York, NY 10019.

2. BISBEE, JOYCE E. (1981), "Business Sponsored Educational Materials: A Perspective," The Teacher's Guide, National Association for Industry-Education Cooperation, 235 Hendricks Blvd., Buffalo, NY 14226.

3. BYMERS, GWEN J. (1982), "On Being Consumer Educators in the 1980's, in American Council on Consumer Interests, ed., Proceedings of ACCI, Columbia, MO: 32-37.

4. BROBECK, STEPHEN (1982), "CFA's Challenge to Business," Mobius, The Journal of the Society of Consumer Affairs Professional in Business, 4900 Leesburg Pike, Suite 311, Alexandria, VA 22302, October.

5. COCA-COLA USA (1983), The Bottom Line Benefits of Consumer Education, P.O. Drawer 1734, Atlanta, GA 30301.

6. GENERAL ELECTRIC COMPANY (1982), The Information Challenge, Consumer Products Sector, P.O. Box 5236, New York, NY 10022.

7. GOODMAN, JOHN (1984), "The Bottom Line Benefits of Consumer Education," Mobius, October/November.

8. HARTY, SHEILA (1979), Hucksters In The Classroom, Center for Study of Responsive Law, Washington, DC.

9. JUDGE, JEAN F. Corporate Consumer Education Programs, Remarks presented by Jean F. Judge, President, Jean Judge Associates, Inc., 125 Prospect Avenue, Hackensack, NJ 07601, The Public Relations Society of America.

10. SOCIETY OF CONSUMER AFFAIRS BUSINESS (1982), Guidelines for Business Sponsored Consumer Education Materials, 4900 Leesburg Pike, Suite 311, Alexandria, VA 22302.

11. US OFFICE OF CONSUMER AFFAIRS (1984), First National Consumer Education Roundtable, Washington, D.C. 20201.

ABOUT THE AUTHOR

Charlotte Baecher has been Education Director of Consumers Union since 1974. After taking a B.A. in English from LeMoyne College in 1967 and teaching high school, Baecher started a career in education publishing with the Paulist Press in New York. In 1971 she moved to Consumers Union where she participated in the Consumer Education Materials Project under David Schoenfield. Baecher has been the Editor of Penny Power since its inception in 1980.

THE ROLE OF CONSUMERS UNION (CU)

Charlotte M. Baecher

CONSUMER EDUCATION: WHOSE RESPONSIBILITY?

An episode at an Educational Press Association Conference several years ago illustrates what I view as a central problem of consumer education. Secretary of Education William Bennett, when asked what priority he would give to consumer education and what leadership his Office could provide, responded by saying that government "could not pay for everything." Hence, consumer education becomes the responsibility of parties that can.

This philosophy of shifting the responsibility for consumer education from the Government -- where it belongs -- to the "highest bidder," i.e., the party most able to pay for it is unacceptable. To my knowledge no other discipline has had to rely so completely on the private sector. While business's willingness to support consumer education is laudable if not always a good idea, business cannot and should not assume the leadership role that Government has relinquished.

Today consumer education suffers from a confusion of roles. And leadership is not the only "problem role." The second consists of a mismatch between the organizations best qualified to teach consumer education and the organizations that have the money to do so.

It seems obvious that experts in the consumer interest are best qualified to design effective and unbiased teaching programs in consumer education. Unfortunately, organizations with this expertise typically lack the financial resources to produce programs that "could make a difference." Further, like CU, they may be reluctant to join forces with business sponsors, whose affiliation could damage the credibility of the programs -- and even that of the participating organization. This is a major problem that needs to be addressed, if consumer education is to grow.

It is worth noting, at the outset, the inherent advantage CU has in consumer education as compared with its counterparts in business or government. As a consumer-controlled organization whose allegiance is wholly to the consumer, CU can comment without suffering any conflict of interest on the entire range of consumer problems. In particular, CU can comment impartially on evaluations of products and consumer policies affecting business without being accused of a conflict of interest. Not so consumer educators from business. Because of their built-in allegiance to the brands and product variants their companies control and/or produce, they are effectively disbarred from commenting impartially on matters involving inter-firm or inter-brand differences, whether it be with respect to product evaluations, business practices, or policies followed by or affecting business.

The position of consumer educators in government is different. They suffer from no inherent conflict of interest. But, in the United States it has been traditional for consumer educators in government to avoid discussion of inter-firm or inter-brand differences. (This is not the case everywhere. The German Consumers Union, Stiftung Warentest, was established and receives financial support from the government of the German Federal Republic. It publishes brand-by-brand comparisons of quality just as CU does.) Do a content analysis of government consumer publications -- whether they emanate from Cooperative Extension, FTC, FDA, the Federal Reserve Board -- and you can make your own confirmation of this proposition. On this basis, I claim a unique role for CU in promoting consumer education.

CONSUMERS UNION'S ROLE

My organization, Consumers Union, is first and foremost a provider of information. It is the publisher of Consumer Reports (circulation: 3.8 million), Penny Power (circulation: 125,0000 to 140,000) -- our "junior" CR targeted to school children, and many other consumer materials. As the country's largest non-profit voice in the consumer interest, CU undertakes a variety of activities from advocacy to education. CU's commitment to consumer education is so extensive that it is difficult to measure. It starts with Consumer Reports whose main purpose is to educate and inform. Other publications, especially Penny Power, represent efforts to teach new groups of consumers.

Most of what I have to say pertains to CU and should not be generalized to "consumer organizations."

CU's consumer education activities over the past 20 or so years have been diverse, reflecting CU's search for the ways in which it could have the greatest impact nationwide, especially with groups most in need of consumer education.

The Scope of CU's Role in Consumer Education

CU's commitment to consumer education has grown considerably over the last two decades. The Education Division has grown from a two-person operation (Director and Secretary) to its current five-person staff (Director, three Editors, Secretary) abetted by extensive consulting time from staffers in Technical, Editorial and other departments.

But it would be a mistake to think that CU's education activities are restricted to the Education Division alone. Other divisions have been undertaking major educational programs as well, e.g., our November, 1986 Conference on Poverty.

CU's budgetary arrangements reflect CU's commitment to consumer education. As a non-profit organization supported by sale of its publications, CU expects most of its publications to break even. Education programs, however, are specifically exempted from this restriction. Their mandate is to reach and teach the greatest number of people. Compare the price of Consumer Reports delivered for classroom use ($0.50 per issue) with the subscription price ($1.50 per issue) or the newstand price ($2 per issue) and the message is clear. The $0.50 classroom price is barely enough to cover the cost of materials, shipping, and handling. Similarly, Penny Power is priced at $4.50 for a classroom subscription vs. $11.95 for a home subscription. In the same vein the Education Division has run a deficit year after year, taking account only of direct costs and not counting the indirect costs involved by staff time and contributions of other divisions within CU.

The History of Consumer Education at CU

In the 1960's when James Mendenhall was CU's Education Director, CU's role was mainly that of a consumer education advocate and facilitator. Mendenhall strongly promoted consumer education and also provided support services to educators who were teaching it. His speeches and workshops introduced many teachers to this "new" subject area while his reduced price subscriptions to

CU for teachers and School Order Plan, which offered a teaching guide for Consumer Reports, provided some of the tools they needed.

Developing Education Materials and Services For Teachers

When David Schoenfeld succeeded Mendenhall in the early 1970's, he expanded CU's consumer education by providing materials for consumer education. As a pioneer in the consumer education movement of the late 60's and early 70's, Schoenfeld obtained a grant from the Office of Education to conduct a landmark survey of consumer education at all levels. The publication of findings from the survey was viewed as a means of helping teachers start their own programs. The six Consumer Education Materials Project books created by this Program were instrumental in launching many new programs.

During this same period, a monthly CU publication for teachers, "Teaching Tools for Consumer Ed," was reaching about 1,000 teachers, along with classroom copies of Consumer Reports.

Despite the popularity of this program, CU at this time did not view the production and dissemination of materials as the most effective vehicle for furthering consumer education. Instead Schoenfeld gave priority to the promotion of consumer education through speaking engagements, workshops, and networking. As a national spokesperson for consumer education, Schoenfeld pleaded the case for the short-lived Office of Consumers' Education, legislative mandates, and other governmental activities that could foster the growth of consumer education.

Restructuring to Survive

With the 1974-75 recession CU's finances plummented, necessitating drastic belt-tightening throughout CU. This was a turning point for CU's educational programs. Harsh realities of the marketplace forced CU to curb deficit programs, seeking ways by which they could cover at least part of their costs. Educational Services was one such program.

Overall, consumer education services were cut back in favor of the development of publications which would have the dual potential of influencing greater numbers and becoming financially self-sustaining.

This was the first of several instances in which funding problems would have an impact on CU's educational activities.

Developing Classroom Materials for Children

CU's major innovation at this time was the development in 1980 of Penny Power (hereafter PP), a children's consumer education magazine. PP was created to teach children while they are in the process of forming consumer attitudes and habits. We believed that young people needed the kind of consumer information and insights they were not getting from television and other commercial media. PP helps children to question advertising, evaluate products, understand peer pressure, and manage money. Some titles of articles will convey more graphically the type of message that we seek to deliver. "The Robots Are Coming," (on Toys), "Where's the Best Beef?" (on Fast Food Restaurants) "Keys to the Keys: Computer Programs that Teach Typing," "Battle of the Network Show," "Tracing Down Terrific Trivia Games," "Making Music: Which Instrument Is Right for You?" "Talking with Young Consumers Around the World," "Kids in Business," "Fruit Snack Surprises."

From a larger educational perspective, we at CU hoped Penny Power would be widely used to teach not only consumer education but also reading and math. CU also saw Penny Power as a way to reach low-income children via widespread classroom use.

A teaching guide for each issue and a videotape teacher workshop helped show teachers how Penny Power might be used to teach reading and math as well as consumer education. The videotape was an effort to provide workshop support services "on a budget," conducting "workshops" nationwide via television instead of in person. This program has been used in dozens of workshops around the country.

Once again, funding played a critical role in the development of this program. Two grants in 1978 and 1979 from the U.S. Office of Consumers' Education enabled CU to develop Penny Power initially. Unfortunately, CU's finances at the time prevented CU from pricing Penny Power as low as other classroom magazine programs, which limited its classroom circulation.

To extend the circulation and influence of PP, we reduced classroom subscription rates from $6 to $4.50 in 1986. In addition we have expanded the Teaching Guide (to accompany PP) from 4 to 8 pages.

Home circulation of Penny Power helped. It increased volume and lowered unit costs. It also helped subsidize school copies, which sold at a substantially lower price. And it greatly expanded the number of children who would get a consumer education, albeit at home instead of at school.

Penny Power has had limited success in the schools, but greater success in teaching children directly through home subscription. Penny Power has been in classrooms since 1980, and is reaching more than four students per classroom copy (1984 survey). More than 120,000 children learn from it at home.

WHAT CU IS DOING NOW

CU's current efforts are still directed to expanding consumer education via producing classroom materials. In our view Penny Power has been a good start, but is just a beginning.

Our main problem is a marketing problem: (1) how to develop interest in consumer education among school authorities and (2) how to distribute these materials. Seeking solutions to these problems is a current priority.

Looking To The Future

There is much that needs to be done to bring consumer education to a position of prominence in this country both within and outside the schools.

As Education Director for CU, I would like to see CU assume a stronger leadership role in consumer education. Yet our own history teaches us that such leadership cannot make significant and lasting progress without major publication programs to back them up.

The interest and fervor awakened at workshops and conferences need to be nurtured by making available tools for putting consumer education ideas into action.

And the tools need to be the right ones. They should not biased or compromised by promotional "shadows." They should identify issues that can truly help consumers. They should consist of long-run programs, not "one-shot" packages that are quickly forgotten.

In conclusion, it is my hope that the critical questioning begun at the Wingspread Conference will continue and that the roles that each of our organizations plays in furthering consumer education will become part of an overall mosaic. If we confuse our roles or relinquish them, the growth of consumer education in this country will be impeded.

ABOUT THE AUTHOR

Josephine Turner is National Program Leader for Family Resource Management in the Home Economics and Human Nutrition Division of the Cooperative Extension Service in Washington. She received her Ph.D. in Family Economics and Home Management from Purdue University in 1975. Her career has been marked by variegated activities with stints in the N.A.S.A. Spacecraft Center in Houston and the Girl Scouts. She moved to academia in 1968, holding teaching positions at several universities before going to Purdue. From 1978 to 1985 Turner was a Family Economics Specialist with the Albama Cooperative Extension Service at Auburn University. While in Alabama, she held leadership positions in professional associations both for Home Economics and for Extension Specialists.

THE ROLE OF COOPERATIVE EXTENSION

Josephine Turner

COOPERATIVE EXTENSION SERVICE: BACKGROUND

To define the role of Cooperative Extension in consumer education, it is necessary to explain the Cooperative Extension Service itself.

The Cooperative Extension Service (CES) was established in 1914 as a partnership between the U.S. Department of Agriculture and the Land Grant Universities, which had been authorized under the Morrill Acts of 1862 and 1890. Subsequent state legislation enabled local governments to become the third partner in Cooperative Extension.

The Congressional charge to the CES through the Smith-Lever Act is far-ranging and extremely broad. The Act specifies audiences, general subject areas, and educational approaches for this unique public partnership. The simple, yet enduring charge of the act is:

> "...to aid in diffusing among the people of the United States useful and practical information on subjects relating to agriculture,... home economics, and rural energy and to encourage the application of the same...extension work shall consist of the development of practical applications of research knowledge and giving of instruction and practical demonstrations of improved practices on technologies, in

> agriculture...home economics, and rural energy and subjects relating to persons not attending or resident in said colleges in the several communities and imparting information on said subjects through demonstrations, publications, and otherwise and for the necessary printing and distribution of information..."[5].

Further direction was specified in the 1935 Federal Bankhead-Jones Act:

> "...the establishment and maintenance of a permanent and effective agricultural industry including...the development and improvement of the rural home and rural life, and the maximum contribution of agriculture to the welfare of the consumer and the maintenance of maximum employment and national prosperity..."[5].

The Cooperative Extension Service was created as a dynamic institution, with multiple audiences, subject matters, and methodologies, thus creating a national system of education with broad objectives. This new educational system came close to the national university that George Washington, our first President, had envisioned.

By its very charter, the CES was established as an entity that would modify its programs and outreach in response to such factors as new knowledge, changes in its clientele's needs, and alterations in the socio-economic landscape. And, over the years, Cooperative Extension Service has changed in accordance with changing surroundings [11].

In FY 1986 this educational system includes professionals in each of America's sixty-six Land Grant Universities in the 50 states, Puerto Rico, the Virgin Islands, Guam, American Samoa, Micronesia, and the District of Columbia.

The CES is indeed a cooperative effort. Estimates of funding for the total Cooperative Extension System from all sources equal $1.042 billion in FY 1986. Funds are received from: federal, $330 million (31.7 percent); states, $487 million (46.7 percent); local, $193 million (18.5 percent); and private contributions, $32 million (3.1 percent). For each dollar of Federal funds provided for CES programs in 1986, $2.15 of state, county and private dollars were contributed. Public funds for the Cooperative Extension System are matched by the contributed time of more than 2.5 million volunteers as well as cash and in-kind donations. The service contributions by volunteers to CES exceed government appropriations by a ratio of 4 1/2 to 1. Together the value of resources contributed or appropriated annually to CES totals $5.4 billion [3, 10].

Staffing in the Federal Government consists of 177 full-time equivalents (FTE'S). This number is dwarfed by the approximately 16,745 state and county extension agents and specialists who develop and deliver educational programs. In addition, another 5,000 nutrition aides are working with low-income families on nutrition, diet, and health. These two sets of professionals are supplemented by thousands of paraprofessional staff and nearly three million volunteer leaders. This unique federal-state-local partnership has functioned effectively for more than seven decades [3].

Thus, the basic mission of the Cooperative Extension System is to disseminate and to encourage the application of research-generated knowledge and leadership techniques for individuals, families, and communities [2]. The Cooperative Extension System:

- Is an integrated partnership with federal, state,and county levels of government, research, and the private sector.

- Has an educational, not a regulatory or financial role. Thus, CES is administratively attached directly to the Land Grant Universities.

- Provides informal, non-credit education conducted for the most part outside the formal classroom for people of all ages.

- Is practical, problem-centered and situation based. CES's helps people to identify and understand their needs and problems and to use new technology or information in solving them.

- Features the objective presentation and analysis of factual information for decision making by people themselves. CES is typically research-based, drawing on the research, extension, and resident resources of the state universities as well as the United States Department of Agriculture and other agencies.

- Functions as a nationwide educational network through local, semi-autonomous offices accessible to and partly controlled by local citizens.

- Requires cooperative sharing of program development and funding among federal, state, and county or local governments.

- Involves funding and administrative relationships which permit educational programs to be directed toward broad national purposes, such as the energy crisis and/or the farm/rural crises. The Programs also serve specific local priorities such as how to utilize the family's income and other resources more effectively.

- Is staffed professionally by college trained personnel specifically qualified for their positions.

This American innovation of farmers and households with qualified scientists has made the United States the greatest food producing country the world has ever known [4]. To a lesser extent it may have improved the functioning of families and consumers, particularly those in rural areas.

Since CES is part of the Department of Agriculture, its role is limited to citizen education. CES does not conduct formal classroom instruction. Neither does it lobby or assume an advocacy role.

CES is unique, probably the only organization with the education potential to reach every family in the United States.

CES'S ACCOMPLISHMENTS

Consumer Education As A Major Activity of CES. Consumer education programs organized around such concerns as Food, Nutrition and Health, Family Economic Stability and Security, Family Strengths and Social Environment, Energy and Environment, Volunteer Leadership Development, 4-H, Agriculture, and Community Resource Development are offered in every county, in state, and territory. The goal is to use current research, new knowledge and emerging technology to improve consumer competence, marketplace performance, and consumer affairs participation of individuals in targeted audiences [7].

Delivery is achieved by a bewildering array of methods: mass media (radio, television, cable television, newspapers, newsletters, fact sheets, bulletins and magazines), group meetings, seminars, workshops, personal contacts, fairs, exhibits, shows, correspondence courses, home study courses, newsletter series, computer-assisted instruction, video and audio tapes, taped telephone messages, consumer call-in services, master volunteer programs, tele-conferences, and in one-on-one counseling sessions.

The CES cooperates with other organizations in sponsoring workshops, fairs, programs, and publications. For examples, CES has cooperated with the White House Office of Consumer Affairs in sponsoring National Consumers Week, with various military installations in offering consumer programs, with the American Council of Life Insurance in developing and distributing of education materials on life insurance.

In 1985, six million people received information and training directly from one or more of CES's consumer education programs while messages sent through media efforts reach millions more. Some specific program emphases are highlighted below.

- Consumer News Service. In most states a consumer news packet is sent from the state's CES office to each county office weekly or monthly. The county agent(s) localizes the information in the packet and releases it through the local news media.

- Encouragment of Home-Based Businesses. In 10 states job skills training programs were provided by CES. Two-thirds of Illinois's participants found jobs. Oregon's program resulted in the start up of a number of home-based businesses such as "Bed and Breakfast". Colorado's program redirected unemployed textile workers into "sew-for-profit" businesses. Michigan assisted 3,200 unemployed with crises management and a retooling program. Indiana reached 95,000 citizens through publications and media. Maryland provided a newsletter for those interested in home-based businesses. In Puerto Rico 2,500 workshop participants reported profits of $2.5 million from sales of home produced goods, or about $1,000 per participant.

- Enhancement of Consumer Skills. In 26 states emphases were placed on programs in food buying, housing, and maintenance of resources. These programs saved or extended income an estimated $44 million in addition to improving the family's health. Consumer food buying programs helped 919,015 families to save an average of $30.30 per month at the grocery store.

- Energy and Environment. In 1984 consumer programs in energy and environment in 41 states reached 1.9 million people directly and 34.5 million through the media. Resources were extended by $37.2 million, with an additional savings of $1.626 million in reduced energy use.

- Money Management. Several states train volunteers to carry CES's messages. One example is Alabama's Master Money Manager program which gave intensive training in money management to 127 volunteers in 1985. These volunteers contributed 2,774 hours of their own time, reaching 8,350 other people with money management information.

- Media Support for Cooperative Extension. In addition to the direct financial support given CES by county governments, CES usually receives support in the form of free air time on radio and television as well as free space in newspapers and magazines. In Missouri last year CES was given $60,000 worth of free radio time to reach farm families.

- CES and Local Crises. CES seeks to help with the emergencies some communities face. Two recent examples: programs to assist (1) families managing limited resources during the period of high unemployment and (2) farm families faced with financial crises, e.g., forclosure. From 1983-85, at least 95,600 farm families benefitted directly from this CES effort [9].

CES'S FUTURE

Knowledge is not developed to be published and hidden away on a library shelf or in some scholar's files. It is CES's role to see that knowledge is used to help consumers/citizens.

CES needs to work with researchers in identifying worthwhile research questions, translating research into usable knowledge, disseminating this knowledge to clients. The CES-research is critical for CES to carry out its consumer education role in the future [6].

REFERENCES

1. ALABAMA COOPERATIVE EXTENSION SERVICE (1982), Program Development, Circular EX-3, Auburn University.

2. EXTENSION SERVICE, U.S.D.A. (April 1983), Challenge and Change---A Blueprint for the Future, Extension Service, Washington D.C., U.S.D.A.

3. _________ (Feb. 1986), Extension Resources. The Cooperative Extension System, Washington, D. C., U.S.D.A.

4. _________ (Feb. 1986), The Collaborative Role of Research and Extension, Washington, D.C., U.S.D.A.

5. FOOD SECURITY ACT OF 1985, Section 1435.

6. LEWIS, LOWELL (Dir Ag Experiment Station) (Mar-Apr 1982), California Agriculture.

7. MANN, OPAL H. (Oct 1980), Speech at Martha's Vineyard, Mass.

8. SANDERS, H.C. (ed.) (1966), The Cooperative Extension Service, NJ: Prentice Hall.

9. TURNER, JOSEPHINE and HEFFERAN, COLIEN (1984-85), "Synthesis of National Accomplishment Reports".

10. UNIVERSITY OF WISCONSIN (1984), Local Volunteers and Cooperative Extension Agents: Partners in Action. University of Wisconsin-Madison, November: pg. 1.

11. U.S.D.A. and NASULGA COMMITTEE (1983), Extension in the '80's USDA and NASULGA Committee Report on the Future of Cooperative Extension, May.

12. WARNER, PAUL D. and CHRISTENSON, JAMES A. (1984), The Cooperative Extension Service: A National Assessment, CO: Westview Press.

Chapter 35

ABOUT THE AUTHOR

Jean R. Robinson is Professor and Chairman in the Department of Consumer Economics and Housing at Cornell University. After an undergraduate degree from Beloit College, Robinson received her Ph.D. in Economics from Radcliffe College in 1953. Devoting most of her time after her doctorate to family matters, Robinson became engaged again professionally in 1965 when she became a Lecturer in Consumer Economics at Cornell, teaching large undergraduate courses half-time with an interim administrative assignment (Acting Chairman, 1973). In 1981 she was appointed Professor and Chairman, a role that she has held since. In Fall, 1987 she served as Acting Associate Dean of the College of Human Ecology. Robinson's administrative flair has been called on frequently as she served as Chairman and Member of some of the most influential committees in both College and University.

THE CONTENT OF A COLLEGE-UNIVERSITY COURSE IN CONSUMER EDUCATION[1]

Jean R. Robinson

INTRODUCTION

My task is to review the content of current consumer education text at the college or university level and to make suggestions for new directions. My views, of course, reflect my own values and prejudices. To define the basic consumer education course, one must set certain boundaries. I make four assumptions about the role of this course in a college program.

First, as all education should be, a course in consumer education is only the start of a continuing process. It is important, therefore, for the content to be general and durable, providing not information or solutions, but the framework for analyzing problems and choosing solutions under ever-changing conditions.

Second, this is a course that stands alone and is accessible to students from a variety of academic backgrounds. Inevitably all will be consumers, entering the market to buy a substantial portion of

---

[1]Basic courses in consumer education courses are offered under different labels: consumer economics, consumer science, consumer affairs, etc. This paper is intended to apply to a basic, first or only course in consumer education, whatever its label.

the goods and services they require. They will have been prepared for earning a living and in this course they will be introduced to the skills they need to translate the returns from their efforts in the labor force into desired consumer goods.

This is not primarily a course for students majoring in consumer economics. The material which is included will duplicate components of microeconomics, personal financial management and/or decision making, and consumers and the law. Nor is this a course for those who intend to go beyond the practice of careful consumption for themselves to adopt the principles to different audiences and teach in informal and formal settings. The needs of the consumer educator go well beyond what might be considered basic consumer education. In addition to content, consumer educators must master communication and interpersonal relations skills, and develop knowledge of the characteristics of particular subgroups in the population. Thus, preparation for the role of consumer educator would include greater depth in economics, American government, family resource management, family sociology, knowledge of the ways people learn, and communication skills, as well as consumer education, per se.

Finally, any text must choose between (1) providing examples and allowing the instructor to supply the appropriate theory or (2) providing the theory and expecting the instructors to illustrate the principles with examples. My approach emphasizes the theory and general framework.

I begin by commenting on the continuing need and principal objectives for consumer education. Then I turn to a discussion of the role of the three institutions that I consider important in consumer education: household, market, and government. Here I comment on the contributions and limitations of several types of consumer education texts. In conclusion I note some areas where research might reinforce the efforts of consumer educators and the success of consumers in dealing in markets.

The Need for Consumer Education

In a simple economy where few goods were offered and the ties of consumer and producer were close, informed choice of consumer goods may have been achieved relatively easily. In modern times, however, informed choice has become increasingly difficult, made so by the enormous number of complex products on the market, the non-local control of the production and sale of goods and services, uninformed sales persons, and the unequal power of sellers/producers versus consumers in pursuing information and redress.

Colston Warne, the "Father" of the consumer movement, put the problem of the consumer cogently [19]: "The task of becoming an intelligent consumer has become ever more difficult because of the anarchistic nature of the American market, the spectacular development of new products, and the pervasive influence of advertising. The consumer is asked to choose wisely under circumstances which often baffle even the trained technician. He is faced with product differentiation, brand differentiation, model differentiation, price differentiation." An article in the Wall Street Journal in April 1986, supports this, noting that food companies introduce 20 to 30 new products a week [18].

For the last sixty years at least, educational efforts on behalf of consumers have been undertaken to assure that economic activity under these more difficult conditions does deliver the goods and services that will bring the greatest satisfaction to individuals and households and send the correct signals to the market. The early work of Benjamin Andrews [1], Henry Harap [6], Hazel Kyrk [7], and Margaret Reid [14] sought to equip consumers with the concepts and understandings that would enable them to function more effectively in the market. Socially, it reinforced efforts to establish standards of quality, informative labeling, access to information from government and industry testing, and organizations to strengthen the voice of consumers. Then as now, the goals of consumer education included the parochial needs of the households themselves as well as the broader social good as reflected in conditions for workers and the welfare of others.

In reviewing these activities on behalf of consumers over the years, one can be impressed with the prescience of these writing in recognizing the difficulties that consumers face. Alternatively, one may despair that, given these efforts, there has been so little progress toward the goal of wise consumption.

Here is a sampler of various writers' views from 1912 to the present regarding the plight and prospects of consumers. They deplore the failure of consumers in the market, whether failure stems from misguided values, inept decision-making, exploitation by sellers, or the peculiar nature of the household in the market.

Economist Wesley Mitchell writing in 1912 on "The Backward Art of Spending Money," [12]:

> "Important as the art of spending is, we have developed less skill in its practice than in the practice of making money. Common sense forbids our wasting dollars earned by irksome efforts; and yet we are notoriously extravagant. Ignorance of qualities, uncertainty of taste, lack of accounting, carelessness about prices--faults that would ruin a merchant--prevail in our housekeeping. Many of us scarcely know what becomes of our money, though well-schooled citizens of a money economy ought to plan for their outgoes no less carefully than for their incomes." p. 3
>
> "To spend money is easy, to spend it well is hard. Our faults as spenders are not wholly due to wantonness, but largely to broad conditions over which as individuals we have slight control." p. 14.

Thomas McCraw, summarizing Supreme Court Justice Louis D. Brandeis' caustic views of consumer performance [11, p. 107]:

> "The consumer himself Brandeis judged to be 'servile, self-indulgent, indolent, ignorant.' Even worse, the consumer had abrogated his role as a countervailing power against bigness. 'Isn't there among your economists,' he once inquired of Felix Frankfurter, 'some one who could make clear to the country that the greatest social-economic troubles arise from the fact [that] the consumer has failed absolutely to perform his function? He lies not only supine, but paralyzed and deserves to suffer like others who take their lickings 'lying down'. He gets no worse than his just desserts."

Consumer journalist Sidney Margolius, writing in 1967 [10, pp. 1-2]:

> "'Exploitation' is not too strong a word to describe the consumer situation. Never in the 30 years I have been reporting on consumer problems has the public been as widely and steadily exploited as today, from the children manipulated by TV toy ads and the teenagers by disc jockeys, to their parents manipulated into habitual installment buying at startling charges for the financing, and often for the merchandise as well.
>
> "This is serious business. It involves much more than mere irritations. It really involves a massive waste of family money and a diversion of family resources that are

> helping to frustrate vital personal and national goals such as advanced education, the rehabilitation of our cities, better housing and more adequate health care."
>
> "The fact is, and this may seem a little strong to swallow at first taste, consumer exploitation has to a large extent replaced labor exploitation as the real problem of our times. We would not
> permit the things to be done to people as workers that we allow to be done to them as consumers."

Paper presented at the <u>Conference on Quality Control and the Consumer</u> [13, p. 108]:

> "The central point....is that, considering the pitfalls to which American consumers are subjected as well as the lack of adequate buying aids, we have developed a remarkably alert contingent of buyers at one end of our purchasing spectrum--a group which on the whole makes pretty good use of its money and purchases with circumspection and after considerable deliberation, particularly in the acquisition of durable goods and items in which quality characteristics loom as especially important. At the other end of the spectrum, we have an equally substantial group which is constantly being victimized by high-pressure selling and advertising techniques and represents a manipulated mass, possessed of scant discernment and accorded little protection against its own failure to comprehend the new forces of hidden persuasion which mold its actions."

Economist J.K. Galbraith arguing the "oversupply" of goods provided by demand-manipulating oligopolists versus the "undersupply" of publicly provided services in his influential book, <u>The Affluent Society</u> [4, p. 253]:

> "The family which takes its mauve and cerise, air conditioned, power-steered, and power-braked automobile out for a tour passes through cities that are badly paved, made hideous by litter, blighted buildings, billboards, and posts for wires that should long since have been put under ground. They picnic on quantity packaged food from a portable icebox by a polluted stream and go on to spend the night at a park which is a menace to public health and morals. Just before dozing off on an air mattress, beneath a nylon tent, amid the stench of

> decaying refuse, they may reflect vaguely on the curious unevenness of their blessings."

There has been no shortage of books and periodicals offering consumers education, information, and/or advice. The advice they proffer ranges from excessively specific and hence highly perishable recommendations to theoretical analyses that could prove quite unhelpful to households trying to get on with the business of living well, according to their own preferences and within their limited resources.

The criticism of consumers by friendly observers has not abated, perhaps with good reason. Consumers follow fads and fashions, make inadequate provision for the future, are swayed by advertising for quack cures, are ignorant of price variability, and are unwilling to get the most from products they purchase by using and maintaining them properly. It is, of course, more interesting to cite the foolishness and failures of the consumer, than to acknowledge the evolution of a group of discerning consumers who are using their education and skills to acquire and evaluate information, organize for effective lobbying, and lead business into the development of consumer "hot lines," consumer action panels, and consumer representation in management.

Given the mixed results of consumer education so far, it seems worthwhile to explore the developmennt of a course that would build on the successes of present programs and, by affecting additional consumers and the market, bring improvements in individual and social well-being. Better informed choices clearly present the possibility of substantial returns both to individuals and society. Unfortunately, individuals continue to make poor choices, for a variety of reasons. For many the exercise of even rudimentary care in choice-making could substantially improve the quality of their life without requiring much by way of additional resources.

The Goal of Consumer Education

The fundamental goal of consumer education is to enable the individual and household to achieve a more satisfying level of living both for the present and in the future. This includes the satisfaction derived from the goods and services they purchase. But it also takes account of the goods and services they do not purchase, due to their awareness of possible damaging effects of their consumption activities on other people and on the natural environment.

The problem for the individual lies in the nature of the household. The household consumer is, and will for the foreseeable future remain, a small-scale, unspecialized buyer for whom the benefits from a "good" purchase may be very small whatever the combined benefits to society as a whole might be. Household and society losses stemming from uninformed buying are difficult to measure. The diversity of wants and the vast differences among consumers in the money, effort, and time of finding "best buys" make it impossible to obtain simple objective measures of net gains from "better" choices. Nonetheless, it is clear that many individuals and households do not realize how much they could improve their level of living by making better choices in the marketplace.

How then can consumer education be defined with some hope that a program which fulfills its requirements will assist a consumer in making informed choices in the marketplace?

Components of Consumer Education--An Overview

Consumer education develops a process, with strong roots in the concepts of economics, that prepares individuals and households to follow optimizing procedures that will enable them to obtain from the market the goods and services that provide the decision makers with the greatest satisfaction. Thus, consumer education teaches a way of discovering preferences, identifying available resources, investigating alternatives in the market or in home production, evaluating choices, and understanding the role of government in assisting and protecting consumers.

There are basically three components of consumer education. The first component, household choicemaking, seeks to provide individuals and households with "family management" skills that will help them arrive at preferences that will determine the goals and services they desire. For those goods to be acquired in the market, household choicemaking provides the motivation to make the best or satisfactory choice.

The second component, the consumer and the market or consumer decisionmaking, deals with understanding the functioning of the market and the discovery of the market options available. Understanding the process of price determination and the structure of markets should help individuals to judge the credibility of the information received from business and identify the situations where quality and price dispersion is likely to be significant and the search for reliable price and quality information will yield the greatest return.

The third component, government and the consumer, deals with the way in which government intervenes with the market and sellers/producers to provide information, goods and services, and protection. The government may try to protect consumers in situations where the consumer cannot be expected to judge products accurately on the basis of experience and current information, for example, in health and safety questions. The economic consequences of government's protection and regulation role and the advantage of government facilitating informed choice through the provision of information in an organized and manageable fashion should be covered in consumer education programs.

It is common to define as texts in consumer education, both those dealing with personal financial management and those dealing with "economics for consumers" or consumer issues. Personal financial management texts generally cover choicemaking rather cursorily. Instead, the focus is on providing detailed information regarding particular purchases, for example, housing, insurance, or financial investments. The principal weakness of the personal finance books is their failure to emphasize economic principles. On the other hand, books emphasizing consumer economics/consumer decision making or consumer issues commonly fail to address adequately the issue of what goods or services to purchase. The concentration of these texts on efficiency in the market may well lead to a least cost, but inappropriate purchase.

Neither financial management nor consumer economics texts deal effectively with the economic consequences of government in protection and regulation. Nor do they discuss the advantage government possesses in facilitating informed choice through the provision of organized and manageable information. Chapters on government typically describe institutions and perhaps procedures for redress.

Consumer education has tended to pay too little attention to social concerns, reaching back to the conditions under which goods are produced and forward to the environmental consequences of consumption choices. This is an appropriate topic for consumer education.

Underlying Economic Concepts. Three basic economic concepts affect the status of consumers and therefore should be included in a consumer education program. The first, the circular flow of economic activity, joins the individual to business and government and highlights the joint role of the individual as producer and consumer. "The circular flow can be a starting point for individuals to see how the roles of consumer, wage earner, and citizen interrelate. As consumers, the goods and services purchased affect who is to be employed. The quality of output and the wages demanded by workers will affect the cost of goods and services available to the consumer. The income workers earn will affect their standard of living. As citizens, the officials we elect and the issues we decide upon affect the goods and services provided by the government. These decisions also affect our taxes and the amount of disposable personal income we have to spend."[8, p. 42]

The second concept is opportunity cost. With limited resources the decision by the consumer to acquire one good is simultaneously a decision not to acquire something else. The decision might be to give up leisure activities to earn the income necessary for the purchase or to engage in household production. Opportunity cost provides the basis for assigning priorities for alternative uses of the household resources of income and time.

The third concept, present value, makes possible the comparison of alternatives with a different stream of benefits or with different periods over which the benefits will accrue to consumers. Present value is the amount in dollars a rational person would pay now for some future benefit, e.g., the receipt of a lump sum or a flow of income. The calculation of present value takes into account the effect of interest, inflation, and income tax rates. Despite uncertainty about the future, comparing present values enables one to make more satisfactory decisions regarding saving or borrowing and human capital or financial investments.

Information or Education. Consumer information is not consumer education. In fact, a major hazard for consumer education is the tendency to become too specific concerning products or markets. The more specific the information, the more likely it is to become dated: products change, new products appear, and new uses of products are developed. Information can quickly become obsolete. But where consumer education concentrates on developing skills in acquiring and interpreting information, these skills can be applied to the new circumstances. "Without consumer education, the customer will be overwhelmed with information and unable to assemble it in a manner that will aid in making an intelligent market decision. Without educating the consumer on how to use it, consumer information is of little use."[15, p. 1] But to place greater weight on the general in consumer education, is not to belittle the specific. Ultimately consumer education is worthless unless it leads the consumer to the acquisition of particular information relevant to important decisions.

THE DEVELOPMENT OF HOUSEHOLD PREFERENCES

What should be considered in the course in consumer education regarding the development of household preferences? How does the knowledge of the household and its "management" lead to improved choices in the market? Essentially this is an examination of the household looking inward to determine its values and goals and, where appropriate, its preferences for various goods and services, provided either through the market or through home production, which will create the greatest satisfaction for the members of the household. Wesley Mitchell [12] makes the point in what might now be considered a sexist comment, but one containing a basic truth often ignored in the financial management literature. "(But) to women of conscience and insight the ends of living will always be a part of the problem of spending money--the part that is most inspiring and most baffling. In this aspect the art of spending money differs from the technical pursuits of business and science, and is allied to philosophy and ethics. There is a scheme of values embodied in every housewife's work, whether she knows it or not, and this scheme affects for good or ill the health, the tastes, the character of those for whom she cares and those with whom she associates." Personal financial management texts frequently cover the identification of values and goals in an introductory chapter or two along with some comments about the economic environment. Weirich, Personal Financial Management [20] and Winger and Frasca, Personal Finance [22] are typical. Courses on "family resource management" typically devote more attention to this aspect of decisionmaking. This is true of texts such as Gross, Crandall and Knoll, Management for Modern Families [5] and Deacon and Firebaugh, Family Resource Management [2]. For consumer education courses their treatment of values is too detailed.

What is important to cover are the essentials of resource management:

-- understanding individual and household values and setting goals;

-- identifying and developing resources;

-- allocating particular resources to the achievement of goals, that is, taking the actions which lead to meeting the goals set forth;

-- evaluating the outcomes of the management process.

A household will develop consistent patterns of behavior in the market if there is a clear understanding of the values of the members of the household, individually and collectively. These values are made explicit in the establishment of the short and long run goals which the household will seek to fulfill. Knowing what is wanted and why will prevent the household from proceeding in one direction and then another, not satisfactorily meeting any goal. It is through this exercise of value clarification and goal setting that the motivation to function efficiently in the market is also developed.

Households have a variety of resources for use in meeting goals, including income, wealth, credit, human capital, household capital, time, and community resources. Depending on the preferences of the household, these can be allocated to a variety of goals. There are alternative combinations of resources that can be applied to meeting goals and there is a wide range of quality and price for similar goods and services in the marketplace. Changing family composition, the state of the economy, new government policies, or a different emphasis in the enforcement of existing regulations all affect household preferences and resources and lead to the necessity to reconsider values, goals, and priorities.

In the identification of resources and their allocation to particular ends, the household interacts with the market. In seeking to acquire the "best buy", the household uses some resources in search to assure that the remaining resources are spent efficiently.

Household Search Costs

One of the issues in consumer education that needs to be pursued further is the economics of search from the household point of view. The individual seeks information from outside the household concerning the combination of goods and services to achieve maximum satisfaction from the market. From the point of view of the household, the search is a use of resources to be pursued only so long as the expected increased satisfaction from the search exceeds the expected cost of the search.

Search involves three different kinds of costs--money, time, and effort. The money outlay includes subscriptions to periodicals and the cost of transportation or communication to seek price, quality, and service information. The time cost is valued according to the alternative activities that might have been pursued--the opportunity cost of the market work, home production, or leisure foregone. The time cost will be determined not only by the duration of time spent in search, but also by whether the search can be conducted only at certain hours. The effort cost may be the most limiting. Individuals whose jobs or other activities involve substantial mental effort may already be mentally overloaded and unable to cope with seeking and interpreting additional information.

For some the enjoyment of shopping may be an offset to the cost of search. These individuals take satisfaction from the process as well as from the improved outcome. Hence, the net cost will vary greatly among different individuals and for the same individual at different times, depending on the value placed on the specific activities given up. Thus, the search for information will cease at different points for different individuals. (See [17] for a further discussion of household search costs.)

The final element in the decision making process is the evaluation of the satisfaction flowing from the goods or services purchased to determine whether the decisions were indeed appropriate. The evaluation may permit the development of habitual choices which are satisfactory, reducing the number of decisions which must be made regularly and, therefore, the cost of decision making in total. The cost of search may also be significantly lowered over time as the accumulation of knowledge and experience in the market reduces the number of alternatives that need to be researched.

Consumers and The Market

Presumably, the internal household decision making establishes the preferences and the motivation to seek information which will lead to an efficient choice. Then the individual/household looks outward to the market and is transformed into a consumer seeking information to arrive at the most satisfactory decision on resource use. The theory underlying consumer choice presents the analysis of preferences and resources in indifference curves and budget lines. (See [3])

Whether consumers will search sufficiently depends heavily on their expectations of gain from search and their ability to obtain the desired information. A general underestimation of price dispersion in markets leads to a general underestimation of the gains from search. Differences in production and selling costs in different firms, the ability to control price through product differentiation or supply control, geographic dispersion of sellers and buyers, and market instability all lead to a variety of prices for equivalent quality. The economic framework for understanding price dispersion in markets is an analysis of supply and demand and the determination of price in various market types. Knowledge of markets can direct the consumer to the types of goods and services more likely to yield a significant return for search. (See [9] for numerous examples especially Chaps. 2-4.)

The effect of government intervention in setting consumer prices, for example, fares, interest rates, or rents, and the role of government as a provider of goods and services as an alternative to the private sector may be discussed.

The quality of information provided by firms and alternative private information sources affects the outcome of market searches and the contribution of the well known consumer periodicals such as Consumer Reports, Consumers Research Magazine, Changing Times, Money, is generally dealt with fully in consumer education texts. Whether the newly developing, sophisticated institutions can provide local price/quality information at a cost to the consumer commensurate with the benefits is still to be determined.

If individuals can set their priorities in some consistent fashion, taking account of their values and goals, then they will tend to select the combination of goods and services, within the limits of their resources, which rank highest on their preference scale. Any individual finding new information or new sources of supply may obtain an advantage in the market. Furthermore, if a significant body of consumers function intelligently, businesses will be forced to respond or fail. These "Information Seekers", discussed by Thorelli and Thorelli [17], "are also the opinion leaders of the marketplace. They, rather than the average consumer, are keeping producers on their toes. They, more than others, fight the battle for better products, for honesty and decency in business practice, and for more truthful and informative advertising. In effect, their role relative to the average consumer is that of St. George, ombudsman, and proxy purchasing agent, all in one." Thus, informed consumers are essentially a resource for all consumers, providing potentially greater satisfaction from resources available to the household for themselves and for the uninformed or incompetent consumer also.

Government and Consumer Education

Actions of the government cannot remove the need for consumer education and awareness. "Essentially the consumer must be in a position to take care of himself in the marketplace. At that critical moment when a person is about to make a purchase or investment decision, the presence of all the regulation and the legislation in the world will do very little to protect him if he is unaware of it -- or keep him from making a decision which is wrong for his personal situation [21]."

The history of the role of the government in consumer choice lies in two different directions. On the one hand, the government has facilitated informed choice by requiring the disclosure of certain relevant information. For example, legislation has provided for labeling of ingredient and fabric content, grade labeling, unit pricing, and energy ratings for appliances. An extension of that role might explore the effects of publishing product test results obtained by the purchasing agencies of the government. For the Federal government, gains from quantity purchases justify testing that is uneconomic and unfeasible for the individual household (though surely the evidence of efficient purchasing by some U.S. agencies is mixed!). To assure the publication of this information will require all the lobbying resources of the consumer movement. Support of this proposal by consumer groups and vehement opposition by producer groups highlight the conflict between producer and consumer interests. The range of products for which information could be provided would vastly exceed the number of products tested regularly by Consumers Union and its "cousins" elsewhere. Search costs are significantly reduced when information through the market and/or government is readily available, reasonably truthful, relevant to decision making, and intelligible to the non-specialist.

On the other hand, as a protector or regulator to prevent fraud and to protect the health of consumers, governments have intervened in varying degrees where even information seeking consumers as non-specialists are unable to evaluate qualities of products and services independently. This has taken the form of licensing of professionals, testing the accuracy of weights and measures, providing disclosure standards for securities, and either preventing certain products from coming to the market or removing dangerous products from the market. Thus, government is poised between offering information that leaves consumers free to make their own choices intelligently and creating freedom <u>from</u> choice by limiting goods and services available.

Problems arise when the government, as protector, removes goods from the market whether it be to assure health and safety, to limit purchases solely to technically superior products, or to prevent the purchase of inferior goods by some other definition (design). Not only will choice be limited, but also the costs of goods and services will rise, due to the costs of investigation and enforcement as well as the costs of the additional features necessary to meet the standards set. How extensive are the costs and the limitation on choice will depend on the type of "average" consumer the regulations aim to protect. The more intelligent consumers are assumed to be, the narrower the role of government needs to be. The more incompetent the "average" consumer, the more limited the range of products which can be acquired by any consumer. If the government sets very restrictive standards, costs are raised for everyone. Furthermore, this may effectively eliminate an item from the choice sets of lower income households, if the only item available becomes too costly because of the required features. Although this may not be common, government in its zeal to protect its citizens may reduce the role for intelligent, individual response and may reduce consumers' levels of living.

Thus, consumer education, if successful, can assist individuals and households to achieve a more satisfactory level of living through better use of their own resources and also serve society by permitting the widest range of choices to co-exist in the market, allowing households to make the choices right for them.

Social Consequences of Household Decisions

Consumer education appropriately includes a discussion of consumer responsibilities to the society at large, as well as to the individual household. Even in 1923, Andrews [1] was concerned about the economic conditions under which goods were produced and the obligation of consumers to choose those items produced under healthy, safe conditions with adequate pay for the workers. Recent concerns relate less to conditions of employment, assuming these are regulated by fair labor laws, than to issues of the depletion and/or waste of resources and pollution. There are conflicts between those seeking increasing output to assure goods and services for those in poverty and those who are more concerned about preserving resources for the next generation or protecting the environment. These value laden topics are appropriate for inclusion as a part of the education of the consumer/citizen.

Future Research

To promote the consumer interest, it is appropriate to highlight some areas where further research might improve the knowledge base for consumer education. The important research questions are those that lead to lower search costs by identifying ways to acquire and use information more effectively. The following are just a few examples.

1. What evidence can be obtained about how households of varying composition use information to make decisions? Would any differences lead to altering the media chosen to provide information and education to different household types?

2. What simplified rules or practices might provide satisfactory results for household members having little time or limited skills?

3. Are there alternative ways for the independent research organizations to present their recommendations to enable households to meet a variety of individual needs and to reach a wider audience?

4. How effective are various consumer affairs arrangements in business and government in assuring effective redress of consumer grievances?

5. And a final question to which we might not want an answer: Is there a connection between decisions judged "good" after the fact and the time, money, or effort expended in making them? Is there a measurable return to search as perceived by the buyer?

CONCLUSION

Presenting a consumer education course may be like working in a mature industry. The participants are not likely to discover something dramatically new that revolutionizes the ways in which consumers make choices. This does not mean that the content is irrelevant or unimportant. Despite the fact that the basic problems of consumers have been known, and have changed little over the past 50 years, today's consumers continue to have difficulties in arriving at optimal decisions. Hence, there is a continuing role for consumer education in aiding students of all ages to make effective decisions as consumers. This is best achieved by teaching principles. Principles are versatile, retaining their usefulness over long periods of time as circumstances and lifestyles change.

REFERENCES

1. ANDREWS, BENJAMIN (1923), Economics of the Household, New York: Macmillan.

2. DEACON, RUTH E. and FRANCILLE M. FIREBAUGH (1981), Family Resource Management, Boston, Mass.: Allyn and Bacon, Inc..

3. EASTWOOD, DAVID B. (1985), The Economics of Consumer Behavior, Boston, Mass.: Allyn and Bacon, Inc.

4. GALBRAITH, J.K. (1958), The Affluent Society, Boston, Mass.: Houghton Mifflin Company.

5. GROSS, IRMA H., ELIZABETH W. CRANDALL, and MARJORIE M. KNOLL (1980), Management for Modern Families, Englewood Cliffs, N.Y.: Prentice-Hall, Inc..

6. HARAP, HENRY (1924), The Education of the Consumer, New York: Macmillan.

7. KYRK, HAZEL (1923), A Theory of Consumption, Boston, Mass.: Houghton Mifflin Co.

8. MACDOWELL, MICHAEL A. and JOHN CLOW (1983), "Integrating Economic Concepts into Consumer Education," in NASSP Bulletin, Vol. 67, No. 467, December.

9. MAYNES, E. SCOTT (1976), Decision Making for Consumers, New York: MacMillan Company.

10. MARGOLIUS, SIDNEY (1967), The Innocent Consumer vs. The Exploiters, New York: Trident Press.

11. MCCRAW, THOMAS K. (1984), Prophets on Regulation, Cambridge, Mass.: Harvard University Press.

12. MITCHELL, WESLEY C. (1950), "The Backward Art of Spending Money," American Economic Review, June, 1912, Vol. II, pp. 269-281, reprinted in Wesley Mitchell, The Backward Art of Spending Money and Other Essays, New York, Augustus M. Kelley.

13. PROCEEDINGS ON THE QUALITY CONTROL AND THE CONSUMER CONFERENCE (1957), September 5-6, New Brunswick, N.J.: Rutgers University.

14. REID, MARGARET G. (1942), Consumers and the Market, New York: Appleton-Century-Crofts, Inc.

15. TECHNICAL ASSISTANCE RESEARCH PROGRAMS, INC. (1983), "The Bottom Line Benefits of Consumer Education," Washington, D.C., July 14.

16. THORELLI, HANS B. and SARAH V. (1977), Consumer Information Systems and Consumer Policy, Cambridge, Mass.: Ballinger Publishing Company.

17. THORELLI, HANS; HELMUT BECKER, and JACK ENGLEDOW (1975), The Information Seekers, Cambridge, Mass.: Ballinger Publishing Co.

18. WALL STREET JOURNAL (1986), Thursday, April 10, Section 2, p. 35, CLCCVII, No. 70.

19. WARNE, COLSTON E. (1957), "How Backward Is the Art of Spending Money?" in Conference on Quality Control and the Consumer, New Brunswick, N.J.: Rutgers University.

20. WEIRICH, JEAN LUTTNELL (1983), Personal Financial Management, Boston, Mass.: Little, Brown and Company.

21. WILLIAMSON, IRENE K. (1984), "Whither Consumerism?" At Home With Consumers, Vol. 5, No. 4, December.

22. WINGER, BERNARD J. and RALPH R. FRASCA (1986), Personal Finance, Columbus, Ohio: Chas. E. Merrill Publishing Company.

Chapter 36

ABOUT THE AUTHOR

Gordon E. Bivens is Mary B. Welch Distinguished Professor of Home Economics at Iowa State University. After receiving his Ph.D. in Economics from Iowa State University in 1957, Bivens served on the faculties of Iowa State University, University of Wisconsin-Milwaukee, Pennsylvania State University, and the University of Missouri before returning to Iowa State. Bivens has been a long time leader in the American Council on Consumer Interests. He was founding Editor of the Journal of Consumer Affairs, served as President of ACCI in 1967-68, and was elected Distinguished Fellow in 1982. Widely published, he is the author of Consumer Choice, The Economics of Personal Living (Harcourt, Brace, Jovanovich, 1977) with Andrew Allentuck.

A COLLEGE COURSE IN CONSUMER EDUCATION: COMMENTS AND EXTENSIONS

Gordon E. Bivens

I agree with most of Professor Robinson's main themes. My contribution will be to underline and extend.

Professor Robinson's emphasis of the following is especially meritorious. Consumer education should be concerned with:

1. Decisions to consume or not to consume, as well as development of decision-making skills useful for the consumer in the market;

2. Emphasis on the present value of a stream of services flowing over time;

3. Behavior that results in consumer equilibrium (or something approaching it), based on clarified long- and short-run goals.

These points are important in many ways. They help avoid wasteful consumption, improve consumer decision making in a dynamic environment, and introduce consumer assertiveness vis-a-vis sales and advertising pressures.

TOPICS WORTHY OF EMPHASIS

Ethical Considerations

It seems unlikely that ethical frameworks per se will ever be a part of consumer education courses. But it does seem appropriate to set consumer decisions against a back-drop of ethical considerations. Is it not appropriate to think of "stewardship" of resources, to use an old-fashioned but still powerful term? As Kenneth Boulding has suggested, stewardship implies minimization of throughput with a view to conservation of resources for future generations. Is it not appropriate to ask individuals how their consumption might or might not harm others? (Unmuffled motor vehicles come to mind along with other forms of noise pollution). Should one consider how one's consumption helps or hinders one's own -- and possibly one's family's -- development? Examples: people who over eat or under-exercise. In essence, I am suggesting that consumer education should be cast in a human resource development framework.

Search: Cost Vs. Leisure Components

Robinson rightly identifies search time and effort as part of the cost of choosing goods and services. The extent to which search is a cost or leisure activity is as yet an unexplored issue, worthy of future research.

Macro Considerations

Many events and conditions external to the consuming unit and its market decisions are worthy of inclusion in a consumer education course. Examples: (1) The "external" effects of one's own consumption on others; (2) The social effects of military spending on the availability of consumer goods, inflation, and levels of trust; (3) The effect of aggregate consumption in the U.S. on consumers in other countries -- their access to goods and services, potential for employment, etc. (4) Appropriate government intervention to ensure the accountability of large business to the public/consumer interest. Admittedly, these matters lie far beyond the "today" concerns of consumers. But, as Professor Robinson points out, college level consumer education courses should do more than provide information for immediate use which soon will be obsolete.

Unperceived Complementaries

When consumers enter the market, they often face uncertainty and risks. It is important to alert consumers to uncertainty and risks to show them how to cope. One uncertainty worth attention is the string of purchases which may ensue from a decision to buy one product; the joint products in the form of repairs and maintenance, which come with the purchase of a durable; the complements of the purchased product, e.g., the sailing togs and yachting club membership that follow the purchase of a sailboat; the lift tickets and clothing purchases that ensue from the purchase of skis. Consumers need to be alerted to the extent that a single purchase may encumber future income. They must learn that the purchase price may not be the only cost.

Philanthropy, Gifts, Grants

It would be inappropriate for a consumer education course to prescribe or even suggest a norm for expenditures on philanthropy. But it is my view that individuals should be encouraged to consider philanthropy as a category of claims on income. Otherwise, gift-giving may be overlooked or, at best, treated as a residual. If philanthropy can further movement toward peace on the international level or contribute to domestic social stability, does it not contain a potential benefit for consumers?

The Blurring Distinction: Goods and Services

In general, we continue to discuss goods and services as though they were distinct entities. However, it appears to me they are blurring realities. Services are linked to goods acquisition to a greater and greater extent -- for example, the acquisition of the services of many more products through leasing mechanisms, a trend that is likely to continue. In other ways, too, services are a facilitating mechanism for acquisition of the flow of services which goods provide. Consumers need to see this. And, as in the case of goods, they need to learn to appraise the quality of and price differences of various competing services.

CONCLUSION

In general, a college-level consumer education course must develop skills that enhance the student's ability to make and implement decisions in markets. Development of such skills involves informational material. That serves an important purpose.

Courses with such a primary focus would necessarily be of short-term value. The longer, staying value of these courses lies in development of the student's ability to understand his/her consumer decision-making in both its micro-level dimensions and its related macro-level, or societal, circumstances. Although difficult and often less enticing at the moment for students, these more elusive components establish a foundation on which individuals can build and modify their behavior as consumers over a lifetime.

REFERENCES

1. ALLENTUCK, ANDREW J. and BIVENS, GORDON E. (1977), Consumer Choice: The Economics of Personal Living, NY: Harcourt & Brace Jovanovich, Inc.

2. BIVENS, GORDON E. (1972), "Dimensions of Consumerism: Ethical Considerations," The Distaff, XL(1): 36-42.

3. LEE, STEWART M. & ZELENAK, MEL J. (1982), Economics for Consumers, Belmont, CA: Wadsworth Publishing Co.

4. MAYNES, E. SCOTT (1976), Decision-Making for Consumers, NY: MacMillan Publishing Co.

5. SWAGLER, ROGER M. (1979), Consumers and the Market, 2nd Ed., Lexington, MA: D.C. Heath.

6. TROELSTRUP, ARCH W. and HALL, E. CARL (1978), The Consumer in American Society: Personal and Family Finance, 6th Ed., NY: McGraw-Hill.

ABOUT THE AUTHOR

Edward J. Metzen is Professor and Chairman of Family Economics and Home Management at the University of Missouri-Columbia. Metzen received his Ed. D. from the University of Missouri in 1963. Starting as a high school teacher in Alden, Minnesota, he turned quickly to college teaching, first at Stephens College (1954-63) and then at the University of Missouri (1963--). Metzen has been a longtime leader of the American Council on Consumer Interests, serving as Executive Director from 1965 to 1975 and as President for 1975-76. He was elected Distinguished Fellow of ACCI in 1982. He has been a member of the Policy Board of The Journal of Consumer Affairs since 1984.

A COLLEGE COURSE IN CONSUMER EDUCATION: A CRITIQUE

Edward J. Metzen

While Professor Robinson's paper does not provide a direct, structured assessment of consumer education texts or existing courses, it does provide an array of recommendations for the nature and substance of such courses, and, by implication, textbook content.

I agree with much of the philosophy and many of the specific ideas presented by Robinson. Her focus on mastery of basic concepts, orientations, and strategies rather than acquisition of a body of facts -- the emphasis on the timeless rather than the timely -- is certainly sound. It is the kind of education with the greatest potential long-run payoff for students and for society. And most of the constructs she suggests as central for consumer education seem appropriate. Beyond that, the paper presents a solid rationale for consumer education. However, there are some propositions, inconsistencies, and omissions which merit attention and/or challenge. To these I now turn.

THEORY VERSUS APPLICATIONS

Robinson's framework that divides the content of consumer economics into (1) analysis of problems vs. (2) information or solutions imposes too tight a box of mutual exclusivity. I see no need for texts to be designed to provide either theory/general framework or examples. I concur that sound educational principles call for organizing around basic frameworks and concepts. But surely courses and textbooks can provide some of both. Indeed, they must, in order to be maximally effective. Will a consumer education course or text that is skimpy in covering relevant facts and examples be attractive to non-specialists who seek to enhance their expertise as consumers? Most undergraduates suffer from an inability to apply general concepts and principles unless these concepts and principles are illuminated by examples.

THE SAME COURSE FOR MAJORS AND NON-MAJORS?

Why cannot a common first course in Consumer Economics serve both majors in consumer economics and non-majors? Both groups share a common interest as consumers. Further, majors in consumer economics would gain valuable insights from the experiences, concerns, and misconceptions of students coming with a variety of backgrounds, orientations, degrees of understanding, appreciation, and sensitivities. Finally, as a practical matter it must be recognized that the small size of many programs in consumer economics will mandate that some courses serve dual purposes. In my view the first course should serve both as a general education course and an introductory professional course. If implemented effectively, it should be a prime vehicle for recruiting majors.

While Robinson specifies elements of microeconomics, personal financial management and/or decision-making, and consumer and the law as components of consumer economics, it is unclear as to how far Robinson would go in incorporating elements of personal finance and consumer law. Existing textbooks also reflect diversity and ambiguity on this matter. It seems to me that it is desirable to include some elements of macroeconomics in the basic course.

BREADTH OF FOCUS: A LOOK BEYOND THE MARKET?

Should the course focus upon market transactions or deal with consumer activities more broadly construed? The prevailing suggestion is for the broader focus, but there is occasional reversion to the perspective that consumer education is to prepare people to make optimizing choices from the market. For myself, I believe that the prevailing American tendency to ballyhoo the private sector and commercially-produced goods and services as contrasted with the public sector, non-market production, and nonconsumption experiences is much in need of reassessment and adjustment. A course of the type proposed could make a valuable contribution by helping students gain perspective through careful analysis and reflection regarding the role and contribution of the public and private sectors.

Let me suggest the voluntary sector as meriting attention in a consumer economics course. The rationale: it is a neglected avenue for satisfying consumer wants and needs and for enhancing life satisfaction through both consumption and production.

WHAT PERCEIVED ROLE FOR GOVERNMENT INTERVENTION?

A cautionary stance against the public sector permeates Robinson's paper although the role of government as both appropriate protector of consumer interests and supplier of public goods and services is forthrightly acknowledged. In my judgment the expressed concern about government interference in the marketplace to the detriment of consumer choice is conceptually valid, but I do not find the empirical evidence overwhelming. A marketplace in which tobacco companies spend millions of dollars on role modeling and habit formation, arguing that there still is no substantive evidence of linkage between smoking and illness and that tobacco advertising does not induce tobacco smoking, is hardly a marketplace in which government interference in the form of product limitations looms as a major element of consumer concern!

I agree with the pervasive emphasis in Robinson's paper on informed consumers, the focus on choice making in the marketplace, and in particular the importance given to the economics of information search. These fit my view of what a consumer course and text should bring to students. But, to repeat, I sense in the paper some reticence regarding the potential of government action for enhancing the well-being of consumers. While it is true that "actions of the government cannot remove the need for consumer education and awareness," it is also true that all the consumer education in the world cannot accomplish what certain government actions can accomplish in the interests of consumer well-being. Or, at the very least, consumer education cannot match the degree of efficiency and effectiveness that government regulation achieves in some domains. Robinson does point out in several places how government facilitates informed consumer choice by requirements for information disclosure that make not only for effectiveness but also for efficiency. Similar results apply to safety standards and prohibitions against certain practices. Such regulations benefit and safeguard the interests of even the uninformed consumer, at least when he is dealing with legitimate players in the marketplace. These regulations may not consistently lead ineffective consumers to utility-maximizing choices, but they at least rule out disastrous options.

What Considerations Beyond the Purchase Stage?

Robinson points out the willingness of consumers to maximize utility from products purchased through proper use and maintenance. Yet she excludes this topic from her model consumer education course. This is a topic that deserves attention along with household choice-making, consumer decision making, and government and the consumer. The framework for analysis of use and maintenance behavior resembles that for information search. I believe this topic could be given attention without drifting into the unworthy mundane.

In cautioning that "Their [consumers'] concentration on efficiency in the market may well lead to a least cost, but inappropriate purchase," Robinson would seem to be doing a disservice to textbook authors, or at least the consumer educators who use the texts. Surely most consumer educators will introduce benefit-cost and present-future concepts as they engage students, thus avoiding the bad choices Robinson warns against.

Robinson's admonition that attention be given to the social concerns related to consumption -- environmental pollution, depletion of nonrenewable resources, labor conditions in production -- merits applause. This domain -- the present-future tradeoffs between satisfactions for today's consumers and the needs of future consumers -- is the only instance where consumer interests might potentially be at odds with the long-run general public interest. The issues are not easy ones with which to cope, and answers to the inherent problems are anything but simple. But they are of tremendous significance and must be brought into the conscience of consumers.

For purchase decisions by individual consumers, the concept of present value is most important and appropriate. But I have some misgivings that students may become so embroiled in the mathematics of finance, getting bogged down in formulae and calculations, that they ignore other important topics.

WHAT ROLE FOR THEORY?

I have misgivings, too, as to whether "translating consumer preferences and resources into economic terms in the theory of consumer choice through indifference curves and budget lines" should be "a first step" in such a course. The general concept of preferences and trade-offs can be introduced and understood well without immersing students in the arcane details, the arid rigor, the complexities, and underlying assumptions of the indifference curve apparatus. For most students practical applications of the basic concepts of consumer economics are likely to generate greater enthusiasm and insight than are subtle exercises in consumer theory. It would be better to reserve the subleties of theory for more advanced students specializing in the field.

I wonder, too, whether a single course in consumer economics can adequately incorporate "an analysis of supply and demand and the determination of price in various market types" that goes beyond students' first course in economics, while still providing the meaningful experiences they seek in a consumer education course. It is very important that students come to appreciate the central and crucial role of consumer choice in a market economy, the centrality and tenuousness of the heroic assumptions regarding perfectly rational and informed consumers that underly so much of the theory, and the vulnerability of the consumers in real-world markets. Students also need to take to heart the point Robinson emphasizes -- that informed consumers, through their ability to make markets work, are a potential resource for all consumers, including the uninformed. This is a role and responsibility that should be communicated to all students. It is a message that can be delivered without resort to sophisticated theoretical refinements.

NEED FOR A PRACTIVE ORIENTATION

Finally, there exists a theme that seems to bob beneath the surface of the Robinson paper: that the consumer course should be proactive, advocacy-oriented regarding consumer interests, and normative regarding marketplace conditions and behavior. This, rather than being merely descriptive or even merely analytical. This, with respect to both individual actions and public policy. The prevailing societal orientations, marketplace realities, public policy orientations (particularly in recent times), and even the bias of our educational system, demand such a perspective. Only with this perspective can we hope to improve the societal condition and enhance consumer well-being to the fullest extent possible with the resources we have to commit to the task.

NO CONSENSUS YET ON FIELD AND COURSE CONTENT

Robinson confronts us with two quandaries that characterize the field, its courses, its curricula, and its textbooks. The first one is how all the desirable objectives in consumer education can be packaged into a single course, given the limited time, energies, and ingenuity of faculty members. This "budget constraint" of limited time, energies, and ingenuity results in a wide diversity of course configurations and textbook content, each version intended to satisfy the purposes of a college course in consumer education. All of this is affected by the broader curriculum structure within which this particular course is embedded on a particular campus.

(Let me digress to discuss for a moment texts related to our field. A perusal of my book shelves reveals a market saturated with personal finance books, and relatively undersupplied with new books in which the consumer is the central focus. While the amount of attention given in the personal finance books to direct personal investing in individual securities is probably out of proportion to its relevance to the lives of most students, many include some consumer focus. This suggests that consumer consciousness has become somewhat pervasive, a natural part of our society's orientation. The personal finance texts also give greater attention than formerly to the macro context, environmental considerations, and basic value assessment and choice-making, along with varying attention to consumer frauds and protection, commodity information, and buying techniques.)

Our second quandary relates to the definition of our field and the delineation between consumer education and related areas. Robinson's statement that consumer education "fundamentally conveys a way of discovering preferences, identifying available resources, generating alternative ways to satisfy wants and needs and evaluating choices" (while I concur) brings to mind definitions I have encountered of "home management" courses. These definitional problems do not end at the course level. They came to light clearly, almost hilariously, at the National Invitational Symposium on Consumer Science in Institutions of Higher Education, held at the University of Wisconsin five years ago. There a select group of erudite professionals, finding that definitional nuances and the inability to agree even on the definition of "science" obstructed the flow of communication, finally solved the dilemma by agreeing to refer to the field by the auspicious title, "Consumer _Whatever_"!

While the matter has its humorous side, it is reflective of the fact that our field has a long way to go in delineating and articulating its content. The problem is made more complex by the diversity of settings in which our courses exist. The discussion above shows why we must still grapple with the question of appropriate structure, style, and content for even a general-interest consumer education course. It shows also why we encounter so much diversity in textbooks intended basically for "the same course." Hopefully, Dr. Robinson's paper and the several review papers will contribute to a healthy evolution of the field via course and curriculum development.

ABOUT THE AUTHOR

Carole J. Makela is Professor of Consumer Sciences and Housing at Colorado State University. She has held the administrative positions of Department Head and Interim Associate Dean of the College of Applied Human Sciences. An original member of the ACCI Research Committee, Dr. Makela worked through the development of the efforts that culminated in The Frontier. She was the President of ACCI in 1981-82. Her research, publications and service have emphasized consumer issues and personal financial management.

CONTENT IS NOT ENOUGH

Carole J. Makela

The content of the college consumer education course discussed by Professor Robinson gives one little to challenge. Her major elements are similar to the often cited concepts classified by Bannister and Monsma [2]. Though any of us may prefer a different emphasis, the reality of one course "accessible to students with a variety of academic interests,...who all will be consumers" is easy to accept. Some consumer education for the college student is better than little or none. Developing a course that can contribute to, let alone, assure competent, mature and effective implementation of the consumer role from the perspective of the household, the marketplace, government and society is a challenge.

I applaud Robinson for not undertaking a detailed content analysis of the texts in consumer education. What actually is included or emphasized in a course may not be a reflection of textbook contents, course syllabi or even students' class notes. By focusing on what she sees as important in a course, Robinson challenges educators to compare their courses for similarities to and differences from her proposal. Using the proposed course content as a comparative standard can be useful to educators in refocusing, refining and developing their courses. Now that we have settled the content, we need the students.

NEEDED: HIGHER ENROLLMENTS

My discussion is based on acceptance of the proposed course. A course with similar content is available on many college campuses though one may find personal finance courses with larger enrollments more common. As to consumer education courses, I express two concerns. First it bothers me that relatively few students take a consumer education course. Professors of consumer education can all compare numbers. But, unless we are speaking of one of the few universities that has accepted consumer education as part of general education, enrollment is far from universal. It is time we become more concerned about the number of students we do not have rather than those that we have. Each of us, from our current background, can identify subject matter of lesser impact on the quality of life that is in high demand by students. Yes, a few are the "easy grade" courses, but others have prestige, appeal, challenge, necessity, or other qualities that attract and hold students.

The resurgence of general education poses an opportunity to become part of "educating students for living" with perhaps less concentration on the consumer major. It is important to review the qualities of the educated person. The educated person can deal with life and the world today and tomorrow while respecting the past. Employability is not the sole criteria by which to judge outcome. An educated person gains "skills and knowledge...needed...at different times of their lives to cope with the voluntary and involuntary tasks of everyday living, with the chores and challenges of work, and with the activities associated with self improvement" [5]. Further as Bailey [1] argued, the educated person must be able to function in a series of political, economic and social systems.

In Investment in Learning: The Individual and Social Value of American Higher Education, Bowen [3], after reviewing more than 1000 goal statements of educational philosophers, critics, commissions, faculty and institutions, included a consumer-role-related goal. "Consumer efficiency" was one of his seven goals under "practical competence." Specifically, he included "sound choice of values relating to style of life. Skill in stretching consumer dollars. Ability to cope with taxes, credit, insurance, investments, legal issues, etc. Ability to recognize deceptive sales practices and to withstand high-pressure sales tactics." Five of the other "practical competence" goals also related to the content of the course described by Jean Robinson. These are citizenship, economic productivity, sound family life, fruitful leisure and health. From this goal segment for individual students in higher education and our own commitment to educating "effective consumers," there should be little question as to the role of consumer education in general education. No doubt there will be much debate.

Higher education currently divides the undergraduate curriculum into thirds--general education, major requirements and electives [5]. This gives us at least two opportunities to fit consumer education into the curriculum. The first occurs in the general education portion. Of course, this depends on the definition of general education adopted by a particular college or university and whether you and I can make the case for consumer education as a component of "general education." Even if we are unsuccessful here, there is the alternative of making consumer education such an exciting and valued course that it becomes a widely sought-after elective. We should also make the case for consumer education as a valuable background in preparing for consumer related careers, e.g., in marketing, sales, and business management.

FAVORABLE RECOGNITION FOR THE CONSUMER ROLE

My second concern is public perception of the consumer role. Is it viewed as positive and worthwhile? When was the last time you acknowledged or recognized someone for being a "competent consumer"? When were you so acknowledged? The following examples are more typical: <u>astonishment</u> that individuals could be effective consumers with few resources available to them; <u>surprise</u> that individuals could possibly be satisfied with older, high mileage autos; <u>curiosity</u> that individuals could have made a "good" purchase by spending much less money than is normal or usual. We recognize and honor people for excellence as students, athletes, citizens, drivers, parents. By contrast, we give "excellent" consumers little support or credit for effective use of their skills, knowledge, and effort. I am not suggesting that we have a "Ten Best Consumers of the Year" contest. But I think it is time that we recognize excellence so that we can motivate people to aspire to "excellence" as consumers. Should one be proud of a job well done as a consumer? We need only note the cartoons and comic strips that make light of the problems and weaknesses of consumers (especially women) and the labels given to persons on the consumer continuum to grasp the underappreciation of the effective consumer. At one extreme are the "Penny Pincher," "so tight that they squeak," or "Scotch," etc. Each of these labels expresses a derisive attitute towards unwillingness to spend (which may be a "good" thing) and/or compulsive care in consumer decisions (information seeking and processing as an end rather than a means). At the other extreme, we label people as "materialistic," "impulse buyers," "conspicuous consumers," etc. Here again the buying behavior of the targets is given a pejorative label. There often lies behind these expressions the underlying view that information search, decision making, and problem solving skills are little valued.

This concern is raised here since it may throw light on why students are not waiting in line to take courses in consumer education. The consumer role is pervasively viewed as one that people easily and effectively play. Effective performance of the consumer role <u>per se</u> is not held in high esteem.

The passage of time is likely to change the quality of decisions made -- some for the better, some for the worse. Time also brings new and unfamiliar choices. Many take the view that "best guesses" will be as effective as wading through conflicting, incomplete or inconclusive information. With these views widely held, why would consumer education be deemed beneficial or necessary?

The book, In Search of Excellence, has caught the attention of the business world as well as the public as its authors sought to find those characteristics of corporations that brought success. Likewise we have heard challenges to develop excellence in education. To bring consumer education to its full stature, it now may be the time to identify the value of excellence in the consumer role and to effect a plan for its acceptance. Consumer competence can be the next wave of excellence. Robinson has laid out a college course which we can use as part of the effort. Many of us are affiliated with institutions of higher education. As individuals, we may not be in the position to teach courses in consumer education. We should not, however, be the obstacles to their availability, accessibility and attractiveness to students. We can provide valuable insights to course development and refinement, help sell the course(s) to administrators, faculty and students, and do research that will improve effective consumer education and information for many people. Much can be done in altering attitudes so that the consumer role is not viewed primarily as a "daily necessity." What needs to be acknowledged is the idea that the consumer role makes a difference in both the quality of daily living and also in helping to make economic, political and social systems work effectively.

The essence of these broadened perspectives was reported from the Dearborn Conference in 1985, "Should There be a National Agenda for Consumer Education?"

> Essentially, all individuals are consumers. The consumer role includes both one's own choices and actions, and one's influence on others. The consumer role is inescapable in our society. To satisfy our needs, we make choices in a complex, dynamic marketplace. The scope of consumer concerns and need is broader than marketplace decisions on personal and household purchases. The interdependence of peoples and nations with the physical environment, demands that we must balance our quest for quality of personal life with a consideration of the effects of our decisions on future generations. This interrelationship

> creates natural partnerships among all sectors of the economy in making critical decisions. Consumer education is therefore an essential part of both basic and continuing education for all. Society will not have the benefits of the consumer perspective unless we invest appropriate resources for consumer education [4].

One course for one segment of the population is not enough. Therefore, I challenge each of you to take a part in making consumer education courses (like that described by Robinson) a high demand product for the education of most students in our universities and colleges. We have a responsibility to educate people "to live" as well as "to make a living." Only if consumer education is an integral part of higher education will it make the necessary impact at other levels of education, affecting the majority of citizens of all nations. We need to start some place. Why not in our own backyards?

REFERENCES

1. BAILEY, S.K. (1976), The Purposes of Education, Bloomington, IN: Phi Delta Kappa.

2. BANNISTER, R. and MONSMA, C. (1982), Classification of Concepts in Consumer Education, Monograph 137, Cincinnati, OH: South-Western Publishing Co.

3. BOWEN, H.R. (1977), Investment in Learning: The Individual and Social Value of American Higher Education, San Francisco, CA: Jossey-Bass Publishing.

4. "SHOULD THERE BE A NATIONAL AGENDA FOR CONSUMER EDUCATION?" (1985), New York: Avon Products, Inc.

5. THE CARNEGIE FOUNDATION FOR THE ADVANCEMENT OF TEACHING (1977), Missions of the College Curriculum: A Contemporary Review with Suggestions, San Francisco, CA: Jossey-Bass Publishers.